W9-BVI-726

◆ FOURTH EDITION ◆

THEORY AND PRACTICE OF GROUP COUNSELING

GERALD COREY, is a professor of human services and counseling at California State University at Fullerton and a licensed psychologist. He received his doctorate in counseling from the University of Southern California. He is a Diplomate in Counseling Psychology, American Board of Professional Psychology; a National Certified Counselor; a Fellow of the American Psychological Association (Counseling Psychology); and a Fellow of the Association for Specialists in Group Work. He was the coordinator of the Human Services Program at California State University at Fullerton from 1983 to 1994 (except for a two-year period).

Jerry received the Outstanding Professor of the Year Award from California State University at Fullerton in 1991 and was the recipient of an honorary doctorate in humane letters from National-Louis University in 1992. He teaches both undergraduate and graduate courses in group counseling, as well as courses in experiential groups, the theory and practice of counseling, and professional ethics. With his colleagues he has conducted workshops in the United States, Canada, Germany, Belgium, Scotland, Mexico, and China, with a special focus on training in group counseling. He often presents workshops for professional organizations and at various universities. Along with his wife, Marianne Schneider Corey, and other colleagues, Jerry offers weeklong residential personal-growth groups and residential training and supervision workshops each summer in Idyllwild, California. In his leisure time, Jerry likes to travel, hike and bicycle in the mountains, and drive his 1931 Model A Ford.

Other books by Gerald Corey:

- *Becoming a Helper,* 2nd Edition
  (1993, with Marianne Schneider Corey)
- *I Never Knew I Had a Choice,* 5th Edition
  (1993, with Marianne Schneider Corey)
- *Issues and Ethics in the Helping Professions,* 4th Edition
  (1993, with Marianne Schneider Corey and Patrick Callanan)
- *Groups: Process and Practice,* 4th Edition
  (1992, with Marianne Schneider Corey)
- *Group Techniques,* 2nd Edition
  (1992, with Marianne Schneider Corey, Patrick Callanan, and J. Michael Russell)
- *Case Approach to Counseling and Psychotherapy,* 3rd Edition
  (1991)
- *Theory and Practice of Counseling and Psychotherapy,* 4th Edition
  (and *Manual*) (1991)

♦ FOURTH EDITION ♦

THEORY AND PRACTICE OF GROUP COUNSELING

GERALD COREY

California State University, Fullerton

Diplomate in Counseling Psychology,
American Board of Professional Psychology

Brooks/Cole Publishing Company
Pacific Grove, California

I(T)P ™
The trademark ITP is used under license.

 A CLAIREMONT BOOK

Brooks/Cole Publishing Company
A Division of Wadsworth, Inc.

Printed in the United States of America

10   9   8   7   6   5   4   3

Library of Congress Cataloging-in-Publication Data

Corey, Gerald.
    Theory and practice of group counseling / Gerald Corey. — 4th ed.
        p.   cm.
    Includes bibliographical references and indexes.
    ISBN 0-534-24066-6
    1. Group counseling.   2. Small groups.   I. Title.
BF637.C6C576   1994
158' .35—dc20   94-1915
                                                                    CIP

Sponsoring Editor: *Claire Verduin*
Editorial Associate: *Gay C. Bond*
Production Coordinator: *Fiorella Ljunggren*
Production: *Cecile Joyner, The Cooper Company*
Manuscript Editor: *William Waller*
Interior Design: *E. Kelly Shoemaker*
Cover Design and Illustration: *Lisa Thompson*
Typesetting: *Kachina Typesetting, Inc.*
Cover Printing: *Color Dot Graphics, Inc.*
Printing and Binding: *R. R. Donnelley & Sons Company,
Crawfordsville Manufacturing Division*

To the special groups in my life:

◆ *My family group*

◆ *My group of friends*

◆ *My professional colleagues*

◆ *The human-services student group*

◆ *The members of our weeklong residential groups*

◆ *The group at Brooks/Cole who work on our books*

CONTENTS

◆ PART ONE ◆

BASIC ELEMENTS OF GROUP PROCESS: AN OVERVIEW 1

CHAPTER ONE
Introduction to Group Work   **3**

The Increasing Use of Groups   3
About This Book   5
Overview of the Counseling Group   6
Other Types of Groups   10
Group Counseling in a Multicultural Context   15

CHAPTER TWO
Ethical and Professional Issues in Group Practice   **26**

The Rights of Group Participants   26
The Issue of Psychological Risks in Groups   33
The Ethics of Group Leaders' Actions   35
The Issue of the Group Leader's Competence   43

CHAPTER THREE
Group Leadership   **53**

The Group Leader as a Person   53
Special Problems and Issues for Beginning Group Leaders   57
The Group Leader as a Professional   63

Co-Leading Groups 79
Developing Your Style of Group Leadership 81

CHAPTER FOUR
Early Stages in the Development of a Group **84**

Pregroup Issues: Formation of the Group 85
Stage 1: Initial Stage—Orientation and Exploration 95
Stage 2: Transition Stage—Dealing with Resistance 103
Concluding Comments 109

CHAPTER FIVE
Later Stages in the Development of a Group **110**

Stage 3: Working Stage—Cohesion and Productivity 110
Stage 4: Final Stage—Consolidation and Termination 123
Postgroup Issues: Follow-Up and Evaluation 127
Concluding Comments 130
REFERENCES AND SUGGESTED READINGS FOR PART ONE 131

◆ PART TWO ◆
THEORETICAL APPROACHES
TO GROUP COUNSELING   137

CHAPTER SIX
The Psychoanalytic Approach to Groups **139**

Introduction 139
Key Concepts 142
Basic Techniques 151
Role and Functions of the Group Leader 157
Developmental Stages and Their Implications for Group Work 159
Contemporary Trends in Psychoanalytic Group Theory 171
Evaluation of the Psychoanalytic Model 177
Where to Go from Here 182
RECOMMENDED SUPPLEMENTARY READINGS 182
REFERENCES AND SUGGESTED READINGS 183

CHAPTER SEVEN
Adlerian Group Counseling **186**

Introduction 186

Key Concepts 187
Application of Adlerian Principles to Group Work 193
Phases of the Adlerian Group 194
Role and Functions of the Adlerian Counselor 198
Evaluation of the Adlerian Approach to Groups 199
Where to Go from Here 202
RECOMMENDED SUPPLEMENTARY READINGS 203
REFERENCES AND SUGGESTED READINGS 204

CHAPTER EIGHT
Psychodrama **206**

Introduction 206
Key Concepts 207
Basic Components of the Psychodramatic Method 212
Phases of the Psychodramatic Process 216
Techniques of Psychodrama 222
Evaluation of Psychodrama 228
Where to Go from Here 233
RECOMMENDED SUPPLEMENTARY READINGS 233
REFERENCES AND SUGGESTED READINGS 234

CHAPTER NINE
The Existential Approach to Groups **236**

Introduction 236
Key Concepts 238
Role and Functions of the Group Leader 253
Evaluation of the Existential Approach 254
Where to Go from Here 259
RECOMMENDED SUPPLEMENTARY READINGS 259
REFERENCES AND SUGGESTED READINGS 260

CHAPTER TEN
The Person-Centered Approach to Groups **263**

Introduction 263
Key Concepts 267
Role and Functions of the Group Leader 276
The Person-Centered Group Process 279
Evaluation of the Person-Centered Group Approach 282
Where to Go from Here 288
RECOMMENDED SUPPLEMENTARY READINGS 289
REFERENCES AND SUGGESTED READINGS 290

CHAPTER ELEVEN
Gestalt Therapy   **293**

Introduction   293
Key Concepts   294
Role and Functions of the Group Leader   302
Applications and Techniques   305
Evaluation of the Gestalt Approach   317
Where to Go from Here   322
RECOMMENDED SUPPLEMENTARY READINGS   322
REFERENCES AND SUGGESTED READINGS   323

CHAPTER TWELVE
Transactional Analysis   **325**

Introduction   325
Key Concepts   327
Role and Functions of the Group Leader   336
Therapeutic Procedures and Techniques   336
Evaluation of Transactional Analysis   339
Where to Go from Here   342
RECOMMENDED SUPPLEMENTARY READINGS   343
REFERENCES AND SUGGESTED READINGS   343

CHAPTER THIRTEEN
Behavioral Group Therapy   **345**

Introduction   345
Key Concepts   346
Role and Functions of the Group Leader   349
Stages of a Behavior-Therapy Group   351
Applications and Techniques   358
Evaluation of Behavioral Group Therapy   370
Where to Go from Here   377
RECOMMENDED SUPPLEMENTARY READINGS   377
REFERENCES AND SUGGESTED READINGS   378

CHAPTER FOURTEEN
Rational Emotive Behavior Therapy in Groups   **381**

Introduction   381
Key Concepts   382
Suitability of REBT for Groups   386
Role and Functions of the Group Leader   389

Therapeutic Techniques and Procedures   390
Evaluation of Rational Emotive Behavior Therapy   398
Where to Go from Here   403
RECOMMENDED SUPPLEMENTARY READINGS   405
REFERENCES AND SUGGESTED READINGS   405

CHAPTER FIFTEEN
Reality Therapy in Groups   **409**

Introduction   409
Key Concepts   410
Role and Functions of the Group Leader   413
The Practice of Reality Therapy in Groups   415
Evaluation of Reality Therapy   429
Where to Go from Here   435
RECOMMENDED SUPPLEMENTARY READINGS   436
REFERENCES AND SUGGESTED READINGS   437

◆ PART THREE ◆

APPLICATION AND INTEGRATION   439

CHAPTER SIXTEEN
Illustration of a Group in Action: Various Perspectives   **441**

The Model Group   441
The Emerging Themes   442
Theme: Clarifying Personal Goals   442
Theme: Creating and Maintaining Trust   445
Theme: Dealing with Fears and Resistances   447
Theme: Coping with Loneliness and Isolation   449
Theme: Resolving Dependence/Independence Conflicts   451
Theme: Overcoming the Fear of Intimacy   453
Theme: Dealing with Depression   455
Theme: Searching for Meaning in Life   458
Theme: Challenging and Clarifying Values   461
Theme: Dealing with the Termination of the Group   464

CHAPTER SEVENTEEN
Comparisons, Contrasts, and Integration   **469**

The Goals of Group Counseling: Various Perspectives   470
Role and Functions of the Group Leader: Various Perspectives   470

Degree of Structuring and Division of Responsibility:
Various Perspectives   472
The Use of Techniques: Various Perspectives   474
Group Work in a Multicultural Context: Various Perspectives   475
Applications of the Integrated Eclectic Model   476
Summary and Review Charts   485

NAME INDEX   495
SUBJECT INDEX   498

PREFACE

Group counseling is an increasingly popular form of therapeutic intervention in a variety of settings. Although many textbooks deal with groups, very few of them present an overview of various theoretical models and describe how these models apply to group counseling. This book outlines the basic elements of group process, deals with ethical and professional issues special to group work, and presents an overview of the key concepts and techniques of ten approaches to group counseling. The book also attempts an integration of these approaches and encourages students to develop a framework that leads to their own synthesis.

Theory and Practice of Group Counseling is written in a clear and simple style, so that students will have no difficulty understanding the theoretical concepts and their relationship to group practice. Of course, many readers will have taken a course in counseling theories before their group-counseling course, and that background will be useful in understanding and applying the material in this book.

This updated fourth edition emphasizes the *practical applications* of the theoretical models to group work. Its focus is on helping readers develop their own syntheses of various aspects of these approaches. It also has two detailed chapters on the stages of a group's development, providing a guide for leaders in the practice of counseling.

Part One presents an overview of the various types of groups and discusses some general principles that can be applied in working with the reality of cultural diversity in groups. It also covers ethical and professional issues in group work; the stages in the evolution of a group, from its formation to its termination and follow-up; and some basic issues in group membership and group leadership. In this new edition, the sections dealing with group counseling in a multicultural context have undergone considerable updating. There is new material on perspectives on multiculturalism, on the need for a multicultural focus in group work, on the challenges of a multicultural perspective, and on general guidelines for group practitioners serving multicultural populations. Also, the sections covering ethical issues in multicultural group counseling and the skills required for becoming an effective multicultural group counselor have been considerably expanded. The topic of ethical and professional issues in group practice has been rewritten to reflect the revisions of the ethical guidelines for group counselors and the professional standards for training of group workers, both developed by the Association for Specialists in Group Work (ASGW). The coverage of the stages of the development of a group has been revised by condensing and reorganizing some material. Finally, the references and suggested readings for Part One have been updated and expanded.

Part Two examines ten theoretical approaches to group counseling. In this fourth edition, some of the chapters have been largely rewritten to reflect recent trends, whereas other chapters have undergone only minor revisions. The chapters that have been extensively revised are those on Adlerian group counseling, psychodrama, the existential approach to groups, behavioral group therapy, rational emotive behavior therapy, and reality therapy. These revisions were based on the recommendations of expert reviewers, who provided suggestions for updating the discussions of the various theories with regard to current trends, new studies, and recent developments in the practice of the approach.

The chapters in Part Two follow a common organizational pattern, so that students can easily compare and contrast the various models. A typical chapter introduces the rationale for the model and its unique characteristics; discusses the model's key concepts and their implications for group process, as well as the model's basic procedures and techniques; defines the role and functions of the group leader; and, when applicable, describes the stages of development of that particular group process. Near the end of each of these theory chapters is an updated evaluation section, which is primarily devoted to my personal assessment of the approach under discussion. These evaluation sections have been largely rewritten, expanded, and reorganized, using the following format in each chapter: contributions and strengths of the approach, limitations, and applications with multicultural populations. This new organization makes comparing the theories easier. Also, the discussions of the multicultural applications of each theory have been rewritten to reflect recent trends. The necessity for flexibility and a willingness to adapt techniques to fit the client's cultural background is emphasized in each chapter. Students are given recommendations regarding where to look for further training in each of the theoretical approaches. Updated annotated lists of reading suggestions and extensive references at the end of these chapters are offered to stimulate students to expand on the material and broaden their learning through further reading.

In the two chapters in Part Three, I have applied the ten models to a group in action in order to illustrate how practitioners of different orientations would view a particular group and how they might deal with certain typical themes that emerge in groups. These illustrative samples of group work are intended to make the theoretical perspectives come alive and to provide some flavor of the differences and similarities among the approaches. The final chapter compares and contrasts the various group approaches with respect to the goals of group counseling, the role and functions of the group leader, the degree of structuring and division of responsibility in groups, the use of techniques, and the contributions of the various approaches to group work in a multicultural society. The chapter concludes with a description of an "integrated eclectic model of group counseling," which combines concepts and techniques from all the approaches that have been examined and which should help students attempt their own personal integration. The model I present integrates "thinking," "feeling," and "doing" perspectives, with varying emphases at each stage of a group's development. My purpose is to show on which aspects of each theory I draw at the various stages of the group, as well as to offer a basis for blending what may look like diverse approaches to the practice of group work. Readers are given some guidance in thinking about ways to develop their own synthesis of the various group approaches. For the purpose of getting a general overview of basic issues and of comparisons among the ten theories, I recommend that students read Part Three (Chapters 16 and 17) early in the course as a way to get a general overview of the approaches. Of course, these two chapters will be most important as tools for integrating and synthesizing concepts after readers have studied the contemporary approaches in Part Two. The revisions in Part Three are relatively minor.

This book is for graduate or undergraduate students in any field involving human services. It is especially suitable for students enrolled in any of the courses under the general designation of "Theory and Practice of Group Counseling." The book is also for practitioners who are involved in group work or for students and trainees who are interested in leading various types of groups. Those who may find this book useful are psychiatric nurses, ministers, social workers, psychologists, marriage and family counselors, rehabilitation counselors, community-agency counselors, school counselors, and mental-health professionals who lead groups as a part of their work.

A fourth edition of the *Student Manual for Theory and Practice of Group Counseling* is available to help students gain maximum benefit from this book and actually experience group process and techniques. The manual includes questions for reflection and discussion, suggested activities for the whole class and for small groups, ideas for supervised training groups, summary charts, self-inventories, study guides, comprehension checks and quizzes, self-tests, group techniques, and examples of cases with open-ended alternatives for group-counseling practice. The manual has also been updated and includes new supplementary materials for the ten theories. An *Instructor's Resource Manual* is also available; it has been revised to reflect the changes in both the textbook and the student manual.

Acknowledgments

Many of the revisions that have become a part of this textbook since its original edition in 1981 have come about in the context of discussions with students, colleagues, and professors who use the book. Those students and professionals whom I teach continue to teach me in return, and most of my ideas are stimulated by the interactions with them. The supportive challenge of my friends and colleagues (with whom I offer classes and workshops and with whom I co-lead groups) continues to keep my learning fresh and provides me with encouragement to keep practicing, teaching, and writing. These friends and colleagues are Patrick Callanan, Mary Moline, J. Michael Russell, Veronika Tracy, and George Williams, all of whom teach at California State University at Fullerton; I especially want to recognize the influence on my life and my books of my wife and colleague, Marianne Schneider Corey, with whom I regularly work professionally. Her critique and feedback have been especially valuable in preparing these revisions, and many of the ideas in the book are the product of our many hours of discussions about group work.

The comments of those who provided reviews either before or after the manuscript was revised have been most helpful in shaping up the final product. Those who reviewed the entire manuscript of the fourth edition and offered both supportive and critical feedback are Susan J. Ezell, Marymount University; Penina Frankel, National-Louis University; Barbara Herlihy, University of Houston–Clear Lake; Joseph R. Morris, Western Michigan University; and David G. Zimpfer, Kent State University.

The following people reviewed the sections dealing with multicultural issues and provided critical comments and useful suggestions for ways to incorporate the role of cultural diversity in the practice of group counseling: Victoria D. Coleman, Purdue University; Farah A. Ibrahim, University of Connecticut; Frederick T. L. Leong, The Ohio State University; Don C. Locke, University of North Carolina at Asheville; Noreen Mokuau, University of Hawaii; Zehra Mooman, undergraduate student in human services, California State University, Fullerton; Paul B. Pedersen, Syracuse University; Ronnie Priest, Memphis State University; Derald Wing Sue, California State University, Hayward; Sandra Wathen, doctoral student in counseling, Indiana University, Southeast; and Julia R. J. Yang, California State University, Fresno.

I value the detailed commentaries I received from single-chapter reviewers. Many people contributed by sharing their expertise in certain areas. I thank the following for their assistance in updating the various theory chapters:

- ◆ Chapter 6: William Blau, California School of Professional Psychology at Los Angeles; and J. Michael Russell, California State University, Fullerton
- ◆ Chapter 7: James Bitter, California State University, Fullerton
- ◆ Chapter 8: Adam Blatner, University of Louisville
- ◆ Chapter 9: J. Michael Russell, California State University, Fullerton; Emmy van Deurzen-Smith, Regent's College, London
- ◆ Chapter 10: David J. Cain, founder of the Person-Centered Association, Carlsbad, California
- ◆ Chapter 13: Arnold A. Lazarus, Rutgers University; and Sheldon Rose, University of Wisconsin–Madison

◆ Chapter 14: Albert Ellis, President of the Institute for Rational-Emotive Therapy, New York
◆ Chapter 15: Robert E. Wubbolding, Xavier University.

This book is the result of a team effort, which includes the combined talents of several people in the Brooks/Cole family. I appreciate the opportunity to work with Claire Verduin, publisher in counseling and psychology, who continues to provide a balance between challenge and support; with Gay Bond, editorial associate, who has always been most efficient and helpful in getting reviewers' input; with Fiorella Ljunggren, production services manager, who oversees the production of our books; with William Waller, the manuscript editor, who gives careful attention to making sure that our books have a concise and readable quality; and with Cecile Joyner, The Cooper Company, who carried out the production of the book with skill and efficiency. I also appreciate the careful work that Glennda Gilmour did in preparing the index. Their talents, efforts, dedication, and extra time certainly have contributed to the quality of this text. With the professional assistance of these people, the ongoing task of revising this book continues to bring more joy than pain.

Gerald Corey

◆ PART ONE ◆

BASIC ELEMENTS
OF GROUP PROCESS:
AN OVERVIEW

CHAPTER ONE
Introduction to Group Work

CHAPTER TWO
Ethical and Professional Issues in Group Practice

CHAPTER THREE
Group Leadership

CHAPTER FOUR
Early Stages in the Development of a Group

CHAPTER FIVE
Later Stages in the Development of a Group

**REFERENCES AND SUGGESTED READINGS
FOR PART ONE**

◆ **Chapter One** ◆

Introduction to Group Work

Today more than ever, mental-health practitioners are being challenged to develop new strategies for both preventing and treating psychological problems. Although there is still a place in a community agency for individual counseling, limiting the delivery of services to this model is no longer practical, especially in these tight financial times. From my perspective, group counseling offers real promise in meeting this challenge. Not only do groups let practitioners work with more clients, but the group process also has unique learning advantages. Group counseling may well be the treatment of choice for many populations. If group work is to be effective, however, practitioners need a theoretical grounding and will have to find ways to use these theories creatively in practice.

The Increasing Use of Groups

As my colleagues and I conduct workshops around the United States, we are finding a surge of interest in group work. Professional counselors are creating an increasing variety of groups to fit the special needs of a diverse clientele. In fact, the types of groups that can be designed are limited only by one's imagination. This expanded interest underscores the need for broad education and training in both the theory and the practice of group counseling. This book attempts to provide you with a fundamental base of knowledge applicable to the many kinds of groups you will be leading.

Groups can be used for either therapeutic or educational purposes or for a combination of the two. Some groups deal primarily with helping people make fundamental changes in their ways of thinking, feeling, and behaving. Other groups, with an educational focus, teach members specific coping skills. This chapter provides a brief overview of various types of groups and the differences among them.

You will be expected in the human-services field to be prepared to use group approaches with a variety of clients for a variety of purposes. In a psychiatric hospital, for example, you may be asked to design and lead groups for patients with various problems, for those who are about to leave the hospital and reenter the community, or for patients' families. Insight groups, remotivation groups, assertion-training groups, bereavement groups, and recreational/vocational-therapy groups are commonly found in these hospitals.

If you work in a community mental-health center, a college counseling center, or a day-treatment clinic, you will be expected to provide therapeutic services in a wide range of group settings. Your client population will most likely be diverse with respect to age, problems, socioeconomic status, level of education, race or ethnicity, and cultural background. Community agencies are making increased use of groups, and it is not uncommon to find groups for women, consciousness-raising groups for men, groups for children of alcoholics, support groups, parent-education groups, groups for cancer patients, eating-disorders groups, groups for people in crisis, groups for senior citizens, groups for people who are HIV-positive, AIDS support groups, and groups aimed at reducing substance abuse. The theoretical approach may be based primarily on a single system, such as reality therapy or one of the many forms of behavior therapy done in a group setting. Increasingly, however, practitioners are becoming more eclectic as they draw techniques from various approaches.

Special groups in schools are designed to deal with students' educational, vocational, personal, or social problems. If you work in a school, you may be asked to form a test-anxiety-reduction group, a career-exploration group, a self-esteem group, a group for children of divorce, a group of acting-out children, a group aimed at teaching interpersonal skills, or a self-awareness or personal-growth group. Elementary school counselors are now leading therapeutic groups as well as educational groups. On the high school level, groups are aimed at helping students who are on drug rehabilitation, who have been victims of crime, or who are going through a crisis.

In sum, a group approach has been designed to help people meet almost any need. One of the main reasons for this popularity is that the group approach is frequently more effective than the individual approach. This effectiveness stems from the fact that group members can practice new skills both within the group and in their everyday interactions outside of it. Moreover, members of the group benefit from the feedback and insights of other group members as well as those of the practitioner. Groups also offer many opportunities for modeling. Members learn how to cope with their problems by observing others with similar concerns. There are practical reasons for the popularity of groups, too, such as lower costs and a broader distribution of the available counselors and therapists.

One problem, however, is that even practitioners with an advanced degree in one of the helping professions have often had very little exposure to the theory and techniques of group work. Many of these professionals find themselves thrust into the role of group leader without adequate preparation and training. It is not surprising that some of them panic and don't know where to begin. Although this book is not intended to be an exclusive means of preparing competent group leaders, it is aimed at providing some preparation for coping with the demands of group leadership.

About This Book

Theory and Practice of Group Counseling will introduce you to some basic issues of group leadership and group membership, and it will show you how groups function. The remainder of Part One treats the basic elements of group process and practice that you'll need to know regardless of the types of groups you may lead or the theoretical orientation you may hold. In Chapter 2 you are introduced to important *ethical and professional issues* that you will inevitably encounter as you lead groups. The emphasis is on the rights of group members and the responsibilities of group leaders. Chapter 3 deals with basic concerns of group *leadership,* such as the personal characteristics of effective leaders, the problems they face, the different styles of leadership, and the range of specific skills required for effective leading. In Chapters 4 and 5 you are introduced to the major developmental tasks confronting a group as it goes through its various *stages,* from its formation to its termination, evaluation, and follow-up. The central characteristics of the stages that make up the life history of a group are examined, with special attention paid to the major functions of the group leader at each stage. These chapters also focus on the functions of the members of a group and the possible problems that are associated with each stage in the group's evolution.

Part Two of the text is designed to provide you with a good overview of a variety of theoretical models underlying group counseling, so that you can see the connection between theory and practice. Ten models have been selected to present a balanced perspective. More specifically, the *psychoanalytic* model was selected because it is the theory from which most other approaches have developed. Even though you may find some of the psychoanalytic techniques limited, you can still draw on psychoanalytic concepts in your work. The *Adlerian* approach to groups is included because there appears to be a resurgence of interest in Adlerian concepts and procedures in group counseling. The inclusion of *psychodrama* is based on my belief that the action-oriented methods of role playing can be integrated into most forms of group work. The relationship-oriented therapies—which include the *existential* approach, the *person-centered* approach, and the *Gestalt* approach—are important because they stress the experiencing of feelings and interpersonal relationships in group practice. *Transactional analysis* is included because it provides a cognitive structure for group work and can be integrated into a variety of other group approaches. The behavioral and cognitive-behavioral therapies—*behavior therapy, rational emotive behavior therapy,* and *reality therapy*—stress action methods and behavior change.

To provide a framework that will help you integrate the theoretical models, these ten chapters follow a common outline. They present the key concepts of each theory and their implications for group practice; outline the role and functions of the group leader according to the particular theory; discuss how each theory is applied to group practice; and describe the major techniques employed under each theory. Illustrative examples make the use of these techniques more concrete. Each chapter contains my evaluation of the approach under discussion—an evaluation based on what I consider to be its major strengths and limitations—and a brief description of how these approaches can be applied with diverse groups.

From this text you will learn only some essential aspects of the therapies explored. The book is *not* designed to make you an expert in any one group approach. Its aim is to provide you with an understanding of some of the significant commonalities and differences among these theoretical models. My hope is that you will become sufficiently motivated to select some approaches and learn more about them by doing additional reading (there are suggestions after each chapter in Part Two) and by actually experiencing some of these group approaches as a participant. The ultimate goal is that you achieve your own theoretical perspective and personal style of group leadership.

Part Three focuses on the practical application of the theories and principles covered in Parts One and Two. To make such applications more vivid and concrete, Chapter 16 follows a group in action and discusses how the various therapeutic approaches apply to the case. In this way you'll get some idea of how practitioners with differing orientations work with the same group and with the same themes. This comparative view will also demonstrate some of the techniques of group leadership in action. Chapter 17 is designed to help you pull together the various methods and approaches and look for commonalities and differences among them. This chapter also presents my own version of an integrated eclectic model for group practice.

I invite you to keep an open mind, yet to read critically. By being an active learner and by raising questions, you'll gain the necessary foundation for becoming an effective group leader. A *Manual for Theory and Practice of Group Counseling* has been designed as a supplement to the textbook, so that you can actually experience the techniques that you are studying. Your active involvement in the manual's exercises and activities will make what you read in this textbook come alive for you.

Overview of the Counseling Group

This book focuses on *counseling* groups. There are other types of therapeutic groups, and most of them share some of the goals, procedures, techniques, and processes of counseling groups. They differ, however, with respect to specific aims, the role of the leader, the kind of people in the group, and the emphasis given to issues such as prevention, remediation, treatment, and development. To make these similarities and differences clear, the discussion of group counseling in this section is followed by brief descriptions of group psychotherapy, structured groups, and self-help groups.

Group counseling has preventive as well as remedial aims. Generally, the counseling group has a specific focus, which may be educational, vocational, social, or personal. The group involves an interpersonal process that stresses conscious thoughts, feelings, and behavior. Often counseling groups are problem oriented; their content and focus are determined largely by the members, who are basically well-functioning individuals who don't require extensive personality reconstruction and whose concerns relate to the developmental tasks of the life span. Group counseling tends to be growth oriented in that its focus is on discovering internal resources of strength. The participants may be facing situational crises and temporary conflicts, or they may be trying to change self-defeating behaviors. The group provides the empathy and support necessary to create the atmosphere of trust that leads to the sharing and exploration of these concerns. Group counseling is often carried out in institutional settings, such as schools, university counseling centers, community mental-health clinics, and other human-services agencies.

The group counselor uses verbal and nonverbal techniques as well as structured exercises. Common techniques include reflection (mirroring the verbal and nonverbal messages of a group member), clarification (helping members understand more clearly what they are saying or feeling), role playing, and interpretation (connecting present behaviors with past decisions). Other common techniques used in group counseling are described in more detail in Chapter 3. Basically, the role of the group counselor is to facilitate interaction among the members, help them learn from one another, assist them in establishing personal goals, and encourage them to translate their insights into concrete plans that involve taking action outside of the group. Counselors perform this role largely by teaching the members to focus on the here and now and to identify the concerns they wish to explore in the group.

Goals

Ideally, the members decide for themselves the specific goals of the group experience. Some of the general goals shared by members of counseling groups are these:

- ◆ to learn to trust oneself and others
- ◆ to achieve self-knowledge and develop a sense of one's unique identity
- ◆ to recognize the commonality of the participants' needs and problems and develop a sense of universality
- ◆ to increase self-acceptance, self-confidence, and self-respect in order to achieve a new view of oneself
- ◆ to find alternative ways of dealing with normal developmental issues and of resolving certain conflicts
- ◆ to increase self-direction, autonomy, and responsibility toward oneself and others
- ◆ to become aware of one's choices and to make choices wisely

- ◆ to make specific plans for changing certain behaviors and to commit oneself to follow through with these plans
- ◆ to learn more effective social skills
- ◆ to become more sensitive to the needs and feelings of others
- ◆ to learn how to confront others with care, concern, honesty, and directness
- ◆ to move away from merely meeting others' expectations and to learn to live by one's own expectations
- ◆ to clarify one's values and decide whether and how to modify them

Advantages

Group counseling has a number of advantages as a vehicle for helping people make changes in their attitudes, beliefs about themselves and others, feelings, and behaviors. One advantage is that participants can explore their styles of relating with others and learn more effective social skills. Another is that members can discuss their perceptions of one another and receive valuable feedback on how they are being perceived in the group.

In many ways the counseling group provides a re-creation of the participants' everyday world, especially if the membership is diverse with respect to age, interests, background, socioeconomic status, and type of problem. As a microcosm of society the group provides a sample of reality, for members' struggles and conflicts in the group are no different from those they experience outside of it. The diversity that characterizes most groups also results in unusually rich feedback for the participants, who can see themselves through the eyes of a wide range of people.

The group offers understanding and support, which foster the members' willingness to explore the problems they have brought with them to the group. The participants achieve a sense of belonging, and through the cohesion that develops they learn ways of being intimate, of caring, and of challenging. In this supportive atmosphere members can experiment with alternative behaviors. They can practice these behaviors in the group, where they receive encouragement as well as suggestions on how to apply what they are learning in the outside world.

Ultimately, it is up to the members themselves to decide what changes they want to make. They can compare the perceptions they have of themselves with the perceptions others have of them and then decide what to do with this information. In essence, the members get a clearer glimpse of the kind of person they would like to become, and they come to understand what is preventing them from becoming that person.

Value for Specific Populations

Group counseling can be designed to meet the needs of specific populations such as children, adolescents, college students, or the elderly. Examples of these counseling groups are described in the book *Groups: Process and Practice* (M. Corey & Corey, 1992), which offers suggestions on how to set up these groups and on what techniques to use for dealing with the unique problems of each of them. Following is a brief discussion of the value of counseling groups for several specific populations.

COUNSELING GROUPS FOR CHILDREN. Counseling groups for children can serve preventive or remedial purposes. In schools, group counseling is often suggested for children who display behaviors or attributes such as excessive fighting, inability to get along with peers, violent outbursts, chronic tiredness, lack of supervision at home, and neglected appearance. Small groups can provide children with the opportunity to express their feelings about these and related problems. Identifying children who are developing serious emotional and behavioral problems is extremely important. If these children can receive psychological assistance at an early age, they stand a better chance of coping effectively with the developmental tasks they must face later in life.

COUNSELING GROUPS FOR ADOLESCENTS. The adolescent years can be extremely lonely ones, and it is not unusual for an adolescent to feel that no one is there to help. Adolescence is also a time of deep concerns and key decisions that can affect the course of one's life. Dependence/independence struggles, acceptance/rejection conflicts, identity crises, the search for security, pressures to conform, and the need for approval are all part of this period. Many adolescents are pressured to perform and succeed, and they frequently experience severe stress in meeting these external expectations.

Group counseling is especially suited for adolescents because it gives them a place to express conflicting feelings, explore self-doubts, and come to the realization that they share these concerns with their peers. A group allows adolescents to openly question their values and to modify those that need to be changed. In the group, adolescents can learn to communicate with their peers, can benefit from the modeling provided by the leader, and can safely experiment with reality and test their limits. Another, unique value of group counseling for adolescents is that it offers them a chance to be instrumental in one another's growth. Because of the opportunities for interaction available in the group situation, the participants can express their concerns and be heard, and they can help one another on the road toward self-understanding and self-acceptance.

COUNSELING GROUPS FOR COLLEGE STUDENTS. Counseling groups are a valuable vehicle for meeting the developmental needs of the many students who feel that their college or university is preoccupied with their intellectual development to the exclusion of their emotional and social growth. It was during the years I spent working in the counseling centers at two universities that I became aware of the need for groups on campus. At those universities the existing groups were designed for the relatively healthy students who were experiencing developmental crises. The main purpose of these groups was to offer the participants an opportunity for growth and a situation in which they could deal with issues concerning career decisions, male/female relationships, identity problems, educational plans, isolation feelings on an impersonal campus, and other concerns related to becoming an autonomous person.

Many university and college counseling centers now offer a wide range of structured groups to meet the diverse needs of the students, a few of which are assertion groups, consciousness-raising groups for women and men, groups for minorities, groups for the physically handicapped, stress-reduction groups, groups for middle-aged returning students who are considering career and lifestyle changes, and test-anxiety-reduction groups. These structured groups will be examined briefly in the next section.

COUNSELING GROUPS FOR THE ELDERLY.　Counseling groups can be valuable for the elderly in many of the same ways that they are of value to adolescents. As people grow older, they often experience isolation, and many of them, seeing no hope of meaning—let alone excitement—in their future, may resign themselves to a useless life. Like adolescents, the elderly often feel unproductive, unneeded, and unwanted. Another problem is that many older people accept myths about aging, which then become self-fulfilling prophecies. An example is the misconception that old people can't change or that once they retire, they will be doomed to depression. Counseling groups can do a lot to help older people challenge these myths and deal with the developmental tasks that they, like any other age group, must face in such a way that they can retain their integrity and self-respect. The group situation can assist people in breaking out of their isolation and offer the elderly the encouragement necessary to find meaning in their lives so that they can live fully and not merely exist.

Other Types of Groups

Group Psychotherapy

A major difference between group *therapy* and group *counseling* lies in their goals. Whereas counseling groups focus on growth, development, enhancement, prevention, self-awareness, and releasing blocks to growth, therapy groups typically focus on remediation, treatment, and personality reconstruction. Group psychotherapy is a process of reeducation that includes both conscious and unconscious awareness and both the present and the past. Some therapy groups are primarily designed to correct emotional and behavioral disorders that impede one's functioning. The goal may be a minor or a major transformation of personality structure, depending on the theoretical orientation of the group therapist. Because of this goal, therapy groups tend to be of relatively long duration. The people who make up the group may be suffering from severe emotional problems, deep neurotic conflicts, or psychotic states, and some may exhibit socially deviant behavior. Therefore, many of these individuals are in need of remedial treatment rather than developmental and preventive work.

Group therapists are typically clinical or counseling psychologists, psychiatrists, and clinical social workers. They use a wide range of verbal modalities (which group counselors also use), and some employ techniques to induce regression to earlier experiences, to tap unconscious dynamics, and to help members reexperience traumatic situations so that catharsis can occur. As these experiences are relived in the group, members become aware of and gain insight into past decisions that interfere with current functioning. The group therapist assists members in developing a corrective emotional experience and in making new decisions about the world, others, and themselves. Working through unfinished business from the past that has roots in the unconscious is a primary characteristic of group therapy. This focus on past material, unconscious dynamics, personality reconstruction, and development of new patterns of behavior based on insight also accounts for the longer duration of group therapy.

Structured Groups

Structured groups, or groups characterized by some central theme, seem to be gaining in popularity. When my colleagues and I conduct group-process workshops, the practitioners we meet are often very creative in designing short-term groups that deal with a specific theme or particular population. These group workers perceive needs in the community and address these needs by creating groups. Such groups serve a number of purposes: imparting information, sharing common experiences, teaching people how to solve problems, offering support, and helping people learn how to create their own support systems outside of the group setting.

It is clear that structured groups—as opposed to counseling groups or ongoing personal-growth groups—are finding a place in many settings. They appear to be increasingly used in community agencies and in schools. Many college and university counseling centers offer a variety of special groups for particular populations in addition to their unstructured personal-growth groups and counseling groups. For example, the structured groups offered by the Counseling-Psychological Services Center at the University of Texas at Austin include the following: Mid-Life Transitions: Values and Life Decisions; Gaining Control of Your Lifestyle and "Work-style"; Stress Management; Depression-Management Training; Managing Relationships/Ending Relationships; Strategies for Building Self-Confidence for Graduate Women; Learning to Cope with Speech Anxiety; Developing Assertive Behavior; Women in Transition: Shifting Gears; Perfectionism: The Double-Edged Sword; The Aftermath of Suicide: A Special Kind of Grief; Jealousy: Taming the Green-Eyed Monster; and Students with an Alcoholic Parent.

For another example, consider the group-counseling programs available for students at Colorado State University. There are both therapy groups for adult children of alcoholics and also education and support groups for these clients. This counseling center also offers an anxiety-management group, an eating-disorders group, a family-issues group, a group for students of non-traditional age, a relationship-concerns group, a self-esteem group, a group for adult female survivors of childhood sexual abuse, and a personal-identity group for women.

The above list gives you some idea of the scope of topics for structured groups. These groups help people develop specific skills, understand certain themes, or go through difficult life transitions. Although the topics obviously vary according to the interests of the group leader and the clientele, such groups have a common denominator of providing members with increased awareness of some life problem and tools to better cope with it. Typically, the sessions are two hours each week, and the groups tend to be relatively short term. They may last only four or five weeks, up to a maximum of one semester.

Members are generally asked to complete a questionnaire at the beginning of the group that pertains to how well they are coping with the particular area of concern. Structured exercises and homework assignments are typically introduced as ways of teaching new skills to group members. Another questionnaire is often used at the final session to assess the members' progress. A contract is frequently drawn up as a way of helping members pinpoint specific goals that will guide their participation in the group and stimulate them to practice new skills outside of the group.

Many structured groups are based on a learning-theory model and use behavioral procedures. Chapter 13 provides detailed descriptions of such groups, including social-skills-training and assertiveness-training groups, stress-management groups, self-directed groups, and multimodal-therapy groups.

Self-Help Groups

The last 20 years have seen a burgeoning of self-help groups, which allow people with a common problem or life predicament to create a support system that protects them from psychological stress and gives them the incentive to begin changing their lives. These groups serve a critical need for certain populations that is not met by professional mental-health workers. The members share their experiences, provide one another with emotional and social support, learn from one another, offer suggestions for new members, and provide some direction for people who do not see any hope for their future. Typically, self-help groups meet in a community setting such as a school or a church. The core of the self-help process is members helping themselves by assuming personal responsibility and taking action to resolve their concern, rather than placing the blame for the problem or the responsibility for solving it on someone else (Borkman, 1991).

The two terms *self-help group* and *support group* are often used interchangeably. *Self-help groups* tend to emphasize their autonomy and internal group resources (Katz, 1981). In many self-help groups the original intent was to use the leader as a model to demonstrate the universality of the need for members to help themselves. *Support groups,* in contrast, are often begun by a professional helping organization or individual. To expedite the description, categorization, and comparison of self-help groups,

Schubert and Borkman (1991) have created a typology that provides for a recognition of similarities and differences in the organizational structure of these groups. They describe the following ten self-help groups:

1. On the Street: a group for persons affected by imprisonment
2. Families Adopting Children Everywhere (FACE): a group aimed at those who wish to adopt or have adopted children from other countries
3. Mending Hearts: a group for individuals before and after heart surgery
4. Taking Off Pounds Sensibly (TOPS): a group geared for people concerned about weight loss or weight control
5. Seasons: a group for people who have lost a loved one to suicide
6. Alliance for the Mentally Ill (AMI): a group for those affected by mental illness that stresses educating the public
7. New Beginnings: a group for people who are separated or divorced from a spouse or lover
8. Reach to Recovery: a group for women with breast cancer
9. Alcoholics Anonymous (AA): a group for people struggling with abuse of alcohol
10. Parent Educational Advocacy Training Center: a group for parents of children with special needs

This list is merely a sample of the range of groups designed for sharing a common distressing problem.

ATTITUDES TOWARD SELF-HELP GROUPS. What are the attitudes of mental-health professionals and future professionals toward self-help groups? Riordan and Beggs (1987) reviewed the growth of self-help groups and made recommendations on ways in which counselors could use these groups as adjuncts to their practices. From their review of the literature, it is clear that self-help groups are now playing a significant role in this regard. According to Meissen, Mason, and Gleason (1991), given the reductions in traditional mental-health services coupled with the growth of the consumer movement, it is likely that self-help groups could become as important to the mental-health system as AA and related groups have become to the substance-abuse field.

Meissen and his colleagues (1991) examined the attitudes toward self-help groups of graduate students in social work and clinical psychology. They found that almost 40% of the students had had personal experience with self-help groups. Those with such experience expressed more positive attitudes about these groups than those without it. Some research supports the conclusion that future professionals will be more amenable to collaborating with self-help groups. Meissen and his colleagues maintain that professional training regarding self-help is a priority. They add that safeguards will be important to prevent unintentional professional influence on self-help groups. In their view, students should be taught respect for the self-help ethos and for the autonomy and independence of groups, as well as the appropriate professional roles.

DIFFERENCES BETWEEN THE SELF-HELP GROUP AND THE THERAPY GROUP. Self-help groups and therapy groups have some common denominators. Lakin (1985) notes that both place emphasis on expressing and sharing emotions. This emphasis is grounded in the assumption that people suffer from unexpressed feelings and thoughts and that maladaptive attitudes and behaviors result from these bottled-up feelings. Both types of groups encourage support, stress the value of affiliation, and aim for behavioral change.

Despite these commonalities between self-help and therapy groups, there are some critical differences (Riordan & Beggs, 1988). One basic difference involves the goals of the group. As mentioned, self-help groups have as their central issue a single topic such as addiction, cancer, or obesity, whereas therapy groups have more global goals such as improving general mental health or one's interpersonal functioning (Riordan & Beggs, 1987). Moreover, self-help groups emphasize inspiration, persuasion, and support, whereas therapy groups employ self-understanding, reinforcement, and member feedback (Lakin, 1985).

Another difference between self-help groups and therapy groups involves the nature of the problems that are explored in the groups. In the study conducted by Meissen and his associates (1991), graduate students in clinical psychology and social work perceived the following as appropriate problems for self-help groups: addictions, alcohol dependency, parenting, weight control, and bereavement. Almost half of these students thought that mental illness and serious problems related to mental health were inappropriate for self-help groups. To a lesser degree, chronic depression and issues related to suicide were also seen as inappropriate topics.

A further difference between the two types of groups involves the kind of leadership employed. Self-help groups are generally led by individuals who are struggling with the same issues as the members of the group. In most self-help groups the leadership emerges rather than being designated. In one study, participants were asked to identify appropriate professional roles when practitioners work with self-help groups (Meissen et al., 1991). These roles were listed: consultant, facilitator, speaker, researcher, source of members, leader, member, and group therapist. There are differences of opinion regarding how and to what degree professionals should be involved in self-help groups.

With counseling groups and therapy groups, as we have seen, a basic assumption is that the group represents a *social microcosm*. These groups attempt to reflect in some ways all of the dimensions of the members' real social environment. The therapeutic factor that accounts for change in the participants is the group process as a sample of the interpersonal conflicts that members confront in their daily lives. In contrast, self-help groups are not a social microcosm. The interactions of members within the group are not viewed as the primary catalyst for change. Instead, attention is placed on providing an accepting and supportive climate in the group itself. The group becomes a means of helping people modify their beliefs, attitudes, and feelings about themselves. Self-help groups stress a common identity based on a common life situation to a far greater extent than do most other groups.

Another difference between self-help groups and therapy groups deals with the issue of politics. Self-help groups have become increasingly political, as evidenced by particular groups organized within the women's movement. For example, many self-esteem groups and consciousness-raising groups for women are aimed at both personal and sociopolitical change (Enns, 1992). Other populations, such as ethnic and racial minorities and gays and lesbians, who feel that they are subjected to social and political oppressions, are also using groups in this way (Lakin, 1985). Thus, self-help groups focus on the external causes of their members' problems and on developing strategies to deal with environmental barriers. Therapy groups tend to focus on ways in which the individual can change even if certain environmental factors do not change.

Riordan and Beggs (1987, 1988) maintain that practitioners must be aware of the differences between self-help and therapy groups so they can assess the potential benefits of each type for different clients. They suggest that although self-help groups have been a source of valuable help for thousands of people, they are not appropriate for everyone. Thus, in suggesting such a group, it is important to explore the client's expectations and the possible benefits and risks.

THE FUTURE OF SELF-HELP GROUPS. People seem to have an increasing interest in banding together to find ways of helping themselves. Although professionally led counseling and therapy groups still serve a vital role, perhaps it is a healthy sign that people are seeking other methods. Many self-help groups serve a unique function, one that cannot always be met in professionally led counseling and psychotherapy groups. The challenge is to train future professionals how best to collaborate with self-help groups.

In addition to recognizing the need to train future helping professionals in self-help approaches, practitioners are showing an increased interest in research in the self-help field. In addressing the advances in research on self-help groups, Borkman (1991) writes that research tools have become more sophisticated, thus yielding more valuable information. Borkman also points out that an increasing number of graduate students are investigating self-help groups and that research on these groups is becoming institutionalized. Clearly, both self-help groups and therapy groups have a distinct contribution to make in our society.

Group Counseling in a Multicultural Context

This book assumes that for group counseling to be effective, it must take into consideration the cultural backgrounds of both the members and the leader. Pluralism is an ideal state in which the reality of diversity is recognized, respected, and encouraged. In this sense, multicultural group work involves strategies that cultivate understanding and appreciation of diversity in such areas as culture, ethnicity, race, gender, class, religion, and lifestyle. The group, with its varied worldviews of both the group leader and the members, is a natural place to acknowledge and promote pluralism.

Group counselors, in addition to understanding the range of clients' cultural similarities and differences, must be willing and able to challenge the traditional view of a group's structure, goals, techniques, and practices. A fundamental step for group counselors is reexamining the underlying assumptions of all the major theories in light of their appropriateness in a multicultural context. It is likely that culturally skilled group counselors will need to revise their theories and techniques if they hope to better serve individuals from diverse cultural backgrounds. In Chapters 6–15, I identify some of the major strengths and limitations of the ten major theories from a multicultural perspective. The following pages deal with general principles of effective multicultural group counseling.

Multiculturalism: Some Definitions and Implications

In *multicultural counseling* two or more people with different ways of perceiving their social environment attempt to work together in a helping relationship (Pedersen, 1994). The term *multicultural* refers to the complexity of culture as it pertains to delivery of services. Other terms that are used in discussing group practice in a multicultural context include race, ethnicity, minority, and culture. Pedersen defines these terms as follows: *Race* pertains to a shared genetic history or physical characteristics. *Ethnicity* involves a shared sociocultural heritage of religion, history, or common ancestry. *Culture,* broadly defined, includes race, ethnicity, affectional orientation, class, religion, sex, and age. *Minority* identifies a group that has received differential and unequal treatment because of collective discrimination. Multicultural counseling focuses on understanding not only racial and ethnic minority groups (African Americans, Asian Americans, Hispanics, Native Americans, and white ethnics) but also women, gay men and lesbians, the handicapped, the elderly, and other special-needs populations.

According to Pedersen (1991), the multicultural perspective seeks to provide a conceptual framework that both recognizes the complex diversity of a pluralistic society and suggests bridges of shared concern that link all people, regardless of their differences. This perspective looks both at the unique dimensions of a person and at how this person shares themes with those who are different. Such a perspective respects the needs and strengths of diverse client populations, and it recognizes the experiences of these clients. Mere knowledge of certain cultural groups is not enough; it is important to understand the variability within groups. Each individual must be seen against the backdrop of his or her cultural group, the degree to which he or she has become acculturated, and the level of development of racial identity.

Pedersen (1994) emphasizes the importance of understanding both group and individual differences in making accurate interpretations of behavior. Whether practitioners pay attention to cultural variables or ignore them, culture will continue to influence both group members' and group leaders' behavior, and the group process as well. Group counselors who ignore culture will provide less effective services.

Two Perspectives on Multiculturalism

In the multicultural field there are two approaches to understanding and working with the diverse worldviews of client populations: (1) the universal, or transcultural, perspective is grounded on the premise that basic human dimensions are important regardless of culture (Fukuyama, 1990); (2) the focused approach argues for the necessity of gaining an in-depth knowledge of specific cultures (Locke, 1990).

The universal approach to multicultural counseling explores the commonalities of the experiences of people of color and proposes transcultural models for training effective multicultural counselors. Fukuyama (1990) proposes training programs that involve the following:

- an understanding of the concept of culture as a whole as it affects the individual, society, and the helping process
- a broad view of culture that encompasses gender, lifestyle, age, ethnicity, and race
- providing of information on all forms of oppression, such as racism, sexism, and homophobia
- exploring the importance of gender roles
- facilitating the individual's identity development as a member of a culture
- facilitating an understanding of one's own worldview and how it relates to family and one's cultural background
- encouraging loyalty and pride in one's own culture and family ties

According to Fukuyama, overemphasis on the differences that separate one cultural group from another may promote stereotyping. She contends that her students have been able to adapt universal concepts covered in a multicultural counseling course and apply these notions to a variety of counseling situations.

Locke (1990), in contrast, argues for a provincial perspective as a requisite for an adequate philosophy of multicultural counseling. In his challenge of the universal, or broad, approach, he asserts that counselors must gain cultural expertise about specific groups that they are likely to encounter in their practice. This narrow approach rests on three key assumptions:

1. a willingness by counselors to examine their racial beliefs and attitudes as they relate to specific culturally different individuals or groups
2. a willingness to discuss specific racially relevant issues at an institutional level

3. a willingness to view clients both as individuals and as members of a group

The Need for a Multicultural Focus in Group Work

Clients in your groups will bring with them specific values, beliefs, and actions that are influenced by their culture, race or ethnicity, gender, religion, historical experiences with the dominant culture, socioeconomic status, education, political views, lifestyle, and geographic region. D. W. Sue (1992) reminds us that the complexion of the U.S. population is rapidly changing and that counselors will be confronted with making a choice at the crossroads. The road more frequently traveled is that of monoculturalism and ethnocentricism, which offers some comfort and security. The other road is multiculturalism, which recognizes and values diversity. This path provides a picture of this society as a cultural mosaic rather than a melting pot. It offers a basis for helpers to develop new structures, paradigms, policies, and practices that are responsive to all groups in society. The changing demographics of North America make it imperative that counselors assume a proactive stance on cultural diversity. According to Comas-Diaz (1992), these demographic changes will alter the sociological, political, and economic realities of people of color. Pluralism will become the blueprint of North American society. This reality will lead to flexibility and increased choices in psychotherapeutic practice.

It is not possible to apply the assumptions that suit a monocultural society to a multicultural society. Counselors need to take a broad multicultural perspective, for these reasons: because our perceptions of the world are learned within the context of a culture, because people from different cultural backgrounds perceive their world differently, and because counseling requires an accurate and profound understanding of the world of each client (Pedersen, 1991). We are ethically bound to acquire the knowledge and skills necessary to work effectively in multicultural situations (Ibrahim & Arredondo, 1990).

The topic of cultural diversity in group counseling is being given more attention in the psychological literature. For example, the November 1992 special issue of the *Journal for Specialists in Group Work* is entirely devoted to group counseling with multicultural populations. The articles deal with how group workers can be sensitive to diversity in clients and adapt theoretical orientations, techniques, and styles to match clients' worldviews and needs. The challenge of a group is to adapt to the needs and beliefs of each member. The degree to which this challenge is met is the degree to which a group will be effective in helping a diverse range of clients (DeLucia, Coleman, & Jensen-Scott, 1992).

In an article on group counseling with Asian clients, Yu and Gregg (1993) take the position that cultural awareness and sensitivity should be an integral part of any group-counseling experience. They contend that through the 1990s and into the next century, group workers will need to address the unique concerns that clients from diverse backgrounds bring to the group experience.

The Challenges and Rewards of a Multicultural Perspective

The literature dealing with multicultural counseling indicates that ethnic and minority clients underuse mental-health services and social services (Atkinson, Morten, & Sue, 1993; Chu & Sue, 1984; Ho, 1984; Lee, Juan, & Hom, 1984; Leong, 1992; Mokuau, 1985, 1987; Pedersen, 1994; D. W. Sue, 1992). There are a number of reasons for this failure to make full and appropriate use of existing counseling services. One explanation involves the failure of mental-health providers to assess, monitor, and address cultural issues. At times, counselors may be insensitive to cultural realities. In addition, clients' cultural values may inhibit the utilization of services, for in some cultures informal helping processes are used more than professional resources. Some clients hold values that call for them to work out their problems by themselves, and doing so indicates greater maturity than seeking help from others (Ho, 1984). Other explanations for the underuse of services include a lack of knowledge of available services, language difficulties, stigma and shame, geographic or community inaccessibility, and conflicts between a client's value system and the values underlying contemporary Western therapeutic approaches (Mokuau, 1985). Because this pattern of underutilization will not be changed in the short term, it seems important to explore the nature and effectiveness of helping mechanisms utilized by the various cultural groups in North America.

Practitioners writing about multicultural counseling often assert that many counseling approaches fail to meet the complex needs of various ethnic and minority clients because of stereotyped narrow perceptions of those needs. Asian Americans, African Americans, Hispanics, Native Americans, and members of other minority groups leave counseling significantly earlier than do Euro-American clients. This tendency is often caused by cultural barriers such as language difficulties, class-bound values, and culture-bound values that hinder the formation of a good counseling relationship (Atkinson et al., 1993; Mokuau, 1987; Pedersen, 1994; D. W. Sue & Sue, 1990).

If you expect to have diversity within your groups, which is the case in most work settings, it will be important to accept the challenge of modifying your strategies to meet the unique needs of special populations. The American Psychological Association ([APA], 1993), has developed *Guidelines for Providers of Psychological Services to Ethnic, Linguistic, and Culturally Diverse Populations*. These rules underscore the responsibility of counselors to know their clients' cultural values before delivering mental-health services. They stress the importance of having a sociocultural framework from which to consider diverse values, interactional styles, and cultural expectations. An effective multicultural practice requires both knowledge and skills. This issue will be considered in more detail in Chapter 3.

Although it is unrealistic to expect that you will have an in-depth knowledge of all cultural backgrounds, it is feasible for you to have a comprehensive grasp of general principles for working successfully amid cultural diversity. While upholding a belief in your own values, you must avoid assuming a stance of superiority that leads you to impose your values unthinkingly on others. Indeed, some clinicians use differences in values as justification for excluding a range of clients from their practice. If you are able to appreciate cultural differences and do not associate them with superiority or inferiority, diversity can indeed expand your group members' perceptions of problems, increase your psychological resourcefulness, and result in a sense of community.

Pedersen (1994) asserts that adopting a multicultural perspective allows one to think about diversity without polarizing issues into "right" or "wrong." When two people's arguments are based on culturally different assumptions, they can disagree without one being right and the other being wrong. Depending on the cultural perspective from which a problem is considered, there can be several appropriate solutions. Culture is complicated, rather than being simple; it is dynamic, rather than being static. Nevertheless, the tapestry of culture that is woven into the fabric of all helping relationships need not be viewed as a barrier through which you must break. As Pedersen says, multiculturalism can make your job as a helper easier and more fun; it can also improve the quality of your life if you adopt a perspective that cultural differences are positive attributes that add richness to relationships.

TRANSCENDING CULTURAL ENCAPSULATION. Cultural encapsulation, or provincialism, can afflict both group members and the group leader. As group counselors, we have to confront our own distortions as well as those of the members. Culture-specific knowledge about a client's background should not lead counselors to stereotype him or her. Culturally competent group leaders recognize both differences among groups and differences within groups. It is essential that you do not get into the trap of perceiving individuals as simply belonging to a group. Indeed, the differences between individuals within a group are often greater than the differences among the various groups (Pedersen, 1994). Not all Native Americans have the same experiences, nor do all African Americans, Asians, women, the elderly, or people with disabilities. Thus, counselors need to be prepared to deal with the complex differences among individuals from every cultural group. Effective group work from a multicultural perspective involves challenging stereotypes about an individual within a given group and modifying them to fit reality.

Practitioners may encounter resistance from some people of color because they are using traditional white, middle-class values to interpret these clients' experiences. Such culturally encapsulated practitioners are not able to view the world through the eyes of all of their clients. Wrenn (1985) defines the "culturally encapsulated counselor" as one who has substituted stereotypes for the real world, who disregards cultural variations among clients, and who dogmatizes technique-oriented definitions of counseling and therapy. Such individuals, who operate within a monocultural framework, maintain a cocoon by evading reality and depending entirely on their own internalized value assumptions about what is good for society and the individual. These encapsulated people tend to be trapped in one way of thinking, believing that their way is the universal way. They cling to an inflexible structure that resists adaptation to alternative ways of thinking.

Western models need to be adapted to serve the members of certain ethnic groups, especially those clients who live by a different value system. In the Western orientation, for example, there are frequently three core cultural values—freedom, responsibility, and achievement—each of which has implications for the practice of counseling (Sampson, 1988). As Sampson has noted, self-contained individualism helps sustain the core values and institutions that represent North American society today. Freedom, responsibility, and achievement are all assumed to require this individualism for their realization. Freedom, autonomy, and independence are prime values from the perspective of individualism.

Yet many clients from non-Western cultures, members of ethnic minorities, and women from nearly all cultural groups tend to value interdependence more than independence, social consciousness more than individual freedom, and the welfare of the group more than their own welfare. Western psychological thought emphasizes self-sufficiency, independence from family, and self-growth. However, many Asian Americans emphasize the collective good and make plans with the family in mind (Chu & Sue, 1984; Leong, 1992). In Asian cultures, moreover, family roles tend to be highly structured, and "filial piety" exerts a powerful influence; that is, obligations to parents are respected throughout one's life, especially among the male children. The roles of family members are highly interdependent. The family structure is arranged so that conflicts are minimized while harmony is maximized. Traditional Asian values emphasize reserve and formality in most social situations, restraint and inhibition of intense feelings, obedience to authority, and high academic and occupational achievement. The family structure is traditionally patriarchal in that communication and authority flow vertically from top to bottom. The inculcation of guilt and shame are the main techniques used to control the behavior of individuals within a family (D. Sue & Sue, 1993).

These traditional values are shared by other cultural groups. For instance, the values of Latinos emphasize the cultural context. *Familismo* stresses interdependence over independence, affiliation over confrontation, and cooperation over competition. Parents are afforded a great deal of respect, and this respect governs all interpersonal relationships. The role of fate is often a pervasive force governing behavior. Hispanics typically place a high value on spiritual matters and religion (Comas-Diaz, 1990).

If the group experience is largely the product of values that are alien to certain group members, it is easy to see that such members will not embrace the group. Group counselors who practice exclusively with a Western perspective are likely to meet with a considerable amount of resistance from clients with a non-Western worldview. Culturally sensitive group practice implies that leaders are willing to reveal the underlying values of the group process and also to determine whether these values are congruent with the cultural values of the members. Group members can also be encouraged to express their values and needs. The major challenge for group leaders is to determine what techniques are culturally appropriate.

As you study the ten theories explored in Part Two of this book, give careful consideration to the underlying value issues that are likely to have a clear impact on your practice. It is apparent that the direct application of many contemporary models of therapy is inappropriate for some clients. However, certain concepts and techniques drawn from the various therapeutic schools do have cultural relevance. As a group practitioner, you will use a range of concepts and techniques. It is important to develop selection criteria that will enable you to systematically integrate those tools that best meet the needs of diverse client populations. You will also need to assess the particular attributes that your clients bring to you, and you will have to tailor the particular interventions that you make in a group to those attributes. In working with diverse populations, counselors will be challenged to develop eclectic strategies.

ADVANTAGES OF GROUP WORK WITH MULTICULTURAL POPULATIONS. One factor that makes group work valuable is cross-cultural universality. In groups, people learn that they are not alone in their struggles. Everyone experiences psychological pain in life. Regardless of cultural variations, people who seek professional help are concerned with alleviating their suffering. Because of these underlying human commonalities, it is a mistake to fashion highly specialized groups to accommodate every possible cultural mix. Although the multicultural perspective fosters an awareness of differences among people, this focus should not overshadow the universal human themes that unite all people (Fukuyama, 1990). In Chapter 9, on the existential approach, we will consider some of these universal human themes.

SOME LIMITATIONS OF GROUP WORK IN A MULTICULTURAL CONTEXT. Along with the advantages of group counseling with multicultural populations, there are certain disadvantages. Some individuals may be reluctant to disclose personal material or to share family conflicts (Ho, 1984). They may see it as shameful even to have personal problems and all the more shameful to talk about them in front of strangers. In fact, some cultures value relying on members of one's extended family for help. Rather than seeking professional services, these individuals may be more likely to turn to their own support groups. As a group worker, you need to find ways to reach clients who want help but do not know where to find it, or who are reluctant to seek it from a professional. It will be essential to accept the difficulties that clients experience in talking to you about themselves in personal ways, so that the foundation of a therapeutic relationship can be formed.

A related problem in group work with culturally diverse populations pertains to conflicts between members' values and what goes on in a group. In some groups, for example, touching and other physical contact are common. Some cultures do not take physical contact so lightly, however, especially heterosexual contact. Clients may make a distinction between displaying physical affection in private and doing so in public (Chu & Sue, 1984). It is easy to see that some clients would be both offended and intimidated by the spontaneous touching that often occurs in groups.

In Chapters 6–15, some of these limitations of the ten theoretical frameworks are discussed. I would caution against too quickly discounting the potential value of any of these approaches, for I think they all have something of value to offer in working with diverse individuals in a group. What is essential is the willingness of practitioners to examine how well the key concepts of these theories fit with the value systems of the group members. It is also critical that practitioners subscribing to any theoretical orientation be flexible in employing a range of techniques. Many of the group methods can be creatively applied if modifications are made depending on the client population.

General Guidelines for Group Workers Serving Multicultural Populations

Racial and ethnic minority clients may display behavior that group leaders interpret as resistance. It is important to make a distinction between uncooperative behavior as a manifestation of resistance and as a hesitation to participate fully in the group process. Often, these clients are not so much *resistant* as they are *reluctant* or, in some cases, simply politely respectful. Such clients are not helped to participate more actively by leaders or other members who demonstrate little understanding or appreciation of these clients' underlying cultural values. For example, silence in a group should not always be interpreted as a refusal to participate. Quiet clients may think that being silent is better than talking excessively or than verbalizing without careful thought. Their quietness could reflect their fear of being perceived as seeking attention. They may be waiting to be called on by the group leader, whom they view with respect because of his or her status as an authority figure. Some clients may be hesitant to talk about members of their family. This hesitation should not necessarily be interpreted as a stubborn refusal to be open and transparent. Instead, such clients may be influenced by taboos against openly discussing family matters.

PREPARING CLIENTS FOR A GROUP EXPERIENCE. Multicultural group counseling demands adequate preparation by members. Screening and selecting members and orienting them to group procedures are especially critical in working with clients from certain cultural groups. This preparation is so critical because many of the behaviors expected in a group are often foreign to what people do in their everyday lives. For example, their culture may value indirect communication. When they are in a group, they are told to be direct as they speak to one another. In daily life, people are often encouraged to mask their real feelings so that they will not offend people. They probably are not encouraged to express their feelings openly, to talk about their personal problems with people whom they do not know well, or to tell others what they think about them. Yet in a group situation they are expected to abide by norms of openness, honesty, and directness, and they are expected to make themselves emotionally vulnerable. Depending on one's cultural background, some of the expected group behaviors may be most demanding and may certainly go against the grain of one's cultural conditioning.

It is important for group leaders to help members clearly identify *why* they are in a group. Clients need to identify what they want to get for themselves from this process. Group leaders can help by focusing them on where they are now and where they want to go. It is important that members fully realize that group counseling involves change. They should be made aware of the possible consequences of change, not only for themselves but also for others in their lives. Some clients may be shunned by family members if they become too outspoken or move toward individualism.

Adequate preparation of members is one of the best ways to increase the chances of a successful group experience for all clients. The preparation can include a discussion of members' values and how the group can help them achieve their personal goals. It is essential for clients with diverse cultural backgrounds that the goals and the purposes of the group be appropriate for their cultural context. This is why a discussion of the aims of a group and the importance of members' establishing their own goals is most important. At times, the goals may be consistent with the clients' cultural values, but the process or methods used to attain these goals can be antagonistic to these values.

SELF-DISCLOSURE AND CONFRONTATION IN GROUPS. Pushing for early disclosure of highly personal material or expecting members to be completely open can entrench resistance in certain clients. Some individuals from a variety of cultural backgrounds may take longer to develop trust and to participate in the disclosure that is based on this trust. Group leaders who understand the worlds of their clients are better able to be patient in helping these clients begin to speak. If such clients feel that they are respected, there is a greater chance that they will begin to challenge their hesitation.

Part of the group process is confrontation. Confrontation is therapeutic when it invites clients to more deeply explore a particular issue in their lives and when it is appropriate and well timed. On the other hand, confrontation that is harsh, attacking, hostile, and uncaring does not have a beneficial impact. Even therapeutic confrontation may not always be appropriate for clients from certain cultures, especially if it is done too soon. In fact, confronting client resistance too quickly and too directly can often be counterproductive. Certain clients may perceive the directness associated with confrontation as a personal attack (Ho, 1984; Leong, 1992). For some individuals, confrontation would cause a significant loss of face, making it difficult for them to return to the group setting. If such individuals feel insulted, the chances are that they will also feel rejected or angry, and such feelings may cement their resistance to becoming involved in the group. For such clients, confrontation may be a factor in premature termination from the group.

SOME POINTS TO REMEMBER. Reflecting on the following guidelines may increase your effectiveness in serving diverse client populations:

- Learn more about ways that your own cultural background has an influence on your thinking and behaving. Become familiar with some of the ways that you may be culturally encapsulated. What are some specific steps you can take to broaden your base of understanding both of your own culture and of other cultures?

- Identify your basic assumptions—especially as they apply to diversity in culture, ethnicity, race, gender, class, religion, and lifestyle—and think about how your assumptions are likely to affect your practice as a group counselor.

- Learn to pay attention to the common ground that exists among people of diverse backgrounds. What are some of the ways that we all share universal concerns?

- Realize that it is not necessary to learn everything about the cultural backgrounds of your clients before you begin working with them. Allow them to teach you how you can best serve them.

- Spend time preparing clients for a successful group experience, especially if some of their values may differ from some of the values that undergird a group. Teach clients how to adapt their group experience to meet the challenges they face in their everyday lives.

- Recognize the importance of being flexible in applying the methods you use with clients. Don't be wedded to a specific technique if it is not appropriate for a given group member.

- Remember that practicing from a multicultural perspective can make your job easier and can be rewarding for both you and your clients.

CHAPTER TWO

Ethical and Professional Issues in Group Practice

In my view, those who seek to be professional group leaders must be willing to examine both their ethical standards and their level of competence. The ethical issues treated in this chapter include the rights of group members, including informed consent and confidentiality; the psychological risks of groups; personal relationships with clients; socializing among members; the impact of the group leader's values; working sensitively and ethically with diverse clients; the uses and misuses of group techniques; and legal liability and malpractice. In my opinion, a central ethical issue in group work pertains to the group leader's competence. Thus, I give special attention to the following topics: ways of determining competence, identifying professional training standards, and adjuncts to academic preparation of group counselors. Also highlighted are ethical issues involved in training group workers.

As a responsible group practitioner, you are challenged to clarify your thinking about the ethical and professional issues that are discussed in this chapter. Ethical guidelines for group leaders, as well as professional training standards, have been established by the Association for Specialists in Group Work ([ASGW], 1989, 1991). Although you are obligated to be familiar with, and bound by, the ethical code of your professional organization, many of these codes offer only general guidelines. Thus, you will be challenged to learn ways of making ethical decisions in practical situations. The guidelines will give you a general framework from which to operate, but you will need to apply principles to concrete cases. As you will see when you study them, the guidelines provide a starting point for practitioners of group work, and they offer a focal point for discussion in group-counseling classes. Much of this chapter deals with specific ethical and professional issues that group workers typically face. It is a good idea to develop an ethical awareness and reflect on these issues *before* you actually begin to lead groups.

The Rights of Group Participants

My experience has taught me that those who enter groups are frequently unaware either of their basic rights as participants or of their responsibilities. It is your function as a group leader to help prospective members learn what their rights are. Therefore, this section offers a detailed list of group participants' rights.

A Basic Right: Informed Consent

If basic information about the group is discussed at the initial session, the participants are likely to be far more cooperative and active. A leader who does this as a matter of policy demonstrates honesty and respect for the members and fosters the trust necessary if group members are to be open and active. Such a leader has obtained the *informed consent* of the participants. Following is a consideration of basic information that members have a right to receive *before* joining a group. I then list what clients have a right to expect *during* the course of the group.

INFORMATION CLIENTS DESERVE BEFORE JOINING A GROUP. The following is a list of what group participants have a right to expect before they make the decision to join a group:

- ◆ a clear statement regarding the purpose of the group
- ◆ a description of the group format, procedures, and ground rules
- ◆ a pregroup interview to determine whether this particular group with this particular leader is at this time appropriate to their needs
- ◆ an opportunity to seek information about the group, to pose questions, and to explore concerns
- ◆ a statement describing the education, training, and qualifications of the group leader
- ◆ information concerning fees and expenses and whether the fee includes a follow-up session; also, information about length of group, frequency and duration of meetings, group goals, and techniques being employed
- ◆ information about the psychological risks involved in group participation
- ◆ knowledge of the circumstances in which confidentiality must be broken because of legal, ethical, or professional reasons
- ◆ clarification of what services can and cannot be provided within the group
- ◆ help from the group leader in developing personal goals
- ◆ a clear understanding of the division of responsibility between leader and participants
- ◆ a discussion of the rights and responsibilities of group members

CLIENTS' RIGHTS DURING THE GROUP. Following is a list of what members have a right to expect during the course of the group:

- ◆ instructions concerning what is expected of them
- ◆ the freedom to leave the group if it doesn't appear to be what they expected or what they want or need

- notice of any research involving the group and of any tape recording or videotaping of group sessions
- if recording does take place, the right to stop it if it restricts member participation
- assistance from the group leader in translating group learning into action in everyday life
- opportunities to discuss what one has learned in the group and to bring some closure to the group experience, so that participants are not left with unnecessary unfinished business
- a consultation with the group leader should a crisis arise as a direct result of participation in the group, or a referral to other sources of help if further help is not available from the group leader
- the exercise of reasonable safeguards on the leader's part to minimize the potential risks of the group
- respect for member privacy with regard to what the person will reveal as well as to the degree of disclosure
- freedom from undue group pressure concerning participation in group exercises, decision making, disclosure of private matters, or acceptance of suggestions from other group members
- observance of confidentiality on the part of the leader and other group members
- freedom from having values imposed by the leader or other members
- the opportunity to use group resources for growth
- the right to be treated as an individual and accorded dignity and respect

The leader should stress that participation in groups carries certain responsibilities as well as rights. Some of these responsibilities are attending regularly, being prompt, taking risks, being willing to talk about oneself, giving others feedback, maintaining confidentiality, and asking for what one needs.

Issues in Involuntary Groups

When participation is mandatory, informed consent is particularly important. Much effort needs to be directed toward fully informing involuntary members of the nature and goals of the group, the procedures to be used, their rights and responsibilities, the limits of confidentiality, and what effect their level of participation in the group will have on critical decisions about them outside of the group. When groups are involuntary, every attempt should be made to enlist the cooperation of the members and encourage them to continue attending voluntarily.

An alternative would be for the group leader to accept involuntary group members only for an initial limited period. There is something to be said for giving reluctant members a chance to see for themselves what a group is about and then eventually (say, after three sessions) letting them decide whether they will return. Of course, there may be consequences for clients who elect not to continue treatment. Ethical practice would seem to require that group leaders fully explore these issues with clients who are sent to them.

The Freedom to Leave a Group

Leaders should be clear about their policies pertaining to attendance, commitment to remaining in a group for a predetermined number of sessions, and leaving a particular session if they do not like what is going on in the group. If members simply drop out of the group, it makes it extremely difficult to develop a working level of trust or to establish group cohesion. The topic of leaving the group should be discussed during the initial session, and the leader's attitudes and policies should be clarified from the outset.

In my view, group members have a responsibility to the leaders and other members to explain why they want to leave. There are a number of reasons for such a policy. For one thing, it can be deleterious to members to leave without having been able to discuss what they considered threatening or negative in the experience. If they simply leave when they become uncomfortable, they are likely to be left with unfinished business, and so are the remaining members. A member's dropping out can surely damage the cohesion and trust in a group, for the remaining members may think that they in some way "caused" the departure. It is a good practice to tell members that if they are even thinking of withdrawing, they should bring the matter up for exploration in a session. It is critical that members be encouraged to discuss their departure, at least with the group leader. The ASGW's (1989) guideline on leaving the group is:

> Members have the right to exit a group, but it is important that they be made aware of the importance of informing the counselor and the group members prior to leaving the group. The counselor discusses the possible risks of leaving the group prematurely with a member who is considering this option.

If a group is counterproductive for an individual, that person should have a right to leave the group. Ideally, both the group leader and the members will work cooperatively to determine the degree to which a group experience is productive or counterproductive. My position is that if, at a mutually agreed-upon time, members still choose not to participate in a group, then they should be allowed to drop out without being subjected to pressure by the leader and other members to remain.

Freedom from Coercion and Undue Pressure

Members can reasonably expect to be respected by the group and not to be subjected to coercion and undue group pressure. On this matter the ASGW's (1989) guideline is "Group leaders protect member rights against physical threats, intimidation, coercion, and undue peer pressure insofar as it is reasonably possible."

On the one hand, some degree of group pressure is inevitable, and it is even therapeutic in many instances. People in a group are confronted with some of their self-defeating beliefs and behaviors and are challenged to admit what they are doing and determine whether they want to remain the way they are. Further, there is pressure in sessions to speak up, to make personal disclosures, to take certain risks, to share one's reactions to the here-and-now events within the group, and to be honest with the group. It is essential for group leaders to differentiate between destructive pressure and therapeutic pressure. People may need a certain degree of pressure to aid them in breaking through their usual forms of resistance.

On the other hand, it is well to keep in mind that the purpose of a group is to help participants find their own answers, not to pressure them into doing what the group thinks is the appropriate course. Members can easily be subjected to needless anxiety if they are badgered to behave in a certain way. Members may also be pressured to take part in communication exercises or nonverbal exercises designed to promote interaction. It is essential that leaders be sensitive to the values of members who decline to participate in certain group exercises. Leaders must make it genuinely acceptable for members to abstain by mentioning this option periodically whenever it is appropriate. It is a good practice for group leaders to teach members how to resist undue group pressure and how to decline gracefully from participating in activities they dislike.

The Right to Equitable Treatment

Members have a right to expect that they will be able to make optimum use of the resources within a group. At times certain members may display problematic behaviors such as monopolizing the group's time, storytelling, asking many questions, making interpretations for others, chronically jumping in, or giving advice or reassurance when it is not appropriate. Such behavior leaves little time for those members who want to work on their concerns. The ASGW's (1989) guideline here is "Group counselors ensure equitable use of group time for each member by inviting silent members to become involved, acknowledging nonverbal attempts to communicate, and discouraging rambling and monopolizing of time by members."

Although group counselors do not have to assume complete responsibility for intervening to stop members who are disrupting the group, leaders should notice the situation and work with the group in such a way that one member does not sap group energy and make it difficult for others to do productive work. I see it as the leader's function to teach rambling members to become aware of how they present themselves to others in the group. Without being sharp or overly critical, leaders can help members learn how to be specific and to avoid getting lost in the details of a story. They can teach members how to share the responsibility so that the resources in the group are maximized. This includes teaching members how to ask for what they want, developing a sense of limitations of time during the sessions, and confronting others appropriately if they see them disrupting the group process.

Part of treating group members equitably involves the counselor's recognition of and respect for individual differences in racial and cultural background, religious views, lifestyle orientation, age, disability, and gender. Any of these factors can influence a member's ability to profit from a group experience. What is especially important is that leaders help members identify and sort out difficulties they have as the group progresses due to one or more of these variables. It is also essential that all members develop an awareness of the reality that others in their group are likely to have a different worldview from theirs. The members can be encouraged to welcome diversity as a rich source of personal learning.

The Right to Confidentiality

Confidentiality is a central ethical issue in group counseling. Not only are you as a leader required to keep the confidences of group members; you have the added responsibility of impressing on the members the necessity of maintaining the confidential nature of whatever is revealed in the group. This matter bears reinforcement, from the initial screening interview to the final group session. Confidentiality, as one of the key norms of behavior in a group, is best arrived at through negotiation rather than by a dictate from the leader (Lakin, 1985). If the rationale for confidentiality is clearly presented to each individual during the preliminary interview and again to the group as a whole at the initial session, there is less chance that members will treat this matter lightly. Confidentiality is often on the minds of people when they join a group, so it is timely to fully explore this issue.

A good practice is to remind participants from time to time of the danger of inadvertently revealing confidences. My experience continues to teach me that members rarely gossip maliciously about others in their group. However, people do tend to talk more than they should outside the group and can unwittingly offer information about fellow members that should not be revealed. If the maintenance of confidentiality seems to be a matter of concern, the subject should be discussed fully in a group session. Clearly there is no way to ensure that group members will respect the confidences of others. As a group leader, however, you can discuss the matter, express your feelings about the importance of maintaining confidentiality, have members sign contracts agreeing to it, and even impose some form of sanction on those who break it. Realize that your own modeling and the importance that you place on maintaining confidentiality will be crucial in setting norms for members to follow. If the members sense that you take confidentiality seriously, there is a greater likelihood that they will also be concerned about the matter. Ultimately, it is up to the members to respect the need for confidentiality and to maintain it.

The ASGW's *Ethical Guidelines for Group Counselors* (1989) have several principles related to the issue of confidentiality, including the injunction that "group counselors protect members by defining clearly what confidentiality means, why it is important, and the difficulties involved in enforcement." Other aspects of this guideline are:

◆ The limits of confidentiality should be addressed. For instance, leaders can explain to members when they are legally required to break confidentiality.
◆ Group leaders can assure confidentiality on their own part but not on the part of other members.
◆ Members can be encouraged to bring up matters pertaining to confidentiality whenever they are concerned about them.

With respect to tape recordings and videotapes of group sessions, members have the right to know of any that might be made and for what purpose they will be used. Their written permission should be secured before any recording of a session. If the tapes will be used for research purposes or will be critiqued by a supervisor or other students in a group-supervision session, the members have the right to deny permission.

EXCEPTIONS TO CONFIDENTIALITY. The proposed ethical standards of the American Counseling Association ([ACA], 1993) specify exceptions to the general norm of confidentiality, which have implications for group members' disclosures: "The general requirement that Professional Counselors keep information confidential does not apply when the best interests of clients, welfare of others, obligations to society, or legal requirements demand that confidential information be revealed. Professional Counselors consult with other mental health professionals when they are unsure of whether an exception to confidentiality exists" (p. 17).

Group workers often give a written statement to each member setting forth the limitations of confidentiality and spelling out specific situations that would demand the breaching of confidences. It seems that such straightforwardness with members from the outset does a great deal to create trust, for at least members know where they stand.

Of course, it is imperative that those who lead groups become familiar with the state laws that have an impact on their practice. Counselors are legally required to report clients' threats to harm themselves or others. This requirement also covers cases of child abuse or neglect, incest, or child molestation. Taking an extreme case, if one of your group members convincingly threatens to seriously injure another person, you may have to consult your supervisor or other colleagues, warn the intended victim, and even notify the appropriate authorities. The threat need not involve others; clients may exhibit bizarre behavior, such as having "visions" or "hearing voices" telling them to maim themselves, that requires you to take steps to have them temporarily hospitalized.

If you lead a group at a correctional institution or a psychiatric hospital, you may be required to act as more than a counselor; for instance, you may have to record in a member's file certain behaviors that he or she exhibits in the group. At the same time, your responsibility to your clients requires you to inform them that you are recording and passing on certain information. Generally speaking, you will find that you have a better chance of gaining the cooperation of group members if you are candid about a situation than if you hide your disclosures and thereby put yourself in the position of violating their confidences.

CONFIDENTIALITY WITH MINORS. Another delicate problem related to confidentiality involves group counseling with children and adolescents. Do parents have a right to information that is disclosed by their children in a group? The answer to that question depends on whether you are looking at it from a legal, ethical, or professional viewpoint. Before any minor enters a group, it is a good practice to require written permission from the parents. It is useful to have this permission include a brief statement concerning the purpose of the group, along with comments regarding the importance of confidentiality as a prerequisite to accomplishing such purposes and your intention not to violate any confidences. Clearly, it may be useful to give the parents information about their child, but this can be done without violating confidences. One useful practice to protect the privacy of what goes on in the group is to provide feedback to parents in a session with the child and one or both parents. In this way the child will have less cause to doubt the group leader's integrity in keeping his or her disclosures private.

Group leaders have a responsibility in groups that involve children and adolescents to take measures to increase the chances that confidentiality will be kept. It is important to work cooperatively with parents and guardians as well as to enlist the trust of the young people. It is also useful to teach minors, in terms that they are capable of understanding, about the nature, purposes, and limitations of confidentiality. In summary, group leaders would do well to continue to remind members to bring up their concerns about confidentiality for discussion whenever the issue is on their minds.

The Issue of Psychological Risks in Groups

Since groups can act as powerful catalysts for personal change, they can also pose definite risks for group members. The nature of these risks—which include life changes that cause disruption, hostile and destructive confrontations, scapegoating, and harmful socializing among members—and what the leader can do about them are the subject of this section. It is unrealistic to expect that a group will not involve risk, for all meaningful learning in life involves taking risks. However, it is the ethical responsibility of the group leader to ensure that prospective group members are aware of the potential risks and to take every precaution against them.

An ASGW ethical guideline specifies that group leaders stress the personal risks involved in any group, especially regarding potential life changes, and help group members explore their readiness to face these risks. A minimal expectation is that group leaders discuss with members the advantages and disadvantages of a given group, that they prepare the members to deal with any problems that might grow out of the group experience, and that they be alert to the fears and reservations that members might have.

It is also incumbent on group leaders to have a broad and deep understanding of the forces that operate in groups and how to mobilize those forces for ethical ends. Unless leaders exert caution, members not only may miss the benefits of a group but also could be harmed by it psychologically. Ways of reducing these risks include knowing members' limits, respecting their requests, developing an invitational style as opposed to a pushy or dictatorial style, avoiding assaultive confrontations, describing behavior rather than making judgments, and presenting hunches in a tentative way rather than forcing interpretations on members. The next chapter describes group-leadership skills that provide a basis for dealing with some of the issues that have been mentioned here.

Following are a few of the problems that group leaders can warn members about and work toward minimizing:

1. Members should be made aware of the possibility that participating in a group (or any other therapeutic endeavor) may disrupt their lives. As members become increasingly self-aware, they may make changes in their lives that, although constructive in the long run, create crisis and turmoil along the way. For example, changes that a wife makes as a result of what she gains in a group may evoke resistance, even hostility, in her husband, with a resulting strain on their marriage. Furthermore, the rest of her family may not appreciate her changes and may prefer the person she was before getting involved in counseling.

2. Occasionally an individual member may be singled out as the scapegoat of the group. Other group members may "gang up" on this person, making him or her the object of hostility or other forms of negativity. Clearly, the group leader can and should take firm steps to eliminate such occurrences.

3. Confrontation, a valuable and powerful tool in any group, can be misused, especially when it is employed to destructively attack another. Intrusive interventions, overly confrontive leader tactics, and pushing of members beyond their limits often produce negative outcomes. Here, again, leaders (and members as well) must be on guard against behavior that can pose a serious psychological risk for group participants. To lessen the risks of nonconstructive confrontation, leaders can model the type of confrontation that focuses on specific behaviors and can avoid making judgments about members. They can teach members how to talk about themselves and the reactions they are having to a certain behavior pattern of a given member.

One way to minimize psychological risks in groups is to use a contract, in which the leader specifies his or her responsibilities and the members specify their commitment by stating what they are willing to explore and do in the group. Such a contract reduces the chances that members will be exploited or will leave the group feeling that they have had a negative experience.

Another safeguard against unnecessary risk is the ability of leaders to recognize the boundaries of their competence and to restrict themselves to working only with those groups for which their training and experience have properly prepared them. Ultimately, it is the group leader who is responsible for minimizing the inevitable psychological risks associated with group activity. To best assume this responsibility, the leader will undergo the supervised practice and course work that is described later in this chapter.

The Ethics of Group Leaders' Actions

Being a group practitioner demands sensitivity to the needs of the members of your group and to the impact that your values and techniques can have on them. It also demands an awareness of community standards of practice, the policies of the agency where you work, and the state laws that govern group counseling. In the mental-health professions in general there is a trend toward accountability and responsible practice. Graduate programs in counseling and social work are increasingly requiring course work in ethics and the law. In part, these trends may have something to do with the increased vulnerability of mental-health practitioners to malpractice suits.

Almost all of the professional organizations have gone on record as affirming that their members should be aware of prevailing community standards and of the impact that conformity to or deviation from these standards will have on their practice. These organizations state explicitly that professionals will avoid exploitation of the therapeutic relationship, will not damage the trust that is necessary for a relationship to be therapeutic, and will avoid dual relationships if they would interfere with the primary therapeutic aims. Typically, the ethical codes caution against attempting to blend social or personal relationships with professional ones.

Personal Relationships between Leaders and Members

What criteria can a group counselor use to determine whether personal and social relationships with group members are appropriate? A key factor is whether such a social relationship is interfering with the therapeutic relationship. There is an ASGW (1989) guideline on this issue: "Group counselors avoid dual relationships with group members that might impair their objectivity and professional judgment, as well as those which are likely to compromise a group member's ability to participate fully in the group." One of the subprinciples of this general concept cautions counselors about misusing their role and power to meet their personal needs. The core issue in this guideline deals with using power appropriately. When group leaders meet their personal needs for power and prestige at the expense of what is best for the members, there is an ethical violation. For example, if group leaders rely on their professional role to make friends and satisfy their personal and social needs by becoming personally involved with members or former members, the abuse of power becomes an issue. Their role is to help members meet their goals, not to become friends with their clients.

Two other subprinciples to this guideline alert leaders to the potential dangers of engaging in dual relationships—professional and personal—with members:

1. "Group counselors do not use their professional relationship with group members to further their own interest either during the group or after the termination of the group."
2. "Sexual intimacies between group counselors and members are unethical."

On the issue of intimacies between therapists and current or former therapy clients, the revised ethical code of the APA (1992) states clearly:

◆ "Psychologists do not engage in sexual intimacies with current patients or clients."
◆ "Psychologists do not accept as therapy patients or clients persons with whom they have engaged in sexual intimacies."
◆ "Psychologists do not engage in sexual intimacies with a former therapy patient or client for at least two years after cessation or termination of professional services."

It is interesting to note that in its proposed standards of practice, the ACA (1993) would prohibit sexual intimacies with former clients regardless of the time elapsed since termination: "Professional Counselors must avoid any type of sexual intimacies with current and former clients" (p. 15). The rationale for what might seem like an extreme standard regarding intimacies with former clients is that a sexual relationship has the potential to undermine the positive results that were accomplished in therapy.

Socializing among Group Members

A related issue is whether socializing among group members hinders or facilitates the group process. This concern can become an ethical issue if members are forming cliques and gossiping about others in the group or if they are banding together and talking about matters that are best explored in the group sessions. If hidden agendas develop through various splinter groups within the group, it is likely that the progress of the group will come to an abrupt halt. Unless the hidden agenda is brought to the surface and dealt with, it seems very likely that many members will not be able to use the group therapeutically or meet their personal goals.

Yalom (1985) writes that a therapy group teaches people *how to form* intimate relationships but does not *provide* these relationships. He also points out that members meeting outside of the group have a responsibility to bring information about their meeting into the group. The type of out-of-group socialization that interferes with the functioning of the group is counterproductive and should be discouraged. This is especially true in those situations in which participants discuss issues relevant to the group and avoid bringing up the same issues in the group itself.

One of the best ways for the group leader to prevent inappropriate and counterproductive socialization among group members is to bring this issue up for discussion. It is especially timely to explore the negative impact of forming cliques when the group seems stuck and getting nowhere or when it appears that members are not talking about their reactions to one another. The members can be taught that what they do not say in the group itself might very well prevent their group from attaining any level of cohesion.

The Impact of the Leader's Values on the Group

In all controversial issues related to the group process, the leader's values play a central role. Your awareness of how your values influence your leadership style is in itself a central ethical issue. Sometimes group counselors are taught to be neutral and are urged to attempt to keep their values separate from their leadership function. My position is that it is neither possible nor desirable for counselors to be scrupulously neutral with respect to values in the therapeutic relationship. Although it is not the proper function of counselors to persuade clients to accept a certain value system, it is critical that they be clear about their own values and express them openly when it is relevant to the work of the group. But leaders must keep in mind how these values influence their therapeutic work and, ultimately, the directions taken by their clients.

In my view, the crux of the ethical concern in this area involves leaders who use their group to advance their personal agenda, or to meet their own needs at the expense of the members. Group counseling is not a forum in which leaders impose their worldview on the members, but a way to assist members in exploring their own cultural values and beliefs. The ASGW's guideline here is that "group counselors develop an awareness of their own values and needs and the potential impact they have on the interventions likely to be made."

There is a real difference between *imposing* and *exposing* one's values. When leaders impose their values, they are showing disrespect for the members' integrity. They are implying that members are incapable of discovering a meaningful set of values and acting on them by themselves. When leaders expose their values, in contrast, the members are free to test their own thinking against the background of the leader's beliefs, but they can still make their own choices without being burdened with guilt that they are not meeting the leader's expectations. For myself, I am inclined to expose my values when they conflict with a member's values. It does not seem therapeutic to feign acceptance or to pretend that no difference of opinion exists. Expressed values are less likely to interfere with the process of a group than values that are concealed.

Members are best served if they learn to evaluate their behavior to determine how it is working for them. If they come to the realization that what they are doing is not serving them well, it is appropriate for the counselor to challenge them to develop alternative ways of behaving that will enable them to reach their goals.

It is also critical that group counselors increase their awareness of how their personal reactions to members may inhibit the group process. This involves becoming aware of their basic assumptions and values that influence the way they facilitate a group, monitoring their countertransference, and recognizing the danger of stereotyping individuals on the basis of race or ethnicity, gender, age, and sexual orientation.

Ethical Issues in Multicultural Group Counseling

Related to the matter of recognizing how leaders' values influence the group process is the issue of group practitioners taking into account the reality of human diversity. If leaders ignore some basic differences in people, they can hardly be doing what is in the best interests of these clients. An ASGW (1989) guideline specifies that "group counselors are aware of their own values and assumptions and how these apply in a multicultural context." If group counselors do not understand how their cultural background influences their own thinking and behavior, there is little chance that they can work ethically and effectively with members who are culturally different from themselves.

D. W. Sue, Arredondo, and McDavis (1992) have developed a comprehensive set of specific attitudes, awarenesses, and skills that help group counselors come to terms with their own cultural values. Their guidelines are addressed in the following chapter, on group-leadership skills. Ibrahim (1985) asserts that counselors can begin understanding the values and beliefs of diverse client groups once they understand their own cultural values. She maintains that if counselors lack an understanding of their own or their clients' value systems and worldviews, frustration and anxiety result for both parties: "Effectiveness in cross-cultural counseling and psychotherapeutic encounters is determined by how well the helper is aware of his or her world view and can understand and accept the world view of the client. Without these conditions there cannot be a viable therapeutic relationship" (p. 633).

Although there is a clear trend toward acknowledging the importance of a multicultural perspective in training practitioners, the ethical standards of many of the professional organizations do not concretely address this imperative. The codes tend to be rather general in dealing with matters of cultural diversity, and many are concerned with a minimal level of ethical functioning. For example, the newly revised *Ethical Principles of Psychologists and Code of Conduct* of the APA (1992) takes the following position on the ethics of recognizing human differences:

> Where differences of age, gender, race, ethnicity, national origin, religion, sexual orientation, disability, language, or socioeconomic status significantly affect psychologists' work concerning particular individuals or

groups, psychologists obtain the training, experience, consultation, or supervision necessary to ensure the competence of their services, or they make appropriate referrals.

In my view, this brief statement on human differences does not go far enough. This position refers more to situations where psychologists are not able to work effectively because of differences they have with a particular individual or group. Unfortunately, the APA code still reflects a minimal level of ethical functioning, rather than promoting a higher level of ethical practice. Pedersen (1994) maintains that the ethical principles of both the APA (1992) and the ACA (1988) are culturally biased. With respect to the APA guideline on human diversity cited above, Pedersen asserts that its conditional language conveys the message that human differences are not always important. He contends that the APA principles provide examples of cultural encapsulation through implicit assumptions, inconsistencies, and contradictions when these guidelines are applied to multicultural settings. For instance, one principle discourages multiple relationships and bartering with clients. Pedersen contends such rules disregard cultural patterns in those cultures that place a higher value on collectivistic relationships than on a monetary economy. Pedersen also asserts that the ACA *Ethical Standards* (1988) do not reflect clients' diversity in race, culture, class, and gender. He contends that these standards demonstrate presumptions that favor the dominant culture's perspective and put minority groups at a disadvantage regarding judgments of ethical behavior.

Although the standards of the APA and the ACA still need to give more specific attention to the ethical implications of working with culturally diverse clients, the APA's Office of Ethnic Minority Affairs has developed a useful set of guidelines in this area that are intended to raise standards (APA, 1993). Even though these guidelines are not specifically designed for group counselors, group facilitators can use them. The following list represents an adaptation of these guidelines:

- ♦ Group leaders acquire the knowledge and skills they need to effectively work with the diverse range of members in their groups. If they do not have this essential background, they fill in these gaps by seeking consultation, supervision, and further education and training.
- ♦ Group leaders are aware of how their own cultural background, attitudes, values, beliefs, and biases influence their work, and they make efforts to correct any prejudices they may have.
- ♦ Group leaders acknowledge that ethnicity and culture influence behavior.
- ♦ Group leaders respect the roles of family and community hierarchies within a client's culture.
- ♦ Group leaders respect members' religious and spiritual beliefs and values.
- ♦ Group leaders assist members in determining those instances when their difficulties stem from others' racism or bias, so that they do not inappropriately personalize problems.

◆ Group leaders consider the impact of adverse social, environmental, and political factors in assessing problems and designing interventions.

◆ Group leaders make an effort to eliminate biases, prejudices, and discriminatory practices. In their practice they develop sensitivity to issues of oppression, sexism, and racism.

It is a good practice for leaders to inform members about basic values that are implicit in the group process. For example, some groups operate on the following value assumptions: taking risks is essential for growth and change; self-determination is preferable to living by the standards of others; expressing emotions is healthier than repressing them; being open and expressing vulnerability can lead to intimacy; self-disclosure is a key to building solid relationships; striving for independence and autonomy is a primary goal; directness in communicating what you want and need from others is valued; and trust in a group is attained by investing oneself in the group. Some of these values may conflict with those of individual members. Certainly, ethical practice implies that members become aware of these values and what will be expected of them. It is useful to explore potential value conflicts during the early group sessions. Ethical group leaders spend time in the initial sessions clarifying their cultural assumptions and the clients' cultural values and beliefs. Furthermore, leaders need to establish goals and processes that match the cultural values of the members of the group.

For an interesting article that examines ways in which Islamic values are relevant to group work, the positive and negative impacts on counseling groups, and practical applications for leaders with Muslim group members, see Banawi and Stockton (1993).

Uses and Misuses of Group Techniques

It is important for leaders to have a clear rationale for each technique they use in their groups. This is an area in which theory is a useful guide for practice. As you will see, the ten theories at the core of this book give rise to many therapeutic strategies and techniques. Such techniques are a means to accomplish change or to promote exploration and interaction. They can certainly be used ethically and therapeutically, yet they can also be misused. Some of the ways in which leaders can practice unprofessionally are using techniques with which they are unfamiliar, using them merely as gimmicks, using them to serve their own hidden agendas or to enhance their power, and using them to pressure members. Lakin (1985) considers the core ethical issue to be whether the leader can use the emotional arousal stimulated by the group without exploiting it. Many techniques that are used in a group do facilitate an intense expression of emotion. For example, guided fantasies into times of loneliness as a child can lead to deep psychological experiences. If leaders use such techniques, they must be ready to deal with any emotional release. What is crucial is to use these techniques properly for the benefit of the members and to avoid the exploitation that occurs when members are pushed to "get into their emotions." Some group leaders measure the efficacy of their group by the level of catharsis, and members can be exploited by a leader who has a need to see them experience intense emotions. This expression of emotion can sometimes be more important in meeting the leader's needs than in meeting the member's. If members do not have a "good catharsis," some leaders (and members) feel that the group is "not getting anywhere."

Techniques have a better chance of being used appropriately when there is a rationale underlying their use. Techniques should foster the client's self-exploration and self-understanding. At their best, they are invented in each unique client situation, and they assist the group member in experimenting with some form of new behavior. It is critical that techniques be introduced in a timely and sensitive manner, with respect for the client, and that they be abandoned if they are not working.

In working with culturally diverse client populations, leaders must modify their interventions so that they suit the client's cultural and ethnic background. For example, if a client has been taught not to express his feelings in public, it may be inappropriate to quickly introduce techniques aimed at bringing out his feelings. It would be useful to find out if this member was interested in exploring what he has learned from his culture about expressing his feelings. Take another situation of a woman who has been socialized to obey her parents without question. It could be inappropriate to introduce a role-playing technique that would have her confronting her parents directly. Leaders can respect the cultural values of members and at the same time encourage them to think about how these values and their upbringing have a continuing effect on their behavior. In some cases, members will decide to modify certain behaviors because the personal price of retaining a value is too high. In other cases, they will decide that they are not interested in changing certain cultural values or behaviors. The techniques used by leaders can help such members examine the pros and cons of making these changes. For a more detailed discussion of ethical considerations in using group techniques, see G. Corey, Corey, Callanan, and Russell (1992).

Legal Liability and Malpractice

Group leaders are expected to practice within the code of ethics of their particular profession and to abide by legal standards. Practitioners are subject to civil penalties if they fail to do right or if they actively do wrong to another. If group members can prove that personal injury or psychological harm was caused by a leader's failure to render proper service, either through negligence or ignorance, the leader is open to a malpractice suit. Negligence consists of departing from the standard and commonly accepted practices of others in the profession. Practitioners who are involved in a malpractice action may need to justify the techniques they use. If their therapeutic interventions are consistent with those of other members of their profession in their community, they are on much firmer ground than if they employ uncommon techniques.

Leaders need to keep up to date with the laws of their state as they affect their professional practice. Those leaders who work with groups of children and adolescents, especially, must know the law as it pertains to matters of confidentiality, parental consent, the right to treatment or to refuse treatment, informed consent, and other legal rights of clients. Such awareness not only protects the group members but also protects group leaders from malpractice suits arising from negligence or ignorance.

STRIVING FOR PROFESSIONAL PRACTICE. The best way to protect yourself from getting involved in a malpractice suit is to take preventive measures, which means not practicing outside the boundaries of your competence. Following the spirit of the ethical standards of your professional organization and the ethical guidelines for group leaders such as those developed by the ASGW is also important. The key to avoiding a malpractice suit is maintaining *reasonable, ordinary,* and *prudent* practices. Below are some guidelines for professional standards of practice that make these terms more concrete:

- ◆ Give the potential members of your groups enough information to make informed choices about group participation. Do not mystify the group process. Professional honesty and openness with group members will go a long way toward building a trusting climate.
- ◆ Become aware of local and state laws that limit your practice, as well as the policies of the agency for which you work. Inform members about these policies and about legal limitations (such as exemptions to confidentiality, mandatory reporting, and the like).
- ◆ Restrict your practice to client populations for which you are prepared by virtue of your education, training, and experience.
- ◆ Be alert for symptoms of psychological debilitation in group members, which may indicate that their participation should be discontinued. Be able to put such clients in contact with appropriate referral resources.
- ◆ Don't promise the members of your group anything that you can't deliver. Help them realize that their degree of effort and commitment will be key factors in determining the outcomes of the group experience.
- ◆ In working with minors, secure the written permission of their parents, even if this is not required by state law.
- ◆ Always consult with colleagues when you are in doubt. Realize that the willingness to consult and to seek supervision implies a high level of professionalism. Find sources of ongoing supervision.
- ◆ Learn how to assess and intervene in cases in which clients pose a threat to themselves or others.
- ◆ Be willing to devote the time it takes to adequately screen, select, and prepare the members of your group.

◆ Avoid mixing professional relationships with social ones.
◆ Avoid engaging in sexual relationships with either current or former group members.
◆ Remain alert to ways in which your personal reactions might inhibit the group process, and monitor your countertransference. Although your personal needs may be met through your professional work, be careful of meeting these needs at the expense of the members of your group. Avoid using the group as a place where you work through your personal problems.
◆ Keep yourself informed about research findings, and be able to apply this information to increase the effectiveness of your groups.
◆ Be able to explain the techniques that you regularly use in your groups. Have a rationale that is tied to some theoretical perspective.

The Issue of the Group Leader's Competence

Determining One's Own Level of Competence

The ASGW's (1989) basic ethical principle is that "group counselors do not attempt any technique unless thoroughly trained in its use or under supervision by a counselor familiar with the intervention." How can leaders determine whether they have the competence to use a certain technique? Although some leaders who have received training in the use of a technique may hesitate to use it (out of fear of making a mistake), other overly confident leaders without training may not have any reservations about trying out new methods. It is a good policy for leaders to have a clear rationale for any technique they use. Further, it is useful if leaders have experienced these techniques as members of a group. The issue of whether one is competent to lead a specific group or type of group is an ongoing question that faces all professional group leaders. You will need to remain open to struggling with questions such as the following:

◆ Am I qualified through education and training to lead this specific group?
◆ What criteria can I use to determine my degree of competence?
◆ How can I recognize the boundaries of my competence?
◆ If I am not as competent as I'd like to be as a group worker, what specifically can I do?
◆ How can I continue to upgrade my leadership abilities?
◆ What techniques can I skillfully employ?
◆ With what kinds of clients do I work best?
◆ With whom do I work least well, and why?
◆ How far can I go with clients?
◆ When and how should I refer clients?
◆ When do I need to consult with other professionals?

There are no simple answers to these questions. Different groups require different leader qualities. For example, you may be fully competent to lead a group of relatively well-adjusted adults or of adults in crisis situations yet not be competent to lead a group of seriously disturbed people. You may be well trained for, and work well with, adolescent groups, yet you may not have the skills or training to do group work with younger children. You may be successful leading groups dealing with substance abuse yet find yourself ill-prepared to work successfully with family groups. In short, you need specific training and supervised experience for each type of group you intend to lead.

Degrees and credentials may be necessary but are not sufficient in themselves; all they indicate is a certain background of content and experience, which usually means that you have completed a *minimum* number of years of training and experience. The breadth and quality of training and experience indicated by credentials vary greatly.

Most practitioners have had their formal training in one of the branches of the mental-health field, including counseling psychology, clinical psychology, community counseling, educational psychology, marriage and family counseling, nursing, pastoral psychology, rehabilitation counseling, mental-health counseling, psychiatric social work, and psychiatry. Generally, however, those who seek to become group practitioners find that formal education, even at the master's or doctoral level, doesn't give them the practical grounding they require to effectively lead groups. Thus, practitioners often find it necessary to take a variety of specialized group-therapy training workshops.

Professional Training Standards for Group Counselors

Effective group-leadership programs are not developed by legislative mandates and professional codes alone. For proficient leaders to emerge, a training program must make group work a priority. Unfortunately, in some master's programs in counseling not even one group course is required, and in others such a course is still an elective. In those programs that do require course work in group counseling, there is typically one course that covers both the didactic and experiential aspects of group process. It is a major undertaking to train group counselors adequately in a single course!

The ASGW (1991) has published expanded *Professional Standards for the Training of Group Workers,** which specify two levels of competencies and related training. First is a set of core *knowledge* competencies and *skill* competencies that provides the foundation on which specialized training is built. At a minimum, one group course should be included in a training program, and it should be structured to help students acquire the basic knowledge and skills needed to facilitate a group. These group skills are

---

*Adapted from *Professional Standards for the Training of Group Workers,* adopted April 20, 1991, and reproduced by permission of the Association for Specialists in Group Work, a division of the American Counseling Association, 5999 Stevenson Avenue, Alexandria, VA 22304.

best mastered through supervised practice, which should include observation and participation in a group experience. Second, the standards contain a set of guidelines for integrating the new provisions with the accreditation standards of the Council for Accreditation of Counseling and Related Educational Programs (CACREP).

Areas of knowledge that are considered basic include identifying one's strengths and weaknesses and one's values, being able to describe the characteristics associated with the typical stages in a group's development, being able to describe the facilitative and debilitative roles and behaviors of group members, knowing the therapeutic factors of a group, understanding the importance of group and member evaluation, and being aware of the ethical issues special to group work.

Skill competencies that group leaders should have include being able to open and close group sessions, modeling appropriate behavior for group members, engaging in appropriate self-disclosure in the group, giving and receiving feedback, helping members attribute meaning to their experience in the group, helping them integrate and apply their learning, and demonstrating the ability to apply the ASGW ethical standards in group practice.

The ASGW standards state that these group-work skills are best mastered through supervised practice, which should include observation and participation in a group experience. Although there is a minimum of 10 hours of supervised practice, 20 hours are recommended as part of the core training.

Once counselor trainees have mastered the core knowledge and skill domains outlined above, they can acquire training in group-work specializations in one or more of these four areas: (1) task/work groups, (2) guidance/psychoeducational groups, (3) counseling/interpersonal-problem-solving groups, and (4) psychotherapy/personality-reconstruction groups. The standards detail specific knowledge and skill competencies for these specialties and also specify the recommended number of hours of supervised training for each.

The training for *task/work groups* involves course work in the broad area of organizational development and management. It also includes course work in consultation. Specialist training requires a minimum of 30 hours of supervised experience in leading or co-leading a task/work group.

The specialist training for *guidance/psychoeducational groups* involves course work in the broad area of community psychology, health promotion, marketing, consultation, and curriculum design. This specialty requires an additional 30 hours of supervised experience in leading or co-leading a guidance group in field practice.

The specialist training for *counseling/interpersonal-problem-solving groups* should ideally include as much course work in group counseling as possible, with at least one course beyond the generalist level. For this specialization there is a minimum of 45 hours of supervised experience in leading or co-leading a counseling group.

The specialist training for *psychotherapy groups* consists of courses taken in the area of abnormal psychology, psychopathology, and diagnostic assessment to ensure capabilities in working with more disturbed populations. For this specialization, there is a minimum of 45 hours of supervised experience in working with therapy groups.

The guidelines for integrating the ASGW standards with the CACREP accreditation standards call for supervised clinical experience that should be obtained in both practicum and internship programs. For the master's practicum, at least 15 hours should be spent in supervised leadership or co-leadership in a group work specialty as outlined by the ASGW. For the internship in a master's degree program, at least 90 hours should be spent in supervised group leadership. For a doctoral internship, at least 450 (of the 1200 hours stipulated) should be spent in supervised clinical work with groups. The current trend in training of group workers focuses on learning group process by becoming involved in supervised experiences. Certainly, the mere completion of one graduate course in group theory and practice does not equip one to lead groups. Both direct participation in planned and supervised small groups and clinical experience in leading various groups under careful supervision are needed to provide leaders with the skills to meet the challenges of group work.

I want to give recognition to the generally outstanding job done by the ASGW committee that revised the professional training standards. Now, at least, the group-work field has a set of basic guidelines for determining a minimal level of competence for practitioners. However, I view these training standards not as a finished product but as guidelines that are open for revision. One area that is not given sufficient attention, in my view, is the specific knowledge and skills needed for becoming an effective multicultural counselor. My hope is that future revisions will include these competencies required for dealing effectively with diversity in groups.

In addition, I agree with Pate and Bondi (1992), who maintain that religious beliefs and values are an aspect of clients' cultural background that should be considered a vital component of counselor training programs. I also support their stand that counseling students need to be taught the importance of religious beliefs in the lives of many of their clients. They indicate that a CACREP standard requires the inclusion of religious and spiritual values in the multicultural component of counselor-education programs. A client's spirituality is an important part of culture that group counselors need to consider if they expect to serve culturally, ethnically, racially, and religiously diverse client populations. Of course, it is essential that group counselors have clarity on their own spiritual beliefs and values if they hope to acquire a sensitivity to dealing with these issues with group members. Chapter 3 includes a further discussion of this topic.

Three Adjuncts to the Training of Group Counselors

From an ethical perspective, if you expect to lead groups, you will want to be prepared for this work, both personally and academically. If your program has not provided this preparation, it will be necessary for you to seek in-service workshops in group processes. It is not likely that you will learn how to lead groups merely through reading about them and listening to lectures.

I recommend at least three experiences as adjuncts to a training program for group workers. First, undergoing their own counseling makes students better able to perceive any countertransference feelings and to use their personal attributes effectively in groups. Second, I highly recommend participation in group counseling or a personal-growth group. Third, by participating in a training and supervision group, one can develop the skills needed for effective intervention. Leaders in training can bring into their supervision the problems they are encountering with group members, and they can be exposed to various ways of looking at their concerns. Following is a discussion of these three adjuncts to the professional preparation of group counselors.

PERSONAL PSYCHOTHERAPY FOR GROUP LEADERS. I agree with Yalom's (1985) recommendation that extensive self-exploration is necessary if trainees are to perceive countertransference feelings, recognize blind spots and biases, and use their personal attributes effectively in groups. Although videotapes, work with a co-leader, and supervision all are excellent sources of feedback, Yalom maintains that some type of personal therapy is usually necessary for fuller understanding and correction. Group leaders should demonstrate the courage and willingness to do for themselves what they expect members in their groups to do: expand their awareness of self and the effect of that self on others.

Increasing self-awareness is a major reason to seek out personal counseling. In leading a group, you will encounter many instances of transferences, both among members and toward you. Transference refers to the unconscious process whereby clients project onto their therapist past feelings or attitudes that they had toward significant people in their lives. Of course, group leaders can easily become entangled in their own feelings of countertransference, or unconscious emotional responses to group members. Leaders also have their unresolved personal problems, which they can project onto the members of their group. Through personal counseling, trainees can work through some of their unfinished business, which could easily interfere with their effective functioning as a group leader.

SELF-EXPLORATION GROUPS FOR GROUP LEADERS. Being a member of a variety of groups can prove to be an indispensable part of training for group leaders. By experiencing their own resistances, fears, and uncomfortable moments in a group, by being confronted, and by struggling with their problems in a group context, practitioners can experience what is needed to build a trusting and cohesive group.

In addition to helping interns resolve personal conflicts and increase self-understanding, a personal-growth group can be a powerful teaching tool. One of the best ways to learn how to assist group members in their struggles is to participate yourself as a member of a group.

Yalom (1985) strongly recommends a group experience for trainees. Some of the benefits that he suggests are experiencing the power of a group, learning what self-disclosure is about, coming to appreciate the difficulties involved in self-sharing, learning on an emotional level what one knows intellectually, and becoming aware of one's dependency on the leader's power and knowledge. Yalom cites surveys indicating that 60% to 70% of group-therapy training programs offer some type of personal-group experience.

PARTICIPATION IN EXPERIENTIAL TRAINING WORKSHOPS. I have found training workshops most useful in helping group counselors develop the skills necessary for effective intervention. The trainees can also learn a great deal about their response to criticism, their competitiveness, their need for approval, their concerns over being competent, and their power struggles. In working with both university students learning about group approaches and with professionals who want to upgrade their group skills, I have found an intensive weekend workshop effective. In these workshops the participants have ample opportunity to lead their small group for a designated period. After a segment in which the participants lead their group, my colleagues and I intervene by giving feedback and by promoting a discussion by the entire group. By the end of the weekend each participant has led the group at least twice (for an hour each time) under direct supervision. My wife, Marianne Corey, and I (1986) describe a framework for such a weekend or weeklong residential workshop for training and supervision using experiential and didactic methods to help participants refine their skills as group leaders. This type of workshop is a regular part of my own group-counseling courses on both the undergraduate and graduate levels. One of the best ways to learn how to facilitate groups is to get extensive experience as both a group member and a group leader, with supervised feedback and teaching. The training workshop provides for this type of learning.

Ethical Issues in Training Group Counselors

Training programs differ on whether participating in a group is optional or required. *Requiring* participation in a therapeutic group as a part of a training program can present some practical and ethical problems of its own. One of the ethical standards of the ACA (1988) is that learning that focuses on self-understanding or personal growth should be voluntary or, if it is required as a part of the educational program, should be made known to prospective students before they enter. A related ACA ethical guideline deals with accommodating students who do not wish to take part in personal-growth experiences: "The member [counselor educator] will at all times provide students with clear and equally acceptable alternatives for self-understanding or growth experiences. The member will assure students that they have a right to accept these alternatives without prejudice or penalty."

I have difficulty with the above ACA guidelines. If an educational program requires a therapeutic group and if students know of this requirement before they enter, I do not see why an "equally acceptable alternative" should be provided. Although some will complain that group participation causes them anxiety, because they are expected to disclose personal issues, candidates who are not willing to deal with this anxiety should probably ask themselves why they are choosing this profession. After all, most programs require a course in statistics and research methods, and for many (including myself) this obstacle is far more anxiety-provoking than being a member of a group.

One controversial ethical issue in the preparation of group workers involves the combining of experiential and didactic training methods. I consider an experiential component to be essential in the teaching of group-counseling courses. Admittedly, there are inherent problems in teaching students how groups function by involving them on an experiential level. Such an arrangement entails their willingness to engage in self-disclosure, to become active participants in an interpersonal laboratory, and to engage themselves on an emotional level as well as a cognitive one. Time and again, however, my colleagues and I hear both students and professionals who participate in our group-training workshops comment on the value of supervised experience in which they have both leadership and membership roles. Through this format, group-process concepts come alive. Trainees experience firsthand what it takes to create trust and what resistance feels like. They often say that they have gained a new appreciation for the resistance of their clients.

In talking with many other counselor educators throughout the country who teach group courses, I find that it is common practice to combine the experiential and didactic domains. In those group classes that are taught both experientially and didactically, the first half of the class typically deals with counseling theories and group-process issues. The content of the discussions may be very similar to the material in this textbook. During the second half of the session many instructors conduct a group in which the students have an opportunity to be a member. Sometimes students co-lead a small group with a peer and are supervised by the instructor. Of course, this arrangement is not without problems. Students may fear that their grade will be influenced by their participation (or lack of it) in the experiential part of the class. Clear guidelines need to be established so that students know what their rights and responsibilities are. This arrangement does put a bit more pressure on both the instructor and the students. It calls for honesty, maturity, and professionalism.

In grading and evaluating students in group courses, the professionalism of the instructor is crucial. Ethical practice requires instructors to spell out their grading criteria clearly. The criteria may include the results of written reports, oral presentations, essay tests, and objective examinations. Students' performance in the experiential group should not be graded, but they can be expected to attend regularly and to participate. The ASGW (1989) ethical guideline on this matter is:

Students who participate in a group as a partial course requirement for a group course are not evaluated for an academic grade based on their degree of participation as a member in a group. Instructors of group counseling courses take steps to minimize the possible negative impact on students when they participate in the group course by separating course grades from participation in the group and by allowing students to decide what issues to explore and when to stop.

Such a group might well focus on here-and-now interactions. Even if members choose not to bring up matters such as their childhood, there is plenty to talk about if they deal with their reactions to other people in the group. If they openly and honestly learn to deal with one another, they are making great strides in learning how to facilitate a group.

Having presented my personal views on the ethical aspects of training group counselors, let me briefly review the literature on this subject. Donigian (1993) considers dual relationships in training group counselors to be "the issue that won't go away." In summarizing the views of a panel of counselor educators, Donigian identifies the controversy as being related to what constitutes a group experience and what its content and process should be. Donigian concludes that the ASGW needs to identify what is to be taught, why it is to be taught, and what the criteria are for group workers' readiness for practicing group counseling.

Merta and his associates have researched the ethical dilemmas involved in employing experiential groups in training. Merta and Sisson (1991) report that the use of the experiential group has come under increasing criticism because of the existence of dual relationships and the potential for unethical practices such as invasion of privacy, conflict of interest, and abuses of power. They write that counselor educators need to consider the needs of the students, the program, and the profession. They do view experiential groups as being an indispensable component in training, and they offer recommendations for ethical practice in preparation of group workers.

A national survey identified five models being used by counselor educators in preparing group counselors (Merta, Wolfgang, & McNeil, 1993). This survey also evaluated how consistent the various training models were with the ethical standards of the ACA and the ASGW. Merta and his colleagues found that although the majority of counselor educators made use of the experiential group in training group workers, there was significant diversity in the way they employed various training models. The researchers remind us that an ethical dilemma really has no perfect solution, and they conclude:

> No one training model or combination of safeguards is apt to solve the dilemma of protecting students from adverse dual relationships while still providing them with appropriate training and protecting the profession and public from ill-suited group counselors. The existence of diversity in the use of the experiential group is evidence that counselor educators are grappling with this dilemma; greater awareness of their choices and the motivation behind their choices is needed [p. 207].

Pierce and Baldwin (1990) address the ethical issues involved in protecting student privacy while requiring personal-growth experiences as a part of the training of group counselors. They contend that student participation in a personal-growth experience is essential. At the same time, they address ways of coping with the ethical dilemma that group trainers and supervisors face in evaluating their students' use of leadership skills. Their key points are summarized below:

◆ Students should be given information about what to expect before they enter a program. A written statement on the rationale for participation in personal-growth activities is likely to improve student participation.
◆ Students can be given guidelines regarding appropriate and useful self-disclosure. It is helpful to train students about the specific risks and benefits of self-disclosure, using a combination of didactic methods and modeling on the trainer's part.
◆ Trainers need to demonstrate sensitivity to the privacy needs of the students in their group courses. Certain probing questions are likely to open up highly personal material that may not be relevant in the group.
◆ Trainers can provide exercises and assignments to establish individual goals for the course. Students can be involved in selecting topics for themes that they would be willing to explore in a group context.

Remley (1992) is one critic of professors' providing counseling for their students. Yet he is also convinced that teaching a group course without a concurrent group experience for students is unsatisfactory. To avoid the ethical problem, he combines didactic and experiential approaches in his group-counseling courses, but he does *not* lead the experiential group. He teaches the didactic half of the course by using a variety of standard teaching methods. The experiential half of the course consists of an encounter group that is led by an experienced counselor who does not teach in the graduate program. Other professionals who sometimes lead these groups are graduates from the program who want additional credits in advanced group counseling, counselors from local centers who are willing to lead groups in exchange for his consulting services, and professionals from the university counseling center. Remley's students do, however, reveal personal information in their papers for his course. He sees value in the self-reflective nature of these papers and does not recommend changing these assignments to avoid the problem of students' unintentionally disclosing private information. He reports that both he and his students are satisfied with this approach to the group course.

Forester-Miller and Duncan (1990) have identified some guidelines that they contend will reduce the potential risks associated with combining a personal-growth experience with a group course:

- ◆ The personal-growth experience should not be related to the process of screening for entering or continuing in the program.
- ◆ No aspects of the student's personal life, value system, or behavior in the group may be considered in evaluating the student's performance in the group experience. Students should be evaluated only on their acquisition of group skills.
- ◆ Students are not allowed to lead a personal-growth group of their peers without the presence of a professional staff member.

The challenge of educators is to provide the best training available, keeping in mind the safeguards mentioned above. If you are interested in further information on this topic, I suggest that you consult the standards of the ASGW (1989, 1991). For a more detailed discussion of various perspectives on dual-relationship controversies in the preparation of group counselors, see Herlihy and Corey (1992) and the articles that were cited in this section. These sources will give you more help in formulating your own position and guidelines on these topics.

◆ CHAPTER THREE ◆

Group Leadership

This chapter focuses on the influence of the group leader, as a person and as a professional, on the group process. After discussing the personal characteristics of effective leaders, I analyze the skills and techniques that are necessary for successful leadership and the specific functions and roles of group leaders. This chapter will give you enough information about these crucial topics to allow you to benefit fully from the discussion in the next two chapters of the stages in a group's development. The topics covered in this chapter also represent an important prelude to the theory chapters in Part Two.

The Group Leader as a Person

Group-counseling techniques cannot be divorced from the leader's personal characteristics and behaviors. Thus, I don't agree with those who attribute the success or failure of a group mainly to the characteristics of the participants or to the specific techniques being used to get the group moving. These are no doubt important variables, but I don't see them, by themselves, as determining the outcome of a group.

Group leaders can acquire extensive theoretical and practical knowledge of group dynamics and be skilled in diagnostic and technical procedures yet be ineffective in stimulating growth and change in the members of their groups. Leaders bring to every group their personal qualities, values, and life experiences. In order to promote growth in the members' lives, leaders need to live growth-oriented lives themselves. In order to foster honest self-investigation in others, they need to have the courage to engage in self-appraisal. If they hope to inspire others to break away from deadening ways of being, they need to be willing to seek new experiences themselves. In short, the most effective group direction is found in the kind of life the group members see the leader demonstrating and not in the words they hear the leader saying.

I am not implying that group leaders must be self-actualized beings who have successfully worked through all of their problems. The issue is not whether leaders have personal problems but whether they are willing to make serious attempts to live the way they encourage members to live. More important than being a finished product is the willingness to continually look at oneself to see whether one's life reflects life-giving values. The key to success as a group leader is the commitment to the never-ending struggle to become more effective as a human being.

Personality and Character

The following personal characteristics are vitally related to effective group leadership, since their presence or absence can facilitate or inhibit the group process. Keep these descriptions in mind as you evaluate your own characteristics.

PRESENCE. Being emotionally present means being moved by the joy and pain that others experience. If leaders recognize and give expression to their own emotions, they can become more emotionally involved with others. Leaders' ability to draw on these experiences makes it easier for them to empathize with and be compassionate toward group members. Presence also has to do with "being there" for the members, which involves genuine caring and a willingness to enter their psychological world. Being present implies that leaders are not fragmented when they come to a group session, that they are not preoccupied with other matters, and that they are open to their reactions in the group.

PERSONAL POWER. Personal power involves self-confidence and an awareness of one's influence on others. If group leaders do not feel a sense of power in their own lives (or if they do not feel in control of their destiny), it is difficult for them to facilitate members' movement toward empowerment. In short, it is not possible to give to others what one does not possess. It should be stressed that power does *not* mean domination and exploitation of others, which are abuses of power. Truly powerful leaders use the effect they have on group participants to encourage them to get in contact with their own unused power, not to foster their dependency. Personal power is accompanied by the recognition that one does not need to keep others in an inferior position to maintain one's own power. If members risk change, the bulk of the credit belongs to them. Yet group leaders are at times a key source of inspiration for members who are struggling to become the powerful people that they are capable of being.

COURAGE. Effective group leaders are aware that they need to exhibit courage in their interactions with group members and that they cannot hide behind their special role as a counselor. They show courage by taking risks in the group and admitting mistakes, by being occasionally vulnerable, by confronting others and revealing their own reactions to those they confront, by acting on intuitions and beliefs, by discussing with the group their thoughts and feelings about the group process, and by being willing to share their power with the group members. They can model important lessons to members by taking a stance toward life and acting in spite of the fact that they are imperfect. When members push themselves to leave familiar and secure patterns, they often report being anxious and scared. Group leaders can demonstrate, through their own behavior, the willingness to move ahead in spite of being uncertain about the terrain and somewhat fearful.

WILLINGNESS TO CONFRONT ONESELF. One of the leader's central tasks is to promote self-investigation in clients. Since group counselors cannot expect participants to do something that they themselves are not prepared to do, they must show that they are willing to question themselves. Self-confrontation can take the form of posing and answering questions such as the following:

◆ Why am I leading groups? What am I getting from this activity?
◆ Why do I behave as I do in a group? What impact do my attitudes, values, biases, feelings, and behaviors have on the people in the group?
◆ What needs of mine are served by being a group leader?
◆ Do I ever use the groups I lead to satisfy my personal needs at the expense of the members' needs?

Self-confrontation is an ongoing process, and there are no simple answers to these questions. The main issue is the *willingness* to continually raise questions in order to determine how honest you are with yourself about your motivations for being a group leader.

Self-awareness is a concomitant of the willingness to confront oneself. This essential characteristic of effective leadership includes awareness not only of one's needs and motivations but also of personal conflicts and problems, of defenses and weak spots, of areas of unfinished business, and of the potential influence of all of these on the group process. Leaders who are self-aware are able to work therapeutically with the transferences that emerge within the group setting, both toward themselves and toward other members. Furthermore, they are aware of their own vulnerabilities, especially their potential countertransference. They do not make the members responsible for their reactions, nor do they use the group as a place to seek their own therapy.

SINCERITY AND AUTHENTICITY. One of the leader's most important qualities is a sincere interest in the well-being and growth of others. Since sincerity involves being direct, it can also involve telling members what they don't want to hear. For a group leader, caring means challenging the members to look at parts of their lives that they are denying and discouraging any form of dishonest behavior in the group.

Authenticity is a close cousin to sincerity. Authentic group leaders do not live by pretenses and do not hide behind masks, defenses, sterile roles, and facades. Authenticity entails the willingness to appropriately disclose oneself and share feelings and reactions to what is going on in the group. But, as we will examine in more detail, authenticity does not imply indiscriminately "letting it all hang out." It is surely possible to be authentic without sharing every fleeting thought, perception, fantasy, and reaction. For instance, even though a leader might initially be sexually attracted to a member, it would not be wise to disclose this reality at the initial session. Such "holding back" does not imply inauthenticity.

SENSE OF IDENTITY. If group leaders are to help others discover who they are, they need to have a clear sense of their own identity. This means knowing what one values and living by internally derived standards, not by what others expect. It means being aware of one's own strengths, limitations, needs, fears, motivations, and goals. It means knowing what one is capable of becoming, what one wants from life, and how one is going to get what one wants.

A major part of the group-counseling experience involves members sorting out for themselves who they are and what identities they have assumed without conscious thought. When people live by outworn identities, their lives become meaningless. An effective group can be instrumental in providing a challenge to members to create projects that will bring a new level of meaning to their lives. Through the group experience, members see that their identity is not cast in stone but that they can reshape the purpose of their life. Group leaders who themselves continue to reshape their personal meanings can be an encouragement to the members.

BELIEF IN GROUP PROCESS AND ENTHUSIASM. The leader's deep belief in the value of the group process is essential to the success of the group. Why should members believe that the group experience will be of value to them if the leader is without enthusiasm for it? Too often practitioners lead groups in an agency simply because they are expected to without being convinced that group interventions make a difference.

The enthusiasm that group leaders bring to their groups can have an infectious quality. If leaders radiate life, the chances are slim that they will be consistently leading "dead groups." If group leaders lack enthusiasm for what they are doing, however, it is unlikely that they will inspire members and provide them with an incentive to work. This is not to say that practitioners should adopt a "cheerleading" style. What I am suggesting is that leaders need to show that they enjoy their work and like being with their groups. A leader's lack of enthusiasm is generally reflected in members' lack of excitement about coming to group sessions and in their resistance to doing significant work.

INVENTIVENESS AND CREATIVITY. Leaders need to avoid getting trapped in ritualized techniques and programmed presentations that are void of life. It may not be easy to approach each group with new ideas. Inventive and creative leaders are open to new experiences and to lifestyles and values that differ from their own.

One of the main advantages of group work is that it offers so many avenues for being inventive. Many groups with a special focus grow out of a leader's willingness to brainstorm. If fact, group leaders often develop an idea for a special group because of a concern in their life. For instance, group leaders who are struggling with stress in their personal and professional lives might create a support group for professionals with similar concerns. In addition, the very structure of groups encourages creativity in devising a wide range of approaches.

A Concluding Comment

As you review the characteristics of effective group leaders, do not burden yourself with thinking that you have to possess all of these qualities to the utmost. Consider such qualities on a continuum. For instance, it is not a matter that either you have traits such as courage, self-awareness, and a clear sense of identity or you don't. Instead, as your self-awareness increases, it will be easier for you to facilitate members' self-exploration. The challenge is for you to take an honest look at your personal qualities and make an assessment of your ability as a person to inspire others. Your own commitment to living up to your potential is a key tool. Your best way of leading others is by demonstrating what you believe in through your own life. Experiencing your own therapy (either individually or in groups) is one way to remain open to looking at the direction of your life. It is certainly not a matter of being the perfectly integrated group leader who has "arrived." Once you have arrived, after all, there is no place to go!

From my perspective the personal dimensions described in the preceding pages are essential. Yet they are not sufficient for successful leadership. Specialized knowledge and skills, as identified by the ASGW's (1991) *Professional Standards for Training of Group Workers* and described in the previous chapter, are central to effective group leadership. Later in this chapter we will examine these leadership skills in greater detail.

Special Problems and Issues for Beginning Group Leaders

Through my work in training and supervising group leaders and providing in-service workshops, I have come across a number of issues with special relevance for beginning leaders. Although these issues must be faced by all group leaders regardless of their experience, they are especially significant for those who are relatively inexperienced.

You may wonder whether you have what it takes to be an effective leader. My advice is to be patient with yourself and not to demand that you immediately become the "perfect group leader." Most practitioners I know (including myself) struggled over their competence when they began leading groups and still have difficult times. Such self-doubts are less of a problem if you are willing to continue to seek training and to work under supervision.

Initial Anxiety

Before you lead your first group, you will no doubt be anxious about getting the group started and about keeping it moving. In other words, you will probably be asking yourself questions like these with a certain degree of trepidation:

- ◆ Do I know enough to lead a group yet?
- ◆ What do the participants really expect of me?
- ◆ Will I be able to get the group started? How?
- ◆ Will I run out of things to say or do well before the end of the session?
- ◆ Should I take an active role, or should I wait for the group to start on its own?
- ◆ Should I have an agenda, or should I let the group members decide what they want to talk about?
- ◆ What techniques shall I use during the early stages of the group?
- ◆ What if nobody wants to participate? And what if too many people want to participate? How will I be able to take care of those who want to get involved?
- ◆ Will the group members want to come back?

In supervising and training beginning leaders, I encourage them to recognize that these doubts and concerns are perfectly normal and that moderate anxiety can be beneficial, because it can lead to honest self-appraisal. Anxiety can be counterproductive, however, if it begins to feed on itself and is allowed to freeze one into inactivity. Therefore, I encourage beginning leaders to voice their questions and concerns and to explore them in the course of the training sessions. Their very willingness to do this can allay some unnecessary anxiety, for the trainees discover that their peers share their concerns. Students frequently say that their peers appear to be so much more knowledgeable, skilled, talented, and self-confident than they themselves are. When they hear their peers express anxieties and feelings of inadequacy, these students realize that those who appear to be extremely self-confident are also struggling with self-doubts. The interchanges that occur when trainees are willing to openly discuss their anxieties offer invaluable opportunities for personal and professional growth. Exploring these feelings with peers and a supervisor can help the beginning leader distinguish between realistic and unrealistic anxiety and thus defuse unwarranted and counterproductive anxiety.

Self-Disclosure

Regardless of their years of experience, many group leaders struggle with the problem of self-disclosure. For beginning leaders the issue is of even greater concern. Although *what* to reveal and *when* are factors in determining the appropriateness of self-disclosure, the issue centers on *how much*. It is not uncommon to err on either extreme, disclosing too little or disclosing too much.

TOO LITTLE SELF-DISCLOSURE. If you try very hard to maintain stereo-typed role expectations and keep yourself mysterious by hiding behind your professional facade, you can lose your personal identity in the group and allow very little of yourself to be known. The reasons for functioning in a role (rather than as a person who has certain functions to perform) are many. One may be the fear of appearing unprofessional or of losing the respect of the members. Another may be the need to keep a distance or to maintain a "doctor/patient" relationship.

In addition to being unwilling to share your personal life, you may also be hesitant to disclose how you feel in the group or how you feel toward certain members. As a way of avoiding sharing your own reactions to what is occurring within the group, you might limit your interventions to de-tached observations. Such "professional" aloofness may be expressed by making interpretations and suggestions, asking questions rather than mak-ing personal statements, acting as a mere coordinator, providing one struc-tured exercise after another to keep the group moving, and clarifying issues. Although these functions are important, they can be carried out without keeping you from revealing what you are presently experiencing in the group.

In my opinion, the most productive form of sharing is disclosure that is related to what is going on in the group. For instance, if you have a persistent feeling that most members are not very motivated and are not investing themselves in the session, you are likely to feel burdened by the constant need to keep the meetings alive all by yourself, with little or no support from the participants. Disclosing how you are affected by this lack of motivation is generally very useful and appropriate.

TOO MUCH SELF-DISCLOSURE. At the other end of the continuum are the problems associated with excessive self-disclosure. Most beginning group leaders (and many experienced ones) have a strong need to be approved of and accepted by the group members. It's easy to make the mistake of "paying membership dues" by sharing intimate details to prove that you are just as human as the members. There is a fine line between appropriate and inappropriate self-disclosure. It is a mistake to assume that "the more disclosure, the better." It is also inappropriate to "let it all hang out" without evaluating the reasons for your disclosures, the readiness of the members, the impact that your sharing of intimate details is likely to have on them, and the degree to which your disclosures are relevant to the here-and-now process of the group.

You may be tempted to submit to group pressure to share more of yourself. Members often say to leaders: "We don't know much about you. Why don't you say more about yourself? For example, tell us about your hang-ups. *We* talk about ourselves, and now we'd like to see you come down to our level and open up too!" The members can exert more subtle, but no less strong, pressures for you to "become a member" of the group you are leading. Out of your attempt to avoid getting lost in a professionally aloof role, you may try too hard to be perceived as a friend and a fellow group member. If you decide to share personal concerns, it should be for the benefit of your clients. The place to explore these concerns (and thus serve your own needs) is a group in which you are a participant yourself. Group leading is demanding work, and you can make this work even more difficult by confusing your role and functions with those of the participants.

APPROPRIATE AND FACILITATIVE LEADER SELF-DISCLOSURE. Facilitative and appropriate self-disclosure is an essential aspect of the art of group leading. It is not necessary to disclose details of your past or of your personal life in order to make yourself known as a person or to empathize with the participants. A few words can convey a great deal, and nonverbal messages—a touch, a look, a gesture—can express feelings of identification and understanding. Appropriate disclosure does not take the focus away from the client and is never a contrived technique to get the group members to open up. Your sensitivity to how people respond can teach you a lot about the timeliness and value of your disclosures. Timeliness is a truly critical factor, for what might be inappropriate to disclose during the early stages of a group could be very useful at a later stage.

Yalom (1983, 1985) stresses that a leader's self-disclosure must be instrumental in helping the members attain their goals. He calls for selective disclosure that provides members with acceptance, support, and encouragement. For Yalom, group leaders who disclose here-and-now reactions, rather than detailed personal events from their past, facilitate the movement of the group.

Dealing with Difficult Group Members

Many students in group-counseling classes want to talk about the "difficult" members in the groups they are leading. Learning how to deal therapeutically with resistance and the many forms it takes is a central challenge for group leaders. When beginning counselors encounter members who are highly resistant, they often take the matter personally. They seem to view themselves as not being competent enough to cope with certain problematic members. If they were able to "break through" the layers of defenses of some of these difficult members, they believe, they would then feel competent. When I encounter such attitudes, I encourage my students to look at how they are being personally affected by the wide variety of problem behaviors. I suggest that they avoid categorizing people in their groups as "problem types" and instead attempt to understand the meaning of certain forms of resistance. A few of these forms are intellectualizing, emotionalizing, questioning, giving advice, being overly silent, monopolizing, storytelling, demanding answers and direction from others, dependency, hostility, aggression, and haughtiness. The fact is that many of us would display a variety of avoidance strategies if we were in a group. As old patterns are challenged and as we experience the anxiety that accompanies personal change, we are likely to be very creative in devising a pattern of resistive strategies. Remember, resistance does make sense and emerges from members for a purpose. My way of working with students is to teach them to take into account their own reactions to resistant members rather than focusing entirely on strategies for dealing with "problem members." For a more in-depth discussion of this topic, see M. Corey and Corey (1993b).

Dealing with Your Own Reactions to Member Resistance

When group members exhibit what you consider to be problematic behavior, you need to be aware of the tendency to respond with strong feelings. In the previous chapter you saw the importance of becoming aware of your own countertransference and learning how to deal effectively with your feelings. You may be threatened by those members who dominate and attempt to control the group, you may be angered by members who display resistive behavior, you may blame certain clients or the group as a whole for the slow pace or lack of productivity of the group, and you may take any signs of resistance personally.

If you ignore your own reactions, you are in essence leaving yourself out of the interactions that occur in the group. Your own responses—be they feelings, thoughts, or observations—are often the most powerful resource at your disposal in effectively handling resistant behaviors. As you've seen, a rationale for group leaders to experience their own group therapy is that this kind of self-exploration increases the chances that they will gain awareness of their own blind spots and potential vulnerabilities. Frequently, the "difficult" members who affect us the most are those who remind us of aspects of ourselves that we would just as soon deny.

In dealing with countertransference, supervision is most helpful. As a trainee you have the opportunity to explore with your supervisor and fellow group leaders your feelings of attraction or dislike toward certain members and learn a lot about yourself in the process. If you are leading a group alone and no longer have supervision, it is important that you be willing to consult with a qualified professional so that you can work through unresolved problems that may lie behind your feelings of countertransference. One of the advantages of working with a co-leader is that the partner can offer valuable feedback from an objective point of view and thus help you see things that may be blocked from your awareness. The topic of handling countertransference is discussed further in Chapter 6.

The Challenges of Dealing with a System

Most groups that you lead will be under the auspices of some type of institution—a school system, a community mental-health organization, a state mental hospital, a clinic, or a local or state rehabilitation agency. When conducting groups in an institutional setting, one quickly discovers that mastering group-leadership theory and practice doesn't guarantee successful groups. Being able to deal effectively with institutional demands and policies may at times be as important as being professionally competent.

A common problem among those who regularly do group work in an institutional setting is the constant struggle to retain dignity and integrity in a system where the administrators are primarily concerned with custodial care or with putting out "crisis fires" and are relatively indifferent to the pursuit of genuine group therapy or counseling. Another common problem besetting counselors in an institution relates to demands that they function as leaders of groups that they are unequipped or ill-equipped to handle. This problem is intensified by the fact that few institutions provide the training needed for the type of group leadership they demand and burden their counselors with such a work load that they don't have time for continuing education during their regular working hours. Thus, many institutional counselors are forced to take courses or attend workshops on their own time and at their own expense.

The point is that these problems exist and that it is up to you to deal with them and to work within the system while, at the same time, maintaining your professional standards and integrity. Ultimately, the responsibility for conducting successful groups is yours. Beware of blaming external factors for failures in your group-counseling programs. Watch out for statements that absolve you of responsibility and lead you to a sense of personal powerlessness:

- ◆ "My administrator is not sympathetic toward my attempts to develop groups."
- ◆ "The bureaucratic structure hampers my development of innovative and meaningful programs."
- ◆ "I'm prevented from doing any real counseling because of office policies."
- ◆ "The system doesn't reward us for our efforts."
- ◆ "We don't have the funds to do what is necessary."
- ◆ "The people in this community are not receptive to the idea of any type of group therapy; they won't come for help even when they need it."

I'm not implying that these complaints don't reflect real obstacles. I know from personal experience how taxing and draining any battle with a bureaucracy can be. There are times when the hassle of merely trying to get a group started in some institutions may overwhelm us to the point of questioning whether the effort is worth it. My point is that whatever the external obstacles, it is our responsibility to face them and not allow them to render us powerless.

Professional impotency of any kind is a condition that feeds on itself. When counselors abdicate their own power, they assume the role of victims, or they develop the cynical attitude that all their proposals and efforts are doomed—that nothing they do matters or makes any difference. So, by way of summary and restatement, when we surrender our power by placing all the responsibility for the failure of our programs outside of ourselves, we are in jeopardy of having our work devitalize us when it should be having the opposite effect.

The Group Leader as a Professional

Group-Leadership Skills

It is a mistake to assume that anyone with certain personal qualities and a desire to help will be an effective group leader. Successful leadership requires specific group-leadership skills and the appropriate performance of certain functions. Like most skills, leadership skills need to be learned and practiced.

ACTIVE LISTENING. Active listening involves paying total attention to the speaker and being sensitive to what is being communicated at both the verbal and nonverbal levels. Your ability to hear what is being communicated improves as your expertise improves. Many leaders make the mistake of focusing too intently on the content and, in doing so, don't pay enough attention to the way in which group members express themselves. Being a skilled group leader entails picking up the rich cues provided by members through their style of speech, body posture, gestures, voice quality, and mannerisms. (The topic of active listening will be dealt with in greater detail in Chapter 10, since attending and listening are key concepts of the person-centered approach to group work.)

RESTATING. In a sense, restating (or paraphrasing) is an extension of listening. It means recasting what someone said into different words so that the meaning is clearer to both the speaker and the group. Effective restating zeroes in on the core of a person's message, brings into sharper focus the meaning of what was said, and thus eliminates ambiguity. By capturing the essence of a member's message and reflecting it back, the leader helps the person continue the self-exploration process on a deeper level.

Restating is not an easy skill to master. Some group leaders, for example, confine themselves to simply repeating what was said, adding little new meaning and not really clarifying the message. Others overuse the technique, with the result of sounding mechanical and repetitive. The value of accurate and concise restating is twofold: it tells the participants that they are being understood, and it helps them see more clearly the issues they are struggling with and their own feelings and thoughts about these issues.

CLARIFYING. Clarifying, too, is an extension of active listening. It involves responding to confusing and unclear aspects of a message by focusing on underlying issues and helping the person sort out conflicting feelings. Often members say that they have ambivalent feelings or are feeling many things at once. Clarification can help the participants sort out their feelings so that they can focus more sharply on what they are actually experiencing. The same procedure applies to thinking. In clarifying, the group leader stays within the individual's frame of reference but, at the same time, helps the client put things into perspective; this, in turn, may lead to a slightly deeper level of self-exploration on the part of the client.

SUMMARIZING. The skill of pulling together the important elements of a group interaction or part of a session is known as summarizing. This ability is particularly useful when making a transition from one topic to another. Rather than merely proceeding from issue to issue, it is valuable to identify common elements in order to increase learning and maintain continuity.

Summarizing is especially needed at the end of a session. It is a mistake for a group leader to end a session abruptly, with little attempt to pull the session together. One of the leader's functions is to help members reflect on and make sense of what has occurred in their group. Summarizing encourages participants to think about what they have learned and experienced in a session and about ways of applying it to their everyday lives. At the end of the session group leaders may offer their own brief summary or ask each member in turn to summarize what has taken place, what the highlights of the session were, and how they responded to the interaction.

QUESTIONING. Questioning is probably the technique that novice group leaders tend to overuse most. Bombarding members with question after question does not lead to productive outcomes and may even have a negative impact on the group interaction. There are several problems with the ineffective use of questioning. Members feel violated, as if they had been subjected to the "third degree." The questioner probes for personal information while remaining safe and anonymous behind the interrogation. Also, a low-level questioning style on the leader's part provides a poor model for the members, who soon begin to imitate the leader's ineffective questioning style when they deal with one another.

Not all questioning is inappropriate. It is closed questions, which require a mere "yes" or "no" response, that are generally fruitless. And so are "why" questions, because they usually lead to intellectual ruminating. Instead, open questions—questions that open up alternatives and new areas of self-investigation—can be of real value. "*What* are you experiencing right now?" "*What* is happening with your body at this moment?" and "*How* are you dealing with your fear in this group?" are questions that can help the participants become more focused and feel their emotions more deeply. Therefore, it is important that leaders ask questions that, instead of merely probing endlessly, explore issues in greater depth. (The topic of questioning will be dealt with in greater detail in Chapter 15 as a special procedure used in reality group therapy.)

INTERPRETING. The leader interprets when he or she offers possible explanations for a participant's thoughts, feelings, or behavior. By offering tentative hypotheses concerning certain patterns of behavior, interpreting helps the individual see new perspectives and alternatives. Interpreting requires a great deal of skill. Interpreting too soon, presenting an interpretation in a dogmatic way, and encouraging the members to become dependent on the leader to provide meanings and answers are some of the common mistakes. Timing is especially important. Interpretations not only have to be made at a time when the person is likely to be willing to consider them but also need to be expressed in a tentative way that gives the person a chance to assess their validity. Although an interpretation may be technically correct, it may be rejected if the leader is not sensitive to the client's willingness or unwillingness to accept it. (I will return to the topic of interpreting in Chapters 6 and 7.)

CONFRONTING. Confrontation can be a powerful way of challenging members to take an honest look at themselves. If it is handled poorly, it also has the potential of being detrimental both to the person being confronted and to the group process. Many beginning leaders shy away from confrontation, because they fear its possible repercussions: blocking the group interaction, hurting someone, or becoming the target of retaliation. The problem with confrontation is that it can easily be seen as an uncaring attack. That's why skilled group counselors confront only when they care about the person, and they do so in a way that gives the person ample opportunity to consider what is being said. Skillful confrontation specifies the behavior or the discrepancies between verbal and nonverbal messages that are being challenged, so that no labeling can possibly occur.

It is useful for leaders to bring their own reactions into the act of confrontation. Thus, skilled counselors would not say, "George, you're a boring person." Instead, they might say: "George, I find it difficult to pay attention to what you say. I'm aware that I get impatient and that I tend to tune you out. I really don't like this, and I'd like to be able to focus on what you're saying." (Confrontation is a skill I will discuss in more detail in Chapters 11, 14, and 15.)

REFLECTING FEELINGS. Reflecting feelings is the skill of responding to the essence of what a person has communicated. The purpose is to let members know that they are being heard and understood. Although reflection entails mirroring certain feelings that the person has expressed, it is not merely a bouncing-back process. Reflection is dependent on attention, interest, understanding, and respect for the person. When reflection is done well, it fosters further contact and involvement; feeling understood and achieving a clearer grasp of one's feelings are very reinforcing and stimulate the person to seek greater self-awareness.

SUPPORTING. Supporting means providing group members with encouragement and reinforcement, especially when they are disclosing personal information, when they are exploring painful feelings, and when they are taking risks. A leader can provide support by being fully present at the appropriate time. This full presence requires a combination of skills: listening actively to what is being said, being psychologically present with the client, and responding in a way that encourages the client to continue working and to move forward.

The essence of this skill is knowing when it will be facilitative and when it will be counterproductive. Some group leaders make the mistake of being overly supportive, of supporting without challenging, or of supporting too soon. If leaders limit themselves to a style that is almost exclusively supportive, they deprive the members of potentially valuable challenges. Leaders who offer support too quickly when someone is exploring painful material tend to defuse the intensity of the experience and pull group members away from their feelings.

Support is particularly appropriate when people are faced with a crisis, when they are venturing into new territory, when they are trying to rid themselves of unconstructive behavior and establish new behaviors, and when they are attempting to implement what they are learning in the group to situations in their daily lives. (We will return to this topic in Chapter 10.)

EMPATHIZING. The core of the skill of empathy lies in the leader's ability to sensitively grasp the subjective world of the participant and yet retain his or her own separateness. In order to empathize effectively, a leader needs to care for and respect the group members. A background that includes a wide range of experiences can help the leader identify with others. (Empathy, too, is discussed in more detail in Chapter 10.)

FACILITATING. Facilitating is aimed at enhancing the group experience and enabling the members to reach their goals. Facilitation skills involve opening up clear and direct communication among the participants and helping them assume increasing responsibility for the direction of the group. Since facilitating is a vital tool in the person-centered approach, it will be explored in more depth in Chapter 10. Here I briefly list some specific ways in which group leaders can facilitate the group process:

◆ focusing on resistances within the group and helping members realize when they are holding back and why
◆ encouraging members to express their feelings and expectations openly
◆ teaching members to focus on themselves and their feelings
◆ teaching members to talk directly and plainly to one another
◆ working to create a climate of safety that will encourage members to take risks
◆ providing support for members as they try new behaviors
◆ fostering a member-to-member, rather than member-to-leader, interactional style
◆ encouraging open expression of conflict
◆ assisting members in overcoming barriers to direct communication

◆ helping members integrate what they are learning in the group and find ways to apply it to their everyday lives

◆ helping members achieve closure by taking care of any unfinished business in the group

INITIATING. Good initiating skills on the leader's part keep the group from floundering without direction. These skills include using catalysts to get members to focus on meaningful work, knowing how to employ various techniques that promote deeper self-exploration, and providing links among the various themes being explored in the group. Whereas appropriate leader direction can give the group a focus and keep it moving, too much direction can lead to passivity on the part of members.

SETTING GOALS. Productive goal setting is at the core of group counseling. Note that group leaders do not set goals for the clients; they help group members select and clarify their own specific goals. Although goal setting is especially important during the initial stages of a group, throughout the group's life leaders need to encourage the participants to take another look at their goals, to modify them if necessary, and to determine how effectively they are accomplishing them. Leaders who don't develop the intervention skills of challenging members to formulate concrete goals often find that their groups are characterized by aimless and unproductive sessions. (This topic is dealt with in more detail in Chapters 13 and 15.)

EVALUATING. Evaluating is an ongoing process that continues for the duration of a group. After each session the leader needs to assess what is happening in the group as a whole and within individual members. Leaders must also teach participants how to evaluate themselves and how to appraise the movement and direction of their group. For example, if at the end of a session most participants agree that the session was superficial, they can be challenged to find the reasons for the unsatisfactory outcome and to decide what they are willing to do to change the situation. (This topic is also explored in more depth in Chapters 13 and 15.)

GIVING FEEDBACK. A skilled group leader gives specific and honest feedback based on his or her observation of and reaction to the members' behaviors and encourages the members to give feedback to one another. One of the great advantages of groups is that the participants can tell other members their reactions to what they observe. The purpose of feedback is to provide a realistic assessment of how a person appears to others. The skill involved in productive feedback relates to the ability to present the feedback so that it is acceptable and worthy of serious consideration. Feedback that is specific and descriptive rather than global and judgmental is the most helpful.

SUGGESTING. Suggestion is a form of intervention designed to help participants develop an alternative course of thinking or action. It can take many forms, a few of which are giving information and advice, giving "homework assignments," asking members to think of experiments they might try inside and outside of the group, and encouraging members to look at a situation from a different perspective. Giving information and providing appropriate suggestions for alternative plans of action can hasten the progress members make in a group. Suggestions need not always come from the leader; members can make suggestions for others to consider.

The overuse of persuasion, suggestions, and advice entails some dangers. One is that members can be led to believe that simple and neat solutions exist for complex problems. Another is that members may remain dependent on other people to suggest what they should do in the face of future problems, instead of growing toward autonomy. There is a fine line between suggesting and prescribing, and the skill consists in using suggestions to enhance an individual's movement toward independence.

PROTECTING. Without assuming a parental attitude toward the group, leaders need to be able to safeguard members from unnecessary psychological or physical risks associated with being in a group. Although the very fact of participating in a group does entail certain risks, leaders can step in when they sense that psychological harm may result from a series of group interactions. For example, intervention is called for when a member is being treated unfairly or when an avalanche of feelings from the group is directed toward one person.

It takes skill for a leader to warn members of the possible dangers inherent in group participation without "setting them up" by implanting unnecessary fears about these risks. If leaders are overprotective, the members' freedom to experiment and learn for themselves is unduly restricted. If leaders fail to be protective enough, members may suffer from negative outcomes of the group experience.

DISCLOSING ONESELF. When leaders reveal personal information, as we have seen, they usually have an impact on the group. The skill consists of knowing what, when, how, and how much to reveal. If the leader shares appropriately, the effects on the group are likely to be positive, because the members may imitate his or her willingness and try to make themselves known. If the leader shares too much too soon, the effects are likely to be adverse, because the members may not be able yet to handle such openness comfortably. The most productive disclosure is related to what is taking place within the group. The skill involved in appropriate self-disclosure lies in the ability to present the information in such a way that the members are encouraged to share more of themselves.

MODELING. Group members learn by observing the leader's behavior. If leaders value honesty, respect, openness, risk taking, and assertiveness, they can foster these qualities in the members by demonstrating them in the group. From a leader who shows respect by really listening and empathizing, members learn a direct and powerful lesson in how respect is shown behaviorally. In short, one of the best ways to teach more effective skills of interpersonal relating is by direct example. (Modeling is discussed more fully in Chapter 13.)

LINKING.   One way of promoting interaction among the members is to look for themes that emerge in a group and then to connect the work that members do to these themes. Group leaders with an interactional bias—that is, those who develop the norm of member-to-member rather than leader-to-member communication—rely a great deal on linking. They encourage members to address others in the group directly, rather than looking at the leader and talking about others who are present. Members often have shared concerns, and through effective linking they can be helped to work through their problems by talking to others with similar concerns. By being alert for common concerns, the leader can promote interaction and increase the level of group cohesion. Through linking several members together, the leader is also teaching them how to take responsibility for involving themselves in the work of others. If the members learn how to bring themselves into group interactions, they become more independent of the leader and are also likely to feel a greater sense of belongingness by being connected to others.

BLOCKING.   Blocking refers to the leader's intervention to stop counterproductive behaviors within the group. It is a skill that requires sensitivity, directness, and the ability to stop the activity without attacking the person. The focus should be on the specific behavior and not on the person as a whole, and labeling should be avoided. For example, if a member is invading another member's privacy by asking probing and highly personal questions, the leader will point to this behavior as unhelpful, without referring to the person as a "peeping Tom" or an "interrogator." Some of the behaviors that need to be blocked are:

- *Scapegoating.* If several people gang up on an individual and begin dumping their feelings on the person in an accusatory manner, the leader can intervene and ask the members involved to turn their attention to what is going on inside them.
- *Group pressure.* Group leaders need to be aware of subtle or not-so-subtle attempts on the part of some members to pressure others to take a specific course of action or to make certain changes. It is one thing to offer feedback and another to demand that others change and accept standards imposed by the group.
- *Questioning.* Members who habitually interrogate others or ask too many closed questions can be invited to try to make direct statements instead of asking questions.

Other behaviors that group leaders need to watch for and block when necessary include making excuses to justify failure to make changes, breaking confidences, invading a member's privacy, perpetually giving advice, storytelling, gossiping, offering support inappropriately, and making inaccurate or inappropriate interpretations. Whatever the behavior, blocking must be carried out gently and sensitively.

TERMINATING. Group leaders need to learn when and how to terminate their work with individuals as well as groups. The skills required in closing a group session or ending a group successfully include providing members with suggestions for applying what they've learned in the group to their daily lives, preparing the participants to deal with the problems they may encounter outside of the group, providing for some type of evaluation and follow-up, suggesting sources of further help, and being available for individual consultation should the need arise.

An Integrated View of Group-Leadership Skills

It is not unusual for beginning group counselors to feel somewhat overwhelmed when they consider all the skills that are necessary for effective group leadership. If you, too, feel overwhelmed and discouraged, think about what it was like when you were learning to drive a car. If you had tried to think of all the rules and all the dos and don'ts simultaneously, you would have become frustrated and incapable of responding appropriately. The same applies to developing specific leadership skills. By systematically learning certain principles and practicing certain skills, you can expect to gradually refine your leadership style and gain the confidence you need to use these skills effectively. Participating in a group as a member is one way of developing these skills, for you can learn a lot through observing experienced people. Of course, you also need to practice these skills by leading groups under supervision. Feedback from group members, your co-leader, and your supervisor is essential to the refinement of your leadership skills. Seeing yourself in action on a videotape playback can be a powerful source of feedback that allows you to note the specific areas that are most in need of strengthening.

Like all skills, group-leadership skills exist in degrees, not on an all-or-nothing basis. They may be developed only minimally, or they may be highly refined and used appropriately. But through training and supervised experience these skills can be constantly improved. Table 3-1 presents an overview of the group-leading skills discussed in the preceding pages.

Becoming an Effective Multicultural Group Counselor

Until recently, little had been written specifically on the topic of training effective multicultural *group* counselors. In addition to the list of group-leadership skills already discussed, special knowledge and skills are required for dealing with culturally diverse groups. As I have said, acquiring this competency begins with group leaders' awareness of any cultural values, biases, and attitudes that may be hindering their development of a positive view of pluralism. Greeley, Garcia, Kessler, and Gilchrest (1992) contend that this awareness includes knowledge of the development of their own racial, cultural, gender, and sexual identity.

In writing about the future of psychotherapy with ethnic minorities, Comas-Diaz (1992) makes the point that sensitivity, understanding, and competence in working within a multicultural perspective will benefit both minority clients and therapists. She calls for providing training that encourages students to explore their own experiences with oppression and powerlessness. She asserts that developing skills in working with culturally diverse clients will be essential as our society becomes increasingly pluralistic.

As you study the contemporary theories and apply them to group counseling, strive to think about the cultural implications of the techniques that grow out of them. Consider which techniques may be more appropriate with specific client populations and in specific contexts. Even more important, think about ways to adapt the techniques you will be learning to a group member's cultural background. Perhaps most important of all, give consideration to ways in which you might acquire the personal characteristics required for becoming a culturally effective group counselor.

Counseling is by its very nature diverse in a multicultural society. Because there may be many different types of clients within a given group, it is easy to see that there are no ideal therapeutic approaches. Instead, different theories have distinct features that have appeal for different cultural groups. In addition, some theoretical approaches have distinct limitations, both in their concepts and their techniques, when they are applied to certain populations. Effective multicultural practice demands an open stance on the part of the practitioner, a flexibility, and a willingness to modify strategies to fit the needs and situations of the individuals within the group. It is clear that there is no one "right" technique that can be utilized with all clients, irrespective of their cultural background. It is important to realize that it takes time, study, and experience to become an effective multicultural group counselor. Multicultural competence cannot be reduced simply to cultural awareness and sensitivity, to a body of knowledge, or to a specific set of skills. This multicultural expertise requires that counselors have sufficient breadth and depth in all three areas (Leong & Kim, 1991).

Thomason (1991) offers useful advice to counselors who work with Native Americans, advice that also applies to other populations:

> A good counselor is, in a sense, like an artist who studies light and color and design and then deliberately forgets all rules in the act of creating a painting. In a similar way, the counselor interested in serving Native Americans should learn as much as possible about Native Americans in general and specific local tribes and then forget it in the live encounter with the client, who is the best teacher [p. 184].

D. W. Sue and his colleagues (1992), as you may recall, have developed a conceptual framework of competencies and standards for multicultural counseling. It includes three areas: beliefs and attitudes, knowledge, and skills. What follows is a condensed version adapted for group practitioners.

◆ **TABLE 3-1** ◆

Overview of Group-Leadership Skills

SKILL	DESCRIPTION	AIMS AND DESIRED OUTCOMES
Active listening	Attending to verbal and non-verbal aspects of communication without judging or evaluating.	To encourage trust and client self-disclosure and exploration.
Restating	Paraphrasing what a participant has said, to clarify its meaning.	To determine if the leader has understood correctly the client's statement; to provide support and clarification.
Clarifying	Grasping the essence of a message at both the feeling and the thinking levels; simplifying client statements by focusing on the core of the message.	To help clients sort out conflicting and confused feelings and thoughts; to arrive at a meaningful understanding of what is being communicated.
Summarizing	Pulling together the important elements of an interaction or session.	To avoid fragmentation and give direction to a session; to provide for continuity and meaning.
Questioning	Asking open-ended questions that lead to self-exploration of the "what" and "how" of behavior.	To elicit further discussion; to get information; to stimulate thinking; to increase clarity and focus; to provide for further self-exploration.
Interpreting	Offering possible explanations for certain thoughts, feelings, and behaviors.	To encourage deeper self-exploration; to provide a new perspective for considering and understanding one's behavior.
Confronting	Challenging members to look at discrepancies between their words and actions or their bodily and verbal messages; pointing to conflicting information or messages.	To encourage honest self-investigation; to promote full use of potentials; to bring about awareness of self-contradictions.
Reflecting feelings	Communicating understanding of the content of feelings.	To let members know that they are being heard and understood beyond the level of words.
Supporting	Providing encouragement and reinforcement.	To create an atmosphere that encourages members to continue desired behaviors; to provide help when clients are facing difficult struggles; to create trust.
Empathizing	Identifying with clients by assuming their frames of reference.	To foster trust in the therapeutic relationship; to communicate understanding; to encourage deeper levels of self-exploration.

◆ **TABLE 3-1** ◆

(continued)

SKILL	DESCRIPTION	AIMS AND DESIRED OUTCOMES
Facilitating	Opening up clear and direct communication within the group; helping members assume increasing responsibility for the group's direction.	To promote effective communication among members; to help members reach their own goals in the group.
Initiating	Promoting participation and introducing new directions in the group.	To prevent needless group floundering; to increase the pace of the group process.
Setting goals	Planning specific goals for the group process and helping participants define concrete and meaningful goals.	To give direction to the group's activities; to help members select and clarify their goals.
Evaluating	Appraising the ongoing group process and the individual and group dynamics.	To promote better self-awareness and understanding of group movement and direction.
Giving feedback	Expressing concrete and honest reactions based on observation of members' behaviors.	To offer an external view of how the person appears to others; to increase the client's self-awareness.
Suggesting	Offering advice and information, direction, and ideas for new behavior.	To help members develop alternative courses of thinking and action.
Protecting	Safeguarding members from unnecessary psychological risks in the group.	To warn members of possible risks in group participation; to reduce these risks.
Disclosing oneself	Revealing one's reactions to here-and-now events in the group.	To facilitate deeper levels of group interaction; to create trust; to model ways of revealing oneself to others.
Modeling	Demonstrating desired behavior through actions.	To provide examples of desirable behavior; to inspire members to fully develop their potential.
Linking	Connecting the work that members do to common themes in the group.	To promote member-to-member interactions; to encourage the development of cohesion.
Blocking	Intervening to stop counterproductive group behavior.	To protect members; to enhance the flow of group process.
Terminating	Preparing the group to close a session or end its existence.	To help members assimilate, integrate, and apply in-group learning to everyday life.

Note: The format of this chart is based on Edwin J. Nolan's article "Leadership Interventions for Promoting Personal Mastery," *Journal for Specialists in Group Work,* 1978, *3*(3), 132–138.

BELIEFS AND ATTITUDES OF CULTURALLY SKILLED GROUP WORKERS.
First, effective group leaders recognize and understand their own values, biases, ethnocentric attitudes, and assumptions about human behavior. They do not allow their personal values or problems to interfere with their work with clients who are culturally different from them. They seek to understand the world from the vantage point of their clients. They respect clients' religious and spiritual beliefs and values and are comfortable with differences between themselves and others in race or ethnicity, culture, and beliefs. They value bilingualism and do not view another language as an impediment to counseling.

Effective group workers monitor their functioning through consultation, supervision, and continuing education. They realize that group counseling may not be appropriate for all clients or for all problems. If necessary, they are willing to refer a client if it becomes evident that group counseling is not an appropriate form of treatment for the client or if, for example, a more homogeneous support group seems warranted.

KNOWLEDGE OF CULTURALLY SKILLED GROUP WORKERS. Second, culturally effective group practitioners possess certain knowledge. They know specifically about their own racial and cultural heritage and how it affects them personally and professionally. Because they understand the dynamics of oppression, racism, discrimination, and stereotyping, they are aware of the institutional barriers that prevent minorities from utilizing the mental-health services available in their community. They possess knowledge about the historical background, traditions, and values of the groups with whom they are working. They have knowledge of minority family structures, hierarchies, values, and beliefs. Because they understand the basic values underlying the therapeutic group process, they know how these values may clash with the cultural and family values of various minority groups. Furthermore, these practitioners are knowledgeable about community characteristics and resources. They know how to help clients make use of indigenous support systems. In areas where they are lacking in knowledge, they seek resources to assist them. The greater their depth and breadth of knowledge of culturally diverse groups, the more likely they are to be effective group workers.

SKILLS AND INTERVENTION STRATEGIES OF CULTURALLY SKILLED GROUP WORKERS. Third, effective group counselors have acquired certain skills in working with culturally diverse populations. Multicultural counseling is enhanced when practitioners use methods and strategies and define goals consistent with the life experiences and cultural values of their clients. Such practitioners modify and adapt their interventions in a group so as to accommodate cultural differences. They do not force their clients to fit within one counseling approach. They are able to send and receive both verbal and nonverbal messages accurately and appropriately. They are willing to seek out educational, consultative, and training experiences to enhance their ability to work with culturally diverse clients.

RECOGNIZING YOUR OWN LIMITATIONS. Although group practitioners can acquire general knowledge and skills that will enable them to function effectively with a variety of clients, it is not realistic to expect that they will know everything about the cultural background of all their clients. There is much to be said for letting group members teach the leader about relevant aspects of their culture. It is a good idea for leaders to ask members to provide them with the information they will need to effectively work with them. It helps to assess a client's degree of acculturation and identity development. This is especially true for individuals who have the experience of living in several cultures. They often have allegiance to their own home culture, and yet they may also find certain characteristics of their new culture attractive. They may experience conflicts in integrating the two cultures in which they live. These core struggles can be very productively explored in the context of an accepting group if the leader and the other members respect this cultural conflict.

Practitioners who truly respect the members in their group will patiently attempt to enter the world of their clients as much as they can. It is not necessary for practitioners to have the same experiences as their clients; what is more important is that they attempt to be open to a similar set of feelings and struggles. If this respect exists, all of the members benefit from cultural diversity within a group.

Special Skills for Opening and Closing Group Sessions

In training and supervising group leaders, I have found that many of them lack the skills necessary to open and close a group session effectively. For example, some simply select one member and focus on that person while the rest of the group sits passively back. Because of the leader's anxiety to "get things going," any member who raises a question is likely to receive attention, without any attempt to involve the other participants in the interaction. The problem is that when a group session begins poorly, it may be difficult to accomplish any sustained work during the rest of the meeting.

The way each session is closed is as important as the way it is initiated. I have observed group leaders who simply allow the time to elapse and then abruptly announce, "Our time is up; we'll see you all next week." Because of the leader's failure to summarize and offer some evaluation of the session, much of the potential value of the meeting is lost. The effective opening and closing of each session ensure continuity from meeting to meeting. Continuity makes it more likely that participants will think about what occurred in the group when they are outside of it and that they will try to apply what they have learned to their everyday lives. Together with encouragement and direction from the leader, it also facilitates the members' task of assessing their own level of participation at each session.

PROCEDURES FOR OPENING A GROUP SESSION. With groups that meet on a weekly or other regular basis, group leaders can follow a number of procedures to open the session:

1. Participants can be asked to briefly state what they want to get from the session. I prefer a quick "go-around" in which each group member identifies issues or concerns that could be explored during the session. Before focusing on one person, it is a good procedure to give all members a chance to at least say what they want to bring up during the meeting. In this way a loose agenda can be developed, and if a number of people are concerned with similar issues, the agenda will allow the repeated involvement of several members.

2. It is useful to give people a chance to express any thoughts that they may have had about the previous session or to bring up for consideration any unresolved issues from an earlier meeting. Unresolved issues among members themselves or between members and the leader can make progressing with the current agenda most difficult, since the hidden agenda will interfere with productive work until it has surfaced and been dealt with effectively.

3. Participants can be asked to report on the progress or difficulties they experienced during the week. Ideally, they have been experimenting with other ways of behaving outside of the group, they are getting involved in carrying out "homework assignments," and they are working on concrete plans that are action oriented. Even if not all of these desirable activities have taken place, time can be profitably used at the beginning of a session to share successes or to bring up specific problems.

4. The group leader may want to make some observations about the previous meeting or relate some thoughts that have occurred to him or her since the group last met.

PROCEDURES FOR CLOSING A GROUP SESSION. Before closing a session, allow time for integrating what has occurred, for reflecting on what has been experienced, for talking about what the participants may do between now and the next session, and for other summarizing. The leader may also find it useful to check with the group around the midpoint of the session and say something like this: "I'm aware that we still have an hour left before we close today. So I want to check with you to see if there are any matters you want to bring up before we close"; or this: "I'd like each of you to give me an idea of how you feel about this session. So far, have you gotten what you wanted from it?" Although these assessments in the middle of a session don't have to be made routinely, doing so from time to time can encourage members to evaluate their progress. If they are not satisfied with either their own participation or what is going on in the session, there is still time to change the course of the group before it ends.

Generally, members do not automatically evaluate the degree of their investment in the group or the extent of the gains they have made. The leader can do a great deal to guide participants into reflecting on the time limitations of their group and on whether they are satisfied with their participation. Members also need guidance in appraising how fully their goals are being achieved and how effectively the group is operating. If this periodic appraisal is done well, members have a chance of formulating plans for changes in the group's direction before it is too late. Consequently, it is less likely that they will leave the group feeling that they didn't get what they had hoped for when they joined.

In sum, the leader's closing skills bring unity to the group experience and consolidate the learning that has occurred during a session. The following is a list of steps that group leaders can take toward the end of each weekly session to help members evaluate their participation and bridge the gap between the group and their daily existence:

1. Group leaders should strive to close the session without closing the issues raised during the session. Although the anxiety that results from "leaving people hanging" may be counterproductive, it is not therapeutic to wrap up an issue too quickly. Many leaders make the mistake of forcing resolution of problems prematurely. Being task oriented, they feel uncomfortable about allowing members the time they need to explore and struggle with personal problems. In such instances, the leader's intervention has the effect of resolving quite superficially what may be complex matters that need to be fully explored. It is good for people to leave a session with unanswered questions, so that they will be motivated to think more about their concerns and come up with some tentative solutions on their own. Leaders need to learn the delicate balance between bringing temporary closure to an issue at the end of a session and closing the issue completely. The following comment, for example, indicates that the leader knows how to achieve such a balance: "I'm aware that the matter you worked on today has not been resolved. I hope, however, that you'll give further thought to what we did explore and to what you did learn about yourself today. I'm willing to work further with you on this issue in future sessions."

2. Summarizing can be effective at the end of each session. It is helpful to ask members to summarize both the group process and their own progress toward their goals. Comments can be made about common themes and issues that have emerged. The group leader can add summary comments, especially as they pertain to group process, but it is even better to teach members how to integrate what they have learned for themselves.

3. Participants can be asked to tell the group how they perceived the session, to offer comments and feedback to other members, and to make a statement about their level of investment in the session. By doing this regularly, members share in the responsiblity of deciding what they will do to change the group's direction if they are not satisfied with it. For example, if participants report week after week that they are bored, they can be asked what they are willing to do to relieve their boredom.

4. It is helpful to focus on positive feedback, too. Individuals who got involved should be recognized and supported for their efforts by both the leader and other participants.

5. Members can report on their homework assignments, in which they tried to put into practice some of their new insights; they can briefly discuss what they are learning about themselves through their relationships in the

group context; and they can make plans about applying what they have learned to problem situations outside the group.

6. Participants can be asked whether there are any topics or problems that they would like to put on the agenda for the next session. Besides linking sessions, this procedure prompts the participants to think about ways of exploring these concerns in the next meeting—that is, to work between sessions.

7. Group leaders may want to express their own reactions to the session and make some observations. These reactions and comments about the direction of the group can be very useful in stimulating thought and action on the part of the members.

In summary, the leader interventions that I have described illustrate that careful attention to opening and closing group sessions facilitates learning. It has the effect of challenging members to recognize their role in determining the outcomes of the group.

Procedures for Keeping a Session Moving

As you will see in the chapters on the various theories of group counseling, some approaches make extensive use of exercises and structured techniques to keep group sessions moving, whereas other approaches (such as person-centered therapy) reject any reliance on such exercises to promote interaction. Depending on how, when, and why they are used, structured exercises can enhance interaction and provide a focus for work, or they can promote member dependence on the leader for continuing to provide direction. In their eagerness to get a group moving and keep it moving, some leaders try one exercise after another in a hit-or-miss fashion. In my view exercises that relate to the overall plan of the group and are appropriately applied in a timely manner can be a useful tool for promoting change; lacking proper application, they can be counterproductive to the enhancement of the group process and of an individual's growth. A more detailed review of this subject is found in *Group Techniques* (G. Corey, Corey, Callanan, & Russell, 1992).

Group leaders should be careful not to overuse structured exercises. These exercises foster interaction among group members, and members can quickly become overly dependent on them. If whenever members encounter an impasse they are rescued with some kind of exercise, they will not learn to struggle on their own and draw on their own responses to get through the impasse. A typical misuse of structured exercise occurs when the group energy level is low and the members seem to have little investment in the group. If the leader continually plugs in an exercise as a kind of psychological pep pill, the group members will never make the effort to take a look at what is producing this boredom and apathy. Indeed, in this case, the exercise can encourage avoidance behaviors in the members.

I think that structured exercises can be very useful, especially during the initial and the final stages of a group. At the beginning of a group I use certain exercises designed to assist members in focusing on their personal goals, in dealing with their expectations and fears, and in building trust. These exercises consist of asking members to work in dyads, triads, and small groups on some selected topic—for example, what they hope to get from the group. During the closing phase of a group, I rely on some be-havior-rehearsal exercises, use contracts, suggest homework assignments, and use a variety of other procedures designed to help consolidate learning and facilitate its generalization.

Generally, I don't use techniques to actually stir up the members' desire to work. But once participants commit themselves to work—particularly when they have clearly identified issues to explore and have shown a willingness to penetrate their problems more deeply—I have found that a technique or an exercise can help them deepen their explorations and lead to new awareness and action.

Co-Leading Groups

There are pluses for both you and your group if you are able to arrange to be a co-leader. Leading a group alone can be a lonely experience at times, and the value of meeting with a co-leader for planning and processing should not be underestimated. The co-leadership style has many advantages and a few disadvantages. Here are some of the advantages:

- ◆ Group members can benefit from the life experience and insights of two therapists; the leaders may have different perspectives on any given situation.
- ◆ Two leaders can complement each other; a group can benefit from the combined strengths of the co-leading team.
- ◆ If one of the leaders is female and the other is male, they can re-create some of the original dynamics involved in the members' relation-ships with their parents; the opportunities for role playing are vari-ous.
- ◆ Co-leaders can serve as models for the participants with respect to how they relate to each other and to the group.
- ◆ The co-leaders can provide each other with valuable feedback; they can discuss what happened in the session and how to improve their skills.
- ◆ Each leader can grow from observing, working with, and learning from the other.
- ◆ Co-leaders provide more opportunities to facilitate linking among the work of members. While one leader is working with a particular member, the other leader can scan the group to get a sense of how other members are involved.
- ◆ The participants have the opportunity of getting feedback from two leaders instead of one; occasional differing reaction may inject vital-ity into the group and other opportunities for reflection and further discussion.

Most of the disadvantages of the co-leading model arise when the two leaders fail to create and maintain an effective working relationship. A central factor in determining the quality of this relationship is *respect*. The two leaders are likely to have their differences in leadership style, and they may not always agree or share the same perceptions or interpretations. But if there is mutual respect, they will be open and direct with each other, will trust each other, will work cooperatively instead of competitively, and will be secure enough not to need to "prove" themselves. If this trust is lacking, the members are bound to sense the absence of harmony, and the group will be negatively affected.

The choice of a co-leader, therefore, is an important one. A power struggle between incompatible co-leaders can have the effect of dividing the group. If the co-leaders do not work as a harmonious team, the group may follow their example and become fragmented. If the co-leaders evidence even subtle ongoing friction, they are providing a poor model of interpersonal relating. This friction can lead to unexpressed hostility among the members, which interferes with effective group work. If there are conflicts between leaders, it might be helpful to explore them openly in the group session, but ideally the two leaders have talked about any emerging differences between them in their private meetings. It is not helpful to a group for the co-leaders to pretend that everything is fine when, in fact, there is a strained relationship between them.

Although co-leaders do not necessarily have to work from the same theoretical approach, there are bound to be problems if they have vastly different perceptions about what the purpose of a group is or about their own role and function. For example, consider the situation in which one leader is intent on intervening with a great deal of advice aimed at providing answers for every problem a member raises, whereas the other leader is not interested in quick problem solving but, rather, encourages the members to struggle and to find their own direction. It is likely that they will be working at cross purposes and that their clients will get different messages about the purpose of the group.

It is important that co-leaders get together regularly to discuss any matters that may affect their work—for example, how they feel about working together, how they see their group, and how they can enhance each other's contribution. Ideally, they will spend time together before and after each session, so that they can plan for the upcoming session, share their perceptions, and iron out any difficulties that arise between them. In the two chapters that follow, I suggest specific issues that co-leaders might talk about in their meetings at each of the various stages of a group.

I prefer the co-leadership model both for leading groups and for training and supervising leaders. Co-leading offers a certain safety, especially when practitioners are leading a group for the first time. It is typical for beginning group leaders to experience self-doubt and anxiety. Facing a group for the first time with a co-leader whom you trust and respect can make what might seem like an onerous task a delightful learning experience.

Developing Your Style of Group Leadership

I said at the beginning of this book that my goal was to help you develop a leadership style that is your own and that expresses your uniqueness as a person. I believe that if you attempt to copy someone else's style, you can lose much of your potential effectiveness as a group leader. Surely you will be influenced by supervisors, co-leaders, and leaders of groups and workshops that you attend as a participant. But it is one thing to be influenced by others—most leaders borrow from many resources in developing their style of group leadership—and another to deny your own uniqueness by copying others' therapeutic styles, which may work well for them but may not be suited to you. The theoretical stance that each therapist needs to develop must be closely related to the therapist's values, beliefs, and personal characteristics. Thus, the first step in developing one's own approach is to come to an increased awareness of self.

In essence, there are as many methods of group counseling as there are leaders; and even those leaders who subscribe to a primary therapeutic model, such as behavior therapy or transactional analysis, show considerable variation in the way they lead groups. As a group leader, you bring your background of experiences and your personality, value systems, biases, and unique talents and skills to the group you lead. You also bring to it your theoretical preferences. You may advocate an approach that emphasizes thinking, one that stresses experiencing and expressing feelings, or one that focuses on action-oriented methods. On the other hand, your approach may be an eclectic one that integrates the thinking, feeling, and acting dimensions. Regardless of the approach you favor, your theoretical preferences will no doubt influence your style, especially with regard to the aspects of the group interaction on which you choose to focus.

Two Poles of a Continuum

Shapiro (1978) describes two types of group-leadership styles: the intrapersonally oriented and the interpersonally oriented. They can be best understood as ranging on a continuum from strictly intrapersonal to strictly interpersonal. Those group leaders who are *intrapersonally oriented* tend to deal with group members in a one-to-one manner. This style has often been referred to as individual counseling (or therapy) in a group situation. The focus is on intrapsychic concerns, or the conflicts and dynamics that exist within the individual. There is an interest in one's past, in the development of insight, and on the resolution of internal conflicts. In sum, the style of the intrapersonal leader focuses on the individual rather than on the group's dynamics or on the process of interaction among members.

At the other end of the continuum are those group leaders with an *interpersonal orientation*. They focus on the interactions among the members and on the relationships that are formed in the group. They are less interested than their intrapersonal counterparts in the individual's past, unconscious processes, and intrapsychic conflicts. This style of leadership emphasizes the here and now, the interactions among members, the group as a whole, the ongoing group dynamics, and the obstacles to the development of effective interpersonal relationships within the group.

I agree with Shapiro's contention that successful group leaders are able to incorporate both approaches into their style of leadership. Shapiro also stresses that effective group leaders have an orientation that fits their own personality, regardless of whether it leans toward the interpersonal or the intrapersonal pole. A crucial aspect of a leader's style is knowing when and to what degree each of these two orientations is appropriate with certain members or with a particular group. Learning how to integrate the best features of each orientation into a style that is personally your own is an ongoing process that depends heavily on your actual experience in the practice of leading groups. Of course, practice in leading groups under supervision, with the benefits of feedback, is one of the best ways to gradually develop a style that can be somewhat distinctive for you.

The Role of Theory in Developing a Personal Leadership Style

One way to build a foundation for a personal leadership style is to know the diverse range of theories of group counseling and their implications for styles of leading. Leading a group without an explicit theoretical rationale is somewhat like flying a plane without a map and instruments. Some students think of a theoretical model as a rigid structure that prescribes step by step what to do in specific situations. That's not my understanding of theory. I see theory as a set of general guidelines that you can use in your practice. A theory is a map that provides direction and guidance in examining your basic assumptions about human beings, in determining your goals for the group, in clarifying your role and functions as a leader, in explaining the group interactions, and in evaluating the outcomes of the group.

Developing a theoretical stance involves more than merely accepting the tenets of any one theory. It is an ongoing process in which group leaders keep questioning the "what," "how," and "why" of their practice. I encourage my students to take a critical look at the key concepts of the various theories and to also consider the theorists behind them, since a theory is generally a personal expression of the person who developed it. I further encourage them not to blindly follow any theory in totality, so that they will remain open and seriously consider the unique contributions as well as the limitations of the different approaches. If someone swallows a theory whole, the theory never gets properly digested and integrated. When practitioners settle on one theory and don't recognize its limitations, they are likely to misuse it and to assume that it is an axiom and a set of proven facts rather than a tool for inquiry. If your theoretical perspective causes you to ignore all others, you may force your clients to fit its confines instead of using it to understand them. The problem with adopting a theory in full is that one can become a "true believer." And the problem with true believers is that they limit their vision by screening out anything that doesn't fit their preconceived structures. Also, since they assume that their approach contains the whole truth, they are likely to try to impose it on others and to expect the same complete acceptance from them.

I also warn my students of the danger of discarding a theory in its entirety because of their objections to some aspects of it. For example, some students initially see little practical relevance in the psychoanalytic approach. They object to the lengthy period of time required by analysis, they consider the analysis of unconscious material as being beyond their scope of competence, and they typically don't appreciate the anonymous role of the therapist. I encourage these students to examine the model to see what concepts they *can* incorporate.

As you study in Part Two the ten chapters on theoretical models of group counseling, you will become aware of the commonalities and differences among these models and of the ways in which the various perspectives can shape your style as a group leader.

CHAPTER FOUR

Early Stages
in the Development
of a Group

This chapter and the next one are meant to be a road map of the stages through which a group progresses. This map is based on my own experience, as well as on the experience and writings of others, and describes the essential issues that characterize the development of a group.

A point that needs to be clarified right away is that the stages described in this chapter don't correspond to discrete and neatly separated phases in the life of a real group. There is considerable overlap between the stages, and groups don't conform precisely to some preordained time sequence that theoretically separates one phase from the next. Also, the content of the group process varies from group to group, and different aspects of the process may be stressed depending on the theoretical orientation of the leader, the purpose of the group, and the population that makes up the group. In spite of these differences, however, there does seem to be some generalized pattern in the evolution of a group.

A clear grasp of the stages of group development, including an awareness of the factors that facilitate group process and of those that interfere with it, will maximize your ability to help the members of your groups reach their goals. By learning about the problems and potential crises of each stage, you learn *when* and *how* to intervene. As you gain a picture of the systematic evolution of groups, you become aware of the developmental tasks that must be successfully met if a group is to move forward, and you can predict problems and intervene therapeutically. Finally, knowledge of the developmental sequence of groups will give you the perspective you need to lead group members in constructive directions by reducing unnecessary confusion and anxiety.

Several authors have discussed the stages of group-process development, and from these descriptions it is clear that although the specific *content* of groups varies considerably, the trends and *process* are very similar. In other words, regardless of the nature of the group and the leader's theoretical orientation, some generalized trends become apparent in most groups that meet over a period of time. Gazda (1989) observes that the stages through which counseling groups progress are most clearly visible in closed groups—those that maintain the same membership for the duration of the group. Schutz (1973b) writes about three stages: inclusion, control, and affection. Mahler (1969) describes in detail five stages: the formation, involvement, transition, working, and ending stages. Gazda's four stages are similar to Mahler's: exploration, transition, action, and termination. Hansen, Warner, and Smith (1980) write about five stages: initiation of the group, conflict and confrontation, development of cohesiveness, productivity, and termination. Yalom (1985) identifies three stages. The initial stage is characterized by orientation, hesitant participation, and the search for meaning; the second, by conflict, dominance, and rebellion; and the third, the stage of cohesion, by an increase of morale, trust, and self-disclosure.

This chapter begins with an examination of the leader's concerns in forming a group: getting prepared, announcing the group, screening and selecting the members, and preparing them for a successful experience. *Stage 1* of a group, under my four-stage breakdown, is the *orientation phase,* a time of exploration during the initial sessions. *Stage 2,* the *transition stage,* is characterized by dealing with conflict, defensiveness, and resistance. In Chapter 5 we will continue with *stage 3,* called the *working stage.* This phase is marked by action—dealing with significant personal issues and translating insight into action both in the group and outside of it. In *stage 4,* the *consolidation stage,* the focus is on applying what has been learned in the group and putting it to use in everyday life. I will conclude with an examination of postgroup concerns, including follow-up and evaluation. The description of these stages is based on models presented by various writers as well as on my own observations of the ways in which groups evolve.

Pregroup Issues: Formation of the Group

If you want a group to be successful, you need to devote considerable time to planning. In my view planning should begin with the drafting of a written proposal. The issues that need to be dealt with in the proposal include the basic purposes of the group; the population to be served; a clear rationale for the group—namely, the need for and justification of that particular group; ways to announce the group and recruit members; the screening and selection of members; the size and duration of the group; the frequency and time of meetings; the group structure and format; the methods of preparing members; whether the group will be open or closed; whether membership will be voluntary or involuntary; and the follow-up and evaluation procedures.

It cannot be overstressed that leader preparation at this formative phase is crucial to the outcome of a group. Thus, wise leaders spend time thinking about what kind of group they want and by getting themselves psychologically ready. If your expectations are unclear and if the purposes and structure of the group are vague, the members will surely engage in unnecessary floundering.

Announcing a Group and Recruiting Members

How a group is announced influences the way it will be received by potential members and the kind of people who will be attracted to it. It is imperative that you say enough to give prospective members a clear idea about the group's rationale and goals.

Although printed announcements have their value if they can reach the population they are intended for, they have their limitations. Regardless of how specific you are in these announcements, people—at least some of them—are likely to misunderstand them. Because of this risk, I am in favor of making direct contact with the population that is most likely to benefit from the group. For example, if you are planning a group at a school, it is a good idea to make personal visits to several classes to introduce yourself and tell the students about the group. You could also distribute a brief application form to anyone who wanted to find out more about the group.

Screening and Selecting Group Members

Both the ACA and the ASGW have ethical guidelines pertaining to screening group members. The ACA's (1988) existing guideline on this subject is as follows: "The member [counselor] must screen prospective group participants, especially when the emphasis is on self-understanding and growth through self-disclosure. The member must maintain an awareness of the group participants' compatibility throughout the life of the group." The ACA's (1993) proposed guideline for screening states: "Professional Counselors screen prospective group participants and maintain an awareness of group participants' suitability throughout the life of the group" (p. 17). The ASGW's (1989) guideline is: "The group counselor screens prospective group members (when appropriate to their theoretical orientation). Insofar as possible, the counselor selects group members whose needs and goals are compatible with the goals of the group, who will not impede the group process, and whose well-being will not be jeopardized by the group experience."

The setting in which leaders work may make it difficult to screen members individually. There are alternative ways of accomplishing the same purposes. For example, leaders can have prospective members complete a written questionnaire and can then arrange group interviews with them. If these methods of screening are not realistic, the initial group meeting can be used as an information and screening session. This idea of a pregroup meeting has particular relevance in settings where it is not practical to interview potential members individually.

In keeping with the spirit of this guideline, the leader, after recruiting potential members, must next determine who (if anyone) should be excluded. Careful screening will lessen the psychological risks of inappropriate participation in a group (discussed in Chapter 2). During the screening session, the leader can spend some time exploring with potential members any fears or concerns they have about participating in a group.

The leader can help them make an assessment of their readiness for a group and discuss the potential life changes that might come about. Members should know that there is a price for remaining the way they are as well as for making substantive changes. If they go into a group unaware of the potential impact of their personal changes on others in their lives, their motivation for continuing is likely to decrease if they encounter problems with their family. The efforts that the leader devotes to member selection and orientation can result in a group that is motivated and ready to work and contribute.

The following questions will also help you screen and select group members: "How can I decide who is most likely to benefit from the group I plan to create?" "Who is likely to be disturbed by group participation or become a negative influence for the other members?"

Screening should be a two-way process. Therefore, the potential members should have an opportunity at the private screening interview to ask questions to determine whether the group is right for them. Group leaders should encourage prospective members to be involved in the decision concerning the appropriateness of their participation in the group.

Of course, there is always the possibility that the leader has real reservations about including some people who are quite determined to join the group. Ultimately it is the group leader's task to make the decision. It is a difficult decision, and I recognize that screening and selection procedures are subjective. Yet certain guidelines can help a leader make this and other decisions wisely. I find that it is often difficult to determine which candidates will benefit from a group. During the private interview people are often vague about what they hope to get from the group. They may be frightened, tense, and defensive, and they may approach the personal interview as they would a job interview, especially if they are anxious about being admitted to the group. It is not uncommon in my experience to find people actually trying to be vague in their answers and attempting to say what they think I expect of them, much as they might in a job interview.

The basic criterion for the selection of group members is whether they will contribute to the group or whether they will be counterproductive. Some people can quite literally drain the energy of the group so that little is left for productive work. Also, the presence of certain people can make group cohesion difficult to attain. This is especially true of individuals who have a need to monopolize and dominate, of hostile or aggressive clients with a need to act out, and of people who are extremely self-centered and who seek a group as an audience. Others who should generally be excluded from most groups are people who are in a state of extreme crisis, who are suicidal, who have sociopathic personalities, who are highly suspicious, or who are lacking in ego strength and are prone to fragmented and bizarre behavior. It is difficult to say categorically that a certain kind of person should be excluded from all groups, for a guiding principle is that the type of group should determine who is accepted. Thus, an alcoholic might be excluded from a personal-growth group but be an appropriate candidate for a homogeneous group of individuals who suffer from addiction problems, be it addiction to alcohol, to other drugs, or to food.

If the private screening session is an opportunity for the leader to evaluate the candidates and determine what they want from the group experience, it is also a chance for the prospective members to get to know the leader and develop a feeling of confidence. The manner in which this initial interview is conducted has a lot to do with establishing the trust level of the group. This is why during the interview I stress the two-way exchange, hoping that members will feel free to ask questions that will help them determine whether they want to join this group at this particular time. Some questions I consider are: Does this person appear to want to do what is necessary to be a productive group member? Has the decision to join the group been made by the person, or has it been influenced by someone else's opinion? Does the candidate have clear goals and an understanding of how a group might help him or her attain them? Is the individual open and willing to share something personal?

The selection of members to ensure optimum group balance often seems an impossible task. Yalom (1985) proposes that cohesiveness be the main criterion in the selection of participants. Thus, the most important thing is to choose people who are likely to be compatible, even though the group may be a heterogeneous one.

In the context of group psychotherapy, Yalom argues that unless careful selection criteria are employed, clients may end up discouraged and unhelped. He maintains that it is easier to identify the people who should be excluded from a therapy group than it is to identify those who should be included. Citing clinical studies, he lists the following as poor candidates for a heterogeneous, outpatient, intensive-therapy group: brain-damaged people, paranoid clients, hypochondriacs, those who are addicted to drugs or alcohol, acutely psychotic individuals, and sociopathic personalities. In terms of criteria for inclusion, Yalom contends that the client's level of motivation to work is the most important variable. From his perspective groups are useful for people who have interpersonal problems such as loneliness, an inability to make or maintain intimate contacts, feelings of unlovability, fears of being assertive, and dependency. Clients who lack meaning in life, who suffer from diffuse anxiety, who are searching for an identity, who fear success, and who are compulsive workers might also profit from a group experience.

The key point is that screening needs to be done within the context of the type of group that a practitioner is offering. Whether a client is to be included or excluded has much to do with the purposes of the group.

Practical Concerns in the Formation of a Group

OPEN VERSUS CLOSED GROUPS.   Whether the group will be open or closed may in part be determined by the population and the setting. But the issue needs to be discussed and decided at the initial session. There are some distinct advantages to both kinds of groups. In the closed group no new members are added for the predetermined duration of its life. This practice offers a stability of membership that makes continuity possible and fosters cohesion. A problem with closed groups is that if too many members drop out, the group process is drastically affected.

In an open group, new members replace those who are leaving, and this can provide for new stimulation. A disadvantage of the open group is that new members may have a difficult time becoming a part of the group, because they are not aware of what has been discussed before they joined. Another disadvantage is that the changing of group membership can have adverse effects on the cohesion of the group. Therefore, if the flow of the group is to be maintained, the leader needs to devote time and attention to preparing new members and helping them become integrated.

VOLUNTARY VERSUS INVOLUNTARY MEMBERSHIP. Should groups be composed only of members who are there by their own choice, or can groups function even when they include involuntary members? Obviously, there are a number of advantages to working with a group of clients who are willing to invest themselves in the group process. As we have seen, Yalom (1985) maintains that in order to benefit from the group experience, a person must be highly motivated. Attending a group because one has been "sent" there by someone greatly curtails the chances for success. Yalom believes that people with a deeply entrenched unwillingness to enter a group should not be accepted. However, he thinks that many of the negative attitudes that involuntary candidates have about groups can be changed by adequately preparing members for a group.

In line with Yalom's view, I have found that many involuntary members learn that a group-counseling experience can help them make some of the changes they want to achieve. In many agencies and institutions, practitioners are expected to lead groups with an involuntary clientele. It is therefore important for these counselors to learn how to work within such a structure rather than holding on to the position that they can be effective only with a voluntary population. If by presenting the group experience in a favorable light the leader can help involuntary members see the potential benefits of the experience, the chances of productive work taking place will be increased. The key to successful participation lies in thorough member orientation and preparation, as well as in the leader's belief that the group process has something to offer to these prospective members.

HOMOGENEOUS VERSUS HETEROGENEOUS GROUPS. Group leaders need to decide the basis for the homogeneity of their groups. By homogeneous I mean composed of people who, for example, are similar in ages, such as a group for children, for adolescents, or for the elderly. Other homogeneous groups are those based on a common interest or problem. Thus, there are groups designed for people with a weight problem or for those who are overdependent on drugs or alcohol, as well as consciousness-raising groups for women or for men. Some school groups are especially designed for children and adolescents with learning difficulties or for those who have serious problems adjusting to the classroom environment.

For a given population with certain needs, a group composed of homogeneous members is more functional than one composed of people from different populations. Consider, for example, a group for adolescents. Such a group can focus exclusively on the unique developmental problems adolescents face, such as those related to interpersonal relationships, sexual development and identity, and the struggle toward autonomy. In a group designed for and composed exclusively of adolescents, the participants are encouraged to express many feelings that they have kept to themselves; through interaction with others of their same age, they can share their concerns and receive support and understanding.

While homogeneous membership can be more appropriate for certain target populations with definite needs, heterogeneous membership has some definite advantages for many personal-growth groups. A heterogeneous group, by representing a microcosm of the social structure that exists in the everyday world, offers the participants the opportunity to experiment with new behavior, develop social skills, and get feedback from many diverse sources. If a simulation of everyday life is desired, it is well to have a range of ages, backgrounds, and interests and concerns.

GROUP SIZE. The desirable size for a group depends on factors such as the age of the clients, the type of group, the experience of the group counselors, and the type of problems explored. Another element to be taken into consideration is whether the group has one leader or more. For ongoing groups with adults, about eight members with one leader seems to be a good size. Groups with children may be as small as three or four. In general, the group should have enough people to afford ample interaction so that it doesn't drag and yet be small enough to give everyone a chance to participate frequently without, however, losing the sense of "group."

FREQUENCY AND LENGTH OF MEETINGS. How often should groups meet? And for how long? These issues, too, depend on the type of group and, to some extent, on the experience of the leader. Once a week is a typical format for most counseling groups. With children and adolescents it is usually better to meet for more frequent and shorter sessions. For adults who are functioning relatively well a two-hour group each week is long enough to allow for some intensive work.

GROUP DURATION. In my opinion it is wise to set a termination date at the outset of a closed group, so that members have a clear idea of the time limit. The duration varies from group to group, depending on the type of group and the population. In private practice, groups can run for 30 to 50 weeks. Many college and high school groups typically run for the length of a semester (about 15 weeks). The group should be long enough to allow for cohesion and productive work yet not so long that it seems to drag on interminably.

MEETING PLACE. Another pregroup concern is the setting. Privacy, a certain degree of attractiveness, and a place that allows for face-to-face interaction are crucial. Since a poor setting can set a negative tone that will adversely affect the cohesion of the group, an effort should be made to secure a meeting place that will make it possible to do in-depth work.

The Uses of a Pregroup Meeting or the Initial Session

After the group membership has been established, another question needs to be raised: what is the group leader's responsibility in preparing members to get the maximum benefit from their group experience? My bias is that systematic preparation is essential and that it begins at the private screening interview and continues during the first few sessions. Preparation consists essentially of exploring with members their expectations, fears, goals, and misconceptions; the basics of group process; the psychological risks associated with group membership and ways of minimizing them; the values and limitations of groups; guidelines for getting the most from the group experience; and the necessity of confidentiality. This preparation can be done through a preliminary meeting of all those who will be joining a group.

In addition to the private interview with each person before the group is formed, I use the initial session as a group-screening device. The initial session is a good place to talk about the purposes of the group, to let members know how they will be using group time, to explore many of the possible issues that might be considered in the group, to discuss the ground rules and policies, and to begin the getting-acquainted process. Because I prefer to have people decide early if they are ready for a group and willing to become active members, I encourage the participants to consider the first session as an opportunity to help them make such a decision.

The structuring of the group, including the specification of norms and procedures, should be accomplished early in the group's history. Although some of this structuring will have been accomplished or at least begun at the private intake session, it will be necessary to continue this process the first time the group actually meets. In fact, structuring is an ongoing process, one that will be a vital part of the early phases of your group.

Preparation is particularly important for ethnic and minority clients, for many of them hold values that make it difficult for them to participate fully in a group experience. For example, the free participation and exchange of views in therapy groups appear to be in conflict with Asian values of humility and modesty. Furthermore many Asians do not share Western values of independence, individualism, directness of communication, expressiveness of feelings, and assertiveness (Lee, Juan, & Hom, 1984; Leong, 1992). Such clients may be threatened in a group experience, especially if they are expected to make deeply personal disclosures too quickly. Therefore, adequate preparation will be essential for Asian-American clients who have had no prior therapeutic experience in a group setting. Careful preparation will reduce the dropout rate of these clients and will help them maximize their gains (Ho, 1984). For individuals of other ethnic groups, preparation is no less important. It is essential that they know the purpose of the group as well as how the group experience can be of personal value to them. Group workers need to be aware that reluctance or resistance may be more the result of cultural background than of an uncooperative attitude.

Bowman and DeLucia (1993) maintain that there is increasing support for preparation methods that reduce clients' initial anxiety, clarify their expectations, and educate them about the group process. Their study found that preparation can have a positive impact on clients' beliefs, attitudes, and expectations about therapy. They also conclude that it can help members acquire skills that contribute to a successful group experience. Finally, preparation can give beginning group leaders a greater understanding of the group process and thus give them increased confidence in their leadership role.

Another advocate of systematic preparation for group members is Yalom (1985). His preparation includes explaining his theory of group work, exploring misconceptions and expectations, predicting early problems and stumbling blocks, discussing how the participants can best help themselves, talking about trust and self-disclosure, and exploring the risks associated with experimenting with new behavior. Yalom also discusses matters such as the goals of group therapy, confidentiality, and extragroup socialization.

Although I strongly believe in the value of systematic and complete preparation of group members, I also see the danger of overpreparation. For example, I typically ask members to talk early in the group about any fears or reservations they might have. I also explore a few common risks of participating in a group. In this particular area, however, if the leader becomes overspecific, the members may end up developing concerns or even fears that they never had before and that may become self-fulfilling prophecies. Also, too much structure imposed by the leader can stifle any initiative on the part of the members. The risks inherent in overpreparation should be balanced against those that accompany insufficient preparation. Excessive floundering and useless conflict during the group's later stages are often the result of a failure to acquire basic skills and understanding of group process.

My Guidelines for Orientation and Preparation of Members

I begin my preparation program at the time of screening each potential member, and I devote most of the first group meeting (what I call the pregroup meeting) to orientation about group process. This orientation continues during the initial phase of the group. As group-process issues emerge naturally while the group is taking shape, these concerns are dealt with.

I start by discussing with the participants the importance of their own preparation for group work. I stress that what they get from their group will depend largely on their level of investment. During the pregroup meeting and continuing into the initial group sessions, I view my role as helping members examine and decide on their level of commitment. We focus on what they want to get from participating in a group, and I assist them in defining clear, specific, and meaningful personal goals. After they have decided on some personal goals that will guide their work in the group, they are asked to refine these goals by developing a contract. (For details on ways of helping members define personal goals and formulate contracts, see the discussions of transactional analysis, behavioral group therapy, rational emotive behavior therapy, and reality therapy in Chapters 12–15.)

At the pregroup meeting I ask members to talk about their expectations, their reasons for being in the group, their fears about participating, and their hopes. I also provide them with some pointers on what they can do to maximize the benefit of the group in enabling them to make the changes they desire in their lives. I talk with them about appropriate self-disclosure. They hear that it is their decision to select the life issues that they want to explore in the group. They are also told that it is critical that they be willing to share persistent reactions they are having to here-and-now group interactions. My purpose is to teach them that the group will function only if they are willing to express what they are thinking and feeling about being in the group. In fact, their reactions provide the direction in which we typically proceed during the first few sessions. I also encourage them to bring up any questions or concerns they have about group process.

I ask the members to give some thought before they come to each session about personal issues that they are willing to bring up for exploration. Although they may have a specific agenda when they come to a group meeting, I also encourage them to remain flexible by being willing to work on other issues that may emerge spontaneously as others are interacting in the group. Because I continue to find that reading, reflecting, and writing do help members focus on themes for themselves, I attempt to get them to read selected books. They are typically asked to keep a journal, which allows them to spontaneously write about a range of reactions they have while they are in the group as well as reactions to what they experience between the sessions. They are encouraged to bring into the group the gist of what they have been writing in their journals. In this way they are taught about the value of continuing work that was begun during a session. Members hear over and over about the importance of using the group to practice new behaviors. I continually remind them that the group is not an end in itself but only a means to help them acquire new ways of thinking, feeling, and behaving. Thus, they are continually invited to try out new styles of behavior during the sessions to see if they might want to make certain changes.

In Chapter 1 of the student manual that accompanies the book, I have a set of suggestions entitled "Ways of Getting the Most from Your Group Experience." These guidelines serve as one method of teaching members how to become active participants.

Summary of Pregroup Issues

MEMBER FUNCTIONS AND POSSIBLE PROBLEMS. Before joining a group, individuals need to have the knowledge necessary for making an informed decision concerning their participation. Members should be active in the process of deciding if a group is right for them. Following are some issues that pertain to the role of members at this stage:

◆ Members should know all the specifics about a group that might have an impact on them.
◆ Members need to learn how to interview the group leader to determine if this group with this particular leader is appropriate for them at this time.
◆ Members can profit by preparing themselves for the upcoming group by thinking about what they want from the experience.

Problems can arise if members:

◆ are coerced into a group.
◆ do not have adequate information about the nature of the group.
◆ are passive and give no thought to what they want or expect from the group.

LEADER FUNCTIONS. The main tasks of group leaders during the formation of a group include these:

◆ developing a clearly written proposal for the formation of a group
◆ presenting the proposal to the proper authorities and getting the idea accepted
◆ announcing the group so as to provide as much information as possible to prospective participants
◆ conducting pregroup interviews for screening and orientation purposes
◆ making decisions concerning the selection of members
◆ organizing the practical details necessary to launch a successful group
◆ getting parental permission, if appropriate
◆ preparing psychologically for leadership tasks and meeting with co-leader (if appropriate)
◆ arranging for a preliminary group session for the purposes of getting acquainted, presenting ground rules, and preparing the members for a successful group experience
◆ making provisions for informed consent and exploring with participants the potential risks involved in a group experience

FINAL COMMENTS. Many groups that get stuck at an early developmental stage do so because the foundations were poorly laid at the outset. What is labeled as "resistance" on the part of group members is often the result of the leader's failure to give them adequate orientation. The nature and scope of pregroup preparation are determined largely by the type of group, yet there are common elements that can be addressed in most groups: member and leader expectations, basic procedures of the group, misconceptions about groups, and the advantages and limitations of group participation. This preparation can begin at the individual screening and can be continued during the initial session. Although building pregroup preparation into the design of a group takes considerable effort, the time involved pays dividends as the group evolves. Many potential barriers to a group's progress can be avoided by careful planning and preparation.

Stage 1: Initial Stage—Orientation and Exploration

Characteristics of the Initial Stage

The initial stage of a group is a time of orientation and exploration: determining the structure of the group, getting acquainted, and exploring the members' expectations. During this phase members learn how the group functions, define their own goals, clarify their expectations, and look for their place in the group. At the initial sessions members tend to keep a "public image"; that is, they present the dimensions of themselves they consider socially acceptable. This phase is generally characterized by a certain degree of anxiety and insecurity about the structure of the group. Members are tentative, because they are discovering and testing limits and are wondering whether they will be accepted.

Typically, members bring to the group certain expectations, concerns, and anxieties, and it is vital that they be allowed to express them openly. At this time the leader needs to clear up the participants' misconceptions and, if necessary, demystify groups. I see this initial phase as akin to the first few days one spends in a foreign land, having to learn the rudiments of a new language and different ways of expressing oneself.

Primary Tasks of the Initial Stage: Inclusion and Identity

Finding an identity in the group and determining the degree to which one will become an active group member are the major tasks of the initial stage. Schutz (1973a) says that this phase involves finding a balance between maintaining one's individuality within the group and making commitments. The following questions are the kind members often ask themselves at the initial sessions:

- "Will I be in or out of this group?"
- "How much do I want to reveal of myself?"
- "How much do I want to risk?"
- "How safe is it to take risks?"
- "Can I really trust these people?"
- "Do I fit and belong in here?"
- "Whom do I like, and whom do I dislike?"

◆ "Will I be accepted or rejected?"
◆ "Can I be myself and, at the same time, be a part of the group?"

The Foundation of the Group: Trust

Most writers agree that establishing trust is vital to the continued development of the group. Without trust, group interaction will be superficial, little self-exploration will take place, constructive challenging of one another will not occur, and the group will operate under the handicap of hidden feelings.

It is a mistake to assume that people will "naturally" trust one another as soon as they enter a group. And why should they trust without question? How do they know that the group will offer a more accepting and safer climate than society at large? My view is that people make a decision whether to trust a group. Such a decision depends in part on the leader's ability to demonstrate that the group can be a safe place in which to be oneself and reveal who one is. Also, by encouraging members to talk about any factors that inhibit their trust, the leader supports the therapeutic atmosphere necessary for openness and risk taking on the part of the members.

WAYS OF ESTABLISHING TRUST. The manner in which leaders introduce themselves can have a profound effect on the group's atmosphere. Is the leader enthusiastic, personable, psychologically present, and open? To what degree does the leader trust himself or herself? To what degree does the leader show trust and faith in the group? I have often heard members comment that it felt good to be trusted by their leaders.

The leader's success in establishing a basic sense of trust and security depends in large part on how well he or she has prepared for the group. Careful selection of members and efforts to make sure that the group is appropriate for them are very important, and so is the way in which the leader presents the ground rules of the group. Leaders who show that they are interested in the welfare of individual members and of the group as a whole engender trust. Talking about matters such as the rights of participants, the necessity of confidentiality, and the need for respecting others demonstrates that the leader has a serious attitude toward the group. If leaders care, chances are that the members will also care enough to invest themselves in the group to make it successful.

These comments, however, should not be interpreted to mean that trust building is the exclusive province of group leaders. True, leaders can engender trust by their attitudes and actions, but the level of trust also depends in large part on the members—individually and collectively.

Members usually bring to the group some fears as well as hopes. Participants will trust the group more if they are encouraged to expose their fears, because talking about them is likely to reveal that the fears are shared by others. If one member, for example, is concerned about not being able to express herself effectively and someone else expresses the same concern, almost invariably a bond is established between the two.

Silences and awkwardness are characteristically part of the beginning session. The more unstructured the group, the greater the anxiety and ambiguity about how one is to behave in a group. The members are floundering somewhat as they seek to discover how to participate. As the sessions progress, the members generally find it easier to raise issues and participate in the discussion. More often than not, these issues tend to be safe ones (at the beginning), and there is some talking about other people and there-and-then material. This is one way that the members go about testing the waters. It is as though they were saying "I'll show a part of myself—not a deep and sensitive one—and I'll see how others treat me."

WAYS OF MAINTAINING TRUST.   Another characteristic aspect of this initial phase is the tendency for some participants to jump in and try to give helpful advice as problems are brought up. It is the leader's task to make sure that these "problem-solving interventions" do not become a pattern, since they will cause enough irritation in other members to precipitate a confrontation with those who are quick to offer remedies for everyone's troubles.

The group's atmosphere of trust is also affected by the negative feelings that members often experience at the initial stage toward certain other members or toward the leader and over the fact that the group is not proceeding the way they would like to see it proceed. This is an important turning point in a group, and trust can be lost or enhanced depending on the manner in which negative feelings are dealt with. If conflict is brought out into the open and negative feelings are listened to nondefensively, there's a good chance that the situation producing these feelings can be changed. Members need to know and feel that it is acceptable to have and express negative feelings. Only then can the group move ahead to a deeper level of work. The members feel secure enough to take greater risks and are able to focus on struggles that are personally significant and to express here-and-now feelings.

As members reveal more of themselves to one another, the group becomes cohesive; in turn, this emerging cohesion strengthens the trust that exists in the group and creates the right atmosphere for members to try new ways of behaving in the group. When the members trust one another, they also trust the feedback they receive, which they can use as they try to carry these newly acquired behaviors into their daily lives.

Role of the Group Leader at the Initial Stage

MODELING.   When you lead a group, you set the tone and shape the norms as a model-setting participant as well as a technical expert (Yalom, 1985). It is important that you state your own expectations for the group openly during the first session and that you model interpersonal honesty and spontaneity. You need to be aware of your own behavior and of the impact you have on the group and to practice the skills that create a therapeutic milieu.

To be effective, a leader must be able and willing to be psychologically present in the group and to be genuine. Genuineness implies a level of enthusiasm and involvement in one's work as a leader. How can you expect the participants to get involved and believe in the potential of your group if you don't believe in what you are doing or if you are apathetic?

With regard to empathy—both cognitive and affective—you can create a therapeutic situation by being able to see and understand the world from the internal vantage point of the members. Another key characteristic is your sensitivity in attending and responding not only to what is said but also to the subtle messages conveyed beyond words. This applies to individual members as well as to the group as a whole. Finally, the people who make up your group need to sense that you have respect and positive regard for them.

All of these comments acquire special meaning if you keep in mind that at the initial stage, the participants depend very much on you. They turn to you for direction and structure and often focus so much on you that they neglect their own resources. This situation, which exists in most groups, requires that you be constantly aware of your own need to be seen as an authority figure and to keep tight control on the group. If you are not aware of these needs in yourself, you may keep the members of your group from becoming autonomous.

HELPING IDENTIFY GOALS. Another of your main tasks as a group leader is to help the participants get involved. You can do a lot to motivate, inspire, and challenge people to *want* to get the most from their group. At this stage you do it mostly by helping them identify, clarify, and develop meaningful goals. There are *general group goals,* which vary from group to group because they depend on the purpose of the group, and there are *group-process goals,* which apply to most groups. Some examples of these process goals are staying in the here and now, making oneself known to others, challenging oneself and others, taking risks, giving and receiving feedback, listening to others, responding to others honestly and concretely, dealing with conflict, dealing with feelings that arise in the group, deciding what to work on, acting on new insights, and applying new behavior in and out of the group.

In addition to establishing these group-process goals, you need to help members establish their own goals. Typically, people in the early stages of a group have vague ideas about what they want from a group experience. These vague ideas need to be translated into specific and concrete goals with regard to the desired changes and to the efforts the person is actually willing to make to bring about these changes. It is during the initial phase that this process needs to take place if the members are to derive the maximum benefit from the group. As I said earlier, you can do much to promote this process by assuming the responsibility of practicing and modeling the skills and attitudes that are necessary for effective group interaction.

One of the leader's basic tasks, and a most challenging one, is to bring hidden agendas out into the open. For example, some members may have hidden goals that are at cross-purposes with group goals. They may have an inordinate need to be the center of attention, or they may sabotage intimacy in a group because of their discomfort with getting close to others. A leader's function is to do what is needed to make these hidden agendas explicit. If such personal goals remain hidden, they are bound to undermine the effectiveness of the group.

THE DIVISION OF RESPONSIBILITY. A basic issue that group leaders must consider is responsibility for the direction and outcome of the group. Is a nonproductive group the result of the leader's lack of skill, or does the responsibility rest with the group members?

One way of conceptualizing the issue of leader responsibility is to think of it in terms of a continuum. At one end is the leader who assumes a great share of the responsibility for the direction and outcomes of the group. Such leaders tend to have the outlook that unless they are highly directive, the group will flounder. They see their role as that of the expert, and they actively intervene to keep the group moving in ways that they deem productive. A disadvantage of this extreme form of responsible leadership is that it robs the members of the responsibility that is rightfully theirs; if members are perceived by the leader as not having the capacity to take care of themselves, they soon begin to live up to this expectation by being irresponsible, at least in the group.

At the other end of the responsibility continuum is the leader who proclaims: "I am responsible for me, and you are responsible for you. If you want to leave this group with anything of value, it is strictly up to you. I can't do anything for you—make you feel something or take away any of your defenses—unless you allow me to."

Ideally, each leader will discover a balance, accepting a rightful share of the responsibility but not usurping the members' responsibility. This issue is central because a leader's approach to other issues (such as structuring and self-disclosure) hinges on his or her approach to the responsibility issue. The leader's personality is involved in the determination of how much responsibility to assume and what, specifically, this responsibility will include.

STRUCTURING. Like responsibility, structuring exists on a continuum. The leader's theoretical orientation, the type of group, and the membership population are some factors that determine the amount and type of structuring employed. Providing therapeutic structuring is particularly important during the initial stage, when members are typically confused about what behavior is expected in the group and are therefore anxious. Structure can be either useful or inhibiting in a group's development. Too little structure results in members' becoming unduly anxious, inhibiting their spontaneity. Too much structuring and direction, on the other hand, can foster dependent attitudes and behavior. The members may wait for the leader to "make something happen" instead of taking the responsibility for finding their own direction.

In my own groups the type of structure provided in the initial stage is aimed at assisting members to identify and express their fears, expectations, and personal goals. For example, members participate in dyads, go-arounds, and structured questions as ways of making it easier for them to talk to one another about their life issues. After talking to several people on a one-to-one basis, they feel more comfortable talking openly to the entire group. From the outset I try to help them become aware of what they are thinking and feeling in the here and now and encourage them to express their reactions. My interventions are aimed at promoting a high degree of interaction within the group, as opposed to creating the norm of having a few individuals do prolonged work while other members merely observe. This type of structuring is designed to let members assume increased responsibility for getting the most out of the group. As they learn basic norms, they tend to take the initiative rather than waiting for my direction.

What does research teach us about the value of providing structure during the initial stages of a group? Yalom (1983, 1985) cites a body of evidence indicating that ambiguity with respect to the goals and procedures of the group and to the behavior expected of members increases members' anxiety, frustration, and disengagement. Yalom found that either too much or too little leader activity or leader management was detrimental to the members' growth as well as to the autonomy of the group. Too much leader direction tends to limit the growth of members, and too little results in aimless groups. Yalom sees the basic task of the group leader as providing enough structure to give a general direction to the members while avoiding the pitfall of fostering dependency on the leader. His message to leaders is to structure the group in a way that promotes each member's autonomous functioning. Instead of inviting or calling on members to speak, for example, leaders can show them how to bring themselves into the interactions without being called on.

Research has shown the value of an initial structure that builds supportive group norms and highlights positive interactions among members. The leader must carefully monitor and assess this therapeutic structure throughout the life of a group, rather than waiting to evaluate it during the final stage. Structuring that offers a coherent framework for understanding the experiences of individuals and the group process will be of the most value. When therapeutic goals are clear, when appropriate member behaviors are identified, and when the therapeutic process is structured to provide a framework for change, members tend to engage in therapeutic work more quickly (Dies, 1983b). In agreement with the findings of Dies, another summary of the research indicates that leader direction during the early phases of a group tends to foster cohesion and the willingness of members to take risks by making themselves known to others and by giving others feedback (Stockton & Morran, 1982).

Another leader task during the early stage of a group involves being aware of the nature of members' concerns about self-disclosure. Leaders can intervene by helping members identify and process their concerns early in the life of a group. Robison, Stockton, and Morran (1990) cite research indicating that early structure imposed by the leader tends to increase the frequency of therapeutically meaningful self-disclosure, feedback, and confrontation. It appears that this structuring can also reduce negative attitudes about self-disclosure.

In summary, although many variables are related to creating norms and trust during the early phase of development, the optimum balance between too much and too little leader direction is one of the most important. The art is to provide structuring that is not so tight that it robs the group members of the responsibility of finding their own structure. Involving the group members in a continual process of evaluating their own progress and that of the group as a whole is one effective way of checking for the appropriate degree of structure. Members need to be taught specific skills of monitoring group process if they are to assume this responsibility.

Summary of the Initial Stage

STAGE CHARACTERISTICS.   The early phase of a group is a time for orientation and determining the structure of the group. Some of the distinguishing events of this stage are as follows:

◆ Participants test the atmosphere and get acquainted.
◆ Members learn the norms and what is expected, learn how the group functions, and learn how to participate in a group.
◆ Members display socially acceptable behavior; risk taking is relatively low, and exploration is tentative.
◆ Group cohesion and trust are gradually established if members are willing to express what they are thinking and feeling.
◆ Members are concerned with whether they are included or excluded, and they are beginning to define their place in the group.
◆ A central issue is trust versus mistrust.
◆ There are periods of silence and awkwardness; members may look for direction and wonder what the group is about.
◆ Members are deciding whom they can trust, how much they will disclose, how safe the group is, whom they like and dislike, and how much to get involved.
◆ Members are learning the basic attitudes of respect, empathy, acceptance, caring, and responding—all attitudes that facilitate trust building.

MEMBER FUNCTIONS AND POSSIBLE PROBLEMS.   Early in the course of the group, some specific member roles and tasks are critical to the shaping of the group:

◆ taking active steps to create a trusting climate
◆ learning to express one's feelings and thoughts, especially as they pertain to interactions in the group
◆ being willing to express fears, hopes, concerns, reservations, and expectations concerning the group
◆ being willing to make oneself known to others in the group
◆ being involved in the creation of group norms
◆ establishing personal and specific goals that will govern group participation
◆ learning the basics of group process, especially how to be involved in group interactions

Some of the problems that can arise are these:

◆ Members may wait passively for "something to happen."
◆ Members may keep to themselves feelings of distrust or fears pertaining to the group and thus entrench their own resistance.
◆ Members may keep themselves vague and unknown, making meaningful interaction difficult.
◆ Members may slip into a problem-solving and advice-giving stance with other members.

LEADER FUNCTIONS.* The major tasks of group leaders during the orientation and exploration phase of a group are these:

◆ teaching participants some general guidelines and ways to participate actively that will increase their chances of having a productive group
◆ developing ground rules and setting norms
◆ teaching the basics of group process
◆ assisting members in expressing their fears and expectations and working toward the development of trust
◆ modeling the facilitative dimensions of therapeutic behavior
◆ being open with the members and being psychologically present for them
◆ clarifying the division of responsibility
◆ helping members establish concrete personal goals
◆ dealing openly with members' concerns and questions
◆ providing a degree of structuring that will neither increase member dependence nor promote excessive floundering
◆ assisting members to share what they are thinking and feeling about what is occurring within the group
◆ teaching members basic interpersonal skills such as active listening and responding

---

*Exercises and activities designed to help students develop specific skills for each of the stages of a group are found in the student manual accompanying this book.

- assessing the needs of the group and facilitating in such a way that these needs are met
- showing members that they have a responsibility for the direction and outcome of the group

Stage 2: Transition Stage—Dealing with Resistance

Before a group can begin doing productive work, it must typically go through a somewhat difficult transition phase. During this stage members deal with their anxiety, resistance, and conflict, and the leader helps them learn how to begin working on their problems.

Characteristics of the Transition Stage

ANXIETY. The transition stage is generally characterized by increased anxiety and defensiveness. These feelings normally give way to genuine openness and trust in the stages that follow. Often the participants articulate their anxieties in the form of statements or questions to themselves or to the group, such as these:

- "I wonder whether these people really understand me and whether they care."
- "What good will it do to open myself up in here? Even if it works, what will it be like when I attempt to do the same outside of this group?"
- "What if I lose control? What if I cry?"
- "I see myself standing before a door but unwilling to open it for fear of what I'll find behind it. I'm afraid to open the door into myself, because once I open it a crack, I'm not sure I'll be able to shut it again. I don't know whether I'll like what I see or how you'll respond if I show you what is locked within me."
- "How close can I get to others in here? How much can I trust these people with my inner feelings?"

Anxiety grows out of the fear of letting others see oneself on a level beyond the public image. Anxiety also results from the fear of being judged and misunderstood, from the need for more structure, and from a lack of clarity about goals, norms, and expected behavior in the group situation. As the participants come to trust more fully the other members and the leader, they become increasingly able to share of themselves, and this openness lessens their anxiety about letting others see them as they are.

CONFLICT AND STRUGGLE FOR CONTROL. Many writers point out the central role that conflict plays during the transition stage of a group. Yalom (1985) sees this stage as characterized by negative comments and criticism. People may be quite judgmental of others and yet unwilling to open up to the perceptions that others have of them. In Yalom's eyes the transition stage is a time of struggling for power—among the members and with the leader—and establishing a social pecking order. The struggle for control is an integral part of every group: "It is always present, sometimes quiescent, sometimes smoldering, sometimes in full conflagration" (Yalom, 1985, p. 304).

Schutz (1973a), too, sees control as the central issue in the second stage of a group. Characteristic group behaviors include competition, rivalry, a jockeying for position, a struggle for leadership, and frequent discussions about the procedure for decision making and division of responsibility. Schutz contends that at this point the primary anxieties of participants relate to having too much or too little responsibility and too much or too little influence.

Before conflict can be dealt with and constructively worked through, it must be recognized. Too often both the members and the leader want to bypass conflict, out of the mistaken assumption that it is negative and indicates a poor relationship. If conflicts are ignored in a group, what originally produced the conflicts festers and destroys the chance for genuine contact. When conflict is recognized and dealt with in such a way that those who are involved can retain integrity, the foundations of trust between the parties are established. Recognizing that conflict is inevitable and that it can strengthen trust is likely to reduce the probability that members and the leader will try to dodge the conflicts that are a natural part of a group's development.

Ignoring conflicts and negative feelings requires energy, and that energy can be better employed to develop an honest style of facing and working through inevitable conflicts. Rogers (1970) observes that the first expression of significant here-and-now feelings is frequently related to negative attitudes toward other group members or toward the leader. According to Rogers, expressing negative feelings is one way to test the freedom and trustworthiness of the group. Members are discovering whether the group is a safe place to disagree, to have and express negative feelings, and to experience interpersonal conflict. They are testing the degree to which they can be accepted when they are not "being nice." The way conflict is recognized, accepted, and worked with has critical effects on the progress of the group. If it is poorly handled, the group may retreat and never reach a productive working stage. If it is dealt with openly and with concern, the members discover that their relationships are strong enough to withstand an honest level of challenge.

Certain group behaviors tend to elicit negative feelings that reflect conflict:

◆ remaining aloof and hiding behind the stance of observer
◆ talking too much and actively interfering with the group process through questioning, giving abundant advice, or in other ways distracting people from their work
◆ dominating the group, using sarcasm, belittling the efforts that are being made, and demanding attention

Intermember conflict is often the result of transference. Members may have intense reactions to one another; through exploring these reactions to specific individuals in a group, they can discover some important connections to the ways in which they transfer feelings from significant people in their lives to others. Below are some statements that can represent transference reactions:

◆ "You seem so self-righteous. Every time you begin to talk, I want to leave the room."
◆ "You bother me because you look like a well-functioning computer. I don't sense any feeling from you."
◆ "Your attempts to take care of everyone in here really bother me. You rarely ask anything for yourself, but you're always ready to offer something."

CHALLENGING THE GROUP LEADER.   Conflicts also often involve the group leader. You may be challenged on professional as well as personal grounds. You may be criticized for being "too standoffish" and not revealing enough of yourself, or you may be criticized for being "one of the group" and revealing too much of your private life. Here are some of the comments you may hear from your group members:

◆ "You're judgmental, cold, and stern."
◆ "No matter what I do, I have the feeling that it'll never be enough to please you. You expect too much from us."
◆ "You really don't care about us personally. I sense that you're just doing a job and that we don't count."
◆ "You don't give us enough freedom. You control everything."
◆ "You push people too much. I feel you aren't willing to accept a no."

It is helpful to distinguish between a *challenge* and an *attack*. An attack can take the form of "dumping" or "hit-and-run" behavior. Members who attack group leaders with statements like "This is how you are" don't give them much chance to respond, since the leaders have already been judged, categorized, and dismissed. It is quite another matter to openly confront leaders with how the members perceive and experience them. A member leaves room for dialogue when she says: "I'm aware that I'm not opening up in here. One reason is that if I do, I feel that you'll push me beyond where I want to go." This member openly states her fears but leaves enough room for the leader to respond and to explore the issue further. This is a challenge, not an attack.

Challenging the leader is often a participant's first significant step toward autonomy. Most members experience the struggle of dependence versus independence. If the members are to become free of their dependency on the leader that is characteristic of the initial group stage, the leader must allow and deal directly with these revealing challenges to his or her authority.

The way in which you accept and deal with challenges to you personally and to your leadership style greatly determines your effectiveness in leading the group into more advanced levels of development. Because I value the opportunities that challenges from group members offer, I attempt to deal with these challenges directly and honestly, to share how I am affected by the confrontation, to ask members to check out their assumptions, and to tell them how I see myself in regard to their criticism. I believe in keeping the lines of communication open, and I consistently try to avoid slipping into a "leader role" that entails diluting the challenge as a means of self-defense.

RESISTANCE. Resistance is behavior that keeps oneself or others from exploring personal issues or painful feelings in depth. It is an inevitable phenomenon in groups, and unless it is recognized and explored, it can seriously interfere with the group process. Resistance, however, is not merely something to be overcome. Since it is an integral part of one's typical defensive approach to life, it must be recognized as a way of protecting oneself from the anxieties I just examined. For group leaders not to respect the members' resistances is akin to their not respecting the members themselves. An effective way of dealing with resistances is to treat them as an inevitable aspect of the group process; that is, the leader acknowledges that resistance is a member's natural response to getting personally involved in a risk-taking course. An open atmosphere that encourages people to acknowledge and work through whatever hesitations and anxieties they may be experiencing is essential. The participants must be willing to recognize their resistance and to talk about what might be keeping them from full participation.

Before we proceed with our discussion, two points need to be made. One is that the members' unwillingness to cooperate is not always a form of resistance in the proper sense of the term. There are times when member "resistance" is the result of factors such as an unqualified leader, conflict between co-leaders, a dogmatic or authoritarian leadership style, a leader's failure to prepare the participants for the group experience, and a lack of trust engendered by the leader. In other words, group members may be unwilling to share their feelings because they don't trust the group leader or because the group is simply not a safe place in which to open up. It is imperative that those who lead groups look honestly at the sources of resistance, keeping in mind that not all resistance stems from the members' lack of willingness to face unconscious and threatening sides of themselves.

The second point is a warning against the danger of categorizing people and reducing them to labels such as "the monopolist," "the intellectualizer," "the dependent one," or "the quiet seducer." Although it is understandable that prospective leaders will be interested in learning how to handle "problem members" and the disruption of the group that they can cause, the emphasis should be on actual *behaviors* rather than on labels. Regardless of the type of behavior a member exhibits as a characteristic style, he or she is more than that particular behavior. If you see and treat a person just as a "monopolizer" or an "advice giver" or a "help-rejecting complainer," you contribute to cementing that particular behavior instead of helping the person work on the problems behind the behavior.

For example, if Maria is treated as a "monopolizer" and is not encouraged to explore the impact she has on the group, she will continue to see herself as others see her and respond to her. You can help Maria, as well as the entire group, by investigating the reasons for her need to keep the spotlight on herself and the effects of her behavior on the group. People need to become aware of the defenses that may prevent them from getting involved in the group and of the effects of these defenses on the other members. However, they should be confronted with care and in such a way that they are *challenged* to recognize their defensive behaviors and *invited* to go beyond them.

Another limitation of identifying "problem members" rather than problem behaviors is that most of those who participate in groups exhibit, at one time or another, some form of resistance. Occasional advice giving, questioning, or intellectualizing is not in itself a problem behavior. As a matter of fact, the group leader needs to be aware of the danger of letting participants become overly self-conscious of how they behave in the group. If clients become too concerned about being identified as "problem group members," they won't be able to behave spontaneously and openly.

Summary of the Transition Stage

STAGE CHARACTERISTICS. The transitional phase of a group's development is marked by feelings of anxiety and defenses in the form of various resistances. At this time members are:

- ◆ wondering what they will think of themselves if they increase their self-awareness and wondering about others' acceptance or rejection of them.
- ◆ testing the leader and other members to determine how safe the environment is.
- ◆ struggling with whether to remain on the periphery or to risk getting involved.
- ◆ experiencing some struggle for control and power and some conflict with other members or the leader.
- ◆ learning how to work through conflict and confrontation.
- ◆ feeling reluctant to get fully involved in working on their personal concerns because they are not sure others in the group will care about them.
- ◆ observing the leader to determine if he or she is trustworthy and learning from this person how to resolve conflict.
- ◆ learning how to express themselves so that others will listen to them.

MEMBER FUNCTIONS AND POSSIBLE PROBLEMS. A central role of members at this time is to recognize and deal with the many forms of resistance. Tasks include these:

- ◆ recognizing and expressing the range of feelings
- ◆ respecting one's own resistances but working with them
- ◆ moving from dependence to independence
- ◆ learning how to confront others in a constructive manner
- ◆ recognizing unresolved feelings from the past as they are being acted out in relation to the group leader
- ◆ being willing to face and deal with reactions toward what is occurring in the group
- ◆ being willing to work through conflicts, rather than avoiding them

Some problems can arise with members at this time:

- ◆ Members can be categorized as a "problem type," or they can limit themselves with a self-imposed label.
- ◆ Members may refuse to express persistent negative feelings, thus contributing to the climate of distrust.
- ◆ If confrontations are poorly handled, members may retreat into defensive postures, and issues will remain hidden.
- ◆ Members may collude by forming subgroups and cliques, expressing negative reactions outside of the group but remaining silent in the group.

LEADER FUNCTIONS. Perhaps the central challenge that leaders face during the transition phase is the need to intervene in the group in a sensitive manner and at the right time. The basic task is to provide both the encouragement and the challenge necessary for the members to face and resolve the conflicts that exist within the group and their own resistances and defenses against anxiety. As I indicated earlier, the genuine cohesion that allows for productive work to develop demands that this difficult phase of defensiveness and conflict be experienced and dealt with successfully.

The following are some of the major tasks that you need to perform during this critical period in a group's development:

- ◆ teaching group members the importance of recognizing and expressing their anxieties
- ◆ helping participants recognize the ways in which they react defensively and creating a climate in which they can deal with their resistances openly
- ◆ noticing signs of resistance and communicating to the participants that some of these resistances are both natural and healthy
- ◆ teaching the members the value of recognizing and dealing openly with conflicts that occur in the group
- ◆ pointing out behavior that is a manifestation of the struggle for control and teaching the members how to accept their share of responsibility for the direction of the group
- ◆ providing a model for the members by dealing directly and honestly with any challenges to you as a person or as a professional
- ◆ assisting the group members in dealing with any matters that will influence their ability to become autonomous and independent

Leaders need to be especially active during the first and second stages of a group. During the transition stage, active intervention and structuring are important, because generally the participants have not yet learned to work effectively on their own. If a conflict arises, for example, some members may attempt to move on to more pleasant topics or in some other way ignore the conflict. Group leaders need to teach members the value of expressing their feelings, thoughts, and reactions.

Destructive confrontations, with an attacking quality, can lead to an entrenchment of resistance and breed hostility and mistrust. But confrontation is appropriate even during the early stages of a group if it is done with sensitivity and respect. In fact, trust is often facilitated by caring confrontations on the leader's part. To avoid challenging a group in its early phases is to treat the members as though they were fragile. How leaders deal with conflict, resistance, anxiety, and defensiveness does much to set the tone of the group. In my view members have a tendency to follow the leader's manner of confronting.

Concluding Comments

This chapter has addressed various issues of group membership and group process that are central to your effectiveness as a group leader. I have focused on key concerns as the group is being formed, at its initial phase, and at the transitional period in a group's history. Emphasis has been placed on the central characteristics of the group at each phase, the member functions and possible problems, group-process concepts, and the leader's key tasks. It has been mentioned several times that your approach to leadership functions and skills hinges on your understanding of the roles that members play at the various stages in the group. Only if you are clear in your own mind about the various aspects of productive and unproductive member behaviors can you help group participants acquire the skills necessary for a successful group experience and correct behaviors that hinder self-exploration and involvement in the group. The next chapter continues this account of the unfolding of a group.

◆ CHAPTER FIVE ◆

Later Stages
in the Development
of a Group

Continuing the discussion of the evolutionary process of a group in action, this chapter focuses on the working stage, the final stage, and the postgroup issues of follow-up and evaluation. We will look at the major characteristics of the group at each phase, the member functions and possible problems that are likely to occur, and the group leader's key functions.

Stage 3: Working Stage—Cohesion and Productivity

The working stage is characterized by a more in-depth exploration of significant problems and by effective action to bring about the desired behavioral changes. This is the time when participants need to realize that they are responsible for their lives. Thus, they must be encouraged to decide what issues to explore in the group, they need to learn how to become an integral part of the group and yet retain their individuality, and they must filter the feedback they receive and decide what they will do about it. Consequently, it is very important at this stage that neither the group leader nor other members attempt to decide on a course of action or make prescriptions for a client.

Development of Group Cohesion

NATURE OF GROUP COHESION. Cohesion involves the group's attractiveness to the participants and a sense of belonging, inclusion, and solidarity. Although it may begin to develop in the early stages of a group, at this stage it becomes a key element of the group process. If trust has been established and if conflict and negative feelings have been expressed and worked through, the group becomes a cohesive unit. It is, in a sense, as if the group had gone through a testing period and the members had said to themselves "If it's OK to express negative reactions and conflict, then maybe it's OK to get close."

I have found that cohesion occurs when people open up and take risks.

The honest sharing of deeply significant personal experiences and struggles binds the group together, because the process of sharing allows members to identify with others by seeing themselves in them. Since cohesion provides the group with the impetus to move forward, it is a prerequisite for the group's success. Without a sense of "groupness" the group remains fragmented, the members become frozen behind their defenses, and their work is of necessity superficial. Groups do not become cohesive automatically. Cohesion is the result of a commitment by the participants and the leader to take the steps that lead to a group-as-a-whole feeling.

Although group cohesion is not in itself a sufficient condition for effective group work, in a sense all the characteristics of a well-functioning group are contingent on it. Cohesion fosters action-oriented behaviors such as self-disclosure, immediacy, mutuality, confrontation, risk taking, and translation of insight into action. Also, without group cohesion the participants don't feel secure enough to maintain a high level of self-disclosure.

Yalom (1985) maintains that research evidence shows cohesion to be a strong determinant of a positive group outcome. If members experience little sense of belongingness or attraction to the group, there is little likelihood that they will benefit, and they may well experience negative outcomes. According to Yalom, groups with a here-and-now focus are almost invariably vital and cohesive. By contrast, groups in which members merely talk about issues with a "there-and-then" focus rarely develop much cohesiveness.

COHESION AS A UNIFYING FORCE.   Although cohesiveness is usually necessary for effective group work, it can also actually hinder the group's development. When cohesiveness is not accompanied by a challenge to move forward by both the members and the leader, the group can reach a plateau. The group enjoys the comfort and security of the unity it has earned, but no progress is made.

In many of the adult groups that I lead, there are common human themes that most of the members can relate to personally, regardless of their age, sociocultural background, and occupation. Whereas members are likely to be aware in the earlier stages of the group of the differences that separate them, it is quite common as the group reaches a level of cohesion for members to comment on how alike they are in the feelings that connect them. Some of these responses are as follows:

- ◆ "I'm not alone in my pain and with my problems."
- ◆ "I'm more lovable than I thought I was."
- ◆ "I used to think that I was too old to change and that I'd just have to settle for what I have in life. Now I see that what I feel is no different from what the younger people in here feel."
- ◆ "I'm hopeful about my future, even though I know that I have a long way to go and that the road will be rough."
- ◆ "There are a lot of people in here I feel close to, and I see that we earned this closeness by letting others know who we are."
- ◆ "Intimacy is frightening, but it's also rewarding."

◆ "People can be beautiful once they shed their masks."
◆ "I learned that the loneliness I felt was shared by most people in this group."

As a group becomes cohesive, it is not uncommon for a woman in her early 20s to discover that she is very much like a man in his late 50s. Both of them may still be searching for parental approval, and they may both be learning how futile it is to look outside of themselves for confirmation of their worth. A man learns that his struggles with masculinity are not too different from a woman's struggles with her femininity. A woman learns that she is not alone when she discovers that she feels resentment over the many demands her family makes on her. An older man sees in a younger male member "his son" and allows himself to feel tenderness and compassion that he did not let himself experience earlier.

Other common themes evolving in this stage lead to an increase of cohesion: remembering painful experiences of childhood and adolescence, becoming aware of the need for and fear of love, becoming able to express feelings that have been repressed, discovering that one's worst enemy lives within oneself, struggling to find a meaning in life, feeling guilt over what one has done or failed to do, longing for meaningful connections with significant people, and beginning a process of finding one's identity. The leader can foster the development of cohesion by pointing out the common themes that link members of the group.

Characteristics of an Effective Working Group

Stage 3 is characterized by productiveness that builds on the effective work done in the initial and transition stages. Now that the members have truly become a group and have developed relationship skills that allow them a greater degree of autonomy, they are less dependent on the leader. Mutuality and self-exploration increase, and the group is focused on producing lasting results. Although the specific characteristics of a cohesive and productive group do vary somewhat with the type of group, there are some general trends that identify a group in its working stage:

◆ There is a here-and-now focus. People have learned to talk directly about what they are feeling and doing in the group sessions, and they are generally willing to have meaningful interactions. They are talking *to* one another, not *about* one another. They focus more on what is going on in the group than on stories about people outside of the group. When outside issues are brought up, they are often related to the group process. If Henry explores his fears of intimacy, for example, he will typically be asked to talk about being frightened of intimacy in the group as well as in his relationships in the real world.

◆ Members more readily identify their goals and concerns, and they have learned to take responsibility for them. They are less confused about what the group and the leader expect of them.

◆ Members are willing to work and practice outside the group to achieve behavioral changes. They are carrying out "homework assignments," and they bring into the sessions any difficulties they have had in practicing new ways of thinking, feeling, and behaving. They are willing to try to integrate thoughts, emotions, and behaviors in their everyday situations. They are better able to catch themselves when they are thinking and acting in old patterns.

◆ Most of the members feel included in the group. Those who are not active know that they are welcome to participate, and their lack of participation does not discourage others from doing meaningful work. Members who are having a difficult time feeling a sense of connection or belonging are free to bring this problem up in the sessions, and ideally it becomes a focal point for productive work.

◆ The group has almost become an orchestra, in that individuals listen to one another and do productive work together. Although the participants may still look to the leader for direction, as musicians look to the conductor for cues, they also tend to initiate a direction in which they want to move.

◆ Members continually assess their level of satisfaction with the group, and they take active steps to change matters if they see that the sessions need changing. In a productive group, members realize that they have a part in the outcomes. If they are not getting what they want, they generally say so.

Therapeutic Factors of a Group

The following brief overview offers a summary of the specific factors that ensure that a group will move beyond the security of cohesiveness into productive work. Three major aspects of the working stage, self-disclosure, confrontation, and feedback, are addressed in some detail.

TRUST AND ACCEPTANCE. Group members at the working stage trust one another and the leader, or at least they openly express any lack of trust. Trust is manifested in the participants' attitude of acceptance and in their willingness to take risks by sharing meaningful here-and-now reactions. Feeling that they are accepted, the members recognize that in the group they can be who they are without risking rejection. They dare to assert themselves, for example, because they know that they don't have to please everybody. At the working stage trust is generally high, because members have been willing to deal with any barriers to its establishment and maintenance. As is the case with other interpersonal relations, however, trust is not a static entity. Even during the advanced stages of a group, trust may ebb and flow, and there is an ongoing challenge for members to talk about how safe they feel in their group.

EMPATHY AND CARING. Empathy involves a deep capacity to recall, relive, and tap one's feelings through the intense experiences of others. By understanding the feelings of others—such as the need for love and acceptance, hurt about past experiences, loneliness, joy, and enthusiasm—members come to see themselves more clearly. Empathy means caring, and caring is expressed in a group by genuine and active involvement with the other members. It is also expressed by compassion, support, tenderness, and even confrontation. As people open themselves to others by showing their pain, struggles, joy, excitement, and fears, they make it possible for others to care for them. It is empathy that bridges the gap between peoples of different ethnic and cultural groups and allows them to share in universal human themes. Although clients' specific life circumstances may differ depending on their cultural background, groups allow a diverse range of people to come to realize what they have in common.

HOPE. If change is to occur, members must believe that change is possible, that they need not remain trapped in their past, and that they can take active steps to make their lives richer. Hope is therapeutic in itself, for it gives members the confidence to commit themselves to the demanding work that a group requires and motivates them to explore alternatives. Hope is characteristic of effective group leaders and underlies their beliefs about their clients, themselves, and the basic purposes to be achieved through group counseling (Couch & Childers, 1987).

As Yalom (1985) has indicated, the instillation and maintenance of hope are crucial in group therapy, so that members will remain in the group and other therapeutic factors can take effect. He cites research demonstrating that clients' high expectations that therapy will help them are significantly correlated with positive outcomes. Research also substantiates that the therapist's belief in the group process is critical to motivating clients.

A number of leadership strategies for fostering hope have been proposed (Couch & Childers, 1987). Some of these are using the pregroup interview as an opportunity to instill hope in members by creating positive (but realistic) expectations, acknowledging and validating concerns common to many of the participants, calling attention to improvements that members make, encouraging any signs of subtle and positive movement, letting members acknowledge one another's progress, and helping them assume responsibility for their own progress.

FREEDOM TO EXPERIMENT. Experimentation with different modes of behavior is a significant aspect of the working stage. The group is a safe place in which to try out novel behavior. After such experiments members can decide what behaviors they want to change. In everyday transactions people often behave in rigid and unimaginative ways, for they don't dare deviate from familiar and predictable ways of behaving. With group support participants can practice more functional ways of being. Role playing is often an effective way to practice new skills in interpersonal situations; then these skills can be applied to out-of-group situations. This topic is explored more fully in the discussions of psychodrama (Chapter 8) and Gestalt groups (Chapter 11).

COMMITMENT TO CHANGE. I said earlier that, for change to occur, a person must believe that change is possible. But hope alone is not enough. Constructive change requires a firm resolve to actually do whatever is necessary in order to change. This means deciding *what* to change as well as *how* to change it. Participants need to formulate a plan of action, commit themselves to it, and use the tools offered by the group process to explore ways of carrying it out. The support offered by the group is invaluable in encouraging the members to stick with their commitments even when they experience temporary setbacks. An inherent advantage of groups is that members can use one another to help themselves maintain their commitments. They can agree to call another member when they encounter difficulties in carrying out their plans, or they can call when they have made a successful breakthrough. A "buddy system" can be instrumental in teaching members how to ask for help and how to give this help to others, valuable social skills that they can also apply to relationships outside of the group. The topic of commitment in group counseling is discussed in more detail as it applies to reality group therapy (Chapter 15).

INTIMACY. Genuine intimacy develops in a group after people have revealed enough of themselves for others to identify with them. I've found that intimacy increases as people work through their struggles together. Members see that regardless of their differences, they all share certain needs, wants, anxieties, and problems. When members learn that others have similar problems, they no longer feel isolated; identification with others eventually brings about closeness, which allows the members to help one another work through fears related to intimacy. The group setting provides an ideal arena for members to discover their fears of intimacy and their resistances to getting close to others. The ultimate goal is to understand how one has avoided intimacy outside of the group and how one can accept intimacy in life without fear.

During the working phase members ideally not only recognize their resistances to interpersonal intimacy but also demonstrate a willingness to work through the fears associated with getting close to others. Such members tend to fear that if they do get close, they will not be able to control their impulses; if they care, they may suffer abandonment again; if they allow intimacy, they will merge with others and lose a sense of their own identity; and if they experience intimacy, they are opening themselves up to being emotionally wounded in various ways by others. A productive group offers many opportunities for members to face and challenge these fears. They are able to use the here-and-now group experience as a way of working through past hurts and early decisions that block intimacy. Old and unfinished issues are relived in the group context, and new decisions are made possible. Members are able to see connections between ways in which they are avoiding interpersonal intimacy both in the group and with significant others. What occurs within a group as the members develop mature forms of intimacy is detailed as follows by Ormont (1988): members make emotional space for one another; talk is simple and direct; there are no hidden agendas in the group; members are openly taking risks with one another; powerful feelings are present; members regard one another with a freshness that they have not shown before; and they are able to live in the moment, for the lingering remnants of their past hurts have been worked through successfully.

CATHARSIS.   The expression of pent-up feelings can be therapeutic, because it releases energy that has been tied up in withholding certain threatening feelings. This emotional release, which often occurs in an explosive way, leaves the person feeling freer. Also, keeping a lid on anger, pain, frustration, hatred, and fear means preventing spontaneous feelings such as joy, affection, delight, and enthusiasm from emerging. This emotional release plays an important part in many kinds of groups, but both group leaders and members sometimes make the mistake of concluding that mere catharsis implies "real work." Some disappointed members who do not have emotional releases are convinced that they are not really getting involved. It is not uncommon to witness members who experience "problem envy," or who are convinced that they are not getting as much from the group as others who have had more catharses than they have. Although it is often healing, catharsis by itself is limited in producing long-lasting changes.

Yalom (1985) notes that catharsis is an interpersonal process, for people do not get enduring benefits from ventilating feelings in an empty closet. He stresses that although catharsis is related to a positive outcome and that it is often necessary for change, it is certainly not enough. He puts the impact of catharsis into perspective: "The open expression of affect is without question vital to the group therapeutic process; in its absence a group would degenerate into a sterile academic exercise. Yet it is only a part of the process and must be complemented by other factors" (p. 85).

My experience has taught me that catharsis *may* be a vital part of a person's work in a group, especially if the client has a reservoir of unrecognized and unexpressed feelings. I have also learned that it is a mistake to assume that no real work occurs without a strong ventilation of feelings, since many people appear to benefit in the absence of catharsis. After catharsis has occurred, it is extremely important to work through the feelings that emerged, to gain some understanding of the meaning of the experience, and to make new decisions based on such understanding.

COGNITIVE RESTRUCTURING.   A central part of the work done in a group consists of challenging and exploring beliefs about situations. Understanding the *meaning* of intense emotional experiences is essential to further self-exploration. This cognitive component includes explaining, clarifying, interpreting, providing the cognitive framework needed for change, formulating ideas, and making new decisions. Groups offer members many opportunities to evaluate their thinking and to adopt constructive beliefs in place of self-limiting ones. This process of cognitive restructuring forms a central role in several therapeutic approaches, including Adlerian groups (Chapter 7), transactional analysis (Chapter 12), cognitive-behavioral groups (Chapter 13), and rational emotive behavior therapy (Chapter 14).

SELF-DISCLOSURE. Disclosure is not an end in itself; it is the means by which open communication can occur within a group. If disclosure is limited to safe topics or if it is equated with exposing secrets, the group cannot move beyond a superficial level. There are many barriers within us that keep us from self-disclosure—for example, fear of the intimacy that accompanies self-revelation, avoidance of responsibility and change, feelings of guilt and shame, fear of rejection, and cultural taboos. The willingness to overcome these barriers and make oneself known to others is a basic requirement at every stage of a group. During the working stage most members have developed enough trust to risk disclosing threatening material.

Since self-disclosure is the principal vehicle of group interaction, it is critical that group participants have a clear understanding of what self-disclosure is and is not. One level of self-disclosure involves sharing one's persistent reactions to what is happening in the group. Another level entails revealing current struggles, unresolved personal issues, goals and aspirations, joys and hurts, and strengths and weaknesses. If people are unwilling to share of themselves, they make it very hard for others to care for them. In the process of talking about concerns that occurred outside of the group or in the past, it is important for members to relate these issues to the here and now. By focusing on the here and now, participants make direct contact with one another and generally express quite accurately what they are experiencing in the present. The interactions become increasingly honest and spontaneous, because members are more willing to risk revealing their reactions to one another.

On the other hand, self-disclosure does *not* mean revealing one's innermost secrets and digging into one's past. Nor does it mean "letting everything hang out" or expressing every fleeting reaction to others. Self-disclosure should not be confused with telling stories about oneself or with letting group pressure dictate the limits of one's privacy. At times, in striving to be "open and honest" or in perceiving pressure from others in the group, some members say more than is necessary for others to understand them. They disclose so much that nothing remains private, and as a result they may feel deprived of their dignity.

In working with culturally diverse populations, keep in mind that self-disclosure is highly valued in most of the traditional counseling approaches that are covered in this book. However, self-disclosure is foreign to the values of some cultural groups. This premium that is placed on self-disclosure by most therapeutic approaches is often in conflict with the values of some European ethnic groups that stress that problems should be kept "in the family." Culturally different clients may be slow to self-disclose until they are fairly certain that it is safe to do so, which usually involves some testing of the leader and of other group members.

Unless clients challenge the obstacles to disclosure, their participation in a group will be very limited. As a group leader, you can recognize that some individuals with certain ethnic and cultural backgrounds will have difficulties in readily sharing their feelings and reactions, let alone revealing their deeper struggles. You can help such clients by demonstrating respect for their cultural values and at the same time encouraging them to express what they want from you and from the group. With your support and the understanding of other members, they are in a position to clarify their values pertaining to self-disclosure and can decide the degree to which they are willing to make themselves known to others. A good starting point is for them to talk about their difficulty in revealing themselves in a group setting.

CONFRONTATION. Like self-disclosure, confrontation is a basic ingredient of the working stage; if it is absent, stagnation results. Constructive confrontation is an invitation to examine discrepancies between what one says and what one does, to become aware of unused potential, and to carry insights into action. When confrontation takes place in the supportive environment of a group, it can be a true act of caring.

In a successful group, confrontation occurs in such a way that the confronters share their reactions to the person being confronted rather than their judgments of the person. A negative style of confrontation—that is, confrontation done in a hostile, indirect, or attacking way—is avoided, because it may leave people feeling judged and rejected. Done with care and sensitivity, confrontation by others ultimately helps members develop the capacity for the self-confrontation necessary to work through the problems they need to resolve.

Confrontation is an issue that group members, as well as group leaders, frequently misunderstand; it is often feared, misused, and seen as a negative act to be avoided at all costs. In my opinion, although support and empathy are certainly essential to group process, they can become counterproductive if carried to an excess. In other words, a group can cease to be effective if its members have colluded to interact only on a supportive level and agreed to focus almost exclusively on strengths and positive feedback. Unwillingness to challenge the others to take a deeper look at themselves results in overly polite and supportive exchanges that bear little resemblance to everyday interactions and that provide no incentive to extend oneself.

Group leaders can productively devote time to helping the participants clear up their misconceptions regarding confrontation and learn *what* to confront and *how* to confront in a constructive way. One of the most powerful ways of teaching constructive and caring confrontation is for leaders to model this behavior in their interactions in the group. By being direct, honest, sensitive, respectful, and timely in their confrontations, leaders provide the members with valuable opportunities to learn these skills through observing the leader's behavior.

I typically emphasize the following points about effective confrontation:

◆ Remember that confrontation must be based on respect for others and that it is aimed at challenging others to look at unrecognized and unexplored aspects of themselves.

◆ Use confrontation only if you want to get closer to a client and only if you are willing to stay with the person after the confrontation.

◆ Learn to discriminate between what may be a judgmental attack and a caring challenge. For example, instead of saying "All you do is take from the group; you never give anything of yourself," you may say: "I miss hearing from you. I'm wondering whether you'd like to be saying more. Are you aware of anything that's preventing you from expressing your feelings and thoughts?"

◆ When you confront a person, address his or her specific behaviors that affect others in the group, and explain exactly what the effect is.

◆ Take responsibility for your behaviors instead of blaming others for how you respond. Thus, instead of saying "You make me angry when you go off on your tangents," say, "I get impatient and angry when you digress." Instead of saying "You're boring," say, "I have a hard time staying with you when you speak, and I find that I'm becoming bored."

In sum, confrontation should be done so as to preserve the dignity of the one being confronted, without prejudice to the client, and with the purpose of helping the person identify and see the consequences of his or her behavior. Most importantly, confrontation should open up the channels of communication and not close them.

BENEFITING FROM FEEDBACK. Although I treat the topics of self-disclosure, confrontation, and feedback separately for the purpose of discussion, these therapeutic factors have some degree of overlap in actual practice. Most feedback entails self-disclosure, and sometimes feedback can be confrontational. Take, for example, the group member who says to another member: "I was very affected by the way you role-played talking to your father. It reminded me of my own father and the way I struggle with getting close to him." This is an example of both giving feedback and self-disclosing. Now consider the group member who says:" "When you talked about your father, your fists were clenched, yet you were smiling. I don't know which to believe—your fists or your smile." This type of feedback illustrates a confrontation, as well as some degree of self-disclosure. The person giving feedback disclosed some here-and-now reactions to another member.

The exchange of feedback among group members is widely considered to be a key element in promoting interpersonal learning (Morran, Stockton, & Bond, 1991). One study found that incorporating structured feedback exercises into a group contributed to the attainment of members' goals (Rohde & Stockton, 1992). For members to benefit from feedback, they need to be willing to listen to a range of reactions that others have to their behavior. It is important that there be a balance between "positive" feedback and corrective feedback (sometimes referred to as "negative" feedback). If members give one another their reactions and perceptions honestly and with care, all participants are able to hear what impact they have had on others and can decide what, if anything, they want to change. Such feedback is one of the most important ways in which learning takes place in a group. It can be of great help to the person who is exploring a problem, attempting to resolve a difficult situation, or trying different ways of behaving. Following are some points that can help members learn how to give and receive feedback:

◆ Global feedback is of little value. Reactions to specific behavior in the group, in contrast, provide clients with an immediate, independent assessment that they can compare with their own view.

◆ Concise feedback given in a clear and straightforward manner is more helpful than qualified statements and interpretive or mixed feedback (Stockton & Morran, 1980).

◆ Positive feedback is almost invariably rated as more desirable, more acceptable, more influential, and more conducive to change than corrective feedback. Such feedback focuses on the person's strengths as well as behaviors that might be a source of difficulty (Dies, 1983b; Morran, Robison, & Stockton, 1985; Morran & Stockton, 1980; Morran, Stockton, & Harris, 1991).

◆ Difficult feedback must be timed well and given in a nonjudgmental way, or else the person receiving it is likely to become defensive and reject it.

◆ Corrective feedback seems to be more credible and helpful when it is focused on observable behaviors and when it comes at a later phase of the group; it is also more likely to be accepted when it has been preceded by positive feedback (Stockton & Morran, 1981; Morran, Stockton, & Harris, 1991).

◆ Group members are often more reluctant to deliver corrective feedback than positive feedback. This reluctance is due partly to fears of rejection by other members and partly to fears of causing harm to the feedback recipient (Morran, Stockton, & Bond, 1991). Thus, it can be helpful for members to explore their fears about giving and receiving feedback. Members need to be taught the value of giving a range of feedback, as well as ways to deliver their reactions.

◆ Negative feedback is easier to take if the speaker says how he or she has been affected by the other member's behavior. This practice lessens the chances that members will be judged, for those who give feedback are focusing on themselves at the same time that they are talking to others about their behavior.

◆ Feedback with a quality of immediacy—that is, feedback given as a here-and-now reaction—is especially valuable and is far better than "stored up" reactions.

◆ Leader feedback is generally of higher quality than member feedback, but it is not more readily accepted (Morran et al., 1985).

Members sometimes make a global declaration such as "I'd like feedback!" If such clients have said very little, it is difficult to give them many reactions. Members need to learn how to ask for specific feedback and how to receive it. There is value in listening nondefensively to feedback, in really hearing what others want to say to us, and then in considering what we are willing to do with this information. As the group progresses to a working stage, members are typically more willing to freely give one another their reactions.

COMMENTARY. As my colleagues and I have written elsewhere (G. Corey, Corey, Callanan, & Russell, 1992), not all groups reach the working stage that is being described here. This does not necessarily mean that the leader is ineffective. Changing membership in a group can block its progress. Some populations simply may not be ready for the level of intensity that is often part of a working phase. If the tasks of the initial and transition stages were never mastered, the group can be expected to be stuck. For instance, some groups don't get beyond the hidden agendas and unspoken conflicts that were typical of earlier sessions. Or the members may simply not be willing to give much of themselves beyond safe and superficial encounters. They may have made a decision to stop at a safe level characterized by mutual support, rather than also challenging one another to move into unknown territory. Early interchanges between members and the leader or among members may have been abrasive, thus creating a climate of hesitancy and unwillingness to trust others. The group may be oriented toward solving problems or patching up differences. This orientation can discourage self-exploration, for as soon as a member raises a problem, other members may rush in with advice on how to remedy the situation. For reasons such as these and others, some groups never progress beyond the initial stage or the transition stage.

My colleagues and I have also observed that when a group does get to the working stage, it doesn't necessarily progress as tidily as the above characterization may suggest. Earlier themes of trust, unconstructive conflict, and the reluctance to participate surface time and again in a group's history. As one member put it, "There is no trust heaven in groups!" Trust is not a matter that is dealt with once and for all during the early stages of development. As the group faces new challenges, deeper levels of trust have to be earned. Also, considerable conflict may be resolved during the initial stage or transition stage, but new conflicts emerge in the advanced phases and must be faced and worked through. As is true with any intimate relationship, the relationships in the group are not static. Utopia is never reached, for the smooth waters may well turn into stormy seas for a time. Commitment to functioning as a group is necessary to do the difficult yet rewarding work of progressing.

Summary of the Working Stage

STAGE CHARACTERISTICS. When a group reaches the working stage, the central characteristics include the following:

- ◆ The level of trust and cohesion is high.
- ◆ Communication within the group is open and involves an accurate expression of what is being experienced.
- ◆ Members interact with one another freely and directly.
- ◆ There is a willingness to risk threatening material and to make oneself known to others; members bring to the group personal topics they want to discuss and understand better.
- ◆ Conflict among members is recognized and dealt with directly and effectively.
- ◆ Feedback is given freely and accepted and considered nondefensively.
- ◆ Confrontation occurs in a way in which those doing the challenging avoid slapping judgmental labels on others.
- ◆ Members are willing to work outside the group to achieve behavioral changes.
- ◆ Participants feel supported in their attempts to change and are willing to risk new behavior.
- ◆ Members feel hopeful that they can change if they are willing to take action; they do not feel helpless.

MEMBER FUNCTIONS AND POSSIBLE PROBLEMS. The working stage is characterized by the exploration of personally meaningful material. To reach this stage, members have certain tasks and roles:

- ◆ bringing into group sessions issues that they are willing to discuss
- ◆ giving others feedback and being open to receiving it
- ◆ sharing how they are affected by others' presence and work in the group
- ◆ practicing new skills and behaviors in daily life and bringing the results to the sessions
- ◆ offering both challenge and support to others and engaging in self-confrontation
- ◆ continually assessing their satisfaction with the group and actively taking steps to change their level of involvement in the sessions if necessary

Some problems may arise at this time:

- ◆ Members may collude to relax and enjoy the comfort of familiar relationships and avoid challenging one another.
- ◆ Members may gain insights in the sessions but not see the necessity of action outside of the group to bring about change.
- ◆ Members may withdraw because of anxiety over others' intensity.

LEADER FUNCTIONS. Some of the central leadership functions at this stage are these:

- ◆ providing systematic reinforcement of desired group behaviors that foster cohesion and productive work

- looking for common themes among members' work that provide for some universality
- continuing to model appropriate behavior, especially caring confrontation, and disclosing ongoing reactions to the group
- supporting the members' willingness to take risks and assisting them in carrying this behavior into their daily living
- interpreting the meaning of behavior patterns at appropriate times so that members will be able to reach a deeper level of self-exploration and consider alternative behaviors
- being aware of the therapeutic factors that operate to produce change and intervening in such a way as to help members make desired changes in thoughts, feelings, and actions
- focusing on the importance of translating insight into action; encouraging members to practice new skills
- encouraging members to keep in mind what they want from the group and to ask for it

Stage 4: Final Stage—Consolidation and Termination

Of all the group-leadership skills perhaps none is more important than the capacity to assist members in transferring what they have learned in the group to their outside environments. It is during the termination phase that consolidation of learning occurs; this is a time for summarizing, pulling together loose ends, and integrating and interpreting the group experience.

I see the initial and final stages as the most decisive times in the group's life history. If the initial phase is effective, the participants get to know one another and establish their own identity in the group. An atmosphere of trust develops, and the groundwork is laid for later intensive work. The final stage of a group's development is critical, because it is at this time that members engage in the cognitive work necessary to make decisions regarding what they have learned about themselves. If this phase is poorly handled by the group leader, the chances that the members will be able to use what they have learned are greatly reduced. Worse yet, members can be left with unresolved issues and without any direction how to bring these issues to closure.

It is essential that termination issues be brought up early in the course of a group's history. In every beginning the end is always a reality, and members need periodic reminders from the leader that their group will eventually end. Unless leaders recognize their own feelings about termination and are able to deal with them constructively, however, they are in no position to help members deal with separation issues. Some group leaders find endings difficult, for a variety of reasons, and they tend to ignore feelings of sadness or grief that some will experience as a group comes to an end.

There is a danger that as group members become aware that the end of the group is nearing, they will isolate themselves so that they do not have to deal with the anxiety that accompanies separation. Work generally tapers off, and new issues are rarely raised. If members are allowed to distance themselves too much, they will fail to examine the possible effects of their group experience on their out-of-group behavior. Thus, it is crucial that leaders help the participants put into meaningful perspective what has occurred in the group.

Effective Ways of Terminating a Group

This section deals with ways of terminating the group experience by exploring questions such as these: How can members best complete any unfinished business? How can members be taught, as they leave the group, to carry what they have learned with them and to use it to deal more effectively with the demands of their daily existence? What are the relevant issues and activities in the closing phases of a group? Because of space limitations, most of my discussion focuses on the termination of a closed group—that is, a group that consists of the same members throughout its life and whose termination date has been decided in advance.

DEALING WITH FEELINGS. During the final stages of the group it is a good practice for the leader to remind members that there are only a few sessions remaining, so that they can prepare themselves for termination and achieve successful closure of the group experience. Members need help in facing the reality that their group will soon end. Feelings about separation, which often take the form of avoidance or denial, need to be fully brought out and explored. It is the leader's job to facilitate an open discussion of the feelings of loss and sadness that accompany the eventual termination of an intense and highly meaningful experience. The members can be helped to face separation by the leader's disclosure of his or her own feelings about terminating the group.

During the initial phase, members are often asked to express their fears of *entering* fully into the group. Now, they should be encouraged to share their fears or concerns about *leaving* the group and having to face day-to-day realities without the group's support. It is not uncommon for members to say that they have developed genuine bonds of intimacy and have found a trusting and safe place where they can be themselves without fear of rejection. They may dread the prospect of being deprived of this intimacy and support. Also common are concerns of not being able to be so trusting and open with people outside the group. The leader's task is to remind the participants that if their group is special—close, caring, and supportive—it is because the members made the choice and the commitment to work together. Therefore, they can make similar choices and commitments, and be equally successful, in their relationships outside the group. This "boost of confidence" is not intended to deny the sense of loss and the sadness that may accompany the ending of a group. On the contrary, mourning the separation can be an enriching experience if the members of the group are encouraged to fully express their grief and anxiety.

EXAMINING THE EFFECTS OF THE GROUP ON ONESELF. Toward the end of the group it is useful to give all members an opportunity to put into words what they have learned from the entire group experience and how they intend to apply their increased self-understanding. To be fruitful, this examination must be concrete and specific. Statements such as "This group has been great. I really grew a lot, and I learned a lot about people as well as myself" are so general that the person who made the comments will soon forget what specifically was meaningful about the group experience. When someone makes this kind of sweeping statement, the leader can help the person express his or her thoughts and feelings more concretely by asking questions: "How has the group been good for you? In what sense have you grown a lot? What do you mean by 'great'? What are some of the things you actually learned about others and yourself?" I believe that focusing on the specific, conceptualizing, and sharing feelings and impressions increase the chances that members will retain and use what they have learned.

GIVING AND RECEIVING FEEDBACK. The giving and receiving of feedback are crucial during the final phases. Although members of an effective group have been sharing their perceptions and feelings at each session, the opportunity to give and receive summary feedback has a value of its own. To help participants take advantage of this opportunity, during one of the last few sessions I generally ask the members to give a brief summary of how they have perceived themselves in the group, what conflicts have become clearer, what the turning points were, what they expect to do with what they have learned, and what the group has meant to them. Then the others in the group say how they have perceived and felt about that person. I have found that concise and concrete feedback that also relates to the hopes and fears that the person has expressed is most valuable. Vague comments such as "I think you're a neat person" are of scarce long-term value. I've found that it is useful to ask members to write down specific feedback in their journals. If they do not record some of the things that people say to them, they tend to forget quickly. If they make a record, they can look months later at what others told them to determine if they are progressing toward their goals.

COMPLETING UNFINISHED BUSINESS. Some time needs to be allotted to working through any unfinished business relating to transactions between members or to the group process and goals. Even if some issues cannot be resolved, members should be encouraged to talk about them. For example, a member who has been silent throughout most of the group may say that she never felt safe enough to talk about her real concerns. Although it may be too late to work through this issue to everyone's satisfaction, it is still important to look at it and not leave it dangling.

CARRYING THE LEARNING FURTHER. I routinely discuss the various ways in which participants can go further with what they've learned in the group. These ways may include participation in other groups, individual counseling, or some other kind of growth experience. Participation in a successful group generally results in awareness of a number of specific issues. Members are not always able to work through these issues thoroughly; thus, they need to continue the process of exploration by finding other avenues of personal growth.

Summary of the Final Stage

STAGE CHARACTERISTICS. During the final phase of a group the following characteristics are typically evident:

- ◆ There may be some sadness and anxiety over the reality of separation.
- ◆ Members are likely to pull back and participate in less intense ways, in anticipation of the ending of the group.
- ◆ Members are deciding what courses of action they are likely to take.
- ◆ There may be some fears of separation as well as fears about being able to implement in daily life some of what was experienced in the group.
- ◆ Members may express their fears, hopes, and concerns for one another and tell one another how they were experienced.
- ◆ Members may evaluate the group experience.
- ◆ There may be talk about follow-up meetings or some plan for accountability so that members will be encouraged to carry out their plans for change.

MEMBER FUNCTIONS AND POSSIBLE PROBLEMS. The major task facing members during the final stage of a group is consolidating their learning and transferring what they have learned to their outside environment. This is the time for them to review and put into some cognitive framework the meaning of the group experience. Some tasks for members at this time are:

- ◆ to deal with their feelings about separation and termination
- ◆ to prepare for generalizing their learning to everyday situations
- ◆ to give others a better picture of how they are perceived
- ◆ to complete any unfinished business, either issues they have brought into the group or issues that pertain to people in the group
- ◆ to evaluate the impact of the group
- ◆ to make decisions and plans concerning what changes they want to make and how they will go about making them

Some problems can occur at this time:

- ◆ Members may avoid reviewing their experience and fail to put it into some cognitive framework, thus limiting the generalization of their learning.
- ◆ Due to separation anxiety, members may distance themselves.
- ◆ Members may consider the group an end in itself and not use it as a way of continuing to grow.

LEADER FUNCTIONS. The group leader's central tasks in the consolidation phase are to provide a structure that allows participants to clarify the meaning of their experiences in the group and to assist members in generalizing their learning from the group to everyday situations. Tasks at this period include these:

- ◆ assisting members in dealing with any feelings they may have about termination
- ◆ giving members an opportunity to express and deal with any unfinished business within the group
- ◆ reinforcing changes that members have made and ensuring that members have information about resources to enable them to make further changes
- ◆ assisting members in determining how they will apply specific skills in a variety of situations in daily life
- ◆ working with members to develop specific contracts and homework assignments as practical ways of making changes
- ◆ assisting participants to develop a conceptual framework that will help them understand, integrate, consolidate, and remember what they have learned in the group
- ◆ providing opportunities for members to give one another constructive feedback
- ◆ reemphasizing the importance of maintaining confidentiality after the group is over

Postgroup Issues: Follow-Up and Evaluation

Just as the formation of a group and the leader's preparatory activities greatly affect the group's progress through its various stages, the work that confronts the leader once the group has come to an end is also highly important. Two issues are dynamically related to the successful completion of a group's development: follow-up and evaluation. The questions that need to be raised are: What kind of follow-up should be provided after the termination of a group? What is the group leader's responsibility in evaluating the outcomes of a group? How can the leader help members evaluate the effectiveness of their group experience?

The Follow-Up Session

It is wise at the the final session of a group to decide on a time for a follow-up session to discuss the group experience and put it in perspective. This session is valuable not only because it offers the group leader an opportunity to assess the outcomes of the group but also because it gives the members the chance to gain a more realistic picture of the impact that the group has had on them and their peers.

At the follow-up session members can discuss the efforts they have made since the termination of the group to implement their learning in the real world. They can report on the difficulties they have encountered, share the joys and successes they have experienced in life, and recall some of the things that occurred in the group. A follow-up session also provides people with the opportunity to express and work through any afterthoughts or feelings connected with the group experience. At this time the mutual giving of feedback and support is extremely valuable.

I believe that the element of accountability that a follow-up session encourages maximizes the chances of long-lasting benefits from the group experience. Many people have reported that simply knowing that they would be coming together as a group one, two, or three months after the group's termination and that they would be giving a self-report provided the stimulus they needed to stick with their commitments. Finally, the follow-up session offers leaders another opportunity to remind participants that they are responsible for what they become and that if they hope to change their situation, they must take active steps to do so.

After the termination of a group, some of the participants may seek other avenues to further the process of growth begun in their group. Having been away from the group for some time, the former members may be more amenable to the idea of joining another group or seeking individual counseling to work through certain areas that they believe need further exploration. Thus, the follow-up session is an ideal place to discuss other avenues for continued growth.

Individual Follow-Up Sessions

Besides the group follow-up, I endorse the idea of leaders' arranging for a one-to-one follow-up session with each member. These postgroup individual interviews, which may last only 20 minutes, help the leader determine the degree to which members have accomplished their goals, because in the individual session members may reveal reactions that they would not share with the entire group. Also, this one-to-one contact tells the participants that the leader is concerned and does care. The individual interview provides ideal opportunities to discuss referral sources and the possible need for further professional involvement—matters that are probably best handled individually. Furthermore, the combination of individual postgroup interviews and a group follow-up session gives leaders much valuable information about the level of effectiveness of the group and provides the opportunity to discuss how future groups could be improved.

Although it is ideal to conduct individual follow-up sessions, I realize that this may not be practical in some settings. In a community mental-health clinic, for example, it might be difficult to arrange for this kind of follow-up. One option is a telephone call.

Evaluating Results

I have referred several times to the need for the leader to evaluate the results of a group. Personally, I find it difficult to objectively assess outcomes by using empirical procedures. I have made attempts at objective assessment by administering a variety of tests and inventories both before and after a group experience to determine the nature and degree of change in participants. But in my experience none of these measures is adequate to detect subtle changes in attitudes, beliefs, feelings, and behavior. Consequently, I have come to rely on subjective measures that include a variety of self-reports.

Generally I ask people before they enter a group to put down in writing what their concerns are and what they expect from the group. I strongly encourage members to keep an ongoing journal of their experiences in the group and in their everyday lives between sessions. This writing process helps participants focus on relevant trends and on the key things they are discovering about themselves and others through group interaction. After the group ends, I ask members to write a couple of reaction papers before our follow-up group meeting. These postgroup papers give participants a chance to recall significant occurrences in the group and provide them with an opportunity to discuss what specifically they liked most and least about the group. Now that the group has ended, participants can evaluate its impact differently. Many people have told me that these postgroup reaction papers are very useful, because they provide the impetus necessary to continue on their own the work initiated in the group situation. The writing process is a useful tool for self-evaluation and is in itself therapeutic.

Finally, I often give a brief questionnaire that members fill out when we come together for the postgroup meeting. The members evaluate the techniques used, the group leader, the impact of the group on them, and the degree to which they think they have changed because of their participation in the group. The following questions are designed to get information on key matters:

◆ Did the group have any negative effects on you?
◆ How has the group influenced you in relation to others?
◆ Have your changes been lasting so far?

The questionnaire is a good way to get members focused before the exchange of reactions that occurs in the follow-up session. It also provides useful data for evaluating the group. (This text's manual contains sample questionnaires for both member and leader evaluation of a group.)

Summary of Postgroup Issues

MEMBER FUNCTIONS AND POSSIBLE PROBLEMS. After their group has ended, the members' main functions are applying what they have learned to an action program in their daily lives, evaluating the group, and attending a follow-up session (if appropriate). Some key postgroup tasks for members are

◆ finding ways of reinforcing themselves so that they will continue to grow

- ◆ keeping some record of their changes, including progress and problems
- ◆ attending an individual session to discuss how well their goals were met or a follow-up group session to share with fellow members what they have done with their group experience

Some problems can occur at this time:

- ◆ If members have difficulty applying what they learned in the group to everyday situations, they may become discouraged and discount the value of the group.
- ◆ Members may have problems in continuing with new behaviors without the supportive environment of the group.
- ◆ Members may forget that change demands time, effort, and practice, and thus they may not use what they've learned.

LEADER FUNCTIONS. The last session of the group is not a signal that the leader's job is finished, for there are important considerations after termination. Follow-up and evaluation procedures should be implemented. Leaders have the following tasks after a group ends:

- ◆ if applicable, providing for a follow-up group session or individual interviews to assess the impact of the group
- ◆ finding out about specific referral resources for members who want or need further consultation
- ◆ encouraging members to find some avenues of continued support and challenge so that the ending of the group can mark the beginning of a search for self-understanding
- ◆ meeting with the co-leader to assess the overall effectiveness of the group

Concluding Comments

I have mentioned more than once that the stages in the life of a group do not generally flow neatly and predictably in the order described in the last two chapters. In actuality there is considerable overlap between stages, and once a group moves to an advanced stage of development, there may be temporary regressions to earlier developmental stages.

Knowledge of the major tasks that confront participants and leader during the different phases of the group's evolution allows you to intervene at the right time and with a clear purpose. Knowledge of the group's critical turning points enables you to assist the members in mobilizing their resources, so that they can successfully meet the demands facing them as their group progresses. Knowledge of the typical pattern of groups gives you an overall perspective that enables you to determine which interventions are useful and which ones are not. Also, this perspective allows you to predict certain crises in the life of the group and find ways of resolving these crises successfully.

REFERENCES AND SUGGESTED READINGS FOR PART ONE

American Association for Marriage and Family Therapy. (1991). *AAMFT code of ethics.* Washington, DC: Author.

American Counseling Association. (1988). *Ethical standards* (rev. ed.). Alexandria, VA: Author.

American Counseling Association. (1993). ACA proposed standards of practice and ethical standards. *Guidepost, 36*(4), 15–22.

American Group Psychotherapy Association. (1978). *Guidelines for the training of group psychotherapists.* New York: Author.

American Psychological Association. (1992). Ethical principles of psychologists and code of conduct. *American Psychologist, 47*(12), 1597–1611.

American Psychological Association. (1993). Guidelines for providers of psychological services to ethnic, linguistic, and culturally diverse populations. *American Psychologist, 48*(1), 45–48.

Association for Specialists in Group Work. (1989). *Ethical guidelines for group counselors.* Alexandria, VA: Author.

Association for Specialists in Group Work. (1991). Professional standards for the training of group workers. *Together: Association for Specialists in Group Work Newsletter, 20*(1), 9–14.

Association for Specialists in Group Work. (1992). *Professional standards for the training of group workers.* Alexandria, VA: Author.

Atkinson, D. R., Morten, G., & Sue, D. W. (1993). *Counseling American minorities: A cross-cultural perspective.* Madison, WI: Brown & Benchmark.

Banawi, R., & Stockton, R. (1993). Islamic values relevant to group work, with practical applications for the group leader. *Journal for Specialists in Group Work, 18*(3), 151–160.

Bednar, R. L., Corey, G., Evans, N. J., Gazda, G. M., Pistole, M. C., Stockton, R., & Robison, F. F. (1987). Overcoming obstacles to the future development of research on group work. *Journal for Specialists in Group Work, 12*(3), 98–111.

Borgers, S. B., & Tyndall, L. W. (1982). Setting expectations for groups. *Journal for Specialists in Group Work, 7*(2), 109–111.

Borkman, T. J. (1991). Introduction to the special issue. *American Journal of Community Psychology, 19*(5), 643–650.

Bowman, V. E., & DeLucia, J. L. (1993). Preparation for group therapy: The effects of preparer and modality on group process and individual functioning. *Journal for Specialists in Group Work, 18*(2), 67–79.

Brabender, V., & Fallon, A. (1993). *Models of inpatient group psychotherapy.* Washington, DC: American Psychological Association.

Brown, L. S., & Brodsky, A. M. (1992). The future of feminist therapy. *Psychotherapy, 29*(1), 51–57.

Chu, J., & Sue, S. (1984). Asian/Pacific-Americans and group practice. In L. E. Davis (Ed.), *Ethnicity in social group work practice* (pp. 23–35). New York: Haworth Press.

Cole, S. A. (1983). Self-help groups. In H. I. Kaplan & B. J. Sadock (Eds.), *Comprehensive group psychotherapy* (2nd ed.). Baltimore: Williams & Wilkins.

Comas-Diaz, L. (1990). Hispanic/Latino communities: Psychological implications. *Journal of Training and Practice in Professional Psychology, 4*(1), 14–35.

Comas-Diaz, L. (1992). The future of psychotherapy with ethnic minorities. *Psychotherapy, 29*(1), 88–94.

Corey, G. (1991a). *Case approach to counseling and psychotherapy* (3rd ed.). Pacific Grove, CA: Brooks/Cole.

Corey, G. (1991b). *Theory and practice of counseling and psychotherapy* (4th ed.) and *Manual.* Pacific Grove, CA: Brooks/Cole.

Corey, G., & Corey, M. (1993). *I never knew I had a choice* (5th ed.). Pacific Grove, CA: Brooks/Cole.

Corey, G., Corey, M., & Callanan, P. (1990). Role of group leader's values in group counseling. *Journal for Specialists in Group Work, 15*(2), 68–74.

Corey, G., Corey, M., & Callanan, P. (1993). *Issues and ethics in the helping professions* (4th ed.). Pacific Grove, CA: Brooks/Cole.

Corey, G., Corey, M., Callanan, P., & Russell, J. M. (1992). *Group techniques* (2nd ed.). Pacific Grove, CA: Brooks/Cole.

Corey, M., & Corey, G. (1986). Experiential/didactic training and supervision workshop for group leaders. *Journal of Counseling and Human Service Professions, 1*(1), 18–26.

Corey, M., & Corey, G. (1992). *Groups: Process and practice* (4th ed.). Pacific Grove, CA: Brooks/Cole.

Corey, M., & Corey, G. (1993a). *Becoming a helper* (2nd ed.). Pacific Grove, CA: Brooks/Cole.

Corey, M., & Corey, G. (1993b). Difficult group members—Difficult group leaders. *New York State Journal for Counseling and Development, 8*(2), 9–24.

Couch, R. D., & Childers, J. H. (1987). Leadership strategies for instilling and maintaining hope in group counseling. *Journal for Specialists in Group Work, 12*(4), 138–143.

Council for Accreditation of Counseling and Related Educational Programs. (1988, July). *Accreditation procedures manual and application.* Alexandria, VA: Author.

DeLucia, J. L., Coleman, V. D., & Jensen-Scott, R. L. (1992). Cultural diversity in group counseling. *Journal for Specialists in Group Work, 17*(4), 194–195.

Dies, R. R. (1983a). Bridging the gap between research and practice in group psychotherapy. In R. R. Dies & K. R. MacKenzie (Eds.), *Advances in group psychotherapy: Integrating research and practice* (pp. 1–16). New York: International Universities Press.

Dies, R. R. (1983b). Clinical implications of research on leadership in short-term group psychotherapy. In R. R. Dies & K. R. MacKenzie (Eds.), *Advances in group psychotherapy: Integrating research and practice* (pp. 27–78). New York: International Universities Press.

Dies, R. R. (1992). The future of group therapy. *Psychotherapy, 29*(1), 58–64.

Donigian, J. (1993). Duality: The issue that won't go away. *Journal for Specialists in Group Work, 18*(3), 137–140.

Donigian, J., & Malnati, R. (1987). *Critical incidents in group therapy.* Pacific Grove, CA: Brooks/Cole.

Dufrene, P. M., & Coleman, V. D. (1992). Counseling Native Americans: Guidelines for group process. *Journal for Specialists in Group Work, 17*(4), 229–234.

Enns, C. Z. (1992). Self-esteem groups: A synthesis of consciousness-raising and assertiveness training. *Journal of Counseling and Development, 71*(1), 7–13.

Forester-Miller, H., & Duncan, J. A. (1990). The ethics of dual relationships in the training of group counselors. *Journal for Specialists in Group Work, 15*(2), 88–93.

Fukuyama, M. A. (1990). Taking a universal approach to multicultural counseling. *Counselor Education and Supervision, 30*(1), 6–17.

Fukuyama, M. A., & Coleman, N. C. (1992). A model for bicultural assertion training with Asian-Pacific American college students: A pilot study. *Journal for Specialists in Group Work, 17*(4), 210–217.

Gainor, K. A. (1992). Internalized oppression as a barrier to effective group work with black women. *Journal for Specialists in Group Work, 17*(4), 235–242.

Gazda, G. M. (1989). *Group counseling: A developmental approach* (4th ed.). Boston: Allyn & Bacon.

Greeley, A. T., Garcia, V. L., Kessler, B. L., & Gilchrest, G. (1992). Training effective multicultural group counselors: Issues for a group training course. *Journal for Specialists in Group Work, 17*(4), 196–209.

Hansen, J. C., Warner, R. W., & Smith, E. M. (1980). *Group counseling: Theory and process* (2nd ed.). Chicago: Rand McNally.

Helms, J. E. (1984). Toward a theoretical explanation of the effects of race on counseling: A black and white model. *The Counseling Psychologist, 12*(4), 153–165.

Henry, S. (1992). *Group skills in social work: A four-dimensional approach* (2nd ed.). Pacific Grove, CA: Brooks/Cole.

Herlihy, B., & Corey, G. (1992). *Dual relationships in counseling.* Alexandria, VA: American Association for Counseling and Development.

Higgs, J. A. (1992). Dealing with resistance: Strategies for effective groups. *Journal for Specialists in Group Work, 17*(2), 62–73.

Ho, M. K. (1984). Social group work with Asian/Pacific-Americans. In L. E. Davis (Ed.), *Ethnicity in social group work practice* (pp. 49–61). New York: Haworth Press.

Huhn, R. P., Zimpfer, D. G., Waltman, D. E., & Williamson, S. K. (1985). A survey of programs of professional preparation for group counseling. *Journal for Specialists in Group Work, 10*(3), 124–133.

Ibrahim, F. A. (1985). Effective cross-cultural counseling and psychotherapy: A framework. *The Counseling Psychologist, 13,* 625–683.

Ibrahim, F. A. (1991). Contribution of cultural worldview to generic counseling and development. *Journal of Counseling and Development, 70*(1), 13–19.

Ibrahim, F. A., & Arredondo, P. (1990). Ethical issues in multicultural counseling. In B. Herlihy & L. Golden (Eds.), *Ethical standards casebook* (4th ed.). Alexandria, VA: American Counseling Association.

Ivey, A. E., Ivey, M. B., & Simek-Morgan, L. (1993). *Counseling and psychotherapy: A multicultural perspective.* Boston: Allyn & Bacon.

Jacobs, E. E., Harvill, R. L., & Masson, R. L. (1994). *Group counseling: Strategies and skills* (2nd ed.) Pacific Grove, CA: Brooks/Cole.

Johnson, D. W. (1990). *Reaching out: Interpersonal effectiveness and self-actualization* (4th ed.) Englewood Cliffs, NJ: Prentice-Hall.

Katz, A. H. (1981). Self-help and mutual aid: An emerging social movement? *American Review of Sociology, 7,* 129–155.

Kottler, J. A. (1986). *On being a therapist.* San Francisco: Jossey-Bass.

Kottler, J. A. (1992). *Compassionate therapy: Working with difficult clients.* San Francisco: Jossey-Bass.

Kottler, J. A. (1994). *Advanced group leadership.* Pacific Grove, CA: Brooks/Cole.

Lakin, M. (1985). *The helping group: Therapeutic principles and issues.* Reading, MA: Addison-Wesley.

LeCluyse, E. E. (1983). Pretherapy preparation for group members. *Journal for Specialists in Group Work, 8*(4), 170–174.

Lee, P. C., Juan, G., & Hom, A. B. (1984). Group work practice with Asian clients: A sociocultural approach. In L. E. Davis (Ed.), *Ethnicity in social group work practice* (pp. 37–47). New York: Haworth Press.

Leong, F. T. L. (1986). Counseling and psychotherapy with Asian-Americans: Review of the literature. *Journal of Counseling Psychology, 33*(2), 196–206.

Leong, F. T. L. (1992). Guidelines for minimizing premature termination among Asian American clients in group counseling. *Journal for Specialists in Group Work, 17*(4), 218–228.

Leong, F. T. L., & Kim, H. H. W. (1991). Going beyond cultural sensitivity on the road to multiculturalism: Using the intercultural sensitizer as a counselor training tool. *Journal of Counseling and Development, 70,* 112–118.

Levine, B. (1991). *Group psychotherapy: Practice and development.* Prospect Heights, IL: Waveland Press.

Libo, L. (1977). *Is there a life after group?* New York: Anchor Books.

Lieberman, M. A. (1980). Group methods. In F. H. Kanfer & A. P. Goldstein (Eds.), *Helping people change* (2nd ed.). New York: Pergamon Press.

Lieberman, M. A., & Borman, L. D. (1979). *Self-help groups for coping with crisis.* San Francisco: Jossey-Bass.

Locke, D. C. (1990). A not so provincial view of multicultural counseling. *Counselor Education and Supervision, 30*(1), 18–25.

Luft, J. (1984). *Group processes: An introduction to group dynamics* (3rd ed.). Palo Alto, CA: Mayfield.

Mahler, C. Q. (1969). *Group counseling in the schools.* Boston: Houghton Mifflin.

McFadden, J. (Ed.). (1993). *Transcultural counseling: Bilateral and international perspectives.* Alexandria, VA: American Counseling Association.

Meissen, G. J., Mason, W. C., & Gleason, D. F. (1991). Understanding the attitudes and intentions of future professionals toward self-help. *American Journal of Community Psychology, 19*(5), 699–714.

Merta, R. J., & Sisson, J. A. (1991). The experiential group: An ethical and professional dilemma. *Journal for Specialists in Group Work, 16*(4), 236–245.

Merta, R. J., Wolfgang, L., & McNeil, K. (1993). Five models for using the experiential group in the preparation of group counselors. *Journal for Specialists in Group Work, 18*(4), 200–207.

Mokuau, N. (1985). Counseling Pacific Islander-Americans. In P. Pedersen (Ed.), *Handbook of cross-cultural counseling and therapy* (pp. 147–155). Westport, CT: Greenwood Press.

Mokuau, N. (1987). Social workers' perceptions of counseling effectiveness for Asian American clients. *Journal of the National Association of Social Workers, 32*(4), 331–335.

Morran, D. K. (1982). Leader and member self-disclosing behavior in counseling groups. *Journal for Specialists in Group Work, 7*(4), 218–223.

Morran, D. K., Robison, F. F., & Stockton, R. (1985). Feedback exchange in counseling groups: An analysis of message content and receiver acceptance as a function of leader versus member delivery, session, and valance. *Journal of Counseling Psychology, 32,* 57–67.

Morran, D. K., & Stockton, R. (1980). Effect of self-concept on group member reception of positive and negative feedback. *Journal of Counseling Psychology, 27,* 260–267.

Morran, D. K., & Stockton, R. (1985). Perspectives on group research programs. *Journal of Specialists for Group Work, 10*(4), 186–191.

Morran, D. K., Stockton, R., & Bond, L. (1991). Delivery of positive and corrective feedback in counseling groups. *Journal of Counseling Psychology, 38*(4), 410–414.

Morran, D. K., Stockton, R., & Harris, M. (1991). Analysis of group leader and member feedback messages. *Journal of Group Psychotherapy, Psychodrama, and Sociometry, 43,* 126–135.

National Association of Social Workers. (1990). *Code of ethics.* Silver Spring, MD: Author.

National Board for Certified Counselors. (1989). *Code of ethics.* Alexandria, VA: Author.

Nolan, E. (1978). Leadership interventions for promoting personal mastery. *Journal for Specialists in Group Work, 3*(3), 132–138.

Ohlsen, M. M., Horne, A. M., & Lawe, C. F. (1988). *Group counseling* (3rd ed.). New York: Holt, Rinehart & Winston.

Ormont, L. R. (1988). The leader's role in resolving resistances to intimacy in the group setting. *International Journal of Group Psychotherapy, 38*(1), 29–46.

Pate, R. H., & Bondi, A. M. (1992). Religious beliefs and practice: An integral aspect of multicultural awareness. *Counselor Education and Supervision, 32*(2), 108–115.

Pedersen, P. (1981). Triad counseling. In R. Cornisi (Ed.), *Innovative psychotherapies* (pp. 840–855). New York: Wiley.

Pedersen, P. (Ed.). (1985). *Handbook of cross-cultural counseling and therapy.* Westport, CT: Greenwood Press.

Pedersen, P. (1991). Multiculturalism as a generic approach to counseling. *Journal of Counseling and Development, 70*(1), 6–12.

Pedersen, P. (1994). *A handbook for developing multicultural awareness* (2nd ed.). Alexandria, VA: American Counseling Association.

Pedersen, P., & Ivey, A. (1993). *Culture-centered counseling and interviewing skills: A practical guide*. Westport, CT: Praeger.

Pierce, K. A., & Baldwin, C. (1990). Participation versus privacy in the training of group counselors. *Journal for Specialists in Group Work, 15*(3), 149–158.

Pope, K. S., Sonne, J. L., & Holroyd, J. (1993). *Sexual feelings in psychotherapy: Explorations for therapists and therapists-in-training*. Washington, DC: American Psychological Association.

Pope, K. S., Tabachnick, B. G., & Keith-Spiegel, P. (1987). Ethics of practice: The beliefs and behaviors of psychologists as therapists. *American Psychologist, 42*(11), 993–1006.

Reid, K. E. (1991). *Social work practice with groups: A clinical perspective*. Pacific Grove, CA: Brooks/Cole.

Remley, T. (1992). A model for teaching a graduate course in group counseling. *Together: Association for Specialists in Group Work Newsletter, 20*(2), 10–11.

Riordan, R. J., & Beggs, M. S. (1987). Counselors and self-help groups. *Journal of Counseling and Development, 65*(8), 427–429.

Riordan, R. J., & Beggs, M. S. (1988). Some critical differences between self-help and therapy groups. *Journal for Specialists in Group Work, 3*(1), 24–29.

Robison, F. F., Stockton, R., & Morran, D. K. (1990). Anticipated consequences of self-disclosure during early therapeutic group development. *Journal of Group Psychotherapy, Psychodrama, and Sociometry, 43*(1), 3–18.

Robison, F. F., Stockton, R., Morran, D. K., & Uhl-Wagner, A. N. (1988). Anticipated consequences of communicating corrective feedback during early counseling group development. *Small Group Behavior, 19*(4), 469–484.

Rogers, C. R. (1970). *Carl Rogers on encounter groups*. New York: Harper & Row.

Rohde, R., & Stockton, R. (1992). The effect of structured feedback on goal attainment, attraction to the group, and satisfaction with the group in small group counseling. *Journal of Group Psychotherapy, Psychodrama, and Sociometry, 44*(4), 172–180.

Root, M. P. P. (1985). Guidelines for facilitating therapy with Asian American clients. *Psychotherapy, 22*, 349–356.

Rosenbaum, M., Lakin, M., & Roback, H. B. (1992). Psychotherapy in groups. In D. K. Freedheim (Ed.), *History of psychotherapy: A century of change* (pp. 695–724). Washington, DC: American Psychological Association.

Sampson, E. E. (1988). The debate on individualism: Indigenous psychologies of the individual and their role in personal and societal functioning. *American Psychologist, 43*(1), 15–22.

Schubert, M. A., & Borkman, T. J. (1991). An organizational typology for self-help groups. *American Journal of Community Psychology, 19*(5), 769–787.

Schutz, W. (1973a). *Elements of encounter*. Big Sur, CA: Joy Press.

Schutz, W. (1973b). Encounter. In R. Corsini (Ed.), *Current psychotherapies*. Itasca, IL: F. E. Peacock.

Shapiro, J. L. (1978). *Methods of group psychotherapy and encounter: A tradition of innovation*. Itasca, IL: F. E. Peacock.

Stockton, R., & Hulse, D. (1981). Developing cohesion in small groups: Theory and research. *Journal for Specialists in Group Work, 6*(4), 188–194.

Stockton, R., & Morran, D. K. (1980). The use of verbal feedback in counseling groups: Toward an effective system. *Journal for Specialists in Group Work, 5*, 10–14.

Stockton, R., & Morran, D. K. (1981). Feedback exchange in personal growth groups: Receiver acceptance as a function of valence, session, and order of delivery. *Journal of Counseling Psychology, 28*, 490–497.

Stockton, R., & Morran, D. K. (1982). Review and perspective of critical dimensions in therapeutic small group research. In G. M. Gazda (Ed.), *Basic approaches to group psychotherapy and group counseling* (3rd ed.) (pp. 37–85). Springfield, IL: Charles C Thomas.

Stockton, R., Morran, D. K., & Harris, M. (1991). Factors influencing group member acceptance of corrective feedback. *Journal for Specialists in Group Work, 16*(4), 246–254.

Stockton, R., Rohde, R. I., & Haughey, J. (1992). The effects of structured group exercises on cohesion, engagement, avoidance, and conflict. *Small Group Research, 23*(2), 155–168.

Sue, D., & Sue, D. W. (1993). Ethnic identity: Cultural factors in the psychological development of Asians in America. In D. R. Atkinson, G. Morten, & D. W. Sue, (Eds.), *Counseling American minorities: A cross-cultural perspective* (pp. 199–210). Madison, WI: Brown & Benchmark.

Sue, D.W. (1990). Culture-specific strategies in counseling: A conceptual framework. *Professional Psychology: Research and Practice, 21*(6) 424–433.

Sue, D. W. (1992). The challenge of multiculturalism: The road less traveled. *American Counselor, 1*(1), 6–14.

Sue, D. W., Arredondo, P., & McDavis, R. J. (1992). Multicultural counseling competencies and standards: A call to the profession. *Journal of Counseling and Development, 70*(4), 477–486.

Sue, D. W., & Sue, D. (1990). *Counseling the culturally different: Theory and practice* (2nd ed.). New York: Wiley.

Thomason, T. C. (1991). Counseling Native Americans: An introduction for non-Native American counselors. *Journal of Counseling and Development, 69*(4), 321–327.

Tollerud, F. R., Holling, D. W., & Dustin, D. (1992). A model for teaching in group leadership: The pre-group interview application. *Journal for Specialists in Group Work, 17*(2), 96–104.

Wrenn, C. G. (1985). Afterward: The culturally encapsulated counselor revisted. In P. Pedersen (Ed.), *Handbook of cross-cultural counseling and therapy* (pp. 323–329). Westport, CT: Greenwood Press.

Yalom, I. D. (1983). *Inpatient group psychotherapy.* New York: Basic Books.

Yalom, I. D. (1985). *The theory and practice of group psychotherapy* (3rd ed.). New York: Basic Books.

Yu, A., & Gregg, C. H. (1993). Asians in groups: More than a matter of cultural awareness. *Journal for Specialists in Group Work, 18*(2), 67–79.

◆ PART TWO ◆

THEORETICAL APPROACHES TO GROUP COUNSELING

CHAPTER SIX

The Psychoanalytic Approach to Groups

CHAPTER SEVEN

Adlerian Group Counseling

CHAPTER EIGHT

Psychodrama

CHAPTER NINE

The Existential Approach to Groups

CHAPTER TEN

The Person-Centered Approach to Groups

CHAPTER ELEVEN

Gestalt Therapy

CHAPTER TWELVE

Transactional Analysis

CHAPTER THIRTEEN
Behavioral Group Therapy

CHAPTER FOURTEEN
Rational Emotive Behavior Therapy

CHAPTER FIFTEEN
Reality Therapy in Groups

♦ CHAPTER SIX ♦

The Psychoanalytic Approach to Groups

Introduction

Psychoanalytic theory has influenced most of the other models of group work presented in this textbook. Some of these other approaches are basically extensions of the analytic model, some are modifications of analytic concepts and procedures, and some have emerged as a reaction against psychoanalysis. It is fair to say that most theories of group counseling have borrowed concepts and techniques from psychoanalysis. As a group counselor you may have neither the training nor the motivation to conduct analytic groups. Even if you do not have command of the techniques required for uncovering unconscious material and reconstructing personality, however, the basic psychoanalytic concepts can become an integral part of your own theoretical approach.

This chapter is devoted to an overview of the psychoanalytic and psychosocial perspectives and to a brief introduction to contemporary trends in psychoanalytic thinking. I also outline the stages of development in an individual's life. Although Sigmund Freud made significant contributions to our understanding of the individual's *psychosexual development* during early childhood, he wrote little about the *psychosocial* influences on human development beyond childhood. Therefore, I have given special emphasis to Erik Erikson's (1963, 1982) psychosocial perspective, which provides a comprehensive framework for understanding the individual's basic concerns at each stage of life from infancy through old age. Erikson can be considered a psychoanalyst as well as an ego psychologist, who built on Freudian concepts by continuing the story of human development where Freud left off.

In discussing the key concepts and basic techniques that characterize a psychoanalytic group, this chapter draws on some of Freud's major themes. Although he focused on individual psychodynamics and on the dyadic

I want to acknowledge the contributions of William Blau and J. Michael Russell to the updating of the ideas in this chapter, especially in the area of contemporary trends.

relationship between a patient and an analyst, his ideas and contributions do have implications for the practice of analytic group therapy.

The person credited with first applying psychoanalytic principles and techniques to groups is Alexander Wolf, a psychiatrist and psychoanalyst. He began working with groups in 1938 because he did not want to turn away patients who needed but could not afford intensive individual therapy. His experiences increased his interest in this approach, and he made it his primary mode of therapy. Wolf stresses psychoanalysis *in* groups (as opposed to psychoanalysis *of* groups), since he has consistently maintained that he does not treat a group. Rather, his focus is on each individual in interaction with other individuals.

Goal of the Analytic Group

The goal of the analytic process is the restructuring of the client's character and personality system. This goal is achieved by making unconscious conflicts conscious and examining them. Specifically, psychoanalytic groups reenact the family of origin in a symbolic way via the group, so that the historical past of each group member is repeated in the group's presence. Wolf (1963, 1975) developed group applications of basic psychoanalytic techniques such as working with transference, free association, dreams, and the historical determinants of present behavior. He stresses the re-creation of the original family, so that members can work through their unresolved problems. Their reactions to fellow members and to the leader are assumed to reveal symbolic clues to the dynamics of their relationships with significant figures from their family of origin. Although these reactions are taken from the here and now, there is a constant focus on tracing them back to the early history of the members (Tuttman, 1986). Wolf's approach is aimed at a controlled and systematic regression of the personality in the service of strengthening the ego.

Mullan and Rosenbaum (1978) speak of the process of re-creating one's family as the *regressive-reconstructive* approach to psychoanalytic group therapy. This term refers to a regression into each member's past in order to achieve the therapeutic goal of a reconstructed personality that is characterized by social awareness and the ability to be creatively involved in life. The group in many respects duplicates the original family. The group leader applies understanding to the familylike connections that arise among the members and between the members and the therapist. The leader imposes a minimum of structure, and the group, like a family, is heterogeneous. Members reexperience conflicts that originated in the family context.

The thrust of analytic groups, according to Wolf and Kutash (1986), rests with the creative growth of the individual ego, or self. The authors see the term *group therapy* as a misnomer, for the focus is on the treatment of ailing individuals rather than ailing groups. Further, Wolf (1983) asserts that a group's preoccupation with group dynamics, with here-and-now interactions, and with cohesion can distract from the central core of analytic work. However, he believes that the group atmosphere allows for a deeper analytic searching than is possible in individual analysis because the group ego supports and facilitates deeper exploration. He believes that the exploration of intrapsychic processes enables the members to develop a detailed understanding of the nature of their submission to the significant people in their nuclear family and to the other members in their analytic group.

The Therapeutic Process

The therapeutic process focuses on re-creating, analyzing, discussing, and interpreting past experiences and on working through defenses and resistances that operate at the unconscious level. (*Working through* is a psychoanalytic concept that refers to repetition of interpretations and overcoming of resistance, thus allowing the client to resolve dysfunctional patterns that originated in childhood and to make choices based on new insights.) Insight and intellectual understanding are important, but the feelings and memories associated with self-understanding are crucial. Because clients need to relive and reconstruct their past and work through repressed conflicts in order to understand how the unconscious affects them in the present, psychoanalytic group therapy is usually a long-term and intensive process.

Most practitioners with a traditional analytic orientation value the anonymous role of the leader, because they believe that such a role encourages members to project toward the leader the feelings they had for significant people in their lives. Many analytically oriented group therapists, however, place less value on the nondisclosing role of the leader and tend to share their personal reactions with the group's members. All analytic and analytically oriented therapists consider the process of analyzing and interpreting transference feelings as the core of the therapeutic process, since it is aimed at achieving insight and personality change.

A group format that utilizes psychoanalytic concepts and techniques has some specific advantages over individual analysis:

◆ Members are able to establish relationships that are similar to those that existed in their own families; this time, however, the relationships occur in a group setting that is safe and conducive to favorable outcomes.

◆ Group participants have many opportunities to experience transference feelings toward other members and the leader; they can work through these feelings and thus increase their self-understanding.

◆ Participants can gain more dramatic insight into how their defenses and resistances work.

◆ Dependency on the authority of the therapist is not as great as in individual therapy, for group members also get feedback from other members.

◆ From observing the work of others in a group, the members learn that it is acceptable to have and express intense feelings that they may have kept out of awareness.

◆ In the group setting members have many opportunities to learn about themselves and others, in fact and in fantasy, through interactions with peers as well as with the leader. The material for analysis is available not only in terms of historical recollection but also on the basis of interaction with fellow members.

◆ The group setting encourages members to examine their projections. It is difficult for them to cling to some of their resistances and distortions when others in the group confront them on the ways in which they are misrepresenting reality. Furthermore, observing similar conflicts in others can help ease defensiveness and show them that they are not alone. Resistance melts away in the atmosphere of mutual revelation and exploration in a group to a greater extent than is typically true of one-to-one therapy.

◆ Analysis in groups immediately confronts a member's idealistic expectation of having an exclusive relationship with the therapist. The experience of supporting others and the discovery of universal struggles encourage a fuller range of responses than does individual therapy.

Key Concepts

Influence of the Past

Psychoanalytic work focuses on the influence of the past on current personality functioning. Experiences during the first six years of life are seen as the roots of one's conflicts in the present. When I consider typical problems and conflicts of group members, the following come to mind: an inability to freely give and accept love; a difficulty in recognizing and dealing with feelings such as anger, resentment, rage, hatred, and aggression; an inability to direct one's own life and resolve dependence/independence conflicts; a difficulty in separating from one's parents and becoming a unique person; a need for and a fear of intimacy; a difficulty in accepting one's own sexual identity; and guilt over sexual feelings. According to the psychoanalytic view, these problems of adult living have their origin in early development. Early learning is not irreversible; but to change its effects, one must become aware of how certain early experiences have contributed to one's present personality structure.

Although practitioners with a psychoanalytic orientation focus on the historical antecedents of current behavior, it is a mistake to assume that they dwell on the past to the exclusion of present concerns. A common misconception about psychoanalytic work is that it resembles an archaeological digging out of relics from the past. As Locke (1961) points out, psychoanalytic group work consists of "weaving back and forth between past and present, between present and past" (p. 30). "It is essential that the therapist move back and forth in time, trying always to recapture the past or to see the repetition in the present and to become aware of the early traumatic event which made for the neurotic pattern of the individual today" (p. 31).

Thus, it is essential that participants understand and use historical data in their group work. At the same time, they also need to be aware of the pitfalls of getting lost in their past by recounting endless and irrelevant details of their early experiences. In the view of Wolf and Kutash (1986), the recital of yesterday's events can be uselessly time-consuming and can inhibit progress. They see this use of history as essentially a form of resistance, and they suggest that talking about events in one's childhood is not as useful as dealing with the past in relation to here-and-now interactions within the group.

The Unconscious

The concept of the unconscious is one of Freud's most significant contributions and is the key to understanding his view of behavior and the problems of personality. The unconscious consists of those thoughts, feelings, motives, impulses, and events that are kept out of awareness of the conscious ego. From the Freudian perspective, most of human behavior is motivated by forces outside conscious experience. What we do in everyday life is frequently determined by these unconscious motives and needs. Painful experiences during early childhood and the feelings associated with them are buried in the unconscious. The early traumas are such that conscious awareness would cause intolerable anxiety to the child. The child's repression of them does not automatically lift with time, and the client reacts to threats to the repression as if the anxiety associated with the early events would still be intolerable if these were recalled. Thus, the "shadow of the past" haunts the present. But the trauma was intolerable only to the *child;* with an adult perspective on the world the client can handle the memory with relative ease. Therefore, the therapist helps make the unconscious conscious, and the anxiety is not intolerable; hence, the client is helped to be free of the tyranny of the past repressions.

Unconscious experiences have a powerful impact on our daily functioning. Indeed, Freud's theory holds that most of our "choices" are not freely made; rather, they are determined by forces within us of which we are not aware. Thus, we select mates to meet certain needs that may have never been satisfied; we select a job because of some unconscious motive; and we continually experience personal and interpersonal conflicts whose roots lie in unfinished experiences that are outside the realm of our awareness.

According to the psychoanalytic theory, consciousness is only a small part of the human experience. Like the greater part of the iceberg that lies below the surface of the water, the larger part of human experience exists below the surface of awareness. The aim of psychoanalysis is to make the unconscious material conscious, for it is only when we become conscious of the motivations underlying our behavior that we can choose and become autonomous. The unconscious can be made more accessible to awareness by working with dreams, by using free-association methods, by learning about

transference, by understanding the meaning of resistances, and by employing the process of interpretation. Analytic therapists move back and forth
between reality and fantasy, the conscious and the unconscious, the rational
and the nonlogical, and thought and feeling.

The concept of the unconscious has deep significance for analytic group
therapy. In the psychoanalytic view a group that ignores the role of the
unconscious and focuses exclusively on conscious here-and-now interactions
among participants is more an encounter group than a therapy group.
Although it is true that exhaustive work with the unconscious determinents
of behavior and personality reconstruction is beyond the scope of group
counseling as it is generally practiced, group counselors need to have an
understanding of how unconscious processes operate. This understanding
provides counselors with a conceptual framework that helps them make
sense of the group interactions, even if the unconscious is not directly dealt
with by the members.

Anxiety

In order to appreciate the psychoanalytic model, one must understand the
dynamics of anxiety. Anxiety is a feeling of dread and impending doom that
results from repressed feelings, memories, desires, and experiences bub-
bling to the surface of awareness. It is triggered by something in the
environment or within the individual. Anxiety stems from the threat of
unconscious material breaking through the wall of repression. We experience anxiety when we sense that we are dealing with feelings that threaten
to get out of our control. Anxiety is often "free-floating"; that is, it is vague
and general, not yet having crystallized into specific form. In the section of
this chapter dealing with basic techniques, I will expand on the management of anxiety. The following section deals with the function of the ego-
defense mechanisms, which are an integral part of the individual's attempt
to cope with anxiety.

Ego-Defense Mechanisms

The ego-defense mechanisms were first formulated by psychoanalytic
theory as a way of explaining behavior. These defense mechanisms protect
the ego from threatening thoughts and feelings. Conceptually, the ego is
that part of the personality that performs various conscious functions,
including keeping in contact with reality. When there is a threat to the ego,
anxiety is experienced. Although we may be interested in the growth that
comes from facing reality directly, we attempt to protect ourselves from
experiencing anxiety. The ego defenses enable us to soften the blows that
come with emotional wounding, and they are one way of maintaining a
sense of personal adequacy. Although the ego defenses do involve self-
deception and distortion of reality, they are not considered essentially
pathological. It is only to the degree that they impair a person's ability to
deal effectively with the tasks of life that their use becomes problematic.

Even though these mechanisms are learned and become a habitual mode of defense against anxiety, they do operate outside one's consciousness.

In a group situation there are many opportunities to observe a variety of defensive behaviors. In many cases the defenses that we used in childhood when we were threatened continue when we feel threatened in the group. A main therapeutic value of a group is that through feedback from the leader and the other members, clients can become increasingly aware of their defensive styles of interaction. With awareness, members are eventually able to choose direct forms of dealing with anxiety-producing situations as they emerge in a group.

Several common ego defenses are typically manifested in the pattern of interactions in the therapeutic group:

◆ *Repression* involves excluding from consciousness threatening or painful thoughts and desires. By pushing thoughts or feelings that are distressing into the unconscious, people manage the anxiety that grows out of situations involving guilt and conflict. In groups, adults often have no recollection of the details of incestuous events that occurred in early childhood. If adults were physically or emotionally abused in childhood, they might well have blocked out the pain and anxiety associated with these events by pushing the memories into the unconscious. As other members experience a catharsis and work through the pain associated with incest, however, a member who has repressed the experience may be emotionally triggered, and unconscious material may surface to awareness.

◆ *Denial* plays a defensive role similar to that of repression, yet it generally operates at the preconscious or conscious level. In denial there is an effort to suppress unpleasant reality. It consists of coping with anxiety by "closing our eyes" to the existence of anxiety-producing reality. In a therapy group, members sometimes stubbornly refuse to accept that they have any problems. They may attempt to fool both themselves and others by saying that they have "worked on" certain problems and that they therefore no longer have any concerns to deal with in the group. A common form of denial can be heard in this member's statement: "I really don't have any more issues with my father, who died when I was 7 years old, because I worked on the pain over this event a couple of times in prior groups."

◆ *Regression* involves returning to a less mature developmental level. In the face of severe stress or crisis we sometimes revert to old patterns that worked for us earlier. For instance, a man in a therapy group may retreat to childlike behaviors and become extremely frightened and dependent as he faces a crisis precipitated by his wife's decision to leave him for another man.

◆ *Projection* involves attributing our own unacceptable thoughts, feelings, behaviors, and motives to others. In a group setting members may be very able to see the faults of others. They may also attribute to other members certain feelings and motives that would lead them to feel guilty if they owned these feelings and motives. Of course, groups offer many opportunities to view projection in action. Members often reexperience old feelings that were common in their family of origin. They typically project feelings onto the group leaders that they had toward their parents, and they "see" their siblings in certain group members. Projection is the basis of transference, which is a useful process to explore within the group context. Chronic advice giving can be a form of projection.

◆ *Displacement* entails a redirection of some emotion (such as anger) from a real source to a substitute person or object. Group members who are frustrated are likely to feel angry. If members are not allowed to get away with pouting or employing some other attention-seeking behaviors, for example, they may lash out in a hostile way toward some member who is relatively nonthreatening. Although their anger may be a result of a group leader's confrontation, they may pick a safer target on whom to vent their hostility.

◆ *Reaction formation* involves behaving in a manner that is opposite to one's real feelings. It serves as a defense against anxiety that would result from accepting feelings that one is striving to disown. This defense is exhibited in a group by the woman who is "sugary sweet" yet really harbors many hostile feelings that she dares not express. It is also displayed by the man who tries to convince himself and others in his group that he does not care if others reject him, either in this group or at home (yet who underneath very much wants the acceptance of others). These behaviors cover up one's real feelings, for dealing with hostility or rejection would be painful. In these cases there is an exaggeration of being sweet or of being emotionally indifferent to rejection. The excessive quality of these behaviors is what makes them a form of defense.

◆ *Rationalization* is a defense mechanism whereby we try to justify our behavior by imputing logical and admirable motives to it. Some people manufacture "good" reasons to explain away a bruised ego. This defense involves an attempt to minimize the severity of disappointment over losses or failures. In groups there are many opportunities to observe this behavioral pattern in action. Members may devote a great deal of energy to focusing on "others out there" as the source of their problems. Some men may be quick to blame their mother's coldness as the reason that they avoid getting close to the women in the group. Such members may have a well-developed rationale for how their problems would be nonexistent if only their daughter or wife would change.

Although the ego-defense mechanisms have some adaptive value, their overuse can become problematic. It is true that self-deception can soften harsh reality, but the fact is that reality does not change through the process of distorting those aspects of it that produce anxiety. In the long run, when these defensive strategies do not work, the result is even greater anxiety. The group situation is ideal for enabling individuals to learn to recognize the indirect methods that they resort to when they feel emotionally threatened. To avoid judging such behavior, it is possible to work with members in therapeutic ways so that they can increase their tolerance for coping with anxiety and can learn direct ways of dealing with difficult interpersonal situations.

Resistance

In psychoanalytic therapy resistance is defined as the individual's reluctance to bring into conscious awareness threatening unconscious material that has been previously repressed or denied. It can also be viewed as anything that prevents members from dealing with unconscious material, thus keeping the group from making progress. Resistance is the unconscious attempt to defend the self against the high degree of anxiety that the client fears would result if the material in the unconscious were uncovered. As Locke (1961) puts it, group members need to protect themselves against the "flooding of the conscious by the forbidden feeling, fantasy, or memory" (p. 72). Resistance is the "fight to maintain the defense"; thus, it is "the defense of the defense."

One method of therapeutically dealing with resistance is through free association, an uncensored and uninhibited flow of ideas produced by the client that offers clues about the person's unconscious conflicts. According to Wolf (1983) and Wolf and Schwartz (1962), resistances emerge with clarity as members continue to free-associate with one another and as old feelings recur in the present. When these defenses surface, they are observed, analyzed, and interpreted. Support offered by the group helps the person break through his or her defenses. Durkin (1964) stresses that resistance is a basic part of the analytic group, and she warns group leaders not to be surprised by or impatient with it. She also warns leaders not to view resistance, which is a natural phenomenon of all groups, as a sign of their own ineptness.

There are many kinds of resistances, some relating to apprehension about joining a group, some to participation in the group process, and some to the desire to leave the group (Locke, 1961). One common resistance stems from the belief that one cannot benefit from the group situation, because help cannot come from people who are themselves in trouble. Wolf (1963) lists other sources of resistance in group members: fear that one's privacy will be invaded; need to "own" the therapist exclusively; fear of "meeting" again one's original family in the group—namely, recognizing one's parents or siblings in some of the participants—and having to deal with the anxiety produced by these encounters; unconscious fear of giving up neurotic trends; and anxiety about the freedom that a group offers—including the freedom to discuss anxiety.

Wolf (1963) also explores other forms of resistance, which surface during the advanced stages of group analysis. Members may "go blank" when they are asked to free-associate about other group members, or they may escape personal exploration by simply watching others and refusing to participate. Some members hide behind the analysis of other members, and some engage in lengthy recitations of their life histories, thus avoiding the challenge of facing the present. Additional manifestations of resistance include these:

- ◆ always arriving late or not showing up at all
- ◆ maintaining an attitude of complacency or indifference
- ◆ hiding behind a wall of silence or talking incessantly
- ◆ intellectualizing
- ◆ exhibiting an exaggerated need to help others in the group
- ◆ showing distrust
- ◆ behaving uncooperatively
- ◆ acting out
- ◆ using the group for mere socializing

These are by no means the only manifestations of resistive behavior; what they all have in common is the fear of recognizing and dealing with that part of oneself that is locked in the unconscious.

How do group analysts deal with resistance? Durkin (1964) maintains that in order to penetrate and work through resistances, the therapist needs to enlist the cooperation of members. Therefore, he or she must start with the client's immediate problems as they are manifested through resistive behaviors. Durkin stresses the importance of dealing with disappointments and resentments, because members will otherwise become increasingly angry, less desirous of opening up, and more resistant. Thus, resistances are not just something to be overcome. Because they are valuable indications of the client's defenses against anxiety, they should be acknowledged and worked through by therapist and client together, with the clear understanding that they are both working toward the same ends. Generally, it is best to call attention to those manifestations of resistance that are most readily observable and to work with these behaviors first. In doing so, leaders should take care not to label or censure group members, because unacceptable criticism will only increase resistive behaviors. It can also be useful to bring other group members into the analysis of individual members' resistances.

Transference

Transference is a basic concept of the psychoanalytic approach. It refers to the client's unconscious shifting to the therapist of feelings, attitudes, and fantasies (both positive and negative) that stem from reactions to significant persons from the client's past. The key issue of transference is the distortion imposed on the therapeutic relationship by prior relationships, usually childhood ones. Analytic technique is designed to foster the client's transference. But the therapeutic setting, unlike the original situation, does not punish the person for experiencing or expressing these feelings. If a client perceives the therapist as a stern and rejecting father, he or she does not receive from the therapist the expected negative responses. Instead, the therapist accepts the client's feelings and helps the client understand them.

By reliving their past through the transference process, clients gain insight into the ways in which the past is obstructing present functioning. Insight is achieved by working through unresolved conflicts that keep the person fixated and that make full emotional growth impossible. Basically, the negative effects of painful early experiences are counteracted by working through similar conflicts in the therapeutic setting.

Since transference also manifests itself in groups through the members' attempts to win the approval of the leader, these attempts can be explored to find out whether they reflect the client's need for universal approval and how such a need governs the person's life. Remember that groups can provide a dynamic understanding of how people function in out-of-group situations.

Group therapy also offers the possibility of multiple transferences. In individual therapy the client's projections are directed toward the therapist alone; in group therapy they are also directed toward other members. The group constellation provides rich possibilities for reenacting past unfinished events, especially when other members stimulate such intense feelings in an individual that he or she "sees" in them a father, mother, spouse, ex-lover, boss, and so on.

The element of rivalry that often exists in a group can also be valuable therapeutic material to explore. Group participants tend to compete for the attention of the leader—a situation reminiscent of earlier times, when they had to vie for their parents' attention with their brothers and sisters. Thus, sibling rivalry can be explored in group as a way of gaining increased awareness of how the participants dealt with competition as children and how their past success or lack of it affects their present interactions with others.

The opportunity that psychoanalytic groups offer for multiple transferences is stressed by several authors. The group is a conducive milieu in which to relive significant past events because "the group of today becomes the family of yesterday" says Locke (1961, p. 102). Wolf (1963) and Wolf and Schwartz (1962) observe that the group members serve as transference figures for other members and that the main work of the analytic group consists of identifying, analyzing, and resolving these projections onto family surrogates in the group. The leader has the task of helping members discover the degree to which they respond to others in the group as if they were their parents or siblings. By interpreting and working through their transferences, participants become increasingly aware of their fixations and deprivations and of the ways in which past events interfere with their ability to appraise and deal with reality.

Mullan and Rosenbaum (1978) call the focusing on and using of transference reactions the "hallmarks of psychoanalysis." These authors also discuss the value of using a man and a woman as co-therapists. This arrangement replicates faithfully the original nuclear family, and it enables members to reenact early expectations of their father and mother.

Countertransference

From time to time the therapist's own feelings become entangled in the therapeutic relationship, obstructing or even destroying objectivity. According to psychoanalytic theory, countertransference consists of a therapist's unconscious emotional responses to a client, resulting in a distorted perception of the client's behavior. Wolf (1983) makes it clear that no analytic leader is totally free of involvement in transference or countertransference. Kutash and Wolf (1983) describe countertransference as the leader's "unconscious, involuntary, inappropriate, and temporarily gratifying response to the patient's transference demands" (p. 135).

To the degree that countertransference is present, group therapists react to members as if they were significant figures of their own original family. Group leaders need to be alert to signs of unresolved conflicts within themselves that could interfere with the effective functioning of a group and create a situation in which members are used to satisfy their own unfulfilled needs. If, for example, group leaders have an extreme need to be respected, valued, and confirmed, they can become overdependent on the members' approval and reinforcement. The result is that much of what they do is designed to please the group members in order to ensure their continued support. It is important to differentiate between appropriate emotional reactions and countertransference. For example, if a member typically shows up late for the group and finds all sorts of reasons to justify his lateness, the group leader may become angry with him. Her anger toward his behavior is not necessarily unrealistic. However, if her father had a trait of justifying his behavior and if a common thread exists between the group member and her father, her emotional reactions are likely to represent countertransference. There are other manifestations of countertransference:

◆ seeing oneself in certain clients and overidentifying with them to the point of becoming unable to work effectively with them
◆ projecting onto clients some traits that one despises in oneself and regarding such clients as not amenable to treatment or impossible to work with
◆ engaging in seductive behavior and taking advantage of the leader's role to win the special affection of certain group members

Group therapists' unresolved conflicts and repressed needs can seriously interfere with the group process and can lead them to abuse their position of leadership. The difficulty in recognizing one's own countertransference and the necessity that such reactions be acknowledged and therapeutically dealt with provide a rationale for group leaders to experience their own therapy. The analytic approach requires that therapists undergo psychoanalysis to become conscious of their own dynamics and of the ways in which these dynamics can obstruct therapeutic tasks.

As noted by Brabender (1987), countertransference can be an avenue for understanding the dynamics of a group. She reminds us that group therapists are not immune to feelings such as hate, envy, guilt, admiration, and love. Her position is that "the full experience and tolerance of all of these therapist feelings within the inpatient group enables group members to realize the richness of their humanity in relation to one another" (p. 566).

But it is essential that the therapist's feelings be conscious and self-acknowledged.

Basic Techniques

Exploring Anxiety in the Group Situation

How the group leader recognizes and deals with anxiety, both within the individual and within the group as a whole, can be considered a key technique in the psychoanalytic group. Wolf (1983) points out that anxiety emerges when ego defenses or resistances are attacked. He writes that many members experience anxiety over the idea of joining an analytic group. During the course of the group, anxiety is revealed in many ways in the members' interactions. Mullan and Rosenbaum (1978) view anxiety as a necessary part of regressive-reconstructive group therapy. Therapeutic regression involves a reexperiencing of primitive patterns associated with earlier developmental stages. Some regression is a necessary element of the analytic group process. In a sense, the members must take one step backward in order to advance therapeutically. This regression involves some dissolving of the members' ego defenses, which also results in an increase in their experience of anxiety. Thus, anxiety is not something merely to bypass, and it is essential to recognize, understand, and explore the function that the defenses against it serve. Anxiety is a necessary by-product of taking risks in the group, a process that eventually leads to constructive changes.

Wolf and Kutash (1986) conceptualize anxiety as it is manifested in a group from the perspective of the equilibrium/disequilibrium theory. In their model, individuals feel anxiety, or a state of disequilibrium, when they are not experiencing the optimal level of stress for their needs. The interpersonal environment of the group can be characterized by three patterns of interaction: (1) a generally destructive balance ("group disequilibrium"), (2) a generally constructive balance ("group equilibrium"), or (3) a generally comfortable but stultifying balance ("group malequilibrium").

Group disequilibrium exists when members experience either too little intimacy (isolation) or too much intimacy (engulfment). Individuals then feel anxiety as the result of this imbalance. This anxiety has its roots in the family of origin, and in the group situation, members participate unconsciously in the process of re-creating anxiety-arousing patterns. Kutash and Wolf (1983) point out that just as individuals may re-create their pathogenic family, there is a danger that the group itself can become as pathogenic as their original family. Without skillful management by the group therapist, dependency can bind members together as neurotically as they were their original family.

Group equilibrium is achieved when the members constructively re-create their family, but with a new look. The members provide familial surrogates for bringing out transference reactions. They eventually realize the extent to which they are re-creating their own childhood family in every social setting and inappropriately investing others with qualities that characterized their earlier relationships.

Group malequilibrium exists when group members become so comfortable with one another that they avoid challenging one another's defenses. Members attempt to control and reduce their anxiety by avoiding conflict, and they unconsciously negotiate to bypass anxiety-arousing topics and ignore stressful but potentially growth-inducing material.

Free Association

The basic tool for uncovering repressed or unconscious material is free association: communicating whatever comes to mind, regardless of how painful, illogical, or irrelevant it may seem. Group members are expected to report feelings immediately, without trying to exercise censorship, and the group discussion is left open to whatever the participants may bring up, instead of revolving around an established theme. Foulkes (1965) refers to this process as "free-floating discussion," or "free group association."

One adaptation of free association to groups is the so-called "go-around technique," which uses free association to stimulate member interaction (Wolf, 1963). After a good rapport has developed in the conducive atmosphere fostered by sharing dreams and fantasies, members are encouraged to free-associate about each person in the group. Each participant goes around to each of the other members and says the first thing that comes to mind about that person. According to Wolf, the go-around method makes all the members adjunct therapists; that is, instead of remaining passive recipients of the leader's insights, the participants actively contribute to the interpretation of key meanings. Wolf contends that if group members say whatever comes into their heads about another, "they will intuitively penetrate a resistive facade and identify underlying attitudes" (1963, p. 289). As a result, the participants reveal inner feelings, become less guarded, and often develop the ability to see underlying psychic conflicts. Also, all group members have an opportunity to know how the other participants view them.

Wolf and Kutash (1986) suggest that it is useful when a client reports a dream to ask other members to free-associate with it. In this way they are being active and do not feel excluded as they listen to the details of another member's dream. The group can explore not only the dreamer's but also the other members' associations.

In summary, free association encourages members to become more spontaneous and to uncover unconscious processes, so that they can achieve keener insights into their psychodynamics. This procedure also promotes unity and active participation in the group process.

Interpretation

Interpretation is a therapeutic technique used in the analysis of free associations, dreams, resistances, and transference feelings. In making interpretations, the group therapist points out and explains the underlying meaning of behavior. Interpretations are designed to accelerate the therapeutic process of uncovering unconscious material. The assumption is that well-timed and accurate interpretations can be used by the client to integrate new data that will lead to new insights. Interpretation requires considerable skill. If therapists force their interpretations on clients in a dogmatic fashion, clients are likely to close off and become increasingly defensive. If clients are presented with an accurate interpretation at an inappropriate time, they may fight the therapeutic process and resist other interventions.

Scheidlinger (1987) maintains that an interpretation is simply a hypothesis and that no matter how elegantly conceived, it is still subject to confirmation or refutation. He suggests that when group members reject a therapist's interpretation, it may mean that the interpretation is inaccurate, not that they are being resistant. He writes that the correct timing of an interpretation in group therapy involves both a given member's readiness to understand and accept it and also the readiness of other group members. He adds that premature interpretations are likely to promote undue anxiety and lead to considerable resistance. The way interpretations are phrased and their manner of presentation, according to Scheidlinger, will certainly affect the degree to which they are considered by members. He formulates his interpretations in the form of questions, a practice that conveys the notion that they are merely hypotheses.

Interpretations that are presented as hypotheses and not as facts are more likely to be considered by clients. For example, Sam keeps making inappropriate interventions when other members express intense feelings and thus causes the others to lose contact with their feelings. The leader finally intervenes and says: "Sam, you seem to want to reassure Julie by trying to convince her that everything will work out for her. I have a hunch that you become uncomfortable when you see a person in pain; so you rush in, trying to take that person's pain away. Could it be that you're trying to avoid painful experiences yourself?" This comment alerts Sam to a possible reason for his behavior in the group. If he thinks about the leader's interpretation, he may discover other meanings of which he is not now conscious. Whether he will respond nondefensively has a lot to do with the manner in which the interpretation is made. In this case, the leader's tentative approach doesn't pose a threat and doesn't push Sam into accepting something that he may not be ready to accept.

In making interpretations, a few other general rules are useful:

- ◆ Interpretation should deal with material that is close to the client's awareness. In other words, the therapist needs to interpret material that clients have not yet seen for themselves but that they are ready and able to incorporate.
- ◆ Interpretation should begin from the surface and go as deep as the client can emotionally tolerate.
- ◆ It is best to point out a form of defense or resistance before interpreting the feeling or conflict that lies underneath it.

SHARING OF INSIGHTS BY MEMBERS. One of the advantages of the psychoanalytic method in groups is that members are encouraged to share their insights about other participants. This process can be very supportive and can accelerate progress. Even though the members do not systematically make interpretations, leaving that function to the therapist, they can have a deep effect on other members by being direct, unrehearsed, and confrontive. As members become more familiar with one another, they become increasingly able to recognize defensive strategies and offer perceptive observations. Fellow members' reactions may elicit more consideration and thought than those coming from an expert, but they may also be resisted with more tenacity. Some group therapists are concerned that a member may make inappropriate comments—that is, insights that the person in question is not ready to handle. This concern is somewhat lessened by what typically happens when someone is presented with an insight that is timed poorly or inaccurately: generally the person rejects the insight or in some way discounts it on the ground that it comes from a peer rather than from an expert.

Wolf, Schwartz, McCarty, and Goldberg (1972) observe that the therapist's interpretation of dreams, fantasies, transference, resistance, defensiveness, slips of tongue, and free associations allows the group members to become aware of these phenomena both in themselves and in others. Here, too, as in free association, the members are adjunct therapists as well as patients, for they interpret the manifestations of the unconscious in themselves and in others in the group. Elsewhere, Wolf (1963) writes that successful analysts learn to value the useful contribution of the group members to mutual insight. The group can greatly benefit from the sharing of interpretations, because "patients sometimes show themselves to be closer to the unconscious truth than their physician" (p. 313).

INTERPRETATION OF THE GROUP PROCESS. Interpretations can be directed to the group as a whole as well as to individual participants. For example, group members may be operating under the unspoken agreement that they will be polite and supportive and that they will not challenge one another. By observing the group process and sharing these observations with the group, the therapist can be instrumental in helping the members see their hidden motives and reach a deeper level of interaction. Here, too, *how* the leader presents the observations is crucial.

The interpretation of the group as a whole was developed by W. R. Bion, a British psychiatrist. Bion (1959) observed three basic assumptions that groups develop on their way to becoming a "work group": dependency, fight/flight, and pairing. The dependency-oriented group attempts to coax the professional leader to do for it what it feels it cannot do for itself. The fight/flight group resists structure by the leader or another member by rebelling against or ignoring the person. Members of the pairing group form dyads and hope that these pairings will do the work that they need to do as individuals. It was Bion's goal to help the participants achieve the ability to function effectively in work groups. Toward this goal, all of the interpretations were group interpretations. Although group-as-a-whole phe-nomena and group-process interpretations are valuable, Bion has been accused of overemphasizing group interpretations at the expense of other curative factors in group therapy (Yalom, 1985).

Dream Analysis

Analysis of dreams is an essential procedure for uncovering unconscious material. Freud saw dreams as "the royal road to the unconscious," because they express unconscious needs, conflicts, wishes, fears, and repressed expe-riences. When a dream is shared in a group and worked through, the participant gains new insight into the motivations and unresolved problems behind it. Some motivations are so unacceptable to the person that they can be expressed only in disguised or symbolic form. Thus, an advantage of working with dreams in a group is that it allows members to deal in a concrete way with feelings and motivations that otherwise they couldn't face. After exploring the various facets and possible meanings of a dream in a supportive group, members may be more willing to accept themselves and explore other unresolved problems that elicit feelings of guilt and shame.

It should be noted that dreams have both a *manifest* (or conscious) content and a *latent* (or hidden) content. The manifest content is the dream as it appears to the dreamer; the latent content consists of the disguised, unconscious motives that represent the hidden meaning of the dream. A psychoanalytic group works at both levels. Since dreams are viewed as the key that unlocks what is buried in the unconscious, the goal is to search for the latent beneath the manifest and to gradually uncover repressed con-flicts.

In the first session, group members are told that the sharing of their dreams, fantasies, and free associations is essential to the analysis and understanding of the dynamics behind confused thinking, feeling, and be-having. Even though therapists may have a great deal of insight into clients' dreams, they generally give little analysis during the early stages of a group. Instead, the members are encouraged to offer their own analyses (Mullan & Rosenbaum, 1978).

In her article "The Dream in Psychoanalytic Group Therapy," Kolb (1983) takes the position that dreams can be viewed from both an in-trapersonal and an interpersonal perspective. She contends that the dream experience itself, often without interpretation, taps unconscious mental activity in a manner unequaled by most other clinical experiences.

According to Wolf (1963), the interpretation of dreams is an essential aspect of the analytic process and should continue throughout the various stages of a group. It is an essential technique because the unconscious material that dreams reveal has a liberating effect on the participants. Members are encouraged to interpret and free-associate with one another's dreams in order to reach the deepest levels of interaction. Wolf reports that the entire group becomes "engrossed in dream analysis with its attendant associations, catharsis, sense of liberation and mutuality, all of which contribute toward the group unity which is so important in the first stages of treatment" (p. 287). He stresses the importance of a nonjudgmental attitude on the part of the leader toward the emerging unconscious material. The leader's tolerant approach encourages a similar attitude in the members, and the group soon becomes a compassionate and supportive family.

Besides their value for unblocking unconscious material from the client's past, dreams also contain a wealth of meaningful material concerning what is going on in the group, since the members' dreams reveal their reactions to the therapist and to the other members (Locke, 1961). The dreamer reports the dream and tells the group what meanings and associations it has for him or her. Then the group as a whole responds; other group members give their reactions to the dream and suggest cross-associations. The result is stimulation within the group.

The exploring of dreams in a group has another valuable aspect. As members analyze the dreams of others and offer their own associations, they also project significant dimensions of themselves. In other words, the group members are both interpreting *and* projecting, a process that often leads to extremely valuable insights. Wishes, fears, and attitudes are revealed as members associate with one another's dreams. One person's dream becomes the dream of the whole group, a process that is the "true essence of dream work in group psychoanalysis" (Locke, 1961, p. 133). Readers interested in a more detailed discussion of dream work in an analytic group are referred to Wolf and Schwartz (1962, pp. 135–161) and to Kolb (1983).

Insight and Working Through

Insight means awareness of the causes of one's present difficulties. In the psychoanalytic model insight is also an awareness, intellectual as well as emotional, of the relationship between past experiences and present problems. As clients develop keener insight, they become increasingly able to recognize the many ways in which these core conflicts are manifested, both in the group and in their daily lives. New connections are formed, and dominant themes begin to emerge. For example, if in the course of group work some members discover that they need to please everyone at all costs, they come to see the effects of their need for approval on their lives.

But the analytic process doesn't stop at the insight level; working through core problems and conflicts is an essential aspect of analytically oriented group and individual therapy. Thus, if group members hope to change some aspect of their personality, they must work through resistances and old patterns—typically, a long and difficult process. Working through is one of the most complex aspects of analysis, and it requires deep commitment. The working-through process involves reexperiencing the unfinished business in the context of transference (multiple transference, in group analysis).

Working through represents the final phase of the analytic group and results in increased consciousness and integration of the self. According to Wolf and Schwartz (1962), the leader, after discovering the dynamics of an individual's problems and symptoms, carefully maps a course of action to deal with them. These authors maintain that participants make progress and change as a result of a cooperative effort between the group leader and the client within the context of a thoughtful and flexible treatment plan.

It should be mentioned that early conflicts are rarely completely worked through. Most individuals may, from time to time, have to deal again with these deeply rooted issues. Thus, it is a mistake to think of working through as a technique that frees the individual from any vestige of old patterns.

The Alternate Session

Wolf and his colleagues (1972) write about two goals of psychoanalytic groups that are characteristic of the final stages of a group's development: helping members find more effective ways of relating to other people and encouraging them to grow as persons so that they can think independently and stand by themselves. The technique of the *alternative session* has proven quite successful in the pursuit of both these goals. The alternate session takes place, without the group leader, at the home of one of the members. These leaderless sessions are aimed at contributing to an intimate atmosphere that stimulates uninhibited participation.

In enumerating the advantages of the alternative session, Mullan and Rosenbaum (1978) mention developing group cohesion, increasing the creative potential of each member, enhancing the group's therapeutic function, and heightening a sense of belonging in the group. Mullan and Rosenbaum see the leader's absence as requiring a shift of responsibility, a search for new goals and values, different relationship patterns, and mutual efforts to cope with problems, all factors that contribute to greater autonomy in the members. The alternate session also provides ways of testing this newly acquired autonomy, since the participants' ability to function without the leader may be an indication of their readiness to separate from the therapist. Finally, the alternate session can enhance the regular sessions because it attests to the leader's faith in the members' ability to use their own resources within the group to work toward personal action and social integration.

Role and Functions of the Group Leader

There are great variations with respect to leadership styles among psychoanalytically oriented group therapists, ranging from leaders characterized by objectivity, warm detachment, and relative anonymity, on one side, to those who favor a role that is likely to result in a collaborative relationship with their members. Some psychoanalytically oriented leaders believe that if they remain more anonymous, members will project onto them more of their own images of what they expect leaders to be, images that are seen as expressions of the members' unconscious needs. Although such analysis of transference is still viewed as a hallmark of psychodynamic therapy, the model of the impersonal therapist is far from ideal and "represents a serious and frequently noxious miscarriage of the therapeutic role" (Strupp, 1992, p. 23). Indeed, one of the most significant developments of psychoanalytically oriented therapy is the growing recognition of the central importance of the therapeutic relationship. In contrast to the classical model of the impersonal and detached analyst, the contemporary formulation places emphasis on the therapeutic alliance, or a working relationship whereby the therapist "communicates commitment, caring, interest, respect, and human concern for the patient" (Strupp, 1922, p. 23).

According to Strupp, the redefinition of the therapeutic climate in more personal terms does not prevent the emergence of transference. He maintains that transference and countertransference still remain the cornerstones of psychodynamic therapy. Both the therapist and the group members react in ways that contain real and transference elements. Transference is a complex phenomenon that manifests itself through the interactions within a group.

A central task of the leader is to work out and work through these transference reactions, toward the leader as well as other members, as they are manifested in the group. As group interaction increases, the leader pursues participants' unconscious motivations and investigates the historical roots of these motivations through analysis and interpretation. Other functions of the leader include:

- giving support when support is therapeutic and the group is not providing it
- helping members face and deal with resistances within themselves and in the group as a whole
- attracting members' attention to the subtle aspects of behavior and, through questions, helping them explore themselves in greater depth

Further functions and tasks of the leader are identified by Wolf (1963) and Wolf and Schwartz (1962):

- making efforts to acknowledge errors and being secure enough to transfer some leadership functions to the group
- welcoming manifestations of transference in the group as opportunities for fruitful work
- guiding members toward full awareness and social integration
- seeing the group as a potentially powerful catalytic agent
- recognizing the participants' potential ability to assist in the interpretation and integration of material produced by other members and their capacity to be close to the unconscious truth of one another
- employing the skills necessary to resolve intragroup conflict
- setting the tone of emotional freedom by being open about one's own feelings
- watching for destructive alliances within the group

To be able to carry out these many functions effectively, group leaders have the paramount obligation to understand their own dynamics throughout the therapeutic process. To do so, they may need consultation and occasional supervision. Their own personal therapy can be most valuable in helping them recognize signs of countertransference and ways in which their own needs and motivations influence their group work.

Wolf and his associates (1972) are representative of those psychoanalytic practitioners who do focus on the therapist/client relationship and on the importance of the group leader's personal characteristics. After working within the framework of analytic group therapy for many years, they have come to the conclusion that success depends not only on the theoretical and technical constructs of psychoanalysis but also on the therapist as a person. They assert that the focus of psychoanalysis has gradually shifted from the patient's psychodynamics to the *relationship* between therapist and client.

Beyond that, according to Wolf (1983), the most significant function of the group therapist is to promote members' interpersonal relationships beyond the one with the therapist. Wolf suggests that an exclusive involvement with the therapist can insulate the client and lead to a symbiotic relationship. The promoting of interaction with others in the group expands the member's choices and fosters growth.

Developmental Stages and Their Implications for Group Work

Introduction

This section describes a developmental model that has significant implications for group work. The model is based on Erikson's eight stages of human development and on the Freudian stages of psychosexual development. Such a combination provides group leaders with the conceptual framework required for understanding trends in development, major developmental tasks at each stage of life, critical needs and their satisfaction or frustration, potentials for choice at each stage of life, critical turning points or crises, and the origins of faulty personality development that can lead to later personality conflicts.

Erikson (1963, 1982) built on and extended Freud's ideas by stressing the psychosocial aspects of development. Although he was intellectually indebted to Freud, he did not accept all of Freud's views. He viewed human development in a more positive light than Freud had and emphasized growth and the rational side of human nature, whereas Freud had stressed the irrational aspects of development. Moreover, psychosocial theory maintains that the ego is the organizing force of human development (Erikson, 1963). The ego is viewed as the component of the self that is in contact with the outside world through cognitive processes such as thinking, perceiving, remembering, reasoning, and attending.

Erikson's theory of development holds that psychosexual and psychosocial growth occur together and that at each stage of life we face the task of establishing an equilibrium between ourselves and our social world. Psychosocial theory stresses the integration of the biological, psychological, and social aspects of development. Erikson describes development in terms of the entire life span, which he divides into eight stages, each of which is characterized by a specific crisis to be resolved. According to Erikson, each *crisis* represents a *turning point* in life. At these turning points we can either achieve successful resolution of our conflicts and move forward, or we can fail to resolve the conflicts and regress. To a large extent, our lives are the result of the choices we make at each stage.

This conceptual framework is useful for all group leaders, regardless of their theoretical orientation. Irrespective of the model underlying one's group practice, the following questions need to be raised as group work proceeds:

◆ What are some of the themes that give continuity to a person's life?
◆ What are the client's ongoing concerns and unresolved conflicts?
◆ What is the relationship between this individual's current problems and significant events in earlier years?
◆ What influential factors have shaped the person's character?
◆ What were the major turning points and crises in the client's life?
◆ What choices did the individual make at these critical periods, and how did he or she deal with these various crises?
◆ In what direction does the person seem to be moving now?

Stage 1: Infancy—Trust versus Mistrust (Birth to 12 Months)

Freud labeled the first year of life the *oral stage*; sucking the mother's breast satisfies the infant's need for food and pleasure. According to the psychoanalytic view, the events of this period are extremely important for later development. Infants who don't get enough love and food may later develop greediness and acquisitiveness, because material things become substitutes for what they really wanted and didn't get. Later personality problems that stem from the oral stage include a mistrustful view of the world, a tendency to reject love, a fear of loving and trusting, and an inability to establish intimate relationships.

According to Erikson (1963), an infant's basic task is to develop a sense of trust in self, others, and the world. Infants need to count on others and to feel wanted and secure. By being held, caressed, and cared for, they learn basic trust. Erikson sees the first year of life in terms of *trust* versus *mistrust*. If the significant others (especially the parents) in an infant's life provide the necessary love and satisfy its physical needs, it develops a sense of trust. If, on the other hand, the parents are not responsive to its needs, it develops an attitude of mistrust toward the world, especially toward interpersonal relationships. Clearly, infants who feel accepted are in a more favorable position to successfully meet future developmental crises than are those who don't receive adequate nurturing. Children who receive love generally accept themselves, whereas children who feel unwanted and unloved tend to experience difficulties in doing so.

Some of the behavioral characteristics of people who have a sense of basic trust are an ability to ask others for emotional support, a focus on the positive aspects of others' behavior, an ability to balance giving and receiving, a willingness to self-disclose, and a generally optimistic worldview (Hamachek, 1988).

IMPLICATIONS FOR GROUP WORK. The connection between these ideas and the practice of group psychotherapy seems quite clear. A common theme explored in groups is the feeling of being unloved and uncared for and the concomitant acute need for someone who will deeply care and love. Time after time, group members recall early feelings of abandonment, fear, and rejection, and many of them have become fixated on the goal of finding a symbolic "parent" who will accept them. Thus, much of their energy is directed to seeking approval and acceptance. The problem is compounded by the fact that being unable to trust themselves and others, they are afraid of loving and of forming close relationships.

Group leaders can assist these clients to express the pain they feel and to work through some of the barriers that are preventing them from trusting others and fully accepting themselves. Erikson (1968) observes that these clients tend to express their basic mistrust by withdrawing into themselves every time they are at odds with themselves, others, or the world.

It should be noted that each stage builds on the psychological outcomes of the previous stage(s). In this regard, establishing a sense of basic trust is a foundation for later personality development. As you will see with the stages to come, when a foundation of trust, autonomy, initiative, and industry is laid, young people are ready for the challenges facing them during adolescence: establishing a clear sense of who they are as individuals and developing a positive self-concept (see Hamachek, 1988).

Problems associated with each of these developmental stages may become manifest in an analytic group in which the family of origin is recapitulated. For example, in this first stage members may project hostile feelings onto the leader or other members. These individuals may feel justified in harboring unrealistic fears and may not have enough trust to check such projections for accuracy. It is essential that leaders do what is necessary to establish a group atmosphere that allows members to feel the safety to explore possible projections. If a member does not develop this trust, he or she could easily become isolated in the group.

Stage 2: Early Childhood—Autonomy versus Shame and Doubt (12 Months to 3 Years)

Freud called the next two years of life the *anal stage,* because the anal zone comes to be of major significance in the formation of personality. The main tasks that children must master during this stage include learning independence, accepting personal power, and learning how to express negative feelings such as jealousy, rage, aggression, and destructiveness. Thus, it is at this stage that children begin their journey toward autonomy. They play an increasingly active role in taking care of their own needs and begin to communicate what they want from others. This is also the time when they continually encounter parental demands; they are restricted from fully exploring their environment, and toilet training is being imposed on them. The Freudian view is that parental feelings and attitudes during this stage have significant consequences for later personality development.

During the anal stage children experience feelings of hostility, rage, and aggression. If they are taught, directly or indirectly, that they are bad merely for having these feelings, they soon learn to bottle up these emotions. Having learned that parental love is conditional and that love is going to be withheld if they express "negative" feelings, they repress anger and hostility. Thus, the process of disowning feelings is set in motion, and it often leads to an inability later in life to accept many of one's own real feelings.

From Erikson's viewpoint the years between age 1 and 3 are a time for developing a sense of *autonomy*. Children who don't master the task of gaining some measure of self-control and the ability to cope with the world develop a sense of *shame* and *doubt* about themselves and their adequacy. At this age children need to explore the world, to experiment and test their limits, and to be allowed to learn from their mistakes. If parents do too much for their children and try to keep them dependent, they are likely to inhibit the children's autonomy and hamper their capacity to deal with the world successfully.

What are some of the characteristics of people who have a sense of autonomy? They can make their own decisions about significant matters, they can deny requests without feeling guilty, they resist being dominated by those who want to control them, they can work well by themselves or with others, they can pay attention to their own inner senses when deciding on a course of action, they have a basic belief in their capabilities, and they feel relatively at ease in group situations (Hamachek, 1988).

IMPLICATIONS FOR GROUP WORK. By understanding the dynamics of this stage of life, the group leader can gain access to a wealth of useful material. Many of those who seek help in a group have not learned to accept their anger and hatred toward those they love and need to get in touch with the disowned parts of themselves that are at the bottom of these conflicting feelings. In order to do this, they may need to relive and reexperience situations in their distant past in which they began to repress intense feelings. In the safe environment of the group they can gradually learn ways of expressing their locked-up feelings, and they can work through the guilt associated with some of these emotions. Groups offer many opportunities for catharsis (expressing pent-up feelings) and for relearning.

Group participants who have a limited degree of autonomy and many self-doubts have developed a lifestyle characterized by leaning on others. These people join a group to reacquire their potential for power and to develop the ability to define who they are and what they are capable of doing—in brief, to gain psychological control of their lives. Here, too, the group offers the opportunity to investigate how one's emotionally dependent style originally developed and to learn concrete ways of becoming more self-reliant.

Stage 3: The Preschool Age—Initiative versus Guilt (3 to 6 Years)

In Freud's *phallic stage* sexual activity becomes more intense. The focus of attention is on the genitals, and sexual identity takes form. Preschool children become curious about their bodies. They explore them and experience pleasure from genital stimulation. And they show increased interest in the differences between the sexes and ask questions about reproduction. The way in which parents respond, verbally and nonverbally, to their children's emerging sexuality and sexual interest is truly crucial in determining the kinds of attitudes, sexual and otherwise, that their children develop.

According to the Freudian view, the basic conflict of the phallic stage centers on the unconscious incentuous desires that children develop for the parent of the opposite sex. These feelings are highly threatening, so they are repressed, yet they remain as powerful determinants of later personality development. Along with the wish to possess the parent of the opposite sex comes the unconscious wish to displace the parent of the same sex.

The boy desires the mother's attention, develops feelings of resentment toward the father, yet also fears that the father will retaliate for his incestuous feelings toward the mother. This psychosexual developmental process is known as the *Oedipus complex*. The process is unconscious, of course, since repression is operating to keep the anxiety in check.

The boy typically develops fears related to his penis, which Freud termed *castration anxiety*. This fear plays a major role in the boy's life at this time. His fear is that his father will punish him by cutting off the offending organ. Because of his fear, the boy is said to repress his sexual desire for his mother. If the Oedipal conflict is adequately resolved, the boy replaces his sexual longings for his mother with more socially acceptable forms of affection. He develops a strong identification with his father, deciding that if he cannot beat his father, he will join him.

Although the *female phallic phase* is not so clearly described by Freud as is the male stage, there is a female counterpart to the Oedipus complex known as the *Electra complex*. The girl's first love object is her mother, but this love is transferred to her father during this stage. She develops negative feelings toward her mother but eventually, when she realizes that she cannot successfully compete for her father's attention, identifies with her mother by assuming some of her behavioral characteristics.

This period sees the development of the *superego,* which is the construct that refers to inner controls or ideals that guide the individual's behavior. During the phallic stage there is a conflict between the impulses of the id and the superego. The *id* is the part of the personality, present at birth, that is blind, demanding, and insistent. Its function is to discharge tension and return to homeostasis. The superego is that part of the personality that represents one's moral training. It strives for perfection, not pleasure. The *ego* has the task of mediating between external reality and inner demands. The ego consists of all modes of thought used by individuals to reach their goals and to defend their self-concepts.

Since this is a time of conscience formation, one critical danger is the parental indoctrination of rigid and unrealistic moral attitudes. Also, if the parents manifest a negative attitude toward their children's increased sexual awareness, the children learn that their sexual feelings are evil and that their curiosity about sexual matters is unacceptable. As a consequence, they become guilty about their natural impulses, afraid of asking questions and thinking for themselves, and prone to blindly accepting parental teachings. Sexual feelings and interest in sexual matters become anxiety provoking and are thus repressed. The denial of one's sexuality established at this age is then carried over into adult life and typically leads to conflicts, guilt, remorse, and self-condemnation. Another critical danger is that parents may be extremely lax in teaching any sense of values or that their modeling may be very poor. Such parents can teach children to act strictly on their own behalf and ignore any sense of concern for others. So, on one side are those individuals whose consciences are harshly punitive, and on the other side are people whose consciences are woefully absent. The latter are sociopathic individuals, whose main personality characteristics include a marked lack of ethical or moral development and an inability to behave in accordance with a framework of social values. Psychoanalytic theory provides a perspective for understanding the differences between these two extremes of conscience development.

Erikson, in contrast, contends that the basic task of the preschool years is to establish a sense of *competence* and *initiative*. This is the time for becoming psychologically ready to pursue activities of one's own choosing. If children are allowed the freedom to select meaningful activities, they tend to develop a positive outlook characterized by the ability to initiate and follow through. But if they are not allowed to make at least some of their own decisions or if their choices are ridiculed, they are likely to develop a sense of *guilt* over taking initiative. Typically, they will refrain from taking an active stance and will increasingly let others make decisions for them.

What are some of the characteristics of people who have a sense of initiative? They like accepting new challenges, they tend to set goals and then do what is necessary to accomplish them, they are self-starters, they have high energy levels, they have a clear sense of personal adequacy, and they have a balanced sense of ethics without being overly moralistic (Hamachek, 1988).

IMPLICATIONS FOR GROUP WORK. Oedipal and Electra dramas are commonly played out in group therapy. Members may set up the leader as a parental ideal who can then be demolished with scathing attacks. Competition for the leader's attention and affection is another common pattern with roots in this stage, as is excessive fear of disapproval by the leader (personal communication, William Blau, February 25, 1992).

In the groups that my colleagues and I conduct, we observe the general theme of symbolically wanting to replace the same-sex parent, so that the opposite-sex parent can be the object of attention. Other themes include wanting to be noticed and valued by the parent of the opposite sex, feelings of attraction to the parent of the opposite sex, and struggles with the parent of the same sex.

In most therapy and counseling groups, participants struggle with issues related to sex-role identity. Many individuals have incorporated stereotypical notions of what it means to be a woman or a man, and they have consequently repressed many of their feelings that don't fit these stereotypes. A group can be the place where individuals challenge such restricting views and become more whole.

Because concerns about sexual feelings, attitudes, values, and behavior are often kept private, people feel very much alone with their sexual concerns. Groups offer the chance to express these concerns openly, to correct faulty learning, to work through repressed feelings and events, and to begin to formulate a different view of oneself as a female or male sexual being. Perhaps the most important function of a group is that it gives clients permission to have feelings and to talk honestly about them.

Stage 4: The School Age—Industry versus Inferiority (6 to 12 Years)

Freudians call middle childhood the *latency stage*. After the torrent of sexual impulses of the preceding years, this period is relatively quiescent. There is a decline in sexual interests, which are replaced by interests in school, playmates, sports, and a whole range of new activities. Around 6, children begin to reach out for new relationships.

Erikson stresses the active, rather than the latent, aspect of this stage and the unique psychosocial tasks that must be met at this time if healthy development is to take place. Children need to expand their understanding of the physical and social worlds and continue to develop appropriate sex-role identities. They must also form personal values, engage in social tasks, learn to accept people who are different from them, and acquire the basic skills needed for schooling. According to Erikson, the central task of middle childhood is the achievement of a sense of *industry*, and the failure to do so results in a sense of *inadequacy* and *inferiority*. Industry refers to setting and achieving goals that are personally meaningful. If children fail at this task, they are unlikely to feel adequate as adults, and the subsequent developmental stages will be negatively influenced.

People who have a sense of industry enjoy learning, have a sense of curiosity, experiment with new ideas and arrive at a new synthesis, feel excitement over being productive, take a sense of pride in doing at least one thing well, accept criticism nondefensively, and have a strong sense of persistence (Hamachek, 1988).

IMPLICATIONS FOR GROUP WORK. The following are some of the clients' problems originating at this stage that group leaders may expect to encounter: a negative self-concept, feelings of inadequacy relating to learning, feelings of inferiority in establishing social relationships, conflicts about values, a confused sex-role identity, unwillingness to face new challenges, dependency, and lack of initiative.

To see how the leader's knowledge of the problems and promises of this period of life can help the therapeutic process, let's look at a participant who suffers from feelings of inferiority. Rachel fears failure so much that she shies away from college because she is convinced that she could never make it. In a group, she can be helped to see possible connections between her feelings of inadequacy and some events that occurred when she was in elementary school. Perhaps she had a series of negative learning experiences, such as being told, openly or not, by her teachers that she was stupid and couldn't learn. Before Rachel can overcome her feelings that she cannot meet the demands of college, she may have to go back to the traumatic events of her childhood, relive them, and express the pain she felt then. Through the support of the group she can experience again many of her buried feelings and begin to put the events of her past in a different perspective. Eventually, she may also come to realize that she doesn't have to wreck her academic career now because of something that happened in grade school.

Rachel could be harmed more than helped by a group experience unless she recognizes a pattern of inferiority in her life that is reenacted in the group situation. She could very well fear that she will also fail as a member. Given her dynamics, she is likely to set herself up for failure and also bias others to view her as a failure and as a "group reject." If the other members eventually come to share her negative feelings about her involvement in the group, a vicious circle may be difficult to break. Yalom (1985) cites compelling evidence that a member who is not accepted as valuable by the members (or by himself or herself) may be harmed by the group experience. It is crucial that members learn to recognize patterns that originated during their childhood and will inevitably unfold in a group.

Stage 5: Adolescence—Identity versus Identity Confusion (12 to 18 Years)

Adolescence is a stage of transition between childhood and adulthood. It is a time for continually testing limits, rejecting ties of dependency, and establishing a new identity. It is most of all a time of conflict, especially between the desire to break away from parental control and the fear of making independent decisions and living with the consequences.

In Freudian theory the final psychosexual stage of development, called the *genital stage,* is the longest and extends far beyond adolescence; it begins at the time of puberty and lasts until senility sets in, at which time the individual tends to regress to earlier stages. In essence, Freud saw the developmental period from birth to age 5 as the foundation on which later personality development was built. Thus, he focused on that period and didn't devote much attention to the events of later childhood or to those of adulthood. Erikson picked up where Freud left off and devoted a great deal of attention to the later stages, especially adolescence. He saw the crisis that characterizes adolescence—the identity crisis—as the most important of life.

What does Erikson mean by *identity crisis?* He means that most conflicts of the adolescent years are related to the development of a personal identity. Adolescents struggle to define who they are, where they are going, and how they will get there. Because all kinds of changes—physical as well as social—are taking place and because society applies diverse pressures, many adolescents have difficulty finding a stable identity. They experience pressure from school, from their parents, from their peer group, from members of the other sex, and from society at large, and these demands are often conflicting. In the midst of this turmoil the adolescent has the task of ultimately deciding where he or she stands in the face of these varying expectations. If the adolescent fails, *identity confusion* results, and the person will lack purpose and direction in later years.

What are some of the characteristic behaviors of people who have a sense of identity? They have a stable self-concept, they have a clear sense of goals, they are less susceptible to peer-pressure, they generally accept themselves, they are able to make decisions without vacillating, they assume a sense of responsibility for what happens to them, and they are able to be physically and emotionally close to selected individuals without losing themselves (Hamachek, 1988).

Clarifying and integrating one's values into an organic system that is personally meaningful is another difficult and anxiety-filled task of adolescence. In order to develop a personal philosophy of life, adolescents must make key decisions in a broad spectrum of areas: ethics and sexual morals, religious beliefs, life expectations, values in intimate relationships, education, and career. In meeting these challenges, young people need adequate models, for most values are learned not by direct instruction but by contact with people who provide inspiration through example. Often the models are inadequate or even nonexistent. Adolescents are especially aware of duplicity in adults, and they have a low tolerance for phoniness. They are influenced more by what they observe than by what they are told they *ought* to be.

IMPLICATIONS FOR GROUP WORK. In my groups a good deal of time is devoted to the exploration and resolution of the dependence/independence conflicts that are so prevalent in adolescence. A central struggle involves the process of separation and individuation. In a therapy group, adolescents may sometimes need to explore a missed period of early development and connection with a significant other. The group therapist could serve as a transference object for a time, by allowing feelings to be projected onto him or her and helping members work through unfinished business from the past.

At times one or several members manifest a rebellious attitude toward the leader. Although challenging the leader is often a sign of a move toward independence, attacking a leader may well be a symptom of rebellion against parents or any other authority. There could be an attempt to psychologically slay the therapist, which is an example of a recapitulation of adolescent themes within the group context. It is essential that leaders be aware of their own dynamics, especially if they are confronted by members. Leaders need to differentiate between rebellious and challenging behaviors of members.

Some group members relive their adolescence in the group, and they often go through experiences that they sealed off during that time. For example, they may have allowed others to make all the major decisions for them. In the group they become conscious of how they have let themselves give up self-direction for the comfort of direction from others. Through a relearning process they take active steps that gradually lead to taking charge of their own lives.

Group counseling is especially suited for adolescents. It provides a forum in which they can express and explore conflicting feelings and discover that they are not alone in these conflicts. A group allows open questioning of and modification of values and an opportunity to practice communication skills with peers and adults. Adolescents can safely experiment with reality, test their limits, express themselves, and be heard.

The unresolved problems of adolescence are manifest in many of the problems that adults bring to a group. In most of the groups I've led, one of the most persistent themes is the search for identity: "Who am I? How did I get this way? What do I really stand for? Where am I going, and how will I get there? If I get there, what will it ultimately mean?" Until adults recognize this unfinished issue from their earlier years, they cannot effectively meet the challenges presented by other stages of life.

Stage 6: Young Adulthood—Intimacy versus Isolation (18 to 35 Years)

In Erikson's view we enter adulthood after we have mastered the conflicts of adolescence and established a firm personal identity. During the sixth stage, young adulthood (ages 18–35), our sense of identity is tested again by the challenge of *intimacy* versus *isolation*.

An essential characteristic of the psychologically mature person is the ability to form intimate relationships. In order to achieve true intimacy with others, we need to have confidence in our own identity, because intimacy involves commitment and the ability to share and to give from our own centeredness. The failure to achieve intimacy leads to alienation and isolation. Young adulthood is also a time for focusing on one's interests, for becoming established in an occupation, and for carving out a satisfying lifestyle. It is a time for dreams and life plans but also a time for productivity.

IMPLICATIONS FOR GROUP WORK. In many adult groups considerable time is devoted to exploring the members' priorities. Participants struggle with concerns of interpersonal intimacy, talk about their unfulfilled dreams, question the meaningfulness of their work, wonder about the future, and reevaluate the patterns of their lives to determine what changes they need to make. Perhaps the greatest value of a group for people engaged in these struggles is the opportunity to take another look at their dreams and life plans and determine the degree to which their lives reflect these aspirations. If the gap is great, the participants are encouraged to find ways of changing the situation.

Typically, young adults bring to a group the problems related to living with another person and establishing a family. The central struggle of this period is the intimacy crisis, a conflict between the need to maintain a sense of one's own separateness and the need to establish close relationships. The successful resolution of the intimacy crisis involves achieving a balance between taking care of oneself and actively caring for others. Those who fail to strike this balance either focus exclusively on the needs of others, thus neglecting their own needs, or are so self-centered that they have little room for concern about others. Of course, the quality of the young adult's ability to form interpersonal relationships is greatly influenced by what took place during early development.

How members deal with intimacy within the group reveals patterns they learned about getting close or keeping distant during their young adulthood. For many people in groups, forming close bonds with others is extremely difficult. This pattern of being uncomfortable and frightened of both receiving and giving love and compassion is bound to unfold in the group sessions. The group is an ideal place for members who are struggling with intimacy issues to recognize and confront their fears. If members are not aware of their tendencies to keep themselves distant from others, they could easily try to mold the therapy group into their family-of-origin group, which had injunctions against intimacy.

Stage 7: Middle Age—Generativity versus Stagnation (35 to 60 Years)

The seventh stage is characterized by a need to go beyond ourselves and our immediate families and be actually involved with helping and guiding the next generation. The mature years can be one of the most productive periods of our lives, but they can also entail the painful experience of facing the discrepancy between what we set out to accomplish in young adulthood and what we have actually accomplished.

Erikson sees the stimulus for continued growth during this stage in the conflict between *generativity* and *stagnation*. Generativity is a broad concept that is manifested in the ability to love well, work well, and play well. If people fail to achieve a sense of personal competence, they begin to stagnate and to die psychologically. When we reach middle age, we become more

sharply aware of the inevitability of our own eventual death. This awareness of mortality is one of the central features of the midlife crisis and colors
our evaluations of what we are doing with our lives. For the first time we
must deal with the fact that we will not achieve all we believed we would,
that we have not lived up to our earlier expectations.

IMPLICATIONS FOR GROUP WORK. The changes that occur during this life
stage and the crises and conflicts that accompany them represent valuable
opportunities for group work. Participants are often challenged to make
new assessments, adjustments, and choices in order to open up new
possibilities and reach new levels of meaning. For example, most parents
have to adjust to the departure of their children. If they focused much of
their effort on their children, they now need to look elsewhere for a sense of
purpose and self-fulfillment. Group participants can explore ways of finding
productive new pursuits. Knowledge of adult development allows the group
leader to watch for the hopelessness that so many people experience during
middle age and to help them go beyond the destructive view that "that's all
there is to life." It takes caring and skilled leadership to inspire people to
look for new meanings and to "invent themselves" in novel ways. It is clear
that these developmental issues are salient to the group process as well as to
an understanding of members' out-of-group behavior.

Stage 8: Later Life—Integrity versus Despair (above 60 Years)

The eighth, and last, stage of life confronts the individual with crucial
developmental tasks, such as adjusting to the death of a spouse or friends,
maintaining outside interests, adjusting to retirement, and accepting losses
in physical and sensory capacities. But the central task of the final stage is
reviewing the past and drawing conclusions.

According to Erikson, the successful resolution of the core crisis of this
stage—the conflict between *integrity* and *despair*—depends on how the
person looks back on the past. *Ego integrity* is achieved by those who feel few
regrets; they see themselves as having lived productive and worthwhile
lives, and they feel that they have coped with their failures as well as their
successes. They are not obsessed with what might have been and are able to
derive satisfaction from what has been. They see death as a part of the life
process and can still find meaning and satisfaction in the time left.

Failure to achieve ego integrity leads to feelings of despair, hopelessness, guilt, resentment, and self-rejection. People with this perspective are
constantly aware of unfinished business; they yearn for another chance at
life that they know they will never have, and they cannot accept the thought
of dying, because they have wasted their lives. Thus, they are desperate.

IMPLICATIONS FOR GROUP WORK. Groups for the elderly are becoming
increasingly popular, as Burnside's (1984) excellent book *Working with the
Elderly: Group Processes and Techniques* indicates. She describes a range of

special groups created to meet the unique needs of the elderly. For example, *reality-oriented groups* are designed for regressed older people who have been diagnosed as suffering from chronic brain syndrome. *Remotivation-therapy groups* focus on simple matters of daily living and emphasize discussion of specific issues of interest to the participants. *Reminiscing groups* help the elderly remember and reconstruct the past. *Counseling groups* explore the problems that are common among older people, provide a supportive milieu, enhance a sense of belonging, and offer opportunities for testing reality.

To work successfully with the elderly in a group situation, the leader must take into account the basic limitations in their resources for change without adopting a fatalistic attitude that would only reinforce their sense of hopelessness. Those who lead groups for the elderly need to have realistic expectations. Although dramatic personality changes are quite unlikely, change—no matter how small and subtle—does occur and has a meaningful and beneficial impact on the participants (Corey & Corey, 1992).

Burnside (1984) notes that group work with the elderly requires more structure and direction than work with other age groups. Because of older people's special physical and psychological problems, group leaders are challenged to devise methods that provide support and encouragement. One of the most important elements of group work with the elderly is, in Burnside's opinion, careful and effective communication between leader and members. (For further reading on the topic of group work with older people, see Burnside, 1984.)

The salient issues of this stage of life have implications not only for group leaders working with older adults but also for those who work with young or middle-aged adults. Often these younger people express the fear of getting older. As they begin to see the years slip by, they feel the increasing pressure of making something of their lives. Some worry about being all alone when they are old, and some are afraid of financial or physical dependency on others. Group leaders can help these people realize that perhaps the only way to deal constructively with these fears is to prepare now for a satisfying life as they grow old. Asking the question "What would you like to be able to say about your life when you reach old age?" is a good way to start. What the members say in answer to this question (to themselves and in the group) can dictate the decisions they need to make now and the specific steps they must take in order to achieve a sense of integrity at a later age.

Contemporary Trends in Psychoanalytic Group Theory

Psychoanalytic theory, rather than being closed or static, is continually evolving. Freud's ideas were based on an id psychology, characterized by conflicts over the gratification of basic needs. Later, writers in the social-psychological school moved away from Freud's orthodox position and contributed to the growth and expansion of the psychoanalytic movement by incorporating the cultural and social influences on personality. Then *ego psychology*, with its stress on psychosocial development throughout the life span, was developed by Erikson, among others. Strupp (1992) writes that the notion of unconscious conflict is still fundamental to psychodynamic thought. However, more attention is now being given to internal structures of personality that are significantly influenced by experiences with significant figures during one's infancy and early childhood. Strupp notes that the Oedipus complex is no longer considered a universal phenomenon. Instead, there is an increased focus on disturbances and arrests in infancy and early childhood that stem from deficiencies in the mother/child relationship.

Object-Relations Theory

The evolution of psychoanalytic theory and practice did not cease with the development of the psychosocial perspective. A new trend in psychoanalytic thinking characterized the 1970s and the 1980s. These newer approaches are often classified in terms of *self psychology* and *object-relations theory*. Object relations are interpersonal relationships as they are represented intrapsychically. The term *object* was used by Freud to refer to that which satisfies a need, or to the significant person or thing that is the object or target of one's feelings or drives. It is used interchangeably with the term *other* to refer to an important person to whom the child and, later, the adult become attached. At birth, the infant has no sense of separateness; self and other are fused. The process of separation/individuation begins when the infant perceives that pleasure and discomfort are related to objects external to the self. The infant at this stage will typically make an attachment to the mother's breast before any recognition of her as a whole person.

The classical psychoanalysts held that rather than perceiving individuals as having a separate identity, developing infants perceive others as objects for gratifying their needs. In contrast, psychoanalytic thinkers today maintain that very young infants are already involved in an interpersonal world (Stern, 1985). Virtually all psychoanalytic thinkers believe that there is a continuity in the development of self/other relations from their infantile origins to mature involvement with other persons. Thus, object relations are interpersonal relationships that shape the individual's current interactions with people. Relating to others as objects in a primitive or infantile sense represents a failure of individuation. Object-relations theories diverge from orthodox psychoanalysis, although some theorists attempt to integrate the increasingly divergent trends that characterize this school of thought (St. Clair, 1986).

These contemporary theoretical trends in psychoanalytic thinking center on predictable developmental sequences in which the early experiences of the self shift in relation to an expanding awareness of others. Once self/other patterns are established, it is assumed, they influence later interpersonal relationships. This influence occurs through a process of searching for a type of experience that comes closest to the patterning established by the early experiences. For example, people who are either overly dependent or overly detached can be repeating patterns of relating that they established with their mother when they were toddlers (Hedges, 1983). These newer theories provide insight into how an individual's inner world can cause difficulties in living in the actual world of people and relationships (St. Clair, 1986).

Mahler's Perspective on Early Development

Mahler (1968) is a key figure in the evolution of the object-relations approach. She focused her studies on the interactions between the child and the mother in the first three years of life and formulated theories about the intrapsychic events of these early years. Mahler believes that the individual begins in a state of psychological fusion with the mother and progresses gradually to separation. The unfinished crises and residues of the earlier state of fusion, as well as the process of individuating, have a profound influence on later relationships. Object relations of later life build on the child's search for a reconnection with the mother (St. Clair, 1986).

Psychological development can be thought of as the evolution of the way in which individuals differentiate themselves from others. In group work participants can experience how they are bringing very early patterns into their present interactions. For example, a group member who appears closely involved with others at one meeting may seem distant and removed at the next, leaving everyone wondering what happened to the level of work that seemed to have been achieved. This pattern might repeat what Mahler calls the "ambitendency" of an infant who goes back and forth between wanting to be held by its mother and wanting to be left free to roam and explore.

Dealing with Borderline and Narcissistic Personalities

Perhaps the most significant developments of recent psychoanalytic theory involve borderline and narcissistic personality disorders. The essential features of the *borderline* personality are an unstable view of one's self and instability in relating to others. The essential features of the *narcissistic* personality disorder are a pervasive pattern of grandiosity, hypersensitivity to the evaluations of others, and a lack of empathy. Both of these personality patterns begin by early adulthood. Among the most significant theorists in this area are Kernberg (1975, 1976) and Kohut (1971, 1977, 1984). Kohut maintains that people are their healthiest and best when they can feel both independence and attachment, taking joy in themselves and also being able to idealize others.

From the perspective of object-relations theory, new light is shed on the understanding of personality disorders. According to St. Clair (1986), borderline and narcissistic disorders seem to result from traumas and developmental disturbances during separation/individuation. However, the full manifestations of the personality and behavioral symptoms tend to develop in adolescence or early adulthood. Narcissistic and borderline symptoms such as omnipotence, splitting (a defensive process of keeping incompatible feelings separate), and grandiosity are behavioral manifestations of developmental tasks that were disturbed or not completed earlier.

IMPLICATIONS FOR GROUP WORK WITH THE BORDERLINE PERSONALITY. A borderline personality disorder is characterized by bouts of irritability, self-destructive acts, impulsive anger, and extreme mood shifts. People with borderline dynamics typically experience extended periods of disillusionment, punctuated by occasions of euphoria. Interpersonal relations are often intense and unstable, with marked changes of attitude over time. There is frequently impulsive and unpredictable behavior that can cause physical harm. A marked identity disturbance is generally manifested by uncertainty about life issues pertaining to self-image, sexual orientation, career choice, and long-term goals. Kernberg (1975) describes the syndrome as including a lack of clear identity, a lack of deep understanding of other people, poor impulse control, and the inability to tolerate anxiety. In recent years a great deal more clarity about individuals with borderline dynamics has emerged, especially due to the work of Kernberg and other theorists. They may be more disorganized than neurotics but more integrated than psychotics. People who manifest borderline dynamics have not fully achieved separation/individuation and tend to have a chaotic, primitive personality structure.

One reviewer of this chapter (William Blau, personal communication, February 25, 1992) points out that the diagnosis of a borderline personality is being applied rather broadly in clinical settings. Although such a diagnosis originally referred to individuals occupying a border area between neurosis and psychosis, the diagnosis is now applied to many people who have fully intact reality testing but serious problems in the classic Freudian areas of love and work. Blau believes that these clients are amenable to treatment, although their difficulties may be more difficult to resolve than simple neuroses because they are embedded in relatively permanent personality patterns. He also prefers to refer to borderline "dynamics" rather than borderline "personalities."

In group work these borderline dynamics often show up in the countertransference experience that one is "walking on eggshells" with a group member, so that it appears all too easy to say the wrong thing and precipitate a crisis. Here Mahler's ideas about the "symbiotic" phase of the separation/individuation process can help us compare the potentially problematic group member to the infant who seems to expect the mother (or group leader) to be exactly attuned to his or her every feeling or need and who is ready to fly into a rage at any sign of failure to have this perfect attunement.

In working with borderline clients from ethnic minorities, Comas-Diaz and Minrath (1985) have found that integrating of a psychoanalytic theoretical model with a sociocultural context is essential for effective psychotherapy. Sociocultural factors tend to complicate the borderline dynamics, which revolve around the dimension of identity. Many of these clients experience pervasive feelings of loneliness, and there is an underlying theme of "Where do I belong?" Because socioeconomic and political factors permeate the lives of these clients, Comas-Diaz and Minrath contend, therapy cannot rely exclusively on an insight orientation. The authors maintain that it is essential for therapists to enter the client's life as a real person and to attempt to fully understand the client's life circumstances. It appears that these identity issues can appropriately be dealt with in group therapy. From a psychoanalytic perspective, group work is often more a matter of providing new experiences than of searching for insight into old experiences.

Kretsch, Goren, and Wasserman (1987) found that borderline individuals showed a consistent and significant improvement through their involvement in group therapy, especially in the area of ego functioning: "The group is either a stronger stimulant or a more appropriate setting [than individual therapy] for eliciting pronounced changes in ego functioning" (p. 110).

Yalom's (1985) view of group therapy with borderline clients is consistent with the study just cited. For him, their core problem lies in the area of intimacy, and the group offers the therapeutic factors of cohesiveness and of reality testing. He contends that if these individuals can accept feedback and observations provided by other members and if their behavior is not highly disruptive, the group can offer them supportive refuge from daily stresses. Although individuals with borderline dynamics may express primitive, chaotic needs and fears, they are continually confronted with reality through the group process, which helps keep these feelings somewhat under control. If the group begins to ignore borderline members, they assume deviant roles and act out in the group, and therapy fails.

IMPLICATIONS FOR GROUP WORK WITH THE NARCISSISTIC PERSONALITY. Children who lack the opportunity either to differentiate or to idealize others while also taking pride in themselves may later suffer from narcissistic personality disorders. This syndrome is characterized by an exaggerated sense of self-importance and an exploitive attitude toward others, which serves the function of masking a frail self-concept. Such individuals tend to display exhibitionistic behavior, they seek attention and admiration from others, and they tend toward extreme self-absorption. Narcissism may also present itself as very low self-esteem and an overreadiness to idealize others (see Gabbard, 1990).

Kernberg (1975) characterizes people with narcissistic dynamics as focusing on themselves in their interactions with others, having a great need to be admired, possessing shallow affect, and being exploitive and at times establishing parasitic relationships with others. He writes that individuals who are narcissistically oriented have a shallow emotional life, enjoy little other than tributes received from others, and tend to depreciate those from whom they expect few narcissistic pleasures.

There is also a growing trend of seeing narcissism as a striking lack of self-esteem. Kohut (1971) characterizes narcissistically oriented people as being highly threatened in maintaining their self-esteem and as having feelings of emptiness and deadness. These individuals are typically searching for someone who will serve as an object to feed the famished self. Kohut uses the term *selfobject* to refer to a person who is used to foster the narcissist's self-esteem and sense of well-being. These clients look for people whom they can admire for their power, because they see themselves as worthwhile only if they are associated with such selfobjects. Yet their inner void cannot be filled, so their search for confirmation by others is never-ending. These people attempt to merge with powerful or beautiful self-objects. Because of their impoverished sense of self and their unclear boundaries between self and others, they have difficulty in differentiating between their own thoughts and feelings and those of the selfobject.

A group leader may foster a healthier sense of self and a more successful process of differentiation by focusing interpretations on providing empathetic mirroring of the member's narcissistic disappointments. The assumption underlying this intervention is that differentiation has not been successful because of a failure of childhood efforts to gain a sense of self through adequate parental appreciation. So now the therapeutic emphasis can be on acknowledging current disappointments, thus promoting a manageable new round of differentiation. There will inevitably be moments when such clients' vulnerable sense of self-esteem is dealt a defeat by the failure of other members (or the leader) to appreciate them in just the way they might wish. When the leader verbalizes this disappointment on behalf of a group member, the narcissistic wound is better dealt with, the need for defensively inflated (or deflated) narcissism is reduced, and movement toward more genuine relating is enhanced (J. Michael Russell, personal communication, October 13, 1992).

Yalom (1985) discusses the problems that arise when individuals with narcissistic dynamics enter group therapy. They typically have difficulties in sharing group time, in understanding and empathizing with others, and in forming relationships with other members. These clients have a constant need for center stage. They often assess a group's usefulness to them in terms of how much time is devoted to them and how much attention they receive from the therapist. They are likely to be bored and impatient while other members are working, and they also tend to divert the discussion back to themselves. These individuals have unrealistic expectations of the other members, for they feel that they are special and deserve the group's attention, yet they are not willing to give to others. According to Yalom, a major task of the therapist is to manage such highly vulnerable members in the group. The leader must focus on the nature of the current forces, both conscious and unconscious, that are influencing the way members who display narcissistic traits relate to others in the group.

Future of Psychoanalytically Oriented Therapy

In his article forecasting the future of psychodynamic therapy, Strupp (1992, p. 25) contends that the various modifications of psychoanalysis "have infused psychodynamic psychotherapy with renewed vitality and vigor." He suggests that this approach will undergo further revisions and that it will maintain its prominence in individual, group, marital, and family therapy. Although contemporary psychodynamic forms diverge considerably in many respects from the original Freudian emphasis on drives, the basic concepts of unconscious motivation, influence of early development, transference, countertransference, and resistance are still central to the newer modifications. Strupp notes a decline in practices based on the classical analytic model, due to reasons such as time commitment, expense, limited applications to diverse client populations, and questionable benefits. He acknowledges that the realities stemming from *managed care* will mean increasing emphasis on short-term treatments for specific disorders, limited goals, and containment of costs. Some of the current trends and directions in psychodynamic theory and practice that Strupp identifies are summarized below:

◆ The emphasis on treatment has shifted from the "classical" interest in curing neurotic disorders to the problems of dealing therapeutically with chronic personality disorders, borderline conditions, and narcissistic personality disorders. There is also a movement toward devising specific treatments for specific disorders.

◆ There is increased attention on the establishing of a good therapeutic alliance early in the course of psychodynamic therapy. A collaborative and working relationship is now viewed as a key factor related to a positive therapeutic outcome.

◆ There is a renewed interest in the development of briefer forms of psychodynamic therapy, largely due to societal pressures for accountability and cost-effectiveness. The indications are that time-limited therapy will receive increasing attention in the future.

◆ Psychodynamic group therapy is becoming more popular; it has received widespread acceptance for several reasons: it is more economical, it provides clients with opportunities to learn how they function in groups, and it offers a unique perspective on understanding problems and working them through therapeutically.

Evaluation of the Psychoanalytic Model

Contributions and Strengths of the Approach

There is much in the psychoanalytic approach that I consider of great value. The analytic model provides a conceptual framework for understanding an individual's history, and in this regard group practitioners can learn to think psychoanalytically even if they do not practice psychoanalytically. Although some psychoanalytic techniques may have limited utility for the group counselor, many analytic concepts help explain the dynamics operating both in individuals and in the group as a whole.

It is important to consider one's past in order to fully understand one's present behavior. Many of the conflicts brought to a group are rooted in early childhood experiences. Although I am not advocating that one become preoccupied with the past by digging it up and then dwelling on it, I contend that ignoring the influence of the past leads to superficial group work. Understanding this influence gives people more control over their present behavior.

Another psychoanalytic concept I find of particular importance is resistance. Even when members are in a group by their own choice, I observe stubborn resistances, especially during the early development of the group. These resistances are manifestations of various fears; unless they are dealt with, they are not going to go away. In fact, I typically ask members to share with the group the ways in which they expect their own resistance to interfere with their group work. Even though resistance is typically unconscious, group members will often be surprisingly revealing. Some members seem to know quite well that they will sabotage themselves and resist change by intellectualizing, by being overly nurturing or overly hostile to fellow members, or by convincing themselves that their problems are not really very pressing. If members can recognize their resistant behaviors when they occur, they have a chance to do something about them. Some of the more subtle forms of defense may become evident over time, such as displacing feelings and projecting.

The psychoanalytic concepts of anxiety and the ego-defense mechanisms that emerge as a way to cope with this anxiety are most useful for group practitioners. Although in some groups the leader may not interpret and work through these defensive structures, it is essential to learn to respect defenses and to recognize how they develop and how they manifest themselves in the group interactions. Dealing with the defenses against anxiety provides a useful framework for intense group work. Members have the opportunity to challenge some of their defensive strategies, and in the process of learning how to communicate in nondefensive ways, they can also learn new ways of responding.

Transference and countertransference have significant implications for group work. Although not all feelings between members and the leader are the result of these processes, a leader must be able to understand their value and role. I find the analytic concept of projection quite useful in exploring certain feelings within the group, because projections onto the leader and onto other members are valuable clues to unresolved conflicts within the person that can be fruitfully worked through in the group.

The group can also be used to re-create early life situations that are continuing to have an impact on the client. In most groups individuals elicit feelings of attraction, anger, competition, avoidance, aggression, and so forth. These feelings may be similar to those that members experienced toward significant people in the past. Thus, members will most likely find symbolic mothers, fathers, siblings, and lovers in their group. These transferences within the group and the intense feelings that often characterize them are fruitful avenues to explore.

MODIFICATIONS OF CLASSICAL ANALYTIC PRACTICE. An approach that integrates Freud's psychosexual stages of development with Erikson's psychosocial stages is, in my view, most useful for understanding key themes in the development of personality. I do not think that working solely on an insight level will result in changes; it is essential to explore sociocultural factors as they pertain to the struggles of individuals at the various phases of their development. Unless group practitioners have a good grasp of the major tasks and crises of each stage, they have little basis for determining whether developmental patterns are normal or abnormal. Also, a synthesis of Freud's and Erikson's theories offers a general framework for recognizing conflicts that participants often explore in groups.

The newer developments, object-relations theories and self psychology, offer valuable conceptions for group therapists. There have been a number of breakthroughs in working with borderline and narcissistic dynamics in group therapy. As we have seen, the group offers some unique advantages over the one-to-one relationship in working with borderline personalities. According to Strupp (1992), the focus of psychoanalytic therapy has shifted toward understanding and working with personality disorders, such as borderline and narcissistic conditions. Many practitioners who were trained in classical psychoanalysis have modified analytic concepts and techniques to fit group situations. I have encountered a number of therapists who think in psychoanalytic terms but draw on other therapeutic models. They work with analytic concepts such as the unconscious, defenses, resistances, transference, and the significance of the past, but they also borrow techniques from other approaches.

Limitations of the Approach

From a feminist perspective, there are distinct limitations to a number of Freudian concepts, especially the notion of the Oedipus and Electra complexes and the assumptions about the inferiority of women. In her review of feminist counseling and therapy, Enns (1993) notes that the object-relations approach has been criticized for its emphasis on the role of the mother/child relationship as a determinant of later interpersonal functioning. The approach gives great responsibility to mothers for deficiencies and distortions in development, whereas fathers are conspicuously absent from the hypothesis. Enns writes that some feminist therapists have addressed the limitations of psychoanalysis by incorporating family-systems work within their psychoanalytic model.

In addition to the criticisms of psychoanalysis from feminist writers, the approach is accused of failing to adequately address the social, cultural, and political factors that result in an individual's problems. There are likely to be some difficulties in applying a psychoanalytic approach with low-income clients. This is especially true in working within the framework of long-term, in-depth analysis, which may be in direct conflict with some clients' social framework and interpersonal and environmental perspective. Psychoanalytic therapy is less concerned with short-term problem solving than it is with long-term personality reconstruction. Poor people generally do not have the time, resources, or inclination to begin and maintain the extended and expensive journey of psychoanalytic self-exploration. Instead, they are likely to be motivated more by the need to have psychological security and provide for their family. If they seek professional help, they are generally concerned with dealing with a crisis situation and with finding answers, or at least some direction, in addressing survival needs pertaining to housing, employment, and child care.

The increasing number of economically disadvantaged people raises the question of the relevance of traditional psychoanalytic approaches to group work. A systems perspective, including the role of the family, one's network of friends and extended family, and social and environmental factors, may be more compatible with the socioeconomic and cultural backgrounds of some client groups.

In his critique of long-term psychodynamic therapy, Strupp (1992) acknowledges that this approach will clearly remain a luxury for most people in our society. Recognizing that most practitioners have been influenced by an eclectic spirit, he predicts the following outlook for psychodynamic practice: "This [new] movement reflects a decisive departure from orthodoxy, together with much greater openness by most therapists to adapt to changing circumstances and to tailor techniques to the changing needs of patients as well as to the demands of our multifaceted society" (p. 25).

Applying the Psychoanalytic Approach with Multicultural Populations

Regardless of the theoretical orientation, it is important to specify the criteria that determine whether a given theory is appropriate for ethnic-minority clients. One key criterion is the consistency between the key concepts and principles of a theory and the cultural values of the clients being served (Julia Yang, personal communication, June 14, 1993). The basic question to be asked is: How can group counseling be more effective than traditional healing methods or individual counseling? In evaluating all the theories in this book, it will be important to consider how well the underlying assumptions and key concepts of each theory mesh with the cultural values of diverse client groups.

Psychoanalytically oriented group therapy, if modified, can be appropriate for culturally diverse populations. De La Cancela (1985) mentions specifically the value of preparing minority clients during the preliminary phase of therapy. He also suggests that therapists reduce the social distance between themselves and their clients, that they work toward establishing rapport, and that they educate and motivate clients to reflect on feelings and to reveal themselves.

Comas-Diaz and Minrath (1985) recommend that the diffused sense of identity prevalent among minority clients with borderline dynamics be examined from both a sociocultural and a developmental perspective. They believe that one aid to helping clients rebuild their identity is to emphasize strengths rather than deficiencies. They also suggest that exploring the meaning of ethnicity and race within the therapeutic relationship is essential for working through the clients' diffused sense of identity. Erikson's psychosocial approach seems to have particular relevance here.

Many cultural groups place a high priority on family history. A review of a client's past and of how this past is having an important bearing on current functioning may be appropriate as a conceptual framework. Working in symbolic ways can also be powerful, especially with clients who are reluctant to talk about their personal problems. For example, there is value in using pictures of the family at different periods of the client's childhood. The leader might say: "Select a picture that has particular meaning for you. Tell me what you remember during these times. As you look at the picture, what thoughts and feelings come to you?" Once group members begin talking to one another about their memories based on pictures, they are likely to be more open in dealing with emotional material.

As we have seen, group therapists need to be aware of the ways in which the interpretations they make are influenced by their cultural background and their theoretical assumptions. Although practitioners can still conceptualize the struggles of their clients from an analytic perspective, it is critical that they adopt a stance of flexibility. Group counselors need to exercise vigilance lest they misuse their power by turning the group into a forum for pushing clients to adjust by conforming to the dominant cultural values at the expense of losing their own worldviews and cultural identities.

Group practitioners also need to be clear about their own potential sources of bias. The concept of countertransference can be expanded to include unconfronted bias and prejudices that may be conveyed unintentionally through the group therapist's interventions (Julia Yang, personal communication, June 14, 1993).

Comas-Diaz and Minrath (1985) emphasize that the conflicts of minority clients result from the interplay of intrapsychic and sociocultural forces and that therapists may at times feel overwhelmed with the myriad of problems presented by these clients. These authors suggest that it is the therapist's role to address the pervasiveness of these factors in the client's daily life. If these sociocultural forces are not acknowledged, many ethnic minorities are likely to feel alienated from both the therapist and the therapeutic process. Ultimately, this recommendation affirms the deepest and oldest concept of psychoanalysis, which is that we are to listen very carefully to what our clients have to tell us (Casement, 1991).

Atkinson, Thompson, and Grant (1993) suggest that problems of racial- and ethnic-minority clients stem more often from past experiences with discrimination than from internal dynamics. Consider these examples:

◆ An African-American man's behavior may be interpreted by the therapist as a manifestation of paranoia, when in reality his reactions are justified in his dangerous social environment.

◆ A Hispanic student may exhibit low self-esteem, yet her feelings of inadequacy may well be due to teachers who have consistently given her negative feedback or to children who have teased her.

If there is no balance between the external and internal sources of problems, the client will be blamed for his or her condition.

Where to Go from Here

If you would like to learn more about psychoanalytic groups, you would do well to join the American Group Psychotherapy Association. Membership includes a subscription to an excellent journal, the *International Journal of Group Psychotherapy,* which is published four times a year. The journal contains a variety of articles dealing with both the theory and practice of group therapy, and many of the articles relate to psychoanalytic groups. The AGPA has a training program for group therapists and graduate students; successful completion results in a certificate. The program entails taking 90 hours of didactic instruction about group therapy, leading therapy groups for at least 60 hours, having at least 25 hours of qualified supervision in group leadership, and participating as a member of a group or groups for at least 60 hours. Each year in February the AGPA sponsors a five-day annual meeting that features a variety of institutes, seminars, open sessions, and workshops. Although psychodynamic groups are featured, other group orientations are offered as well. Many of these full-day and half-day workshops are directed toward issues of interest to psychodynamic practitioners. The AGPA does have a student-member category. For further information about journal subscriptions and membership requirements contact:

American Group Psychotherapy Association, Inc.
25 East 21st Street, 6th Floor
New York, NY 10010
TELEPHONE: (212) 477-2677

RECOMMENDED SUPPLEMENTARY READINGS

Object Relations and Self Psychology: An Introduction (St. Clair, 1986) provides an overview and critical assessment of two streams of psychoanalytic theory and practice: object-relations theory and self psychology. An introductory chapter describes the basic concepts and deals with some core issues. Especially useful are the chapters discussing the approaches of Margaret Mahler, Otto Kernberg, and Heinz Kohut. There are also chapters devoted to the models of Klein, Fairbairn, Winnicott, and Jacobson. The issues and concepts of these models are presented relatively clearly (considering that the primary sources are difficult to read). The book looks at how these different theorists vary from one another and how they depart from the classical Freudian model. This is a good place to start if you want an update on the contemporary trends in psychoanalysis.

Psychoanalysis in Groups (Wolf & Schwartz, 1962) offers an excellent overview of the stages of development of an analytic group, the role of the group analyst, and the practical aspects of the analytic group process. This book also discusses the alternate session, acting out, dreams, working through, and the misuse of the group.

Beyond the Couch: Dialogues in Teaching and Learning Psychoanalysis in Groups (Wolf, Schwartz, McCarty, & Goldberg, 1970) presents basic psychoanalytic concepts that apply to the theory and technique of analytic groups. Specific issues such as the training experience, the alternate session, extragroup socialization, transferences in the group, the nature of supervision, transference theory, and termination are explored.

Group Psychotherapy: Theory and Practice (Mullan & Rosenbaum, 1978) is written mainly from a psychoanalytic perspective. Part II deals with the psychoanalytic method and innovations. Stages of group development, the alternate session, conceptual foundations of the analytic group, transference and countertransference, and the group organization are a few of the topics covered. I highly recommend this book for both beginning and advanced group practitioners.

REFERENCES AND SUGGESTED READINGS*

American Psychiatric Association. (1987). *Diagnostic and statistical manual of mental disorders* (4th ed.). Washington, DC: Author.

Atkinson, D. R., Morten, G., & Sue, D. W. (1993). *Counseling American minorities: A cross-cultural perspective* (4th ed.). Madison, WI: Brown & Benchmark.

Atkinson, D. R., Thompson, C. E., & Grant, S. K. (1993). A three-dimensional model for counseling racial/ethnic minorities. *The Counseling Psychologist, 21*(2), 257–277.

Bacal, H. A. (1985). Object relations in the group from the perspective of self-psychology. *International Journal of Group Psychotherapy, 35*(4), 483–501.

Bion, W. R. (1959). *Experience in groups and other papers.* New York: Basic Books.

*Brabender, V. M. (1987). Vicissitudes of countertransference in inpatient group psychotherapy. *International Journal of Group Psychotherapy, 37*(4), 549–567.

Brown, L. S., & Brodsky, A. M. (1992). The future of feminist therapy. *Psychotherapy, 29*(1), 51–57.

Burnside, I. M. (Ed.). (1984). *Working with the elderly: Group processes and techniques* (2nd ed.). Boston: Jones & Bartlett.

Casement, P. J. (1991). *Learning from the patient.* New York: Guilford Press.

*Comas-Diaz, L., & Minrath, M. (1985). Psychotherapy with ethnic minority borderline clients. *Psychotherapy, 22*(25), 418–426.

Corey, G., & Corey, M. S. (1993). *I never knew I had a choice* (5th ed.). Pacific Grove, CA: Brooks/Cole.

Corey, M. S., & Corey, G. (1992). *Groups: Process and practice* (4th ed.). Pacific Grove, CA: Brooks/Cole.

De La Cancela, V. (1985). Toward a sociocultural psychotherapy for low-income ethnic minorities. *Psychotherapy, 22*(25), 427–435.

Eagle, M. N., & Wolitzky, D. L. (1992). Psychoanalytic theories of psychotherapy. In D. K. Freedheim (Ed.), *History of psychotherapy: A century of change* (pp. 109–158). Washington, DC: American Psychological Association.

*Durkin, H. (1964). *The group in depth.* New York: International Universities Press.

Enns, C. Z. (1993). Twenty years of feminist counseling and therapy: From naming biases to implementing multifaceted practice. *The Counseling Psychologist, 21*(1), 3–87.

*Erikson, E. (1963). *Childhood and society* (2nd ed.). New York: Norton.

Erikson, E. H. (1968). *Identity: Youth and crisis.* New York: Norton.

Erikson, E. H. (1982). *The life cycle completed.* New York: Norton.

Foulkes, S. H. (1965). *Therapeutic group analysis.* New York: International Universities Press.

*Books and articles marked with an asterisk are suggested for further study.

Foulkes, S. H., & Anthony, E. J. (1965). *Group psychotherapy: The psychoanalytic approach* (2nd ed.). London: Penguin.

*Freud, S. (1955). *The interpretation of dreams*. New York: Basic Books.

Gabbard, G. O. (1990). *Psychodynamic psychiatry in clinical practice*. Washington, DC: American Psychiatric Press.

Grotjahn, M. (1984). The narcissistic person in analytic group therapy. *International Journal of Group Psychotherapy, 34*(2), 243–256.

*Hamachek, D. F. (1988). Evaluating self-concept and ego development within Erikson's psychosocial framework: A formulation. *Journal of Counseling and Development, 66*(8), 354–360.

*Hamachek, D. F. (1990). Evaluating self-concept and ego status in Erikson's last three psychosocial stages. *Journal of Counseling and Development, 68*, 677–683.

Hannah, S. (1984). Countertransference in in-patient group psychotherapy: Implications for technique. *International Journal of Group Psychotherapy, 34*(2), 257–272.

Hedges, L. E. (1983). *Listening perspectives in psychotherapy*. New York: Aronson.

*Kernberg, O. F. (1975). *Borderline conditions and pathological narcissism*. New York: Aronson.

Kernberg, O. F. (1976). *Object-relations theory and clinical psychoanalysis*. New York: Aronson.

Kohut, H. (1971). *The analysis of the self*. New York: International Universities Press.

Kohut, H. (1977). *The restoration of the self*. New York: International Universities Press.

Kohut, H. (1984). *How does psychoanalysis cure?* Chicago: University of Chicago Press.

*Kolb, G. E. (1983). The dream in psychoanalytic group therapy. *International Journal of Group Psychotherapy, 33*(1), 41–52.

Kretsch, R., Goren, Y., & Wasserman, A. (1987). Change patterns of borderline patients in individual and group therapy. *International Journal of Group Psychotherapy, 37*(1), 95–112.

*Kutash, I. L., & Wolf, A. (1983). Recent advances in psychoanalysis in groups. In H. I. Kaplan & B. J. Sadock (Eds.), *Comprehensive group psychotherapy* (2nd ed.). Baltimore: Williams & Wilkins.

Liff, Z. A. (1992). Psychoanalysis and dynamic techniques. In D. K. Freedheim (Ed.), *History of psychotherapy: A century of change* (pp. 571–586). Washington, DC: American Psychological Association.

Locke, N. (1961). *Group psychoanalysis: Theory and technique*. New York: New York University Press.

Mahler, M. S. (1968). *On human symbiosis and the vicissitudes of individuation*. New York: International Universities Press.

Mahler, M. S. (1971). A study of the separation and individuation process. In *The psychoanalytic study of the child: Vol. 26* (pp. 403–422). New York: Quadrangle.

Mullan, H., & Rosenbaum, M. (1978). *Group psychotherapy: Theory and practice* (2nd ed.). New York: Free Press.

Ormont, L. R. (1988). The leader's role in resolving resistances to intimacy in the group setting. *International Journal of Group Psychotherapy, 38*(1), 29–46.

*St. Clair, M. (1986). *Objects relations and self psychology: An introduction*. Pacific Grove, CA: Brooks/Cole.

Scheidlinger, S. (1987). On interpretation in group psychotherapy: The need for refinement. *International Journal of Group Psychotherapy, 37*(3), 339–352.

Stern, D. N. (1985). *The interpersonal world of the infant*. New York: Basic Books.

*Strupp, H. H. (1992). The future of psychodynamic psychotherapy. *Psychotherapy, 29*(1), 21–27.

Tuttman, S. (1986). Theoretical and technical elements which characterize the

American approaches to psychoanalytic group psychotherapy. *International Journal of Group Psychotherapy, 36*(4), 499–515.

*Wolf, A. (1963). The psychoanalysis of groups. In M. Rosenbaum & M. Berger (Eds.), *Group psychotherapy and group function.* New York: Basic Books.

Wolf, A. (1975). Psychoanalysis in groups. In G. M. Gazda (Ed.), *Basic approaches to group psychotherapy and group counseling* (2nd ed.). Springfield, IL: Charles C Thomas.

*Wolf, A. (1983). Psychoanalysis in groups. In H. I. Kaplan & B. J. Sadock (Eds.), *Comprehensive group psychotherapy* (2nd ed.). Baltimore: Williams & Wilkins.

Wolf, A., & Kutash, I. L. (1985). Di-egophrenia and its treatment through psychoanalysis in groups. *International Journal of Group Psychotherapy, 35*(4), 519–530.

*Wolf, A., & Kutash, I. L. (1986). Psychoanalysis in groups. In I. L. Kutash & A. Wolf (Eds.), *Psychotherapist's casebook* (pp. 332–352). San Francisco: Jossey-Bass.

*Wolf, A., & Schwartz, E. K. (1962). *Psychoanalysis in groups.* New York: Grune & Stratton.

*Wolf, A., Schwartz, E. K., McCarty, G. J., & Goldberg, I. A. (1970). *Beyond the couch: Dialogues in teaching and learning psychoanalysis in groups.* New York: Science House.

*Wolf, A., Schwartz, E. K., McCarty, G. J., & Goldberg, I. A. (1972). Psychoanalysis in groups: Contrasts with other group therapies. In C. J. Sager & H. S. Kaplan (Eds.), *Progress in group and family therapy.* New York: Brunner/Mazel.

Wong, N. (1983). Fundamental psychoanalytic concepts: Past and present understanding of their applicability to group psychotherapy. *International Journal of Group Psychotherapy, 33*(2), 171–191.

*Yalom, I. D. (1983). *Inpatient group psychotherapy.* New York: Basic Books.

*Yalom, I. D. (1985). *The theory and practice of group psychotherapy* (3rd ed.). New York: Basic Books.

◆ CHAPTER SEVEN ◆

Adlerian Group Counseling

Introduction

While Freud was developing his system of psychoanalysis, a number of other psychiatrists also interested in the psychoanalytic approach were independently studying the human personality. Two of these were Alfred Adler and Carl Jung. These three thinkers attempted to collaborate, but it became evident that Freud's basic concepts of sexuality and biological determinism were unacceptable to Adler and Jung. Whereas Freud believed that sexual repression caused neurotic disorders, Adler contended that the basic problem pertained to the struggle of individuals to become all that they might become. Adler emphasized a psychology of growth, rather than a psychology of the abnormal personality. After about nine years of association, the three parted company, with Freud taking the position that the others had deserted him.

Another major difference between Freud and Adler involves the populations with which they worked. Freud focused on the individual psychodynamics of a neurotic population, and Freudian psychoanalysis was largely confined to more affluent clients. By contrast, Adler was a politically and socially oriented psychiatrist who showed great concern for the common person; part of his mission was to bring psychotherapy to the working class and to translate psychological concepts into practical methods for helping a varied population meet the challenges of life.

Because of Adler's basic assumption of the all-important social nature of human beings, he was interested in working with clients in a group context. He combined his social interests and his concern with the personality by becoming an educator and establishing family-education and child-guidance clinics. He devoted much time to lecturing on the application of his principles to treating children and demonstrating them to both parents and professional groups. He pioneered live demonstrations by interviewing children, adults, teachers, and parents in front of a group.

To fully appreciate the development of the practice of Adlerian psycholo-

I appreciate James Bitter's collaboration with me on revising this chapter.

186

gy, one must recognize the contributions of Rudolf Dreikurs, who was largely responsible for transplanting Adler's ideas to the United States. It was Dreikurs who developed and refined Adler's concepts into a clear-cut, teachable system with practical applications for family life, education, preventive mental health, and, especially, group psychotherapy (Terner & Pew, 1978). Dreikurs was a key figure in developing the Adlerian child-guidance clinics in the United States. Work with children and their parents in a group setting paved the way for Dreikurs's pioneering group psychotherapy. He introduced groups into his busy psychiatry practice in 1928 as a time-saving measure, yet he soon found that they were a more effective way of reaching people than individual therapy. He was perhaps the first to employ group therapy as a way of facilitating insights into each participant's lifestyle (Terner & Pew, 1978).

Key Concepts

Overview of the Adlerian View of the Person

Adler's system emphasizes the social determinants, rather than the biological aspects, of behavior, its goal directedness, and its purposeful nature. This "socioteleological" approach implies that people are primarily motivated by social forces and are striving to achieve certain goals. Paramount is the striving for significance, "a movement toward the fulfillment of the goal to achieve unique identity and to belong" (Dinkmeyer et al., 1987, p. 16). The search for significance is related to our basic feelings of inferiority with regard to others, which motivate us to strive for mastery, superiority, power, and, ultimately, perfection. Inferiority feelings can thus be the wellspring of creativity; perfection, not pleasure, is the goal of life.

Freud's historical/causal approach sees behavior as governed by forces within us that are beyond our control. Adler's system, instead, stresses self-determination and consciousness (rather than the unconscious) as the center of personality. We are not the victims of fate but creative, active, choice-making beings whose every action has purpose and meaning. Movement toward goals and our anticipation of the future are far more important than what has happened to us in the past. Behavior can be understood only if one takes a holistic approach and looks at all actions from the perspective of the individual's chosen style of life. Each of us has a unique lifestyle, or personality, which starts to develop in early childhood to compensate for and overcome some perceived inferiority. Our lifestyle influences our experience of life and interactions with others. It consists of our views about ourselves and the world and of the distinctive behaviors we use to pursue our goals.

Because of its stress on responsibility, on the striving for superiority, and on the search for value and meaning in life, Adler's approach is basically a growth model. The striving for superiority is best conceived of as a "moving from a perceived minus to a perceived plus" (Ansbacher & Ansbacher, 1956). Adlerians reject the idea that some individuals are psychologically "sick" and in need of a "cure." Instead, they view their work as teaching people better ways to meet the challenges of life tasks, providing direction, helping people change their mistaken notions, and offering encouragement to those who are discouraged.

Holism

The Adlerian approach, also known as *Individual Psychology,* is based on a holistic view of the person. (The word *individual* does not imply a focus on the individual client as opposed to people in groups.) In Individual Psychology, holism refers to viewing the person as a unified, indivisible whole. Holism also refers to the unity of personality, which occurs after an individual has selected a life goal (Ansbacher & Ansbacher, 1956, p. 189). Individuals are always more than the sum of their parts. Thoughts, feelings, beliefs, convictions, attitudes, and actions are all expressions of the uniqueness of the person. One implication of this view is that the client is seen as an integral part of a social system. There is more focus on *inter*personal factors than on *intra*personal ones. The therapist is oriented toward understanding the client's social situation and the attitudes he or she has about it. Viewing people in relationship to social systems is basic to group and family therapy.

Teleology

According to Adler, all forms of life are characterized by a trend toward growth and expansion. He rejected Freud's causal determinism in favor of teleological explanations: humans live by goals and purposes, they are moved by anticipation of the future, and they create meaning. Very early in life, people begin to envision what they might be like if they were perfect. They set this vision as a fictive life goal and consistently act as if they will one day reach it.

Individual Psychology contends that we can be understood best by looking at where we are going and what we are striving to accomplish (Corsini, 1987). Thus, in contrast to the Freudian psychoanalytic emphasis on the past, Adlerians are more interested in the future. The three aspects of time are dynamically interrelated: our decisions are based on what we have experienced in the past, on our present situation, and on what we are moving toward. In short, Adlerians look for a continuity, or a pattern, in a client's life, but always with the emphasis on the goal-directed nature of all behavior.

Phenomenology

Adler was perhaps the first major theorist to stress a phenomenological orientation toward therapy. His psychology is phenomenological in that it pays attention to the subjective fashion through which people perceive their world. This personal perspective includes the individual's views, beliefs, perceptions, and conclusions. People give meaning to their experiences. Furthermore, each individual is both the creator and the creation, "the painter and the painting," of his or her own life. Humans are creative beings who decide on their actions based on their subjective perceptions (Sherman & Dinkmeyer, 1987, p. 8).

As you will see in chapters that follow, many contemporary theories have incorporated this notion of the client's subjective perception of reality, or personal worldview, as a basic factor explaining behavior. Some of the other group approaches that have a phenomenological perspective are psychodrama, existential therapy, person-centered therapy, Gestalt therapy, the cognitive therapies, and reality therapy.

Creativity and Choice

From the Adlerian perspective, humans are not merely determined by heredity and environment; rather, these are the foundations, or building blocks, of life. People have the capacity to influence and create events. Adler believed that *what* we are born with is not as crucial as the *use* we make of our natural endowment. Adlerians do recognize, however, that biological and environmental conditions limit our capacity to choose and to create. Although they reject the deterministic stance of Freud, they do not go to the other extreme by maintaining that individuals can become whatever they want. This approach is based on the premise that within a framework of limitations a wide range of choices is open to us.

From the Adlerian viewpoint healthy people strive toward perfection but are not perfectionistic. They attempt to become the master of their fate. Adlerians base their practice on the assumption that people are creative, active, and self-determining. They have little sympathy with perspectives that cast a client in the role of a passive victim. As an illustration of the implications of this view, consider the Dreikurs's typical remark to a man who complained about his wife's behavior and who tried to play a helpless role. Dreikurs (1967) confronted him with the question "And what did you do?" He developed a style of challenging clients to become aware of the ways in which they were active participants in situations they perceived as problematic. His therapy was aimed at showing clients that although they could not directly change the behavior of others, they did have power to change their own reactions and attitudes toward others.

Social Interest

According to Manaster and Corsini (1982), social interest, from the German *Gemeinschaftsgefühl,* is possibly the single most distinctive and valuable concept in Individual Psychology. The term *social interest* refers to an individual's attitudes in dealing with other people in the world, and it includes striving for a better future for humanity. Adler equates social interest with a sense of identification and empathy with others. Quoting a phrase from an unidentified English author, he says that social interest means "to see with the eyes of another, to hear with the ears of another, to feel with the heart of another" (Ansbacher & Ansbacher, 1956, p. 135).

Individual Psychology rests on a central belief that our happiness and success are largely related to a social connectedness. As social beings we have a need to be of use to others and to establish meaningful relationships in a community. Because we are embedded in a society, we cannot be understood in isolation from that social context. We are primarily motivated by a desire to belong. Only within the group can we actualize our potentialities.

Adler (1964) writes that we have strong needs to feel united with others and that only when we do so can we act with courage in facing and dealing with life's problems. He contends that we must successfully master three main tasks: building friendships, establishing intimacy, and contributing to society (generally through work). Dreikurs and Mosak (1966, 1967) discuss two additional life tasks: the self-task (getting along with ourselves) and the spiritual task. Adler maintains that the degree to which we successfully share with others and are concerned with the welfare of others is an index of our overall personality adjustment and level of maturity. In other words, social interest is the measure of mental health, insofar as it is reflected in our capacity to give and receive and in our willingness to cooperate for the common benefit of all (Sherman & Dinkmeyer, 1987, p. 12).

This key concept of social interest has significant implications for group counseling; the general goals of the group are to increase self-esteem and to develop social interest. The group focuses on discovering the members' mistaken assumptions that are keeping them from feeling adequate and from being interested in others. This concept is applied to group counseling by structuring the group so that members can meet some of their needs for affiliation with others. Self-centeredness and the alienation it produces are the opposite of social interest and are seen as a major problem in contemporary society. It is hoped that one of the outcomes of a group experience will be that members grow to accept themselves and others, even though all of us are imperfect. For this reason, most Adlerians are against prescreening in groups, since the process tends to destroy heterogeneity and works against an acceptance of different levels of imperfection common in the larger society. Groups, Adlerians believe, ought to welcome all who want to join and not exclude people who need it most (James Bitter, personal communication, September 17, 1992). Out of establishing meaningful relations with others and of being productive members of society, members will gain a greater ability to express social interest.

Inferiority/Superiority

In his earlier writings Adler speaks about feelings of inferiority, which are typically associated with children's early recognition of their dependent position vis-à-vis adults and nature. From the very beginning our recognition of helplessness is characterized by feelings of inferiority. Adler does not view this inferiority as a negative force. On the contrary, out of our basic inferiority comes the motivation to master our environment. We attempt to compensate for feelings of inferiority by finding ways in which to control the forces in our lives, as opposed to being controlled by them. As Bitter (1987) has noted, when inferiority feelings become so exaggerated that they constrict our movement and our sense of self-worth, they become an inferiority complex. Such a complex can be a reaction to perceived negative influence or can result from mistaken notions and faulty interpretations.

Our striving for goals involves moving from a feeling of inferiority to one of superiority. According to Ansbacher (1974), inferiority feelings and compensation lost their primary importance for Adler over the years. In his later writings Adler speaks more of the goal of success and the urge toward perfection and self-mastery, or becoming what we are able to become.

Role of the Family

Adlerians place great emphasis on family processes, which play a significant role in the development of the personality during childhood. The climate of relationships among family members is known as the *family atmosphere*. The term *family constellation* describes the social configuration of the family group. It is the system of relationships in which self-awareness develops. This system includes and is maintained by oneself, by one's parents and siblings, and by any others living in the household (Powers & Griffith, 1987).

Children incorporate many of the personal characteristics of their parents, and they learn a great deal about life by observing and interacting with their parents (Sherman & Dinkmeyer, 1987). Dreikurs takes the position, however, that sibling relationships are more influential in personality development than relationships between the child and the parents. In addition, the meaning that people give to their own position in the family constellation and the positions of their siblings is more important than the actual chronological ages of the siblings. The personality characteristics of each person in the family, the emotional bonds between family members, the size of the family, and the sex of the siblings are all factors in the family constellation. The child's position and role in the family influence later personality development (Powers & Griffith, 1987).

Powers and Griffith write that the young family members rehearse a way of relating to others that will become a vital part of their style of life. They add that the family is not an encapsulated system apart from the community. Once material is gathered about the client's family constellation, a summary is developed so that interpretations can be made. The summary contains the client's strengths and weaknesses, and it is used in helping clients gain a fuller understanding of the current influence of their family on them.

Specifically, Powers and Griffith mention the following as crucial topics to include in the summary of the family constellation: birth order, family atmosphere, family values, masculine guiding line (the characteristics, attitudes, interests, and competencies ascribed to the father and not shared by the mother), feminine guiding line (the characteristics, attitudes, interests, and competencies ascribed to the mother and not shared by the father), the role of the client in the family, the role of the siblings in the family, role models and alliances, the experience of neighborhood and school in childhood and adolescence, the experience of the sexual challenge in adolescence, and major unresolved issues remaining from childhood and adolescence. It is also important to take into account the ethnic, religious, social, and economic milieu reported by the client. These factors serve as the material for one's self-perception and one's view of the world, rather than the cause of them.

Lifestyle

Lifestyle refers to the individual's basic orientation to life and the themes that characterize the person's existence. As already mentioned, it is drawn first from one's family constellation and family atmosphere. The formative experiences within the family, particularly among siblings, contribute to establishing guidelines for understanding life that eventually make up the lifestyle (Sherman & Dinkmeyer, 1987). In striving for goals that are meaningful to us, we develop this unique approach to life (Ansbacher, 1974). This concept helps explain how all our behavior fits together so that there is some consistency to our actions. Everything we do is related to our fictive goal of perfection. Adlerians refer to this process as *fictional finalism,* which is the imagined central goal that gives direction to behavior and unity to the personality. It is an image of what people would be like if they were perfect and perfectly secure.

No two persons develop exactly the same style. In striving for the goal of success, some people develop their intellect, others develop their physical being, and so on. Our style of life is learned primarily during the first six years of life. Adler asserts, along with Freud, that our earliest impressions lay the foundation of our lifestyle. But he stresses that these childhood experiences in themselves are not crucial; rather, it is our *interpretation* of these events that is significant. Adler emphasizes that our interpretations of early influences may lead to the developing of a faulty lifestyle. Although we are not determined by our past, we are significantly influenced by our perceptions and interpretations of these past events. Once we become aware of the patterns and continuity of our life, especially of certain mistaken notions that we have developed, we are in a position to modify those faulty assumptions and thus make basic changes. We can use childhood experiences to *consciously* create our own lifestyle.

Behavioral Disorders

Adler sees emotional disorders as "failures in life." Psychological and behavioral disorders can be considered erroneous ways of living, or mistaken assumptions. They can include a faulty lifestyle, a mistaken goal of success, and an underdeveloped social interest. Since Adlerians maintain that clients do not suffer from a disease but from discouragement and a failure to solve the problems and tasks set by life, therapy is based on an educational model, not a medical model. Applied to group counseling, this emphasis means that much of what goes on in a group is a process of encouraging clients and teaching them a better approach so that they can succeed.

Application of Adlerian Principles to Group Work

Adler and his co-workers used a group approach in their child-guidance centers in Vienna as early as 1921 (Dreikurs, 1969). As noted earlier, Dreikurs extended and popularized Adler's work, especially with regard to group applications, and used group psychotherapy in his private practice for over 40 years. His rationale for groups is the following: "Since man's problems and conflicts are recognized in their social nature, the group is ideally suited not only to highlight and reveal the nature of a person's conflicts and maladjustments but to offer corrective influences" (1969, p. 43). Inferiority feelings can be challenged and counteracted effectively in groups, and the mistaken concepts and values that are at the root of social and emotional problems can be deeply influenced by the group, since it is a value-forming agent.

The group provides the social context in which members can develop a sense of belonging and a sense of community. Dinkmeyer (1975) writes that group participants come to see that many of their problems are interpersonal in nature, that their behavior has social meaning, and that their goals can best be understood in the framework of social purposes. Some of the specific therapeutic factors that Dinkmeyer finds operating in Adlerian groups are these:

♦ The group provides a mirror of the person's behavior.
♦ Members benefit from feedback from other members and the leaders.
♦ Members both receive help from others and give help.
♦ The group provides opportunities for testing reality and for trying new behavior.
♦ The group context encourages members to take action to change their life.
♦ Transactions in the group help members understand how they function at work and at home and also reveal how they seek to find their place in society.
♦ The group is structured in such a way that members can meet their need for belonging.

According to Dinkmeyer and his colleagues (1987), Adlerian counseling has four major objectives, which correspond to four phases of the therapeutic process:

1. establishing an empathic relationship based on mutual respect
2. understanding beliefs, feelings, motives, and goals

3. developing insight into mistaken goals and self-defeating behaviors
4. seeing alternatives and making new choices

Phases of the Adlerian Group

Like the psychoanalytic approach to groups, Adlerian group counseling involves the investigation and interpretation of one's early life. As the following discussion indicates, however, there are some fundamental differences between Adlerians and Freudians.

In writing about the characteristics of the Adlerian approach to group work, Dreikurs (1969) and Sonstegard, Dreikurs, and Bitter (1982) outline four phases of group counseling, which correspond to the four goals of counseling just listed and which overlap to some extent:

1. establishing and maintaining the proper therapeutic relationship
2. exploring the dynamics operating in the individual (assessment)
3. communicating to the individual an understanding of self (insight)
4. seeing new alternatives and making new choices (reorientation)

Phase 1: Establishing and Maintaining the Relationship

In the initial phase the emphasis is on establishing a good therapeutic relationship based on cooperation and mutual respect. Group participants are encouraged to be active in the process, for they are responsible for their own participation in the group. It is not always easy to create an active atmosphere, because even those clients who are most eager to make progress may be unwilling to do the work required for effective group participation and may be determined to prove that they are helpless (Dreikurs, 1969). Dreikurs sees the group as conducive to a good client/counselor relationship. In the group situation there is ample opportunity to work on trust issues and to strengthen the relationship between member and leader. Also, by witnessing positive changes in peers, participants can see how well the group works.

The Adlerian therapeutic relationship is one between equals. A democratic atmosphere prevails, and the effective group-counseling relationship is based on mutual respect. This does not imply that members do anything they please, however, for firmness in a spirit of kindness is necessary in all group counseling (Sonstegard et al., 1982). Sonstegard and his colleagues point out that winning the client's cooperation is essential for effective group counseling. Therapist and client work together toward mutually agreed-on goals. Adlerians believe that counseling, individual or group, progresses only when the therapeutic process focuses on what *clients* see as personally significant and on areas that *they* want to explore and change. This is what Dreikurs (1967) says of the collaborative nature of the Adlerian therapeutic relationship and of the necessity for aligning the client's and the therapist's goals:

Therapeutic cooperation requires an alignment of goals. When the goals and interests of the patient and therapist clash, no satisfactory relationship can be established. Winning the patient's cooperation for the common task is a prerequisite for any therapy; maintaining it requires constant vigilance. What appears as "resistance" constitutes a discrepancy between the goals of the therapist and those of the patient [p. 65].

Phase 2: Analysis and Assessment— Exploring the Individual's Dynamics

The aim of the second phase is twofold: understanding one's lifestyle and seeing how it is affecting one's current functioning in all the tasks of life (Mosak, 1989). The leader may begin by exploring how the participants are functioning at work and in social situations and how they feel about themselves and their sex-role identities.

According to Dreikurs (1969), the individual's goals and current lifestyle become much more obvious in interactions with others in the group. Also, clients may respond differently when they are confronted by fellow participants than when they are confronted by the counselor alone.

Adlerian group counselors use a number of assessment techniques. Process assessments of the members' family constellation, relationship difficulties, early recollections, dreams, and art work produce clues to each person's life goal and lifestyle (Sonstegard et al., 1982). Analysis and assessment rely heavily on the exploration of the client's family constellation, which includes evaluating the conditions that prevailed in the family when the person was a young child in the process of forming lifestyle convictions and basic assumptions. Dinkmeyer and his associates (1987) describe a family-constellation questionnaire that provides insight into clients' self-perception, sibling relationships, significant forces in their life, and key decisions they have made.

Another assessment procedure is asking clients to report their early recollections along with the feelings and thoughts that accompanied these childhood incidents. These early recollections are more than a report; they reveal beliefs, "basic mistakes," self-defeating perceptions, and unique laws of psychological movement (Dinkmeyer et al., 1987). Adlerians contend that people remember only those past events that are consistent with their current views of themselves (Adler, 1958). Dreikurs (1969) adds that once people develop such views, they perceive only that which fits their views. This self-perception strengthens the person's "private logic," which in turn helps the individual maintain his or her basic convictions. Early recollections provide an understanding of how we view and feel about ourselves, how we see the world, what our life goals are, what motivates us, what we believe in, and what we value.

The lifestyle investigation, which includes exploration of one's family background and life story, reveals a pattern of *basic mistakes*. Mosak (1989) writes that the lifestyle can be conceived of as a personal mythology; people behave as if the myths were true, because, for them, they are true. Mosak lists five basic mistakes: (1) overgeneralizations, (2) impossible goals, (3) misperceptions of life and its demands, (4) denial of one's basic worth, and (5) faulty values.

During the assessment phase the counselor's main task is to integrate and summarize data from the lifestyle investigation and to interpret how the mistaken notions and personal mythology are influencing the client. This is done in a clear and concise way so that clients can recognize their own dynamics and pinpoint their assets. The analysis of the lifestyle is an ongoing process and helps client and counselor develop a plan for counseling. According to Dreikurs (1969), analysis of the lifestyle and of its psychodynamic forces can be carried out in both individual and group settings, but the group format offers certain definite advantages:

> The patient's goals and movements become much more obvious in the interaction with his fellow group members than in the limited interaction between him and the therapist. Furthermore, the therapist no longer depends entirely on the verbal reports by the patient about his interaction with others outside of the therapeutic session; he sees him in action during the session. Not infrequently, the patient appears in a quite different light when confronted by other members of the group, than when he is alone with the therapist. Certain facades of his personality may become more pronounced, or visible [pp. 44–45].

Phase 3: Insight

Whereas the classical analytic position is that personality cannot change unless there is insight, the Adlerian view is that insight is only a step toward change and not a necessary prerequisite for it (Dreikurs, 1969). Insight, then, is not an end in itself but a means to an end. People can make abrupt and significant changes without much insight. Mosak (1989) defines insight as "understanding translated into constructive action." He contends that the Freudian notion that insight must precede behavioral change frequently results in extended treatment and encourages clients to postpone taking action to change. Mere intellectual insight can lead to the endless "Yes, but" game of "I know I should stop, but . . ."

According to Sonstegard and his colleagues (1982), groups are more effective than individual counseling in helping people gain insight and redirect their mistaken goals and mistaken notions. These authors write that the interaction within a group provides an ideal setting for learning about oneself. Furthermore, the sense of social connectedness that develops in groups enables members to see parts of themselves in others. The writers contend that the personal disclosures and interpretations during the group sessions are of value both for the person to whom they are directed and for the others in the group, who learn from these disclosures. One of the advantages of a group is that the insights and statements of other members often carry more weight than observations and interpretations provided by the leader.

In a group context the insight phase is concerned with helping participants understand *why* they are functioning as they are. Members learn about themselves by exploring their own goals, personal mythology, and lifestyle. The group facilitates the process of gaining insight, because as members experience resistance in themselves, they can also observe resistance in other members. There is enough similarity in basic mistaken attitudes and faulty motivations among all participants to allow the members to observe themselves in others and to help one another.

Interpretation is a technique that facilitates the process of gaining insight into one's lifestyle. Interpretation deals with members' underlying motives for behaving the way they do in the here and now. By offering an outside frame of reference, the counselor helps participants see their behaviors from a different perspective and thus gain access to a wider range of alternatives (Dinkmeyer et al., 1987). Interpretations are never forced on the client; they are presented tentatively in the form of hypotheses: "Could it be . . . ?" "I have a hunch that I'd like to share with you . . ." "It seems to me that . . ." Therefore, interpretations are open-ended sharings that can be explored in group sessions. The ultimate goal of this process is that clients will come to understand their own role in creating a problem, the ways in which they are maintaining the problem, and what *they* can do to improve the situation.

Phase 4: Reorientation

The end product of the group process is reorientation. The reorientation phase involves considering alternative attitudes, beliefs, goals, and behaviors. Members are helped to redirect their mistaken goals and mistaken notions. One of the aims is teaching participants how to become more effective in dealing with the tasks of life. Another aim is challenging and encouraging clients to take risks and make changes.

Dreikurs (1969) believes that groups are especially useful during the reorientation phase, because they stimulate action and new orientations. The group becomes an agent in bringing about change because of the improved interpersonal relationships among members. The group process allows members to see themselves as others do and to recognize faulty self-concepts or mistaken goals that they are pursuing (Sonstegard et al., 1982).

Encouragement is a basic aspect of this phase. Through encouragement, clients begin to experience their own inner resources and the power to choose for themselves and direct their own lives. The encouragement so necessary at this stage is found in the support of the group and in its egalitarian nature, which removes social distance and reduces the risk of self-disclosure. In Dreikurs's words, "It is this social atmosphere of equality which characterizes a therapy group and which exerts one of the most effective therapeutic influences on each one of its members" (1969, p. 47).

Reorientation is the action phase of a group, during which new decisions are made and goals are modified. To challenge self-limiting assumptions, members are encouraged to act *as if* they were the persons they wanted to be. They are asked to "catch themselves" in the process of repeating old patterns that have led to ineffective behavior. Commitment is an essential ingredient of the reorientation phase; if clients hope to change, they must be willing to set tasks for themselves and do something specific about their problems. Commitment is also needed to translate new insights into concrete action.

Role and Functions of the Adlerian Counselor

The concept of the anonymous counselor is not part of the Adlerian view. An anonymous counselor would increase the distance from the client and interfere with the egalitarian, person-to-person relationship basic to the Adlerian approach. As Mosak (1989) writes, the Adlerian counselor has feelings and opinions and is free to express them.

Other Adlerian writers stress the active role of the counselor as a participant in a collaborative therapeutic effort. Dinkmeyer and his colleagues (1987) view the role of the group leader as establishing and maintaining the group process. They write that the members expect the leader to assume responsibility for the group's movement: "The leader must participate actively in the development of norms that facilitate growth and interpersonal learning. He intentionally establishes a structure for the group and indicates guidelines for behavior, such as congruence, open interaction, involvement, nonjudgmental acceptance, confrontation, and commitment" (p. 198). The leader assumes the functions of a facilitator who both creates and encourages the development of therapeutic conditions, such as universality, support, opportunities to experiment with new behavior, and feedback. These processes promote interpersonal learning, individual growth, and a sense of group cohesiveness.

Another evidence of the Adlerian counselor's strong role is the commitment to active procedures such as confrontation, self-disclosure, interpretation, and analysis of prevailing patterns. The counselor challenges the clients' beliefs and goals and helps them translate what they have learned in the group process into new beliefs and behaviors. Dinkmeyer and his associates (1987) point out that counselors serve as models for their clients, who often learn more from what counselors do, in the group as well as in their personal lives, than from what they say. This implies that counselors need to have a clear sense of their own identity, beliefs, and feelings. They must also be aware of the basic conditions that are essential for the growth of clients: empathy, respect, care, genuineness, openness, sincerity, positive regard, understanding of the dynamics of behavior, and the ability to use action-oriented techniques that stimulate changes in clients.

Evaluation of the Adlerian Approach to Groups

Contributions and Strengths of the Approach

My group practice has been influenced by several Adlerian concepts, including emphasis on the social forces that motivate behavior and the search for mastery, superiority, and power. The patterns that people develop out of their relationships with their parents and siblings and the notion that we create a unique lifestyle as a response to our perceived inferiority are also intriguing to me.

The Adlerian approach deviates in many ways from the psychoanalytic model. Most Adlerians maintain that much of Adler's work was done independently of Freud. There are, however, some important commonalities between the two approaches, including a focus on critical periods of development, an interest in early recollections, and an emphasis on interpretation.

In my opinion, one of the strengths of the Adlerian approach is its integrative nature. It is a holistic approach that encompasses the full spectrum of human experience, and practitioners have great freedom in working with clients in ways that are uniquely suited to their own therapeutic style. According to James Bitter (personal communication, September 17, 1992), Adlerians use a wide variety of techniques, only a few of which are unique to Adlerian group counseling. One is the use of the family constellation as a means of learning the client's identity interpretations. Another technique is the use of early recollections as a means of discovering people's values and convictions and the meaning they have given to themselves, others, and the world. The last of these techniques involves discovery of how mistaken notions based on faulty goals and values fly in the face of social interest and create problems in people's lives.

Even though all Adlerians accept the same theoretical concepts, they do not have a monolithic view of the therapeutic process. Corsini (1987) writes that the methods of assessment and treatment differ substantially. Some Adlerian group practitioners are very directive, and others are looser. Some are willing to disclose themselves, and others rarely make personal disclosures to their clients. Adlerians who were trained by Adler tend to ask for 1 early recollection, whereas those who were trained by Dreikurs might routinely ask for as many as 6 to 12 recollections as a part of the lifestyle interview. Dreikurs asked for the number of early recollections that allowed the forming of a pattern. As was mentioned, Adlerian group practitioners are not bound to follow a specific procedure, nor are they limited to using certain techniques. There can be almost as many methods as there are Adlerian therapists. The basic criterion is that therapeutic techniques fit the theory and the client. Thus, therapists are encouraged to grow both personally and professionally by being inventive.

INTEGRATION WITH OTHER APPROACHES. One of the strengths of the Adlerian approach is that its concepts have group applications in both clinical and educational settings (Sonstegard et al., 1982). As we have seen, its emphasis on social factors makes it suitable for working with individuals in groups, including parent-education groups, teacher groups, and families.

It is difficult to overestimate the contributions of Adler to contemporary therapeutic practice. His influence has extended beyond group counseling into the community mental-health movement, including the use of paraprofessionals (Ansbacher, 1974). Abraham Maslow, Viktor Frankl, Rollo May, and Albert Ellis have acknowledged their debt to Adler. Both Frankl and May see him as a forerunner of the existential movement because of his position that human beings are free to choose and are entirely responsible for what they make of themselves. This view makes him also a forerunner of the subjective approach to psychology, which focuses on the internal determinants of behavior: values, beliefs, attitudes, goals, interests, personal meanings, perceptions of reality, and strivings toward self-realization. Furthermore, the Adlerian view is congruent with many of the other current psychological schools, such as Gestalt therapy, learning theory, transactional analysis, reality therapy, rational emotive behavior therapy, cognitive therapy, person-centered therapy, and logotherapy. All these approaches are based on a similar concept of the person as purposive and self-determining and as always striving for growth, value, and meaning in this world (Terner & Pew, 1978). In several important respects, Adler seems to have paved the way for the current developments in the cognitive therapies. Adlerians' basic premise is that if they can change clients' thinking, they can change their feelings and behavior.

Adler's contributions to counseling, especially group counseling, are discussed in this separate chapter because of the far-reaching implications of his work and because of the renewed interest in Adlerian theory and practice. This resurgence of interest is attested to by the increasing number of national and international institutes and societies that offer training in Adlerian techniques, including Adlerian group counseling. Dinkmeyer, Dinkmeyer, and Sperry (1987) discuss the applications of Adlerian principles to group work with a wide population: very young children, older children, adolescents, college students, and adults. They also describe Adlerian group counseling for teachers, parent- and family-education groups, family-therapy groups, and marriage counseling.

Limitations of the Approach

The Adlerian approach to group work shares some of the basic limitations of the psychoanalytic approach. Leaders of more structured groups may have difficulty incorporating some of the procedures geared toward understanding members' lifestyles and showing them how earlier experiences are influencing their current functioning. Members in many structured or short-term groups may not be able to appreciate the value of exploring their childhood dynamics, based on a comprehensive assessment.

Another basic limitation pertains to the practitioner. Unless group leaders are well trained, they can make significant mistakes, especially if they engage in interpreting members' dynamics. Leaders who have simply a general understanding of Adlerian concepts could overstep the boundaries of their competence in attempting to teach members about the meaning of factors such as birth order and the family constellation. Using the procedures outlined in this chapter requires training.

Applying the Adlerian Approach with Multicultural Populations

Adlerian theory is well suited to working with culturally diverse clients. Although the Adlerian approach is called Individual Psychology, the focus is on the person-in-the-environment. As Corsini (1987) notes, Adlerian uses of groups are more varied than those in any other system. Adlerians' interest in helping others, in social interest, in pursuing meaning in life, in belonging, and in the collective spirit fits well with the group process. This approach stresses social connectedness and establishing meaningful relationships in a community. The Native American, Hispanic, African-American, and Asian-American cultures likewise stress collectivism over the individual's welfare and emphasize the role of the family.

However, there are some potential problems in applying these Adlerian concepts of belongingness and social interest to group counseling with Asian-American clients. Leong (1992) writes that the collectivist orientation of many Asian Americans implies that there is no clear distinction between individual and family problems. This could make disclosure about family dynamics in a group quite problematic. Many Asian Americans have been socialized to respect their family heritage, and some clients will be reluctant to reveal material that they believe brings dishonor to members of their family. Asian Americans are likely to be less orally expressive than Caucasian Americans in group situations, and they may be hesitant about admitting personal problems due to the shame it may cause. Leong points out that honor and the avoidance of losing face are important values for Asians. These factors need to be considered in an Adlerian group.

Leong also writes that in most Asian cultures, interpersonal relationships tend to be hierarchical, with a strong respect for and loyalty to authority. Asian-American group members will tend to view the group leader as the authority and expect him or her to have special expertise and power and to direct the group process. As was mentioned, the Adlerian approach stresses an egalitarian, person-to-person spirit as a way to reduce social distance and to encourage self-disclosure. Adlerian group leaders may need to adapt some of the techniques, especially their lifestyle-assessment procedures, in working with Asian Americans and with many other racial and ethnic groups as well.

I do not mean to imply that Adlerian concepts are of limited use from a multicultural perspective. The phenomenological nature of the Adlerian approach lends itself to understanding the worldview of clients. The emphasis on the subjective fashion in which people view and interpret their world leads to a respect for clients' unique values and perceptions. Adlerians investigate culture in much the same way that they approach birth order and family atmosphere. Culture is a vantage point from which life is experienced and interpreted; it is also a background of values, history, convictions, beliefs, customs, and expectations that must be addressed by the individual. Adlerians do not decide for clients what they should change or what their goals should be; rather, they work cooperatively to enable them to reach their self-defined goals.

Where to Go from Here

If you find that your thinking is allied with the Adlerian approach, you might consider seeking training in Individual Psychology or becoming a member of the North American Society of Adlerian Psychology. To obtain information on the society and also a list of Adlerian organizations and institutes, contact:

North American Society of Adlerian Psychology
65 East Wacker Place, Suite 400
Chicago, IL 60601
TELEPHONE: (312) 629-8801

The society publishes a newsletter and a quarterly journal (see below), and it maintains a list of institutes, training programs, and workshops in Adlerian psychology.

The quarterly *Individual Psychology: The Journal of Adlerian Theory, Research, and Practice* presents current scholarly and professional research. Columns on counseling, education, and parent and family education are regular features. Information about subscriptions is available by contacting the society.

Alfred Adler Institute of New York
1780 Broadway, Suite 502
New York, NY 10019
TELEPHONE: (212) 974-0431

Americas Institute of Adlerian Studies
Robert L. Powers and Jane Griffith
600 N. McClurg Court, Suite 2502A
Chicago, IL 60611-3027
TELEPHONE: (312) 337-5066

Americas Institute of Adlerian Studies
486 Hillway Drive
Vista, CA 92084
TELEPHONE: (619) 758-4658

If you are interested in pursuing training, postgraduate study, continuing education, or a degree, contact the society for a list of 58 Adlerian organizations and institutes. A few of these training institutes, some of which grant degrees, are listed below:

Adler School of Professional Psychology
65 East Wacker Place
Chicago, IL 60601
TELEPHONE: (312) 201-5900

Adler-Dreikurs Institute of Human Relations
Room 0313, MLK Building
Bowie State University
Bowie, MD 20715
TELEPHONE: (301) 464-7560

Alfred Adler Institute of Minnesota
1001 Highway 7, Suite 344
Hopkins, MN 55305
TELEPHONE: (612) 933-9363

The Union Institute, Graduate School
Adlerian Counseling Coordinator
440 E. McMillan Street
Cincinnati, OH 45206-1947
TELEPHONE: (513) 861-6400

RECOMMENDED SUPPLEMENTARY READINGS

Adlerian Counseling and Psychotherapy (Dinkmeyer et al., 1987) gives a good basic presentation of the theoretical foundations of Adlerian counseling and applies basic concepts to the practice of group counseling. There are excellent chapters dealing with the phases and techniques of the counseling process. There are also chapters on family and marital therapy, consultation with teachers, and parent education.

Understanding Life-Style: The Psycho-Clarity Process (Powers & Griffith, 1987) is one of the best sources of information for doing a lifestyle analysis. This book comes alive with many good clinical examples. Separate chapters deal with interview techniques, lifestyle assessment, early recollections, the family constellation, and methods of summarizing and interpreting information.

Systems of Family Therapy: An Adlerian Integration (Sherman & Dinkmeyer, 1987) explains family organization and dynamics from an Adlerian perspective. The structure of Adlerian family therapy and the basics of change are discussed within the framework of an integrative theory. There is a useful chapter on Adlerian family therapy techniques.

Individual Psychology (Manaster & Corsini, 1982) is a very readable overview of Adlerian psychology. The authors trace the approach's history, describe its current status, present a clear summary of key concepts, including the dynamics of personality, and discuss the application of these concepts to the practice of both individual and group counseling. Several excellent chapters are devoted to descriptions of Adlerian techniques.

The Individual Psychology of Alfred Adler (Ansbacher & Ansbacher, 1956) is a comprehensive collection of Adler's writings that shows the development and refinement of his thinking. This is one of the definitive sources of the Adlerian approach.

Superiority and Social Interest: A Collection of Later Writings, edited by H. L. Ansbacher and R. R. Ansbacher (1973), contains various writings by Adler on topics such as his basic assumptions, his theory of the neuroses, case studies, and his views of religion and mental health. It also has a biographical essay on Adler and a chapter on the increasing recognition of his influence on current practice.

REFERENCES AND SUGGESTED READINGS*

Adler, A. (1958). *What life should mean to you.* New York: Capricorn.

Adler, A. (1964). *Social interest: A challenge to mankind.* New York: Capricorn.

Ansbacher, H. L. (1974). Goal-oriented individual psychology: Alfred Adler's theory. In A. Burton (Ed.), *Operational theories of personality.* New York: Brunner/Mazel.

*Ansbacher, H. L., & Ansbacher, R. R. (Eds.). (1956). *The Individual Psychology of Alfred Adler.* New York: Basic Books.

*Ansbacher, H. L., & Ansbacher, R. R. (Eds.). (1973). *Superiority and social interest: A collection of later writings* (3rd rev. ed.). New York: Viking Press.

Bitter, J. (1979). An interview with Heinz Ansbacher. *Journal of Individual Psychology, 35*(1), 95–110.

Bitter, J. (1987). Communication and meaning: Satir in Adlerian context. In R. Sherman & D. Dinkmeyer (Eds.), *Systems of family therapy: An Adlerian integration* (pp. 109–142). New York: Brunner/Mazel.

*Corsini, R. J. (1987). Adlerian groups. In S. Long (Ed.), *Six group therapies.* New York: Plenum.

Dinkmeyer, D. (1975). Adlerian group psychotherapy. *International Journal of Group Psychotherapy, 25*(2), 219–226.

*Dinkmeyer, D. C., Dinkmeyer, D. C., & Sperry, L. (1987). *Adlerian counseling and psychotherapy* (2nd ed.). Columbus, OH: Merrill.

*Dreikurs, R. (1960). *Group psychotherapy and group approaches: The collected papers of Rudolf Dreikurs.* Chicago: Alfred Adler Institute.

Dreikurs, R. (1967). *Psychodynamics, psychotherapy, and counseling: Collected papers.* Chicago: Alfred Adler Institute.

Dreikurs, R. (1969). Group psychotherapy from the point of view of Adlerian psychology. In H. M. Ruitenbeek (Ed.), *Group therapy today: Styles, methods, and techniques.* Chicago: Aldine-Atherton.

Dreikurs, R., & Mosak, H. H. (1966). The tasks of life: 1. Adler's three tasks. *The Individual Psychologist, 4,* 18–22.

Dreikurs, R., & Mosak, H. H. (1967). The tasks of life: 2. The fourth task. *The Individual Psychologist, 4,* 51–55.

Leong, F. T. L. (1992). Guidelines for minimizing premature termination among Asian American clients. *Journal for Specialists in Group Work, 17*(4), 218–228.

Lowe, R. N. (1982). Adlerian/Dreikursian family counseling. In A. M. Horne & M. M. Ohlsen (Eds.), *Family counseling and therapy.* Itasca, IL: F. E. Peacock.

*Manaster, G. J., & Corsini, R. J. (1982). *Individual Psychology: Theory and practice.* Itasca, IL: F. E. Peacock.

Mosak, H. (1979). Adlerian psychotherapy. In R. J. Corsini (Ed.), *Current psychotherapies* (2nd ed.). Itasca, IL: F. E. Peacock.

Mosak, H. (1989). Adlerian psychotherapy. In R. J. Corsini & D. Wedding (Eds.), *Current psychotherapies* (4th ed.). Itasca, IL: F. E. Peacock.

Mozdzierz, G. J., Lisiecki, J., Bitter, J. R., & Williams, A. L. (1984). Role-functions for Adlerian therapists. *Individual Psychology, 42*(2), 154–177.

*Books and articles marked with an asterisk are suggested for further study.

*Powers, R. L., & Griffith, J. (1987). *Understanding life-style: The psycho-clarity process*. Chicago: Americas Institute of Adlerian Studies.

*Sherman, R., & Dinkmeyer, D. (1987). *Systems of family therapy: An Adlerian integration*. New York: Brunner/Mazel.

*Sonstegard, M., Dreikurs, R., & Bitter, J. (1982). The teleoanalytic group counseling approach. In G. M. Gazda (Ed.), *Basic approaches to group psychotherapy and counseling* (3rd ed.). Springfield, IL: Charles C Thomas.

Sweeney, T. J. (1989). *Adlerian counseling: A practical approach for a new decade* (3rd ed.). Muncie, IN: Accelerated Development.

Terner, J., & Pew, W. L. (1978). *The courage to be imperfect: The life and work of Rudolf Dreikurs*. New York: Hawthorn Books.

CHAPTER EIGHT

Psychodrama

Introduction

Psychodrama, created and developed by J. L. Moreno (1889–1974), is a primarily group-therapy approach in which the client acts out or dramatizes past, present, or anticipated life situations and roles in an attempt to gain deeper understanding, achieve catharsis, and develop behavioral skills. Significant events are enacted to help the client get in contact with unrecognized and unexpressed feelings, to provide a channel for the full expression of these feelings and attitudes, and to encourage new behavior. The methods of psychodrama are best thought of as tools for helping people relate to one another more effectively. The term *drama* is not used to refer to theatrics; rather, it pertains to reworking our lives as if they were dramatic situations and we were the playwrights (Blatner with Blatner, 1988b).

Psychodrama had its origins in the Theater of Spontaneity, which Moreno started in Vienna in 1921. People who participated in the Theater were not professional actors, and they didn't have any scripts. Instead, they played out in a spontaneous manner events from the daily newspaper or topics suggested by the audience. After the performance, people in the audience were invited to discuss the experiences they had had while observing it. Moreno found that the personal problems, and thus the reactions, of the audience members influenced not only the choice of the topic but also the way in which the participants played their parts. He also found that both the people involved in the play and the people in the audience experienced a psychological release of pent-up feelings (catharsis). The Theater of Spontaneity led him to develop the group methods and specialized therapeutic techniques that he later incorporated into psychodrama.

Psychodrama is designed to facilitate the expression of feelings in a spontaneous and dramatic way through the use of role playing. One of its values in group work is that it allows a maximum number of people to play various roles and receive feedback about the impact of these roles. The

I want to thank Adam Blatner for his contributions toward revision of this chapter.

techniques of psychodrama lend themselves very well to producing lively group interaction, exploring interpersonal problems, experimenting with novel ways of approaching significant others in one's life, and reducing one's feelings of isolation. (Although psychodramatic therapy is interpersonally oriented, *intra*personal aspects of group members' lives are often explored.) Zerka Moreno, J. L. Moreno's wife, writes that "psychodrama represents a major turning point away from the treatment of the individual in isolation and toward the treatment of the individual in groups, from treatment by verbal methods toward treatment by action methods" (1983, p. 158).

Of all the approaches discussed in this book, psychodrama is the most ideally suited for groups. Nevertheless, its methodology can be adapted for work with families, couples, and even clients in individual psychotherapy.

Key Concepts

Moreno's View of His Approach

Moreno considered himself a philosopher as much as a psychiatrist. He can be thought of as an early existentialist, and he views clients as having been damaged through social acculturation. Moreno rejects Freud's position that only through a lengthy process of psychoanalysis can humans become free of the irrational forces that rule them. Instead, he contends that psychodramatic methods often produce therapeutic breakthroughs suddenly and spontaneously. It is to be noted, however, that these breakthroughs do not necessarily free the client from the bondage of ruling unconscious forces. The working-through and integration aspects of the therapeutic process still take time.

Moreno made no attempt to construct a comprehensive system of human nature but, rather, noted a number of themes that many approaches had tended to ignore: creativity, spontaneity, encounter, the importance of the present, a multidimensional view of personality, and the value of action in promoting catharsis and insight. He also developed methods for operationalizing these key ideas and principles. These methods are best thought of as being tools that can be readily integrated with other approaches. This section elaborates on some of the most important concepts Moreno introduced.

Creativity

Moreno was an "improvisational theologian" (Adam Blatner, 1992, personal communication). In synthesizing the ideas of Friedrich Nietzsche, Henri-Louis Bergson, and others, including the great spiritual teachers of Western culture such as Socrates and Jesus, Moreno in his late adolescence developed his own "religion of encounter." This view emphasized the importance of people expressing their own sense of God's purpose through the vehicle of their own individuality. Moreno envisioned God, the divine force, as being continuously active, not simply as having created the world but as being the archetypal energy functioning within the essence of all existence. God is to be discovered in every moment and in the soul of every being. This metaphor infused Moreno's life and his view of actualized existence with a sense of initiative, experimentation, and creation (Blatner with Blatner, 1988b).

Spontaneity

If creativity is a central theme in human existence, then spontaneity, Moreno asserts, is the way to foster it. Creativity does not usually emerge from careful, reasoned planning but, rather, bursts the bonds of conventional thought and surges from the unconscious to inform and vitalize our experience. Moreno's attitude toward the unconscious is similar to Jung's view that the unconscious is a source of wisdom and creativity as well as a repository of disowned emotions.

From Moreno's perspective, spontaneity is an adequate response to a new situation or a novel response to an old situation. The essential qualities of spontaneity include openness, a freshness of approach, the willingness to take the initiative and take risks, and an integration of the external realities with one's internal world of thinking and feeling. Spontaneity is not to be confused with impulsivity, for it implies the intention to achieve a constructive result (Blatner with Blatner, 1988b).

Most of us can be more creative if we allow ourselves to be spontaneous. Moreno observed that children, in contrast to adults, were relatively more able to enter into role-playing and fantasy situations and to express their feelings freely. As people grow older, they tend to become less and less spontaneous. To remedy this tendency, Moreno developed methods for training spontaneity aimed at freeing people from limiting "scripts" and rigid and stereotyped responses. He adopted techniques that encouraged the participation of the audience, and he stressed the need to get in touch with one's fantasies and feelings by enacting situations that trigger certain emotions. He considered spontaneity training to be a prime way of enabling people to meet new situations from a fresh perspective.

Although the development of spontaneity is valued in psychodramatic groups, Nicholas (1984) cautions against pushing members too quickly to express their spontaneity. She suggests that group members be treated gently and respectfully and that they be allowed to get involved in the group action in ways of their choosing when they feel ready to do so. She believes that the most important teaching tool for the enhancement of the group members' spontaneity is the leader's ability to model spontaneous behavior. For this reason, she recommends that group leaders obtain their own training in psychodrama and that they experience other expressive group approaches. To be able to create a climate that fosters the development of spontaneity, group practitioners must be aware of their own feelings and draw upon them in intuitive ways.

Encounter and Tele

The *encounter* is defined by Greenberg (1974) as that which occurs when individuals immediately and meaningfully confront significant others on the psychodramatic stage. The encounter always occurs in the context of the here and now, regardless of whether the enactment relates to a past event or to an anticipated one.

Moreno wrote a small book entitled *Invitation to Encounter,* from which he often quoted this passage:

> A meeting of two: eye to eye, face to face. . . .
> And I will look at you with your eyes
> And you will look at me with mine.

Encountering is at the very core of psychodrama, for through this process people not only meet but also understand one another on a deep and significant level. By their very nature encounters entail an element of surprise, because they are not rehearsed or forced. The encounter entails dimensions of both transference and empathy, yet it goes beyond them. It fosters a sense of community in a group, which builds the trust that is necessary for productive work.

A related concept is *tele* (TELL-uh), which is enhanced in the course of an authentic encounter. Moreno defines tele as the two-way flow of feelings between people, or "therapeutic love." He calls it a "feeling of individuals into one another, the cement which holds groups together" (1964, p. xi). Other writers on psychodrama have broadened the notion to include that intangible field of attractions and repulsions among people. Where it is reciprocally positive and strong, other phenomena occur, including increased group cohesion and a higher likelihood of empathy. Positive tele may facilitate a person's ability to penetrate and understand another person. Through positive tele there is a strengthening of bonds, a promotion of continuity and stability, and a sense of group cohesion. Tele is the sum total of the feeling aspects of empathy, transference, and countertransference. It is a significant factor affecting the degree of interaction among participants of a group. When tele is positive, people become more spontaneous and thus can more easily find creative alternatives for working out interpersonal conflicts. In this sense, tele is a therapeutic factor related to change. Healing of individuals occurs through a reciprocal empathic feeling.

Dealing with the Present

In psychodrama, clients enact conflicts or crisis situations as if they were occurring in the present moment, as opposed to merely talking about them. A basic tenet of psychodrama is that reliving and reexperiencing a scene from the past gives the participants both the opportunity to examine how that event affected them at the time it occurred and a chance to deal differently with the event *now*. By replaying a past event in the present, individuals are able to assign new meaning to it. Through this process they work through unfinished business and put a new and different ending to that earlier situation.

In practical terms, psychodrama offers encouragement to members to speak in the present tense and to use action words. The placing of members in the present, regardless of when the scenes actually happened, has a tendency to reduce verbal reporting and turns members into actors (Z. T. Moreno, 1987).

Exploring Unexpressed Emotions

According to J. L. Moreno, clients involved in psychodrama present not only what they actually experienced in reality but also what may never have actually occurred except in their own fantasy. Psychodrama offers ways of exploring these unexpressed emotions that are associated with the "reality" in the imagination, or this realm of surplus reality. One of psychodrama's real advantages is to make the powers of the imagination concrete, accentuated by all the devices of the theater. Thus, scenes in the future can be played out, exploring different possible outcomes. Encounters with those not present—a deceased relative, God, a parent, a sibling, or oneself at an earlier age—are just one way of reviewing one's experiences. In a psychodrama, members can vividly experience their hopes, fears, expectations, unexpressed resentments, projections, internalizations, and judgmental attitudes. Clients are assisted in ventilating these feelings and are able to symbolically live through them. They are generally encouraged to maximize all expression, action, and verbal communication, rather than to reduce it (Blatner, 1988).

Catharsis and Insight

Catharsis occurs when stored-up feelings are finally expressed. In psychodrama a client experiences catharsis by verbally and physically acting out an emotion-laden situation. This release of pent-up feelings is more meaningful when participants deal with real-life situations and spontaneously express what they are feeling. Anger, sadness, hatred, rage, and despair, as well as joy and ecstasy, are tapped and released. In writing about the dynamics of catharsis, Blatner (1985) points out that this emotional release reflects an expansion of the sense of self on four levels: abreaction and an awareness of previously disowned feelings, integration of those feelings, experiencing a sense of being a part of a social network, and participating meaningfully in the universe. Although catharsis is often a natural part of the psychodramatic process, it is not in itself a goal but, rather, an indicator of emotional expansion and integration. Blatner suggests that dramatic emotional releases should not become the exclusive focus of psychodrama, for subtle and gentle catharses can also result in healing.

Insight, or gaining an increased awareness of a problem situation, often follows the process of an emotional purging. It might occur during the enactment or at its end, when members are sharing their feelings and reactions to what happened on the stage. Both the participants in a psychodrama and members of the audience can experience catharsis and thus achieve insight. Once people allow themselves the freedom to release intense emotions that have been controlling them, they begin the critical process of gaining control over these feelings. They gradually come to an emotional and cognitive understanding that they do not have to continue living in ways that they did in the past.

Reality Testing

The psychodramatic group provides its members with an opportunity to test reality, because the group consists of real people and real-life situations. Members can assess the assumptions and fantasies of an individual client and can suggest alternatives for action, many of which the client may not have considered.

Consider the following example of how a psychodramatic group offers members ways to test reality. A young woman is in great emotional pain over what she sees as her father's indifference to her and the ways in which he has passed up opportunities to demonstrate whatever love he has for her. After concluding a psychodramatic enactment in which the young woman "tells" her father of her feelings of missing this love, she may still be angry with him and expect him to make the first move to change matters. During the discussion phase, the leader or the members can point out that she is making the assumption that *he* must be the person to initiate a closer relationship. In reality, the father may well be fearful of showing her affection and attention, thinking that she is not interested in such a relationship with him. The group can be instrumental in helping her see that if she wants to change her relationship with him, she may have to make the first move.

Role Theory

We play multiple roles in everyday life; some of them are an extension of our unique identity, and others are stultifying and restrict our identity. Moreno's basic idea is that we have the capacity to become more conscious and creative in how we play our roles. We can examine the roles we play, renegotiate them, and choose different ways to play the roles we choose to keep. In psychodrama, members are given the freedom to try out a diversity of roles, thereby getting a sharper focus on parts of themselves that they would like to present to others. Playing roles also enables participants to get in contact with parts of themselves that they were not aware of. They can challenge stereotyped ways of responding to people and break out of behaving within a rigid pattern, creating new dimensions of themselves. Blatner writes that role theory "suggests that we can become spontaneous, improvisational actors, creating our parts without scripts. We thus become not only actors but also playwrights. We can go further and question which roles we want to take on, as if we were negotiating with an inner agent" (1991, p. 37). Indeed, we have the capacity to break out of roles when we discover that they no longer serve us.

Basic Components of the Psychodramatic Method

The psychodramatic method consists of the following components: a director (the person who "produces" a psychodrama); a protagonist (the person who is presenting a problem to be explored); the auxiliary egos (representatives of persons not present, or the people portraying significant others in the protagonist's life as a way of helping the protagonist explore an enactment); the audience (the others in the group, before whom the problem is actually explored); and the stage (usually a space in a room).

The Stage

The stage is the area where the enactment takes place. It represents an extension of the life space of the protagonist, and as such it should be large enough to allow for movement of the protagonist, the auxiliary egos, and the director. A stage generally has some chairs, a table, and other props that can intensify the dramatic function. When a protagonist emerges from the group, he or she moves to this area to create the psychodrama. If an actual stage is not available, a section of the room can be designated.

The Director's Role and Functions

According to J. L. Moreno (1964), the director has the role of producer, catalyst/facilitator, and observer/analyzer. Directors help in the selection of the protagonist and then decide which of the special psychodramatic techniques are best suited for the exploration of the person's problem. They organize the psychodrama, play a key role in warming up the group, and pay careful attention to what emerges in the drama. Directors function as catalysts/facilitators in that they assist the protagonist in developing a scene and facilitate the free expression of feelings. At times they make therapeutic interpretations to help the protagonist gain a new understanding of a problem. Haskell describes specific functions of psychodramatic directors (1975, pp. 161–164):

- ◆ planning the session so that various members have an opportunity to be the protagonist and so that the problems presented are relevant to the needs and interests of the group
- ◆ providing an accepting and tolerant atmosphere that lends itself to spontaneous expressions of feelings associated with meaningful events

◆ warming up the group so that the participants will be psychologically ready to freely and fully explore personal issues and identify their goals

◆ providing support and direction for the protagonist, including suggesting appropriate techniques designed to enhance the enactments

◆ encouraging spontaneity and catharsis and helping the protagonist interpret what he or she experiences during the psychodrama

◆ suggesting relationships that might be explored, scenes that might be enacted, and experiments that might be tried

◆ stopping the action for clarification whenever necessary, and making sure that the roles are being properly enacted

◆ paying careful attention to the reactions of the group members and, if it seems appropriate, trying to bring other participants into the psychodrama; also, assisting other members in deriving therapeutic benefits from the experience

◆ protecting the protagonist from being verbally attacked by other members of the group or from being subjected to simplistic directives and advice

◆ leading a group discussion after the action is over—a function that entails encouraging members to give the protagonist feedback and share what they experienced during the psychodrama, what they learned from it, and what experiences and feelings they think they have in common with the protagonist

◆ summarizing the experience on the basis of the feedback obtained in the discussion and the enactments, thus providing a good closure for one experience and a direct lead into another area of exploration

Corsini (1966) concludes that effective directors possess both creativity and courage. Asserting that directing role playing involves not only technical skills but also *creativity,* Corsini makes it clear how many variables directors must attend to. They must not only depend on their own resources for being inventive but also find ways of tapping the creativity within the group. They must make decisions about what aspects of a psychodrama to focus on and quickly arrange for reenactment of certain scenes. In addition, they must be able to function as a guide by using their clinical expertise and technical knowledge to help individuals bring to the surface, explore, and work through their personal concerns. Directors must also find ways of involving as many members as possible in the protagonist's work. Effective directors are able to invent techniques that will highlight a member's struggles. They must be able to improvise, and their improvisations must have structure and meaning.

Directors must also have *courage,* for many of the techniques they use involve some degree of risk and of the unknown. It takes courage to run the risk of being found wanting before the public eye as they work with protagonists who are exposing themselves (Greenberg, 1986). Although they are not impulsive, good psychodramatic leaders trust their clinical hunches enough to try techniques that can have a powerful effect on the members.

According to Zerka Moreno (1987) the director's function is complicated and involves a combination of art and science. She contends that it takes approximately two years to train a director. In addition, a certified director must have at least a master's degree in one of the mental-health professions. She maintains that the more fully the director lives, the better he or she will be able to fulfill the functions demanded in a psychodrama.

Since psychodrama is a powerful method, it is essential that directors have theoretical, technical, and practical knowledge of psychodramatic techniques. In order to appreciate fully the potential values and risks inherent in these techniques, directors need to have experienced them as participants. Inept leadership—manifested, for instance, in forcing people into situations with which they are not ready to deal—can have serious negative consequences for the participants. The sensitivity and expertise of the director are crucial if the experience is to be therapeutic.

Perhaps one of the most crucial skills of the psychodramatist is learning how to work *with* any resistance or reluctance on the protagonist's part. Participants are almost never facilitated into deeper expression and exploration of a conflict when their natural resistances are attacked by the therapist. If the leader does not respect the resistance of the members, they will not develop the trust in the leader and the group process necessary for confronting their own fears. Blatner (1988) underscores the value of the director working *with* the resistances as a path toward exploration of deeper conflicts. He cites Moreno's advice on this issue: "We don't tear down the protagonist's walls; rather, we simply try some of the handles on the many doors, and see which one opens" (p. 72).

Group practitioners who are interested in incorporating psychodrama into their style of leadership should realize that they do not have to be perfect in their first attempts to apply its methods. Some beginning leaders become overly intimidated when they think about the personal qualities, skills, and knowledge that are required for effectively using psychodrama. With supervised practice, experience as a member of a psychodramatic group, and specialized training, they can acquire competence in this powerful approach.

The Protagonist

The protagonist selects the event to be explored. He or she either volunteers or is picked by the group and the director. In the case of a past event the protagonist is asked to reenact the substance of the event without attempting to recall the exact transaction or words. The protagonist is the source of the imagery but requires the assistance of the director to explore a problem and to create a psychodrama. As soon as possible, the director encourages the protagonist to move spontaneously into action rather than merely talking about the event. Protagonists are asked to deal with the significant people in their past as though these figures were present. In the enactment the protagonists' fears and fantasies come to life and enable them to modify intrapsychic and interpersonal processes.

It is important that as protagonists act out a situation, they have the freedom to explore any aspect of the scene (and related relationships) that seem significant to them. It is the protagonists, not the director, who examine and explore, and it is crucial that their decisions be respected. Although the director may encourage protagonists to reenact a situation or deal with an anticipated event, they decide whether they are willing to follow the director's suggestions. Also, the director may employ a particular technique, but protagonists always have the right to say that they don't want to move in that direction. Effective psychodrama should never be coerced or pressured; the auxiliary egos and the director are there to serve the protagonist.

At the end of a scene the protagonist or the director may suggest that the protagonist assume a different role in the same scene to determine whether he or she can respond more effectively. Another suggestion is that the protagonist fantasize about the future by acting out how things might be a year afterward, thus sharing private thoughts with the audience.

The Auxiliary Egos

Auxiliary egos often portray the roles of significant others in the life of the protagonist. These persons may be living or dead, real or imagined. Auxiliaries may also play the roles of inanimate objects, pets, or any emotionally charged object or being that is relevant to the protagonist's psychodrama.

The auxiliary egos have other functions: (1) to play out the perceptions held by the protagonist, at least in the beginning; (2) to investigate the interaction between the protagonist and their own roles; (3) to interpret this interaction and relationship; and (4) to act as a therapeutic guide in helping the protagonist develop an improved relationship (Z. T. Moreno, 1987). Effective auxiliary egos can give a psychodrama greater power and intensity. A few ways in which they do this are by helping the protagonist warm up, by intensifying the action, and by mirroring the protagonist. Auxiliaries encourage the protagonist to become more deeply involved in the here and now of the drama, which tends to intensity the involvement of both themselves and the protagonist.

The protagonist generally selects the group members who will serve as auxiliary egos. These choices are made for both conscious and unconscious reasons. Some choices are made of the basis of characteristics of group members that are similar to those of the actual loved ones. When a choice is made on this basis, the interaction between the protagonist and auxiliary egos is likely to be more spontaneous, real, and effective. Directors may take exception to this rule if they want a group member to assume a role with particular therapeutic potential.

Although the protagonist has ideas about a problem, both the protagonist and the director have the job of coaching auxiliary egos how to play their roles. This sometimes entails giving an auxiliary ego some background on the person he or she is to play and a feeling for the style of that person. Protagonists may teach an auxiliary ego the behavioral style of a significant other by acting out that part.

Auxiliary egos use information about significant others that is conveyed to them by the protagonist through role reversal. It is the director's responsibility to assess whether their role playing is working more for the protagonist's benefit or for their own. In the latter case the auxiliaries may be redirected by the director. The director should be sure to discuss this development during the sharing phase of the group, because it usually has significant therapeutic implications for the auxiliaries. It should be underscored that psychodrama is a *group process* and that auxiliary work has great therapeutic potential. It is a good idea to permit auxiliaries some freedom of expression in their role portrayals. Playing someone else's role often serves as a vehicle for getting in touch with parts of the self not uncovered while playing one's own role. However, Zerka Moreno (1987) warns about possible dangers when there is a meshing of the protagonist's psychodrama with the auxiliary ego's drama. She cautions both the auxiliary ego and the director to avoid doing their own psychodrama, thus taking the focus away from the protagonist's drama. It is the director's task to make sure that the spontaneity of the total group involvement is tempered with some degree of purpose and structure.

The Audience

Even when people in the group are not protagonists or auxiliary egos in a psychodrama, they can still benefit in vicarious ways. They can identify with the protagonist, they can experience a release of their own feelings through their empathy, and they can gain insight into some of their own interpersonal conflicts. These other group members—the audience—provide valuable support and feedback to the protagonist. An action scene is generally followed by a discussion that involves the entire group. Other members are asked to share some experiences of their own that are related to the scene they have just observed, and they provide the protagonist with feedback concerning alternative ways of dealing with the situation. Because of the variety in group membership, the audience's reactions can help the protagonist understand the impact he or she has on others.

Phases of the Psychodramatic Process

Psychodrama consists of three phases: (1) the warm-up (or preaction) phase, (2) the action phase, and (3) the discussion, or sharing, phase. These are not rigid categories but frames of references for the practitioner to (1) build the spontaneity, (2) apply it, and (3) integrate the enactment with the group process.

The Warm-Up Phase

Warming up consists of the initial activities required for a gradual increase in involvement and spontaneity. It includes the director's warm-up, establishing trust and group cohesion, identifying a group theme, finding a protagonist, and moving the protagonist onto the stage (Blatner, 1988).

J. L. Moreno emphasizes the necessity of getting the participants ready for the experience. Such readiness involves being motivated enough to formulate one's goals and feeling secure enough to trust the others in the group. There are many ways to conduct a productive warm-up phase. For example:

- ◆ The director gives a brief talk about the nature and purpose of psychodrama, and participants are invited to ask questions.
- ◆ Each member is briefly interviewed by the director. A lead question may be "Is there a present or past relationship that you'd like to understand better?" If each person in the group responds to this question, a basis for group cohesion is being established.
- ◆ Members can form several sets of dyads and spend a few minutes sharing a conflict that they are experiencing and that they'd like to explore in the session.
- ◆ The "go-around" technique can facilitate group interaction. Each member is asked to make some brief comments about what he or she is experiencing in the moment. This making the rounds can also focus the members on personal work they would like to do during the session.
- ◆ In a long-term group with functional people, a nondirective warm-up is often used as a way to get members ready for a session. Members may be simply asked to briefly state what they were aware of as they were coming to the session or to make any comments about their readiness to work.

In addition to structured techniques aimed at warming up a group for action, there are unstructured warm-ups, including the process by which a protagonist emerges from the spontaneous interaction at the beginning of a group session. It is critical that the leader pay close attention to verbal and nonverbal cues as the protagonist describes the issue to be explored. For example, a member may describe himself as reserved and distant from others. He may use some metaphoric or symbolic language that has rich implications. In talking about letting others get close to him, he may allude to "shields" that he has carefully built to protect himself from the pain of rejection.

During the warm-up phase, members need to be reassured that the working environment is a safe one, that they are the ones to decide *what* they will reveal and *when* they will reveal it, and that they can stop whenever they want to. If participants have the impression that they will be pressured to "perform" and badgered to go further than they feel ready or willing to, the morale of the group will suffer, and the members will resist participation. The techniques are less important than the spirit and purpose of the warm-up: anything that facilitates the cohesion of the group and the establishing of trust is a useful tool for this phase.

According to Blatner (1988), the most important issue in the warm-up phase is creating an atmosphere that fosters spontaneity. In his view the necessary conditions for spontaneous behavior to occur include:

◆ a sense of trust and a climate of psychological safety
◆ group norms that allow for the expression of emotions and for the inclusion of intuitive dimensions
◆ an element of playfulness
◆ a willingness to explore and engage in novel behavior

Blatner emphasizes the importance of the director's own warm-up as a key factor in creating a climate that encourages spontaneous behavior. It is during the warm-up period that directors are developing their own spontaneity. By communicating a sense of authenticity and warmth, they foster confidence and trust. Similarly, modeling risk taking, self-disclosure, humor, spontaneity, creativity, empathy, and the acceptability of expressing emotions and acting them out contributes to the group's cohesion. A theme may begin to emerge, and a protagonist may be selected and move onto the stage for action.

The Action Phase

The action phase includes the acting out and working through of a past or present situation or of an anticipated event. The enactment begins when the protagonist enters the stage area. It is important to facilitate the process so that the protagonist can move into action as soon as possible. The director guides the protagonist in establishing the scene in which some significant event took place. In doing this, the leader can draw on important cues that the protagonist gave in presenting his or her situation, including facial expressions, figures of speech, and body posture. The director helps the protagonist get a clear focus on a particular concern. Rather than having the protagonist give lengthy details and risking losing the energy of the psychodrama, the director can ask the protagonist questions such as "With whom in your life are you having the most trouble at this time?" "What few words or phrases would best describe your father [mother]?" "What is the main message that you get from your mother [father]?" "When have you felt the most isolated or abandoned?" "What did you do when you felt rejected and unloved?" "How old are you feeling at this time?" "How do you wish your husband had been different with you?" "When do you feel most criticized by your wife?" "What are the things your husband tells you that upset you the most?" "What are a few lines you'd like to say to your son?" "What would you most like to hear from your daughter?" The point of these questions is to avoid lengthy commentaries on content and instead to focus the protagonist on the process of his or her struggle.

Once the protagonist has a clear sense of what he or she would like to explore, it is possible to create the scene and coach the auxiliary egos. After this focusing process, protagonists act out their problems and relationships on the stage. A single action phase may consist of one to several scenes. Scenes are constructed and enacted as they relate to the protagonist's issues. They may be interpersonal or intrapersonal in nature and usually progress from peripheral issues (presenting problems) to more central issues (the real or deeper problems). The duration of the action phase varies, depending on the director's evaluation of the protagonist's involvement and on the level of involvement of the group.

Fine (1979) observes that sometimes an entire session may be devoted to the group as a whole working through interpersonal issues among members or identifying and modifying norms that have been developing in the group. At other times a common theme such as loneliness, fear of intimacy, and feelings of rejection seems to touch everyone in the group. With skillful facilitation by the group leader each person can become involved with others in here-and-now encounters.

Haskell offers some guidelines for directors during the action phase of psychodrama (1975, pp. 192–193):

◆ The protagonist should be encouraged as soon as possible to enact scenes involving conflicts in relationships.
◆ All the action should be geared to the here and now. Thus, if a person is dealing with a past situation and says, "Then I told him," the director intervenes and says, "You are telling him *now.*"
◆ The protagonist needs the freedom to select the event, time, place, and people involved in the situation.
◆ Generally it is wise to deal first with less significant events and leave the reenacting of more traumatic experiences for later.
◆ Protagonists should be asked to reconstruct a situation as faithfully as possible without, however, being overly concerned with recalling the exact words exchanged, so that the flow of action is not inhibited. Instead, they need to know that the essence of an interaction, *as they recall it,* is what's important.
◆ Protagonists should be encouraged to express themselves as fully as possible, both verbally and nonverbally. However, the director needs to exert caution so that rage is expressed symbolically—for example, by hitting a pillow—and people are not injured.
◆ Protagonists can be given the opportunity to play the role of each person in their scene (role reversal); this can help them develop an understanding of how others perceived and felt about an event.

At the end of the action phase, it is important to help protagonists acquire a sense of closure for any work they accomplished. One useful way to facilitate closure is to arrange for behavioral practice. This allows the protagonist to translate in-group learning to everyday life. The function of behavioral practice is to create a climate that allows for experimentation with a variety of new behaviors. Then the person can implement some of these new behaviors with significant others outside the group and cope with situations more effectively. To facilitate behavioral practice, the protagonist presents the situation as it was originally presented in the action phase. Various techniques, such as role reversal, future projection, mirroring, and feedback, are often used to help the protagonist get a clearer idea of the impact of his or her new behavior. (These techniques are described later in the chapter.)

The Sharing and Discussion Phase

The third phase of psychodrama is the sharing and discussion phase. (For some therapists who use psychodrama, sharing and discussion are separate.) Sharing, which comes first, consists of nonjudgmental statements about oneself; a discussion of the group process follows. The participants are asked to share with the protagonist their observations of and reactions to the psychodrama in a constructive and supportive way, emphasizing what the enactment touched in their lives. Those who played roles in the enactment can also share their reactions to these roles.

Zerka Moreno (1987) has some excellent guidelines for making the sharing session a therapeutic experience:

- ◆ Group members should speak for themselves and not analyze the protagonist.
- ◆ Since the protagonist has engaged in open sharing, he or she deserves more than a cold analysis or critique.
- ◆ Insight by itself rarely has a healing impact. Sharing has healing effects. The disclosure of others' experiences gives people a sense that they are not alone and leads to bonding.
- ◆ Interpretation and evaluation come later, when the protagonist is not so vulnerable.

The director's task is to initiate and lead a discussion that includes as many participants as possible, so that feedback can be maximized. The director needs to watch for attempts by members to analyze the protagonist or confront the person harshly at a time when, having just finished revealing some intimate life experiences, he or she can be most vulnerable. It is important that protagonists be given an opportunity for some form of closure of their experience. If they have opened themselves up and expressed deep feelings, they need to be able to count on the support of the group in order to integrate psychologically what they have just experienced. If no such opportunity is available through sharing and some exploration of the meaning of the experience, the protagonists may leave the session feeling rejected and lost instead of feeling freer and more purposeful. After an intense piece of work, the leader might ask the protagonist any one of these open-ended questions: "What are you experiencing now?" "What are you aware of right now?" "How was it for you to do and say what you just did?" If the protagonist is aware of what others are thinking or feeling, he or she can simply look at the eyes of each of the members in the room. Sometimes remaining silent and "taking in the energy of the group" is much more powerful than using too many words.

It is crucial that the sharing from the audience be personal and nonjudgmental. The director must reinforce the kind of sharing that entails self-disclosure, support, and emotional involvement on the part of the members. The sharing is best structured so that members discuss how they were affected by the session, and in this way their own involvement, transparency, and growth are fostered. This is not a time for giving advice to the protagonist or, worse yet, attempting to "cure" the protagonist by providing insightful interpretations into his or her psychodynamics. If participants attempt to analyze or to provide solutions, the director needs to intervene, for example by asking questions such as these:

◆ "How has Jane's drama affected you?"
◆ "What feelings were stirred up in you as you were participating in her drama?"
◆ "What experiences in your life relate to Jane's situation?"
◆ "Are there any feelings you had toward her that you'd like to share with her?"

During the sharing time, group cohesion is typically increased, for members are able to see commonalities. The participation in universal struggles is a way to bond members. Thus, after an effective sharing of experiences, protagonists are not left feeling as though they are alone in an unfriendly universe. They have a basis for feeling accepted, and the feedback from other members acts as a reinforcement for them to continue revealing personal concerns. Blatner writes that the sharing period gives all the members in a psychodrama group the chance to express their feelings: "The group members need this as much as the protagonist does. The catharsis in the drama may then spread, be reexperienced, and subside as the group realizes its common bond of human feelings" (1988, p. 98).

Closure depends on the client, the situation, and the group. If the group will not meet again, closure is essential; if the group meets on a regular basis, however, there are times when the leader may defer closure to a later session. A period of discussion can be useful for "winding down" the emotional pitch to a more cognitive level and for helping protagonist and audience integrate key aspects of the session. Although the emotional aspects of an enactment are of great therapeutic value, a degree of cognitive integration will maximize the value of the emotional components. Protagonists can be asked to express what they have learned from the particular enactment and the insights they have acquired. It is also a good practice to encourage protagonists to talk about the personal meaning of reliving a situation. They can be stimulated to think of a possible course of action that will permit them to cope with repressed feelings and of practical ways of dealing more effectively with similar problem situations in the future.

Several writers discuss the importance of dealing with unfinished business during the final phase of a psychodrama (Blatner, 1988; Goldman & Morrison 1984; Greenberg, 1986; Leveton, 1992; Z. T. Moreno, 1987). Before ending a session, the director may ask members to verbalize any unspoken feelings that have developed during the psychodrama. As mentioned earlier, it is not always necessary to work things out, but it is important that the existence of unfinished business be mentioned before the session closes. Some problems will probably be opened up and fruitfully explored, yet the protagonist may be far from having resolved the issue. After a successful sharing session, new work is likely to be shaping up as other members identify with what they just experienced. Of course, it is not wise to undertake further work in a given session if there is not ample time to address the issue adequately.

Members need to be warned of the danger of attempting premature and forced closure of an issue. It is essential that protagonists have ample opportunities to express their feelings, experience their conflicts, and explore the meaning of their emotional release. Clinicians, out of their own anxiety for wanting to see problems solved, sometimes suggest behavioral practice and an action plan before members have had a chance to ventilate and identify an area of personal concern. J. L. Moreno suggests: "Enactment comes first, retraining comes latter. We must give the protagonist the satisfaction of act completion first, before considering retraining for behavioral changes" (cited in Blatner, 1988, p. 92).

Leveton (1992) notes that some practitioners expect perfection. Unless everything is settled, these leaders feel that they have failed. In order to avoid such feelings, they may try to force closure in situations where participants are better off if they continue thinking about what has occurred. One of the most challenging tasks for the director is learning to bring closure to a session without curtailing members' further self-exploration, which is necessary for an in-depth resolution of their problems.

An optional part of psychodrama is "postsession rapping," which provides opportunities for some social sharing among the participants. Greenberg (1986) typically invites those who attend a psychodrama to stay for a while and have coffee or tea. This is a time when participants can talk with one another in more informal ways and can say things that they didn't get a chance to say to another person during the psychodrama. This period also provides further opportunities for people to wind down from an experience.

Techniques of Psychodrama

Psychodrama uses a number of specific techniques designed to intensify feelings, lead to catharsis, and bring about increased self-understanding. This understanding of self comes about by a process of working through and integrating material that has surfaced in a psychodrama. These techniques, while instrumental to the success of the psychodramatic process, are not ends in themselves. Thus J. L. Moreno (1978) warns about the misuse of techniques simply to stir up a dramatic performance.

Directors have latitude to invent their own techniques or modify standard ones. Because psychodrama can be powerful, practitioners need to bring caution and commitment to the practice of their technical skills, and they need to know when and how to apply these methods. Effective psychodrama consists of far more than the mere use of certain techniques. Practitioners must learn to know, and work with, the members' psychological worlds in an educated, trained, sensitive, caring, and creative manner.

I suggest that you keep these cautions in mind as you read the following overview of some standard psychodramatic techniques. These techniques are described in detail in the following sources: Blatner (1988), Blatner with Blatner (1988b), Goldman and Morrison (1984), Greenberg (1986), Leveton (1992), J. L. Moreno (1964), J. L. Moreno and Z. T. Moreno (1958), Z. T. Moreno (1959, 1965, 1983, 1987), and Starr (1977).

Below are some principles of psychodramatic techniques that are useful as guidelines to the practitioner (Blatner with Blatner, 1988b):

- ◆ Whenever possible, use physical action rather than talking about a situation.
- ◆ Use direct address, talking to the people most involved (or auxiliaries playing their roles) rather than about them.
- ◆ Look for ways to promote the active behavior of other members by getting them involved in an enactment as much as possible.
- ◆ Make abstract situations more concrete by working with specific scenes.
- ◆ Encourage participants to make affirmative statements about themselves by using sentences beginning with "I."
- ◆ Continue to encourage members to deal with situations in the past or future as if they were happening in the present moment.
- ◆ Recognize and tap the potential for redecisions, renegotiations, and corrective experiences in the present.
- ◆ Pay attention to the nonverbal aspects of communication.
- ◆ Have participants directly exercise empathic skills through role reversal.
- ◆ Include a degree of playfulness, humor, and spontaneity in a situation.
- ◆ Utilize symbols and metaphors, personifying them and making them more vivid.
- ◆ Include other artistic principles and vehicles, such as movement, staging, props, poetry, art, and music.
- ◆ Exaggerate or amplify behavior to explore a wider range of responses.

Behavioral Practice

Behavioral practice is designed for experimenting in the safety of the group with a range of new ways of acting. Protagonists have many opportunities for replaying a scene until they discover a response that fits them personally. They are given support, reinforcement, and feedback on the effectiveness of their new behaviors. As a part of working through a problem, the director typically focuses on acquiring and rehearsing specific interpersonal skills, which are often learned through the modeling of other members. Participants are likely to be coached and to receive role training in situations such as a job interview, with the aim of learning how to manage their anxiety. Not only can they come into contact with their feelings, but they can also gain insight into behaviors that are likely to impede an effective interview. They can get feedback on the way they present themselves in the interview, and they can practice various behavioral styles to prepare themselves psychologically for what they see as a stressful experience. Members work on developing and practicing concrete social skills that will help them deal effectively with a range of interpersonal situations.

Self-Presentation

The protagonist gives a self-portrayal in order to introduce the situation. Let's assume that Jack, the protagonist, wants to explore his relationship with his daughter, Laura. He may do so by demonstrating how he typically approaches her. His self-presentation gives the audience a sense of how he experiences himself in the father/daughter relationship. In the course of the self-presentation he may state the problem as he sees it and may say something about his daughter.

Role Reversal

In role reversal the protagonist takes on the part of another personality portrayed in his or her drama. Once an enactment is set up, the director may wish to have the protagonist use this technique (1) to better portray how he or she imagines or remembers the other personality and (2) to reach a fuller understanding of the viewpoint or situation of the other.

In the setting of a scene, the auxiliary ego chosen to play a particular part (mother, father, sibling, lover, close friend, teacher, or relative) does not know how to enact either the nonverbal or the verbal components of the assigned role. The protagonist is asked to reverse roles to demonstrate this. As the scene unfolds, if the auxiliary ego begins to take the role in a direction that does not apply to the protagonist, the director can again invite a role reversal so that the auxiliary can get back on track. The leader needs to intervene to reduce the chances that the auxiliary will contaminate the process with his or her own dynamics. The auxiliary is instructed to keep the drama true to the protagonist's perception of events.

The second and more important function of role reversal is to encourage protagonists to empathize with a significant person in their life. In assuming the role of that person in the psychodrama, they begin to develop a deeper appreciation for the person's world. This reversal allows them to experience the environment from a different perspective. Typically, the director suggests a role reversal when it appears that the protagonist would benefit by attempting to "walk in the shoes" of the person with whom he or she is experiencing conflict.

Zerka Moreno (1983) makes the point that protagonists must act out the truth as they feel it and from their own subjective stance, regardless of how distorted their presentation may appear to the other members or the leader. For example, Jack presents his daughter. Preferably, he plays the role of Laura and demonstrates how she typically responds. As Jack "becomes" his daughter, another member can assume his role as a father. By playing the role of Laura as he experiences her, Jack may begin to come to a clearer understanding of how *she* feels. As a variation, the director can interview Jack as he plays the role of his daughter. This technique will give the director and the group a clearer picture of how Jack perceives his daughter and how he thinks she perceives him.

Role reversal is considered to be one of the most powerful tools of psychodrama, and it serves other purposes (Fine, 1979):

◆ It allows expansion of the clients' awareness and behavior.
◆ It encourages participants to take responsibility for their behavior and decisions.
◆ It helps protagonists confront the impact of their immediate interpersonal behavior.

Zerka Moreno (1983) maintains that this technique encourages maximum expression in conflict situations. Protagonists' distortions of these relationships can be brought to the surface, explored, and corrected in action. First, clients must "own" their emotions through ventilation, or catharsis. Then by reversing roles, protagonists can reintegrate, redigest, and grow beyond situations that are keeping them unfree. Role reversal allows members to fully express their perceptions of reality, to get feedback from others in the group about their subjective views, and to make modifications of their perceptions to the extent that they discover distortions. It can be used throughout the drama to correct or modify the principal auxiliary's role portrayal and to present additional information to the auxiliary. More importantly, it is used throughout the action phase to increase the protagonist's depth of perception of the significant other.

Double Technique

An auxiliary ego stands behind the protagonist and acts with or even speaks *for* him or her. The double can mirror the inner thoughts and feelings of the protagonist, often expressing preconscious material. Doubling facilitates the client's awareness of internal processes and often leads to an expression of unvoiced thoughts and feelings. The double supports the protagonist and also serves as a link between the director and the protagonist. The double may serve an integrative function and also intensify the interaction between the protagonist and the auxiliary ego. It is useful for doubles to assume both the posture and the attitude of protagonists. However, these are merely tools that doubles use to help them fulfill their purpose. The purpose is to help protagonists increase their awareness of inner conflicts and repressed feelings and even express them. According to Leon Fine (personal communication, June 1988), the double is the agent of the protagonist. The double attends to process events and the immediate moment and is available to the protagonist in role reversals and in other roles. In Jack's case, the double technique might be used if he felt stuck or felt overwhelmed by his daughter. The double would then help Jack stay in contact with and express his feelings. Effective doubling often results in the escalation of an interaction, and it is likely to provide the protagonist with the needed catalyst to say things that until now have remained unexpressed.

Multiple doubles may be used to represent and embody the various sides of the protagonist. They can represent the protagonist's internal conflicts, desires, assets, liabilities, or various roles he or she plays in life (Goldman & Morrison, 1984). With Jack, one double may represent the side of him that misses his daughter and wants to express love, and the other double can be the "cold father," who really wants to have nothing to do with her. The doubles may speak at the same time, or they may take turns. If the doubles are effective, the father's ambivalent feelings toward his daughter can be successfully portrayed on the stage, and Jack may come to see which side within him is stronger. Also, he may get a clearer picture of the feelings and attitudes he'd like to express to Laura.

Soliloquy

At times, protagonists are asked to imagine themselves in a place alone where they can daydream out loud (soliloquize). The director may ask a protagonist to stop the action at some point, turn aside, and express her feelings at the moment. Or the director, on sensing ambivalence on the part of another protagonist, may stop the action and ask him to walk around the stage and say what he is thinking and feeling. The protagonist may be engaged in a solitary activity, such as walking home. As a variation, the protagonist may soliloquize with a double as the two walk together. The double can facilitate the protagonist's expression of feelings and thoughts that would typically be kept hidden.

The soliloquy is valuable in helping protagonists clarify their thinking and experience their feelings more intensely (Greenberg, 1986). This technique facilitates an open expression of what they may be thinking and feeling but not verbally expressing. For example, Jack may be asked to verbalize his thoughts during the course of a role reversal. This soliloquy gives him the chance to get a sense of what he believes Laura is thinking and feeling but perhaps not expressing directly. He can also be asked to soliloquize after he has portrayed himself. He does this by summarizing his uncensored thoughts, expressing his feelings, and examining them more closely.

Mirror Technique

An auxiliary ego assumes the role of the protagonist by mirroring the protagonist's postures, gestures, and words as they appeared in the enactment. During the auxiliary ego's mirroring, the protagonist is not on the stage, so that by observing his own behavior reflected by another person, he can see himself as others do. The protagonist stands back and watches a very live form of videotape playback. This process may help the protagonist develop a more accurate and objective self-assessment. Mirroring is basically a feedback process, because the technique sensitizes protagonists to the reality of how others perceive them. This feedback may help clarify any discrepancies between their self-perception and what they communicate of themselves to others (Goldman & Morrison, 1984). Consider the illustration of Jack. If he is mirrored as demanding, critical, aloof, and cold, he is likely to wonder whether that's the way his daughter perceives him. This technique may be particularly useful if others in the group see Jack differently from the way he sees himself or if he has difficulty presenting himself verbally or in action. Blatner with Blatner (1988b) caution that mirroring can be a powerful confrontation technique and must be used with discretion. It must be given in the spirit of concern and empathy, rather than making the protagonist the object of ridicule.

The Magic Shop

The "magic shop" is often used as a warm-up technique and may also be elaborated on throughout the action phase. This technique is frequently used with protagonists who are unclear about what they value, who are confused about their goals, or who have difficulty assigning priorities to their values. One at a time, the group members bargain with the "storekeeper," who has the power to grant each member his or her most pressing wish. An auxiliary ego or the director is the storekeeper in a magic shop filled with imaginary qualities. These qualities are not for sale, but they can be bartered for. Thus, clients exchange qualities they possess for qualities they desire. Jack, for example, may want to exchange his competitive style for the ability to open up to his daughter in a loving way. This technique can help him assess his priorities and see what is keeping him from getting what he wants from his relationship with Laura.

Future Projection

The technique of future projection is designed to help group members express and clarify concerns they have about the future. These future concerns are not merely discussed, but an anticipated event is brought into the present moment and acted out. These concerns may include wishes and hopes, dreaded fears of tomorrow, and goals that provide some direction to life. Members create a future time and place with selected people, bring this event into the present, and get a new perspective on a problem. Members may act out either a version of the way they hope a given situation will ideally unfold or their version of the most horrible outcome.

Zerka Moreno (1983) contends that the future has typically been a neglected dimension in therapeutic practice. When participants in psychodrama enact anticipated events as though they were taking place in the here and now, they achieve an increased awareness of their available options. In this sense, psychodrama can be considered a rehearsal for life (Starr, 1977).

Once members clarify their hopes for a particular outcome, they are in a better position to take specific steps that will enable them to achieve the future they desire. To return to the case of Jack, he can be asked to carry on the kind of dialogue with his daughter that he would ideally like one year hence. He may even reverse roles, saying all those things that he hopes she will say to him. He can also project himself forward and tell her how he has acted differently toward her during the previous year. If he gets a clearer sense of the kind of relationship that he would like with her and if he accepts his own responsibility for the quality of this relationship, he can begin to modify some of the ways in which he approaches his daughter.

Evaluation of Psychodrama

Contributions and Strengths of the Approach

The action-oriented methods that have been described in this chapter can be integrated into the framework of other group approaches. I value psychodrama's active techniques and role playing mainly because they lead the participants to the direct experience of real conflicts. I have little patience with endless talk about problems, because it has been my experience that members profit very little from talking about themselves in a detached, storytelling manner. For the participants to learn about themselves, it is essential that role playing be designed to fit a specific situation.

I tend to employ psychodramatic methods when a member is undergoing a conflict that can be enacted or dramatized in some form. I see these methods as useful not only for the person who is the focus of the action but for other participants as well. Most of my uses of psychodrama have led to increased participation by other members. This method also binds people together, because it offers opportunities for them to become aware that their own struggles are also the struggles of others.

People often simply don't see alternatives for dealing with the significant people in their lives. In psychodrama, group members can demonstrate other ways of responding and thus provide the person with different frames of reference. In a role-playing situation, for example, Noreen approaches her husband, Roger, with a litany of all his shortcomings: he's selfish, he doesn't care, and he doesn't show his feelings or truly share his life with her. Another member can show Noreen a different way of relating to Roger that is not accusatory and that won't cause him to close up and ignore her complaints.

POTENTIALS FOR INTEGRATION. Integrated into other systems, such as some of the cognitive versions of behavior therapy, psychodrama can provide the exploration of emotions that these other systems often play down.

The psychodramatic group can be enhanced by more emphasis on the cognitive aspects of the process and by deeper investigation of the meaning of the cathartic experience.

Although there is value in catharsis, my experience with groups has taught me time and again how essential it is to provide a context in which members can come to an understanding of how their bottled-up emotions have affected both themselves and their relationships. Yet emotional release and self-understanding alone do not seem sufficient to produce lasting changes in one's way of thinking, feeling, and behaving. I am convinced that such deep changes will come about only if members are taught how to transfer what they have learned in their sessions to everyday situations. It is also critical to teach them ways of maintaining these positive emotional and behavioral changes. This can be done by helping them plan ways of coping effectively when they meet with frustration in the world and when they regress by seeming to forget the lessons they have learned. An excellent time for this cognitive work and formulation of action plans is toward the end of the sharing sessions after each psychodrama has been brought to a close. One excellent way to help members achieve closure on some of their emotional issues is to have them begin to think about the meaning of heightened emotional states. They can be encouraged to formulate their own interpretations of their problem situations. Furthermore, they can reflect on how their beliefs and decisions may be contributing to some of the emotional turmoil that they reexperienced in a psychodrama.

Borrowing techniques from those group approaches that stress a cognitive-behavioral orientation—transactional analysis, behavior therapy, rational emotive behavior therapy, and reality therapy—are especially useful for conceptualizing and acting on new learning. Rehearsals for future encounters, coupled with constructive and specific feedback, can be of real value to those members who want to develop alternative means of relating to significant people in their lives.

According to Blatner (1988), a major contribution of psychodrama is that it supports the growing trend toward technical eclecticism in psychotherapy. Practitioners are challenged to draw on whatever tools will be useful in a given situation. As we have seen, the experiential aspects of psychodrama blend well with cognitive-behavioral approaches. In many ways psychodrama was the precursor of many other group approaches, including Gestalt therapy, family therapy, encounter, and some applications of behavior-therapy groups. These orientations often use techniques that were originally developed by J. L. Moreno or adaptations. It is clear that many psychodramatic techniques can be adapted to work well within the framework of other contemporary theoretical models, including psychoanalytic therapy, behavior therapies, multimodal therapy, Gestalt therapy, Adlerian therapy, play therapy, imagination therapy, Jungian therapy, family therapy, and group therapy. (See Blatner, 1988, and Blatner with Blatner, 1988b, for a more detailed discussion of integrations with other therapies.)

Limitations of the Approach

Blatner (1988) emphasizes that psychodrama is not a panacea. He cautions practitioners against the danger of romanticizing a single approach, thus becoming blind to its limits and to the values of other methods. Blatner reminds us that because psychodramatic techniques can be powerful, practitioners need to acquire humility along with developing skills, and he underscores the importance of the practitioner's training to deal therapeutically with what surfaces. He provides this summary for training leaders:

> The student of psychodrama must balance several aspects of learning: (1) the knowledge that comes with reading and classroom work; (2) the understanding that comes with experiencing a variety of situations through the exercise of role reversal, as auxiliary, as protagonist, and simply in play; (3) the competence that comes with practice to the point of mastery; and (4) the wisdom that comes from integrating into the learning process one's own personal therapeutic journey, and with it the growing capacity to liberate and access one's higher self [p. 155].

Leveton (1992) warns about the irresponsible use of psychodramatic procedures. Skilled directors, she says, are willing to devote the time necessary to develop their skills, and they have undergone a training program under the supervision of an experienced clinician.

J. L. Moreno and Elefthery (1982) write that psychodrama should be used only very carefully, if at all, with acting-out individuals, with a seriously disturbed population, or with a sociopathic population. It is especially important that leaders have the experience and knowledge to deal with underlying psychopathology. In addition, they must have considerable sensitivity so that they do not push disturbed clients past a point that is therapeutic. It is also critical that they exercise good judgment in structuring situations so that members are not likely to open up old wounds without getting some closure to them.

There is a danger of leaders' being attracted to psychodrama primarily to gratify their own psychological needs. It is critical that they be aware of how their own personal problems and needs might interfere with their functioning. In this regard, countertransference issues must be worked through before the leader can hope to have a therapeutic impact on the group. If group practitioners are not secure in their professional competence, they may easily become impatient with what they perceive as the "slow progress" of clients. Out of their desire to see more immediate results, they may resort to a variety of manipulations designed to stir up emotions for the sake of drama.

Although spontaneity is one of the basic concepts of psychodrama, it can be misused. Blatner reminds clinicians that expressing impulses is not the goal of developing spontaneity: "When grossly misused, this kind of expressiveness could be called *pathological spontaneity*" (1988, p. 104). It is imperative that a group leader's spontaneity, inventiveness, and courage to try new techniques be tempered with a measure of caution, respect for the members, and concern for their welfare.

Applying Psychodrama with Multicultural Populations

If practitioners take seriously the cautions that have been mentioned in this chapter, psychodrama can make unique contributions in helping ethnically and culturally diverse populations. Rather than having a mother merely talk about her problems in relating to her children, for example, she can take on the role of some of her children during therapeutic sessions. Of course, it is important not to suggest directive techniques that are likely to open up intense emotional experiencing too quickly, for some members will be frightened of these feelings and may withdraw from the group. Rather than pushing members to emote, leaders can look for clues to when an invitation to move into a role-playing situation would be most appropriate.

For many people who have English as a second language, psychodrama has some interesting applications. My colleagues and I have often asked group members to speak to a significant other in their native language as they are engaged in a role-playing situation (Corey, Corey, Callanan, & Russell, 1992). When they do so, their emotions quickly come to the surface. I recall a German-born group member who was speaking in English to her "father" in a role-playing situation. She did this in a detached manner, and what she said had a rehearsed quality to it. We asked her to continue talking to her father, but to speak in German. She did so and was quickly overcome with emotion. It was difficult for her to keep up her defenses against experiencing her intense feelings when she used her mother tongue. It was not important for the leaders or the other members to understand the exact words spoken. They could understand the underlying emotional message through the protagonist's nonverbal messages and tone of voice. After she finished her psychodrama, we asked her to put some English words to what she had been experiencing. She said that speaking in German had vividly brought back early images, which led to a powerful experience of reliving scenes from her childhood. This helped others who did not understand German to be more tuned into her work, and it also helped her put her emotional work into a cognitive perspective.

Questions such as the following are often useful: "What did your father say to you? What were you able to tell him this time that you had not told him before? When did you get stuck as you were talking to him? What emotions did this bring up for you that were familiar? Did you respond to him in different ways today than you did when you were a child?" A few well-timed and appropriate questions can help members sort out their ambivalent feelings and make more sense out of their work.

If the purpose of the group is to explore intrapersonal and interpersonal problems, the psychodramatic techniques that are aimed at facilitating the expression of feelings are often appropriate for many clients. But if the group has a more didactic, educational, and informational focus, these techniques are more limited. If members demonstrate that they are highly uncomfortable in even talking about personal issues, let alone displaying their emotions in front of others, psychodrama is not the technique of choice. For those members who have grave cultural injunctions against talking about their family in a group, role playing that would involve "talking" to their mother or father would probably be met with resistance. Before attempting such techniques, the leader would have to fully explore the clients' cultural values and resistance. This demands a high level of training and skill on the leader's part. It is easy to see that an untrained and culturally unaware leader could be counterproductive.

Concluding Comments: The Impact of J. L. Moreno

Psychodrama and its development cannot be understood apart from its founder, J. L. Moreno. In many ways, this approach is an extension of his personality. He is sometimes described as having been narcissistic and grandiose. Moreno's dramatic interests can be traced to what he called the healthy megalomania of his childhood play. In his youth, he observed children's activities in the parks around Vienna. He began telling the children stories, which they would then enact. He observed that when they had no scripts, their portrayals of the roles they were playing were highly spontaneous and creative.

The more I learn about the techniques that Moreno pioneered, the more aware I become of his genius as a practitioner. It is an understatement to say that he was far ahead of his time. With his visionary perspective he created methods for integrating feelings, fantasies, and actions.

Moreno's enthusiasm was translated into an active leadership role when he was using psychodramatic methods. Even though his own style was flamboyant, he was also intuitive and warm. His wife, Zerka, has demonstrated that it is possible to use a different type of therapeutic style and still be highly effective. Her style includes more refinement and gentleness than did her husband's. She has carried on as the chief exponent of his work and has made significant contributions to training.

Moreno chose his own epitaph: "Here lies the man who brought laughter back into psychiatry." He approached his death with dignity, creativity, and control. When he was 85, after having led a full and vigorous life, his body failed him, and he elected to die in his own way. He stopped eating and took only water. He showed that even at the time of his death he was the actor and director of his fate, for he died in his own way, at his own pace (Fine, 1979).

As you read about other group-therapeutic approaches, you will see how many of the basic concepts and techniques of psychodrama appear in what are sometimes referred to as "innovative therapies." Learning about psychodrama is of value because of the many ways in which it can be integrated with the therapies that you will study in the remainder of this book.

If you are interested in learning more about the practical values and applications of psychodrama, you can make a good beginning by reading about the approach in journals and books. Also consider seeking out advanced training and supervision and attending reputable workshops where you can experience psychodrama as a group member. You will not only learn how this approach works in a group but also be able to work on some personal concerns and find new ways of dealing with them.

Where to Go from Here

The *American Society for Group Psychotherapy and Psychodrama* (ASGPP) is geared to the needs of professionals who want to learn about the latest developments in the field. It is an interdisciplinary society, in that its members come from all of the helping professions. The goals of the organization are to establish standards for specialists in group therapy and psychodrama and to support the exploration of new areas of endeavors in research, practice, teaching, and training. If you are interested in further information, contact:

American Society for Group Psychotherapy and Psychodrama
6728 Old McLean Village Road
McLean, VA 22101
TELEPHONE: (703) 556-9222

The American Board of Examiners in Psychodrama, Sociometry and Group Psychotherapy was established to serve two basic purposes: (1) to establish national professional standards in the fields of psychodrama, sociometry, and group psychotherapy and (2) to certify qualified professionals on the basis of these standards. Two levels of certification have been established by the board: (1) Practitioner and (2) Trainer, Educator, Practitioner. Applicants must be certified at the first level before becoming eligible for certification at the second. If you are interested in details about certification or if you want a geographic listing of approved trainers, educators, and practitioners in psychodrama, request a copy of the current *Directory of the American Board of Examiners in Psychodrama, Sociometry and Group Psychotherapy*. Contact:

American Board of Examiners
P.O. Box 15572
Washington, DC 20003-0572
TELEPHONE: (202) 483-0514

RECOMMENDED SUPPLEMENTARY READINGS

If you are seriously interested in psychodrama, I encourage you to read the works of J. L. Moreno and Zerka Moreno. Also, current and back issues of the *Journal of Group Psychotherapy, Psychodrama and Sociometry* are important readings. This journal is published quarterly, and the annual subscription rate is $40. Write to:

Heldref Publications
1319 Eighteenth Street, N.W.
Washington, DC 20036-1802

Foundations of Psychodrama: History, Theory, and Practice (Blatner with Blatner, 1988b) is an updated and excellent resource dealing with the historical, philosophical, psychological, social, and practical foundations of psychodrama. If you have time to read only one source, this would be my recommendation. The Blatners have a readable style; and they have succeeded in giving a fine overview of psychodrama. The book has an extensive bibliography.

Psychodrama: Experience and Process (Goldman & Morrison, 1984) is a concise description of the practice of psychodrama. The authors describe specific techniques for the warm-up, action, and sharing phases. Their book also contains a glossary of terms and techniques in the literature of psychodrama.

Acting-In: Practical Applications of Psychodramatic Methods (Blatner, 1988) is a guide for practitioners interested in using psychodramatic techniques in a group setting. This brief book is written very clearly and contains excellent discussions of the basic elements of psychodrama: its methods, stages, principles, and applications as well as some of its pitfalls. Beginners who want a good overview of psychodrama will find this book extremely valuable.

A Clinician's Guide to Psychodrama (Leveton, 1992) offers an excellent and eclectic view of psychodrama. The writing is clear, vivid, and interesting. A number of psychodramatic techniques are described and illustrated through case examples that attest to the author's skills and creativity in applying these techniques. Group leaders can greatly benefit from reading the book and following the author's encouragement to use experiential techniques in group work.

REFERENCES AND SUGGESTED READINGS*

Blatner, A. (1985). The dynamics of catharsis. *Journal of Group Psychotherapy, Psychodrama and Sociometry, 37*(4), 157–166.

*Blatner, A. (1988). *Acting-in: Practical applications of psychodramatic methods* (2nd ed.). New York: Springer.

Blatner, A. (1989). Psychodrama. In R. J. Corsini & D. Wedding (Eds.), *Current psychotherapies* (4th ed.). Itasca, IL: F. E. Peacock.

Blatner, A. (1991). Role dynamics: A comprehensive theory of psychology. *Journal of Group Psychotherapy, Psychodrama and Sociometry, 44*(1), 33–40.

Blatner, A. (1992). Theoretical principles underlying creative arts therapies. *The Arts in Psychotherapy, 18,* 405–409.

Blatner, A., & Blatner, A. (1988a). *The art of play: An adult's guide to reclaiming imagination and spontaneity.* New York: Human Sciences Press.

*Blatner, A., with Blatner, A. (1988b). *Foundations of psychodrama: History, theory, and practice.* New York: Springer.

Blatner, A., & Blatner, A. (1991). Imaginative interviews: A psychodramatic warm-up for developing role-playing skills. *Journal of Group Psychotherapy, Psychodrama and Sociometry, 44*(3), 115–120.

Corey, G., Corey, M., Callanan, P., & Russell, J. M. (1992). *Group techniques* (2nd ed.). Pacific Grove, CA: Brooks/Cole.

Corsini, R. J. (1966). *Roleplaying in psychotherapy.* Chicago: Aldine.

*Fine, L. J. (1979). Psychodrama. In R. J. Corsini (Ed.), *Current psychotherapies* (2nd ed.). Itasca, IL: F. E. Peacock.

Fox, J. (Ed.). (1987). *The essential Moreno: Writings on psychodrama, group method, and spontaneity.* New York: Springer.

*Goldman, E. E., & Morrison, D. S. (1984). *Psychodrama: Experience and process.* Dubuque, IA: Kendall/Hunt.

Greenberg, I. A. (1974). *Psychodrama: Theory and therapy.* New York: Behavioral Publications.

*Books and articles marked with an asterisk are suggested for further study.

*Greenberg, I. A. (1986). Psychodrama. In I. L. Kutash & A. Wolf (Eds.), *Psychotherapist's casebook* (pp. 392–412). San Francisco: Jossey-Bass.

Haskell, M. R. (1975). *Socioanalysis: Self-direction via sociometry and psychodrama.* Long Beach, CA: Role Training Associates.

Holmes, P., & Karp, M. (Eds.). (1991). *Psychodrama: Inspiration and technique.* New York: Routledge.

Kellermann, P. F. (1984, Spring). The place of catharsis in psychodrama. *Journal of Group Psychotherapy, Psychodrama and Sociometry,* 1–13.

Kipper, D. A. (1986). *Psychotherapy through clinical role playing.* New York: Brunner/Mazel.

Leveton, E. (1992). *A clinician's guide to psychodrama* (2nd ed.). New York: Springer.

Moreno, J. L. (1947). *Theatre of spontaneity: An introduction to psychodrama.* Beacon, NY: Beacon House.

Moreno, J. L. (1964). *Psychodrama: Vol. 1* (3rd ed.). Beacon, NY: Beacon House.

Moreno, J. L. (1978). *Who shall survive?* (3rd ed.). Beacon, NY: Beacon House.

Moreno, J. L., & Elefthery, D. G. (1982). An introduction to group psychodrama. In G. M. Gazda (Ed.), *Basic approaches to group psychotherapy and group counseling* (3rd ed.). Springfield, IL: Charles C Thomas.

Moreno, J. L., & Moreno, Z. T. (1958). *Psychodrama: Vol. 2.* Beacon, NY: Beacon House.

Moreno, J. L., & Moreno, Z. T. (1969). *Psychodrama: Vol. 3.* Beacon, NY: Beacon House.

Moreno, Z. T. (1959). A survey of psychodramatic techniques. *Group Psychotherapy,* 12, 5–14.

Moreno, Z. T. (1965). Psychodramatic rules, techniques, and adjunctive methods. *Group Psychotherapy,* 18, 73–86.

*Moreno, Z. T. (1983). Psychodrama. In H. I. Kaplan & B. J. Sadock (Eds.), *Comprehensive group psychotherapy* (2nd ed.). Baltimore: Williams & Wilkins.

*Moreno, Z. T. (1987). Psychodrama, role theory, and the concept of the social atom. In J. K. Zeig (Ed.), *The evolution of psychotherapy* (pp. 341–366). New York: Brunner/Mazel.

Nicholas, M. W. (1984). *Change in the context of group therapy.* New York: Brunner/Mazel.

Starr, A. (1977). *Psychodrama: Rehearsal for living.* Chicago: Nelson-Hall.

Sternberg, P., & Garcia, A. (1989). *Sociodrama: Who's in your shoes?* Westport, CT: Praeger.

Thacker, J. K. (1984, Spring). Using psychodrama to reduce "burnout" or role fatigue in the helping professions. *Journal of Group Psychotherapy, Psychodrama and Sociometry,* 14–25.

Treadwell, T., & Treadwell, J. (1972). The pioneer of the group encounter movement. *Group Psychotherapy and Psychodrama,* 25, 16–26.

Williams, A. (1989). *The passionate technique: Strategic psychodrama with individuals, families, and groups.* Westport, CT: Praeger.

CHAPTER NINE

The Existential
Approach to Groups

Introduction

Existential therapy can best be considered as an *approach,* or *philosophy,* by which a therapist operates. As such, it is not a separate school or a neatly defined, systematic model with specific therapeutic techniques. Group leaders cannot assume that they alone know the purpose of the group; rather, it is up to each participant to create this purpose. This chapter focuses on the basic themes, or universal human concerns, of this approach.

The existential approach rejects the deterministic view of human nature espoused by orthodox psychoanalysis and radical behaviorism. Psychoanalysis sees freedom as restricted by unconscious forces, irrational drives, and past events. Behaviorists see freedom as restricted by sociocultural conditioning. In contrast, while acknowledging some of these realities of the human situation, existential therapists emphasize our freedom to choose what to make of our circumstances. It is a dynamic approach that focuses on four ultimate concerns that are rooted in human existence: death, freedom, isolation, and meaninglessness (Yalom, 1980). It is grounded on the assumption that we are free and therefore responsible for our choices and actions. We are the architect of our life, and we draw up the blueprints for its design. A basic existential premise is that we are not the victim of circumstances, because to a large extent we are what we choose to be. Thus, one of the goals of the therapeutic process is to challenge clients to discover alternatives and choose among them. As van Deurzen-Smith (1988) has indicated, existential therapy is ultimately a process of exploring the value and meaning that we can find in living. The therapist's basic task is to encourage clients to consider what they are most serious about, so that they can pursue a direction in life. The existential approach assumes the individual's capacity to make well-informed choices about his or her life.

Existential counseling involves exploring options to create a meaning-

I want to acknowledge the helpful suggestions of Emmy van Deurzen-Smith and Michael Russell, which enhance this chapter.

ful life. For many of us, the recognition of the ways in which we have kept ourselves in a victimlike stance marks the beginning of change. We can recognize that we do not have to remain the passive victim of our circumstances, and thus we can consciously become the author of our life.

The Focus of Existential Psychotherapy

Existentialism is a branch of philosophical thought that began in Europe. The key existential writers, such as Martin Heidegger (1889–1976) and Jean-Paul Sartre (1905–1980), do not address themselves to psychotherapeutic concerns directly. The existential tradition emphasizes the limitations and tragic dimensions of human existence. It grew out of a desire to help people engage the dilemmas of contemporary life, such as isolation, alienation, and meaninglessness. The focus is on the individual's experience of being in the world alone and facing the anxiety of this isolation. The approach aims at understanding these universal human experiences.

Perhaps one of the key figures responsible for bringing existentialism from Europe and translating key concepts into psychotherapeutic practice is Rollo May. His writings have had a significant impact on existentially oriented practitioners. According to May, becoming a person is not an automatic process, yet people do have a desire to fulfill their potential. It takes courage to be, and our choices determine the kind of person we become. There is a constant struggle within us. Although we want to grow toward maturity and independence, we realize that expansion is often a painful process. Hence, the struggle is between the security of dependence and the delights and pains of growth. Along with May, two other significant contemporary sources of existential therapy in the United States are James Bugental (1987) and Irvin Yalom (1980).

Existentialism focuses on understanding of the person's subjective view of the world and, thus, is a phenomenological approach. Therapy is a journey taken by therapist and client into the world as perceived and experienced by the client. But this quest demands that the therapist also be in contact with his or her own phenomenological world. Bugental (1987) writes about life-changing psychotherapy, which is the effort to help clients examine how they have answered life's existential questions and challenge them to revise their answers in order to begin living authentically.

This approach does not focus on merely applying problem-solving techniques to the complex task of authentic living. Existential counseling does not aim at curing people in the traditional medical sense, because people are not viewed as being ill but as being sick of playing certain roles or being clumsy at living. What clients need is assistance in surveying the terrain so that they can decide which path to pursue. They are not changed by the therapist as much as they are helped in coming to terms with life in all its contradictions. Through the experience of existential therapy, clients acquire a sense of wisdom in learning how to distinguish between those aspects of life that they can change and those they cannot change. They gradually learn how to accept life in all its complexities and paradoxes. This process involves learning to face the inevitable problems, difficulties, disappointments, and crises that are a part of living. Clients come to understand that they are not cemented to a narrow range of responses, and thus they develop flexibility. They are better able to live with the givens and find the courage within themselves to deal with uncertainty. Therapy provides them with the opportunity to contemplate a life that is worthy of commitment (van Deurzen-Smith (1988, 1990a).

The Purpose of an Existential Group

The existential group represents a microcosm of the world in which participants live and function. Its members meet for the purpose of discovering themselves as they are by sharing their existential concerns. An existential group can be described as people making a commitment to a lifelong journey of self-exploration with three goals: (1) enabling members to become truthful with themselves, (2) widening their perspectives on themselves and the world around them, and (3) clarifying what gives meaning to their present and future life (van Deurzen-Smith, 1990a). The group provides the encouragement for members to begin listening to themselves and paying attention to their subjective experience. This process of inner searching gives emphasis to what members discover within their own stream of awareness when this stream is not directed by the therapist. By openly sharing and exploring universal personal concerns, members develop a sense of mutuality. The close ties that they feel with one another give them many opportunities for using the group culture differently from other aspects of their culture. The group becomes a place where people can be together in deeply meaningful ways.

Key Concepts

In this chapter we'll examine some key concepts of the existential approach and their implications for group practice. These concepts are self-awareness, self-determination and responsibility, existential anxiety, death and non-being, the search for meaning, the search for authenticity, and aloneness/relatedness. Rather than focusing on group techniques, this chapter stresses understanding how these key concepts can be applied in a group. Some of the major themes running through various existential writings are summarized and applied to group work.

Self-Awareness

The capacity for self-awareness separates us from other animals and enables us to make free choices. The greater our awareness, the greater our possibilities for freedom. Even though we are subject to the deterministic forces of sociocultural conditioning and to the limitations imposed by our genetic endowment, we are still able to choose based on our awareness of these limiting factors. As May (1961) writes, "No matter how great the forces victimizing the human being, man has the capacity to know that he is being victimized and thus to influence in some way how he will relate to his fate" (pp. 41–42). Furthermore, because of our self-awareness, we come to recognize the responsibility associated with the freedom to choose and to act.

IMPLICATIONS FOR GROUP WORK. As mentioned earlier, the basic goal of existential therapy is to expand self-awareness and thus increase the potential for choice. In groups this goal is pursued by helping members discover their unique "being-in-the-world." By asking themselves key questions, participants seek to define themselves and become aware of the central dimensions of their existence: "To what degree am I aware of who I am and where I am going? How do I experience my world? What meanings do I attach to the events I experience? How can I increase my self-awareness? In what concrete ways does expanded consciousness increase my range of alternatives?"

According to May (1983), the task of therapy is to illuminate existence. Clients try to become aware of their existence as fully as possible, which includes realizing their potentialities and learning to act on the basis of them. A central theme of the existential approach is taking existence seriously.

In the group situation participants have the opportunity to express their own unique feelings and their subjective views of the world. They are also explicitly confronted by others, and they learn to deal with the anxiety that arises from having to choose for themselves when they are stripped of the securities of their everyday roles. As we will see in detail later in the chapter, existentialists view anxiety in positive terms. Anxiety helps "individuate" us, it awakens us to the inauthenticity of merely being who others want us to be, and it reflects the understanding that we are unique.

I believe that group leaders need to alert the members of their groups to the price they must pay for seeking greater self-awareness. As people become more aware, they find it increasingly difficult to "go back home again." If living in ignorance of the quality of one's existence can lead to staleness, it can also bring a certain degree of contentment or, at least, security. As we open doors that were previously closed, we can expect to encounter more struggle as well as the potential for enhancing the quality of our living. The experience can be exciting and joyful but also frightening and at times depressing. This is an issue that should be mentioned during the early phases of a group.

What are the options that a higher degree of self-awareness permits us to recognize? Here are some of them:

- ◆ We can choose to expand our awareness, or we can choose to limit our vision of ourselves.
- ◆ We can determine the direction of our own lives, or we can allow other people and environmental forces to determine it for us.
- ◆ We can use our potential for action, or we can choose not to act.

- ◆ We can choose to establish meaningful ties with others, or we can choose to isolate ourselves.
- ◆ We can search for our own uniqueness, or we can allow our identity to be lost in conformity.
- ◆ We can create and find meaning in our life, or we can lead an empty and meaningless existence.
- ◆ We can engage in certain risks and experience the anxieties that accompany deciding for ourselves, or we can choose the security of dependence.
- ◆ We can make the most of the present by accepting the inevitability of our eventual death, or we can hide from this reality because of the anxiety it generates.

EXAMPLE. The following example is meant to illustrate how participants in a group can gradually achieve a higher level of awareness. This and the examples that illustrate the other key concepts in this chapter are drawn from my experience with the groups I have led. To protect the identity of the clients, I have changed the names and the specific circumstances, and I have chosen examples that have a universal quality—that is, situations that occur frequently in a group.

When Crystal first entered the group, she could see no value in expressing intense emotions and insisted that she *had* to be rational no matter what. She tried very hard to keep her feelings harnessed at all times, because she was afraid that she'd "go crazy" if she allowed herself to feel intensely. This need to tightly control her feelings manifested itself in several ways. For example, when other group members relived painful emotional events, she panicked and tried to leave the room, and she often attempted to defuse the expression of intense emotions by others in the group. During one session, however, another person's work triggered some painful memories in Crystal, which she felt fully because, for some reason, she allowed herself to relive a scene from her childhood related to her parents' divorce. Suddenly she became that frightened child again, pleading with her parents to stay together and letting herself "go emotionally out of control."

This unexpected experience made Crystal aware that she had been keeping a lid on her strong feelings and that her defenses against "hurting too much" had resulted in her difficulty in getting close to others, in expressing anger, and in manifesting the love she claimed she felt for her family now. She also learned that she wouldn't "go crazy" by permitting herself to experience the depth of her feelings. After that experience she chose to open herself to feelings and not to run out of the room when she was afraid she couldn't take the intense emotions of other members.

Self-Determination and Personal Responsibility

Another existential theme is that we are self-determining beings, free to choose among alternatives and therefore responsible for directing our lives and shaping our destinies. The existentialists' view is that although we are thrust into the world, how we live and what we become are the result of our choices. As Sartre (1971) puts it, our existence is a given, but we do not have, and cannot have, a fixed, settled "nature," or "essence." We are constantly faced with having to choose the kind of person we want to become, and as long as we live, we must continue to choose. Sartre remarks: "Man being condemned to be free carries the weight of the whole world on his shoulders; he is responsible for the world and for himself as a way of being" (p. 553). For Sartre, we are free in that we are nothing but what we *do,* and what we do is not the result of our past. However, we are much given to making excuses, thus acting in "bad faith."

Russell (1978) notes that in Sartre's view, nothing in the world has a meaning independent of us, and we are responsible for the world as a significant place. Russell adds: "Each time we act we thereby choose and create ourselves as we want to be, and this is never finished—what we are is never settled—but is created in each of the deeds that constitute us" (p. 262). We are responsible for the consequences of our actions and any failure to act: "I author the meaningfulness of my world in giving significance to my situation. . . . It is when I see myself as the *author* of my actions and (relatedly) of the significance I give my world that I get an enlarged sense of my responsibility for this" (p. 261).

Viktor Frankl, an existential psychiatrist, stresses the relationship between freedom and responsibility and insists that freedom can never be taken from us, because we can at least choose our attitude toward any given set of circumstances. To support this statement, Frankl (1963) draws from his own experiences in a German concentration camp, where the prisoners were stripped of every semblance of outward freedom. He contends that even in a situation of such extreme powerlessness, people can ultimately be their own master, because the attitude they assume toward their suffering is of their own choosing: "Life ultimately means taking responsibility to find the right answer to its problems and to fulfill the tasks which it constantly sets for each individual" (p. 122). Frankl believes that human freedom is not freedom *from* conditions but, rather, the ability to take a stand in the *face* of conditions.

Frankl's brand of existential therapy, *logotherapy (logos* = meaning), teaches that meaning in life cannot be dictated but can only be discovered by searching in our own existential situation. Indeed, we have the will to meaning, and we have the freedom to find meaning in how we think and in what we do. Frankl believes that the goal is not to attain peace of mind but to experience meaning in a healthy striving. This search for meaning, which is our central quest, enables us to make sense of our existence despite guilt, suffering, and the inevitability of death (Gould, 1993). We are also responsible for (but not to blame for) the symptoms that restrict our ability to live freely and fully. It is essential that we recognize and accept our part in creating the quality of our existence, for life does not simply happen to us. We are capable of actively influencing our thoughts, feelings, and actions. Until we accept our capacity for freedom, we will not change. If we wait around for others to change or for the environment to change, we may well increase our misery and hopelessness instead of taking action to make something happen differently.

IMPLICATIONS FOR GROUP WORK. The members of an existential group are confronted over and over with the fact that they cannot escape from freedom and that they are responsible for their existence. Accepting this freedom and this responsibility generates anxiety, and so does the risk associated with making choices. Another goal of the existential group is to help participants face and deal with these anxieties. The main task for the group leader with regard to the issue of self-determination is to confront members with the reality of their freedom and of the ways in which they are restricting or denying it. Group participants sometimes present themselves as victims, talk about their feelings of helplessness and powerlessness, and place the blame for their miseries on others and on external circumstances. A good place for clients to start on the road to greater self-determination is to become aware of the roles they have been programmed to play. When people come to *believe* that they can direct their own destiny, they ultimately assume control of their life.

Lantz (1993) believes that some clients are so externally focused on the requirements of social living that they have limited awareness of their own feelings, goals, thoughts, responsibilities, fantasies, and expectations. He adds that these clients usually benefit from a treatment approach that introduces them to their own strengths and potentials. Because *group logotherapy* promotes internal reflection and develops internal self-awareness, Lantz recommends this approach "for emancipated adults who need to replace old interpersonal patterns that once were useful in the family of origin but now create difficulties for the client away from the original family" (p. 67). He also maintains that group logotherapy is often the treatment of choice for children, adolescents, and adults who are not living in a natural family group or who are living in a group that is unable to support their changes.

Yalom (1980) contends that the group provides the optimal conditions for therapeutic work on personal responsibility. If the group has a here-and-now focus, the members can be encouraged to observe how they are creating a victimlike stance for themselves. In Yalom's view, members are responsible for the interpersonal position they assume in the group, which also gives a glimpse of how they behave in life situations. Members who describe themselves as being victimized by external conditions can be challenged. Through feedback, members learn to see themselves through others' eyes, and they learn the ways in which their behavior affects others. Further, they learn how the group situation represents situations in their everyday life. Building on these discoveries, they can take responsibility for making changes.

From Yalom's perspective, the existential group leader encourages the members to assume genuine responsibility for their functioning as a group.

In this way individual members learn ways to take greater responsibility for their lives:

> The interactional therapy group enhances responsibility assumption not only by making members aware of their personal contribution to their unsatisfying life situations but also by accentuating each member's role in the conduct of the group. The underlying principle is that if members assume responsibility for the functioning of the group, then they become aware that they have the ability (and obligation) to assume responsibility in all spheres of life [p. 240].

It is important to recognize that existentialism represents a way of thinking that influences the members of an existential group. Over time, they are likely to acknowledge their own freedom and responsibility as they have significant moments of insight. However, it is a mistake to conduct the group with the superficial aim of changing the vocabulary of the members. A group leader who preaches the language of freedom and choice, who prematurely coaches members to merely talk about how they are "choosing" this or that, will only encourage people to go through the motions of accepting these ideas (J. Michael Russell, personal communication, March 22, 1992).

EXAMPLE. Edward had reluctantly joined one of my groups. I say "reluctantly" because he had serious misgivings about the value of participating in a group. At 62, Edward had settled into a dull, predictable, but comfortable and safe lifestyle as a successful business executive. When he joined, he presented himself with this statement: "I don't know if this group will do me any good or not. Frankly, I think that I'm too old to change and that what I have is the most I can hope to get from life. I believe that things will probably stay as they are." In spite of his own statement and in spite of the fact that his life was orderly and safe, he felt that he was "drying up" and that life had lost zest. He was ready for a change, even though he was not sure whether change was possible.

Through his involvement in the group, Edward began to realize that he did have options—many more than he had thought possible. All along, he had blamed his wife, his three sons, and his daughter for the fact that he couldn't change jobs and live the kind of life he wanted for himself. He was, of course, avoiding the responsibility for his own problems by focusing on what his family expected, often without ever verifying whether they did expect what he thought they did.

The other members and I challenged Edward to begin thinking for himself about how *he* wanted his life to be different. I asked him questions such as "If you were to continue living for the rest of your life as you are now, with no basic changes, how would you feel about it?" "Assume that your family would be willing to make the changes in lifestyle that you want to make. How would your life be different a year from now? And five years from now?" "What steps can you take today that will help you make some of the changes you want? What is preventing you from taking these steps?"

Another dimension of an existential approach consists of helping people face their own attitude and situation in life. For example, Edward might be encouraged to take note of the way in which he makes himself comfortable by choosing to settle for the same routines and pretending to himself that this is all that there is to life, or at least all that *he* is capable of achieving for himself. Van Deurzen-Smith (1990a) reminds us that we often pretend that life has determined our situation to the degree that we have no real choices left. Crises provide us with evidence to the contrary, however. The safety within a group allows members such as Edward to explore the meaning of crises as a place for rediscovering opportunities and challenges that have been forgotten. An existential group leader could help Edward face the actual process of decay that he is allowing to take place. Once he recognizes his ways of engaging in self-deception and sees that he is choosing to rest on his laurels, he can decide to take a different direction.

Existential Anxiety

From the existential viewpoint, anxiety is a basic characteristic of being human. Thus, it is not necessarily pathological but, on the contrary, can be a strong motivational force toward growth. Anxiety results from having to make choices without clear guidelines and without knowing what the outcome will be and from being aware that we are ultimately responsible for the consequences of our actions. In the words of the Danish philosopher Soren Kierkegaard (1813–1855), existential anxiety is "the dizziness of freedom." At some level we know that for new dimensions of ourselves to emerge, old parts of ourselves must die. The knowledge that in order to grow we must exchange familiar and secure ways for new and unknown ones is in itself a source of anxiety.

From the perspective of van Deurzen-Smith (1988, 1990a, 1991), existential anxiety is basic to living with awareness and being fully alive. In fact, the courage to live fully entails accepting the reality of death and the anxiety associated with uncertainty. Although we may not welcome this anxiety, it is the price we must pay for becoming what we are capable of becoming. Some people dull their sensitivity as a way of avoiding the basic challenges of life, and others find different ways of disguising their anxiety. Yet underneath the surface of their coping styles, people experience anxiety as an ever-present threat.

IMPLICATIONS FOR GROUP WORK. Bugental (1978) describes therapeutic work with existential anxiety as a stripping away of defenses, much like the peeling of an onion. At the core of therapy, clients eventually come to terms with the underlying conditions of being human that are related to the anxiety they experience. These sources of existential anxiety must be faced and worked through in therapy; they involve recognition of our separateness and our need to be with others, of our guilt over not living authentically, of the emptiness in the universe and lack of meaning, of the burden of responsibility associated with choosing for ourselves, and of our fear of death and nonbeing. As therapy progresses and the resistances are peeled away, clients often painfully recognize how much energy they have put into maintaining an idealized image of themselves that is impossible to achieve. They also see that they must let go of old images of themselves that lead to a restricted existence. As clients give up their phony roles, they are able to bring a renewed quality to their living. A death of their old self occurs, which allows room for some kind of breakthrough experience. Yet such a process is typically anxiety provoking, for clients are giving up rigid ways of being that are familiar.

In existential group therapy, members are assisted in coming to terms with the paradoxes of existence such as life and death, success and failure, freedom and necessity, and certainty and doubt. As members recognize the realities of their birth and death, their confrontation with pain and suffering, the need to struggle for survival, and their basic fallibility, anxiety surfaces. Thus, anxiety is an indicator of the level of awareness that group participants allow. Existential anxiety is exposed in a group, especially when members explore ways in which they have adjusted too comfortably to a status quo style of living designed to mask basic insecurity and anxiety. Van Deurzen-Smith (1991) maintains that an essential aim of existential therapy is not to make life seem easier or safer but to encourage clients to be more receptive to recognizing and dealing with the sources of insecurity and anxiety. Facing existential anxiety involves viewing life as an adventure, rather than hiding behind securities that seem to offer protection. As she puts it: "We need to question and scrape away at the easy answers and expose ourselves to some of the anxiety that can bring us back to life in a real and deep way" (1991, p. 46).

It is essential for the group leader to recognize existential anxiety and guide group members in finding ways of dealing with it constructively. Existential therapy does not aim at eliminating anxiety, for doing so would be to cut off a source of vitality. Leaders have the task of encouraging members to deal with their existential anxiety and to develop the courage to face life squarely (van Deurzen-Smith, 1988).

Therefore, one of the leader's tasks is to encourage participants to accept anxiety as growth-producing and to help them find the courage to face and to fully experience their anxieties. The next step is to encourage members to make a commitment to action. Through the support of the leader and of other participants in the group, the individual can be inspired to explore unknown paths and to investigate new dimensions of self. This search can lead to even greater anxiety, but if the person is in the process of growth, he or she knows that anxiety doesn't have to be devastating and that it is the price one must pay for breaking out of constricting modes of existence.

EXAMPLE.   For much of her life Ann had allowed others to make decisions for her. She had uncritically accepted her parents' religious values and had become dependent on her church to make decisions for her. At this time in her life she was struggling with following the values that she had grown up with. Through her work in a group, she came to see more and more clearly that if she wanted to grow, she needed to take more responsibility for her choices. Thus, she decided to look within herself for strength and direction. This decision brought her a great deal of anxiety. She continued to ask herself: "Am I doing the right thing?" and "What if the ethical decisions I'm making now on my own are wrong?"

It took Ann some time to begin to trust herself and even longer to let go of the need to lean on some kind of authority for all her answers and for security. A little at a time, however, she began to experience a new sense of power, the exhilarating feeling that *she* was directing her life, even though she kept struggling all along with conflicts and doubts. Surely she would have been more comfortable had she continued to rely on external guidance. Yet when she realized that she had allowed others to make most of her major decisions, she also saw how she had given up control over her life. In choosing for herself, she still felt anxiety over not having a guarantee that she was doing the right thing.

Death and Nonbeing

The existentialist considers death as essential to the discovery of meaning and purpose in life (Heidegger, 1962). Life has meaning precisely because it must end; the present is precious because it is all we really have (May, 1983). It is our temporal nature that makes us feel the urgency to do something with our life, to make a choice between affirming life by trying to become the person we are capable of becoming and allowing life to slip by us and eventually realizing that we've never been truly alive. Yalom (1980) summarizes this notion as follows:

> Death and life are interdependent: though the physicality of death destroys us, the *idea* of death saves us. Recognition of death contributes a sense of poignancy to life, provides a radical shift of life perspective, and can transport one from a mode of living characterized by diversions, tranquilization, and petty anxieties to a more authentic mode [p. 40].

Mullan (1979) makes the point that death is an inevitability to be dealt with and accepted in the existential group, since it is always present. For members to face this issue and work with the anxiety it brings, the leader cannot ignore it. According to Mullan:

> The death motif is awakening and challenging and not, as some claim, morbid and nihilistic. Through its use patients are bombarded with the insignificance of their ordinary pursuits. Their usual customs, routines, conventions, and habits all come under fire. Once they have faced the certainty of their death, many persons cease to be victims of the past in which their parents' irrational authority was so pronounced. Suddenly they find that they must act now and with greater intensity than before [p. 173].

Thus, humans, as the only creatures with a strong sense of the future, need to deal with the end of life, which Heidegger (1962) calls "cessation of possibility." Because many of us are afraid of facing the reality of our own death and the anxiety that goes with it, we might attempt to escape the awareness of this reality. But the price for trying to flee from the confrontation with nonbeing is awesome. In the words of May (1961): "The price for denying death is undefined anxiety, self-alienation. To completely understand himself, man must confront death, become aware of personal death" (p. 65). Frankl (1963) concurs and adds that it is not *how long* we live but *how* we live that determines the quality and meaningfulness of our life.

IMPLICATIONS FOR GROUP WORK. Awareness of death and the anxiety it generates has significant implications for the practice of group work. The concern with living life fully, rather than merely existing, is a recurrent theme in many groups. Generally I tackle this theme by encouraging group members to ask themselves honestly how they feel about the quality of their lives. Then I ask them to answer this same question as if they knew that they were about to die. How do the two answers differ? Have they made decisions that were not carried through, or have they ignored opportunities for change? By reflecting on their unfinished business, participants may come to realize that they are not living the kind of life they'd like to live, and they may be able to identify the reasons for this unsatisfactory existence. Sometimes dreams about one's dying may symbolize the coming to a close of one phase of life, of some interest, work, or relationship.

I find it valuable to expand the concept of physical death to other kinds of death. Even though we are physically alive, we may be dead or dying in important areas of life. Perhaps we are numb to our feelings or caught up in deadening roles. We may have lost our intellectual curiosity and wonderment about life. Perhaps our relationships with significant people are characterized by routine and devitalizing acts. What we do may have lost meaning. A group can be a good place to recognize the areas in which we have gone stale and to confront ourselves with what we are willing to do in order to change and flourish again.

The process of change always entails allowing parts of us to die in order to make room for new growth. And growth often demands that we be willing to let go of familiar ways of being. We may need to experience a period of mourning over our losses before we can move forward and establish new patterns. Groups offer a safe place to express this sadness, to explore the ambivalence that generally accompanies change, and to experiment with new ways of being.

EXAMPLE. In another book, *I Never Knew I Had a Choice* (Corey & Corey, 1993), I discuss the concept of *freedom in dying*—the notion that even in dying we still have choices concerning how we face and deal with what is happening to us. As I was writing that section of the book, a friend and former group member, Jim Morelock, was dying. He permitted me to use his real name and to share some of the significant moments in his dying.

Jim was 25 years old. He was full of life and seemed to have a bright future when he discovered that he had a rare form of cancer. In the group Jim talked about his fears of dying and expressed his anger about the reality that he wouldn't be able to put to use much of what he had learned about himself, because his time was so limited. As he put it, "I finally learned that I have a lot to offer and that I'm lovable. I'd sure like to hang around and enjoy all those people that love me!"

His own gifts and active interest in life, as well as his counseling and group experience, enabled Jim to face death with courage and to infuse it with meaning. Even after he learned that his illness was terminal, he continued to take a course at the university, because he liked the contact with people there. He decided not to remain in a hospital and not to undergo chemotherapy, primarily because he didn't want to prolong his life if he couldn't live it fully. Jim made a choice to accept God into his life, which gave him peace and serenity. He did many of the things he most wanted to do, maintaining an active interest in life and in the world around him. More than anyone I know, Jim took care of unfinished business. He said everything he wanted to say to his family and close friends and made all the arrangements for his own funeral, including asking my wife, Marianne, to deliver the eulogy.

Jim showed me that his style of dying was no different from his style of living, and through him I have learned much about dying and about living. Shortly before his death, Jim told me that he didn't have regrets about the way he had lived his life, because in those short 25 years he had lived more fully than many older people. He also commented that although we may not have a choice concerning our losses in dying, we can still choose our attitude toward death.

The Search for Meaning

The struggle for a sense of significance and purpose in life is a distinctively human characteristic. We search for meaning and personal identity, and we raise existential questions: "Who am I? Where am I going and why? Why am I here? What gives my life purpose and meaning?" For the existentialists, life does not have positive meaning in itself; it is up to us to create meaning. As we struggle in a world that often appears meaningless and even absurd, we challenge values we never challenged before, we discover new facets of ourselves, we try to reconcile conflicts and discrepancies, and, in so doing, we create our meaning in the world.

Frankl has devoted his career to developing an existential approach to therapy that is grounded on the role of meaning in life. According to him, the central human concern is to discover meaning that will give one's life direction. On the basis of his clinical work and study, Frankl has concluded that a lack of meaning is the major source of existential stress and anxiety in modern times. He views existential neurosis as the experience of meaninglessness. Many people come to therapy because of an *existential vacuum,* or a feeling of inner void that results from not pursuing meaning. Therefore, according to Frankl, therapy should be designed to help clients find meaning in their lives.

Frankl (1963) says that there are many ways of finding meaning— through work, through loving, through suffering, and through doing for others. According to him, the therapist's function is not to tell clients what their particular meaning in life should be but to encourage them to discover meaning for themselves. He believes that even suffering can be a source of growth and that if we have the courage to experience our suffering, we can find meaning in it. Suffering can be turned into achievement by the stand we take in the face of it. By confronting pain, despair, and death and by trying to understand their meaning for us, we turn the negative sides of life into triumph.

IMPLICATIONS FOR GROUP WORK. Both the issue of finding meaning and the related question of challenging and perhaps discarding values that are no longer meaningful are commonly explored in groups. Discarding old values without finding new and more suitable ones to replace them is a concern that many participants share. Some people live by a value system that they have never challenged and that was handed down to them and merely incorporated. Others have lost their own identity by submitting to group pressure, thus denying their inner reality in order to conform to social mores.

One of the tasks of the therapeutic process is to confront clients with evidence of the fact that they are living by unexamined values that no longer contribute to a meaningful existence. We may not be responsible for having acquired values that don't help our quest for meaning, but we are certainly responsible for clinging to them and for failing to find new ones. Some useful questions that can be explored in a group setting are these:

- ◆ "Do you like the direction of your life? If not, what are you doing about it?"
- ◆ "What are the aspects of your life that satisfy you most?"
- ◆ "What is preventing you from doing what you really want to do?"

With the support of the group, participants can find the strength to create an internally derived value system that is consistent with their way of being. This process is likely to generate anxiety, at least for a time, and they will flounder in the absence of clear-cut values. The leader's job is to remind these people that learning to develop the self-trust necessary to look within, discover one's own values, and live by them is a long and difficult process that requires determination and patience.

EXAMPLE. Priscilla was reared with extremely conventional values, and she had never really examined them. She felt compelled to be a "proper lady" at all times, as if her parents were watching over her shoulder. Whenever she was doing something that she thought her parents wouldn't approve of, she seemed to "hear mother and father speaking," telling her what she *should* do and what she *ought* to feel. In various group exercises, she "became" her parents and spoke for them by lecturing each of us about how we ought to change our ways.

At one point I urged her to act as if she had no choice but to remain forever the nice and proper lady her parents expected her to be and asked her to exaggerate this ladylike behavior in the group for several sessions. Afterward she reported that doing so "made her sick" and that she would change, no matter how difficult the task was going to be. Although Priscilla still respected some of the core values she had learned at home, she wanted the freedom to retain some of those values and discard others without feeling guilty. Her work in the group and outside of it gave her new freedom to develop her own set of values—values that were meaningful to her and that allowed her to live by her own expectations and not by those of others.

The Search for Authenticity

The theologian Paul Tillich (1952) uses the phrase "the courage to be" to convey the essence of the spirit it takes to affirm ourselves and to live from the inside. Discovering, creating, and maintaining the core deep within our being is a difficult and never-ending struggle.

According to van Deurzen-Smith (1988), such authentic living is more of a process than a static end result. Briefly put, it means that we are true to ourselves. Living authentically entails engagement in doing what is worthwhile as we see it. This kind of living provides a deep sense of inner peace. Yet authenticity is no easy matter. It is only when we stop trying to be cured of the paradoxes of life, van Deurzen-Smith reminds us, that we can be truly alive. She suggests that "earth is a place somewhere between heaven and hell, where much pain and much joy is to be had and where some degree of wisdom can make all the difference" (1988, p. 238).

When we lead an authentic existence, we are constantly becoming the person we are capable of becoming. Living authentically also entails knowing and accepting our limits. The "Serenity Prayer" offers a good example of this knowledge and acceptance: "God grant me the serenity to accept the things I cannot change, courage to change the things I can, and wisdom to know the difference."

A quote with a different twist, one that Frankl is fond of using, is Goethe's admonition: "If we take man as he is, we make him worse; but if we take him as he should be, we help him become what he can be." Frankl sees it as the therapist's task to challenge clients to become their full and authentic selves by getting engaged in life and making commitments. His logotherapy, since it is concerned with people's spiritual dimensions and higher aspirations, provides inspiration to continually seek the meaning that is necessary to live authentically. The essence of defining oneself is captured in an adage I saw in a church in Hawaii: "Who you are is God's gift to you; what you make of yourself is your gift to God."

Those who typically ignore their inner promptings in a perennial quest for conformity lose themselves in the values and standards of others. One of the most common fears expressed by people in groups is that if they take an honest look at themselves, they will discover that they are just empty shells with no core and no substance. Therefore, they are afraid of shedding masks and pretenses, because, once those are gone, nothing will be left.

A concept related to inauthenticity is guilt. *Existential guilt* grows out of a sense of incompleteness and the realization that we are viewing our life through someone else's eyes. Ultimately, the loss of the sense of being becomes psychological sickness. To the extent that we allow others to design our life, we experience a restricted existence.

IMPLICATIONS FOR GROUP WORK. A group provides a powerful context in which to look at oneself, decide the degree to which one is a fully functioning person as opposed to the reflection of what others expect, and consider what choices might be more authentically one's own. Members can openly share their fears related to living in unfulfilling ways and come to see how they have compromised their integrity. The group offers many opportunities for tackling life's challenges. Members can gradually discover ways in which they have lost their direction and can begin to be more true to themselves. They will learn that others cannot give them easy answers to the problems of living. Certainly, existential group leaders will not prescribe simple solutions, for they know that this is inconsistent with helping members live in authentic ways.

EXAMPLE. The case of Martha, who at 45 had devoted a major portion of her life to her family, represents a situation characteristic of many women who have been members of my groups and personal-growth workshops. For most of her life she had depended almost totally on her roles as wife, mother, and homemaker as sources of identity. As her daughters and sons entered high school and then college and finally left home, she kept asking herself more and more frequently: "Is there more to life than what I've done so far? Who am I besides all the roles I've responsibly filled? What do *I* want to do with the rest of my life?"

Martha returned to the university and obtained a degree in human services and psychology, a critical turning point in her life because of the many new doors that her degree opened for her. She engaged in a number of projects that enriched her life, including specialized work with the elderly. Through her program of studies, she joined several intensive personal-growth workshops, which gave her the opportunity to pose and debate questions such as "Do I have the courage to find out if I can create a new identity for myself? Will I be able to withstand pressures from my family to remain the way they want me to be? Can I give to others and at the same time give to myself?" These questions indicated Martha's growing awareness that she needed to be a person in her own right and that she wanted to live an authentic existence. Her self-questioning also showed that she knew that making choices entails doubts and struggles that one must resolve for oneself.

Aloneness and Relatedness

The existentialists believe that ultimately we are alone—that only we can give a sense of meaning to our lives, decide how we will live, find our own answers, and decide whether we will be or not be. Because awareness of our ultimate aloneness can be frightening, some of us try to avoid it by throwing ourselves into casual relationships and frantic activities, trusting that they will numb our fear and anguish.

We also have the choice of experiencing our aloneness and trying to find a center of meaning and direction within ourselves. Only if we make this choice and succeed at establishing our own identity as an individual can we relate genuinely and meaningfully to others. We must stand alone before we can truly stand beside another.

There is a paradox in the proposition that we are existentially both alone and related. Yet, it is this very paradox that describes the human condition. We are social beings, and we depend on interpersonal relationships for our humanness. We have a desire for intimacy, a hope to be significant in another's world, and a desire to feel that another's presence is important in our world. But unless we can stand alone and find our own strength within ourselves, we cannot have nourishing relationships with others, based on fulfillment and not on deprivation.

IMPLICATIONS FOR GROUP WORK. In groups, participants have the opportunity to relate to others in meaningful ways, learn to be themselves in the company of other people, and find reward and nourishment in the relationships they establish. They also learn that it is not in others that they can find the answers to questions about significance and purpose in life. If their struggle for self-awareness is successful, they come to realize that no matter how valuable the relationships, they are ultimately on their own.

The friendships that participants establish within the group are valuable also because they teach people how to relate to others outside of the group. In a group, people recognize their own struggles in others, and this often results in a bond. Even though they may accept that ultimately they are existentially alone, they also come to realize that they are not alone in their struggles and that others, too, are courageously looking at themselves and trying to establish their own identities.

EXAMPLE. The case of Zeke shows that a person can be with others and at the same time be very much alone. During a group session Zeke said that he felt cut off from everyone in the group and described himself as a "spectator who seems out of place." I asked him if he would be willing to experiment with *really* separating himself from the group and observing us from a distance. He agreed to leave the room, sit outside on the balcony, and observe what was going on through the window. I asked him to be aware of what he was thinking and feeling as he sat out there observing. He was told to return to the group when he was ready to talk about what he had experienced sitting on the outside.

When he returned, Zeke said that for the first time he had realized how safe it was for him to keep himself in a spectator role, that he was beginning to hate this role, and that he was ready to do something different. I asked him if he would go around to each person in the group and complete these two sentences: "One way I have kept you at a distance is by . . ."; "One way I could be closer to you is by . . ." After he had "made the rounds," he described the circumstances in which he typically felt alone, even when surrounded by many people. He spoke of his desire to achieve intimacy and of his fears of approaching people. His work in the group had intensified his attempts to keep himself separate but finally resulted in a desire to change.

Role and Functions of the Group Leader

Unlike many other group approaches the existential model puts more emphasis on experiencing the client in the present moment than on using a particular set of techniques. May (1983) emphasizes that technique follows understanding. This means that the primary concern of the therapist is to be *with* the client and to understand his or her subjective world. Questions concerning therapeutic technique are subordinate to this quest for understanding. There are no "right" techniques in this approach, because the task is accomplished through the therapeutic encounter between client and therapist.

In the existential view therapy is a partnership and a shared venture between the therapist and the client. To develop this partnership, therapists focus on the human side of the person-to-person relationship. From the existential perspective, therapists must bring their own subjectivity into their work, and it is essential that they demonstrate presence if they are to develop an effective working relationship with members. A central role of existential leaders is to create a therapeutic alliance, for it is assumed that change comes from the relationship itself. This climate for change will not come about if the leader maintains a strictly objective orientation, is psychologically absent from the group, and is merely a skilled but impersonal technician. Bugental (1987) puts this idea beautifully:

> The therapeutic alliance is the powerful joining of forces which energizes and supports the long, difficult, and frequently painful work of life-changing psychotherapy. The conception of the therapist here is not of a disinterested observer-technician but of a fully alive human companion for the client. In this regard my view is in marked contrast to the traditional notion of the therapist as a skilled but objective director of therapeutic processes [p. 49].

The existential group leader is free to draw from techniques that flow from many other orientations. In her discussion of the role of the therapist, van Deurzen-Smith (1990a) points out that the existential approach is well known for its antitechnique orientation. She emphasizes the importance of therapists' reaching sufficient depth and openness in their own lives to allow them to venture along with clients in their murky waters without getting lost. She writes that therapists who are fully available to their clients as they explore their deepest issues are implying that their own being is subject to change. In the therapeutic endeavor, both the group members and the group leader are bound to be transformed if they allow themselves to be touched by life.

In the group context, change is brought about not only by the relationship with the leader but also by relationships with other members. Thus, a primary role of the leader is to foster meaningful relationships among participants. This can be done by having them focus on key existential concerns and providing a climate in which these concerns can be fully explored. A therapeutic community is thus established, based on the commonality of shared struggles. The members make a commitment to confront one another about their unused potentials and inauthentic behaviors and to support one another in the common endeavor to open the door to oneself.

The leader sets the tone for the group not by introducing techniques and by *doing something* but, rather, by *being* and *becoming somebody*. Mullan (1978) describes how challenges by the group leader bring about personality changes in members (including changes in thinking, feeling, and behaving). The group sessions tend to shake up the conventional ways in which members view the world. When their status quo is jarred, they have a better chance of facing themselves and of changing.

Evaluation of the Existential Approach

Contributions and Strengths of the Approach

From a conceptual standpoint I value many features of the existential approach and have incorporated them into my practice. I work on the basic assumption that people have the capacity to become increasingly self-aware and that expansion of awareness results in greater freedom to choose their own directions in life. I share the existentialists' view that we are not bundles of instincts or the products of conditioning. Thus, I base my group work on the premises that people do not have to remain victims of their past or of the external world and that they have the power to decide for themselves and take action, so that their lives are their own and not a reflection of the expectations of others. For me, this assumption has implications for conducting a wide range of groups for victims of rape, battering, crime, and various other forms of abuse. Although I agree that people can indeed be victims of forces outside of themselves, I also believe that the existential approach can help such individuals reclaim or acquire a sense of power.

I value the existential approach because it has brought the person back into central focus and because it addresses itself to the central question of what it means to be human. This approach humanizes psychotherapy and reduces the chances of its becoming a mechanical process in the hands of technicians. I especially value the focus on the therapist's being fully present in the therapeutic encounter. This full presence implies having access to one's own feelings and being able to express them appropriately and in a timely way. Bugental (1987) maintains that through the therapist's concern, sensitivity, and presence, clients are invited to disclose the core life issues they are struggling with. If therapists are not humanly involved in their work, their clients will not be supported as they endure the painful and frightening self-confrontations that are necessary for major life changes to occur.

This approach encourages and challenges me as a group leader to tap and bring to my work my own experiences and my very humanness. It leaves my own modes of existence open to challenge, because I couldn't be genuine with others or help them face their existential concerns without doing the same in my own life. My willingness to remain open to my own struggles determines the degree to which I can be a significant and positive influence for others in a group.

I appreciate the existential view that techniques follow understanding, because it lessens the danger of abusing techniques. Too often leaders use techniques merely to "get things going" in a group. When the focus is on understanding the world of the participant, the leader's first concern is with genuinely grasping the core struggles of others and *then* drawing on certain techniques to help the participants explore these struggles more fully in the group. Existentially oriented group leaders can draw from the techniques of most of the other approaches discussed in this book. Van Deurzen-Smith (1990a) agrees that it is possible to combine existential work with approaches such as the psychoanalytic, person-centered, and Gestalt. Although I consider myself as having strong existential leanings, I do employ a wide range of techniques drawn from systems such as psychodrama, Adlerian therapy, Gestalt therapy, the cognitive-behavioral therapies, and reality therapy.

Van Deurzen-Smith (1990a) identifies the clients and problems that are most suited to an existential approach. This is a form of therapy for helping clients who are interested and committed to dealing with their problems about living, rather than for curing pathology or removing symptoms. The approach has particular relevance for people who feel alienated from the current expectations of society or for those who are searching for meaning in their lives. It tends to work well with people who are at a crossroads, coping with the changes of personal circumstances such as bereavement or loss of employment. Van Deurzen-Smith believes that existential therapy works better with individuals who are willing to challenge the status quo in the world. It can be useful for people who are on the edge of existence, such as those who are dying, people who are working through a developmental or situational crisis, and those who are starting a new phase of life.

Bugental and Bracke (1992) write that the value and vitality of a psychotherapeutic approach depend on its ability to help clients deal with the sources of pain and dissatisfaction in their lives. They contend that the existential orientation is particularly suited to offering meaningful assistance to individuals who are experiencing a lack of a centered awareness of being. Cushman (1990) has written about the *empty self*—whose emptiness results from failing to listen to our internal voice or from not trusting our sense of direction. This emptiness is manifested in several ways: through depression, through the absence of a purpose for life, through a lack of clear priorities, through addiction to food or drugs, and through other means of striving to fill the void. Many group members complain that they feel a hole in their lives, and that even though they attempt to fill this emptiness of self, they are not successful. Unless they confront their fears and the sources that are blocking their ability to live fully, they are likely to strive in vain to numb the pain created by this inner void. An existential group can be instrumental in encouraging the members to face themselves courageously and deal with the inauthentic aspects of their living.

Limitations of the Approach

Many of the existentialist concepts are quite abstract and difficult to apply in practice. Existential theorists such as Kierkegaard, Heidegger, and Sartre were not writing for group counselors and therapists! Existentialism began as a formal philosophical movement, and although it eventually led to existential approaches within both psychology and psychiatry, its philosophical nature still dominates. Both beginning and advanced group practitioners who are not of a philosophical turn of mind tend to find many of the existential concepts lofty, abstract, and elusive. Even those group counselors who are sympathetic to the core ideas of this perspective sometimes struggle with knowing how to apply these concepts to the practice of group work. In relationship to this criticism, however, van Deurzen-Smith (personal communication, October 22, 1992) observes that it is not so much a matter of applying existentialist philosophy but one of allowing it to educate group leaders on the concrete and practical issues of life that are relevant to all human beings. In this sense, existential group work has little to do with existentialism but everything to do with life.

What has been said does not mean that the existential approach is about intellectualizing. Indeed, it focuses on subjective phenomena such as a person's basic impressions, ideas, intuitions, and feelings. However, the approach is often misconstrued as being primarily an intellectual one. As van Deurzen-Smith (1990a) points out, some existential therapists tend to emphasize the cognitive aspects of a client's concerns, and some clients are attracted to the approach believing that they can avoid tapping their senses, feelings, and intuitions. She suggests that a good existential therapist would address all these different levels of human experience, believing that openness to exploring these aspects of being is a requisite for self-understanding.

Below is a summary list of some of the other limitations of the existential approach as identified by van Deurzen-Smith (1990a):

◆ It is not particularly relevant for people who are uninterested in examining their basic assumptions and who would rather not explore the foundation of their human existence.
◆ Those clients who want relief from specific symptoms or who are seeking problem-solving methods will generally not find much value in this orientation.
◆ The existential therapist functions in the role of a consultant who can provide clients with support in facing up to the truth of their lives.

For those who are looking for a therapist who will direct them or who will function as a substitute parent, this approach will have little to offer.

♦ Being an effective existential practitioner implies a great deal of maturity, life experience, and intensive supervision and training. It is easy to envision the dangers posed by therapists who have a shallow grasp of this approach and who deceive both themselves and their clients into thinking that they possess the requisite wisdom.

Applying the Existential Approach with Multicultural Populations

According to van Deurzen-Smith (1990a), because the existential approach does not dictate a particular way of viewing or relating to reality, it is very suitable for people living in a foreign culture or for individuals who are diverse with respect to class, ethnicity, and race. One quality of this approach is its flexibility in therapeutic style. Existential therapists are willing to shift their stance when the situation requires it. Furthermore, they attempt to free themselves of their preconceptions and prejudices as much as possible. They respect the uniqueness of the particular situation of each client.

Those clients who are willing to participate in a group experience are frequently experiencing psychological pain, and they are often faced with a crisis and feel helpless. Out of this helplessness they often experience their lives as being out of their control. For example, a woman who is being abused by her husband may be convincing herself that there are no options and that she must accept whatever harsh treatment comes her way. She may be unwilling to even consider leaving an abusive relationship out of fear of what would happen to her children and herself. If she is in a group, this woman may have grave reservations about talking about her abusive partner because others might form the "wrong" impression of him. This would be especially true if she is a minority person in a group with members who are mostly from a different racial, ethnic, or cultural background.

However, if such a woman is able to deal with her fears and reservations about talking about her abusive situation, a group experience can be a force in aiding her to consider alternatives and to examine the price she is paying for remaining in this relationship as well as the price she might pay if she were to leave. In cases such as this it is useful to explore the client's underlying values and to help her determine if they are working for her and for her family. Ultimately, it will be up to her to decide in what ways she might change her situation.

If we pay careful attention to what our clients tell us about what they want, we can operate within an existential framework. Our task then becomes encouraging them to explore the consequences of what they are doing in their lives. Assuming an existential orientation does not mean that we have to preach to group members about the values of self-awareness, choice, and responsibility; it is also not about preaching any other values. An existential approach is particularly relevant for multicultural situations because it does not impose certain values and meanings; rather, it investigates such values and meanings of the client.

One of the strengths of the existential approach for group leaders who work with culturally diverse clients is that it places value on understanding the view of reality these clients hold and the frame of reference they use in attributing meaning to their life experiences. Ibrahim (1985, 1991) emphasizes the importance of therapists' understanding their own worldview and also those of their clients as a requisite for effective cross-cultural counseling. She has developed a framework for understanding various worldviews and the universal existential categories that make them up. The five existential categories pertain to human nature, human relationships, relationship to nature, time orientation, and activity orientation. Five questions posed are:

1. How is human nature characterized and defined? (Is human nature viewed as bad? good and bad? good?)
2. How are human relationships defined? (Are relationships lineal/hierarchical? collateral/mutual? individualistic?)
3. What is the relationship of people to nature? (Is the focus on harmony? subjugation and control? the power of nature?)
4. What is the temporal focus of human life? (Is there a focus on the past? present? future?)
5. What is the modality of human activity? (Is there an emphasis on being? being-in-becoming? doing?)

This model has implications for existentially oriented group counselors, for it helps them respect the different elements that make up a client's philosophy of life. With this understanding of different worldviews, group practitioners are in a position to establish mutually agreed-upon goals with clients that will provide a direction for change.

The existential approach has some limitations as it is applied to multicultural populations in group settings. Some clients simply believe that they do not have a choice or that even if they do have some freedom, societal factors (such as racism, discrimination, and lack of opportunity) are severely restricting their ability to choose for themselves. Existentially oriented group leaders would do well to take into account the sociocultural factors that do restrict choices. In working with clients who come from the barrio or an inner-city environment, for example, it is important to deal with their survival issues. Such clients may be motivated primarily by the need for safety and survival and may thus be seeking help in getting their basic needs met. They may need to know how best to take care of their children, how to cope with a crisis over housing, or how to deal effectively with unemployment. Simply lecturing clients that they have a choice in making their life better will not help, and it is likely to have a negative impact. These real-life issues provide a good focus for group work, assuming that the leader is willing to deal with them. This can be done by developing interventions that can help the client take action, even if it is only small steps toward change. In addition to working toward individual change, the group leader can at the same time do what is possible to change the environmental situations that are contributing the client's problems.

Where to Go from Here

The *Society for Existential Analysis* is a professional organization devoted to an exploration of issues pertaining to an existential/phenomenological approach to counseling and therapy. Membership is open to anyone interested in this approach and includes students, trainees, psychotherapists, philosophers, psychiatrists, counselors, and psychologists. Members receive a regular newsletter and an annual copy of the *Journal of the Society for Existential Analysis*. The society provides a list of existentially oriented psychotherapists for referral purposes. The School of Psychotherapy and Counselling at Regent's College in London offers an advanced diploma in existential psychotherapy as well as short courses in the field. For information on any of the above, contact:

Society for Existential Analysis
School of Psychotherapy and Counselling
Regent's College
Inner Circle, Regent's Park
London, England NW1 4NS

If you want to learn more about the existential approach to groups, give consideration to enrolling in a good philosophy course on existentialism. This will provide the means to get to know the underlying theoretical concepts that were briefly explored in this chapter.

I'd also suggest reading a good anthology of existentialist writings. In the References and Suggested Readings a few of these sources are: Oaklander (1992) and Raymond (1991). Some other books, all of which are annotated in the following Recommended Supplementary Readings, offer useful material that can be adapted to the practice of group work; they include the works of Yalom (1980), van Deurzen-Smith (1988), and Bugental (1987).

A videotaped interview with Irvin Yalom is available, covering the existential approach and his views of group therapy. In another videotape, Yalom works with patients in simulations of an inpatient therapy group. This tape applies Yalom's ideas of dealing with the here and now in a group session, as well as focusing on several key existential themes in the group. These videotapes can be purchased from Brooks/Cole Publishing Company, Pacific Grove, CA 93950.

RECOMMENDED SUPPLEMENTARY READINGS

No books that I am aware of deal explicitly and exclusively with the application of the existential approach to group counseling. Some of the following sources contain related material that group leaders can use to apply this model to their work with groups.

Existential Psychotherapy (Yalom, 1980) is a superb treatment of ultimate human concerns of death, freedom, isolation, and meaninglessness as these issues relate to therapy. This book has depth and clarity, and it is rich with clinical examples that illustrate existential themes. If you were to select just one book on existential therapy, this would be my recommendation.

Existential Counselling in Practice (van Deurzen-Smith, 1988) is highly recommended as a good overview of the basic assumptions, goals, and key concepts of the existential approach. The author clearly puts into perspective topics such as anxiety, authentic living, clarifying one's worldview, determining values, discovering meaning, and coming to terms with life. This book offers practitioners a framework for practicing counseling from an existential perspective.

Existential Therapy (van Deurzen-Smith, 1990a) is an informative booklet that outlines theoretical assumptions, therapeutic goals, qualities of effective therapists, strategies and techniques, the therapeutic process, and the limitations of the approach.

The Art of the Psychotherapist (Bugental, 1987) is an outstanding book that bridges the art and science of psychotherapy, making places for both. The author is an insightful and sensitive clinician who writes about the psychotherapist's and the client's journey from an existential perspective.

Psychotherapy and Process: The Fundamentals of an Existential-Humanistic Approach (Bugental, 1978) is a concise and comprehensive overview. It is highly readable, and the clinical examples provide a sense of reality to the discussion of concepts. An excellent source.

The Discovery of Being: Writings in Existential Psychology (May, 1983) addresses fundamental human concerns that are central to existential therapy.

Man's Search for Himself (May, 1953) is a classic. It deals with key existential themes such as loneliness, anxiety, the experience of becoming a person, the struggle to be, freedom, choice, responsibility, and religion.

I Never Knew I Had a Choice (Corey & Corey, 1993) is a self-help book written from an existential perspective. It contains many exercises and activities that leaders can use for their group work and that they can suggest as "homework assignments" between sessions. The topics covered include our struggle to achieve autonomy; the roles that work, love, sexuality, intimacy, and solitude play in our lives; the meaning of loneliness, death, and loss; and the ways in which we choose our values and philosophies of life. Each chapter is followed by numerous annotated suggestions for further reading.

REFERENCES AND SUGGESTED READINGS*

Atkinson, D. R., Morten, G., & Sue, D. W. (1993). *Counseling American minorities: A cross-cultural perspective* (4th ed.). Madison, WI: Brown & Benchmark.

Atkinson, D. R., Thompson, C. E., & Grant, S. K. (1993). A three-dimensional model for counseling racial/ethnic minorities. *The Counseling Psychologist, 21*(2), 257–277.

Brazier, D. (1992). Eigenwelt and Gegenwelt: Authenticity in counselling and psychotherapy. *Journal of the Society for Existential Analysis, 3,* 84–93.

Bugental, J. F. T. (1978). *Psychotherapy and process: The fundamentals of an existential-humanistic approach.* Reading, MA: Addison-Wesley.

Bugental, J. F. T. (1986). Existential-humanistic psychotherapy. In I. L. Kutash & A. Wolf (Eds.), *Psychotherapist's casebook* (pp. 222–236). San Francisco: Jossey-Bass.

*Bugental, J. F. T. (1987). *The art of the psychotherapist.* New York: Norton.

Bugental, J. F. T., & Bracke, P. E. (1992). The future of existential-humanistic psychotherapy. *Psychotherapy, 29*(1), 28–33.

*Books and articles marked with an asterisk are suggested for further study.

Burton, A. (1967). *Modern humanistic psychotherapy*. San Francisco: Jossey-Bass.

Comas-Dias, L. (1992). The future of psychotherapy with ethnic minorities. *Psychotherapy, 29*(1), 88–94.

*Corey, G., & Corey, M. (1993). *I never knew I had a choice* (5th ed.). Pacific Grove, CA: Brooks/Cole.

Cushman, P. (1990). Why the self is empty: Toward a historically situated psychology. *American Psychologist, 45*(5), 599–611.

*Deurzen-Smith, E. van (1988). *Existential counselling in practice*. London: Sage.

*Deurzen-Smith, E. van (1990a). *Existential therapy*. London, England: Society for Existential Analysis Publications.

*Deurzen-Smith, E. van (1990b). What is existential analysis? *Journal of the Society for Existential Analysis, 1*, 6–14.

Deurzen-Smith, E. van (1991). Ontological insecurity revisited. *Journal of the Society for Existential Analysis, 2*, 38–48.

Deurzen-Smith, E. van (1992). Dialogue as therapy. *Journal of the Society for Existential Analysis, 3*, 15–23.

Dryden, W. (Ed.). (1992). *Hard-earned lessons from counselling in action*. London: Sage.

*Frankl, V. (1963). *Man's search for meaning*. New York: Washington Square Press.

*Gould, W. B. (1993). *Viktor E. Frankl: Life with meaning*. Pacific Grove, CA: Brooks/Cole.

Heidegger, M. (1962). *Being and time* (John Macquarrie & Edward Robinson, Trans.). New York: Harper & Row.

Ibrahim, F. A. (1985). Effective cross-cultural counseling and psychotherapy: A framework. *The Counseling Psychologist, 13*(4), 625–638.

Ibrahim, F. A. (1991). Contribution of cultural worldview to generic counseling and development. *Journal of Counseling and Development, 70*(1), 13–19.

Keen, E. (1970). *Three faces of being: Toward an existential clinical psychology*. New York: Appleton-Century-Crofts.

*Lantz, J. (1993). Treatment modalities in logotherapy. *International Forum for Logotherapy, 16*(2), 65–73.

May, R. (1953). *Man's search for himself*. New York: Norton.

May, R. (Ed.). (1961). *Existential psychology*. New York: Random House.

*May, R. (1983). *The discovery of being: Writings in existential psychology*. New York: Norton.

May, R., & Yalom, I. (1989). Existential psychotherapy. In R. Corsini & D. Wedding (Eds.), *Current psychotherapies* (4th ed.). Itasca, IL: F. E. Peacock.

Mullan, H. (1978). Existential group psychotherapy. In H. Mullan & M. Rosenbaum (Eds.), *Group psychotherapy: Theory and practice* (2nd ed.). New York: Free Press.

Mullan, H. (1979). An existential group psychotherapy. *International Journal of Group Psychotherapy, 29*(2), 163–174.

Oaklander, L. N. (1992). *Existentialist philosophy: An introduction*. Englewood Cliffs, NJ: Prentice-Hall.

Raymond, D. (1991). *Existentialism and the philosophical tradition*. Englewood Cliffs, NJ: Prentice-Hall.

Rice, L. N., & Greenberg, L. S. (1992). Humanistic approaches to psychotherapy. In D. K. Freedheim (Ed.), *History of psychotherapy: A century of change* (pp. 197–224). Washington, DC: American Psychological Association.

Russell, J. M. (1978). Sartre, therapy, and expanding the concept of responsibility. *The American Journal of Psychoanalysis, 38*, 259–269.

Sartre, J.-P. (1971). *Being and nothingness*. New York: Bantam.

Sue, D. W., & Sue, D. (1990). *Counseling the culturally different: Theory and practice* (2nd ed.). New York: Wiley.

Tillich, P. (1952). *The courage to be*. New Haven, CT: Yale University Press.

Vontress, C. E. (1979). Cross-cultural counseling: An existential approach. *Personnel and Guidance Journal, 58*, 117–121.

Vontress, C. E. (1988). An existential approach to cross-cultural counseling. *Journal of Multicultural Counseling and Development, 16*, 73–83.

Wilberg, H. P. (1992). The language of listening: Towards an ontology of communication. *Journal of the Society for Existential Analysis, 3*, 54–68.

*Yalom, I. D. (1980). *Existential psychotherapy.* New York: Basic Books.

◆ CHAPTER TEN ◆

The Person-Centered Approach to Groups

Introduction

The person-centered approach to group counseling (which was originally known as client-centered therapy) was developed by the late Carl Rogers. It is grounded on the assumption that human beings tend to move toward wholeness and self-actualization and that individual members, as well as the group as a whole, can find their own direction with a minimal degree of help from the group leader, or "facilitator." The person-centered approach emphasizes the personal qualities of the group leader rather than techniques of leading, because the primary function of the facilitator is to create a fertile and healing climate in the group. This therapy is best considered as a "way of being" rather than a "way of doing." The essence of the approach is captured by Rogers:

> The person-centered approach, then, is primarily a way of being that finds its expression in attitudes and behaviors that create a growth-producing climate. It is a basic philosophy rather than simply a technique or a method. When this philosophy is lived, it helps the person expand the development of his or her own capacities. When it is lived, it also stimulates constructive change in others. It empowers the individual, and when this personal power is sensed, experience shows that it tends to be used for personal and social transformation [1986b, p. 199].

A therapeutic climate is established in the group by the facilitator's creating a relationship based on certain attitudes such as accurate empathic understanding, acceptance, nonpossessive warmth, caring, and genuineness. As the facilitator projects these attitudes and an accepting and caring climate emerges, it is presumed, members will drop their defenses and work toward personally meaningful goals, a process that will eventually lead to appropriate and useful behavioral change.

The contemporary person-centered approach to group counseling is the result of an evolutionary process that continues to remain open to change and refinement. Certain trends go back more than 50 years. In the early 1940s Rogers developed what was known as *nondirective counseling,* in part

263

as a reaction against more directive and interpretive individual therapy. He caused a furor when he challenged the basic assumption that the counselor was the expert and the client should be in a passive role. Thus, he questioned the validity of such widely used therapeutic procedures as suggestion, giving of advice, teaching, diagnosis, and interpretation. A common theme that originated in his early writings and permeated all of his works is a basic trust in the client's ability to move forward if the appropriate conditions fostering growth are present. According to Rogers, there is a *formative tendency* in nature, or a central source of energy that seeks fulfillment and actualization, involving both maintaining and enhancing the organism. A faith in subjective experience and a belief in the basic trustworthiness of human nature go hand in hand. The whole conceptual framework of Rogers's ideas grows out of his experience that human beings become increasingly worthy of trust once they feel at a deep level that they are understood and respected (Thorne, 1992). Although person-centered therapy has changed over the years, this faith in the person has remained at its foundation.

The Relationship between Existential Therapy and Humanistic Psychology

In the previous chapter, some key concepts of existential therapy were presented, many of which may seem to overlap with the humanistic themes put forth by Rogers and others. Indeed, Rogers constructed his notions of therapeutic practice on some existential principles about what it means to be human, the balance between freedom and responsibility, and the client/therapist relationship as a key to change. Both person-centered therapy and Gestalt therapy, developed by Fritz Perls (the subject of Chapter 11), are experiential and existentially oriented approaches. They are humanistic approaches that are based on a foundation of existential concepts.

THE FOCUS OF HUMANISTIC PSYCHOLOGY. A number of humanistic theorists, who contributed to a movement often referred to as the "third force" in psychology (in reaction to the analytic and behavioral forces), have written on the nature of human existence, on methods for studying human modes of functioning, and on the implications of humanistic assumptions. Synthesizing their theories from many divergent fields and approaches, early humanistic psychologists contended that people could not be studied and understood in segmented fashion. Rather, humans must be studied in complete relation to how they interact with others and with the world. Some key figures in the development of humanistic psychology were Rogers, Rollo May, Abraham Maslow, Sidney Jourard, Perls, and James Bugental. Many of these psychologists have an existential orientation, but they also applied themes to the practice of psychotherapy that focus on the capacities unique to humans: love, freedom, choice, creativity, purpose, relatedness, meaning, values, growth, self-actualization, autonomy, responsibility, ego transcendence, humor, and spontaneity. According to humanistic psychologists, any therapy that aims at growth must take these human capacities into account. To a large extent, the encounter-group movement in the 1960s and 1970s grew out of the humanistic force.

One of the pioneers in humanistic psychology was Maslow (1968, 1970, 1971), who extensively studied the meaning of psychologically healthy people. Maslow's concept of the *self-actualizing* person is compatible with Rogers's notion of the formative tendency. For Maslow, human beings strive for self-actualization, which is the tendency to become all that we are able to become. Though all people have a natural tendency to develop their uniqueness and fulfill their potential, the process is not automatic. Because growth entails a struggle between our desire for security and dependence and our desire for self-actualization, we must decide to which side of the struggle we want to commit ourselves.

Maslow has identified characteristics of self-actualizing people, some of which are inner direction and resistance to being defined by others, the capacity to tolerate and even welcome uncertainty, acceptance of others and of oneself, a fresh perspective on the world, spontaneity and naturalness, autonomy, a need for privacy and solitude, deep caring for others and the capacity to form intimate relationships, a sense of humor, and the absence of artificial dichotomies within oneself (such as weakness/strength, love/ hate, and work/play). The group process can be instrumental in empowering individuals by offering them a place to express their inner characteristics.

In a discussion of the major humanistic approaches to psychotherapy, Rice and Greenberg (1992) identify Rogers's person-centered approach, Perls's Gestalt therapy, and the existential approach as the three major humanistic models of psychotherapy. They also list the following four major themes as of primary importance in all of the humanistic approaches to counseling and therapy:

1. The commitment to a phenomenological approach. This central characteristic involves belief in the uniquely human capacity for reflective consciousness.
2. The actualization, or growth, tendency. Both Maslow and Rogers, as mentioned, have maintained that rather than merely seeking stability, human beings strive to grow.
3. The belief that humans are free, self-determining beings. Individuals may be influenced by their past and by their environment, but they have a role in who and what they become.
4. The concern and respect for each person, whose subjective experience is of the utmost importance. Humanistic therapists attempt to understand and grasp the experiential world of their clients.

SOME DIFFERENCES BETWEEN THE HUMANISTIC AND EXISTENTIAL PER-SPECTIVES. Although the two approaches share common ground, they are not identical. According to Michael Russell (personal communication, March 22, 1992), the central difference between existential psychotherapy and humanistic psychotherapy is philosophical. He traces humanism back to the philosophy of Aristotle in its view that people seek to actualize the essential nature within them. We are seen as having certain basic needs that impel us in this self-actualizing direction. The person-centered approach of the humanist, Rogers, assumes that if positive and nurturing conditions are provided, we will automatically grow in positive ways. In contrast, existential thinkers like Kierkegaard and Sartre would not agree that we even have any sort of essential nature or basic needs, nor would they agree that much of anything will happen in life automatically. Where humanists see needs, existentialists see choices; where humanists see the prospect of positive and automatic growth, existentialists see the anxiety of being free and the equal possibilities for growth and decay. Once these philosophical differences are noted, the bundling together of existentialism and humanism can be seen to be highly problematic.

Historical Background

Beginning in the early 1940s, as we have seen, Rogers's *nondirective* approach focused during its early years on reflecting and clarifying the feelings of individual clients. Rogers believed that through a permissive relationship, clients were able to gain increasing insight into the nature of their problems and then take constructive action based on their new self-understanding. During the 1950s, Rogers developed and refined his basic hypotheses for psychotherapy, and these principles were later applied to therapy groups by Hobbs (1951) and Gordon (1951). Examples of these applications in the 1950s included groups for physically handicapped children and their parents, parents of retarded children, mothers on public assistance, clients who were involved in individual counseling, psychiatric inpatients, residents of homes for the elderly, and mental-health professionals (Raskin, 1986a, p. 277).

Rogers also developed a systematic theory of personality and applied this self theory to the practice of counseling individuals, which led him to rename his approach *client-centered therapy* (Rogers, 1951). The client-centered approach was broadened to the extent that it had applications to the teaching/learning situation, affective/cognitive learning in workshops, and organizational development and leadership.

In the 1960s and 1970s Rogers did a great deal to spearhead the development of basic encounter groups and personal-growth groups. As the fields of application grew in number and variety, the name *client-centered therapy* was replaced by the *person-centered approach*. Rogers also broadened his emphasis beyond the therapist's ability to reflect accurately what clients were expressing to include the therapist's congruence and willingness to become increasingly involved in the therapy. The basic encounter groups made it difficult to distinguish between "therapy" and "growth." The group work that Rogers pioneered was mostly in the form of weekend workshops, although some of his workshops lasted two to three weeks. These small groups did much to revolutionize the practice of group work. (For a detailed review of the development of Rogers's approach over the past 50 years, see Zimring and Raskin, 1992.)

Key Concepts

Trust in the Group Process

Rogers (1986b) makes it clear that the person-centered approach rests on a basic trust in human beings' tendency to realize their full potential. Similarly, person-centered therapy is based on a deep sense of trust in the group's ability to develop its own potential by moving in a constructive direction. For a group to move forward, it must develop an accepting and trusting atmosphere in which the members can show aspects of themselves that they usually conceal and move into new behaviors. For example, they move:

- ◆ from playing roles to expressing themselves more directly
- ◆ from being relatively closed to experience and uncertainty to becoming more open to outside reality and tolerant of ambiguity
- ◆ from being out of contact with internal and subjective experience to becoming aware of it
- ◆ from looking for answers outside of themselves to a willingness to direct their own lives from within
- ◆ from lacking trust and being somewhat closed and fearful in interpersonal relationships to being more open and expressive with others

The Therapeutic Conditions for Growth

The basic tenet underlying the person-centered approach to group work is stated briefly by Rogers (1980): "Individuals have within themselves vast resources for self-understanding and for altering their self-concepts, basic attitudes, and self-directed behavior; these resources can be tapped if a definable climate of facilitative psychological attitudes can be provided" (p. 115). According to Rogers (1986b), the necessary climate that releases our formative, or actualizing, tendency is characterized by three primary attitudes of the therapist: genuineness, unconditional positive regard (now called "nonpossessive warmth" or acceptance), and empathy. These three factors, also known as "core conditions," will be introduced here and then taken up in detail later in this section.

The first element is the *genuineness,* realness, or congruence of the therapist (or facilitator of the group). The greater the extent to which facilitators become involved in the group as persons, putting up no professional front, the greater is the likelihood that the members will change and grow. Genuineness implies that the process of a group is influenced by the person of the facilitator as much as by the individuality of the group participants.

The second element is the attitude called *unconditional positive regard,* which is an acceptance of and caring for the members. When group facilitators display a positive, nonjudgmental, accepting attitude toward their clients, therapeutic change is more likely (Rogers, 1986b). As we will see later, this caring on the facilitator's part is nonpossessive in that the members are prized fully rather than conditionally.

The third facilitative aspect is an *empathic understanding* of the members' internal and subjective frame of reference. Facilitators show this empathy when they are able to sense accurately the feelings and personal meanings that the members are experiencing. It is also important for facilitators to be able to communicate this understanding to the members.

To the extent that therapists experience genuineness, acceptance, and accurate empathy for their clients and to the extent that the clients perceive these conditions, therapeutic personality change and growth will occur (Braaten, 1986; Thorne, 1992). Rogers (1987d) maintains that this hypothesis has been put to the test in a wide variety of situations with very divergent groups, different cultures, and different nations. Rogers stresses that the core conditions are not only necessary for effective therapy but also sufficient.

Rogers (1986b) adds another characteristic of a growth-promoting relationship that he concedes cannot as yet be studied empirically: *presence.* He asserts that when he is at his best as a group facilitator, he is in touch with the unknown in him and that his inner spirit reaches out and touches the inner spirit of the client. The relationship transcends itself and becomes a part of something larger. This presence releases the most profound growth and healing.

Natiello (1987) contends that another therapist condition is integral to the practice of the person-centered approach: *personal power.* This is a state in which individuals are aware of and can act on their own feelings, needs, and values rather than looking outside of themselves for direction. The greater the degree of autonomy of therapists, the less likely they are to attempt to control others, and the more they can help their clients tap into their own source of power for self-direction. Facilitators share power by actively trusting individuals to direct their own lives and to solve their problems. In training other facilitators in the person-centered approach, Natiello finds that they often experience difficulties in translating the concept of personal power into practice. They struggle with how much of themselves to share, and they fear taking over others' power. This fear sometimes leads them to disown their own power or to deny it. To be sure, it is a challenge to learn the balance between accepting one's own power as a therapist and sharing power with clients.

IMPLICATIONS FOR TRAINING GROUP LEADERS. Coghlan and McIlduff (1990) maintain that an important aspect of training group facilitators is teaching them the use of personal power. Because the person-centered approach emphasizes an equalization of power, it is critical that the facilitator's behavior in no way diminishes the power of members. According to

Coghlan and McIlduff, training needs to involve teaching facilitators how to offer alternatives in sensitive ways to group members so that real choice and increased freedom become the property of the group, rather than the instrument of the leader.

However, it is a myth that person-centered therapists are self-abnegating, passive, and uninvolved, merely responding to others by mirroring their responses (Natiello, 1987). Rather, they demonstrate behaviorally the three core therapeutic attitudes, genuineness, acceptance, and empathic understanding. A research review confirms the person-centered assumption that the facilitator's expression of these three conditions is the foundation for positive therapeutic outcomes (Raskin, 1986b). This research implies that emphasis is best placed on the art of listening and understanding, rather than focusing mainly on teaching techniques and strategies. Thorne puts the challenge to clinicians well: "The 'core conditions' of congruence, acceptance, and empathy are simple to state, much more difficult to describe and infinitely challenging to practice" (1992, p. 36).

The person-centered spirit of facilitating groups involves developing a style that is an extension of one's personhood. Boy (1990) maintains that when this personhood is well expressed, members are enabled to become involved in the group process in a natural and spontaneous way. He writes that a member's progress is often proportionate to the facilitator's ability to communicate this personhood. In the following sections I expand on Rogers's three therapeutic conditions as they apply to group leaders' behavior.

Genuineness

Genuineness means that what the therapist expresses externally is *congruent* with his or her inner experience, at least during the time of therapy. In other words, genuine therapists don't pretend to be interested when they are not, don't fake attention or understanding, don't say what they don't mean, and don't adopt behaviors designed to win approval. They can perform their professional functions without hiding behind their professional roles.

According to Natiello (1987), in order to maintain genuineness, therapists need a high level of self-awareness, self-acceptance, and self-trust. Genuineness is the state of authenticity that results from a deep exploration of self and a willingness to accept the truths of this exploration. In her work with helping professionals in a person-centered training program, Natiello finds that congruence is both complex and difficult to achieve and that it is the condition that is most often ignored. She contends that without congruence the other therapeutic conditions are then offered inauthentically and become mere techniques, which are meaningless, manipulative, and controlling.

IMPLICATIONS FOR GROUP LEADERS. Genuine therapists, although they are essentially honest in their encounters in the group, are not indiscriminately open, and they know the boundaries of appropriate self-revelation. Although genuineness implies that leaders are internally congruent (which means that they are not self-deceptive), they do not always share all their feelings and thoughts, since that would not be appropriate or therapeutic at certain times. They realize the importance of taking responsibility for any feelings they express in the group and the importance of exploring with clients any persistent feelings, especially those that may be blocking their ability to be fully present. Through their own authenticity, congruent group leaders offer a model that helps their clients work toward greater realness.

Some group leaders have difficulty with "being themselves." Often that difficulty stems from the misapprehension that genuineness entails expressing *every* immediate thought or feeling or being spontaneous without any restraint or consideration of the appropriateness and timeliness of one's reactions. Another difficulty arises when leaders, in the name of being "authentic," make themselves the focal point of the group by discussing their personal problems in great detail. As Braaten (1986) has noted, not every kind of genuineness is facilitating for clients. Therapist self-disclosure can be overdone in magnitude and kind. Clearly, as indicated above, even the expression of genuineness must be handled with discretion. Leaders need to examine honestly their motivations for discussing their personal issues and ask themselves whether the disclosure serves the clients' needs or their own. If the leader has had an experience similar to that of a client, the sharing of feelings about the experience may be therapeutic for the client. When a group leader does engage in self-disclosure, it is important to focus on the members and not to deter them from exploring their own issues. Leaders who frequently make themselves the focal point of group discussion may be using the group as a platform to air their personal problems.

Unconditional Positive Regard and Acceptance

As we have seen, the goal of person-centered groups is to create a climate in which the basic actualizing tendency can freely express itself in each participant and in the group as a whole. For this growth force to be released within individuals and within a group, unconditional positive regard is the second necessary factor.

As mentioned, positive regard involves communicating a caring that is unconditional and that is not contaminated by evaluation or judgment of the client's feelings and thoughts. In other words, group leaders value and accept members without placing stipulations and expectations on this acceptance; they tell the client, "I accept you as you are," not "I'll accept you when . . ." Acceptance, however, is not to be confused with approval; therapists can accept and value their clients as separate persons, with a right to their separateness, without necessarily approving of some of their behavior.

Associated with this attitude of positive regard is an attitude of nonpossessive caring and warmth—namely, an attitude that is not dependent on the therapist's own need for approval and appreciation and that can be expressed in subtle ways such as gestures, eye contact, tone of voice, and facial expression. A genuine expression of caring can be sensed by clients and will promote their development. Artificial warmth can be as readily perceived and is likely to inhibit the client's change and growth. Obviously, once clients sense that the therapist's expression of warmth is more a technique than a genuine feeling, it becomes difficult for them to trust the genuineness of other reactions of the therapist.

Braaten (1986) has written about his struggle with the concept of unconditional positive regard, or even the term *positive regard.* He substitutes the phrase *warm regard,* which includes an expression of both positive and negative feelings. He believes that this regard must include a willingness to share one's total self with significant others, including one's anger and possible rejection. Rogers (1987b) does contend that there is room in the person-centered approach for therapists to communicate a range of feelings. This means that boredom and anger, as well as compassion, can be expressed.

Thus, a potential conflict arises between being genuine and between maintaining a stance of unconditionally (Lietaer, 1984). It is a rare therapist who can genuinely provide unconditional acceptance for every client on a consistent basis. While unconditionality is not impossible, it is improbable. Unconditional positive regard can best be thought of as an attitude of receptiveness toward the subjective and experiential world of the client. From Lietaer's (1984) perspective, unconditionality means that the therapist values the deeper core of the person. Through the therapist's unconditionality clients sense that the therapist is on their side and that they will not be let down in spite of their current difficulties. In its optimal form unconditionality expresses a deep belief in another person. For a scholarly treatment of the controversial concept of unconditional positive regard, see Lietaer (1984).

Related to the concept of accepting the individual group member with unconditional positive regard, caring, and warmth is the idea of developing an attitude of acceptance of the group as a whole. Just as Rogers believes in the capacity of the individual to find his or her own direction, so does he believe in accepting a group where it is, without attempting to impose a direction on it: "From my experience I know that if I attempt to push a group to a deeper level, it is not, in the long run, going to work" (1970, p. 48).

IMPLICATIONS FOR GROUP LEADERS.   It has been my experience that group leaders in training often struggle with what they see as the monumental task of being able to *feel* accepting or being able to demonstrate positive regard. Some tend to burden themselves with the unrealistic expectation that they must *always* be accepting and that they must consistently respond with warmth in all situations. Thus, it is also my experience that group leaders need to develop an accepting attitude toward themselves as well— an acceptance of the fact that at times they won't feel warmth or unconditional positive regard. It is not necessary to feel a high level of warmth and positive regard all the time in order to be an effective group leader. These attitudes are not an either/or condition; rather, they occur on a continuum of gradations. Being an effective group leader starts by accepting oneself and continues by bearing in mind that the greater the degree of valuing, caring, and accepting of a client, the greater the opportunity to facilitate change in the client.

Empathy

The third central concept in the person-centered group approach, as we have seen, is accurate empathy, Rogers (1961) defines empathy as the capacity to see the world of another by assuming the internal frame of reference of that person: "To sense the client's private world as if it were your own but without ever losing the 'as if' quality—this is empathy, and it seems essential to therapy" (p. 284). But sensing, even understanding, the client's private world is not enough. The counselor must also be able to communicate this understanding effectively to the client.

Rogers (1975) considers empathy as "an unappreciated way of being" for many group practitioners. He makes a case for regarding empathy as one of the most potent factors in bringing about learning and self-directed change, thus locating power in the person and not in the expert. He summarizes some general research findings concerning empathy as follows:

- ◆ Therapists of many different orientations agree that attempting sensitively and accurately to understand others from their viewpoint is a critical factor in being an effective therapist.
- ◆ One of the main functions of empathy is to foster client self-exploration. Clients come to a deeper self-understanding through a relationship in which they *feel* that they are being understood by others. Research has demonstrated that clients who feel understood by their therapists are encouraged to share more of themselves.
- ◆ Empathy dissolves alienation, for the person who receives empathy feels connected with others. Furthermore, those who receive empathy learn that they are valued, cared for, and accepted as they are. Rogers (1975) makes this point: "Empathy gives that needed confirmation that one does exist as a separate, valued person with an identity" (p. 7).
- ◆ The ability to exhibit empathy depends on the personal development of the therapist. Rogers (1975) has come to the conclusion that "the more psychologically mature and integrated the therapist is as a person, the more helpful is the relationship he provides" (p. 5).
- ◆ Being a skilled diagnostician and making interpretations is not related to empathy, which, at its best, is accepting and nonjudgmental. In fact, for Rogers, "true empathy is always free of any evaluative or diagnostic quality" (1975, p. 7).

Our ability to experience anger, joy, fear, and love is what makes it possible to enter the world of another person, even though this person's circumstances may be different from our own. Rogers makes it clear that empathy is an active process, yet it is often superficially regarded as a passive stance involving sitting back and listening:

> To really let oneself go into the inner world of this other person is one of the most active, difficult, demanding things that I know. And yet, it is worth it because it is one of the most releasing, healing things that I have had any occasion to do [1987d, p. 45].

Accurate empathy is central to the practice of the person-centered approach. It is a way for therapists to hear the meanings expressed by their clients that often lie at the edge of their awareness. Thus, clients expand their awareness when these precognitive meanings are understood and communicated by a facilitator who is able to encourage them to experience what they are feeling and thinking more deeply (Natiello, 1987).

A special kind of listening with one's total being is a crucial part of achieving empathy. Sensitive listening involves suspending judgment of others. It is not done to gain personal advantage or with an ulterior motive. Rather, this kind of listening comes from a genuine interest in making significant contact with others by knowing their reality (Barrett-Lennard, 1988). Braaten (1986) finds that his active listening involves grasping the cognitive and affective messages from his clients on a moment-to-moment basis and trying to verify his understanding with his clients. He asserts that person-centered therapists are unique in their careful monitoring to determine whether they have grasped the full message of their clients.

Active and sensitive listening is what Rogers *does* when he facilitates a group. "I listen as carefully, accurately, and sensitively as I am able, to each individual who expresses himself. Whether the utterance is superficial or significant, I *listen*" (1970, p. 47). It is apparent that Rogers "listens" to more than the words; he also hears the meaning behind both the verbal and the nonverbal content. In this regard, he is concerned with facilitating the truest expression of the person's subjective experience. According to Cain (1987a), Rogers's most enduring and pervasive contribution is demonstrating the importance of listening, not only in therapy relationships but also in any other relationship. Rogers broadened the meaning of listening and demonstrated the profound healing effect that it has on others. Cain suspects that Rogers will be best remembered as a warm and sensitive therapist who demonstrated for generations of therapists the vital importance of being present and listening. For a scholarly discussion of the role of empathy in the person-centered approach, see Bozarth (1984), and for a thoughtful discussion of listening, see Barrett-Lennard (1988).

IMPLICATIONS FOR GROUP LEADERS. As suggested earlier, empathic understanding is essential to foster the climate of acceptance and trust necessary for the success of the group. Presupposing the correct attitude, empathy is a skill that can be developed—and it is a skill that an effective group leader needs to develop.

In working with group counselors, I have found that many mistakenly assume that unless they themselves have directly experienced the same problems voiced by group members, they can't be empathic. Such an assumption can severely limit the leader's potential sphere of influence. Clearly, one need not experience incest to empathize with a group member's anguish over reliving painful sexual experiences. One need not have been abandoned by a parent to feel and experience the sadness of abandonment. It is not necessary to have been divorced to share a client's anger, hurt, and sadness of separation. Such experiences come in many forms and, at one level or another, are common to us all. It is not the specific experience that is essential. What is essential is a willingness on the part of the group leader to face his or her own unique life problems. There are situations in every life that trigger feelings of isolation, rage, resentment, guilt, sadness, loss, or rejection—to name a few of the feelings that will be expressed in groups. By remaining open to one's own emotions, by allowing oneself to be touched by the emotions of others, and by reexperiencing certain difficult events, group leaders will increase their capacity to be psychologically present for others.

Barriers to Effective Therapy

In the training workshops that my associates and I conduct, the participants typically lead groups and then receive feedback from the members and ourselves. Many of our students express feelings of inadequacy as group leaders and a sense of frustration and hopelessness; they see little change occurring in the members of their groups, and they perceive that their clients are resistant and don't enjoy coming to groups. In many instances the problems besetting these students can be traced back to the fact that the conditions of active listening, empathy, and positive regard are in some measure lacking in their groups. What follows is a list of specific problems that militate against group progress:

◆ *Lack of attending and empathy.* Often these prospective group leaders show that they don't really listen; they are preoccupied with a message that *they* want to impart to their groups and use the group as a vehicle for indoctrination. Or they ask many closed questions and are preoccupied with problem solving rather than with problem understanding. In short, many of our students talk too much and listen too little. At times we observe that leaders are highly judgmental and critical and that they create a dichotomy between "we," the treatment staff, and "they," the clients. Instead of forming an alliance with their clients, they sometimes see the group members as enemies. These counselors often fail to see any of themselves in those they work with.

◆ *Absence of counselor self-disclosure.* Some agencies and institutions foster, even require, an aloof and undisclosing leader role. Group counselors are given the messages "Avoid being personal," "Don't get involved," and "Avoid sharing anything about yourself, even if it affects the relationship."

Leaders are expected to change the behavior of members, yet they are expected to keep themselves out of their interactions with group members— clearly an unreasonable and self-defeating expectation.

◆ *Lack of positive regard, warmth, and acceptance.* Some group counselors are intolerant of the people they are supposedly helping and cling to assumptions that keep their clientele in stereotyped categories. Such prejudice makes client change difficult, if not impossible. Admittedly, it may be hard to maintain positive regard, warmth, and acceptance toward people who are in a treatment program for acts such as wife beating, child abuse, or murder. It is not necessary to condone such actions, and it may not even be possible to avoid feeling negatively toward those who have committed such acts. But it is important to try to set aside one's reactions at least during the course of the group. And it *is* possible to see these people as more than "child abusers," "antisocial personalities," "criminals," and so on. Related to a lack of positive regard are impatience, coldness, abruptness, put-downs, sarcasm, and hostility toward clients. Unless counselors recognize these attitudes, there is little chance that they will modify them and a large chance that they will continue to lead unsuccessful groups.

◆ *Lack of belief in the therapeutic process.* Underlying the concepts of positive regard and acceptance is the belief that people *can* change and improve their personal condition. In our in-service group-process workshops we have frequently met practitioners who lead groups only because they are required to do so and who do not believe in the effectiveness of group therapy. In a climate in which enthusiasm, motivation, and faith in groups are absent, is it surprising that leaders find that their groups are somewhat less than successful? After all, how can group members be expected to have faith in a process that the group leader does not believe in? No wonder that little change occurs and that the members are resistant and don't enjoy coming to the group.

IMPLICATIONS FOR GROUP LEADERS. It is essential that group leaders examine ways in which their attitudes and behaviors could be barriers to the progress of a group. Some examples of questions that serve as useful catalysts for self-reflection are:

- ◆ "Am I genuinely interested in people?"
- ◆ "What personal needs am I meeting by being a group leader?"
- ◆ "Am I authentically myself in a group, or do I hide behind the role of 'leader'?"
- ◆ "Am I able to accept people, or do I need to direct their lives?" "Do I insist that they look at the world through my eyes?"
- ◆ "Am I willing to take time to understand others, or do I force them to follow my agenda?" "Do I see my main task as helping them get what they want, or getting them to want what I want for them?"
- ◆ "Do I offer a proper model for what I expect the members in my group to become?" "What kind of model am I?"

Role and Functions of the Group Leader

Rogers (1986b) writes that the therapist's role is to become a companion to clients in their journey toward self-discovery. When the person-centered way of life is lived in therapy, it leads to a process of self-exploration and self-development and less focus on mastery of skills, techniques, and leadership strategies (Bozarth & Brodley, 1986).

Rogers did his best to become a person to the members of his groups, rather than assuming a directive role. In his work as a group facilitator, he functioned somewhat like a guide on a journey. Rogers (1970) emphasizes some of the following characteristics of group facilitators:

- ◆ They have a great deal of trust in the group process and believe that the group can move forward without their directive intervention.
- ◆ They listen carefully and sensitively to each member.
- ◆ They do all that is possible to contribute to the creation of a climate that is psychologically safe for the members.
- ◆ They attempt to be empathically understanding and accept individuals and the group; they do not push the group to a deeper level.
- ◆ They operate in terms of their own experience and their own feelings, which means that they express here-and-now reactions.
- ◆ They offer members feedback and, if appropriate, confront members on specifics of their behavior; they avoid judging and, instead, speak about how they are affected by others' behavior.

Rogers maintains that certain functions and procedures are counterproductive: (1) manipulating the group toward a particular, but unstated, goal; (2) using planned exercises designed to elicit certain emotions; (3) encouraging and setting up dramatic performances by members; (4) allowing members to attack one another or consistently insisting on expressing hostility; (5) pressuring members to participate in group exercises; (6) consistently interpreting the motives and behaviors of others; (7) making many comments on the group process; and (8) hiding behind the role of "expert leader" by remaining emotionally distant and anonymous. Although he supports the notion of facilitators being participants in a group by expressing their reactions and concerns, he cautions about the dangers of those with severe problems who use the group to work out their own problems.

Rogers (1970) takes a dim view of the use of techniques to get a group moving. If and when techniques are used, he believes, the group needs to be made a party to them. He also cautions against the facilitator's making interpretive comments. Such comments, he feels, are apt to make the group self-conscious and slow the process down. Thus, he believes that if there are to be group-process observations, they should come from members, a view that is consistent with his philosophy of placing the responsibility for the direction of the group on the members. The term *facilitator* reflects the importance of interactions between group members. The role of the facilitator is to create a climate under which the actualizing tendency will be released. The person-centered group encourages the members to explore the incongruities between their beliefs and behaviors and the urgings of their inner feelings and subjective experiencing. As the members become more aware of these incongruities within themselves, their view of themselves expands.

The person-centered approach assumes that members need the group setting and the time to express what they are ordinarily afraid to express on their own. Given the unstructured approach, along with a facilitator who refuses to do the traditional "leaderly" things, the group members, who are accustomed to following authorities, must eventually rely on themselves to formulate a purpose and a direction. Members are helped to begin listening to themselves and other members by a facilitator who will not act as an expert and save them. They are challenged to struggle and to express themselves, and out of this struggle they have a basis for learning how to trust themselves.

In summary, to help delineate the differences between the person-centered approach and other therapeutic models, I am listing some procedures that are *not* generally considered as part of the facilitator's repertoire:

- ♦ advice giving
- ♦ catalysts and techniques to initiate action
- ♦ diagnosis and evaluation
- ♦ structure and directive intervention
- ♦ tasks given to members to do outside the session

The person-centered approach emphasizes, instead, certain skills as a necessary part of the facilitator's style:

- ♦ listening in an active and sensitive way
- ♦ reflecting
- ♦ clarifying
- ♦ summarizing
- ♦ sharing of personal experiences
- ♦ encountering and engaging others in the group
- ♦ going with the flow of the group rather than trying to direct the way the group is going
- ♦ affirming a client's capacity for self-determination

In fairness, it needs to be mentioned that recent developments in the person-centered approach provide more latitude for therapists to share their reactions, to confront clients in a caring way, and to be active in the therapeutic process (Lietaer, 1984). Effective person-centered facilitators are not bound by rigid rules, and *at times* they do many of the things that I have listed as not being a standard part of the facilitator's repertoire. What is basic to this approach is the focus on the members as being the center of the group, not the leader. Members of the person-centered group are often as facilitative as the leader. Current formulations attach more importance to therapists' bringing in their own here-and-now experiences, which can stimulate clients to explore themselves at a deeper level. Although the therapist's receptive attitude is still viewed as being of central importance, this does not exclude the therapist from taking the initiative at times in order to stimulate a client's experiential process. Lietaer (1984) mentions that even "homework" and other auxiliary techniques can be used in a person-centered manner, if the experience of the client remains as the continuous touchstone.

Coghlan and McIlduff (1990) maintain that it is possible to combine a form of group structuring with a person-centered approach without abandoning the system's principles and philosophical foundations. Indeed, structuring is not an end in itself, but what is more important is the question of whether the structuring that is used results in reinforcing leader-dependent behavior or in empowering the members.

One person-centered therapist, David Cain (1990b), maintains that some therapists are so committed to "empowering" group members that the group becomes extremely frustrated and unproductive. He believes that nondirectiveness does not translate to "freedom" for many participants but, rather, becomes a barrier. He suggests that it is essential that therapists modify their therapeutic approach to accommodate the specific needs of each client. A guiding question that he asks of himself and of his clients is "Does it fit?"

It is evident that Rogers (1970) has faith in the capacity of a group to move on its own initiative, although he does admit that anxiety and irritation may result from the lack of external structure. He gave his groups permission to determine for themselves how they would spend their time, and he might open a session with the statement "We can make the group experience whatever we want it to be."

Given the freedom to choose their own direction, members do not always move toward productive work. For example, a group may be characterized by low energy, and members may choose to stay largely on a superficial and impersonal level. Facilitators may encourage the members to focus on what they are doing and not doing. Furthermore, they can certainly express their reactions to what they see happening in the group. Ultimately, group members have the power to move or not move to a deeper level, yet the leader can encourage them to look at their behavior and decide what they might do differently.

In summary, person-centered group leaders use themselves as instruments of change in a group. Their central function is to establish a therapeutic climate in which group members will interact in honest and meaningful ways. Clearly, the leader's attitudes and behavior are the powerful determinants of the accepting group atmosphere that is conducive to real communication—not any techniques, strategies, or exercises the facilitator may employ.

The Person-Centered Group Process

Characteristics of the Group

The person-centered group may meet weekly for about two hours for an unspecified number of meetings. Another format consists of a personal-growth workshop that meets for a weekend, a week, or longer. The residential aspect of such small personal-growth groups affords members opportunities to become a community as a group.

In organizing and conducting a person-centered group, there are generally no rules or procedures for the selection of members. If both the facilitator and the client agree that a group experience would be beneficial, the person is generally included. When the group initially meets, the facilitator does not present ground rules by which members must abide or provide a great deal of information or orientation. It is up to the group members to formulate the rules for their sessions and to establish norms that they agree will assist them in reaching their goals.

Stages of the Group

On the basis of his experience with numerous groups, Rogers (1970) has delineated 15 process patterns that occur in any type of group employing the person-centered approach when most of the conditions that are discussed in this chapter are present. It needs to be emphasized that the following process patterns, or trends, don't occur in a clear-cut sequence and that they may vary considerably from group to group.

1. *Milling around.* The lack of leader direction inevitably results in some initial confusion, frustration, and "milling around"—either actually or verbally. Questions such as "Who is responsible here?" "What are we here for?" or "What are we supposed to be doing?" are characteristic and reflect the concern felt at this stage.
2. *Resistance to personal expression or exploration.* Members initially present a public self—one they think will be acceptable to the group. They are fearful of and resistant to revealing their private selves.
3. *Description of past feelings.* Despite doubts about the trustworthiness of the group and the risk of exposing oneself, disclosure of personal feelings does begin—however hesitantly and ambivalently. Generally, this disclosure deals with events outside of the group; members tend to describe feelings in a "there-and-then" fashion.
4. *Expression of negative feelings.* As the group progresses, there is a movement toward the expression of here-and-now feelings. Often these expressions take the form of an attack on the group leader, usually for not providing the needed direction.
5. *Expression and exploration of personally meaningful material.* If the expression of negative feelings is seen by the members as acceptable to the group, a climate of trust emerges. Because of this feeling of

trust, members decide to take the risks involved in disclosing personal material. At this point the participants begin to realize that the group is what they make it, and they begin to experience freedom.

6. *Expression of immediate interpersonal feelings in the group.* Members tend to express a full range of feelings toward one another.

7. *Development of a healing capacity in the group.* Next, members begin to spontaneously reach out to one another, expressing care, support, understanding, and concern. At this stage, helping relationships are often formed within the group that offer members aid in leading more constructive lives outside of the group.

8. *Self-acceptance and the beginning of change.* At this stage participants begin to accept aspects of themselves that they formerly denied or distorted; they get closer to their feelings and consequently become less rigid and more open to change. As members accept their strengths and weaknesses, they drop their defenses and welcome change.

9. *Cracking of facades.* Here individual members begin to respond to the group demand that masks and pretenses be dropped. This revealing of deeper selves by some members validates the theory that meaningful encounters can occur when people risk getting beneath surface interaction. At this stage the group strives toward deeper communication.

10. *Feedback.* In the process of receiving feedback, members acquire a lot of data concerning how others experience them and what impact they have on others. This information often leads to new insights that help them decide on aspects of themselves that they want to change.

11. *Confrontation.* Here members confront one another in what is usually an intensely emotional process involving feedback. Confrontation can be seen as a stepping up of the interactions described in earlier stages.

12. *The helping relationship outside the group sessions.* By this stage members have begun making contacts outside the group. Here we see an extension of the process described above in number 7.

13. *The basic encounter.* Because the members come into closer and more direct contact with one another than is generally the case in everyday life, genuine person-to-person relationships occur. At this point members begin to experience how meaningful relationships occur when there is a commitment to work toward a common goal and a sense of community.

14. *Expression of feelings of closeness.* As the sessions progress, an increasing warmth and closeness develops within the group because of the realness of the participants' expression of feelings about themselves and toward others. This therapeutic feeling of closeness leads to the last and most important process.

15. *Behavior changes in the group.* As members experience increased

ease in expressing their feelings, their behaviors, mannerisms, and even their appearance begin to change. They tend to act in an open manner; they express deeper feelings toward others; they achieve an increased understanding of themselves; and they work out more effective ways of being with others. If the changes are effective, the members will carry their new behaviors into their everyday lives.

Some Outcomes of the Group Experience

Rogers (1970) conducted a systematic follow-up study to assess the outcomes of encounter groups that he and his associates had facilitated. The follow-up questionnaire, essentially a self-reporting instrument that identified reactions to group participation as well as the value of applying what had been learned in the group to everyday situations, was sent to 500 group participants. The study was conducted three to six months after the group experience. The following are some of the general findings of Rogers's study: Two individuals felt that the experience had been mostly damaging and had changed their behavior in negative ways. A "moderate number" viewed their group experience as neutral and saw very little behavior change after the group. Another "moderate number" felt that the group had only temporarily changed their behavior. Most of the participants viewed the experience as deeply meaningful and positive, one that had made a significant and continuing impact and that had produced positive results in their behavior. (If you are interested in further details of the self-report method of conducting outcome studies of groups, see Rogers, 1970, pp. 126–134.)

Based on his vast experience in conducting groups and workshops, as well as his process and outcomes studies, Rogers (1987d) has identified and summarized a number of changes that tend to occur within individuals in a successful group experience. Members become more open and honest. As they feel increasingly understood and accepted, they have less need to defend themselves, and therefore they drop their facades and are willing to be themselves. Because they become more aware of their own feelings and of what is going on around them, they are more realistic and objective. They tend to be more like the self that they wanted before entering a group experience. They are not as easily threatened, because the safety of the group changes their attitude toward themselves and others. Within the group there is more understanding and acceptance of who others are. Members become more appreciative of themselves as they are, and they move toward self-direction. They empower themselves in new ways, and they increasingly trust themselves. The members become more creative, because they are willing to accept their own uniqueness. They come to realize that making life change entails both pain and joy.

Other Applications of Person-Centered Groups

Rogers (1980) notes that there are similarities between therapy groups and encounter groups. Whether people come together because they are seeking help for dealing with serious problems (group therapy), or whether they are seeking personal-growth experiences (encounter group), the process is much the same. The person-centered approach to the facilitation of these groups has been applied to diverse populations such as therapy clients, counselors, staff members of entire school systems, administrators, medical students, groups in conflict, drug users and their helpers, people representing different cultures and languages, and job-training groups. As the group movement developed, the person-centered approach became increasingly concerned with reducing human suffering, with cross-cultural awareness, and with conflict resolution on an international basis (Raskin, 1986a, p. 285).

In 1973 Rogers and some of his colleagues initiated a new form of person-centered group known as the *large community group*. These groups, which began at the Center for Studies of the Person in La Jolla, California, eventually were offered in many places in the world. They were large groups whose size often reached 50 to 100 or more people who worked and lived together for two weeks. These workshops were designed to build community, to facilitate the members' self-exploration, and to resolve tensions between members representing diverse cultures. These large community groups provided data for understanding how cross-cultural and international differences can be resolved through the applications of conditions advocated by the person-centered approach (Raskin, 1986a).

Perhaps one of the major contributions of the person-centered model lies in its attempt to promote world peace. In the last few years of his life, Rogers focused much attention on alternatives to nuclear planetary suicide. He sought alternatives that would reduce psychological barriers that impinge on communication between factions (see Rogers, 1987c; Rogers & Malcolm, 1987).

Evaluation of the Person-Centered Group Approach

Contributions and Strengths of the Approach

Because the person-centered approach is very much a phenomenological one, based on the subjective worldview of the client, I consider it an excellent basis for the initial stages of any type of group. This foundation sets the tone that allows a group to meet the challenges at the later stages of its development. The approach encourages members from the outset to assume responsibility for determining their level of investment in the group and deciding what concerns they will raise. The emphasis is on truly listening to and deeply understanding the clients' world from their internal frame of reference. Critical evaluation, analysis, and judgment are suspended, and the focus is on grasping the feelings and thoughts being expressed by the others. I see this form of listening and hearing as a prerequisite to any group approach, particularly during the early stages, when it is essential that members feel free to explore their concerns openly. Unless the participants feel that they are being understood, surely any technique or intervention plan is bound to fail.

Many of the problems I have found among group leaders in training (as discussed earlier in this chapter) stem from their failure to reach an understanding of the members' subjective world, an understanding that can be achieved only by very careful listening and by restraining the tendency to dive in too quickly to solve members' problems. I think a major strength of this approach is the central importance placed on the group counselor's personhood as a critical variable determining the outcome of a group. It is not the leader's ability to provide solutions for group members but the ability to be present for members and encourage them to tell their full story. If the leader can create an open and accepting climate within the group, the members are likely to engage in the kind of work that will enable them to find their own resolutions. Ultimately, group members make their own choices and bring about change for themselves. Yet with the presence of the facilitator and the support of other members, they do not have to do their changing alone.

Whatever techniques one employs or avoids, whatever style one adopts or refrains from, the approach should be adapted to the needs of the group and its members. The diverse range of client populations and the individual differences that characterize members of a group demand that any approach be flexibly applied. It almost goes without saying that some clients function better with a high degree of structure, whereas others need very little structure. In addition to the needs of the members, the leadership approach should fit the personality and style of the leader. Although most person-centered therapists subscribe to the same beliefs about human beings and the desirable characteristics of a therapeutic relationship, they may differ widely in therapeutic style. Rogers's approach allows considerable room for practitioners to develop their own style in applying the basic concepts (Thorne, 1992).

Another contribution of the person-centered approach has been its attempts to apply subjective research methods to study both the process and outcomes of groups. Rogers has consistently demonstrated a willingness to state his formulations as testable hypotheses and to submit his hypotheses to research efforts. His 1957 hypothesis on the core conditions necessary and sufficient to produce therapeutic change probably stimulated more research on the process and outcome of psychotherapy than any other idea before or since that time (Cain, 1987a).

In assessing the contributions of the person-centered approach, Cain (1990a) points out that when Rogers founded it over 50 years ago, there were very few other therapeutic models in use. He notes, "At a . . . time when there are well over 200 therapeutic approaches, it is worth noting that the client-centered approach continues to have a significant place . . . among the major therapeutic systems" (p. 5). The longevity of this approach is certainly a factor in considering its impact.

Limitations of the Approach

Although Rogers and his colleagues engaged in research with personal-growth groups when the group movement had reached its zenith in the 1960s, there has been little recent research into person-centered groups. David Cain, the person-centered therapist who reviewed this chapter, comments that although Rogers valued research, neither he nor his colleagues have written much of significance in over 20 years. The person-centered group of today is not substantially different from the encounter group of the late 1960s. Indeed, there has been little evolution of concepts or methods in the model, even though we know more today about group theory and group process than we did in the 1960s. According to Cain (1993), the major reason that person-centered counseling has failed to thrive is its lack of evolution in theory or practice. The potential of this approach is limited because of the relative paucity of information that is being incorporated. Cain asserts that clients will not receive optimal help from traditional therapists who are practicing in limited and constricted ways. He concludes that the person-centered approach seems to be on the decline in the United States.

My central criticism of the person-centered approach, an approach I see as the foundation for practice, involves not what it includes but, rather, what it omits. I don't subscribe to the notion that technical skills and knowledge are unimportant. It is clear that person-centered group leaders typically do not employ directive strategies, mainly because of their belief that the members can find their own direction in working through the problems they bring to a group session. Person-centered therapists do not support the notion that it is the facilitator's job to devise and introduce techniques and exercises as a way of structuring a group or getting the group to do its work (Boy, 1990). In disagreement with this view, I prefer the value of action; of therapeutic direction, if it is needed by clients; and of more directive skills than are found in this approach. I see both active support and directive interventions as being essential if clients are to make changes.

I have found that I'm most effective, and the group seems to be most productive, when there is a structure that offers some direction yet grants freedom to the members. Thus, I typically provide the most structure at the beginning and ending stages of a group. I generally use techniques to enhance and to highlight the existing material in the group, rather than to get things moving. Although I don't like to use techniques to induce emotions, I generally use them to help members deepen their experience of certain emotions and to explore their feelings or problems. For example, when members talk about a lonely time of their lives and sadness comes up naturally, I am inclined to ask them to do any number of things, a few of which might be looking at another person in the room and talking directly to this person about the sadness, talking to a person as though he or she were a significant other, or reenacting a past event as though it were happening now. When members bring a struggle or some unfinished business with significant people in their lives into the present, whatever they are experiencing is usually intensified. By providing some therapeutic structure, I give them the encouragement and support they need to stay with their personal pain and make a crucial breakthrough. When they say they would like to change how they relate to someone they love, I often suggest that they talk to this person symbolically in the group, in a role-playing exercise. Through this structure members can benefit by trying on various alternatives, and they also profit from the feedback of others. These techniques or experiments grow out of the phenomenological situation and are designed to facilitate deeper self-exploration, which is quite different from pushing members to feel certain emotions.

This leader directiveness is not restricted to the group sessions but extends to helping members practice in daily life what they are learning in the meetings. Because I believe that members can benefit from leader assistance in translating their insights into action programs, I am fond of suggesting homework assignments that are designed to help clients challenge themselves to do difficult things. Although I generally ask clients to come up with their own homework, I am not adverse to making suggestions and presenting them in an invitational manner. These action-oriented interventions are designed to enable members to make decisions about how they want to be different and to gain some practice in thinking, feeling, and behaving differently. My guess is that most person-centered group facilitators would not feel comfortable with the action-oriented methods that I am describing.

Applying the Person-Centered Approach with Multicultural Populations

The person-centered approach, more than other models, has been applied to bringing people of diverse cultures together for the purpose of developing mutual understanding. In 1948 Rogers began developing a theory of reducing tension among antagonistic groups, and he continued until his death in 1987. He conducted workshops involving different types of factional differences in Italy, Poland, Brazil, Japan, Mexico, France, the Philippines, South Africa, the former Soviet Union, and the United States (Rogers, 1987c).

Shortly before his death Rogers conducted four-day workshops with Soviet psychologists, educators, and researchers. He maintained that these sessions had demonstrated that the concerns expressed differed little from those felt by a similar professional group in the United States. He found that a psychological climate produced certain predictable results in the United States, Latin America, European countries, and South Africa as well as Russia (Rogers, 1987a).

Person-centered groups have attained considerable popularity in Japan, and researchers there have conducted numerous studies on these groups. Murayama, Nojima, and Abe (1988) point out that members in these groups commonly experience feelings of inferiority in expressing their point of view during group meetings. The difficulty Japanese people have in expressing themselves when they feel different from others is largely due to a feeling of shame they attach to expressing their differences. Findings of person-centered groups indicate that Japanese clients prefer to hide their feelings rather than to express them. Because of this tendency, group sessions often have intense periods of silence, with members hoping that someone else will begin self-disclosure. Japanese facilitators tend to be more autocratic, partly because members expect them to take the initiative. Murayama and his colleagues conclude: "Person-centered groups have been a great factor in the orientation of persons living in Japanese society. The application of person-centered theory has contributed to the development of a more mature and knowledgeable human being" (1988, p. 490).

As we've seen, a major focus of person-centered therapy lies in active listening, which is a key contribution to effective group work. This approach is grounded on the importance of hearing the deeper messages that clients bring to a group. Empathy, being present, and respecting the values of clients are particularly important attitudes and skills in groups with culturally diverse clients. In working with certain Japanese-American clients, for example, the leader might learn of their hesitation in revealing their feelings. Person-centered leaders would respect the cultural norm pertaining to showing one's feelings and not be inclined to push the value of readily displaying feelings. They would help clients work within the framework of their values.

Although the person-centered approach has made significant contributions to working with groups representing diverse social, political, and cultural backgrounds, there are also some limitations to practicing exclusively within this framework in community agency settings and outpatient clinics. Many of the clients who come to a community mental-health clinic or who are involved in some other type of outpatient treatment may need a more structured group experience. This is especially true of short-term groups, open groups with a rapidly changing membership, task-oriented groups, and groups composed of culturally diverse populations. Clients with a lower socioeconomic status often seek professional help to deal with some current crisis, to alleviate psychosomatic symptoms, or to learn certain coping skills (such as stress management). They are often more concerned with basic security and survival needs than they are in actualization needs. Such clients are likely to have expectations of getting some measure of immediate help from the leader. They often wait for active probing by the group leader or for an expressed invitation to speak. They expect a directive leader who functions in an expert role as an authority, and they can be put off by a leader who does not provide some structuring (Chu & Sue, 1984; Leong, 1986, 1992).

According to Leong (1992), leaders who place a high premium on egalitarian relationships and who provide a low degree of structure are likely to meet with difficulty in working with Asian Americans, for these clients prefer a structured, problem-focused, task-oriented approach to dealing with problems. Such clients may well perceive the person-centered therapist's attempts to create a climate of open and free self-expression as being alien to their cultural values. They are likely to be uncomfortable with this informal and personal style. Leong (1986) cites several studies indicating that Asian Americans perceive counseling as a directive, paternalistic, and authoritarian process. Not only do they expect the professional to take an active and directive role in the counseling process, they also expect the counselor to provide advice and recommend a specific course of action. Moreover, the person-centered approach extols the value of an internal locus of control, and prizes self-determination and autonomy, whereas some cultures place a value on an external locus of evaluation. Such clients may look to family tradition for their answers.

There is a high dropout rate for ethnic-minority clients: as many as 52% of them terminate counseling after the first session (Mokuau, 1987). One explanation for this obvious dissatisfaction with professional counseling is that these clients quickly make the assessment that they will not get the help they are looking for from the counseling relationship. This is why it is so crucial that the issue of clients' expectations and goals be explored during the first meeting. If leaders simply wait for clients to bring up these issues for themselves, it may be too late, because they may not return for another session. Therefore, more activity and structuring may be called for than is usually the case in a person-centered framework, especially in a group. In my opinion, groups can benefit from some teaching by the leader on what groups are about and how best to participate. Members profit from a focused discussion of the general goals and procedures of group process and of how the group might help them deal with their concerns. Leaders who discuss expectations with members will increase the retention rate of their group.

Another limitation of person-centered therapy is that it is difficult to operationalize the core conditions. For example, consider these questions: How is warmth specifically manifested? How do group leaders demonstrate their realness in behavioral ways? How do they demonstrate unconditional positive regard? How are they to know the degree to which the members are experiencing this unconditional acceptance? The way in which a group leader communicates these core conditions to the members needs to be consistent with their cultural framework. Some members may be accustomed to indirect communication and may therefore be uncomfortable with the openness and directness of the person-centered group leader, and they may resist relating to others with openness and directness. Respect can be shown by recognizing and appreciating the rich diversity that exists within any group of people.

The difficulties in applying a person-centered approach apply to other cultural groups besides Asian Americans. African-American, Hispanic, and Native American clients may encounter difficulty in relating to the processes involved in a person-centered group. The communication style emphasizing summarization, reflective listening, and restatement tends to be of limited use in working with many Native American clients (LaFromboise, Trimble, & Mohatt, 1990). In addition to being generally "quiet," Native Americans value restraint of emotion and the acceptance of suffering. Such clients may perceive expressing feelings as a weakness. It would be more consistent with their cultural worldview to treat them within the context of a larger family and community social system.

Cain (1990b) points to a paradox of the person-centered approach. Although the model acknowledges and values the uniqueness of the person, it does not specify how to work with diversity. Cain challenges group facilitators to think of appropriate ways to modify their response styles to meet the specific needs and preferences of the members:

> In my view, clients are most likely to realize their unique potential if therapists remain mindful that each person is different from every other, and that each therapy needs to be individualized if we are to be optimally helpful to our clients. To do so means that the therapist attempts to see with the client's eyes, hear through the client's ears, and learn from the client what fits [p. 99].

Although with certain clients there are distinct limitations to working exclusively within a person-centered perspective, it should not be concluded that this approach is unsuitable for ethnically and culturally diverse populations. Whereas some clients prefer a directive and active style, others respond well to a less directive leader. The research literature suggests that the appropriateness and effectiveness of counseling styles depends largely on the cultural values and worldview embraced by an individual (Mokuau, 1987). It is a mistake to assume that one style of group leadership will be effective for all clients. The potential for therapeutic change is maximized when a counselor works with clients in a way that is compatible with their preferred learning style, which is typically influenced by their cultural background (Cain, 1990b).

Where to Go from Here

You might consider joining the Association for the Development of the Person-Centered Approach, an interdisciplinary and international organization with over 250 members. Membership includes a subscription to the *Person-Centered Journal,* the association's newsletter, a membership directory, and information about the annual meeting. It also provides information about continuing education and supervision and training in the person-centered approach. General membership is $45 a year; student membership is $20 a year. For more information, contact:

David Cain
Person-Centered Association
7212 Plaza De La Costa
Carlsbad, CA 92009
TELEPHONE: (619) 438-0684

Perhaps one of the best ways to evaluate a person-centered group is to participate in one. The La Jolla Program offers residential workshops, training seminars, experiential small groups, and sharing of learning in community meetings. Over 15,000 individuals from 25 nations have attended this program in the last 25 years. If you have an interest in finding out more about the workshops described in *Carl Rogers on Encounter Groups* (1970), you can contact:

David Meador
Center for Studies of the Person
1125 Torrey Pines Road
La Jolla, CA 92037
TELEPHONE: (619) 459-3861

If you are interested in obtaining supervised experience in the person-centered approach, consider the Carl Rogers Institute of Psychotherapy Training and Supervision. Training is designed to maximize the effectiveness of practitioners who work with culturally diverse populations. The didactic and experiential program is for mental-health professionals in individual, family, and group therapy. The institute conducts four training programs each year, including a one-month intensive program. For more information, contact:

Norman E. Chambers
Center for Studies of the Person
1125 Torrey Pines Road
La Jolla, CA 92037
TELEPHONE: (619) 459-3861

RECOMMENDED SUPPLEMENTARY READINGS

Carl Rogers on Encounter Groups (Rogers, 1970) is an excellent introduction to these groups. It is a readable account of their process and outcomes, changes as a result of them, and glimpses of the subjective struggles and experiences of those who participate in them.

On Becoming a Person (Rogers, 1961) is an important work addressing the characteristics of the helping relationship, the philosophy of the person-centered approach, and practical issues related to therapy. I especially recommend Chapters 2–9, 16, and 17.

Carl Rogers on Personal Power: Inner Strength and Its Revolutionary Impact (Rogers, 1977) describes the effectiveness of the person-centered approach in dealing with problems encountered in professions, marriage and family life, education, and even politics. A chapter is devoted to the description of a two-week workshop from the planning stages to its outcome.

A Way of Being (Rogers, 1980) contains a series of updated writings on Rogers's personal experiences and perspectives, as well as chapters on the foundations and applications of a person-centered approach. Especially useful are the chapters on person-centered communities, large groups, and perspectives on the world and person of tomorrow.

Carl Rogers (Thorne, 1992) is an informative book on his life and work. The author focuses on Rogers's overall influence on the counseling field, assesses his major contributions to both theory and practice, and addresses criticisms of his approach. This book is highly recommended for a concise overview of Rogers's thinking.

Three Psychologies: Perspectives from Freud, Skinner, and Rogers (Nye, 1992) contains an excellent discussion of Rogers's humanistic phenomenology. It clearly describes concepts such as the actualizing tendency, the core conditions for change, the fully functioning person, and the encounter-group movement.

REFERENCES AND SUGGESTED READINGS*

Atkinson, D. R., Morten, G., & Sue, D. W. (1993). *Counseling American minorities: A cross-cultural perspective* (4th ed.). Madison, WI: Brown & Benchmark.

Barrett-Lennard, G. T. (1988). Listening. *Person-Centered Review, 3*(4), 410–425.

*Boy, A. V. (1990). The therapist in person-centered groups. *Person-Centered Review, 5*(3), 308–315.

Bozarth, J. D. (1981). The person-centered approach in the large community group. In G. Gazda (Ed.), *Innovations to group psychotherapy* (2nd ed.). Springfield, IL: Charles C Thomas.

Bozarth, J. D. (1984). Beyond reflections: Emergent modes of empathy. In R. F. Levant & J. M. Shlien (Eds.), *Client-centered therapy and the person-centered approach: New directions in theory, research, and practice* (pp. 59–75). New York: Praeger.

Bozarth, J. D., & Brodley, B. T. (1986). Client-centered psychotherapy: A statement. *Person-Centered Review, 1*(3), 262–271.

*Braaten, L. J. (1986). Thirty years with Rogers's necessary and sufficient conditions of therapeutic personality change: A personal evaluation. *Person-Centered Review, 1*(1), 37–50.

Bugental, J. F. T. (1978). *Psychotherapy and process: The fundamentals of an existential-humanistic approach.* Reading, MA: Addison-Wesley.

Bugental, J. F. T. (1986). Existential-humanistic psychotherapy. In I. L. Kutash & A. Wolf (Eds.), *Psychotherapist's casebook* (pp. 222–236). San Francisco: Jossey-Bass.

Bugental, J. F. T. (1987). *The art of the psychotherapist.* New York: Norton.

*Cain, D. J. (1987a). Carl R. Rogers: The man, his vision, his impact. *Person-Centered Review, 2*(3), 283–288.

Cain, D. J. (1987b). Carl Rogers's life in review. *Person-Centered Review, 2*(4), 476–506.

Cain, D. J. (1990a). Fifty years of client-centered therapy and the person-centered approach. *Person-Centered Review, 5*(1), 3–7.

*Cain, D. J. (1990b). Further thoughts about nondirectiveness and client-centered therapy. *Person-Centered Review, 5*(1), 89–99.

*Cain, D. J. (1993). The uncertain future of client-centered counseling. *Journal of Humanistic Education and Development, 31*(3), 133–138.

Chu, J., & Sue, S. (1984). Asian/Pacific-Americans and group practice. In L. E. Davis (Ed.), *Ethnicity in social group work practice.* New York: Haworth Press.

Coghlan, D., & McIlduff, E. (1990). Structuring and nondirectiveness in group facilitation. *Person-Centered Review, 5*(1), 13–29.

Coulson, W. R. (1970). Major contribution: Inside a basic encounter group. *The Counseling Psychologist, 2*(2), 1–27.

Gordon, T. (1951). Group-centered leadership and administration. In C. R. Rogers, *Client-centered therapy.* Boston: Houghton Mifflin.

Hobbs, N. (1951). Group-centered psychotherapy. In C. R. Rogers, *Client-centered therapy.* Boston: Houghton Mifflin.

Ibrahim, F. A. (1991). Contribution of cultural worldview to generic counseling and development. *Journal of Counseling and Development, 70*(1), 13–19.

Jourard, S. (1971). *The transparent self* (rev. ed.). New York: Van Nostrand Reinhold.

*Books and articles marked with an asterisk are suggested for further study.

LaFromboise, T. D., Trimble, J. E., & Mohatt, G. V. (1990). Counseling intervention and American Indian tradition: An integrative approach. *The Counseling Psychologist, 18*(4), 628–654.

Leong, F. T. L. (1986). Counseling and psychotherapy with Asian-Americans: Review of the literature. *Journal of Counseling Psychology, 33*(2), 196–206.

Leong, F. T. L. (1992). Guidelines for minimizing premature termination among Asian American clients. *Journal for Specialists in Group Work, 17*(4), 218–228.

*Lietaer, G. (1984). Unconditional positive regard: A controversial basic attitude in client-centered therapy. In R. F. Levant & J. M. Shlien (Eds.), *Client-centered therapy and the person-centered approach: New directions in theory, research, and practice* (pp. 41–58). New York: Praeger.

Maslow, A. (1968). *Toward a psychology of being* (2nd ed.). New York: Van Nostrand Reinhold.

Maslow, A. (1970). *Motivation and personality* (2nd ed.). New York: Harper & Row.

Maslow, A. (1971). *The farther reaches of human nature*. New York: Viking.

May, R. (1953). *Man's search for himself*. New York: Norton.

May, R. (Ed.). (1961). *Existential psychology*. New York: Random House.

Meador, B. D. (1975). Client-centered group therapy. In G. Gazda (Ed.), *Basic approaches to group psychotherapy and group counseling* (2nd ed.). Springfield, IL: Charles C Thomas.

Mokuau, N. (1987). Social workers' perceptions of counseling effectiveness for Asian American clients. *Journal of the National Association of Social Workers, 32*(4), 331–335.

*Murayama, S., Nojima, K., & Abe, T. (1988). Person-centered groups in Japan: A selected review of the literature. *Person-Centered Review, 3*(4), 479–492.

*Natiello, P. (1987). The person-centered approach: From theory to practice. *Person-Centered Review, 2*(2), 203–216.

Nye, R. D. (1992). *Three psychologies: Perspectives from Freud, Skinner, and Rogers* (4th ed.). Pacific Grove, CA: Brooks/Cole.

*Raskin, N. J. (1986a). Client-centered group psychotherapy, Part 1: Development of client-centered groups. *Person-Centered Review, 1*(3), 272–290.

*Raskin, N. J. (1986b). Client-centered group psychotherapy, Part 2: Research on client-centered groups. *Person-Centered Review, 1*(4), 389–408.

Rice, L. N., & Greenberg, L. S. (1992). Humanistic approaches to psychotherapy. In D. K. Freedheim (Ed.), *History of psychotherapy: A century of change* (pp. 197–224). Washington, DC: American Psychological Association.

Rogers, C. (1951). *Client-centered therapy*. Boston: Houghton Mifflin.

*Rogers, C. (1957). The necessary and sufficient conditions of therapeutic personality change. *Journal of Consulting Psychology, 21*, 95–103.

*Rogers, C. (1961). *On becoming a person*. Boston: Houghton Mifflin.

*Rogers, C. (1970). *Carl Rogers on encounter groups*. New York: Harper & Row.

Rogers, C. (1975). Empathic: An unappreciated way of being. *The Counseling Psychologist, 5*(2), 2–9.

Rogers, C. (1977). *Carl Rogers on personal power: Inner strength and its revolutionary impact*. New York: Delacorte Press.

*Rogers, C. (1980). *A way of being*. Boston: Houghton Mifflin.

Rogers, C. (1986a). Carl Rogers on the development of the person-centered approach. *Person-Centered Review, 1*(3), 257–259.

Rogers, C. (1986b). Client-centered therapy. In I. L. Kutash & A. Wolf (Eds.), *Psychotherapist's casebook* (pp. 197–208). San Francisco: Jossey-Bass.

Rogers, C. R. (1987a). Inside the world of the Soviet professional. *Counseling and Values, 32*(1), 46–66.

Rogers, C. R. (1987b). Rogers, Kohut, and Erikson: A personal perspective on some similarities and differences. In J. K. Zeig (Ed.), *The evolution of psychotherapy* (pp. 179–187). New York: Brunner/Mazel.

Rogers, C. R. (1987c). Steps toward world peace, 1948–1986: Tension reduction in theory and practice. *Counseling and Values, 32*(1), 12–16.

Rogers, C. R. (1987d). The underlying theory: Drawn from experience with individuals and groups. *Counseling and Values, 32*(1), 38–45.

Rogers, C. R., & Malcolm, D. (1987). The potential contribution of the behavioral scientist to world peace. *Counseling and Values, 32*(1), 10–11.

Sue, D. W., & Sue, D. (1990). *Counseling the culturally different: Theory and practice* (2nd ed.). New York: Wiley.

*Thorne, B. (1992). *Carl Rogers*. Newbury Park, CA: Sage.

*Yalom, I. D. (1980). *Existential psychotherapy*. New York: Basic Books.

Zimring, F. M., & Raskin, N. J. (1992). Carl Rogers and client/person-centered therapy. In D. K. Freedheim (Ed.), *History of psychotherapy: A century of change* (pp. 629–656). Washington, DC: American Psychological Association.

CHAPTER ELEVEN

Gestalt Therapy

Introduction

Gestalt therapy, a form of existential therapy developed by the late Fritz Perls, is based on the premise that individuals must find their own way in life and accept personal responsibility. The focus is on what the client experiences in the present moment and on the blocks that the person must overcome to achieve full awareness of the here and now. The basic goal of a Gestalt group is to challenge the participants to become aware of how they are avoiding responsibility for such awareness and to encourage them to look for internal, rather than external, support. Moment-to-moment awareness of one's experiencing, together with the almost immediate awareness of one's blocks to such experiencing, is seen as therapeutic in and of itself.

As clients acquire present-centered awareness and a clearer perception of their blocks and conflicts, significant unfinished business emerges. It is assumed that the way to become an autonomous person is to identify and deal with anything from the past that interferes with current functioning. By reexperiencing past conflicts as if they were occurring in the present, clients expand their level of awareness, sometimes gradually and sometimes explosively, and are able to face and integrate denied and fragmented parts of themselves, thus becoming unified and whole.

The Gestalt view is that we are essentially responsible for our own conflicts and that we have the capacity to deal with our life problems. Therefore, the approach of the Gestalt group is basically noninterpretive. Group members make their own interpretations and statements and discover the meaning of their experiences. Leaders avoid interfering with the clients' interpretations and focus instead on whatever the person seems to be experiencing at the moment. Gestalt leaders tend to be active and use a wide range of action-oriented techniques designed to intensify the members' feelings and experiences.

Group members are constantly being urged to try on a new style of behavior, to give expression to certain dimensions of their personality that are dormant, and to test out alternative modes of behavior so as to widen their ability to respond in the world. According to Zinker (1978), Gestalt experiments are anchored in the experiential life of the members as they present themselves in the situation. Prefabricated exercises that are imposed on the group without having experiential roots are not within the province of Gestalt therapy, since they do not grow out of a living context for the group.

Key Concepts

Therapeutic Goals

The basic aim of Gestalt therapy, as mentioned, is the attaining of awareness, which by and of itself is seen as curative. Without awareness, clients don't possess the tools for personality change. With awareness, they have the capacity to recognize the impasses and blockages that they create and to find within themselves the resources necessary to solve their problems and discover the conditions that will make change possible. It is awareness that allows clients to recognize and reintegrate parts of themselves that they have disowned and, thus, become unified and whole.

The question of therapeutic goals can be considered from the point of view of personal goals for each member and of group-process goals for the group as a whole. Zinker (1980) describes the following individual goals:

- ◆ integrating polarities within oneself
- ◆ achieving contact with self and others
- ◆ learning to provide self-support instead of looking to others for this support
- ◆ becoming aware of what one is sensing, feeling, thinking, fantasizing, and doing in the present
- ◆ defining one's boundaries with clarity
- ◆ translating insights into action
- ◆ being willing to learn about oneself by engaging in creative experiments

Goals for the members to achieve on the group level include these:

- ◆ learning how to ask clearly and directly for what they want or need
- ◆ learning how to deal with one another in the face of conflict
- ◆ learning how to give support and energy to one another
- ◆ being able to challenge one another to push beyond the boundaries of safety and what is known
- ◆ creating a community that is based on trust, which allows for a level of deep and meaningful work
- ◆ learning how to make use of the resources within the group rather than relying on the group leader as the director

The Here and Now

One of Perls's most significant contributions is his emphasis on learning to appreciate and fully experience the present: the present is the most significant tense, for the past is gone, and the future has not yet arrived. He notes, however, that for most people the power of the present is lost because, instead of being in the present, they ruminate about the past or engage in endless plans and resolutions for the future. As they direct their energies toward what might have been or what might be, their capacity to seize the power of the moment diminishes dramatically.

Perls (1973) makes it clear that Gestalt is an *experiential* therapy, not a verbal or interpretive one, and that it is aimed at helping clients make direct contact with their experience in the immediacy of the moment. In the Gestalt view, if we think and talk about an experience, we interrupt the flow of present-centered experiencing and become detached from ourselves.

This focus on the present doesn't indicate a lack of interest in the past. The past *is* important, but only insofar as it is related to our present functioning. In Gestalt groups, participants bring past problem situations into the present by reenacting the situation as if it were occurring now. For example, if a group member begins to talk about the difficulty she had when she was younger and attempted to live with her father, the therapist will typically intervene with a request that she "be here now" with her father and speak directly to him. The therapist might say: "Bring your father into this room now, and let yourself go back to the time when you were a child. Tell him now, as though he were here and you were that child, what you most want to say."

For group leaders, it is useful to know that many problems that members bring up relate to unfinished situations with significant people in their life. In this example the group member may harbor feelings of resentment and mistrust toward men, based on her convictions that men will simply not be there for her in time of need. She may connect this present feeling to old feelings associated with her alcoholic father, who continually let her down and brought much pain into her life. Based on her early decision not to trust men, she may be projecting her negative feelings toward all men now. Concluding that if her own father could not be counted on for love and protection, then surely other men will not be more trustworthy, she now looks for evidence to support her hypothesis. The Gestalt group leader would invite her to deal with her father symbolically in the here and now. She might have a dialogue with him, becoming both her father and herself. She could now say all the things that she wanted to say to her father as a child but, because of her fear, kept deep inside herself. She might tell her father what she most wanted from him then and what she still wants with him now.

Of course, there are many creative possibilities within the group. She could look at the men in the group, expressing to each some of her resentments. In making contact with each man in the group, she could share her fantasies of all the ways in which they would let her down or of what she would like from them now yet is afraid to ask for. The theoretical rationale for this technique is rooted in the assumption that the emotions that were overwhelming to her as a child were dealt with by some form of distortion or denial. The Gestalt leader encourages her to reexperience these past events by reliving them in the here and now so that the emotions that were repressed can come to the surface. With the support of the leader and the group members, she can allow herself to experience feelings that she has sealed off from awareness, and she can now work through some of these feelings that are keeping her stuck. By challenging her assumptions of how men are, she is able to establish a new basis for relating to men.

The technique of making a situation a present one can be applied to future events. If the above group member is afraid of a future confrontation with her father, she can be asked to live her expectations in the here and now by speaking directly to her father in the group and by expressing her fears and hopes. Thus, she may say to her father: "I want to tell you how much I'd like to be close to you, but I'm afraid that if I do so, you won't care. I'm afraid of saying the wrong things and pushing you even further away from me."

Since Gestalt therapy focuses on the power of the present, most Gestalt techniques are designed to put clients into closer contact with their ongoing experiencing and increase their awareness of what they are feeling from moment to moment. Just as there are advantages to focusing on the here and now, there are disadvantages to this exclusive focus if the past and the future are discarded. E. Polster (1987) observes that too tight a focus, with a highly concentrated emphasis on the here and now, will foreclose on much that matters, such as continuity of commitment, the implications of one's acts, dependability, and responsiveness to others.

Awareness and Responsibility

The task of the member of a Gestalt group is to pay attention to the structure of his or her experience and to become aware of the *what* and *how* of such experiencing. Whereas the psychoanalytic approach is interested in why we do what we do and not in how we do it, the Gestalt leader asks "what" and "how" questions but rarely "why" questions. Perls (1969a) says that *why* is a dirty word in Gestalt therapy, because it leads to rationalizations and, at best, to clever explanations but never to understanding. By contrast, he adds, focusing on what people experience in the immediate situation and on how they experience it does lead to increased awareness of the present. By attending to the continuum of awareness—that is, by staying with the moment-to-moment flow of experiencing—clients discover how they are functioning in the world.

According to Perls's colorful description, the two legs on which Gestalt therapy walks are the now and the how. The essence of Gestalt theory hinges on these two words: *now* covers all that exists, and it is the basis of awareness; *how* covers behavior and what is involved in an ongoing process. Perls contends that all else is irrelevant. To help clients get focused on the present and experience more intensely their immediate feelings, the Gestalt leader asks questions that lead to present-centeredness:

◆ "What are you experiencing now?"
◆ "What's going on inside you as you're speaking?"

◆ "How are you experiencing your anxiety in your body?"
◆ "How are you attempting to withdraw at this moment, and how are you avoiding contact with unpleasant feelings?"
◆ "What's your feeling at this moment—as you sit there and try to talk?"
◆ What's happening to your voice as you talk to your father now?"

In order to attain present-centered awareness of our existence, Gestalt therapy focuses on the obvious—on the surface of behavior—by concentrating on the client's movements, postures, language patterns, voice, gestures, and interactions with others. Since many people fail to see what is obvious (Perls, 1969a), the Gestalt therapist challenges clients to learn how to use their senses fully, to become aware of how they avoid the obvious, and to become open to what is here now. Polster and Polster (1973), too, point to the value of focusing on the surface of behavior and stress the need to provide a climate in which clients can become more clearly focused on their changing awareness from moment to moment.

The core of Gestalt therapy relates to helping us assume responsibility for whatever we are experiencing and doing. The crux of assuming responsibility is becoming aware of moment-by-moment experiencing and seeing how we are providing meaning to this experience. It means that we avoid manipulating others by fixing on them the blame for whatever we are feeling and doing. Nobody is *making* us feel any way or take any particular course of action. It also means that we do not keep ourselves helpless by expecting others to support us in a variety of ways when we are able to provide this support to ourselves. One way we can promote an increasing sense of personal responsibility is by becoming aware of the ways in which we give away our power by making others responsible for us. Another way is to separate our own expectations from what we think others expect of us and then to make a conscious decision to live by our own expectations.

Unfinished Business and Avoidance

Unfinished business includes unexpressed feelings—such as resentment, hate, rage, pain, hurt, anxiety, guilt, and grief—and events and memories that linger in the background and clamor for completion. Unless these unfinished situations and unexpressed emotions are recognized and dealt with, they keep interfering with present-centered awareness and with our effective functioning.

A concept related to unfinished business is avoidance, which refers to the means people use to keep themselves from facing unfinished business and from experiencing the uncomfortable emotions associated with unfinished situations. Perls (1969a) says that most people would rather avoid experiencing painful emotions than do what is necessary to change. Therefore, they become stuck and are unable to get through the impasse, blocking their possibilities of growth.

Because we have a tendency to avoid confronting and fully experiencing our anxiety, grief, guilt, and other uncomfortable emotions, the emotions become a nagging undercurrent that prevents us from being fully alive. Perls speaks of the catastrophic expectations that we conjure up and that keep us psychologically stuck: "If I express my pain fully, people will be embarrassed, and they won't have anything to do with me"; "If I were to express my anger to the significant people in my life, they would abandon me"; "If I ever allowed myself to mourn over my losses, I might sink so deep into depression that I'd never get out of that hole."

Perls maintains that these fantasies keep us from living, because we use them to avoid taking the necessary risks that growth demands. Thus, the Gestalt therapist encourages expressing in the therapeutic session intense feelings never directly expressed before. If a client says to the group that she is afraid of getting in touch with her feelings of hatred and spite, she may be encouraged by the therapist to become her hateful and spiteful side and express these negative feelings to each group member. By experiencing the side of herself that she works so hard at disowning, this participant begins a process of integration and allows herself to get beyond the impasse that keeps her from growing.

During a group session, a member says that he feels empty and power-less. The therapist is likely to encourage him to stay with these uncomfort-able feelings, even to exaggerate them—to "be empty," to "be powerless." The theory is that if this person can endure and truly experience the depth of his feelings, he will probably discover that whatever catastrophic ex-pectations he has with regard to those feelings are more of a fantasy than a reality and that his helplessness and void will not destroy him. Experienc-ing dreaded emotions leads to integration and growth. By going beyond our avoidances, we make it possible to dispose of unfinished business that interferes with our present life, and we move toward health and integration.

Layers of Neurosis and Modes of Defense

Perls (1970) has likened the unfolding of adult personality to the peeling of an onion. In order for individuals to achieve psychological maturity, they must strip off five layers of neurosis. These superimposed growth disorders are (1) the phony layer, (2) the phobic layer, (3) the impasse, (4) the implo-sive layer, and (5) the explosive layer. The first level we encounter, the *phony layer,* consists of reacting to others in stereotypical and inauthentic ways. This is the level where we play games and get lost in roles. By behaving as if we are a person that we are not, we are trying to live up to a fantasy that we or others have created. Once we become aware of the phoniness of game playing and become more honest, we experience un-pleasantness and pain.

The next layer we encounter is the *phobic layer.* At this level we attempt to avoid the emotional pain that is associated with seeing aspects of our-selves that we would prefer to deny. At this point our resistances to accept-ing ourselves the way we actually are pop up. We have catastrophic fears that if we recognize who we really are and present that side of ourselves to others, they will surely reject us.

Beneath the phobic layer is the *impasse,* or the point where we are stuck in our own maturation. This is the point at which we are sure that we will not be able to survive, for we convince ourselves that we do not have the resources within ourselves to move beyond the stuck point without environmental support. Typically, this is the time when we attempt to manipulate the environment to do our seeing, hearing, feeling, thinking, and deciding for us. At the impasse we often feel a sense of deadness and feel that we are nothing. If we hope to feel alive, it is essential that we get through the impasse.

If we allow ourselves to fully experience our deadness, rather than denying it or running away, the *implosive level* comes into being. Perls (1970) says that it is necessary to go through this implosive layer in order to get to the authentic self. By getting into contact with this layer, or our deadness and inauthentic ways, we expose our defenses and begin to make contact with our genuine self.

Perls contends that peeling back the implosive layer creates an explosive state. When we contact the *explosive layer,* we let go of phony roles and pretenses, and we release a tremendous amount of energy that we have been holding in by pretending to be who we are not. To become alive and authentic, it is necessary to achieve this release, which can be an explosion into pain and into joy, anger, sadness, or sexuality.

A concept related to these layers of personality is that of resistance and ego-defense mechanisms. From a Gestalt perspective, resistance refers to defenses we develop that prevent us from experiencing the present in a full and real way. The five layers of neurosis represent a person's style of keeping energy pent up in the service of maintaining pretenses. There are also ego-defense mechanisms that prevent people from being authentic. Five major channels of resistance that are challenged in Gestalt therapy are introjection, projection, retroflection, confluence, and deflection.

Introjection involves the tendency to accept others' beliefs and standards uncritically without assimilating them and making them congruent with who we are. These introjects become alien to us, because we have not analyzed and restructured them. When we introject, we passively incorporate what the environment provides, spending little time on getting clear what we want or need. During the early stages of a group, introjection is common, for the members tend to look to the leader to provide structure and direction. At this phase of a group's development members typically do not question the leader's interventions or rules. As the group reaches a working stage, members are less inclined to swallow whole the suggestions of the group leader.

Projection is the reverse of introjection. In projection we disown certain aspects of ourselves by ascribing them to the environment. When we are projecting, we have trouble distinguishing between the inside world and the outside world. Those attributes of our personality that are inconsistent with our self-image are disowned and put onto other people. By seeing in others the very qualities that we refuse to acknowledge in ourselves, we avoid taking responsibility for our own feelings and the person who we are. Of course, projection is the basis of transference. When transference feelings surface early in a group, these dynamics can be fruitfully explored. As members attempt to get a sense of both the leader and other members, they often attribute characteristics to these individuals that really belong to significant others in their lives. During the transition stage, when issues such as the struggle for control and power become central, projection continues to be a primary contacting style. Now participants may disown their own needs to control the group. The conflicts that occur at this phase are difficult to resolve unless those members who are projecting their need to control recognize and own their projections (Frew, 1986).

Retroflection consists of turning back to ourselves what we would like to do to someone else. For example, if we lash out and injure ourselves, we are often directing aggression inward that we are fearful of directing toward others. Typically, these maladaptive styles of functioning are done outside of our awareness; part of the process of Gestalt therapy is to help us discover a self-regulatory system so that we can deal realistically with the world. During the initial phase of a group, retroflection is easily observed in the tendency of some members to "hold back" by saying very little and expressing little emotion.

Confluence involves the blurring of awareness of differentiation between the self and the environment. For people who are confluent, there is no clear demarcation between internal experience and outer reality. Confluence in relationships involves an absence of conflicts, or a belief that all parties experience the same feelings and thoughts. It is a style of contact that is characteristic of group members who have a high need to be accepted and liked. Conflicts can be very anxiety-producing for individuals who rely on confluence as a style of contact (Frew, 1986). Confluence makes it difficult for people to have their own thoughts and to speak for themselves. This condition makes genuine contact next to impossible.

Deflection is the interruption of awareness, so that it is difficult to maintain a sustained sense of contact. People who deflect attempt to diffuse contact through the overuse of humor, abstract generalizations, and questions rather than statements (Frew, 1986). Deflection involves a diminished emotional experience. People who deflect speak through and for others.

Introjection, projection, retroflection, confluence, and deflection represent styles of resisting contact. Terms such as *resistance to contact* or *boundary disturbance* are used to characterize people who attempt to control their environment. The premise in Gestalt therapy is that contact is both normal and healthy. Therefore, a discussion of these styles of resistances to contact focuses on the degree to which these processes are in the individual's awareness. Clients in Gestalt therapy are encouraged to become increasingly aware of their dominant style of blocking contact.

Energy and Blocks to Energy

Because members need energy to work in group sessions, Gestalt leaders pay special attention to where energy is located, how it is used, and how it can be blocked. Blocked energy can be thought of as *resistance,* and there are a number of ways in which it can show up in the body. One member will experience tension in his neck and shoulders, and another member will experience shortness of breath. Another person will typically speak with a restricted voice, by holding back power. A few other ways that these blocks to energy will manifest themselves are keeping one's mouth shut tightly (as though one were afraid what might slip out); slouching; looking at the ground or in the air as a way of avoiding contact with others' eyes, keeping one's body tight and closed; talking in a fast and staccato fashion; being emotionally flat; and experiencing body sensations such as a lump in the throat, a quivering of the mouth, a hot and flushed feeling, shaking movements of the hands and legs, or dizziness.

In commenting on the value of focusing on the client's energy in therapeutic work, Zinker (1978) says that clients may not be aware of their energy or where it is located and may experience it in a negative way. From his perspective, therapy at its best is "a lively process of stoking the client's inner fires of awareness and contact" (p. 24). This process involves a therapeutic relationship that awakens and nourishes the client in such a way that the therapist does not become sapped of his or her own energy. Zinker maintains that it is the therapist's job to help clients locate the ways in which they are blocking energy and to help them transform this blocked energy into more adaptive behaviors. This process is best accomplished when resistance is not viewed as a client's refusal to cooperate and as something simply to be gotten around. Instead, therapists can learn to welcome resistance and use it as a way of deepening therapeutic work. Members can be encouraged to recognize how their resistance is being expressed in their body, and rather than trying to rid themselves of certain bodily symptoms, they can actually delve fully into tension states. By allowing themselves to exaggerate their tight mouth and shaking legs, they are able to discover for themselves how they are diverting energy and keeping themselves powerless.

Although talking can be provocative, the most direct access to feeling involves focusing on bodily experience. With body awareness, clients are asked to report bodily sensations that bespeak areas of diminished aliveness or blocks in the flow of that aliveness (Smith, 1985, p. 103). Using body-awareness work is a way of mobilizing clients and bringing them to take an active responsibility for their therapy. Smith writes about the role of the body in psychotherapy, and many of his ideas have applicability to group work. He describes "soft techniques" in working with the body. For example, if a member sits with a closed posture, the leader can invite him or her to uncross and experience the feeling, and then cross again. By inviting clients to move out of a particular posture and experiment with a new posture, leaders can facilitate awareness. Members who slouch and who also complain about low self-esteem can be invited to stand and walk erect. In a like way, members can be asked to exaggerate a particular gesture or posture as a way of learning more about themselves. In short, paying attention to the body and energy blockages within the body can be a productive way to explore the meaning of a member's experience.

Methods of working with the body can be fruitfully combined with other techniques in a Gestalt group. Reichian body-work concepts and techniques are particularly useful in working with energy and blocks to energy. Wilhelm Reich's (1949) central idea was that emotions were an expression of the movement of body energy and that chronic tensions blocked this flow of energy and thus blocked emotions. He associated forms of resistance with specific patterns of "muscular armoring." He emphasized the value of loosening and dissolving this muscular armor, along with dealing with psychological issues in an analytic way. Reich demonstrated that relaxing these patterns of muscular armoring could release bottled-up emotions. In his therapy work he paid attention to nonverbal behaviors such as the client's general appearance, facial expressions, tensions in various parts of the body, and gestures. As a way of helping his clients increase their awareness of their body and character traits, he asked them to exaggerate certain habitual behaviors that were thought to be a part of character armor. Reichian body work included emphasis on breathing in a spontaneous and relaxed way. Methods that deepened the client's breathing led to an opening of the feelings. His approach focused on working with muscular tensions, such as a tight jaw, neck, or mouth, frowns, and so forth. Reichian work is based largely on a reading of the body and proceeds in a systematic way, beginning with the eyes and ending with the pelvis. Reich's therapeutic work increasingly dealt with freeing intense emotions such as pleasure, rage, fear, pain, and anxiety through working with the body. He found that after repressed emotion was expressed, chronic muscular and psychological tension could also be released.

It is interesting to note that Perls was a patient and a student of Reich's, and in his writings Perls credits Reich with having had a significant influence on the concepts and techniques of Gestalt therapy. It is good to add the caution that before group leaders even consider incorporating some of the Reichian body techniques in a Gestalt group, they should have extensive training and supervision in these techniques. Even though Gestalt leaders might not have had such training, however, they can still make use of some of these concepts by learning how to pay attention to the energy flow and blockage as evidenced by looking at the bodies of the group members. Also, members can be taught how to pay attention to what they are experiencing within their own body, so that they can learn from the messages that their body is sending them.

Role and Functions of the Group Leader

Perhaps the best way to describe the functions of the Gestalt therapist or group leader is to review how Gestalt therapy proceeds. (Note that the following discussion applies to group as well as individual therapy.) According to Perls (1969a), the goal of therapy is the client's maturation and the removal of "blocks that prevent a person from standing on his own feet." In order to achieve this goal, the therapist helps the client make the transition from external to internal support by locating the *impasse*. Perls described the impasse as the place where people avoid experiencing threatening feelings and attempt to manipulate others by playing the game of being helpless, lost, confused, and stupid. These games permit clients to remain stuck and thus avoid doing what they need to do in order to resolve pressing unfinished business.

One of the therapist's functions is to challenge clients to get through the impasse so that growth is possible. It is a difficult function indeed, because at the point of impasse clients think that they have no chance of survival; they simply don't believe that they can find inside themselves the means for going on. So they give up their own eyes and ears and desperately try to manipulate others into doing their seeing and hearing for them. If therapists are not careful, they can easily get caught up in the manipulations of their clients. If they try to be "helpful," they may foster dependency and helplessness and reinforce the belief of clients that they don't have the ability to cope with life. Then clients can give in to their catastrophic expectations and avoid challenging the fears that are keeping them stuck.

The therapist must confront clients so that they will face what they are doing and decide whether they will develop their potential. This confrontation consists of challenging clients to fully experience whatever blockages and barriers are within them and to make contact with the frustration resulting from the feeling of being stuck.

Although Gestalt leaders encourage members to assume responsibility for raising their own level of consciousness, they can nevertheless take an active role in creating experiments to help the members tap their resources. Zinker (1978) writes that the therapist, functioning much like an artist, invents experiments with clients to augment their range of behaviors. The leader's function is to create an atmosphere and structure in which the group's own creativity and inventiveness can emerge. For example, a theme of loneliness may come up in a group. Here a central task of the leader is to orchestrate this theme by connecting members with one another and finding ways to involve the group as a whole in exploring loneliness.

Gestalt therapists employ a wide range of techniques to help clients gain awareness and experience their conflicts fully. It should be made clear, however, that, although the skillful and appropriate use of techniques is an important function of the therapist, Gestalt therapy is much more than a collection of techniques. Techniques cannot be separated from the personality of the therapist who uses them, and overuse of techniques may keep the therapist hidden and lead to "phony therapy that *prevents* growth" (Perls, 1969a, p. 1).

Polster and Polster (1973) see the therapist as nothing less than an artist involved in creating new life. Yet in Gestalt, as in most other approaches, the danger exists that the therapist will lose sight of the true meaning of the therapeutic process and become a mere technician. Therapists should use their own experience as an essential ingredient in the therapy process and never forget that they are far more than mere responders, givers of feedback, or catalysts who don't change themselves (Polster & Polster, 1973). Since the client/therapist relationship is the core of the therapeutic process, the use of techniques should never be allowed to interfere with the authenticity of the relationship. Techniques need to be individually tailored to each client, and they need to be the outgrowth of the therapeutic encounter—an encounter grounded in the mutual experiencing of client and therapist.

M. Polster (1987) describes the nature and purpose of experiments in this way: "Experiment is a Gestalt technique aimed at restoring momentum to the stuck points of a person's life. It is one way to recover the connection between deliberation and spontaneity by bringing the possibilities for action right into the therapy room" (p. 318). Through these experiments clients are able to confront the crises of their lives by playing out their troubled relationships in the safety of the therapeutic setting. Polster mentions some of the forms that Gestalt experiments might take: dramatizing a painful memory, imagining a dreaded encounter, playing one's parent, creating a dialogue between two parts within oneself, attending to an overlooked gesture, and exaggerating a certain posture. One of the therapist's functions is to observe whether the experiment appears too safe or too risky.

Therapists have latitude to invent their own techniques (or experiments), which are basically an extension of their personality. Thus, therapists must be grounded and in tune with themselves, as well as being present for their clients. If clients are to become authentic, they need contact with an authentic therapist on a genuine "I/thou" basis.

For Zinker (1978), creative therapists possess a rich personal background, having opened themselves to a range of life experiences and become able to celebrate life fully. In short, they are able to use themselves as a person as they function as a therapist. In addition to being mature and integrated people, creative therapists also possess certain capacities, abilities, and technical skills. Out of their experimental attitude, they use themselves, other group members, and objects and events in the group environment in the service of inventing novel visions of the members. Some of the specific skills that Zinker mentions as being related to the functioning of creative therapists are the following:

- ◆ the capacity to identify energy within the members and to move with this energy
- ◆ the sensitivity to introduce experiments in a timely and appropriate fashion
- ◆ the ability to be flexible by letting go of some things and moving to other areas that are more lively
- ◆ the willingness to push and confront members so that they will get their work done, along with the ability to know when to back off
- ◆ the ability to help members express their feelings and summarize what they are learning after they complete an experiment
- ◆ the wisdom to know when to let members stay confused so that they can learn to find clarity in their own way

From this discussion of the role and functions of the Gestalt group leader, it should be apparent that skilled leadership entails a great deal more than merely grabbing one technique after another from a Gestalt bag. Who the leader is as a person and how he or she functions in the group, creatively drawing on technical expertise, are the critical factors that determine the potency of leadership.

Applications and Techniques

As was mentioned earlier, Gestalt therapy employs a rich variety of action-oriented techniques designed to intensify what group members are experiencing in the present moment. Gestalt therapy encourages "becoming a conflict" or "being what we are feeling," as opposed to merely talking about conflicts, problems, and feelings. It cannot be overemphasized that these techniques need to be tailored to the individuals within the group and to the unique context of a particular group interaction. Applied mechanically or inappropriately, the techniques become mere gimmicks that can result in increased defensiveness by the members and in even less authentic living on their part.

At the beginning of a session, leaders may ask for a go-around in which each participant makes a brief here-and-now statement of what he or she is aware of. Members may be asked to declare if they have any personal issues they are willing to explore or what they want from the session. In this way session time can be maximized by focusing on common themes.

It is useful to differentiate between a group *exercise* and a group *experiment*. With group exercises, leaders prepare some kind of structured technique before the group meets. Members might be asked to pair up and talk, or a catalyst might be introduced into the group to provide a specific focus for work during a session. In contrast, a group *experiment* is a creative happening that grows out of the group experience; as such it cannot be predetermined, and its outcome cannot be predicted (Zinker, 1978). Therefore, it is essential to keep in mind that the techniques described in this chapter are not arbitrarily imposed on a group to *make* something happen. Rather than being used as catalysts for stirring up action in a group, these techniques are best conceived of as experiments that grow out of the ongoing interplay among the members.

To increase the chances that members will benefit from Gestalt techniques, group leaders need to communicate the general purpose of these techniques and to create an experimental climate. "Let's try something on for size and see how it fits" conveys this experimental attitude on the part of the leader. The message also says that the leader is not trying to prove a point and that the members are free to try something new and determine for themselves whether it's going to work. In discussing the need for a brief explanation of the purpose of the technique, Passons (1975) observes that clients may be puzzled by certain Gestalt exercises—for example, by being asked to talk to an empty chair, or to "be their sadness," or to become aware of what they are "saying" with their bodies—and that a brief explanation can dispel this perplexity and lead to greater willingness to experiment. Occasional explanations also foster trust in the leader by making clear that the exercise has a therapeutic purpose and is not an attempt to "trick" someone.

Zinker (1978) views the experiment as a way of modifying a member's behavior in the group context. He asserts that Gestalt therapy is a combination of phenomenology and behavior modification. He sees therapeutic work as rooted in the subjective perspective of the members; at the same time, experiments are introduced in such a manner that behavior is modified in a timely way. As the cornerstone of experiential learning, the experiment transforms talking about a situation into actual doing and rejects stale theorizing in favor of trying novel behaviors with a sense of excitement and imagination. Zinker emphasizes that each aspect of an experiment is presented at a point of developmental readiness for the client. In this sense experiments can be considered graded activities aimed at specific modifications of behavior.

It is clear that the emphasis is on *inviting* (not commanding) members to examine their behaviors, attitudes, and thoughts. Leaders can encourage members to look at certain incongruities, especially gaps between their verbal and nonverbal expression. Thus, the Gestalt group is characterized by challenge and positive confrontation. This confrontation is aimed at helping the members pay attention to what they are doing and experiencing in the here and now, not in a harsh or critical insistence that they be different than they are. Also, confrontation does not necessarily have to be aimed at weaknesses or negative traits; members can be challenged to recognize the ways in which they are blocking their strengths and ways in which they are not living as fully as they might. In this sense confrontation can be genuine expression of caring that results in positive changes in a member, not a brutal assault on a defenseless member. Of course, it cannot be overstressed that members must be prepared for taking part in experiments. They need to know that they can choose to go along and that they can also decide to stop when they want. Rather than pushing them into experimenting, the spirit is always one of inviting them to discover something new about themselves.

Keep in mind these introductory comments as you read the following pages, which describe several Gestalt techniques, their rationales, and their applications to group situations. As with all other techniques, here, too, it is up to the individual practitioner to integrate the exercises into his or her own therapeutic style, so that they become expressions of the personality of the leader. My discussion is based on a variety of sources—among them, Levitsky and Perls (1970), Passons (1975), Perls (1969a), Perls, Hefferline, and Goodman (1951), Polster and Polster (1973), Stevens (1971), and Zinker (1978). Note that I have modified some of the techniques to fit the needs of the group situation.

Language Exercises

Gestalt emphasizes the relationship between language patterns and personality. It suggests that our speech patterns are often expressions of our feelings, thoughts, and attitudes and that by focusing on our overt speaking habits, we can increase our self-awareness (Passons, 1975). Words can bring us to ourselves, or they can take us away from ourselves. The following Gestalt interventions, by making us more aware of some of our speech patterns, can enhance our self-awareness and bring us closer to ourselves.

It should be noted that the following language exercises require a great deal of skill on the part of the leader. Unless the members, through the leader's help, are able to see the value of paying attention to the impact of their language style, they will come to feel that everything they say and do is subject to unnecessary scrutiny.

IT. "It" talk is a way of depersonalizing language. By using *it* instead of *I*, we keep distant from our experience. When group members say "It's frightening to come to this group," they can be asked to change the sentence to "I'm frightened to come to this group." Substituting personal pronouns for impersonal ones is a way of assuming responsibility for what we say.

YOU. Often group participants say something like "You feel hurt when someone rejects you." By using "you" talk, people detach themselves from whatever they may be feeling. Therefore, members are asked to pay attention to the differences between the above statement and "I feel hurt when someone rebuffs me." By changing a "you" statement to an "I" statement, we reveal ourselves, and *we* take responsibility for what we are saying. Beginning a sentence with the word *you* tends to put others on the defensive and makes us disown our own experience.

QUESTIONS. In a Gestalt group, members are discouraged from asking questions. Questions direct attention to other people and can easily put others on the defensive. Also, questions often demand that those being questioned reveal themselves while those who ask them are keeping themselves safe behind their interrogation. Group members who tend to ask too many questions are asked to experiment with any of the following:

- Instead of asking a question, make a direct statement to the person, and share your own motivation for your question.
- Avoid "why" questions, because they lead to a chain of "why/because" exchanges. Try instead "how" and "what" questions.
- Practice making "I" statements. By doing so, you take responsibility for your position, your opinions, and your preferences.

QUALIFIERS AND DISCLAIMERS. By paying attention to the qualifiers they attach to their statements, group members can increase their awareness of how they diminish the power of their messages. A common example is the use of *but:* "I like you, but your mannerisms drive me up the wall"; "I often feel depressed, but I don't know what to do to change the situation"; "I think that this group is helping me, but people outside are so different from those in here." In each of these cases the word *but* essentially discounts the statement that precedes it. Without making group members excessively self-conscious, the leader can encourage them to pay attention to the impact of the use of qualifiers and disclaimers. Also, participants can be asked to substitute the word *and* for *but* and experiment with omitting qualifiers such as *maybe, sort of, possibly, I guess,* and *I suppose,* thus changing ambivalent messages into clear and direct statements.

"CAN'T" STATEMENTS.   Group members often say "I can't" when they really mean "I won't." Sally says, "I simply can't talk to my father and tell him what I feel; he'd never understand me." It would be more precise and more honest for Sally to say that she *won't* make the attempt to talk with her father. Essentially, Sally is unwilling to (won't) take the risk or sees it as not being worth the effort. If a group leader consistently and gently insists that members substitute *won't* for *can't,* he or she is helping them own and accept their power by taking responsibility for their decisions.

"SHOULDS" AND "OUGHTS."   Some group members seem to be ruled by "shoulds" and "oughts": "I should be interested in what others say in this group"; "I ought to care for everyone, and if I don't, I feel terrible"; "I should express only positive feelings"; and so on. The list of "shouldisms," both in daily life and in a group situation, is endless. Members can at least become aware of the frequency of their "should" and "ought" remarks and of the feelings of powerlessness that accompany their use.

One way of increasing one's awareness of the limitations imposed by a "should" standard is to experiment with changing phrases such as "I have to" or "I should" to "I choose to." For example, if Fred says, "I hate to stay in school, but I *have to* because my parents expect this of me," he could say instead "I don't like school, and I *choose to* stay in school because I don't want to have a hassle with my parents."

Nonverbal Language

Perls maintains that when we block an aspect of our personality, the denied side finds ways of expressing itself—for example, in our movements, gestures, posture, and voice. Therefore, skilled therapists listen not just to the verbal level of communication but also, and even more keenly, to the message behind the words, which is often conveyed in the voice tone, pitch, and volume, in the speed of delivery, and so forth.

The group setting offers many opportunities to explore the meaning of nonverbal messages. Such explorations are especially useful when participants exhibit nonverbal cues that are incongruent with what they are saying verbally. For example, Frank tells the group leader that he is angry at him for passing him over, but as he utters his angry words, he is smiling. The leader is likely to call to Frank's attention the discrepancy between his angry words and his smile. Frank may then be asked to carry on a dialogue between his words and his smile, or he may be asked to "become his smile" and give this smile a voice: "What is your smile saying?" This procedure gives Frank the opportunity to discover for himself the meaning of the discrepancy. In fact he may be saying, "I want to let you know that I'm upset that you passed me by, yet I don't want to risk your disapproval by letting you know how angry I am."

The following are other examples of how the exploration of nonverbal expressions can increase members' awareness of what they are really experiencing in the moment.

◆ Dan typically carries himself in a slouched posture. The leader says: "Become aware of your posture, go around the group, and tell what your posture says about yourself to each member of the group. Complete the sentence 'I am my posture, and what I am telling you about me is . . .'"
◆ Marilyn tends to speak in a soft voice and with a very tight mouth. The leader invites her to give a speech to the group and consciously exaggerate these mannerisms. She could "become her tight mouth" and say something like "I'm holding my words and myself back from you. I'm not going to be open, and if you want something from me, you'll have to pry me open."
◆ John comes across as though he were always delivering a lecture to an audience. Group members have told him that his voice and his style of speaking create a barrier between him and others. He could be asked to stand before the group and give a lecture, perhaps on the value of lecturing people.

Examples of how one deals with nonverbal cues are endless. Creative group leaders can invent a wide variety of spontaneous techniques designed to help participants become increasingly aware of what they are communicating through their eye contact, mannerisms, subtle gestures, tone of voice, and hand movements, as well as through their whole bodies. Group leaders would do well to avoid making bold interpretations—for example, that keeping one's arms crossed means that one is closed—and instead encourage members to merely pay attention to the nonverbal cues they emit.

Techniques Related to Assuming Responsibility

Group members frequently dodge responsibility for their feelings by assigning the blame to others. Thus, they will say that the *group* is boring them or that someone in the group is *making* them angry. A Gestalt exercise designed to help individuals recognize and own their feelings instead of projecting them onto others is known as "I take responsibility for . . ." Pauline says she feels that the group is excluding her and making her feel like an outsider. The leader can suggest to her that she make direct statements to several members, such as "I feel left out of the group, and I take responsibility for feeling excluded" or "I feel like an outsider, and I take responsibility for this feeling."

Unwillingness to assume responsibility is a common problem, both in groups and in life. As long as when we are scared, angry, critical, or confused we say, "You are making me feel this way," we are delegating control to others and refusing to take charge of our own lives. The Gestalt leader keeps confronting participants with their unwillingness to take responsibility, so that they can come to recognize and accept their feelings instead of projecting them onto others.

Experiments with Dialogues

Because a goal of Gestalt therapy is to achieve integrated function and the acceptance of aspects of one's personality that have been disowned and denied, therapists pay close attention to splits and polarities in personality function. Fantasy dialogues are meant to promote awareness of internal splits and eventual personality integration. These dialogues can take many forms—for example, dialogues between opposing sides or polarities within oneself (like tender/tough, masculine/feminine, loving/hateful, aggressive/ passive) and dialogues with a parent or other significant person, fantasized others, or inanimate objects.

Understanding how polarities are related to inner conflicts is central to Gestalt therapy. A variety of experiments with dialogues can help members increase their awareness of the dichotomies within themselves and help them come to terms with dimensions of their personality that seem to oppose each other. Our self-concept often excludes painful awareness of the polarities within us. We would rather think of ourselves as bright than as dull, as kind than as cruel, as loving than as unloving, and as sensitive than as indifferent. Typically, we may resist "seeing" in ourselves those parts that we don't want to accept as being part of who we are. Although we can recognize the altruistic side of ourselves, we might have trouble coming to terms with our self-centered nature. Ideally, as we move closer to becoming psychologically mature and healthy, we are aware of most of the polarities within ourselves, including those thoughts and feelings that society does not sanction. As we become more tolerant of the complexities and seeming contradictions within us, there is less of a tendency to expend energy on fighting to disown those parts of our nature that we don't want to accept.

Dialogue experiments are a powerful method of contacting parts of our nature that we work hard at keeping secret from both ourselves and others. Learning how to carry on a conversation between our feminine and masculine sides, for instance, is one way of bringing to the surface inner conflicts we might have with these polarities. Alternatively, becoming each side as fully as we can is a way to *experience* both of these facets of our personality.

Dialogue experiments are typically used to heighten awareness of introjections and projections. Introjection, as was mentioned earlier, is the process by which we uncritically take in aspects of other people, especially parents, and incorporate them into our personality. The danger of uncritical and wholesale acceptance of another's values as our own is that it can prevent personality integration. Gestalt techniques are aimed at getting these introjections out in the open, so that we can take a good look at what we have been swallowing whole without digesting it.

For example, by experimenting with dialogues, Hal becomes aware of some of the messages that he has bought without question: one must be practical; one ought to cling to security and never set out on a new path unless one has carefully assessed all the odds; only irresponsible people seek fun for the sake of fun—in other words, a long list of "dos," "don'ts," "shoulds," and "shouldn'ts" that keep him from enjoying life. At last, Hal begins to realize that he has listened to these directives from others and given others the power to direct his life. He also becomes aware that he wants to reclaim this power for himself. Some of the fantasy dialogues that help him see his introjections more clearly are dialogues with the different facets of himself.

The dialogues can be carried out with the empty-chair technique or with the two-chair technique. Sitting on one chair, Hal becomes one of his introjects—say, the side of him that doesn't have any fun. Speaking in the present tense, Hal "becomes the serious side" and says: "You can't let yourself go; you may go off the deep end and never accomplish anything. Be serious; be practical; get rid of foolish notions." Then Hal switches chairs and "becomes the fun side." He says to the serious side: "You're dull and demanding. If I listen to you, I'll never feel as if I've done enough to earn the right to play. Let me show you how to loosen up and have fun." The dialogue proceeds back and forth, all for the purpose of giving Hal an increased awareness of which side is dominant and of how it feels to be in either role. The goal is not to get rid of either side but to integrate the polarities. If he reaches this goal, Hall will recognize that he can be *both* serious and light and that *he* is the one who can make this happen through awareness.

Projection, as we have seen, is the attribution of one's ideas, feelings, or attitudes to others—especially those very ideas, feelings, or attitudes one does not want to see and accept in oneself. In working with projections, participants are asked to identify with and become a particular characteristic that they attribute to others. For example, if Cindy says that she cannot trust the group—she feels that, if she opened up, no one would care or even know what she was talking about—she is asked to play the role of the untrustworthy person. By becoming the other, she may be able to discover the degree to which the distrust is due to an inner conflict between the side that wants to trust and the side that cannot trust. In what is known as "playing the projection," Cindy is asked to go to other members in the group and play the role of the untrustworthy person by completing the sentence "You don't trust me because, if you do, I'll . . ." The exercise may enable her to experience the inner conflict more intensely and see more clearly the two sides of herself.

Making the Rounds

In this exercise a person goes around to each of the group members and says something that he or she usually does not communicate verbally. For example, assume that Larry sees himself as a self-made man who needs nothing from others. Although he may not *say* this about himself, the theme of "I can do it by myself" runs through much of his life. For the purpose of seeing how this theme actually determines what he does, he could be asked to stand before each member in the group and tell that person something about himself, and then add, ". . . and [or but] I can do everything by myself." Thus, Larry goes to Sue and says, "I never ask for emotional support from others, and at times I feel lonely . . . but I can do everything by myself." He then goes to Marie and says, "I make all the decisions in my business . . . and I can do everything by myself." The aim of this experiment is to have him feel fully what it's like for him to do everything by himself. Ultimately, he may decide to continue to do things for himself, but with the awareness of the price he pays for doing so. Or he may come to see that he doesn't have to be totally self-reliant and that he can be independent while letting others do things for him from time to time.

The following are a few more examples of the use of making the rounds:

◆ Paul says that he is afraid of women. He could make the rounds and say to each woman, "I'm afraid of you because . . ." or "If I were to get close to you, . . ."
◆ Susan worries about boring people in the group. She might be asked to make the rounds and, for each person, complete the sentence "One way I could bore you is by . . ." or "You would be bored if I . . ."
◆ Pam says that she feels distant from the rest of the group, even though she would like to have a sense of identification. She could make the rounds and experiment with completing the sentence "One way I feel distant from you is . . ." or "The way I am different from you is . . ."

Fantasy Approaches

Experimenting with a diversity of fantasy situations in a group can lead to significant growth. Fantasy can promote personal awareness in a number of ways, as the following brief list suggests.

◆ Fantasy can be used when members are too threatened to deal with a problem in concrete terms. For example, members who are afraid to be assertive can imagine themselves in situations in which they *are* assertive. Thus, they can compare what they feel when they are passive with what they feel when they are able to ask for what they want.

◆ Fantasy approaches are useful in dealing with catastrophic expectations, which often result in a sense of paralysis. Members who are afraid to express what they think and feel to someone they love can be guided through a fantasy situation in which they say everything they want to say but are afraid to express. Essentially the person speaks in the here and now to the loved one (as if he or she were present) in front of the group. The leader may say: "Your mother [or some other significant person] is in this empty chair. Come up to the chair and say what you most want her to hear and that you never told her. What are you feeling now? Are you willing to tell how you feel? Tell her now all the terrible things you imagined would happen if you told her what you kept from her." There is a possible psychological value in working through these feelings in the safety of the fantasy approach, because the person may be able to release submerged feelings that have become split off. Note that it is *not* necessary that the person express these feelings in real life; as a matter of fact, to do so could be unwise.

◆ Fantasy can be used to express and explore feelings of shame and guilt. In the technique known as "I have a secret," the leader asks members to fantasize about a well-guarded secret. They are not asked to reveal the secret in the group but only to imagine themselves disclosing the secret to the others. The leader may ask: "What are people thinking about you?" "How do you feel about letting others know your secret?"

◆ Fantasy is a useful and safe way to explore the members' fears about getting involved in the group. For example, members can be asked to imagine the thing they most fear occurring in the group. If, for example, some members are afraid of being rejected by the group, they can be directed to imagine that everyone is systematically rejecting them and then work with the feelings associated with this fantasy.

There are constructive uses of fantasy that, after having been tried in the group, can be carried outside of it. At times members can be invited to picture themselves as they wish they were in interpersonal situations. They might share their fantasies aloud in the group as they experience themselves in powerful, alive, creative, and dynamic ways. Then they can be asked to try acting in the group as if they were the person they imagined themselves to be. If the experiment is successful, members may feel encouraged enough to try the new behavior in real-life situations.

Rehearsal

For Perls, much of our thinking is rehearsing. We rehearse for roles we think we are expected to play, and we worry that we may not say the "right" thing and perform "properly." Internal rehearsing consumes much energy and frequently inhibits spontaneity. The rehearsal technique invites members to say *out loud* what they are thinking silently. Rehearsal experiments are expecially useful when it is obvious that members are doing a lot of blocking and censoring and when what they say seems carefully measured out for a certain effect. For example, during the initial stages of one of my groups, Joan was quite silent and appeared to be developing an observer's stance. When I asked her if she was indeed saying everything she wanted to say, she shook her head in denial. So I asked her to express aloud some of the random thoughts she had as she was sitting there in silence.

Rehearsal can also be fruitful when a member is anticipating some future confrontation. Assume that Sam wants to tell his boss that he doesn't feel appreciated and that he wants to be recognized for his accomplishments. Sam can, in fantasy, picture himself standing before his boss, ready to tell him what he wants to say. Sam's out-loud rehearsal could go something like: "I'm standing here like a fool. What if I mess up? He won't listen to me, and I don't really have anything to say. How can I let him know what I'm thinking? Right now I feel like running away and apologizing."

In a Gestalt group the participants share their rehearsals with one another in order to become more aware of the many preparations they go through in performing their social roles. By doing so, they become more aware of how they strive to please others, of the degree to which they want to be accepted and approved, and of the extent of their efforts to avoid alienating others. And then they can decide whether this role playing is worth the effort.

Reversal Techniques

Certain symptoms and behaviors often represent reversals of underlying or latent impulses. The reversal technique asks participants to become a side of themselves that they rarely or never express, because they don't want to see it and accept it. They theory underlying the use of this technique is that integration is possible when people allow themselves to plunge into the very thing that produces anxiety and make contact with those parts of themselves that have been submerged and denied. Groups provide plenty of timely opportunities for using reversal techniques.

I remember the case of a young man who was excessively nice, overly polite, and constantly trying to "do things" for other people. I suggested that he experiment with asking other people in the group to do something for him. He had great difficulty carrying out my suggestion, but eventually he succeeded. The exercise made him aware of how uncomfortable he was with accepting something from others. Also, it gave him an increased awareness of the denied side of himself and a chance to integrate it.

Other examples of the reversal method are asking someone who says almost nothing to take on the role of monopolizer and deliberately interrupt the group; inviting someone with inferiority feelings to play the role of being superior; and suggesting to someone who pays compliments to everybody to say something negative to each person in the group. Time and time again, I've found that this and similar techniques truly help people become aware of and reconcile polarities within themselves.

Just as the empty-chair experiment gives members an opportunity to take ownership of opposing forces within themselves, so does experimenting with giving expression to a dimension that is kept hidden often result in a creative integration of polarities. For example, the member who habitually presents a tough exterior may well be afraid of contacting a sensitive side of himself. If he is invited to experiment with being the side that he works so hard at denying, he is likely to find joy in broadening his emotional and behavioral range, and if he does not like the results of the experiment, he can always go back to the "tough-guy" role.

The Exaggeration Exercise

This experiment involves becoming more aware of the subtle signals and cues we send through body language. Movements, postures, and gestures are exaggerated, so that the meanings they communicate become clearer. By exaggerating the movement or gesture repeatedly, the person experiences more intensely the feelings associated with the behavior and becomes more aware of its inner meaning.

For example, if the leader notices that Sandy consistently nods her head in an approving way when people speak, he or she could ask Sandy to go before each group member and really give in to her head nodding while, at the same time, putting words into this action. Other examples of behavior that lends itself to the exaggeration technique are habitually smiling while expressing painful or negative emotions, trembling, clenching one's fists, tapping one's foot, crossing one's arms tightly, and pointing a finger at someone.

Jill, a group member, said, "I feel burdened by listening to everyone's problems in here!" At an earlier session she was confronted by Fred for intervening so quickly and trying to make him feel better when he was working on conflicts he was having with his family. She then revealed that during her childhood years she typically assumed the role of family arbitrator, always doing her best to smooth over the battles in her family. Jill eventually said that she was sick and tired of carrying everyone's burdens, for it weighed her down and gave her a heavy feeling.

A technique for working with the material that Jill was providing involved asking her to pick up some heavy objects and hold them as she looked at each person in the group. She could be invited to allow herself to get into the experience of the heaviness and being burdened. For example, while holding the heavy objects, she might make the rounds and complete the sentence "Looking at you I am burdened by . . ." Or she might say something to each member like "Here, let me take on all your burdens; I really enjoy carrying everyone's problems and I just wouldn't know what to do if I didn't have all these burdens weighing me down!" Even though she said that she was sick and tired of carrying around everyone's burdens, we encouraged her to allow herself to give in to the part of herself that felt burdened and experiment with telling others all the benefits of being this way. The rationale here was that if she could fully experience being burdened, there was a good chance that she could allow herself to experience shedding these burdens and being light, at least for a few moments. Again, this experiment is related to the reversal experiment and the empty-chair experiment in that the member is asked to play with polarities. Often the best way to discover the aspect of ourselves that we say we'd like to experience more of is to allow ourselves to stay with that part of us that we want to avoid.

Dream Work

Consistent with its noninterpretive spirit, the Gestalt approach does not interpret and analyze dreams. Instead, the intent is to bring the dream back to life, to recreate it, and to relive it as if it were happening now. For those readers who are interested in a detailed presentation of the Gestalt approach to dream work, good sources are Downing and Marmorstein (1973), Perls (1969a), Rainwater (1979), and Zinker (1978). A brief description of this approach follows.

Group members don't report their dreams in the past tense: they relive them and act them out in the present, transform key elements of the dream into a dialogue, and become a part of the dream. Perls assumes that each part of a dream is a projection of oneself and that all the different parts are expressions of one's own contradictory and inconsistent sides. Therefore dreams contain existential messages. They represent our conflicts, our wishes, and key themes in our lives. By making a list of all the details in a dream—remembering each person, event, and mood—and then acting out ("becoming") each of these parts as fully as possible, one becomes increasingly aware of one's opposing sides and of the range of one's feelings. Eventually the person comes to appreciate and accept his or her inner differences and integrate the conflicting forces, with each piece of work on a dream leading to further assimilation and integration. By avoiding analyzing and interpreting the dream and focusing instead on becoming and experiencing it in all its aspects, the client gets closer to the existential message of the dream. Freud calls the dream "the royal road to the unconscious"; Perls (1969a) calls it "the royal road to integration" (p. 66).

Rainwater (1979) offers some helpful suggestions to dreamers for exploring their dreams:

◆ Be the landscape or the environment.
◆ Become all the people in the dream. Are any of them significant people?
◆ Be any objects that link and join, such as telephone lines and highways.
◆ Identify with any mysterious object, such as an unopened letter or an unread book.
◆ Assume the identity of any powerful force, such as a tidal wave.
◆ Become any two contrasting objects, such as a younger person and an older person.
◆ Be anything that is missing in the dream. If you don't remember your dreams, then speak to your missing dreams.
◆ Be alert for any numbers that appear in the dream, become these numbers, and explore associations with them.

Rainwater suggests that in working with a dream you notice how you feel when you wake up. Is your feeling state one of fear, joy, sadness, frustration, surprise, anger? Identifying the feeling tone may be the key to finding the meaning of the dream. In working with dreams in Gestalt style, she suggests, dreamers can focus on questions such as the following:

◆ What are you doing in the dream?
◆ What are you feeling?
◆ What do you want in the dream?
◆ What are your relationships with other objects and people in the dream?

◆ What kind of action can you take now? What is your dream telling you?

Group experiments can emerge out of the dream work of individuals in a group. Zinker (1978) has developed an approach he calls *dream work as theater,* which goes beyond working with an individual's dream. After a dream is reported and worked through by a participant, a group experiment is created that allows other members to benefit therapeutically from the original imagery of the dreamer. Based on his assumption that all the members share certain archetypal themes, Zinker suggests that various images within a dream can be used to enhance self-understanding. Each plays out a part of the dream. This offers the group participants many opportunities for enacting certain dimensions of the dream that relate both to the dreamer and to their own life.

For example, assume that one of the members, Joan, has had a dream that contains a broken-down car, a man shooting at people in the car, and a woman trying to save the passengers. One member may choose to take on the identity of the person doing the shooting, another can take on the role of one of the people in the car being shot at, and still another can be the car that doesn't function. Each of the members can play out his or her part, and the dreamer can help them understand the characters or objects in the dream. The group leader can facilitate the production of the dream as a dramatic and therapeutic experience for the entire group. There are many advantages to this approach in increasing group cohesion and linking one member's work with others.

The dreams of group participants may have implications for how they feel in their group (Polster & Polster, 1973). In the example given above, Joan may discover that she feels frightened in the group and would like to escape. She may feel attacked (shot at) by one or more members, with a woman coming to her rescue. In this case she can act out her dream in the group by selecting the person by whom she feels most seriously attacked and talking to that person directly. She can then become the broken-down car—her powerless vehicle of escape—and see what associations this association brings. She can also pick out the woman in the group by whom she feels most supported and have a dialogue with her. She might reverse roles, becoming the person doing the shooting. Working with the dream in this way has rich potential for dealing with unfinished business with others in the group.

Evaluation of the Gestalt Approach

Contributions and Strengths of the Approach

I have incorporated much of the spirit of Gestalt therapy into my own style of group leadership. In working with groups, I make frequent use of Gestalt techniques that facilitate the exploration of intense feelings. These techniques are powerful and often lead to the expression of immediate emotions and the reexperiencing of old feelings. The here-and-now focus does intensify the work of members. Instead of merely talking about their problems, they experience their struggles in the present moment. According to Clarkson and Mackewn (1993), one of Perls's most significant contributions is the techniques that he developed to allow for the completion of past business in the present therapeutic experiment. As is the case with psychodramatic techniques, the Gestalt present-centered methods of reenacting early life experiences bring a certain vitality both to an individual's work and to the participants of the group.

Another distinct feature of Gestalt therapy is its focus on the body. In an excellent book dealing with the role of the body in psychotherapy, Kepner (1993) demonstrates how a client's posture, movements, and bodily experiences can be incorporated into the practice of Gestalt therapy. Perls emphasizes that it is not the therapist's task to interpret bodily processes, because doing so prevents clients from the self-discovery that would lead to a meaningful insight. Thus, without making interpretations for members, leaders can encourage them to pay attention to what they are experiencing bodily. This focus can provide a rich clue to areas that members want to avoid, and it also offers a way for them to come into contact with their anxiety. If the leader avoids telling members the meaning of their gestures, postures, and body symptoms, they are more able to stay with what they are experiencing and eventually find their own meaning.

Since Gestalt therapy is grounded on existential principles, the genuineness of the group leader and the quality of the therapeutic relationships between the leader and members (and among the members themselves) are given primary emphasis. In this respect the Gestalt approach has some common denominators with both the existential and person-centered approaches. I think this is a main strength of Gestalt therapy, for the techniques described in this chapter will be most effective when they are used by group leaders who are genuine and who have a commitment to the welfare of the members. A number of Gestalt therapists emphasize the importance of the therapeutic relationship and view techniques as secondary to the quality of the relationship (see M. Polster, 1987; Polster & Polster, 1973; Rice & Greenberg, 1992; Yontef & Simkin, 1989; Zinker, 1978). The therapist's genuineness, presence, and ability to form good contact with clients are certainly as important as the technical skills described in this chapter. Because Gestalt therapy is part of the existential approach, the mutuality of the I/thou encounter is seen as essential for therapy to succeed. Healing results from these nonexploitive encounters. The best experiments grow out of the trusting relationship that the leader creates. This approach encourages genuine experimentation and allows for a great deal of creativity on the part of leaders and members (see Zinker, 1978).

Limitations of the Approach

One of the limitations of traditional Gestalt therapy in my view is its tendency to discount the cognitive side of counseling. To a large extent Perls adopted an anti-intellectual position by derogating the intellectual aspects of personality. His statement "Lose your mind and come to your senses" reflects his reaction against the cognitive therapy of the psychoanalytic approach and illustrates his focus on the role of feelings in therapy. With his preoccupation with experiencing feelings and the body, Perls went to the other end of the continuum from the traditional therapies of the 1960s. Following this lead, some Gestalt group leaders have ignored the value of conceptualizing in a group.

The emphasis on feelings and the body at the expense of cognitive factors may not provide the optimum therapeutic balance. To seek such an equilibrium, I also draw from the cognitive and behavioral approaches (transactional analysis, behavior therapy, rational emotive behavior therapy, and reality therapy). Helping participants discover the meaning of their emotional experiences is a significant factor in producing personality changes that will extend beyond the group. Although the earlier phase of Gestalt therapy's development did not focus on cognitive processes, there appears to be a current trend to pay more attention to these factors and to integrate the affective and cognitive dimensions of human experiencing (see E. Polster, 1987; M. Polster, 1987; Yontef & Simkin, 1989).

As exciting and dynamic as Gestalt methods are, they are not for everyone. The appropriate application of Gestalt techniques hinges on questions of *when, with whom,* and *in what situation* (Shepherd, 1970). According to Simkin (1982): "Gestalt therapy is the treatment of choice for people who are 'up in their head.' It is not for people who act out their impulses. It is most effective in the hands of competent well-trained clinicians" (p. 377). Shepherd (1970) writes that, in general, Gestalt therapy is most effective with overly socialized, restrained, constricted individuals, who are often described as neurotic, phobic, perfectionistic, ineffective, and depressed. On the other hand, Shepherd asserts, work with less organized, more severely disturbed, or psychotic individuals is more problematic and requires caution, sensitivity, and patience.

A major concern I have about Gestalt therapy is the potential danger for abusing techniques. Typically, Gestalt therapists are highly active and directive, and if they do not have the characteristics mentioned by Zinker (1978)—sensitivity, timing, inventiveness, empathy, and respect for the client—the experiments can easily boomerang. Also, the members can grow accustomed to the leader's assuming the initiative in creating experiments for them instead of coming up with some of their own experiments.

With an approach that can have powerful effects on members, either constructive or destructive, ethical practice requires adequate training and supervision. The most immediate limitation of Gestalt or any other therapy is the skill, training, experience, and judgment of the therapist. Probably the most effective application of Gestalt techniques comes after personal therapeutic experiences have been gained in professional workshops and in work with competent therapists and supervisors (Shepherd, 1970).

The Gestalt approach can be dangerous because of the therapist's power to manipulate the client with techniques. Inept therapists may use powerful techniques to stir up feelings and open up problems that members have kept from full awareness, only to abandon the members once they have managed to have a dramatic catharsis. Such leaders fail to help members work through what they have experienced and bring some closure to it.

It is easy to see that many of the Gestalt techniques offer a tempting place for group leaders to hide their personal responses and forget about the I/thou relationship. Through the use of confrontive techniques they can direct the pressure primarily toward the members. The therapist's willingness to encounter clients with his or her honest and immediate responses and ability to challenge clients' manipulative use of their symptoms without rejecting them are crucial (Shepherd, 1970). It is essential for Gestalt practitioners to learn how to confront in a manner that does not entrench the client's resistance. A blend of support and challenge goes a long way in creating the kind of relationship that enables clients to explore their defensiveness.

Some Gestalt practitioners make the mistake of becoming too rigid, pushing such injunctions as "Always be in the present" or "Take responsibility for yourself." There are some situations in which stopping what members are doing and asking them to bring something into the here and now is quite counterproductive. Gestalt leaders who have truly integrated their approach are sensitive enough to practice in a flexible way. They strive to help clients experience themselves as fully as possible in the present, yet they are not rigidly bound by dictates, nor do they routinely intervene with a directive whenever members stray from the present. Sensitively staying in contact with a member's flow of experiencing entails the ability to focus on the person and not on the mechanical use of techniques for a certain effect.

Applying Gestalt Therapy with Multicultural Populations

There are many opportunities for Gestalt leaders to exercise their creativity with diverse client populations. People in many cultures give attention to expressing themselves nonverbally, rather than emphasizing the content of oral communication. Some clients may express themselves nonverbally to a greater extent than they do with words. For example, group leaders may ask members to focus on their gestures, facial expressions, and the experience within their own body. If a group member, Eduardo, says that he is feeling threatened, the leader may invite him to pay attention to his bodily reactions. Some very creative work can emerge from work with people's gestures and body sensations. If Eduardo is having a struggle between two conflicting parts within himself, one hand could represent one side of the conflict, and the other hand, the other side of the conflict. He might be willing to engage in some Gestalt experiments as a way of heightening his own present experience and of clarifying the nature of his struggle. One of the advantages of drawing on Gestalt experiments is that they can be tailored to fit the unique way in which an individual member perceives and interprets his or her culture. Of course, before Gestalt techniques are introduced, especially with culturally different group members, it is essential that the clients have been adequately prepared.

The use of imagery and fantasy has much potential if members are well prepared and if there is a high degree of trust within the group. Assume that Anita is dealing with unfinished business pertaining to guilt surrounding the death of a loved one. She can make significant inroads into completing this unfinished business by bringing this dead person symbolically into the room and dealing with her in the present. If English is her second language, Anita can be asked to speak in her original language. However, such an exercise may be resisted by the client on two counts: it may be difficult for her to talk about the dead person, let alone "speak directly" to her; she may also argue that it would be more comfortable for her if she spoke in English. Certainly, Gestalt techniques have therapeutic power, and participating in them is often uncomfortable. The degree to which group members are willing to engage in experiential processes is largely a function of how much trust they feel in both the group leader and the other members. The importance of the personhood of the group leader cannot be overemphasized. If the leader is trusted, his or her invitations are much more likely to be accepted by the clients.

To a greater extent than is true of most other approaches, there are definite cautions in too quickly utilizing some Gestalt techniques with ethnic minority clients. As is evident from this chapter, these techniques tend to produce a high level of intense feelings. This focus on affect has some clear limitations with those clients who have been culturally conditioned to be emotionally restricted and reserved. Some clients have been conditioned to believe that expressing feelings openly is a sign of weakness and a display of one's vulnerability. Leaders who push for catharsis are likely to find certain clients becoming increasingly resistant, and these members may eventually terminate. For instance, clients who are reluctant to experience and express their emotions will probably not take kindly to the therapist's suggestion that they "talk to the empty chair."

Sue and Sue (1990) suggest that the Gestalt focus on the here and now appears to be congruent with Native American values. But they caution that many Gestalt techniques, because they are confrontational, may be embarrassing to Native American clients. However, aspects of Gestalt work can be useful in understanding Native Americans. Paying attention to nonverbal behavior, without stereotyping the client, often provides significant leads. Thomason (1991) advises counselors to approach each client as an individual and take the lead from him or her regarding nonverbal communication. He rightly reminds us that some Native Americans avoid eye contact, speak only in a low tone of voice, and have soft handshakes. He suggests that following the client's lead in regard to nonverbal behavior helps prevent misunderstandings and increases rapport.

Even though there are certain limitations to utilizing Gestalt techniques with ethnically diverse group members, this does not mean that they have no value in multicultural settings. Although the resistance of such clients can be escalated by ill-timed interventions on the leader's part, timely Gestalt interventions can be one approach in helping clients work through some of their deeper resistances and struggles. More than the techniques themselves, the manner in which these techniques are presented to members determines the outcomes.

Where to Go from Here

If you have become excited about including Gestalt techniques in your style of group leadership, I encourage you to attend a workshop led by a competent professional. Just as I have real concerns about practitioners' employing psychodramatic techniques if they have not experienced them personally, I worry about leaders who routinely use Gestalt techniques that they have learned about mainly through reading. Although reading is surely of value, I don't think that it is sufficient to produce skillful clinicians.

Some resources for training in Gestalt therapy are:

Gestalt Institute of Cleveland
1588 Hazel Drive
Cleveland, OH 44106
TELEPHONE: (216) 421-0468
(Joseph Zinker is the director.)

Gestalt Training Center
P. O. Box 2189
La Jolla, CA 92038
TELEPHONE: (619) 454-9139
(Erv and Miriam Polster are the codirectors.)

Gestalt Therapy Institute of Los Angeles
1460 7th Street, Suite 301
Santa Monica, CA 90401
TELEPHONE: (310) 458-9747

RECOMMENDED SUPPLEMENTARY READINGS

The Gestalt Journal, published twice yearly, offers articles, reviews, and commentaries of interest to the practitioner, theoretician, academician, and student. A one-year subscription is $30. Contact:

The Center for Gestalt Development, Inc.
The Gestalt Journal
P. O. Box 990
Highland, NY 12528
TELEPHONE: (914) 691-7192

Note: The Center for Gestalt Development, Inc., publishes *The Gestalt Directory* on a yearly basis. It includes information about Gestalt practitioners and training programs throughout the world. The training center's program is described in detail, including admission requirements, costs, length of program, certifications, and other pertinent data. Sample copies of *The Gestalt Directory* are free of charge. Requests for copies must be in writing.

Gestalt Therapy Verbatim (Perls, 1969a), which consists essentially of transcripts of lectures, workshops, seminars, and demonstrations given by Perls, provides a graphic description of his unique and dramatic therapeutic style. It is also an excellent source of information about "affective techniques" based on Gestalt exercises. The first part of the book deals primarily with Gestalt theory. (Note: the new publisher and publication date of this book are the Gestalt Journal Press, 1992.)

Beyond the Hot Seat: Gestalt Approaches to Group (Feder & Ronall, 1994) discusses the application of Gestalt theory to group practice. Separate chapters are devoted to Gestalt group process, family therapy, training groups, intensive workshops, and other clinical applications. (Note: the new publisher and publication date of this book are the Gestalt Journal Press, 1994.)

Creative Process in Gestalt Therapy (Zinker, 1978) is a beautifully written book that is a delight to read. Zinker captures the essence of Gestalt therapy as a combination of phenomenology and behavior modification by showing how the therapist functions much like an artist in creating experiments that encourage clients to expand their boundaries. His concepts are fleshed out with rich clinical examples. The book shows how Gestalt can be practiced in a creative and integrative style.

Gestalt Therapy Integrated: Contours of Theory and Practice (Polster & Polster, 1973) is a scholarly and penetrating treatment of some of the concepts underlying Gestalt practice. Theory and practice are successfully integrated in the personal style of the authors.

Fritz Perls (Clarkson & Mackewn, 1993) provides a detailed overview of the contributions of Perls to the theory and practice of Gestalt therapy. The authors have excellent chapters on the criticisms and rebuttals of the approach and an assessment of the overall influence of Perls.

Body Process: Working with the Body in Psychotherapy (Kepner, 1993) is a well-written book that deals with many basic principles of Gestalt therapy, with an emphasis on the body process as an integral part of practice.

REFERENCES AND SUGGESTED READINGS*

Atkinson, D. R., Morten, G., & Sue, D. W. (1993). *Counseling American minorities: A cross-cultural perspective* (4th ed.). Madison, WI: Brown & Benchmark.

Atkinson, D. R., Thompson, C. E., & Grant, S. K. (1993). A three-dimensional model for counseling racial/ethnic minorities. *The Counseling Psychologist, 21*(2), 257–277.

*Clarkson, P., & Mackewn, J. (1993). *Fritz Perls*. London: Sage Publications Ltd.

Downing, J., & Marmorstein, R. (Eds.). (1973). *Dreams and nightmares: A book of Gestalt therapy sessions*. New York: Harper & Row.

Fagan, J., & Shepherd, I. (Eds.). (1970). *Gestalt therapy now*. New York: Harper & Row (Colophon).

*Feder, B., & Ronall, R. (Eds.). (1994). *Beyond the hot seat: Gestalt approaches to group*. Highland, NY: Gestalt Journal Press.

Frew, J. E. (1986). The functions and patterns of occurrence of individual contact styles during the development phase of the Gestalt group. *Gestalt Journal, 9*(1), 55–70.

*Kepner, J. I. (1993). *Body process: Working with the body in psychotherapy*. San Francisco: Jossey-Bass.

Latner, J. (1973). *The Gestalt therapy book*. New York: Bantam.

*Books and articles marked with an asterisk are suggested for further study.

Levitsky, A., & Perls, F. (1970). The rules and games of Gestalt therapy. In J. Fagan & I. Shepherd (Eds.), *Gestalt theray now*. New York: Harper & Row (Colophon).

*Passons, W. R. (1975). *Gestalt approaches in counseling*. New York: Holt, Rinehart & Winston.

*Perls, F. (1969a). *Gestalt therapy verbatim*. New York: Bantam. (Note: In 1992, published by Gestalt Journal Press, Highland, NY).

Perls, F. (1969b). *In and out of the garbage pail*. New York: Bantam.

Perls, F. (1970). Four lectures. In J. Fagan & I. L. Shepherd (Eds.), *Gestalt therapy now*. New York: Harper & Row (Colophon).

Perls, F. (1973). *The Gestalt approach and eyewitness to therapy*. New York: Bantam.

*Perls, F., Hefferline, R., & Goodman, P. (1951). *Gestalt therapy: Excitement and growth in the human personality*. New York: Dell.

Polster, E. (1987). Escape from the present: Transition and storyline. In J. K. Zeig (Ed.), *The evolution of psychotherapy* (pp. 326–340). New York: Brunner/Mazel.

*Polster, E., & Polster, M. (1973). *Gestalt therapy integrated: Contours of theory and practice*. New York: Brunner/Mazel.

Polster, M. (1987). Gestalt therapy: Evolution and application. In J. K. Zeig (Ed.), *The evolution of psychotherapy* (pp. 312–325). New York: Brunner/Mazel.

*Rainwater, J. (1979). *You're in charge! A guide to becoming your own therapist*. Los Angeles: Guild of Tutors Press.

Reich, W. (1949). *Character analysis*. New York: Noonday Press.

Rice, L. N., & Greenberg, L. S. (1992). Humanistic approaches to psychotherapy. In D. K. Freedheim (Ed.), *History of psychotherapy: A century of change* (pp. 197–224). Washington, DC: American Psychological Association.

*Shepherd, I. L. (1970). Limitations and cautions in the Gestalt approach. In J. Fagan & I. L. Shepherd (Eds.), *Gestalt therapy now* (pp. 234–238). New York: Harper & Row (Colophon).

Simkin, J. S. (1982). Gestalt therapy in groups. In G. M. Gazda (Ed.), *Basic approaches to group psychotherapy and group counseling* (2nd ed.). Springfield, IL: Charles C Thomas.

Smith, E. (1976). *The growing edge of Gestalt therapy*. New York: Brunner/Mazel.

Smith, E. (1985). *The body in psychotherapy*. Jefferson, NC: MacFarland & Co.

Stevens, J. O. (1971). *Awareness: Exploring, experimenting, experiencing*. Moab, UT: Real People Press.

Sue, D. W. (1990). Culture-specific strategies in counseling: A conceptual framework. *Professional Psychology: Research and Practice, 21*(6), 424–433.

Sue, D. W., & Sue, D. (1990). *Counseling the culturally different: Theory and practice* (2nd ed.). New York: Wiley.

Thomason, T. C. (1991). Counseling Native Americans: An introduction for non-Native American counselors. *Journal of Counseling and Development, 69*(4), 321–327.

*Yontef, G. M., & Simkin, J. S. (1989). Gestalt therapy. In R. Corsini (Ed.), *Current psychotherapies* (4th ed.). Itasca, IL: F. E. Peacock.

*Zinker, J. (1978). *Creative process in Gestalt therapy*. New York: Random House (Vintage).

Zinker, J. (1994). The developmental process of a Gestalt therapy group. In B. Feder & R. Ronall (Eds.), *Beyond the hot seat: Gestalt approaches to group*. New York: Brunner/Mazel.

◆ Chapter Twelve ◆

Transactional Analysis

Introduction

Transactional analysis (TA) is an interactional therapy grounded on the assumption that we make current decisions based on past premises—premises that were at one time appropriate to our survival needs but that may no longer be valid. TA emphasizes the cognitive, rational, and behavioral aspects of the therapeutic process. It is oriented toward increasing awareness with the goal of enabling people to make new decisions (redecide) and thereby alter the course of their life. To achieve this goal, TA group participants learn how to recognize the three ego states (Parent, Adult, and Child) in which they function. They also learn how their current behavior is being affected by the rules and regulations they received and incorporated as children and how they can identify the "life script" that is determining their actions. Ultimately, they come to realize that they can now redecide and initiate a new direction in life, changing what is not working while retaining what serves them well.

TA provides an interactional and contractual approach to groups—interactional in that it emphasizes the dynamics of transactions between people, and contractual in that group members develop clear statements of what they will change and how they will go about making these changes. These contracts establish the goals and direction of the group.

Historical Background

Transactional analysis was originally developed by the late Eric Berne (1961), who was trained as a Freudian psychoanalyst and psychiatrist. TA evolved out of Berne's dissatisfaction with the slowness of psychoanalysis in curing people of their problems. Historically, it developed as an extension of psychoanalysis with concepts and techniques especially designed for group treatment. Berne discovered that his clients, by using TA, were making significant improvement. As his theory of personality evolved, he parted

325

ways with psychoanalysis to devote himself full time to the theory and practice of TA (Dusay, 1986).

Berne said he had formulated most of the concept of TA by paying attention to what his clients were saying. He began to see an ego image that related to the childhood experiences of his patients. He concluded that there was a Child ego state that was different from the "grown-up" ego state. Later, he postulated that there were two "grown-up" states: one, which seemed to be a copy of the person's parents, he called the Parent ego state; the other, which was the rational part of the person, he named the Adult ego state.

One of Berne's contributions is his perspective on how young children develop a personal plan for their life as a strategy for physical and psychological survival. His view is that people are shaped from their first few years by a script that they follow during the rest of their life.

As is true of many theories in this book, there is a parallel between the basic concepts of TA and the personal life of its founder. Claude Steiner (1974) has contended that Berne was himself under the influence of a life script that called for an early death of a broken heart. Apparently, Berne had strong injunctions against loving others and accepting the love that others had for him. His life could be characterized as work oriented, and his driving motivations were to write books on the development of a new theory (TA) and to cure people. In writing about Berne's life script, Steiner comments about his interest in people who had a history of heart disease. Berne died of a coronary occlusion when he was 60 years old, which was the age his mother had died of a coronary. Steiner believes that such a limited-life-expectancy script is by design and that in Berne's situation his heart gave way when he had completed the last two books he wanted to write.

Contemporary TA practitioners have moved in various directions and modified many of the basic concepts that Berne formulated. Because there are different models of TA, it is difficult to discuss practices that apply to all of them. But this chapter will highlight the expansion of Berne's approach by Mary and the late Robert Goulding (1979), leaders of the *redecisional school* of TA. The Gouldings differ from the classical Bernian approach in a number of ways. They have combined TA with the principles and techniques of Gestalt therapy, family therapy, psychodrama, and behavior therapy. The redecisional approach helps group members experience their impasse, or the point at which they feel stuck. They relive the context in which they made earlier decisions, some of which were not functional, and they make new decisions that are functional. Redecisional therapy is aimed at helping people challenge themselves to discover ways in which they perceive themselves in victimlike roles and to take charge of their lives by deciding for themselves how they will change.

Basic Assumptions

Underlying the practice of TA group work is the premise that awareness is an important first step in the process of changing our ways of thinking, feeling, and behaving. In the early stages of a group, techniques are aimed at increasing the participants' awareness of their problems and their options for making substantive changes in their life.

Another basic assumption of TA is that all of us are in charge of what we do, of the ways in which we think, and of how we feel. Others do not *make* us feel in a certain way; rather, we respond to situations largely by our choices (R. Goulding, 1987).

Rationale for a Group Approach

The practice of TA is ideally suited for groups. Berne believed that group therapy yielded information about one's personal plan for life much more quickly than individual therapy. Redecision therapy, as introduced by the Gouldings, is done in a group context in which members can experience their script coming to life by reliving early memories and by interacting with others in the group. From a redecisional perspective, group therapy is the treatment of choice. People change more rapidly than they do in individual therapy, and groups seem to add a humanness to therapy (R. Goulding, 1987). There are many avenues of self-understanding through analyzing transactions within the group. In the same way that Gestalt groups function in the here and now, TA groups bring past issues into the present. Group members facilitate action by representing both family members from the past and contemporaries. Because of the interaction within the TA group, members are given many opportunities to review and challenge their past decisions and experiment with new ones. For Robert Goulding, one rationale for a group is that it provides a living experience that members can take out to their family, friends, and community.

Key Concepts

The Ego States

As mentioned, people operate in three dynamic ego states that each encompass important facets of the personality: Parent, Adult, and Child (P-A-C). These ego states are considered to be essential and distinguishing characteristics of TA therapy (Dusay, 1986). According to TA, people are constantly shifting from one of these states to another, and their behavior at any one time is related to the ego state of the moment.

The Parent ego state contains the attitudes and behavior incorporated from external sources, primarily one's parents. Outwardly, this ego state is expressed toward others in critical or nurturing behavior. Inwardly, it is experienced as old parental messages that continue and influence the inner Child. When we are in the Parent ego state, we react to situations as we imagine our parents might have reacted, or we may act toward others the way our parents acted toward us. The Parent contains all the "shoulds" and "oughts" and other rules for living. When we are in that ego state, we may act in ways that are strikingly similar to those of our parents or other significant people in our early life. We may use some of their very phrases, and our posture, gestures, voice, and mannerisms may replicate those that we experienced in our parents. Such behavior occurs when the Parent in us is a positive ego state (a Nurturing Parent) or a negative one (a Critical Parent).

The Adult ego state is the objective and computerlike part of our personality and functions as a data processor; it computes possibilities and makes decisions on the basis of available data. This state is neither emotional nor judgmental but simply works with the facts and with external reality. The Adult is oriented toward current reality, is objective in gathering information, and is not related to chronological age.

The Child ego state consists of feelings, impulses, and spontaneous actions. This state contains all the impulses that come naturally to a child, and it includes "recordings" of early experiences. The Child can be either the Natural Child—that is, the spontaneous, impulsive, open, alive, expressive, often charming but untrained being within each of us—or the Adapted Child—the tamed version of the Natural Child and the part of us that learns to accommodate to the expectations of others in order to gain acceptance and approval.

In a TA group, members are first taught how to recognize in which of the three ego states they are functioning at any given time, with the aim of enabling them to decide consciously whether that state or another state is most appropriate or useful. For example, a member who typically responds to others in a Critical Parent style and who has contracted to become more tolerant toward others must recognize his or her habitual ego state before any steps can be taken to change.

The Need for Strokes

A basic premise of the TA approach is that humans need to receive both physical and psychological "strokes" in order to develop a sense of trust in the world and a basis for loving themselves. There is ample evidence that lack of physical contact can not only impair infant growth and development but also, in extreme cases, lead to death. Psychological strokes—verbal and nonverbal signs of acceptance and recognition—are also necessary to people as confirmations of their worth.

Strokes can be either positive or negative. Positive strokes, which express, warmth, affection, or appreciation either verbally or with a look or a smile, a touch or a gesture, are seen as necessary for the development of psychologically healthy people. Negative strokes, which leave people feeling discounted and diminished as persons, are seen as impairing healthy psychological development. Interestingly, despite their ill effects, negative strokes are considered preferable to no strokes at all—that is, to being ignored. We are all familiar with cases of children who, feeling ignored and dismissed, act to elicit negative strokes from their parents because such responses are the only form of recognition they can get.

TA group members are taught how to recognize the strokes that motivate them and to become sensitive to the ways in which they discount themselves. Take, for example, a group member named Sara who continually puts herself down with self-deprecating remarks. She either doesn't hear or soon forgets the positive feedback she gets from others in her group. When paid a sincere compliment, she finds some way to play it down or make a joke of it. If she is the focus of positive attention or receives any display of tenderness, affection, or caring, she becomes extremely uncomfortable, yet she remembers and stores up any critical remarks and feels depressed. As Steiner (1974) would put it, she collects the "cold pricklies" rather than the "warm fuzzies."

In her TA group Sara is confronted with the fact that she discounts her worth and doesn't allow others to give her positive strokes. She is also challenged to decide whether she wants to change her behavior. If she accepts the challenge to change, the group can help her learn how to ask for and accept positive strokes.

Injunctions and Counterinjunctions

The Gouldings' redecision work is grounded in the TA concepts of injunctions and early decisions (M. Goulding, 1987, p. 288). *Injunctions* are parental messages that stem from the parents' Child ego state. Such messages, which are often expressions of disappointment, frustration, anxiety, and unhappiness, establish the "don'ts" by which children learn to live. Out of their own pathology, parents give injunctions such as the following: "Don't," "Don't be," "Don't be close," "Don't be separate from me," "Don't be the sex you are," "Don't want," "Don't need," "Don't think," "Don't feel," "Don't grow up," "Don't be a child," "Don't succeed,' "Don't be you," "Don't be sane," "Don't be well," and "Don't belong" (M. Goulding, 1987; M. Goulding & Goulding, 1979).

According to Mary Goulding (1987), children decide either to accept these parental messages or to fight against them. If they do accept them, they decide precisely *how* they will accept them. Based on accepting certain injunctions, children then make decisions that become a basic part of their permanent character structure.

The counterpart of injunctions are parental messages that come from the parents' Parent ego state, which are known as *counterinjunctions*. These messages convey the "shoulds," "oughts," and "dos" of parental expectations. Examples of counterinjunctions are "Be tough," "Be perfect," "Work up to your potential," "Do what I expect of you," "Hurry up," "Try hard," "Please me," "Be careful," and "Be polite." The problem with these counterinjunctions is that it is almost impossible to live up to them; thus, no matter how hard people try to please, they are bound to feel that they have not done or been enough.

In TA groups, members explore the "shoulds" and "shouldn'ts," the "dos" and "don'ts" by which they have been trained to live. The first step in freeing oneself from behaviors dictated by the often irrational and generally uncritically received parental messages is awareness of the specific injunctions and counterinjunctions that one has accepted as a child. Once group participants have identified and become aware of these internalized "shoulds," "oughts," "dos," "don'ts," and "musts," they are in a better position to critically examine them to determine whether they are willing to continue living by them.

Decisions and Redecisions

As indicated earlier, transactional analysis emphasizes our cognitive, rational, and behavioral aspects, especially our ability to become aware of decisions that govern our behavior and of the capacity to make new decisions that will beneficially alter the course of our life. This section focuses on the decisions determined by parental injunctions and counterinjunctions and investigates how TA group members learn to relive these early decisions and make new ones.

Following is an example of decision making that has been dictated by parental injunctions. A TA group member, Bill, apparently received the parental injunction "Don't trust anybody." The decisions about behavior resulting from this injunction were implicit in many of Bill's characteristic pronouncements: "If you don't let yourself care, you won't be hurt"; "If I keep to myself, I won't need anything from anyone"; "Whenever I've wanted something from another, I've been hurt. It's just not worth getting involved with, or even close to, others." Indeed, it became clear in group sessions that by accepting his parents' injunctions against trusting people, Bill consistently made decisions that caused him to avoid others. To support these decisions, Bill was able to find plenty of data—both in the group and in his everyday life—to maintain his view that trust would inevitably lead to hurt. Consequently he continued, often unwittingly, to abide by his parents' injunction.

In the TA group Bill not only had the opportunity to become aware of his decisions and of the injunction behind them but was also helped to investigate whether these decisions were still appropriate. At one time the decisions to avoid people might have been necessary for Bill's physical and psychological safety—a matter of sheer survival. In the group Bill was able to question whether such decisions were serving any purpose and determine whether they were, instead, thwarting his development. He made a new decision to trust people and to approach them as friends, not enemies.

The Gouldings (1978, 1979) point out that even though injunctions and counterinjunctions carry the weight of parental authority, the child must *accept* these messages if they are to have an impact on his or her personality. The Gouldings add that many injunctions under which children live are not issued by the parents but derive instead from the children's own fantasies and misinterpretations. It is important to note that a single parental injunction may foster a variety of decisions on the part of the child, ranging from reasonable to pathological. For example, the injunction "Don't be stupid" may give rise to decisions ranging from "I'll never do *that* again" to

"I'll let others make decisions" to "I *am* stupid, and I always *will be* stupid." Similarly, the injunction "Don't be you" may evoke decisions ranging from "I'll hide who I really am" to "I'll be someone else" to "I'll be a nobody" to "I'll kill myself, and then they'll accept me and love me."

Whatever injunctions people have received, and whatever the resulting life decisions were, transactional analysis maintains that people can change by changing their decisions—by learning to redecide. In their groups the Gouldings developed an atmosphere in which members are challenged from the outset to make new decisions for themselves. Early in the course of a group, Robert Goulding (1975) would ask, "What did you decide to do to screw up your life, and what are you going to decide now to unscrew it?" (p. 246).

The group work related to making new decisions frequently requires members to return to the childhood scenes in which they arrived at self-limiting decisions. The group leader may facilitate this process with any of the following interventions: "As you are speaking, how old do you feel?" "Is what you are saying reminding you of any times when you were a child?" "What pictures are coming to your mind right now?" "Could you exaggerate that frown on your face? What are you feeling? What scene comes to mind as you experience your frowning?" Mary Goulding (1987) says that there are many ways of assisting a member to return to some critical point in childhood. "Once there," she adds, "the client reexperiences the scene; and then she relives it in fantasy in some new way that allows her to reject old decisions" (p. 288). After members experience a redecision through this fantasy work, they design experiments so that they can practice new behavior to reinforce their redecision.

Consider the following example of a member named Helga, who relives scenes with her parents when she was positively stroked for failing or was negatively stroked for succeeding. It was apparently at those times that she accepted the injunction "Don't succeed." The group challenges her to examine whether the decision, which may have been functional or even necessary in the past, is currently appropriate. She may redecide that "I will make it, and I am successful, even though it is not what you want from me."

Another group member, Gary, is able to see that he responded to his father's injunction "Don't grow" by deciding to remain helpless and immature. He recalls learning that when he was independent, his dad shouted at him and, when he was helpless, he was given his father's attention. Because he wanted his father's approval, Gary decided, "I'll remain a child forever." During a group session Gary goes back to a childhood scene in which he was stroked for his helplessness, and he talks to his father now in a way that he never did as a child: "Dad, even though I still want your approval, I don't *need* it to exist. Your acceptance is not worth the price I'd have to pay. I'm capable of deciding for myself and of standing on my own two feet. I'll be the man that I want to be, not the boy that you want me to be."

In this redecision work Helga and Gary enter the past and create fantasy scenes in which they can safely give up old and currently inappropriate early decisions, because both are armed with an understanding in the present that enables them to relive the scene in a new way. According to the Gouldings, it is possible to give a *new ending* to the scenes in which original decisions were made—a new ending that often results in a *new beginning* that allows clients to think, feel, and act in revitalized ways.

Games

A transaction, which is considered the basic unit of communication, consists of an exchange of strokes between two or more people. A game is an ongoing series of transactions that ends with bad feelings for at least one player. By their very nature games are designed to prevent intimacy. Games consist of three basic elements: a series of complementary transactions that on the surface seem plausible; an ulterior transaction that is the hidden agenda; and a negative payoff that concludes the game and is the real purpose of the game. Berne described a variety of common games, including "Yes, but," "Kick me," "Harassed," 'If it weren't for you," "Martyr," "Ain't it awful," "I'm only trying to help you," "Uproar," and "Look what you made me do!" Games always have some payoff (or else they wouldn't be perpetuated), and one common payoff is support for the decisions described in the preceding section. For example, people who have decided that they are helpless may play the "Yes, but" game. They ask others for help and then greet any suggestions with a list of reasons why the suggestions won't work; thus they feel free to cling to their helplessness. Addicts of the "Kick me" game are often people who have decided to be rejected; they set themselves up to be mistreated by others so that they can play the role of the victim whom nobody likes.

By engaging in game playing, people receive strokes and also maintain and defend their early decisions. They find evidence to support their view of the world, and they collect bad feelings. These unpleasant feelings that people experience after a game are known as *rackets*. They have much the same quality as feelings the people had as children. These rackets are maintained by actually choosing situations that will support them. Therefore, those who typically feel depressed, angry, or bored may be actively collecting these feelings and feeding them into long-standing feeling patterns that often lead to stereotypical ways of behaving. They also choose the games that they will play to maintain their rackets. When people "feel bad," they often get sympathy from others or control others by their bad moods.

A group situation provides an ideal environment for the participants to become aware of the specific ways in which they choose game-playing strategies as a way of avoiding genuine contact and choose patterns of thinking, feeling, and behaving that are ultimately self-defeating. Group members can learn about their own games and rackets by observing the behavior of others in the group, as well as by analyzing how their responses in the group are connected to their responses to life situations in early childhood. Members can begin by using the games they are currently playing in the group to understand that although games often give the appearance of intimacy, their actual effect is to create distance between people.

Later, as members become aware of the more subtle aspects of game playing, they begin to realize that games prevent close human interaction and that it takes at least two to play a game. Consequently, if the members decide that they want to relate more closely to others, they also have to decide not to play games anymore.

Eventually, members are taught to make connections between the games they played as children and those they play now—for example, how they attempted to get attention in the past and how those past attempts relate to the games they play now in order to get stroked. The aim of this TA group process is to offer members the chance to drop certain games in favor of responding honestly—an opportunity that may lead them to discover ways of changing negative strokes and to learn how to give and receive positive strokes.

Basic Psychological Life Positions and Life Scripts

Decisions about oneself, one's world, and one's relationships to others are crystallized during the first five years of life. Such decisions are basic for the formulation of a life position, which develops into the roles of the life script. Generally, once a person has decided on a life position, there is a tendency for it to remain fixed unless there is some intervention, such as therapy, to change the underlying decisions. Games are often used to support and maintain life positions and to play out life scripts. People seek security by maintaining that which is familiar, even though the familiar may be highly unpleasant. As we have seen earlier, games such as "Kick me" may be unpleasant, but they have the virtue of allowing the player to maintain a familiar position in life, even though this position is negative.

Transactional analysis identifies four basic life positions, all of which are based on decisions made as a result of childhood experiences and all of which determine how people feel about themselves and how they relate to others:

1. I'm OK—You're OK.
2. I'm OK—You're not OK.
3. I'm not OK—You're OK.
4. I'm not OK—You're not OK.

The *I'm OK—You're OK* position is generally game-free. It is characterized by an attitude of trust and openness, a willingness to give and take, and an acceptance of others as they are. In this position there are no losers, only winners.

I'm OK—You're not OK is the position of people who project their problems onto others and blame them, put them down, and criticize them. The games that reinforce this position involve a self-styled superior (the "I'm OK") who projects anger, disgust, and scorn onto a designated inferior, or scapegoat (the "You're not OK"). Briefly, this position is that of the person who needs an underdog to maintain his or her sense of "OKness."

The *I'm not OK—You're OK* position is that of the depressed person, one who feels powerless in comparison with others. Typically such people serve others' needs instead of their own and generally feel victimized. Games supporting this position include "Kick me" and "Martyr"—games that support the power of others and deny one's own.

The *I'm not OK—You're not OK* position is held by those who have given up all hope, who have lost interest in life, and who see life as totally without promise. This self-destructive stance is characteristic of people who are unable to cope in the real world, and it may lead to extreme withdrawal, a return to infantile behavior, or violent behavior resulting in injury or death of themselves or others.

Related to the concept of basic psychological positions is the life script, or plan for life. This script, as we have seen, is developed early in life as a result of parental teaching (such as injunctions and counterinjunctions) and the early decisions we make. Among these decisions is selecting the basic psychological position, or dramatic role, that we play in our life script. Indeed, life scripts are comparable to a dramatic stage production, with a cast of characters, a plot, scenes, dialogues, and endless rehearsals. In essence, the life script is a blueprint that tells people where they are going in life and what they will do when they arrive.

According to Berne (1972), through our early interactions with parents and others we receive a pattern of strokes that may be either supporting or disparaging. Based on this stroking pattern, we make a basic existential decision about ourselves; that is, we assume one of the four positions described above. This existential decision is then reinforced by continuing messages (both verbal and nonverbal) that we receive during our lifetime. It is also reinforced by the results of our games, rackets, and interpretations of events. During our childhood years we also make the decision whether people are trustworthy. Our basic belief system is thus shaped through this process of deciding about ourselves and others. If we hope to change the life course that we are traveling, it helps to understand the components of this script, which to a large extent determines our patterns of thinking, feeling, and behaving.

One function of the TA group is to help members, through a process known as *script analysis,* become aware of how they acquired their life script and to see more clearly their life role (basic psychological life position). Script analysis helps members see the ways in which they feel compelled to play out their life script and offers them alternative life choices. Put in another way, this group process relieves participants of the compulsion to play games that justify behavior called for in their life script.

Script analysis demonstrates the process by which group members acquired a script and the strategies they employ to justify their actions based on it. The aim is to help members open up possibilities for making changes in their early programming. The participants are asked to recall their favorite stories as children, to determine how they fit into these stories or fables, and to see how these stories fit their current life experiences.

The analysis of the life script of a group member is based on the drama of his or her original family. Through the process of acting out portions of their life script in the group sessions, members learn about the injunctions they uncritically accepted as children, the decisions they made in response to these messages, and the games and rackets they now employ to keep these early decisions alive. The group leader can gather information about the family drama by taking a history of the childhood experiences of the members. Members can be asked the kind of drama that would probably result if their family were put on the stage. Other group members can be given a part to play in this family play.

These and other cognitive and emotive techniques often help the group participants recall early events and the feelings associated with them. The group setting provides a supportive place to explore the ways in which these past situations are influencing the participants. By being a part of the process of the self-discovery of other members, each member increases the opportunities for coming to a deeper understanding of his or her own unfinished psychological business.

Didactic procedures such as the Karpman Drama Triangle (see Karpman, 1968) can be employed to help members identify scripts and games. The triangle has a "Persecutor," a "Rescuer," and a "Victim." Persecutors criticize others and invite others to assume the position of Victim. Rescuers depend on helping or "saving" others in order to feel OK. If others do not play the role of Victim, then the Rescuers are not able to play their game of taking care of others. Victims assume a passive and helpless stance, maintaining that they have no power to change unless someone else changes first. It should be noted that the same individual might alternate between all three of these roles at different times in various situations. However, most group members have a favorite position in life, which may become evident in the way they behave in the group sessions. For example, Betty may quickly come to the rescue of any member who experiences sadness. She may do her best to provide such members with ready-made solutions for complex problems. In her life outside of the group she may well depend on others to need her so that she can save them from pain. Another member, Jim, may assume a victimlike stance by continually complaining about how awful his life is and how he could change if only others would make certain changes first. The group situation allows members to analyze the positions they often take and the games they play, both in the group and in everyday life. As a result, group participants gain the capacity to take some initial steps to break out of self-defeating patterns. As the group members analyze their own life from a TA perspective, they can check the accuracy of their self-interpretations by asking for feedback from the leader and the other members.

Script analysis can be carried out by means of a script checklist. Steiner (1967) developed a life-script questionnaire that can be used as a catalyst in group situations to help members explore significant components of their life script—among them, life positions and games. In completing this script checklist, members provide basic information such as the general direction of their life, the models in their life, the nature of their injunctions, the payoffs they seek, and the tragic ending they expect from life.

Role and Functions of the Group Leader

Although TA is designed to develop both emotional and intellectual aware-ness, the focus is clearly on the cognitive aspects. As a teacher, the TA therapist explains concepts such as structural analysis, script analysis, and game analysis. As noted earlier, TA stresses the importance of equality in the client/therapist relationship, an equality that is manifested through contrasts between the group leader and the individual members that make them partners in the therapeutic process. Consequently, the role of the therapist is to apply his or her knowledge to fulfilling the contract that the client initiates.

From the perspective of redecision therapy, the group leader's function is to create a climate in which people can discover for themselves how the games they play are supporting chronic bad feelings and how they hold on to these feelings to support their life script and early decisions. Another func-tion of the TA therapist is challenging group members to discover and experiment with more effective ways of being. In short, the role of the therapist is to help members acquire the tools necessary to effect change.

The therapist's style in a TA group tends to promote individual work within a group setting, rather than facilitating interaction between group members and thus encouraging therapy *by* the members. In TA groups the leader assumes an active role as the primary agent of change (Kapur & Miller, 1987). The focus tends to be on interactions between the group leader and individual members. The therapist occupies a central position in the group and works with each client in turn.

Therapeutic Procedures and Techniques

Contracts: The Structure of the Therapeutic Relationship

Transactional analysis is based largely on the capacity and willingness of the group participants to understand and design a therapeutic contract that requires them to state their intentions and set personal goals. Contracts are the key to all TA groups. They are specific and measurable and contain a concrete statement of the objectives that the group participant intends to attain and how and when these goals are to be met. Contracts place the responsibility on members for clearly defining what, how, and when *they* want to change. Thus, from the very beginning, members learn that therapy is a shared responsibility and that they cannot passively wait for the leader to direct the group. In short, the members' contracts establish the departure point for group activity.

Group members agree to work on specific issues within the group. For example, a woman who reacts to others in a highly critical way can design a contract that will lead to changing such behavior. Her contract describes *what* she will do in the group to change her actions and experiences, *when* she will do it, and *how many times*. The contract can then be expanded to include situations outside the group.

Dusay (1983) asserts that a well-stated treatment contract will make it clear whether clients are obtaining what they want from therapy. He says that such a contract is an acceptable answer to the therapist's question "How will you know and how will I know when you get what you are coming to the group for?" Since everyone in the group knows the other participants' contracts, a productive focus can be developed in the group sessions. The process of TA treatment focuses primarily on change as defined by the contract, and there is an Adult-to-Adult agreement between the therapist and the client about what the process and the desired goal will be (Dusay & Dusay, 1989).

Contracts are intended to be practical tools for helping people change themselves. As such, they cannot be rigid and should be open to revision. Long-term contracts can be limiting; thus, it is often useful to develop contracts in steps, subject to modification as members penetrate more deeply the areas that they are seeking to change.

The Gouldings' Redecisional Approach to Groups

The following is a summary of the redecisional approach to TA groups, based on an adaptation of some of the chief works of the Gouldings (1976, 1978, 1979, 1982, 1987). It should be mentioned that the core of the work in this approach consists of helping clients make redecisions while they are in their Child ego state. This is done by having them reexperience an early scene as if the situation were occurring in the present. Merely talking about past events or understanding early feelings and decisions from the Adult ego state is not sufficient to push them beyond the places where they are stuck. How the leader helps members get into their Child ego state and make a new decision can best be seen in the stages of redecision group therapy, which follow.

THE INITIAL STAGE OF THE GROUP. The first step in the group process consists of establishing good contact. To a large extent, the outcome for group members depends on the quality of the relationship that the group leader is able to establish with the members and on the leader's competence. Even when the group leader makes good contact with the members and is competent, the members' most important symptom is typically not brought forward initially (R. Goulding, 1982). Group participants sometimes tell what they *think* is significant but avoid addressing more pertinent issues. Therefore, the leader attempts to get at the chief complaint of the client. Obviously, the trust factor in the group has a lot to do with the willingness of clients to get to their chief complaint.

The next step in the process consists of making an inquiry into the group member's actual contract for change. A typical question is "What are you going to change about yourself today?" Notice that members are not asked to state what they hope to change or what the therapist will do to bring about change; nor are they asked what changes they want in the future. The emphasis is upon the client's *taking action now* to do something that will bring about change.

THE WORKING STAGE OF THE GROUP. After contracts have been formulated, the Goulding group focuses on rackets that they use to justify their life script and, ultimately, their decisions (M. Goulding & Goulding, 1979). The aim is to expose the rackets of group members and have them take responsibility for them. For example, a person with an "anger racket"—one who is chronically angry—may be asked, "What do you do to maintain your anger?" Beginning with recent events, the person is led back through his or her life in an attempt to remember early situations involving anger. As in Gestalt therapy, members are asked to *be* in these situations—to recall them not as observers but as participants in the here and now. Members are asked to act out both their own responses and the responses of other significant people in the scene.

During this stage of group work the focus is on games. Games are analyzed, mainly to see how they support and maintain rackets and how they fit with one's life script. In this connection much work is devoted to looking for evidence of the participants' early decisions, discovering the original injunction that lies at the base of these early decisions, and determining the kinds of strokes that the person received to support the original injunction.

A major function of the TA group leader is to alert the members to take responsibility for their thinking, feeling, and behaving. Members are challenged when they use "cop-out language," such as "can't," "perhaps," "if it weren't for," "try," and other words that keep members from claiming their own power. The leader also creates a group climate in which the members rapidly become aware of how they maintain their chronic bad feelings by their behavior and fantasy. It is the therapist's task to challenge them to discover alternate choices.

The Gouldings take the position that clients can change *rapidly,* without years of analysis. Consequently, they stress the redecisional aspects of TA therapy on the assumption that when clients perceive that they are responsible for their early decisions, they also have it in their power to change those decisions. This approach emphasizes helping participants reexperience early, highly emotional situations in order to generate the energy to break through the places where they are stuck (M. Goulding & Goulding, 1979). Such breakthroughs, according to the Gouldings, usually require that participants remember and relive situations involving real parenting figures. Through the use of fantasy, in which group members reexperience how their parents sounded, acted, and looked, the therapist creates a psychological climate that allows members to feel the same emotional intensity they felt when, as children, they made their original decisions. The Gouldings stress that if participants are to be successful in going beyond an impasse, they must be in the Child ego state, actually reliving psychologically early scenes, rather than in their Adult ego state, merely thinking about new information and insights.

THE FINAL STAGE OF THE GROUP. Once a redecision is made from the Child ego state, the changes in one's voice, body, and facial expressions are obvious to everyone in the group. However, Robert Goulding (1982) emphasizes the importance of reinforcement of this redecision by the client and by the others in the group. The group process provides support for members who begin to feel and behave in new ways. Group members are encouraged to tell a new story in the group to replace their old story, and they typically receive verbal and nonverbal stroking to support their new decision. Attention is also given to ways that members might devise other support systems outside the group. It is also important for members to plan specific ways in which they will change their thinking, feeling, behavior, and body. The focus during the final phase of group work is challenging the members to transfer their changes from the therapy situation to their daily life and then supporting them in these changes. Before members set out on their own, it is important that they fantasize about how some of their changes are likely to lead to other changes. It is well for them to prepare themselves for the new situations they will face when they leave the group and to develop support systems that will help them creatively deal with new problem situations and new successes when they arise (for example, old anxiety arising from these successes).

Evaluation of Transactional Analysis

Contributions and Strengths of the Approach

Transactional analysis provides a cognitive basis for group process that is often missing in some experientially oriented groups. The insistence of this approach on having members get out of their victimlike positions and realize that they don't have to be chained to early decisions is, I believe, crucial to effective therapy. In my opinion TA, especially redecision therapy, provides a useful conceptual framework for understanding *how* these early decisions are made, how they are related to present self-defeating life stances, how games perpetuate bad feelings, and how our lives are governed by old programs and scripts.

Many people are enslaved by their early decisions; they cling to parental messages, live their lives by unexamined injunctions, and frequently are not even aware that they are living in a psychological straitjacket. Conceptually, redecision therapy offers tools that members can use to free themselves from an archaic life script and achieve a successful and meaningful life.

One of the strengths of the TA approach to group counseling is the emphasis on contracts as a way to guide each member's work. The contractual arrangement places the responsibility for deciding what to change clearly on the group members, rather than the leader. Contracts equalize the power base between the leader and the members; they also remove much of the mystery that surrounds what a group is all about.

A number of factors in TA groups make them particularly useful in working with women. Some of these elements are the use of contracts, the egalitarian relationships between the members and the leader, the emphasis on providing members with knowledge of the TA group process, and the value placed on empowering the group members. Feminist therapists are often concerned about the inappropriate imposition of the therapist's values on clients (Enns, 1993). It appears that a TA group has some distinct advantages in exploring gender concerns and sex-role socialization, including its emphasis on empowering members. Additionally, in a TA group the power differential between the leader and members is less pronounced than in most forms of individual therapy. From a feminist perspective, when women are in groups, they have more opportunities to challenge the therapist's ideas and they are able to compare their reality with those of other women (Enns, 1993).

TA groups allow a range of possibilities for both preventive and remedial work; they also provide for both an educational and a therapeutic structure. I think it is important that the information given in TA groups be balanced by experiential work aimed at involving the members both cognitively and emotionally. Personally, I favor integrating TA concepts and practices with Gestalt techniques. Of course, this is what the Gouldings have accomplished. Working from a theoretical base provided by TA, they have used a combination of therapeutic methods, including psychodrama, fantasy and imagery, Gestalt techniques, behavior therapy, desensitization, family-therapy procedures, and psychosynthesis. They contend that pure Gestaltists may fail to give cognitive feedback and that pure TA therapists seldom encourage the intense emotional work that leads to breaking through those impasses that prevent further growth.

There are interesting possibilities of integrating TA and Gestalt perspectives in working with children in groups (Tudor, 1991). The focus of Tudor's groups is both educational and therapeutic, with the aim of promoting positive mental health. He provides a framework that links child development with the phases of the Gestalt cycle, along with the TA injunctions that are relevant to each age.

Limitations of the Approach

This blending of TA concepts with Gestalt techniques lessens certain objections that I have to both therapeutic approaches. As I see it, Gestalt therapy does not sufficiently emphasize the cognitive factors, so that it tends to leave participants with many experiences that have little meaning attached to them. TA, in contrast, tends to overemphasize cognitive factors, so that it can result in therapy that is intellectually stimulating but emotionally arid.

Like most of the other approaches that have been discussed so far, TA can be criticized on the ground that its theory and procedures have not been adequately subjected to empirical validation. Indeed, many of Berne's concepts were stated in such a manner that it would be impossible to design a research study to test them. It appears that most of the claims of success rest on clinical observations and testimonials. Conducting well-designed research studies to evaluate the process and outcome of group therapy has surely not been one of the strengths of TA. This is not to say that no one has attempted to study the outcomes of TA group therapy. Research studies are described in various issues of the *Transactional Analysis Journal.* Some TA therapists contend that the use of specific contracts provides built-in accountability. Measures can be taken to determine the extent to which members have fulfilled their contract and benefited from group therapy. In my opinion TA could profit by integrating the commitment to research that is characteristic of behavior therapy.

TA group leaders, as mentioned, tend to foster individual work in a group, rather than promoting free interaction among the members. My personal bias is that this style of leadership does not make the optimum use of the interactive qualities inherent in group therapy. Kapur and Miller (1987) suggest that future research could well measure the relative lack of attention paid by TA clinicians to the unique properties of groups. Based on their research, they would like to see TA therapists encourage processes such as cohesiveness and universality by varying their therapeutic technique. They also suggest a decentralized role for the group leader, with more emphasis on promoting spontaneous interaction among members.

A final problem I have with transactional analysis relates to the way in which some practitioners use the structure and vocabulary of this system to avoid genuine contact with their clients or to keep from revealing their reactions. A therapist can use the structure of TA to avoid person-to-person interactions and to focus on labeling ego states, devising contracts, and directing traffic between transactions. I have also observed some group members who seem to be using TA jargon to deceive themselves into believing that they are becoming self-actualized when, in reality, they are only learning new terms to identify old processes. Some TA clients also tend to slip into the use of jargon as an intellectual front behind which they can safely hide. In fairness, I should emphasize that the dangers of becoming lost in the structure and vocabulary of TA can be lessened by a therapist who confronts members when they are misusing the model.

Applying TA with Multicultural Populations

The contractual approach to therapy has much to offer in a multicultural context. As we have seen in this chapter, TA clients decide what they are willing to change. Their contracts act as a safeguard against therapists' imposing their cultural values.

TA also provides a structured approach that allows clients to see connections between what they learned in their family and their attitudes toward others. Many clients are likely to find this type of structure useful, for it helps them understand how their culture has influenced them. Consider some of the following injunctions that you are likely to hear from your clients: "Don't cry, or at least don't shed tears in public." "Don't confront your parents." "Live up to the expectations of your parents and your family." "Don't be too concerned about yourself." "Don't show your weaknesses." "Don't make negative comments in public." "Don't stand out or be noticed." "Always show respect to your elders." "Think of what is best for family [community], rather than focusing on your self-interests." "Don't win at the expense of others." "Don't talk about your family or about family problems with strangers." These cultural injunctions provide a good starting place for exploration in a group.

It is important for group leaders to respect their clients' cultural injunctions, yet at the same time they can create a climate in which members can begin to question the degree to which they have accepted these messages. One caution is that therapists should avoid challenging clients too quickly, so that they lessen the chances of having dropouts. Direct confrontation of these cultural injunctions will be interpreted by many clients as a sign that the therapist does not respect their values or is attempting to impose his or her value system on them.

A limitation of applying TA to multicultural group practice is that the terminology may seem foreign to some clients. Even though TA therapists assert that TA is simple and easy to understand, many clients may have difficulty with the complexity of concepts such as the structure and dynamics of games and the subcomponents of the various ego states. Before TA group leaders challenge the life scripts of group members, which are frequently rooted in their cultural heritage, it is well for them to make sure that a trusting relationship has been established and that these clients have demonstrated a readiness to question their family traditions. In some cultures it is considered taboo to doubt family traditions, let alone talk about such matters in a nonfamily group or have these traditions challenged by others. The contract approach used by most TA group leaders can be useful in empowering these clients by giving them the responsibility for deciding what aspects of their family life they are willing to share as well as deciding which family values they are ready to question. If group members assume this responsibility for defining clear contracts, the chances of inappropriate confrontations by leaders are lessened.

Where to Go from Here

According to Dusay (1986), TA is recognized as a complete theory of personality and an entire system of psychotherapy. Its regulatory body, the International Transactional Analysis Association, certifies the therapists who enroll in its rigorous training program. TA is practiced internationally, both by professionals and paraprofessionals. It is applied to business and organizational development. Prison inmates, schizophrenic patients, and people in drug-rehabilitation programs and outpatient clients from all socio-economic levels have participated in TA treatment programs.

If you want to learn more about TA group work, I encourage you to participate in a workshop or a group as a member. Experiencing TA as a member could benefit you personally by bringing many of the concepts in this chapter to life in a concrete way. Also, you may want to consider attending a teaching workshop where you can apply TA principles in a group setting.

For further information, contact:

International Transactional Analysis Association
1772 Vallejo Street
San Francisco, CA 94123
TELEPHONE: (415) 885-5992

This association provides guidelines for becoming a Certified Clinical Member. Before certification is granted, candidates must pass both a written and an oral examination, in which samples of their work are reviewed by a board of examiners to determine their level of clinical competence.

RECOMMENDED SUPPLEMENTARY READINGS

The *Transactional Analysis Journal* is a good source for keeping current with the developments of TA theory, clinical applications, and research. The subscription rate is $40 annually, and the journal is published quarterly. For information concerning dues for various membership classifications and for journal subscriptions, contact the ITAA office, 1772 Vallejo Street, San Francisco, CA 94123.

Redecision Therapy: Expanded Perspectives (Kadis, 1985) consists of a collection of articles on the theory and technique of redecision therapy as well as the applications of this approach to specific settings.

Changing Lives through Redecision Therapy (M. Goulding & Goulding, 1979) is the work I would recommend to a practitioner who had time to read only one book on the TA approach to group work. The authors describe their successful integration of Gestalt and behavioral techniques into their TA theoretical framework.

Scripts People Live: Transactional Analysis of Life Scripts (Steiner, 1974) is a comprehensive discussion of life scripts that can be applied to group work.

Principles of Group Treatment (Berne, 1966) provides a useful discussion of group structure and process from the TA perspective.

REFERENCES AND SUGGESTED READINGS*

Berne, E. (1961). *Transactional analysis in psychotherapy*. New York: Grove Press.
Berne, E. (1964). *Games people play*. New York: Grove Press.
*Berne, E. (1966). *Principles of group treatment*. New York: Oxford University Press.
Berne, E. (1972). *What do you say after you say hello?* New York: Grove Press.
Clarkson, P. (1991). Group image and the stages of group development. *Transactional Analysis Journal, 21*(1), 36–50.
Dusay, J. M. (1983). Transactional analysis in groups. In H. I. Kaplan & B. J. Sadock (Eds.), *Comprehensive group psychotherapy* (2nd ed.). Baltimore: Williams & Wilkins.
*Dusay, J. M. (1986). Transactional analysis. In I. L. Kutash & A. Wolf (Eds.), *Psychotherapist's casebook* (pp. 413–423). San Francisco: Jossey-Bass.

*Books and articles marked with an asterisk are suggested for further study.

Dusay, J. M., & Dusay, K. M. (1989). Transactional analysis. In R. J. Corsini (Ed.), *Current psychotherapies* (4th ed.). Itasca, IL: F. E. Peacock.

Enns, C. Z. (1993). Twenty years of feminist counseling and therapy: From naming biases to implementing multifaceted practice. *The Counseling Psychologist, 21*(1), 3–87.

Gobes, L. (1990). Ego states—Metaphor or reality. *Transactional Analaysis Journal, 20*(3), 163–165.

Goldhaber, G. M., & Goldhaber, M. B. (1976). *Transactional analysis: Principles and applications*. Boston: Allyn & Bacon.

*Goulding, M. M. (1987). Transactional analysis and redecision therapy. In J. K. Zeig (Ed.), *The evolution of psychotherapy* (pp. 285–299). New York: Brunner/Mazel.

*Goulding, M., & Goulding, R. (1979). *Changing lives through redecision therapy*. New York: Brunner/Mazel.

*Goulding, R. (1975). The formation and beginning process of transactional analysis groups. In G. Gazda (Ed.), *Basic approaches to group psychotherapy and group counseling* (2nd ed.). Springfield, IL: Charles C Thomas.

*Goulding, R. (1982). Transactional analysis/Gestalt/redecision therapy. In G. Gazda (Ed.), *Basic approaches to group psychotherapy and group counseling* (3rd ed.). Springfield, IL: Charles C Thomas.

Goulding, R. (1986). Discussion of therapist transparency. *International Journal of Group Psychotherapy, 36*(1), 25–27.

*Goulding, R. L. (1987). Group therapy: Mainline or sideline? In J. K. Zeig (Ed.), *The evolution of psychotherapy* (pp. 300–311). New York: Brunner/Mazel.

Goulding, R., & Goulding, M. (1976). Injunctions, decisions, and redecisions. *Transactional Analysis Journal, 6*(1), 41–48.

*Goulding, R., & Goulding, M. (1978). *The power is in the patient*. San Francisco: TA Press.

*James, M., & Jongeward, D. (1971). *Born to win: Transactional analysis with Gestalt experiments*. Reading, MA: Addison-Wesley.

*Kadis, L. B. (Ed.). (1985). *Redecision therapy: Expanded perspectives*. Watsonville, CA: Western Institute for Group and Family Therapy.

Kapur, R., & Miller, K. (1987). A comparison between therapeutic factors in TA and psychodynamic therapy groups. *Transactional Analysis Journal, 17*(1), 294–300.

Karpman, S. (1968). Fairy tales and script drama analysis. *Transactional Analysis Bulletin, 7*(26), 39–43.

Massey, R. F. (1990). Berne's transactional analysis as a neo-Freudian/neo-Adlerian perspective. *Transactional Analysis Journal, 20*(3), 173–186.

McCormick, P., & Pulleyblank, E. (1985). The stages of redecision therapy. In L. B. Kadis (Ed.), *Redecision therapy: Expanded perspectives* (pp. 51–59). Watsonville, CA: Western Institute for Group and Family Therapy.

Novellino, M., & Moiso, C. (1990). The psychodynamic approach to transactional analysis. *Transactional Analysis Journal, 20*(3), 187–192.

Steiner, C. (1967). A script checklist. *Transactional Analysis Bulletin, 6*(22), 38–39.

Steiner, C. (1974). *Scripts people live: Transactional analysis of life scripts*. New York: Grove Press.

*Tudor, K. (1991). Children's groups: Integrating TA and Gestalt perspectives. *Transactional Analysis Journal, 21*(1), 12–20.

◆ CHAPTER THIRTEEN ◆

Behavioral Group Therapy

Introduction

Behavioral approaches are becoming increasingly popular in group work. One of the reasons for this popularity is the emphasis these approaches place on teaching clients self-management skills they can use to control their lives, deal effectively with present and future problems, and function well *without* continued therapy. Writers with a behavioral orientation, such as Watson and Tharp (1993), have devoted books to the subject of helping people work toward "self-directed behavior." This goal is achieved through a wide variety of cognitive and behavioral action-oriented techniques. Most of these therapeutic techniques are procedures that clients can use on their own to solve interpersonal, emotional, and decision problems.

The term *behavior therapy* refers to the application of a diversity of techniques and procedures that are rooted in a variety of learning theories. Since no single theory undergirds the practice of contemporary behavior therapy, there is no single group model that, strictly speaking, can be called a "behavioral group." Rather, various types of groups operate on behavioral and learning principles. Behavior therapy is best conceptualized as a general orientation to clinical practice that is based on the experimental approach to the study of behavior.

A basic assumption of the behavioral perspective is that most problematic behaviors, cognitions, and emotions have been learned and that they can be modified by new learning. Although this modification process is often called "therapy," it is more properly an educational experience in which individuals are involved in a teaching/learning process. It is educational in that people are taught how to view their own learning process, develop a new perspective on ways of learning, and try out more effective ways of changing their behaviors, cognitions, and emotions. Many of the techniques employed by groups of different orientations (such as rational emotive behavior therapy, reality therapy, and transactional analysis) share this basic assumption of group therapy as an educational process, and they stress the teaching/learning values inherent in a group.

345

Another assumption of the behavioral orientation is that the behaviors that clients express *are* the problem (not merely symptoms of the problem). Successful resolution of these problematic behaviors resolves the problem, and a new set of problems does not necessarily arise. This behavioral perspective is in contrast to the relationship-oriented and insight-oriented approaches, which place considerable emphasis on clients' achieving insight into their problems as a prerequisite for change. Whereas the insight-oriented approaches assume that if clients understand the nature and causes of their symptoms, they will be better able to control their lives, the behavioral approach assumes that change can take place without insight. Behavior therapists operate on the premise that changes in behavior can occur prior to understanding of oneself and that behavioral changes may well lead to an increased level of self-understanding.

Group leaders who operate from a behavioral perspective draw on a wide variety of interventions that are derived from social-learning theory, such as reinforcement, modeling, shaping, cognitive restructuring, desensitization, relaxation training, coaching, behavioral rehearsal, stimulus control, and discrimination training. However, behavioral group leaders may develop other strategies from diverse theoretical viewpoints, provided that their effectiveness in meeting therapeutic goals can be demonstrated. Therefore, these leaders follow the progress of group members through the ongoing collection of data before, during, and after all interventions. Such an approach provides both the group leader and members with continuous feedback about therapeutic progress. In this sense, the behavioral leader is both a clinician and a scientist who is concerned with testing the efficacy of his or her techniques.

Key Concepts

Behavior therapy has some unique characteristics that set it apart from most of the other group approaches discussed in this book. It relies on the principles and procedures of the scientific method. Its experimentally derived principles of learning are systematically applied to help people change maladaptive behaviors. The distinguishing characteristic of behavioral practitioners is their systematic adherence to specification and measurement. Concepts and procedures are stated explicitly, tested empirically, and revised continually. Assessment and treatment occur simultaneously. Research is considered essential to providing effective treatments and to advancing beyond current therapeutic practices. The specific unique characteristics of behavior therapy are (1) conducting a behavioral assessment, (2) precisely spelling out treatment goals, (3) formulating a specific treatment procedure appropriate to a particular problem, and (4) objectively evaluating the outcomes of therapy.

Behavioral Assessment

Behavioral assessment is a set of procedures used to get information that will guide the development of a tailor-made treatment plan for each client and help measure the effectiveness of treatment. According to Spiegler and Guevremont (1993), behavioral-assessment procedures share five characteristics that are consistent with behavior therapy. They (1) are aimed at gathering unique and detailed information about a client's problem; (2) focus on the client's current functioning and life conditions; (3) are concerned with taking samples of a client's behaviors to provide information about how the client typically functions in various situations; (4) are narrowly focused rather than dealing with a client's total personality; and (5) are an integral and continuous part of therapy.

Kuehnel and Liberman (1986) describe the process of pinpointing a client's behavioral problems as the core of behavior therapy, and they identify six steps in conducting a behavioral assessment. The first step is to identify behaviors that are considered maladaptive or problematic and to assess the frequency, intensity, and duration of such behaviors. The next step consists of determining the client's assets and strengths. The third step is putting the information gathered into the context of situations in which the problem behaviors occur. This includes specifying the probable antecedents and consequences of behavioral problems. The fourth step involves setting up a strategy to measure each of the identified problem behaviors. Assessing the frequency of selected target behaviors produces a baseline evaluation, which can be used as a reference point to determine the effectiveness of the interventions. In the fifth step, the client's potential reinforcers are surveyed to identify those people, activities, and things that can provide motivation for treatment and for maintaining changes after therapy ends. The sixth and final step of the assessment process involves the formulation of treatment goals. Cooperatively, both the client and the clinician explore alternative behaviors that could lead to dealing effectively with the problem situation.

Kuehnel and Liberman note that this assessment includes a client's functioning in all domains of cognitive, affective, behavioral, and interpersonal functioning. They see the therapist's task as applying principles of human learning to facilitate the replacement of maladaptive behaviors with more adaptive ones. Although they are not writing specifically about behavioral group counseling, the assessment process just described can be applied to group work.

Precise Therapeutic Goals

In most behavior-therapy groups the initial stages are devoted to clients' expanding the final step of their assessment by formulating specific statements of the personal goals that they want to achieve. Group members spell out concrete problematic behaviors they want to change and new skills they want to learn. Goals that clients typically set include reducing anxiety in test-taking situations, eliminating phobias that interfere with effective functioning, losing weight, and getting rid of addictions (to smoking, alcohol, or other drugs). New skills that clients typically want to acquire include:

- ◆ learning to ask clearly and directly for what they want
- ◆ acquiring habits that lead to physical and psychological relaxation

- developing specific methods of self-control, such as exercising regularly, controlling eating patterns, and eliminating stress
- learning to be assertive without becoming aggressive
- monitoring their behavior or cognitions as a means to change
- learning to give and receive both positive and negative feedback
- being able to recognize and to challenge self-destructive thought patterns or irrational self-statements
- learning communication and social skills
- developing problem-solving strategies to cope with a variety of situations encountered in daily life
- learning more effective behaviors to cope with stress- or anger-inducing situations

The task of the leader is to help the group members break down broad, general goals into specific, concrete, measurable goals that can be pursued in a systematic fashion. For example, if a group member says that he'd like to feel more adequate in social situations, the leader asks: "In what specific ways do you feel inadequate? What are the conditions under which you feel inadequate? Can you give me some concrete examples of the situations in which you feel inadequate? In what specific ways would you like to change your behavior?" The group can be used to help the members formulate answers to these difficult questions.

Treatment Plan

After members have specified their goals, a treatment plan to achieve these goals is formulated. Behavioral techniques are action oriented; therefore, members are expected to *do* things, not just reflect passively and engage in merely talking about their problems. The most commonly used techniques are those that lend themselves to group interaction, such as modeling, behavioral rehearsal, coaching, homework, feedback, training, and information giving; these are defined and discussed later in this chapter.

Objective Evaluation

Once target behaviors have been clearly identified, treatment goals specified, and therapeutic procedures delineated, the outcomes of therapy can be objectively assessed. Because behavioral groups emphasize the importance of evaluating the effectiveness of the techniques they employ, assessment of clients' progress toward their goals is continual. If a group is going to meet ten weeks for social-skills training, for example, baseline data on these skills are likely to be taken at the initial session. Then, every subsequent session may include an assessment of behavioral changes, so that members can determine how successfully their objectives are being met. Providing members with ongoing feedback is a vital part of behavioral group therapy.

The decision to use certain techniques is based on their demonstrated effectiveness. The range of these techniques is quite wide, and many behaviorally oriented group counselors are very eclectic in their choices of treatment procedures. Arnold Lazarus (1986, p. 65) asserts that lasting change is a function of combined techniques, strategies, and modalities. Although he espouses the virtues of *technical eclecticism,* he adds that it is important to avoid a random melange of techniques based on subjective preferences and impressions. He emphasizes that the aim of behavior therapy is to formulate a consistent conceptual framework that permits (1) specification of goals and problems, (2) specification of treatment techniques to achieve these goals and remedy these problems, and (3) systematic measurement of the relative success of these techniques.

Role and Functions of the Group Leader

Because behavioral group counseling is considered a type of education, group leaders perform teaching functions. They are expected to assume an active, directive role in the group and to apply their knowledge of behavioral principles and skills to the resolution of problems. Thus, they carefully observe behavior to determine the conditions that are related to certain problems and the conditions that will facilitate change.

In discussing the social learning that occurs in therapy through modeling and imitation, Bandura (1969, 1977, 1986) suggests that most of the learning that takes place through direct experience can also be acquired by observing the behavior of others. In Bandura's view one of the fundamental processes by which clients learn new behavior is imitation of the social modeling provided by the therapist. Therefore, group leaders need to be aware of the impact of their values, attitudes, and behaviors on group members. If they are unaware of their power in actually influencing and shaping their clients' ways of behaving, they deny the central importance of their influence as human beings in the therapeutic process.

In addition to these broad functions, the behaviorally oriented group leader is also expected to perform a number of specific functions and tasks:

◆ Group leaders conduct intake interviews with prospective members, during which the preliminary assessment and orientation to the group takes place.
◆ Teaching participants about the group process and how to get the most from the group is another leader function. The leader explains the purpose of the group, orients members to the activities and structure of the sessions, reviews the expectations of the members, and gives them suggestions on how the group can be personally useful.
◆ Group leaders conduct an ongoing assessment of member problems. Through procedures such as the initial interview, selected tests and inventories, and group discussion, the leader helps each member identify target behaviors that will give the group sessions some focus. This assessment includes a summary of the major strengths, interests, and achievements of each member.

- ◆ Leaders draw on a wide array of techniques designed to achieve the members' stated goals.
- ◆ The leader collects data to determine the effectiveness of treatment for each member.
- ◆ A major function of leaders is serving as a model of appropriate behaviors and values. Also, leaders prepare and coach members to model by role-playing for one another how an individual might respond in a particular situation.
- ◆ Leaders provide reinforcement to members for their newly developing behavior and skills by making sure that even small achievements are recognized.
- ◆ Leaders teach group members that they are responsible for becoming actively involved both in the group and outside of therapy. The behavioral approach emphasizes a plan for change. Leaders help members understand that verbalizations and insight are not enough to produce change. To broaden their repertoire of adaptive behaviors, members are urged to experiment in the group and practice homework assignments.
- ◆ The leader helps members prepare for termination well ahead of the group's ending date. Thus, they have adequate time to discuss their reactions, to consolidate what they have learned, and to practice new skills to apply at home and work. Appropriate referrals are made when reasonable goals have not been achieved. Suggestions are given for social activities that can help members generalize their learning in the group.

A basic assumption of behavioral group therapy is that a good working relationship between the leader and members is a necessary, but not a sufficient, condition for change. It is unfair to cast behavior therapists in a cold and impersonal role that reduces them to programmed machines. In his stress-management programs, Meichenbaum (1985) emphasizes the value of establishing a collaborative working relationship between clients and trainers. He asserts that the degree to which treatment is successful is based in large part on the degree to which clients feel accepted, understood, and liked by the trainer.

Lazarus (1989a) writes that it is necessary for therapists to establish a climate of respect and trust so that clients will confide personal and emotionally significant material. He views the client/therapist relationship on a continuum extending from a formal and businesslike approach, on one end, to a close-knit and warm approach, on the other. He suggests that it is appropriate to discuss the client/therapist relationship only when there is reason to think that it is getting in the way of therapeutic progress. Elsewhere, Lazarus (1986) finds certain personality characteristics to be associated with highly successful therapists. Such therapists possess a high and genuine respect for people, flexibility, responsibility, a nonjudgmental perspective, personal warmth, a good sense of humor, the willingness to practice what they preach, and a sense of congruence and authenticity. In short, behavioral group leaders must be skilled technicians who also possess the human qualities that lead to the climate of trust and care necessary for the effective use of these therapeutic techniques.

Stages of a Behavior-Therapy Group

The Multimethod Group Approach

This discussion of stages of a group is especially geared to the "multimethod group approach," which has been developed by Rose and his associates (see Rose, 1989; Rose & Edleson, 1987; Rose, Tallant, Tolman, & Subramanian, 1986). The multimethod group approach is called that because it uses various coping strategies for dealing with specific problems: training group members in systematic problem solving, cognitive restructuring, assertion training, relaxation training, behavioral rehearsal, and other strategies that are appropriate for specific problems. This approach involves gradually increasing members' participation and involvement in setting specific goals, planning, decision making, and mutual helping of others. The process progresses from a high degree of leader structure to a low degree of structure. Each client is helped to establish individualized goals and coping skills. Groups often have a common theme, such as stress management, anger control, or pain management. The goal goes beyond demonstrating change within the group setting. The ultimate goal is the transfer of change into the real world. Later group sessions are structured to make this generalization of learning more likely.

The following material on the stages of a behaviorally oriented group is based largely on the works of Sheldon Rose (1982, 1983, 1986, 1989) and Rose and Edleson (1987).

Initial Stage

Since prospective clients usually know very little about behavioral programs, they are given all the pertinent information about the group process before they join. Pregroup individual interviews and the first group session are devoted to exploring the prospective members' expectations and to helping them decide whether they will join the group. Those who decide to join negotiate a treatment contract, spelling out what the group leader expects from the member over the course of the group, as well as what the client can expect from the leader.

During the early stages of the group the focus is on building cohesiveness, on becoming familiar with the structure of group therapy, and on identifying problematic behaviors that need to be corrected. Since the building of cohesion is the foundation for effective work during each stage of a group's development, the leader has a central role in the establishment of trust. According to Rose (1989), the leader must initially strive to make the group attractive to its members; create group situations that require social competence on the part of the members; create many functional roles that members can play in the group; delegate the leadership responsibility to the members in a gradual and appropriate manner; present situations in which the members function as therapeutic partners for each other; control excessive group conflict; and find ways of involving all members in the group interactions. Assessment is a vital component of these early sessions, because before treatment can begin, problems must be stated in specific behavioral terms. Complex problems are not avoided but are broken down into smaller components.

After the goals have been identified, the group leader begins to select therapeutic strategies to meet these goals. Cormier and Cormier (1991) suggest that counselors obtain a commitment from clients to do the work necessary to reach their goals, preferably in the form of a written contract. This contract specifies the procedure to select goals and the strategy to achieve these goals. There are several reasons for having a written contract. An unambiguous contract promotes trust and thus helps forge the therapeutic alliance. Also, a contract sharpens the clients' awareness of their roles as active participants in the therapeutic process. Finally, it serves to link specific therapeutic procedures to specific goals.

Working Stage: Treatment Plan and Application of Techniques

Treatment planning involves choosing the most appropriate set of procedures from among specific strategies that have been demonstrated to be effective in achieving behavioral change. It should be emphasized that *assessment* and *evaluation* continue throughout the working stage. Group leaders must continually evaluate the degree of effectiveness of the sessions and how well treatment goals are being attained. To make this evaluation during the working stage, they continue to collect data on matters such as participation, member satisfaction, attendance, and completion of agreed-on assignments between sessions. These assessments also include gathering data to determine whether problems exist within the group and the degree to which group goals are being attained. Throughout the course of a group, individuals monitor their behaviors and the situations in which they occur. In this way they can quickly determine those strategies that are effective or ineffective. By means of this continuing evaluation process, both the members and the leader have a basis for looking at alternative and more effective strategies. We now turn to a description of some of these strategies that are typically used during the working stage: reinforcement, contingency contracts, modeling, behavior rehearsal, coaching, feedback, cognitive restructuring, problem solving, and the buddy system.

REINFORCEMENT. Reinforcement is a key intervention procedure in behavioral groups. In addition to the reinforcement provided by the group leader, other members reinforce one another through praise, approval, support, and attention. It is a good idea to begin each session with members reporting their successes, rather than their failures. This sets a positive tone in the group, provides reinforcement to those who did well in everyday life, and reminds the group that change is possible. Reports of success, no matter how modest, are especially important when the members are improving but are still falling short of their expectations and when their changing behavior is being met with disapproval in their everyday environments. In these cases the reinforcement and support of the group are critical if members are to maintain their gains.

If social reinforcement is a powerful method of shaping desired behaviors, so is self-reinforcement. Participants are taught how to reinforce themselves for their progress in order to increase their self-control and become less dependent on others.

CONTINGENCY CONTRACTS. Contingency contracts spell out the behaviors to be performed, changed, or discontinued; the rewards associated with the achievement of these goals; and the conditions under which rewards are to be received. Whenever possible, contracts also specify a time period for achieving the desired behaviors. Effective contingency contracts should have the following features: (1) a clear description of the specific behaviors to be performed in the assignments; (2) a specification of the immediate reinforcement to be received as well as the group reinforcement; and (3) a description of the means by which the assignment is to be observed, measured, and recorded (Rose & Edleson, 1987). Contingency contracts are often used with children, but some adults find them patronizing.

MODELING. Role modeling is one of the most powerful teaching tools available to the group leader. As we have seen with other approaches, an advantage of group counseling over individual counseling is that it offers members a variety of social and role models to imitate. The modeling is performed by both the leader and the participants.

What are the characteristics of effective models? Reviews of research (Bandura, 1969) indicate that a model who is similar to the observer in age, sex, race, and attitudes is more likely to be imitated than a model who is unlike the observer. Models who have a degree of prestige and status are more likely to be imitated. If the client is too different from the model in many of these characteristics, the client tends to perceive the model's behavior as unrealistic. Also, models who are competent in their performance and who exhibit warmth tend to increase modeling effects. As much as possible, models should be reinforced in the presence of the observer, and observers should be reinforced for their imitation of the behavior that is modeled. Modeling of specific behavior is carried out in role playing during the sessions and practiced *in vivo*. For example, Henry has difficulty in initiating contacts with women and would like to feel freer in approaching them in his college classes. He can observe another member modeling at least one way of effectively starting conversations with women. He can then practice in the sessions, using skills he has learned from the model. Then, he can make a contract to initiate several conversations in real life in his classes. Modeling is especially useful in assertion-training groups and in teaching clients how to make more constructive self-statements and change cognitive structures. The effect of modeling is enhanced by three other procedures: behavior rehearsal, coaching, and group feedback (Rose, 1989).

BEHAVIOR REHEARSAL. The aim of behavior rehearsal is to prepare members to perform the desired behaviors outside the group, when modeling cues will not be available. New behaviors are practiced in a safe context that simulates the real world. Not only are members protected from adverse consequences while they are learning, but they can also benefit from positive reinforcement, which is likely to increase their willingness to experiment with the new behavior in their daily life (Rose, 1989). The actual practicing of desirable behaviors should take place under conditions that are as similar as possible to the situations that occur in the client's environment, so that maximum generalization from the group to the real world will take place.

Behavior rehearsal, which can be thought of as a gradual shaping process, is a useful technique in teaching social skills. As Goldfried and Davison (1976) indicate, effective social interaction includes many behavioral components besides simply knowing *what* to say in a particular social situation. Specific factors such as vocal quality, rate of speech, gestures, body posture, eye contact, and other mannerisms are significant aspects. Goldfried and Davison suggest that it is wise to select only a few of these specific behaviors at a given time during a behavior rehearsal. They add that feedback is a useful mechanism of change during behavior rehearsals. This feedback can include the member's own subjective evaluation (which can be aided by either audio or videotaped replays of the rehearsal), the leader's commentary, and the reactions of other group members. As much as possible, Goldfried and Davison would like to see clients evaluate the adequacy of their own behavioral rehearsals, for this can help them learn to become more sensitive to their behavior and take corrective actions between sessions. Once members achieve successful performance in the group situation, they need to be made aware that application in real life is a basic part of behavior rehearsal. This can be accomplished by reminding members of the importance of completing homework assignments, by devoting some time in each session to deciding on appropriate assignments, and by routinely beginning each group session by checking on the assignments of each member.

COACHING. In addition to modeling and behavior rehearsal, group members sometimes require coaching. This process consists of providing the members with general principles for performing the desired behavior effectively. Coaching seems to work best when the coach sits behind the client who is rehearsing. When a member gets stuck and does not know how to proceed, another group member can whisper suggestions. It is important, however, that coaching be reduced in subsequent role playing and that the member rehearse independently before trying out a new role in the real world (Rose, 1989).

FEEDBACK. After members practice a new behavior in a group session, as mentioned, others provide them with verbal reactions to their performances. These impressions can be given by fellow group members or the group leader. There are typically two aspects to feedback: praise and encouragement for the behavior and specific suggestions for correcting or modifying errors. Feedback is a useful part of learning new behaviors, especially if it is constructive, specific, and positive. Rose and Edleson (1987) provide the following guidelines for offering feedback on a group member's rehearsal performance:

- ◆ Before group members are encouraged to offer feedback, they are trained in group exercises how to give and receive it.
- ◆ Positive feedback is given first, so that the member can be reinforced immediately.
- ◆ In criticizing a performance the observer says what could have been done differently.
- ◆ Useful feedback is specific and focuses on behaviors.
- ◆ Either the group leader or a group member reviews the feedback.

COGNITIVE RESTRUCTURING. An individual's cognitive processes have implications for behavior change. Indeed, group members often reveal self-defeating thoughts and irrational self-talk when they find themselves in stressful situations. *Cognitive restructuring* is the process of identifying and evaluating one's cognitions, understanding the negative behavioral impact of certain thoughts, and learning to replace these cognitions with more realistic and appropriate thoughts. Both rational emotive behavior therapy and cognitive therapy utilize cognitive restructuring as a core procedure in changing an individual's interpretations and thinking processes, which have a powerful effect on his or her feelings and actions. The following chapter describes in detail a variety of cognitive-restructuring strategies that are applicable to group counseling.

Rose (1989) describes cognitive restructuring as applied to group work. Initially, members may be taught through group exercises how to differentiate between self-defeating and self-enhancing statements. Typically, they provide one another with feedback and various models of a cognitive analysis. A further step is to encourage participants to devise self-enhancing statements that promote problem solving or effective actions. After clients decide on a set of realistic cognitive statements, cognitive modeling is used, in which the members imagine themselves in stressful situations and substitute self-enhancing statements for self-defeating remarks. Self-defeating thoughts can cause emotional distress and can interfere with performance; constructive self-statements can lead to improved performance. In cognitive rehearsal, members imitate the model and get feedback from others in the group. After several trials in the group they are given the assignment to practice a new set of statements at home before they try out a new style in the real world. In the final step of cognitive restructuring, homework is assigned at the end of each session and then monitored at the beginning of the following session. As members make progress, assignments can be developed at successive levels of difficulty.

PROBLEM SOLVING. Problem-solving therapy is a cognitive-behavioral strategy that teaches individuals ways to deal with problems in their daily lives. The main goal is to identify the most effective solution to a problem and to provide systematic training in cognitive and behavioral skills that will help the client apply it and also cope effectively with future problems. The four stages in the problem-solving process are described by Spiegler and Guevremont (1993):

1. The first stage deals with a definition of the problem and the formulation of specific goals. At this time, clients are helped to understand why certain problem situations are likely to occur and are given the expectation that they can learn ways to cope.
2. In the next stage, clients are taught to brainstorm alternative solutions to the problem. They are discouraged from evaluating any of the possible solutions until after all the suggestions have been presented.
3. The third stage consists of making a decision. After clients have identified most of the available responses, they are ready to decide on the best strategy to pursue. In making their choice, they examine the potential consequences of each course of action.
4. In the final stage, clients implement the chosen solution. They are encouraged to act on this decision and then to *verify* the degree of effectiveness of their course of action. This verification phase consists of having clients observe and evaluate the consequences of their actions in the real world.

Rose (1989) proposes an additional step between the third and fourth stages: preparation for implementation. In this phase, clients have others model and rehearse the solution and get information or training on carrying out their plans.

Procedures such as modeling, coaching, and reinforcement are used during problem-solving training. Throughout the therapy process, clients are taught self-control techniques, and they are encouraged to reinforce their own successful performance. Further, once clients have had an opportunity to observe the therapist (or other models) demonstrate effective problem-solving procedures, they are expected to assume a more active role. At this time, the therapist functions largely as a consultant, providing guidance, giving feedback, and encouraging and evaluating real-life applications (Rose, 1989).

THE BUDDY SYSTEM. Rose (1989) makes reference to the "buddy system" as a form of therapeutic alliance between members. Typically, a client is assigned or chooses another as a monitor and coach throughout the group-treatment process. Thus, the members monitor each other's behavior in the group, remind each other between meetings to stick to their commitments and practice their assignments, and play a supportive role both in and out of the group. Rose has found that in adult groups, clients are sometimes reluctant to choose buddies, especially in the early sessions of therapy. But when it has been established, the buddy system is useful in developing a supportive network in the natural environment. Buddies are trained in giving reinforcement for achievements and in giving and receiving criticism. The most important part of treatment occurs outside of the group with the practice of homework assignments. This arrangement offers members opportunities to be helpful to others and to practice their newly learned leadership skills. The buddy system becomes a self-help network that functions after the group terminates (Rose & Edleson, 1987).

Final Stage

During the final stage of the behavioral group the leader is primarily concerned with having members transfer the changes they have exhibited in the group to their everyday environment. Practice sessions involving simulations of the real world are used to promote this transfer. Members rehearse what they want to say to significant people in their life and practice alternative behaviors. Feedback from others in the group, along with coaching, can be of the utmost value at this final stage. Sessions are systematically designed so that new behaviors are gradually carried into daily life. Although preparation for generalization and maintenance of change is given a special focus in the final stage, it is a characteristic of all phases of the group.

Transferring changes from the therapy group to daily life is accomplished largely by the following actions taken by the group leader (Rose, 1989; Rose & Edleson, 1987):

- ◆ encouraging members to assume an increasing share of responsibility for their own treatment
- ◆ providing many varied practice situations for the members
- ◆ simulating the real world in the training context
- ◆ preparing members for facing a nonaccepting environment and for dealing with possible regressions
- ◆ overtraining members in the desired target behaviors
- ◆ instructing members in practicing generalization

Self-responsibility is emphasized throughout the life of the group, but it is especially critical in planning for termination. The leader changes from a direct therapist to a consultant in the final stage. Members are typically encouraged to join various nontherapeutic groups where they can practice and develop their newly acquired skills under less controlled conditions than those offered in the group. In addition, they are taught self-help cognitive skills such as self-reinforcement and problem solving as a way of preparing them for situations they have not encountered in the group. This move toward member independence from the group is essential if clients are to gain confidence in their ability to cope effectively with new problems. As the time of termination approaches, many of the initial assessment instruments are repeated as a way of evaluating the effectiveness of the group program.

Termination and follow-up are issues of special concern to behaviorally oriented group leaders. Therefore, short- and long-term follow-up interviews are scheduled. Rose and Edleson (1987) assert that follow-up interviews and group sessions serve as "booster shots" for maintaining the changed behaviors and continuing to engage in self-directed change. Follow-up sessions, which are often held two months after the group terminates and then again four to six months later, are finding modest but growing support in the research literature. These sessions provide rich opportunities for members to review what they have learned, to update the group on how they are doing, and to encourage them to be accountable for their changes or lack of them. Knowing that they will be accountable, members feel some pressure to maintain and use the discipline they learned in the group. They are encouraged to make use of their buddies and to discover alternative resources (which may include other groups or other forms of counseling) for continuing their progress.

Applications and Techniques

As mentioned earlier, the behavioral group therapist systematically uses a variety of specific techniques whose results can be objectively evaluated. Thus, the techniques can be continually refined for therapeutic effectiveness. The use of techniques varies with the group's clients or the problems that the group is dealing with. There are behavioral groups for managing anxiety and stress; for dealing with depression; for controlling specific behaviors such as excessive drinking, eating, and smoking; for teaching people how to be more effective in interpersonal relating; and for treating specific fears—to mention a few. Behavior therapy in groups can be applied to a variety of settings, such as schools, mental hospitals, day-treatment centers, community clinics, and prisons.

In this section I describe some common behavioral techniques that are applicable to group work. For the purpose of this discussion the techniques have been grouped under five general types of behavioral groups: (1) social-skills groups, (2) assertiveness groups, (3) stress-management groups, (4) groups for self-directed behavior change, and (5) multimodal group therapy as developed by Lazarus.

Social-Skills-Training Groups

Social-skills training is a broad category that deals with one's ability to interact effectively with others in a variety of social situations. Social-skills training in groups involves the application of many of the behavioral techniques discussed earlier in this chapter. The group offers unique advantages over individual counseling for the development of new social skills. What follows is a summary of the process Rose (1986) uses in structuring social-skills training.

Before beginning the social-skills-training process, the group leader discusses with the members the general purposes of the group and the main procedures that are likely to be used. The members are given a variety of examples and are encouraged to ask questions. The group leader attempts to draw on the experiences of those members who have used these procedures themselves. If the members have had no prior experience with role playing, the leader generally provides them with some training. Then situations are given to the group, and experienced members from previous groups are asked to demonstrate how to role-play. Once members learn role-playing skills, they are then trained to develop situations that lend themselves to social-skills training. After the group is trained in the development of problem situations, the members are asked to keep a diary of situations as they occur during the course of the week. Each week at least one situation of each member is handled by the group. In presenting a situation, the member states his or her goals or is given help in developing goals for the situation. After the goals are established and agreed on, other members are asked to propose the specific things that the client could do or say to achieve his or her goals. After all the suggestions have been presented, the group helps the client evaluate the suggestions with reference to the risks involved in a given course of action, appropriateness, compatability with one's personality, and likelihood of effective outcomes. Even though other members contribute suggestions, it is the client who ultimately decides on an overall strategy.

Either the therapist or some group member models the desired verbal and nonverbal behaviors in a brief demonstration. Clients then practice their roles in the situation by using the agreed-on behaviors. If clients have trouble using a strategy during the rehearsal, they can be coached by the group leader or other members. When coaching is used, it is generally eliminated in later rehearsals. After each rehearsal, clients receive feedback from the group pertaining to their strengths and weaknesses. Clients assign themselves homework to carry out in the real world. As they complete these assignments, they are asked to observe themselves in new situations and to keep a diary of problems. Behavioral procedures such as modeling, rehearsal, and homework are used to restructure cognitions.

Assertiveness-Training Groups

A behavioral approach that has gained increasing popularity is teaching people how to be assertive in a variety of social situations. Alberti and Emmons (1990a) provide the following working definition of assertive behavior: "Assertive behavior promotes equality in human relationships, enabling us to act in our own best interests, to stand up for ourselves without undue anxiety, to express honest feelings comfortably, [and] to exercise personal rights without denying the rights of others" (p. 7).

The basic assumption underlying the practice of assertion training is that people have the right—but not the obligation—to express their feelings, thoughts, beliefs, and attitudes. The goal of assertion training is to increase the group members' behavioral repertoire so that they can make the *choice* of being assertive or not. Another goal of assertion training is teaching people how to express themselves in a way that reflects sensitivity to the feelings and rights of others. Truly assertive individuals do not rigidly stand up for their rights at all costs, riding roughshod over the feelings and opinions of others.

THE PURPOSE OF ASSERTIVENESS-TRAINING GROUPS. Assertiveness training can be helpful for people who cannot ask others for what they want; who are unable to resist inappropriate demands; who have difficulty expressing feelings of love, gratitude, and approval as well as feelings of irritation, anger, and disagreement; and who feel that they don't have a right to have their own feelings and thoughts. Alberti and Emmons (1990a) identify three particularly difficult barriers to self-expression: (1) people may not believe that they have the right to be assertive or to express their thoughts or feelings, (2) people may be highly anxious or fearful about being assertive, and (3) people sometimes lack the skills for effectively expressing to others what they think and feel. Assertion training attempts to equip clients with the skills and attitudes necessary to deal effectively with a wide range of interpersonal situations. The specific outcome goals of the training include:

◆ recognizing and changing self-defeating or irrational beliefs concerning one's right to be assertive
◆ developing an attitude that places value on one's right to express oneself and on respect for the rights of others
◆ learning how to identify and discriminate among assertive, aggressive, and nonassertive behaviors
◆ increasing one's self-esteem to the point of becoming capable of taking the initiative
◆ being able to apply newly learned assertive skills to specific interpersonal situations

GUIDELINES FOR CONDUCTING ASSERTION-TRAINING GROUPS. What follows is a description of procedures that are typically used in assertion-training groups. There are various methods of structuring such groups; the following description is an adaptation of the procedures described by Alberti and Emmons (1990b) in their manual for assertiveness trainers. They use assertiveness/social-skills-training groups in a variety of settings, such as private practice, university counseling centers, and outpatient mental-health clinics.

In the first session of an assertiveness-training group, members hear brief introductory comments about the nature of the training, participate in an exercise to get to know one another, observe a brief demonstration of behavior rehearsal, listen to a presentation on how our thinking affects our behavior, receive a homework assignment, and participate in a relaxation exercise. The behavior-rehearsal demonstration is the core of the initial session. The group leader presents a short common scene and then role-plays a brief segment to demonstrate the differences between nonassertive, aggressive, and assertive behavioral styles. As members watch the demonstration, they are asked to identify specific components of the behavior and to provide feedback on the trainer's effectiveness in each style.

During this first session there is also a brief lecture on the cognitive-restructuring process and how a change in thinking can frequently lead to a change in one's attitude about acting assertively. Members are assigned to keep a log of progress that includes specific and detailed examples. They are asked to keep track of the sources of anxiety in their personal logs between the sessions. Members participate in a relaxation exercise as a way to conclude the first session.

In subsequent meetings the general format is the same, although the focus is more on behavioral rehearsal and practicing newly acquired skills in the sessions. The sessions are divided in the following way:

◆ There is follow-up on the homework completed by each of the members.
◆ There is a didactic presentation that deals with some cognitive issue or technique for each session.
◆ There are many opportunities to practice skills in specific situations.
◆ Members are taught to use exercises in coping with anxiety and stress.
◆ Homework to complete between the sessions is assigned.

As assertion training has gained in popularity in the last few years, responsible practitioners have expressed concern about the possible misuse of this counseling technique. Some of the areas of concern are unqualified trainers, illegitimate purposes, and application in inappropriate circumstances.

For those who are interested in learning the specifics of planning, setting up, conducting, and evaluating assertion-training groups, a number of excellent sources are available and are listed in the reference section of this chapter (see especially Alberti & Emmons, 1990a, 1990b).

ASSERTION TRAINING IN A MULTICULTURAL CONTEXT. It should be clear that assertion training is based on a set of values: that people have a right to express themselves, to ask for what they want, and to be direct in dealing with others. Fukuyama and Coleman (1992) describe Asian cultural norms that may influence levels of assertiveness, such as deference to authority, interpersonal harmony, modesty, and avoidance of public shame. They point out that individuals who grow up in a traditional Chinese family have little opportunity to develop assertiveness or decision-making skills. Instead, the parents and the elderly are invested with the power to make decisions, while children are expected to be obedient and respectful. It is clear that assertion-training groups had better take into consideration cultural values and norms.

In a pilot study of a bicultural assertion-training group with Asian–Pacific American college students, Fukuyama and Coleman (1992) adapted assertion-training strategies to the members' cultural norms. This group was designed to incorporate both Western and Eastern values. The facilitators in this group emphasized two key points: (1) that assertive behavior cannot be considered apart from specific situations, including an assessment of the cultural context, and (2) that individuals are encouraged to develop their personal belief systems as a guide to making choices of how they will behave. A bicultural belief system (which is based on two or more equally important belief systems) enables group members to choose appropriate behaviors in various situations.

The members who made up this pilot-study group were given the freedom to select topics for exploration in the sessions. Some of these topics were making requests and saying no, giving and receiving compliments, dealing with rudeness and prejudice, learning how to relate to authority figures, and practicing conversational skills. Fukuyama and Coleman noted several specific cultural values as being central in understanding the dimensions of assertiveness that were salient to the Asian–Pacific American students in this group. Inhibitions based on the cultural injunction of "saving face" were a strong influence on behaviors. Many of these students were particularly concerned about appearing "stupid" and were fearful of being laughed at by others. These social rules were associated with the notion of public shame. From their perspective, withholding emotional expression was often seen as more culturally appropriate than being emotional.

When the members of this group explored factors that were keeping them from being assertive, it was clear that messages they had received about being humble and modest were playing a role. Many of the group participants needed permission to feel good about themselves or to be able to receive compliments. Based on pride, students were hesitant to make requests of others. Through role-playing exercises, the members had opportunities to practice different types of assertion appropriate for various situations. The members benefited not only from learning how to be more expressive but also from recognizing the complexities of cultural values and challenges they faced as minorities in a culture dominated by white males. The group provided a safe context that allowed them to realize that they were not alone in their experiences with racism, prejudice, and cultural differences (Fukuyama & Coleman, 1992, p. 215).

Stress-Management Training in Groups

ASSUMPTIONS UNDERLYING STRESS-MANAGEMENT PROGRAMS. Stress is a basic part of contemporary life. Since it is not realistic to assume that stress can be eliminated, it is a good idea to devise strategies for helping people cope effectively with the multiple stresses they experience in daily life. As Meichenbaum (1985) has observed, the goal of stress-management programs is not to eliminate stress but to educate clients about its nature and effects and to teach them a variety of intrapersonal and interpersonal skills to deal with it constructively. A basic assumption of stress-management programs is that we are not simply victims of stress; rather, what we *do* and what we *think* actively contribute to how we experience stress. In other words, how we appraise events in life determines whether stress will affect us positively or negatively.

MEICHENBAUM'S STRESS-INOCULATION TRAINING. Meichenbaum (1977, 1985, 1986) is concerned with more than merely teaching people specific coping skills. His program is designed to prepare clients for intervention and motivate them to change, and it deals with issues such as resistance and relapse. Stress-inoculation training (SIT) consists of a combination of elements of information giving, Socratic discussion, cognitive restructuring, problem solving, relaxation training, behavioral and imaginal rehearsals, self-monitoring, self-instruction, self-reinforcement, and modifying environmental situations. This approach is designed to teach coping skills that can be applied to both present problems and future difficulties.

Meichenbaum (1985) has designed a three-stage model for SIT: (1) the conceptual phase, (2) the skills-acquisition and rehearsal phase; and (3) the application and follow-through phase.

During the initial stage of SIT (the *conceptual phase*) the primary focus is on creating a working relationship with clients by helping them gain a better understanding of the nature of stress and reconceptualize it in social-interactive terms. During this phase clients are educated about the transactional nature of stress and coping. They learn about the role that cognitions and emotions play in creating and maintaining stress. After an assessment process in which they take an active role, they determine short-, intermediate-, and long-term goals that will guide treatment. Self-monitoring, which begins at this time, continues throughout all the phases. Clients typically keep an open-ended diary in which they systematically record their specific thoughts, feelings, and behaviors. Many clients begin treatment feeling that they have been victimized by external circumstances that they are powerless to control. Training includes teaching them to become aware of their own role in creating their stress. This provides them with a basis for learning ways to reduce the negative effects of stress.

The second phase of SIT, or *skills acquisition and rehearsal,* focuses on helping clients develop and consolidate a variety of intrapersonal and interpersonal coping skills. Some of these specific techniques include relaxation training, cognitive restructuring, problem solving, social-skills training, time management, self-instructional training, and lifestyle changes such as reevaluating priorities, developing support systems, and taking direct action to alter stressful situations. Clients are introduced to a variety of methods of relaxation and are taught to use these skills to decrease arousal due to stress. Through teaching, demonstration, and guided practice, they learn the skills of progressive relaxation. They are expected to practice these skills regularly. Clients need to learn that it is not a waste of time to relax, and they need to grant themselves permission to participate in activities that are relaxing to them. These activities may include meditation, yoga, tensing and relaxing muscle groups, and breath-control techniques. They can also include walking, jogging, gardening, knitting, or other physical activities. Meichenbaum stresses that it is essential that both clients and trainers understand that relaxation is as much a state of mind as a physical state.

Teaching clients a number of cognitive strategies is a basic part of the second phase of SIT. These interventions include cognitive restructuring, problem-solving strategies, and guided self-dialogue. In cognitive restructuring, clients become aware of the role that their cognitions and emotions play in creating and maintaining stress. The cognitive-restructuring approach used in SIT is based on the work of Beck (1976). The goal of his cognitive therapy is to identify clients' unrealistic, maladaptive thought patterns and to replace them with rational and adaptive modes of thinking. He places emphasis on the clients' capacity and responsibility for discovering these maladaptive thought patterns. He systematically uses strategies such as modeling, behavioral rehearsal, and graded task assignments in teaching constructive cognitive and coping skills. In treating stress-related problems, SIT uses three core techniques (which are described in detail by Beck, Rush, Shaw, and Emery, 1979): (1) eliciting the client's thoughts, feelings, and interpretations of events; (2) gathering evidence with the client to either support or disprove these interpretations; and (3) designing homework assignments to test the validity of the interpretations and to gather more data for discussion. Through cognitive-therapy techniques clients learn to detect negative and stress-engendering thoughts. They also learn to challenge their "automatic thoughts" and their absolutistic thinking, which compounds their stress. Clients are also given self-instructional training, in which they learn guided self-dialogue techniques to replace negativistic self-statements. Through training, clients develop a new set of coping self-statements that they can apply when they encounter stressors. It is assumed that if the thinking of clients can make them worse, they can adopt a different set of self-statements to reduce, avoid, or constructively use stress.

In the third phase of SIT *(application and follow-through)* the focus is on carefully arranging for transfer and maintenance of change from the therapeutic situation to the real world. The assumption is that coping skills that are practiced in the clinic will not automatically generalize to everyday life situations. To consolidate the lessons learned in the training sessions, clients participate in a variety of activities, including imagery and behavioral rehearsal, role playing, modeling, and graduated *in vivo* practice. Clients are asked to write down the homework assignments, or personal experiments, that they are willing to complete. The outcomes of these assignments are carefully checked at subsequent meetings, and if clients do not follow through with them, the trainer and the members collaboratively consider the reasons for these failures. Follow-up and booster sessions typically take place at 3-, 6-, and 12-month periods as an incentive for clients to continue practicing and refining their coping skills. Instead of being considered a limited intervention, SIT can be part of an ongoing stress-management program that extends the benefits of training into the future. For a more detailed discussion of the techniques typically used during this phase of treatment, review the earlier discussion of the techniques described in the final stage of a behavioral group.

IMPLICATIONS FOR PRACTICE. Stress-management training has potentially useful applications for a wide variety of problems and client populations, both for remediation of stress disorders and for prevention. Meichenbaum (1985) summarizes the literature identifying the use of SIT and related procedures with selected populations. Target problems and the populations that have received stress-management training include:

◆ problems with anger: adults and adolescents with anger-control problems, abusive parents
◆ problems with anxiety: test anxiety, interpersonal anxiety, performance anxiety, anxiety of adults reentering school
◆ problems with phobias: animal phobias, fear of flying
◆ general stress reactions: Type A individuals, medical outpatients, clients in community mental-health centers
◆ medical problems: preparing patients for surgery, preparing children for dental examinations, pain management, helping cancer patients deal with fear
◆ victim populations: rape victims, victims of terrorist attacks
◆ professional groups: nurses, teachers, school psychologists, probation officers, police officers, parachutists, drill instructors, scuba divers

Based on their experience in conducting stress-management-training groups, Rose, Tolman, and Tallant (1985a) contend that the training approach is widely applicable. They have conducted stress-management groups with foster parents, abusive spouses, students, patients in a cardiac-rehabilitation program, and clients recruited from the population at large. They have helped social workers manage their stress, as well as teaching them techniques they could use with their clients. Coping-skills training does not have to be done in isolation, for these programs can be integrated with other treatment approaches.

For a detailed description of ways to organize stress-management groups, see the manual by Rose and his associates (1985a); for pain-management groups, see the manual by Rose and Subramanian (1986). Both of these are described in the Recommended Supplementary Readings section of this chapter.

Groups for Self-Directed Behavior Change

There is a trend toward "giving psychology away"—that is, a tendency to teach people how to apply interpersonal skills to their everyday life. This trend implies that psychologists will share their knowledge with consumers so that people can lead increasingly self-directed lives and not be dependent on the experts for the effective management of the problems they encounter. Psychologists who share this perspective are concerned primarily with teaching people the skills they will need for self-direction.

Behaviorally oriented groups offer great promise for those who want to learn the skills necessary for self-management. Areas in which one can learn to control behavior and bring about self-directed change are excessive eating, drinking, and smoking and inadequate self-discipline at work or in school. Some people cannot accomplish certain goals in their work because their efforts are hindered by lack of organization; they don't know where to begin with a project, how to sustain their efforts, and how to avoid the crippling discouragement they experience when they fail to attain their goals. It is in these and similar areas that behavioral groups for self-directed change can provide the guidelines and planning necessary to bring about change. If you are interested in a detailed treatment of self-directed change and self-management strategies, consult Watson and Tharp (1993).

Multimodal Group Therapy

The previously described models of behavioral group therapy tend to be short term (6 to 12 sessions) and tend to deal with a homogeneous population. Assertion-training groups are short term, for example, and the members are alike in wanting to learn ways of being assertive. Stress-management training consists of 8 sessions. Pain-management training is done in 10 sessions. Likewise, many of the self-directed groups are homogeneous, and the treatment program is relatively brief. Members are taught skills they can apply in a program once they complete these specific training groups. In contrast, the multimodal group approach tends to be of longer duration and organizationally more like other forms of long-term group therapy.

A major premise of the broad-spectrum orientation known as multimodal therapy is that the more coping responses a person learns in therapy, the less are the chances for a relapse (Lazarus, 1987a). Although most of the writing about multimodal therapy has been from the perspective of individual psychotherapy, Lazarus's formulation can be applied to group counseling and therapy (see Lazarus, 1982). This approach is included in this chapter because of its potential to encompass all the major areas of personality functioning in group treatment.

Multimodal group therapy takes into consideration the *whole person*. Lazarus stresses that since each client is unique, treatment has to be individually tailored. Care must be taken to avoid fitting clients to a preconceived treatment mode. Instead, a careful attempt is made to determine precisely what relationship with the therapist and what treatment strategies would work best with each particular client and under which particular circumstances. The basic question is who or what is best for this particular client? Therapeutic flexibility and versatility are valued highly in the multimodal orientation (Lazarus, 1987b, 1989a, 1989b, 1992a, 1992b).

The essence of the multimodal approach is the premise that human beings are complex in that they move, feel, sense, imagine, think, and relate. According to Lazarus (1989b), there are seven major areas of personality functioning: behavior, affective responses, sensations, images, cognitions, interpersonal relationships, and biological functioning. Although these modalities are interactive, they can be considered discrete functions and defended as useful divisions.

The multimodal therapist takes the view that a complete assessment and treatment program must account for each of the seven modalities of the BASIC I.D., which stands for *b*ehavior, *a*ffect, *s*ensations, *i*magery, cognition, *i*nterpersonal relationships, and *d*rugs/biology. Thus, the BASIC I.D. is the cognitive map that ensures that each aspect of personality receives explicit and systematic attention. Further, comprehensive therapy entails the correction of irrational beliefs, deviant behaviors, unpleasant feelings, bothersome images, stressful relationships, negative sensations, and possible biochemical imbalances. It is assumed that since clients are troubled by a number of specific problems, it is best to employ a number of specific treatments. If therapists fail to tune in to a client's presenting modality, the client often feels misunderstood. It is axiomatic that therapy should start where the client is and then move into more productive areas of discourse (Lazarus, 1989b). Enduring change is seen as a function of combined techniques, strategies, and modalities. The goal of multimodal therapy is to reduce suffering and promote personal growth as rapidly as possible (Lazarus, 1992b).

Some other basic assumptions underly multimodal therapy. First, therapists must be effective as people. Second, they need a range of skills and techniques to deal with the range of problems posed by their clients. Third, they must be technically eclectic; that is, they should be able to employ techniques from any discipline that have been demonstrated to be effective in dealing with specific problems. Fourth, they need to have a consistent theoretical framework that guides their practice.

In calling for technical eclecticism, Lazarus endorses using a variety of techniques within a theoretical structure that is open to verification and disproof. He adds that useful techniques can be derived from many sources. Technical eclectics draw strategies from a variety of approaches without having to embrace any of the diverse theoretical positions. In espousing technical (or systematic) eclecticism, Lazarus is not arguing in favor of a theoretical eclecticism. Multimodal therapy rests primarily on principles of Bandura's (1986) social- and cognitive-learning theory. The kind of technical eclecticism that Lazarus (1987b) maintains is needed is scientific and has three other qualities: breadth, depth, and specificity. Practitioners can spell out precisely what interventions they might employ with various clients, as well as the means by which they are selecting these procedures.

Multimodal group therapy begins with a comprehensive assessment of all the modalities of human functioning. The BASIC I.D. assessment allows therapists to utilize types of interventions that are most likely to be helpful to clients in particular circumstances. Ideally, multimodal therapists are broadly trained so that they can work with individuals, couples, families, and groups; they are also skilled in specific behavioral, affective, sensory, imagery, cognitive, interpersonal, and somatic techniques. (See Lazarus, 1989b, for a list of the most frequently used techniques.) An adaptation of Lazarus's description of this first phase of group therapy is given below. Members are asked questions pertaining to the BASIC I.D.:

1. *Behavior.* This area refers primarily to overt behaviors, including acts, habits, gestures, and motor reactions that are observable and measurable. Some questions asked are "What would you like to change? What behaviors would you like to decrease or eliminate? What behaviors would you like to increase or acquire? What are your chief strengths? What specific behaviors are keeping you from getting what you want?"

2. *Affect.* This modality refers to emotions, moods, and strong feelings. Questions sometimes asked include "What emotions do you experience most often? What makes you laugh? What makes you sad? What are some emotions that are problematic for you?"

3. *Sensations.* This aspect refers to the five basic senses of touch, taste, smell, sight, and hearing. Examples of questions asked are "Do you suffer from unpleasant sensations, such as pains, aches, dizziness, and so forth? What do you particularly like or dislike in the way of seeing, smelling, hearing, touching, and tasting?"

4. *Imagery.* This modality pertains to ways we picture ourselves, and it includes dreams, fantasies, and vivid memories. Some questions asked are "What are some bothersome recurring dreams and vivid memories? How do you view your body? How do you see yourself now? How would you like to be able to see yourself in the future? What are some past, present, or future mental pictures that are troubling you?"

5. *Cognition.* This aspect refers to insights, philosophies, ideas, and judgments that constitute one's fundamental values, attitudes, and beliefs. Questions include "What are the values that are most significant in your life? What are some ways in which you meet your intellectual needs? What is the nature of your self-talk? What are some of your central irrational beliefs? What are the main 'shoulds,' 'oughts,' and 'musts' in your life? Do they get in the way of effective living for you? How does your thinking influence what you are doing and how you are feeling?"

6. *Interpersonal relationships.* This term refers to interactions with other people (relatives, lovers, friends, and co-workers). Examples of questions are "What do you expect from the significant others in your life? What do they expect of you? What do you give to these people, and what do you get from them? Are there any relationships with others that you want to change? If so, what changes would you like to see?"

7. *Drugs/Biology.* This modality includes more than drugs; it takes into consideration one's nutritional habits and exercise patterns. Some questions asked are "What is the state of your health? Do you have any medical concerns? Do you take any prescribed drugs? What are your diet and exercise habits?"

Lazarus (1992a, 1992b) lists the following five principles that embody the essense of the multimodal perspective: (1) Humans act and interact across the seven modalities of the BASIC I.D.; (2) these modalities are interconnected and must be considered as an interactive system; (3) accurate evaluation is best accomplished by systematically assessing each of the seven modalities and the interaction among them; (4) a comprehensive approach to treatment involves the specific correction of significant problems across the BASIC I.D.; and (5) psychological disturbance is a product of factors such as conflicting feelings, misinformation, lack of interpersonal skills, external stressors, and existential concerns.

According to Lazarus (1992a) the essence of the multimodal position is that treating only one or two significant problems will not result in significant improvement. Indeed, even if change occurs, relapse is likely unless clients identify problem areas in all of the basic modalities. It is not sufficient to target one area for exploration. One of the main advantages of the multimodal orientation is that it offers a seven-pronged approach as the focus of therapeutic work.

A preliminary investigation into a client's BASIC I.D. brings out some central and significant themes that can be productively explored in a group. The preliminary questioning is followed by a detailed life-history questionnaire. Once the main profile of a person's BASIC I.D. has been established, the next step consists of an examination of the interactions among the different modalities. This second phase of work intensifies specific facets of the person's problem areas and permits the group therapist to understand the person more fully as well as devise effective coping and treatment strategies.

Lazarus (1982) believes that it is best to form groups that are relatively homogeneous with respect to problem areas and goals. Examples include people who are interested in learning to become more assertive, people who are concerned with weight loss, couples who are interested in improving the communication in their relationship, and individuals who want to quit smoking. Group therapy is seen as particularly appropriate (and the treatment of choice) when there is some reason to believe that other people will enhance the processes of learning, unlearning, and relearning. If the BASIC I.D. assessment reveals that the client has a negative self-image and feelings of inadequacy, then multimodal group therapy can be useful. Likewise, for clients whose assessment reveals interpersonal difficulties, group therapy would offer some distinct advantages over individual treatment.

It is Lazarus's (1982) position that a time-limited group (of approximately 20 sessions) appears to be the most effective format. When the group ends, members might become involved in individual therapy or become a member of another group. Lazarus has found that this format encourages the most active learning, unlearning, and relearning, the basis of multimodal therapy. In terms of the methods that are used in the group sessions, Lazarus endorses an eclectic position. Thus, discussion, role playing, relaxation exercises, behavior rehearsal, cognitive restructuring, modeling, assertion-training exercises, and identifying feelings are but a few of the techniques employed Lazarus emphasizes, however, that most substantial changes occur outside of the group; therefore, he relies heavily on homework assignments and other performance-based methods, rather than exclusively using verbal and cognitive procedures. (For a more detailed discussion of these procedures, see Lazarus, 1989b.)

The multimodal therapist tends to be very active during group sessions. Leaders function as trainers, educators, consultants, facilitators, and role models. They provide information, instruction, and feedback. Leaders also serve an important function by modeling assertive behaviors in the group, challenging self-defeating beliefs, offering constructive criticism and suggestions, offering positive reinforcements, and being appropriately self-disclosing. The multimodal approach to group work requires that the leader be flexible in using various methods and in conducting the group.

In summary, one of the values of the multimodal approach to group work is that it does provide a comprehensive view of assessment and treatment. It allows for the incorporation of diverse techniques. If a technique is proved effective for a given problem, it can become part of the multimodal therapist's approach. Thus, this model appears to foster an openness on the part of practitioners.

Evaluation of Behavioral Group Therapy

Contributions and Strengths of the Approach

One of the contributions of behavioral group therapy is its specificity, which has implications for assessment, treatment, and research. A strength of behavior therapy is its precision in specifying goals and procedures, which are defined in unambiguous and measurable terms. This specificity allows for links among assessment, treatment, and evaluation strategies.

The behavioral tradition seeks to tailor specific strategies to each client. Consider how specificity applies to a stress-management group. Because behavioral group leaders favor specificity, they take a general term such as *stress* and break it down into its component parts. Thus, they would not say, "I'm treating Fred for stress" but "I'm addressing Fred's unassertiveness at work, his tendency to catastrophize, his habit of placing demands on himself, and his fears of rejection, all of which contribute to his feeling stressed out." Leaders attempt to fit the treatment to the client's primary processing style. As Lazarus and Mayne (1990) write, clients rarely suffer from a unitary problem, which means that unimodal solutions will have little value.

More than any of the other therapies discussed in this book, behavior therapy is to be credited with conducting research to determine the efficacy of its techniques. There is a commitment to the systematic evaluation of the procedures used in a group. Those interventions that do not work are eliminated, and techniques are continually being improved. Among the strengths of the behavioral approach are its effectiveness, its efficiency, and the breadth and complexity of its applications (Spiegler & Guevremont, 1993). Thus, behavioral interventions can be incorporated effectively into both heterogeneous and homogeneous groups, and also with groups that have a wide variety of specific purposes.

A behavioral group is a concrete example of a humanistic approach in action. The members are involved in the selection of both goals and treatment strategies. In many groups, the leader helps members move toward independence by delegating leadership functions to them. Members in a behavioral group typically carry out part of the therapy independently of the group in homework assignments and in transferring what they are learning in the sessions to everyday living. Therapy then becomes a place where members learn how to learn and are encouraged to develop the skills necessary to solve future problems.

Lazarus (personal communication, February 1, 1992) believes that behavioral group therapists select appropriate techniques far more systematically than group leaders with other orientations. Some questions that behavioral leaders are likely to raise are "Should the emphasis be on the present or the past? Is it best to focus on external responses, sensory experiences, automatic thoughts, or errors of logic and perception? What sort of direction and teaching will be required of the group therapist? What homework will be involved?"

The behavioral approach allows for the evolution of intervention methods. With the focus on research, these techniques are made more precise so that they can be used with specific clients with a variety of specific problems. Regardless of which models influence our style of group leadership, the spirit of behavior therapy can encourage us to strive for accountability, rather than simply relying on faith and intuition that our practices are working.

Few approaches to group work have as broad and as a strong an empirical base with a wide variety of populations as does behavior therapy (Spiegler & Guevremont, 1993). There is empirical support for each of the dimensions of group work, and preliminary data suggest that the cognitive-behavioral group model offers a promising set of treatment strategies with various types of clients (Rose, 1989).

ADVANTAGES OF A GROUP APPROACH. According to Brabender and Fallon (1993), even though the focus of a behavioral group is on individual goals, the group setting permits and augments individual behavior changes in ways that are not possible in individual therapy. They add that the group facilitates progress toward individual goals by providing enhanced reinforcement options. Given the protected group environment, the members are encouraged to practice their newly acquired or modified behaviors spontaneously without fear of negative consequences. Because of the level of control of the leader, it is easier to orchestrate the group process so that members respond to one another in accepting rather than rejecting ways.

The population that is suited to behavioral group therapy includes clients with one or more of the following problems: social-skills deficits, depression, phobias, anxiety, stress, sexual disorders, pain, anger, over-weight, substance abuse, psychological trauma, and difficulty managing children (Rose, 1986). To this list Lazarus (1986) adds conflicting feelings, maladaptive habits, interpersonal disturbances, low self-esteem, and biological dysfunctions. Clearly, many complex problems are the focus of treatment in behavioral groups. What follows is a summary of some of the advantages of group therapy over individual treatment, based on the writings of Rose (1983, 1986, 1989) and Rose and Edleson (1987).

◆ The group provides members with an intermediate step between performing newly acquired behavior in therapy and transferring this performance to everyday life. It serves as a laboratory for learning skills that are essential in developing good social relationships.

◆ The group offers powerful norms to control the behavior of individuals. Examples of some positive therapeutic norms are a commitment to regular attendance, a willingness to self-disclose, a commitment to evaluating and working on one's problems, and encouragement by others to stick to a plan leading to behavioral and cognitive change.

◆ Group work provides a setting for accurate assessment, because members can learn how their behavior affects others through the feedback they continually receive. Members can provide powerful feedback to one another about specific behaviors, which is often more readily accepted from peers than it is from the group leader.

◆ A unique characteristic of group therapy is the opportunity for peer reinforcement, multiple modeling, and group brainstorming.

◆ In a group setting a wide variety of interpersonal skills can be practiced and transferred to out-of-group situations.

◆ The leader's control of the group process encourages members to experiment with new behaviors in a nonjudgmental setting; it is acceptable to make mistakes, and learning grows out of the willingness to learn from these mistakes.

◆ There is growing empirical support for the utility of various components of behavioral and cognitive-behavioral group therapy. Group therapy appears to be at least as effective and more efficient in terms of therapist cost than individual therapy (Rose, 1989).

USING BEHAVIORAL METHODS WITH OTHER APPROACHES. There is a trend toward broadening the scope of behavior therapy while retaining its essential features. According to Spiegler and Guevremont (1993), behavior therapists are increasingly recognizing that in many cases optimal treatment may require more than one *behavioral* approach. Moreover, the growing trend toward psychotherapeutic integration involves incorporating treatment strategies from two or more different orientations. In keeping with this trend, behavior therapists are now incorporating *nonbehavioral* methods into the treatment plans they devise. A good example of this trend is the technical eclecticism of multimodal therapy as espoused by Lazarus.

BEHAVIORAL GROUP THERAPY ◆ 373

As was mentioned, multimodal therapy is clearly rooted in behavioral theory, yet it borrows a wide variety of techniques from many different therapeutic orientations. The challenge for behavior therapy is to incorporate nonbehavioral treatments without violating the fundamental behavioral approach (Spiegler & Guevremont, 1993).

Another trend in the practice of behavioral group work is to incorporate cognitive factors. Behavior therapists are reformulating their techniques in cognitive- and social-learning terms instead of the traditional conditioning terms. There have been numerous examples in this chapter of groups designed primarily to increase the client's degree of control and freedom in specific aspects of daily life. For example, the cognitive factors are stressed in the self-control and independence of individuals in groups designed for stress-management training, assertion training, social-skills training, and self-directed behavior change.

A therapist need not subscribe totally to behavior therapy in order to derive practical benefits from the use of specific behavioral techniques. As a matter of fact, I believe that certain experiential and humanistic models can be enhanced by systematically incorporating some of the behavioral techniques into their relationship-oriented frameworks. I am convinced that an understanding of the learning principles that operate within a group is critical for effective group leadership, regardless of one's orientation.

For example, behavioral principles operate behind such therapeutic procedures as modeling and reinforcement, which are used in almost any kind of group. Members are supported (reinforced) in their attempts to be honest, to take risks, to experiment with new behavior, to be active, to take the initiative, and to participate fully in the group. Behavioral principles are instrumental in the fostering of group cohesion, which enables members to feel that they are not alone with their problems. The mutual learning and exploration of personal concerns bind the members of a group in a meaningful way. Also, the specificity of the approach helps group members translate fuzzy goals into concrete plans of action, and it helps the group leader keep these plans clearly in focus. Another strength of the behavioral model is the wide range of techniques that participants can use to specify their goals and to develop the skills needed to achieve these goals. Techniques such as role playing, coaching, guided practice, modeling, feedback, learning by successive approximations, and homework assignments can be included in any group leader's repertoire, regardless of his or her theoretical orientation.

Limitations of the Behavioral Approach

Behavioral groups do have their disadvantages. Antitherapeutic norms can develop, which could work against effective treatment. Group contagion and aggression can be more of a problem in groups than in individual counseling. When groups are too highly structured, as behavioral groups can often become, individual clients can be prevented from meeting their personal needs. Even minimal effectiveness with groups requires that leaders have training and supervision and that they develop an extensive repertoire of skills (Rose, 1986, 1989; Rose & Edleson, 1987).

Some critics of the behavioral approach to group work argue that this model ignores the historical causes of present behavior and does not work with the past in the therapeutic process. There is some truth to this criticism. It seems clear that the behavior therapist opposes the traditional psychoanalytic approach, which assumes that early traumatic events are at the root of present dysfunction. As we have seen, the psychoanalytic theory holds that it is essential to discover the original causes, induce insight in the client, and work through past traumas. Behavior therapists may acknowledge that the deviant responses have historical origins, but they maintain that the responses are still in effect because they are being maintained by reinforcing stimuli. They assume that past events seldom maintain current problems. Therefore, they place most of their emphasis on providing the client with new learning experiences. It is clear that the focus is on learning new responses and changing environmental conditions as a necessary prerequisite for behavior change.

Although I think it is unfair to accuse behavior therapists of ignoring the past or considering it unimportant, I do believe that they fail to work with the past sufficiently. In my own work I have found that most of the contemporary struggles of participants appear to be firmly rooted in their childhood experiences. I see it as particularly important that group members have opportunities to express and explore the feelings that are attached to past traumatic events. I have found that it seems necessary for members to relive certain past experiences and resolve some basic conflicts that have lingered since childhood before new learning can proceed. For this depth of emotional work, techniques from psychodrama and Gestalt therapy are especially useful. I think that there is a tendency of behavioral practitioners to give insufficient attention to the role that unexpressed emotional material plays in behavior.

In addition to giving more attention to the past than most behavior therapists, I also value focusing on subjective experiences (such as dreams) to a much greater extent than they do. One of the reviewers of this chapter, Arnold Lazarus, pointed out that astute behavior therapists know that on occasion dreams can provide clues that may have eluded other avenues of inquiry. Therefore, they are not inclined to ignore dreams, yet they will not pay inordinate attention to them either.

According to Rose (personal communication, February 8, 1993), one of the major weaknesses of the behavioral group-therapy movement has been its historical ignoring of group process. In spite of the fact that practitioners have long noted major group differences in their practice, almost all of the research, though often of high quality, is on the effects of the behavioral procedures on outcome. In a review of all research on the group treatment of depression and anxiety prior to 1985, Rose, Tolman, and Tallant (1985b) found that only one study had considered any group characteristic as a contributor to outcome, and then in a post hoc analysis. Since that time only one additional study has been found in which process has been considered as an independent variable (Whitney & Rose, 1989). Only recently have authors of behavioral group-therapy texts begun to take group process into serious consideration (Rose, 1989; Rose & Edleson, 1987).

Another of the limitations of the behavioral model is that if it is too rigidly applied, it can lead the therapist to lose sight of the people in the group by focusing exclusively on techniques and on the details of the members' specific problems. In my opinion, this focus on problems and symptoms can result in a failure to understand the meaning behind an individual's behavior. This is not to say that group therapy should focus on dealing with "underlying causes" of behavior. However, I prefer to deal with factors both in one's *external* situation that may be eliciting behavioral problems *and* with one's *internal* reactions to these environmental variables. For example, in working with a man who has great anxiety over relating to women, I would be interested in knowing what particular situations in his environment lead to this anxiety, and I would be concerned about his reactions to these situations. How does he feel when he is in the presence of women? What are some things he tells himself when he meets women? How does he perceive women in various situations? What are some historical roots of his fear? Therefore, my aim would not be simply to employ techniques to eliminate his anxiety; rather, I would want to explore with him the *meaning* of this anxiety. I might also encourage him to relive some earlier painful experiences in dealing with women and facilitate deeper expression of his feelings and self-exploration. In fairness, most behavior therapists now look at the situation and the response. They are interested in exploring cognitions and, to some extent, the affective elements in the context of the client's problem. In other words, behavior therapists are interested in more than merely eliminating symptoms of problem behaviors. Certainly, practitioners from any orientation could profit by drawing on behavioral interventions and including them in their group work.

Applying Behavior Therapy with Multicultural Populations

Behavioral group therapy has some clear advantages in work with multicultural populations. As we have seen, clients from certain cultural and ethnic backgrounds hold values that are contrary to the free expression of feelings and sharing of personal concerns about family matters. Since behavioral groups do not place emphasis on experiencing and expressing intense feelings, clients who might find catharsis distasteful are not immediately put off by being expected to emote.

Behavioral groups are often short term and highly structured, and thus clients have a good chance of knowing what they are getting into when they agree to participate. Behavioral practitioners typically spend time in preparing members to participate in the group experience. The group process is not mysterious, for norms are made clear.

Other factors that contribute to the usefulness of the behavioral approach to group work include its specificity, task orientation, focus on objectivity, focus on cognition and behavior, action orientation, dealing with the present more than the past, and problem-solving orientation. Clients learn coping strategies and acquire survival techniques. The attention given to transfer of learning and the principles and strategies for maintaining new behavior in the real world are crucial. Because behavior therapy fits into a short-term group format, it is applicable to a variety of practical problems that certain client populations face, and the time frame makes it possible to deal with day-to-day concerns that these clients bring to therapy. A strength of behavioral interventions in groups is the emphasis given to education and prevention.

However, it is important for group leaders to help their clients assess the possible consequences of some of their newly acquired social skills. For example, as was mentioned, Chinese culture places a premium on compliance with tradition, and being assertive can thus lead to problems. Therefore, group leaders need to be mindful of how cultural values can influence the behaviors of clients, and they will also do well to help these members assess the advantages and disadvantages of developing a more assertive style. Members can learn to use what they already have to their advantage. It is also important that members have opportunities to talk about the problems they encounter as they acquire new attitudes and behaviors in their home and at work.

Although assertiveness training is designed largely to empower the participants, there has been some criticism of this type of group from a feminist perspective. Assertion-training groups have been viewed with optimism by some, for they provide a vehicle for women to learn how to express themselves more fully. Enns (1993) comments that women experience frustration when they adopt new roles and then meet with resistance or are given negative labels. From such experiences, it has been learned that social change does not always follow individual change. Enns cites research suggesting that a traditional masculine model of mental health permeates the culture to such a degree that there are few advantages for women if they incorporate behaviorally expressive traits. Although assertiveness training can be an important feminist intervention to empower women, the training needs to consider sociocultural and political dimensions if it is to be effective. Skill development alone is not enough for many individuals with minority status. Even if they succeed in making significant internal changes, they are likely to meet with frustration if social and cultural conditions remain static.

A final potential problem involves group practitioners who assume that they are in the best position to set goals that will determine the direction a group takes. If the goals are not consistent with the cultural values of the members, it is not likely that these members will benefit from the group process. Behavioral approaches are often instrumental in helping ethnic minorities make specific changes they desire. However, there is also the possibility that they may feel manipulated to change in the group therapist's direction, unless he or she is clear and honest in establishing the premise that clients make their own decisions.

Where to Go from Here

If you have an interest in further training in behavior therapy, sources to contact are:

Behavior Therapy Unit
Temple University Medical School
Eastern Pennsylvania Psychiatric Institute
3300 Henry Avenue
Philadelphia, PA 19129

Association for the Advancement of Behavior Therapy
15 West 36th Street
New York, NY 10018

The Association for the Advancement of Behavior Therapy has published a *Directory of Graduate Study in Behavior Therapy,* which gives complete and up-to-date information on nearly 300 programs in clinical/counseling psychology, psychology internship, psychiatry residency, and social work.

RECOMMENDED SUPPLEMENTARY READINGS

Working with Children and Adolescents in Groups (Rose & Edleson, 1987) and *Working with Adults in Groups* (Rose, 1989) are two outstanding books on behavior therapy in groups. In the first one, the authors present a concrete, step-by-step guide for treating problem behaviors in children and adolescents. Based on empirical research and their own work, the authors show how a variety of approaches can be combined to help children. Separate chapters deal with treatment planning, assessment of problems, setting of goals, choosing problem-solving strategies, intervention methods designed to change behavior, practicing new behavior in daily life, and strategies for generalizing and maintaining new behavior. In the second book, Rose describes a multimethod approach to working with adults. Specific guidelines are given for starting and conducting groups, as are a variety of cognitive-behavioral strategies. Some other specific group strategies described are relaxation, breathing, meditation, and techniques for coping with stress. These are my top recommendations for further reading in this area.

Social-skills training and assertion training are particularly well-suited for group work. The two sources that I consider to be excellent in this are *Your Perfect Right: A Guide to Assertive Living* (Alberti & Emmons, 1990a) and the companion professional edition, *Your Perfect Right: A Manual for Assertiveness Trainers* (Alberti & Emmons, 1990b). The latter book contains many helpful guidelines for trainers of these groups.

Contemporary Behavior Therapy (Spiegler & Guevremont, 1993) is a comprehensive and up-to-date treatment of basic principles and applications of the behavior therapies, as well as a fine discussion of ethical issues. Specific chapters deal with procedures that can be usefully applied to group counseling, a few of which are behavioral assessment, modeling therapy, systematic desensitization, cognitive restructuring, and cognitive coping skills.

The Practice of Multimodal Therapy (Lazarus, 1989b) is an excellent source of techniques and procedures. It represents an attempt to deal with the whole person by developing assessments and treatment interventions for all the modalities of human experience.

Interviewing Strategies for Helpers: Fundamental Skills and Cognitive Behavioral Interventions (Cormier & Cormier, 1991) is a comprehensive and clearly written textbook dealing with training experiences and skill development. Its excellent documentation offers group practitioners a wealth of material on a variety of topics, such as assessment procedures, selection of goals, development of appropriate treatment programs, and methods of evaluating outcomes.

The Behavior Therapist is a journal published by the Association for the Advancement of Behavior Therapy. Articles include reports on topical research and innovative treatment programs, commentaries that discuss controversial issues in behavior therapy, special features on important topics, reviews of the latest significant books in the field, and news of the association. You can subscribe to the journal by writing to the AABT, 15 West 36th Street, New York, NY 10018.

The *Cognitive Behaviorist* is another valuable source for keeping current in this field. For information on getting this newsletter, contact Dr. E. Thomas Dowd, Counseling Psychology Program, 130 Bancroft Hall, University of Nebraska, Lincoln, NE 68588.

A Group Leader's Guide to Stress Management Training is a 75-page manual prepared by Sheldon D. Rose, Richard M. Tolman, and Steven H. Tallant (1985a), which describes specific agendas for an eight-session stress-management group. It provides minilectures and exercises for use in group sessions. Also included is a stress diary sheet, a relaxation sheet, an overview of stress-management groups, and a bibliography. *A Group Leader's Guide to Pain Management Training* is a 106-page manual prepared by Rose and Karen Subramanian (1986), which gives an introduction to pain management in groups. It describes a variety of group exercises, contains case studies and sample forms, and provides a review of relevant research in the field. To order either of these manuals, contact Dr. Sheldon D. Rose, Editor, School of Social Work, 425 Henry Mall, University of Wisconsin, Madison, WI 53706.

REFERENCES AND SUGGESTED READINGS*

*Alberti, R. E., & Emmons, M. L. (1990a). *Your perfect right: A guide to assertive living* (6th ed.). San Luis Obispo, CA: Impact.

*Alberti, R. E., & Emmons, M. L. (1990b). *Your perfect right: A manual for assertiveness trainers.* San Luis Obispo, CA: Impact.

Bandura, A. (1969). *Principles of behavior modification.* New York: Holt, Rinehart & Winston.

Bandura, A. (1977). *Social learning theory.* Englewood Cliffs, NJ: Prentice-Hall.

Bandura, A. (1986). *Social foundations of thought and action: A social cognitive theory.* Englewood Cliffs, NJ: Prentice-Hall.

*Beck, A. T. (1976). *Cognitive therapy and the emotional disorders.* New York: New American Library.

Beck, A. T., Rush, A. J., Shaw, B. F., & Emery, G. (1979). *Cognitive therapy of depression.* New York: Guilford Press.

Berkowitz, S. (1982). Behavior therapy. In L. E. Abt & I. R. Stuart (Eds.), *The newer therapies: A sourcebook.* New York: Van Nostrand Reinhold.

Brabender, V., & Fallon, A. (1993). *Models of inpatient group therapy.* Washington, DC: American Psychological Association.

Brunnell, L. F. (1978). A multimodal treatment model for a mental hospital: Designing specific treatments for specific populations. *Professional Psychology, 9*(4), 570–579.

*Cormier, W. H., & Cormier, L. S. (1991). *Interviewing strategies for helpers: Fun-*

*Books and articles marked with an asterisk are suggested for further study.

damental skills and cognitive behavioral interventions (3rd ed.). Pacific Grove, CA: Brooks/Cole.

Ellis, A. (1962). *Reason and emotion in psychotherapy*. New York: Lyle Stuart.

Ellis, A., & Harper, R. (1975). *A new guide to rational living*. Englewood Cliffs, NJ: Prentice-Hall.

Enns, C. Z. (1993). Twenty years of feminist counseling and therapy: From naming biases to implementing multifaceted practice. *The Counseling Psychologist, 21*(1), 3–87.

Fukuyama, M. A., & Coleman, N. C. (1992). A model for bicultural assertion training with Asian–Pacific American college students: A pilot study. *Journal for Specialists in Group Work, 17*(4), 210–217.

Glass, C. R., & Arnkoff, D. B. (1992). Behavior therapy. In D. K. Freedheim (Ed.), *History of psychotherapy: A century of change* (pp. 587–628). Washington, DC: American Psychological Association.

*Goldfried, M. R., & Davison, G. C. (1976). *Clinical behavior therapy*. New York: Holt, Rinehart & Winston.

*Kanfer, F. H., & Gaelick, L. (1986). Self-management methods. In F. H. Kanfer & A. P. Goldstein (Ed.), *Helping people change: A textbook of methods*. New York: Pergamon Press.

*Kanfer, F. H., & Goldstein, A. P. (Eds.). (1986). *Helping people change: A textbook of methods* (3rd ed.). New York: Pergamon Press.

Kuehnel, J. M., & Liberman, R. P. (1986). Behavior modification. In I. L. Kutash & A. Wolf, (Eds.), *Psychotherapist's casebook* (pp. 240–262). San Francisco: Jossey-Bass.

Lazarus, A. A. (1971). *Behavior therapy and beyond*. New York: McGraw-Hill.

*Lazarus, A. A. (1982). Multimodal group therapy. In G. M. Gazda (Ed.), *Basic approaches to group psychotherapy and group counseling* (3rd ed.). Springfield, IL: Charles C Thomas.

*Lazarus, A. A. (1986). Multimodal therapy. In J. C. Norcross (Ed.), *Handbook of eclectic psychotherapy* (pp. 65–93). New York: Brunner/Mazel.

Lazarus, A. A. (1987a). The multimodal approach with adult outpatients. In N. S. Jacobson (Ed.), *Psychotherapists in clinical practice*. New York: Guilford Press.

*Lazarus, A. A. (1987b). The need for technical eclecticism: Science, breadth, depth, and specificity. In J. K. Zeig (Ed.), *The evolution of psychotherapy* (pp. 164–178). New York: Brunner/Mazel.

Lazarus, A. A. (1989a). Multimodal therapy. In R. J. Corsini & D. Wedding (Eds.), *Current psychotherapies* (4th ed.). Itasca, IL: F. E. Peacock.

*Lazarus, A. A. (1989b). *The practice of multimodal therapy*. Baltimore: Johns Hopkins University.

*Lazarus, A. A. (1992a). The multimodal approach to the treatment of minor depression. *American Journal of Psychotherapy, 46*(1), 50–57.

*Lazarus, A. A. (1992b). Multimodal therapy: Technical eclecticism with minimal integration. In J. C. Norcross & M. R. Goldfried (Eds.), *Handbook of psychotherapy integration* (pp. 231–263). New York: Basic Books.

*Lazarus, A. A., & Beutler, L. E. (1993). On technical eclecticism. *Journal of Counseling and Development, 71*(4), 381–385.

*Lazarus, A. A., Beutler, L. E., & Norcross, J. C. (1992). The future of technical eclecticism. *Psychotherapy, 29*(1), 11–20.

Lazarus, A. A., & Mayne, T. J. (1990). Relaxation: Some proposed limitations, side effects, and proposed solutions. *Psychotherapy, 27*(2), 261–266.

London, P. (1985). *The modes and morals of psychotherapy* (2nd ed.). New York: Hemisphere.

Mahoney, M. J. (1991). *Human change processes*. New York: Basic Books.

Mahoney, M. J., & Lyddon, W. J. (1988). Recent developments in cognitive approaches to counseling and psychotherapy. *The Counseling Psychologist, 16*(2), 190–234.

Mahoney, M. J., & Thoresen, C. E. (1974). *Self-control: Power to the person.* Pacific Grove, CA: Brooks/Cole.

Meichenbaum, D. (1977). *Cognitive behavior modification: An integrative approach.* New York: Plenum.

Meichenbaum, D. (1985). *Stress inoculation training.* New York: Pergamon Press.

Meichenbaum, D. (1986). Cognitive behavior modification. In F. H. Kanfer & A. P. Goldstein (Ed.), *Helping people change: A textbook of methods* (3rd ed.). New York: Pergamon Press.

Roberts, T. K., Jackson, L. J., & Phelps, R. (1980). Lazarus's multimodal therapy model applied in an institutional setting. *Professional Psychology, 11*(1), 150–156.

Rose, S. D. (1977). *Group therapy: A behavioral approach.* Englewood Cliffs, NJ: Prentice-Hall.

Rose, S. D. (1982). Group counseling with children: A behavioral and cognitive approach. In G. M. Gazda (Ed.), *Basic approaches to group psychotherapy and group counseling* (3rd ed.). Springfield, IL: Charles C Thomas.

Rose, S. D. (1983). Behavior therapy in groups. In H. I. Kaplan & B. J. Sadock (Eds.), *Comprehensive group psychotherapy* (2nd ed.). Baltimore: Williams & Wilkins.

Rose, S. D. (1984). The use of data in resolving group problems. *Social Work with Groups, 7,* 119–130.

*Rose, S. D. (1986). Group methods. In F. H. Kanfer & A. P. Goldstein (Eds.), *Helping people change: A textbook of methods* (3rd ed.) (pp. 437–469). New York: Pergamon Press.

*Rose, S. D. (1989). *Working with adults in groups.* San Francisco: Jossey-Bass.

*Rose, S. D., & Edleson, J. (1987). *Working with children and adolescents: A multimodal approach.* San Francisco: Jossey-Bass.

Rose, S. D., & Feldman, R. (Eds.). (1986). *Research on groups.* New York: Haworth Press.

Rose, S. D., & Subramanian, K. (1986). *A group leader's guide to pain management training.* Madison, WI: Interpersonal Skill Training and Research Project.

*Rose, S. D., Tallant, S. H., Tolman, R., & Subramanian, K. (1986). A multimethod group approach: Program development research. In S. D. Rose & R. Feldman (Eds.), *Research in groups.* New York: Haworth Press.

*Rose, S. D., Tolman, R. M., & Tallant, S. H. (1985a). *A group leader's guide to stress management training.* Madison, WI: Interpersonal Skill Training and Research Project.

Rose, S. D., Tolman, R. M., & Tallant, S. H. (1985b). Group process in cognitive-behavioral therapy, *The Behavior Therapist, 8,* 71–75.

*Spiegler, M. D., & Guevremont, D. C. (1993). *Contemporary behavior therapy* (2nd ed.). Pacific Grove, CA: Brooks/Cole.

Thoresen, C. E., & Mahoney, M. J. (1974). *Behavioral self-control.* New York: Holt, Rinehart & Winston.

*Watson, D. L., & Tharp, R. G. (1993). *Self-directed behavior: Self-modification for personal adjustment* (6th ed.). Pacific Grove, CA: Brooks/Cole.

Whitney, D., & Rose, S. D. (1989). The effect of process and structural content on outcome in stress management groups. *Journal of Social Service Research, 13*(2), 89–104.

Wilson, G. T., & Agras, W. S. (1992). The future of behavior therapy. *Psychotherapy, 29*(1), 39–43.

CHAPTER FOURTEEN

Rational Emotive Behavior Therapy in Groups

Introduction

Albert Ellis, who founded rational-emotive therapy (RET) in the mid-1950s, is one of the pioneers in emphasizing the influential role of cognition in behavior. He is also a most energetic and productive individual. In his busy professional life, Ellis conducts about 80 individual and 5 group-therapy sessions weekly, along with about 200 talks and workshops for the public and psychological professionals yearly. He has published more than 50 books and 700 articles. There is no doubt that he has played a central role in the recent interest in cognitive-behavioral therapy.

In the Summer 1993 issue of the "Institute for Rational-Emotive Therapy Newsletter," Ellis announced that he was changing the name of his approach to *rational emotive behavior therapy* (REBT) because the model had always stressed the reciprocal interactions among cognition, emotion, and behavior. It has pioneered a large number of thinking, feeling, and activity-oriented methods.

Ellis (1979c) has described his emotional problems and consequent inhibited behavior during his youth. One of his problems was his fear of speaking in public. As a way of overcoming his anxieties, Ellis developed a cognitive-philosophical approach combined with an *in vivo* desensitization approach and homework assignments that involved speaking in public regardless of how uncomfortable he might initially be. With these cognitive-behavioral methods, Ellis says, he has virtually conquered some of his worst blocks.

As a part of his own psychoanalytic training, Ellis underwent three years of analysis. When he began his practice of psychotherapy, he routinely put his patients on the sofa and proceeded with them in a decidedly orthodox psychoanalytic way. Despite getting generally good results, he reports, he was dissatisfied with this approach. In accordance with classical technique, he would endure long and unhelpful silences and sit idly by with a limply held pencil (Ellis, 1962). He then began deviating from classical psychoanalysis and become more of a neo-Freudian therapist. Yet he was still not satisfied with what he observed. Therefore, he began to persuade and impel his clients to *do* the very things they were most afraid of doing, such as risking the rejection of significant others. Gradually, he became much more eclectic and more active and directive as a therapist. He combined humanistic and behavior therapy, and his pioneering efforts have earned him the right to be known as the father of REBT and the grandfather of cognitive-behavioral therapy. Ellis also acknowledges the heavy existentialist influences on the formulation of his theory, particularly the works of Karen Horney, Alfred Adler, Erich Fromm, and Harry Stack Sullivean (Ellis, 1992c).

REBT is based on the assumption that we are not disturbed by our early or later environments but that we have strong inclinations to disturb ourselves consciously and unconsciously. We do this largely by taking our goals and values, which we mainly learn from our families and culture, and changing them into "shoulds," "oughts," and "musts" (Ellis, 1992b). In order to overcome this self-indoctrination, which has resulted in irrational thinking, REBT therapists employ active/directive techniques such as teaching, suggestion, persuasion, and homework assignments, and they challenge clients to substitute a rational belief system for an irrational one. Ellis is convinced that if clients hope to make a profound philosophical change, they had better both change their basic outlook and act against their irrational, self-defeating belief system (Ellis, 1980, 1992c, 1993).

The rational emotive behavior approach does not consider the relationship between therapist and client to be vitally important to the therapeutic process. What is given primary emphasis is the therapist's ability and willingness to challenge, confront, probe, and convince the client to practice activities (both in and outside of therapy) that will lead to constructive changes in thinking and behaving. The approach stresses action—doing something about the insights one gains in the therapy group. Change, it is assumed, will come about mainly by a commitment to practice new behaviors consistently. REBT lends itself to group-oriented procedures, and practitioners frequently use group processes as a method of choice. The group is seen as offering the participants excellent opportunities for challenging self-destructive thinking and for practicing different behaviors.

Key Concepts

Some Hypotheses and Assumptions of REBT

A number of the basic assumptions of REBT can be categorized under the following main postulates (Ellis, 1986a, 1987a, 1987b, 1992b, 1993):

- ◆ Thinking, feeling, and behaving continually interact with and influence one another.
- ◆ Emotional disturbances are caused or contributed to by a complex of biological and environmental factors.

◆ Humans are affected by the people and the things around them, and they also intentionally affect the people around them. People decide, or choose, to disturb themselves—or not disturb themselves—in response to the influences of the system in which they live.

◆ People disturb themselves cognitively, emotionally, and behaviorally. They often think in a manner that defeats their own best interests as well as those of the others in their social group.

◆ When unfortunate events occur, people tend to create irrational beliefs about these events that are characterized by absolutist and dogmatic thinking. Typically, these irrational beliefs are centered on competence and success, love and approval, being treated fairly, and safety and comfort.

◆ It is not unfortunate events by themselves that cause emotional disturbance; rather, irrational beliefs lead to personality problems.

◆ Most humans have a prodigious tendency to make and keep themselves emotionally disturbed. Thus, they find it virtually impossible to maintain good mental health. Unless they clearly and tough-mindedly acknowledge this reality, they are likely to sabotage their best efforts at changing (Ellis, 1987b).

◆ When people behave in self-defeating ways, they do have the ability to become aware of ways in which their beliefs are negatively affecting them. With this awareness they also have the capacity to dispute their irrational thoughts and change them into rational beliefs. By changing these beliefs about certain events, people also change their inappropriate feelings and self-defeating behaviors.

◆ Once irrational beliefs are discovered, they can be counteracted by using a combination of cognitive, emotive, and behavioral methods. REBT has various techniques of showing people how to minimize their self-sabotaging thoughts, feelings, and behaviors.

◆ Clients must be willing to (1) acknowledge that they are mainly responsible for their own disturbed thoughts, emotions, and actions; (2) look at how they are thinking, feeling, and behaving when they needlessly disturb themselves; and (3) commit themselves to the hard work that it will take to change.

Origins of Emotional Disturbance

A central concept of REBT is the role that absolutist "shoulds" and "musts" play in people's becoming and remaining emotionally disturbed. We forcefully, rigidly, and emotionally subscribe to many grandiose "musts" that result in our needlessly disturbing ourselves (Ellis, 1992b). According to Ellis, feelings of anxiety, depression, rejection, rage, guilt, and alienation are initiated and perpetuated by a belief system based on irrational ideas that were uncritically embraced during early childhood. These self-defeating beliefs are supported and maintained by negative, absolutist, and illogical statements that people make to themselves over and over. Other factors also perpetuate emotional disturbance. Some of these factors include human ignorance, stupidity, unperceptiveness, rigidity, defensiveness, pollyannaism, and focusing on changing the situation rather than on changing oneself.

Ellis (1993) stresses that in addition to taking on dysfunctional beliefs from others, people also invent "musts" on their own. As he puts it: "You, like almost all people, are a born *musturbator* and will almost inevitably take parental, societal, and personal rules and foolishly make them into imperatives. So most—not all—of your profound *musturbation* is self-constructed, self-repeated, self-learned" (p. 6).

Ellis (1980, 1988, 1992b, 1993) contends that most of our dysfunctional beliefs can be reduced to three main forms of *must*urbation:

1. "I *absolutely must* do well and be approved by significant others, and I *must* win their approval, or else I am an inadequate, worthless person."
2. "Other people *must* under all conditions and at all times treat me considerately and fairly. If they don't, they are rotten and horrible, and they deserve to roast in hell for eternity!"
3. Conditions under which I live *absolutely must* be comfortable, so that I can get what I want immediately and without effort. If not, the world is a rotten place, I can't stand it, and life is hardly worth living."

Rational emotive behavior therapy is grounded on existential principles in many respects. Although parents and society play a significant role in contributing to our emotional disturbance, we do not need to be victims of this indoctrination that takes place in our early years. We may not have had the resources during childhood to challenge parental and societal messages. Yet as psychological adults we can become aware of how adhering to negative and illogical beliefs hampers our efforts to live fully, and we are also in a position to modify these beliefs.

The A-B-C Theory

The so-called A-B-C theory of personality and emotional disturbance is central to REBT theory and practice. The A-B-C theory maintains that when people have an emotional reaction at point C (the so-called emotional Consequence), after some Activating event that occurred at point A, it is not the event itself (A) that causes the emotional state (C), although it may contribute to it. It is the Belief system (B), or the beliefs that people have about the event, that mainly creates C. For example, if you feel rejected and hurt (C) over the event of not getting a promotion at work (A), it is not the fact that you weren't promoted that causes your hurt; it is your *belief* (B) about the event. By believing that not having received a promotion means that you are a failure and that your efforts have not been appreciated and that they *should* be, you "construct" the emotional consequence of feeling rejected and hurt. Thus, human beings are largely responsible for creating their own emotional disturbances through the beliefs they associate with the events of their lives.

Ellis (1986a) maintains that people have the capacity to significantly change their cognitions, emotions, and behaviors. According to him, people can best accomplish this goal by avoiding preoccupying themselves with A and by acknowledging and yet resisting the temptation to dwell endlessly on emotional consequences at C. They can choose to examine, challenge, modify, and uproot B—the irrational beliefs they hold about the activating events at A.

Confronting and Attacking Irrational Beliefs

The REBT therapeutic process begins by teaching clients the A-B-C theory. When they have come to see how their irrational beliefs and values are causally linked to their emotional and behavioral disturbances, they are ready to Dispute these beliefs and values at point D. D is the application of scientific principles to challenge self-defeating philosophies and dispose of unrealistic and unverifiable hypotheses. This is a form of *cognitive therapy*. One of the most effective methods of helping people reduce their emotional disturbances is to show them how to actively and forcefully dispute these irrational beliefs until they surrender them. This process of disputation involves three other D's: (1) *detecting* irrational beliefs and seeing that they are illogical and unrealistic, (2) *debating* these irrational beliefs and showing oneself how they are unsupported by evidence, and (3) *discriminating* between irrational thinking and rational thinking (Ellis & Bernard, 1986).

After D comes E, or the Effect of disputing—the relinquishing of self-destructive ideologies, the acquisition of a more rational and realistic philosophy of life, and a greater acceptance of oneself, of others, and of the inevitable frustrations of everyday life. This new philosophy of life has, of course, a practical side—a concrete E, if you wish. In the example I gave above, E would translate into a rational and empirically based conclusion: "Well, it's too bad that I didn't get that promotion. But it's not the end of the world. There may be other opportunities. Besides, not getting the promotion doesn't mean that I'm a failure. So I don't need to keep telling myself all that nonsense." Or a person might make a rational statement such as the following: "I'd like to have gotten the job, but I didn't. I regret that, but it's not awful, terrible, and horrible. It's bad enough that I lost it; I don't have to make myself miserable as well. I'm disappointed, but it's not awful unless I make it awful." And, according to REBT theory, the ultimate result is the elimination of feelings of depression and rejection.

Group members learn to separate their rational beliefs from their irrational beliefs and to understand the origins of their emotional disturbances as well as those of other members. Participants are taught the many ways in which they can (1) free themselves of their irrational life philosophy so that they can function more effectively as an individual and as a relational being and (2) learn more appropriate ways of responding so that they won't needlessly feel upset about the realities of living. The group members help and support one another in these learning endeavors.

Self-Rating and Learning Self-Acceptance

According to Ellis (1980), we have a strong tendency not only to rate our acts and behaviors as "good" or "bad," "worthy" or "unworthy," but also to rate *ourselves as a total person* on the basis of our performances. He contends that people can accept themselves or consider themselves worthwhile simply because they are alive. It is not necessary for them to *prove* their worth by being loved and approved of by others because of their actions.

This self-rating process constitutes one of the main sources of our emotional disturbances. Therefore, the REBT group leader teaches members how to separate the evaluation of their behaviors from the evaluation of *themselves*—their *essence* and their *totality*—and how to accept themselves in spite of their imperfections. Some examples of self-rating are:

- "The fact that I make mistakes means that I'm incompetent."
- "If I don't win universal approval and acceptance, I'm a terrible person."
- "If I fail at something, I'm a failure in life."

Ellis contends that this kind of self-rating inevitably leads to a number of problems—among them, self-centeredness and self-consciousness; low self-esteem; a tendency to prove oneself rather than enjoying oneself; a tendency to damn oneself and others; the feeling that no matter what one accomplishes, it is never enough; attempts to manipulate others; and the sabotaging of one's goals. If people are able to assess their performances honestly and accurately without rating themselves as persons, he hypothesizes, they will experience minimal disturbance and gain the maximum enjoyment from life (Ellis, 1980).

The opposite of self-rating is self-acceptance, which REBT favors. Ellis (1993) identifies the following as a few of the pathways of realistic acceptance:

- accepting the fact that change is the product of hard work and practice
- unwhining acceptance of what we cannot change
- accepting the reality that we are imperfect
- avoiding damnation of ourselves and others
- accepting long-range rather than short-range hedonism

Suitability of REBT for Groups

Goals

The goals in an REBT group are to teach clients how to change their dysfunctional emotions and behaviors into appropriate ones and to cope with almost any unfortunate events that may arise in their lives (Wessler, 1986). Ideally, REBT develops the following characteristics of a mentally and emotionally healthy individual: self-interest, social interest, self-direction, tolerance, acceptance of ambiguity and uncertainty, flexibility, scientific thinking, commitment, risk taking, self-acceptance, long-range hedonism, the willingness to be imperfect, and responsibility for one's own emotional disturbance (Ellis, 1987a).

REBT aims at providing group members with tools for reducing or eliminating inappropriate emotions (such as depression and anxiety), so that they can live a richer and more satisfying life. To accomplish this basic objective, it offers clients practical ways to identify their underlying faulty beliefs and to exchange them for constructive beliefs.

Basically, group members are taught that they are responsible for their own emotional reactions, that they can reduce their emotional disturbances by paying attention to their self-verbalizations and by changing their beliefs and values, and that if they acquire a new and more realistic philosophy, they can cope effectively with most of the unfortunate events in their lives. Although the therapeutic goals of REBT are essentially the same for both individual and group therapy, the two differ in some of the specific methods and techniques employed, as you will see in the pages that follow.

Rationale

More than 35 years of experience in conducting and leading REBT groups has confirmed Ellis's belief that a group is particularly effective in helping participants make constructive personality and behavior changes. Ellis (1977c) discusses many of the advantages of REBT in groups, some of which are briefly summarized below:

- ◆ Group members can remind one another of the desirability of accepting reality and work together to bring about positive changes.
- ◆ Since REBT emphasizes a vigorous attack on self-defeating thinking, other members can play a powerful role in challenging the individual's crooked thinking.
- ◆ Group members can contribute suggestions, comments, and hypotheses and reinforce some of the points made by the leader.
- ◆ The activity-oriented homework assignments that are a vital component of REBT are more effectively carried out in the group context than in one-to-one therapy.
- ◆ The group offers an effective milieu for several active/directive procedures such as role playing, assertion training, behavior rehearsal, modeling, and risk-taking exercises.
- ◆ The group serves as a laboratory in which behavior can be directly observed in action.
- ◆ Clients are often asked to complete homework report forms, which require going over the A-B-C's of upsetting situations and then learning how to correct faulty thinking and behaving. By hearing other

members' reports and learning how they have dealt with the situations in question, participants can better deal with their own issues. The members can then practice together the behaviors they would like to increase or decrease in the real world.

◆ Group members discover that since their problems are far from unique, they don't need to condemn themselves for having these problems.

◆ Through feedback from others in the group, participants begin to see themselves as others see them and notice the behaviors that might be changed. They also gain social skills during the sessions and in the socializing that takes place after the sessions.

◆ When the statements that members make indicate faulty thinking, the other members and the leader can bring these mistakes to the person's attention so that the faulty thinking can be corrected.

◆ By watching other members, participants are able to see that treatment can be effective, that people can change, that they can take steps to help themselves, and that successful therapy is the product of hard and persistent work.

◆ In groups, clients have the opportunity to consider a wider range of alternatives to solving their problems than is possible in one-to-one therapy.

◆ Disclosing intimate problems, some of which the person considers shameful, is therapeutic in itself. Self-disclosure enables participants to realize that taking risks pays off: their "revelations" generally don't have the dire consequences they feared so much, and even if someone does criticize them, it is certainly not catastrophic.

◆ Since REBT is highly educational and didactic, it typically includes information giving and discussion of problem-solving strategies. Economically and practically, this is better done in a group than in an individual setting. The group also encourages participants to become actively involved in their treatment.

◆ The average duration of the group session (2¼ hours with the leader and another hour of postgroup work with an assistant leader) provides enough time to effectively challenge rigidly held self-defeating beliefs.

◆ Group procedures are especially useful for people who are rigidly bound by old patterns of dysfunctional behavior, because the group setting provides the challenge necessary to reevaluate these patterns and adopt healthier ones.

Even though Ellis uses this long list of reasons to support his view that REBT is especially suitable for group work, these same reasons can be adduced to support the group application of most of the other therapeutic models covered in this book. Therefore, the points discussed by Ellis can be usefully considered by any group practitioner who is in the process of developing a rationale for a group-counseling program, even if he or she has an orientation other than REBT.

Role and Functions of the Group Leader

The therapeutic activities of an REBT group are carried out with one central purpose: helping the participants internalize a rational philosophy of life, just as they internalized a set of dogmatic and false beliefs derived from their sociocultural environment and from their own invention. In working toward this ultimate aim, the group leader has several specific functions and tasks. The first task is to show the group members *how* they have created their own misery. This is done by clarifying the connection between their emotional/behavioral disturbances and their values, beliefs, and attitudes. The leader confronts them with the propaganda they originally accepted without questioning, demonstrates how they are continuing to indoctrinate themselves with unexamined assumptions, and persuades them to engage in counterpropaganda activities.

To help members move beyond the mere recognition that they originally incorporated irrational thoughts and that they now keep themselves emotionally upset by continuing to think illogically, the therapist strives to modify their thinking. REBT assumes that people's illogical beliefs are so deeply ingrained that they will not change easily. Thus, it is the role of the leader to teach members how to challenge their assumptions and how to stop the vicious circle of the self-rating and self-blaming process.

But getting rid of symptoms of disturbances is not enough. If only specific problems or symptoms are dealt with, other illogical fears are likely to appear. Thus, the final step in the therapeutic process is to teach members how to avoid becoming victims of future irrational beliefs. The therapist challenges the core of clients' irrational thinking and teaches them how to apply logical thinking when coping with future problems.

REBT employs many cognitive and emotive/dramatic techniques, and Ellis (1993) writes that these methods are best carried out in an active manner. REBT group workers favor interventions such as questioning, challenging, assigning homework, and helping members experiment with new ways of thinking, feeling, and doing. The therapist assumes the role of a teacher and not that of an intensely relating partner. REBT group leaders tend to avoid relating too closely to their members and avoid having them increase their dependency tendencies. They differentiate between *acceptance* and *warmth* or *approval,* and encourage the former (Brabender & Fallon, 1993). However, REBT practitioners demonstrate respect for their clients and also tend to be highly collaborative, encouraging, supportive, and mentoring. A group member learns that the leader is not thinking disapprovingly and can be trusted. REBT emphasizes the therapist's unconditional acceptance of clients, regardless of the irrational tendencies that they manifest both in and out of the group sessions. Such leaders often engage in self-disclosure in cases where doing so would help the members work through their problems (Brabender & Fallon, 1993).

In describing his personal style of conducting a group, Ellis makes it clear that he fully accepts clients as persons at the same time as he pokes at their irrational tendencies:

> So, although I am quite often confrontational with group members, I try to show them that I really care about helping them; that I will work hard during every session to hear, understand, empathize with them; that I have great faith that they can, despite their handicaps, change; that I can poke fun *at their irrationalities* without laughing *at them;* and that I totally accept them as fallible humans, no matter how badly they often think and behave. I also use my *person* in my group sessions, and consequently am informal, take risks, reveal some of my own feelings, tell jokes and stories, and generally am myself as well as a group leader. In this way, I hope to model flexible, involved, nondisturbed behaviors [1992b, p. 68].

REBT group leaders are committed to the concept of efficiency. Ellis writes that the approach "minimizes or avoids, except in unusual cases, long-winded, inefficient methods like free-association, dream analysis, detailed 'explanations' of past history, and other methods that lead nowhere in the short, and often in the long, run" (1993, p. 12). Instead, group leaders are active in teaching the theoretical model, proposing methods of coping, and teaching members strategies for testing hypotheses and solutions. Leaders also orchestrate each session to ensure that no one member dominates, that no one becomes disruptive, and that antitherapeutic statements are not allowed to stand. This active role is clearly evident in every session unless the leader elects to be silent or to function as a coach (Brabender & Fallon, 1993).

REBT practitioners employ a directive role in getting members to commit themselves to practicing in everyday situations what they are learning in the group sessions. They view what goes on during the group as important, but they realize that the hard work in between sessions and after therapy is terminated is even more crucial (Ellis, 1993). The group context provides members with the tools that they can use in learning to become self-reliant and to accept themselves unconditionally as they encounter new problems in daily living.

Therapeutic Techniques and Procedures

Rational emotive behavior therapy lends itself to a wide range of cognitive, emotive, and behavioral methods (Ellis, 1980, 1986a, 1992b, 1993). Like other cognitive-behavioral therapies, REBT blends techniques to change clients' patterns of thinking, feeling, and acting. It is an integrative therapy, since it selectively adapts various methods that are also used in existential, humanistic, and other therapeutic approaches (Ellis, 1993). REBT focuses on specific techniques for changing a client's specific thoughts in concrete situations. In addition to modifying beliefs, REBT helps group members see how their beliefs influence what they feel and what they do; thus, there is also a concern for changing feelings and behaviors that flow from dysfunctional thinking patterns. REBT aims to eliminate symptoms through bringing about a profound change in philosophy.

An REBT group fosters the transfer to other members' personal issues better than some other approaches do, because it focuses on ways to generalize what members learn in groups to their everyday living. While one person is working, everyone else can be learning how to work on his or her own changes at the same time.

Problems Treated in REBT

A wide range of disorders can be addressed in REBT groups: anxiety, depression, anger, marital problems, poor interpersonal skills, parenting skills, character disorders, obsessive/compulsive disorders, eating disorders, psychosomatic disorders, addictions, and psychotic disorders (Warren & McLellarn, 1987). In the case of clients who are involuntarily referred, it is necessary to find ways of motivating them by showing them that they can benefit in some way by taking REBT seriously (Wessler, 1986).

Interventions Used in REBT

An international survey of REBT therapists found that the techniques they most frequently used were humor, didactic presentations of REBT theory, cognitive rehearsal of desired behaviors, and unconditional acceptance (Warren & McLellarn, 1987). This same study found the following in-session techniques also being used: strong and forceful language, disputing methods, assertiveness training, social-skills training, role playing, behavioral rehearsal, teaching rational coping self-statements, rational-emotive imagery, modeling, relaxation training, rational role reversal, problem-solving training, imaginal desensitization, contingency contracting, operant methods, Beck's cognitive therapy, *in vivo* desensitization, and information giving.

Cognitive Methods of REBT

From a cognitive perspective REBT demonstrates to clients that their beliefs and self-talk are keeping them disturbed. It has various techniques for dispelling these self-defeating cognitions and teaching people how to acquire a rational approach to living. In an REBT group there is a heavy emphasis on thinking, disputing, debating, challenging, persuading, interpreting, explaining, and teaching. Some of the cognitive techniques that are often used in an REBT group are described next.

TEACHING THE A-B-C'S OF REBT. The A-B-C theory, mentioned earlier, is taught to clients undergoing individual or group therapy. Members are taught that no matter how and where they originally acquired their irrational "shoulds," "oughts," and "musts," they have the power now to begin to surrender these dysfunctional beliefs. They are shown ways to apply the A-B-C theory to practical problems they encounter in everyday life.

DISPUTING IRRATIONAL BELIEFS. REBT teaches clients how to check and modify their values and attitudes about themselves and others. Therapists show clients how to detect their "awfulizing," and their "self-downing." In their didactic role, REBT leaders focus on disputing the irrational, logically inconsistent, absolutist, catastrophic, and rationalized ideas of clients. They demonstrate how such ideas bring about unnecessary disturbances, and they persuade clients to change or surrender these dysfunctional behaviors. Members learn ways to question and challenge their unrealistic and illogical demands, which enables them to change these demands to preferences. Ellis (1992b, p. 70) does this by teaching members to talk about those things that are bothering them in their lives. With the help of others in the group, he attempts to show them exactly how they are needlessly upsetting themselves and what they can do to incorporate healthier ways of thinking, feeling, and behaving.

TEACHING COPING SELF-STATEMENTS. Group members are taught how irrational beliefs can be countered by sensible coping statements. They are expected to monitor their manner of speaking by writing down and analyzing the quality of their language. For example, a member might tell herself: "I *must* perform well, which means being perfect. If I make any mistakes, it would be *horrible*. I simply *can't stand it* when I don't attain perfection immediately. People will give me approval and love only when I'm perfect, and I *absolutely need* this acceptance from others to feel worthwhile." By becoming aware of the absolutist and demanding quality of her internal and external speech, she can learn how what she tells herself is setting her up for failure. She can replace these self-destructive statements with coping statements: "I can still accept myself in spite of my imperfections. Although I like doing my best, I don't have to drive myself to unrealistically high performances. Besides, even if I were to fail, I could still accept myself. I don't have to have universal approval to feel that I'm a valuable person."

PSYCHOEDUCATIONAL METHODS. Members of REBT groups are encouraged to practice and work hard outside of the therapy sessions as a pathway to personal change. Ellis, Abrams, and Dengelegi (1992) have found that clients who read cognitive-behavioral literature, use REBT audio and video cassettes, and attend lectures and workshops usually learn and use REBT better than those who do not. REBT offers many resources dealing with general emotional problems and specific concerns such as overcoming addictions, dealing with depression, managing anger, understanding and coping with weight problems, becoming assertive, and overcoming procrastination. An example of one of these self-help books is *How to Stubbornly Refuse to Make Yourself Miserable about Anything—Yes, Anything!* (Ellis, 1988). Ellis has made many tapes, a few of which cover ways of refusing to be ashamed of anything, ways to stop worrying, conquering the dire need for love, and overcoming low tolerance for frustration. Sources of REBT materials are listed at the end of this chapter.

COGNITIVE HOMEWORK. Clients participating in REBT groups are given cognitive homework assignments, which consist of ways of applying the

A-B-C theory to many of the problems in daily life. Members may be given the "RET Self-Help Form" (which is reproduced in the student manual of this text). In an adjoining column they write down a disputing statement for each irrational belief. In another column they record an effective rational belief to replace the irrational belief. Finally, they record the feelings and behaviors that they experienced after arriving at an effective rational belief. For example, the statement "I *must* be approved of and accepted by all the significant people in my life" can be disputed with statements such as "Where is it written that I *must* have this approval?" "Why *must* I have their total approval in order to feel like a worthwhile individual?" An effective rational belief might include the statement "There is no evidence that I *absolutely must* have approval from others, though I would like to be approved of by those whom I respect." During the week, group members make the time to record and think about how their beliefs contribute to their personal problems, and they work hard at uprooting these self-defeating cognitions. When they return to the group, they can bring up specific situations in which they did well or in which they experienced difficulty. Group members often teach each other ways of disputing beliefs, based on material that grows out of the "RET Self-Help Form."

REBT group therapy is particularly effective with many resistant clients because in a group other members typically challenge their rigid thinking. Individuals are more likely to surrender their ineffective ways of thinking when they are confronted by both the group leader and their peers. They have opportunities to observe others in the group effectively using REBT cognitive homework methods, and they are consequently encouraged to apply these methods to themselves. Furthermore, assignments given by group members are more likely to be performed than those given by an individual therapist (Ellis, 1984c).

Emotive Methods in REBT Groups

As we have seen, REBT is almost always a multimodal approach to change in that it rarely treats individuals without using several emotive and behavioral, as well as cognitive, methods (Ellis, 1986a). Some of the emotive techniques are unconditional acceptance, rational-emotive imagery, the use of humor, shame-attacking exercises, and rational-emotive role playing.

UNCONDITIONAL ACCEPTANCE. REBT gives clients full and unconditional acceptance, no matter how badly they behave inside and outside of therapy. Group members often burden themselves with fears of being "discovered" for what they *really* are and then being rejected. Group leaders can model an accepting attitude that goes beyond what members have done or felt. The therapist can strongly show group members that even though their behavior might be *immoral* or *foolish,* they are never *rotten people* or *total fools.* This kind of REBT-flavored unconditional acceptance creates a group atmosphere that allows members to feel personally accepted, even though some of their beliefs and behaviors are most likely to be challenged vigorously (Ellis, 1984c).

RATIONAL-EMOTIVE IMAGERY. REBT shows clients how to imagine some of the worst things they can think of and then to train themselves to develop appropriate emotions in place of disruptive ones. Clients are asked to imagine themselves in specific situations where they feel habitually inappropriate feelings. They then work actively on changing these feelings to appropriate ones and, consequently, changing their behavior in the situation. For example, therapists can induce even resistant clients to imagine vividly that they keep failing and keep getting criticized and can thereby produce in them extreme feelings of inadequacy. Then, these clients are induced to change their feelings to mere regret and disappointment instead of worthlessness. Members practice this process for at least 30 days in a row until they have trained themselves to feel regretful and disappointed automatically when they experience failure instead of feeling devastated (Ellis, 1984c). Members might imagine some of their worst fears coming true. Within the group, they can share these fears, gain some emotional insight on how such fears control much of what they do and say, and eventually learn to respond in different ways. Imagery work is a safe prelude to actually confronting one's fears in daily life.

USE OF HUMOR. Humor has both cognitive and emotional benefits in bringing about change. Of the many techniques used by REBT therapists, humor has been ranked as the most popular in-session method (Warren & McLellarn, 1987). Ellis (1993) believes that people take themselves far too seriously. As one of its main techniques to combat the kind of exaggerated thinking that leads people into trouble, REBT employs a good deal of humor. It teaches group members to laugh, not at themselves but at their self-defeating beliefs. It reduces certain ideas to which clients hold tenaciously to absurdity by showing how contradictory and ridiculous these views really are. Although introducing humor inappropriately or too soon in a group can present problems, once trust has been established, the members are generally far more ready to see the folly of some of their ways and can actually enjoy laughing at themselves. One example of employing humor is having group members sing comical songs published by Ellis in his songbook, *A Garland of Rational Songs* (1977b). Some clients find benefit in singing these humorous songs to themselves when they experience anxiety or depression.

SHAME-ATTACKING EXERCISES. The rationale underlying shame-attacking exercises is that anxiety results from shame, guilt, embarrassment, and self-damnation. Thus, the more that people directly face and deal with the irrational beliefs behind these feelings, the less likely they are to remain emotionally disturbed. In REBT group therapy, many kinds of self-disclosing, risk-taking, and shame-attacking exercises are introduced (Ellis, 1980). Members in REBT groups are often encouraged to participate in risk-taking activities as a way to challenge their neurotic fears of looking foolish. Practitioners employ shame-attacking exercises as a way of teaching clients to accept themselves in spite of reactions from others. These exercises are aimed at increasing self-acceptance and mature responsibility, not simply at achieving comfort while doing a specific zany activity (Wessler, 1986). The main thing clients learn from shame-attacking exercises is that they are no different when they are experiencing disapproval than when they are not. In other words, disapproval does not have to affect their worth or change them, nor does the fear of disapproval have to prevent them from doing things they consider right. In the course of doing "shameful" things in a group, members move toward self-acceptance.

Group members frequently admit that they are inhibiting themselves from doing many things they would like to do because of their fear of what others might think. In a group situation other members might exert therapeutic pressure and also provide support for individuals to experiment with risky behaviors, first in the group and then in daily situations. Ellis (1984c) describes a few exercises that clients might be induced to perform in public. These include wearing outlandish clothes, borrowing money from a stranger, and shouting out the stops in the train or bus. Ellis contends that if clients will do these acts over and over and also work on their feelings so that they don't feel ashamed or humiliated, they will then be able to conquer the powerful feelings that paralyze them and keep them from doing things they would like to do. He suggests that it is better to combine cognitive homework with these *in vivo* shame-attacking exercises. A few other examples of possible shame-attacking exercises follow:

- ◆ Walk through a park singing at the top of your voice.
- ◆ In a crowded elevator, tell people that you are glad they could attend this important meeting that you have called.
- ◆ Talk to animals, and pretend that they are talking back to you.
- ◆ Ride in a crowded elevator standing backward (facing the rear).
- ◆ Tie a ribbon around a banana and "walk it" down a street.
- ◆ In public, shout out the exact time by saying, "The time is 11:11 and 20 seconds."
- ◆ Go to a drugstore, and in a loud voice say to the pharmacist, "I want a gross of condoms, and since I use so many of them, you should give me a special discount!" (This is one of Ellis's favorites).
- ◆ After finishing a meal in a restaurant say, "Ah, I feel a fart coming on!" (This is one of my favorites).

ROLE PLAYING. There are both emotional and behavioral components in role playing. One way of assisting clients to experience and cope with feelings of fear is to ask them to reverse roles. For example, if a member is experiencing anxiety over an upcoming job interview, he can assume the role of the interviewer. He can also play himself in both a fearful stance and in a confident manner. Rather than having members simply talk about their problems or think about their beliefs, they can become emotionally involved if they allow themselves to role-play. Of course, some members will be faced with challenging their fears of looking foolish during the role playing or of not engaging in the activity as they think they *should*. Not only can role playing free members up emotionally, but it can also provide them with opportunities to act in a host of new ways. Indeed, role playing can result in modifying a member's way of thinking, feeling, and behaving.

In an REBT group, role playing also involves a cognitive evaluation of the feelings and beliefs that are experienced. Thus, if a member is trying to deal more effectively with a rejecting father who demands perfection, he can adopt a role quite different from his usual one, a role in which he no longer feels victimized by his father's lack of approval. Afterward, this person undertakes a cognitive analysis of the feelings experienced during the role enactment. To that effect, he may try to answer questions such as the following:

- ◆ "Do I need my father's approval to survive?"
- ◆ "Will I ever be able to attain the level of perfection that my father demands?"
- ◆ "Can I accept myself although I'll never be perfect? Can I avoid destructive self-rating and self-blaming because of my imperfection?"
- ◆ "Do I *need* my father's approval, or do I simply *want* it?"
- ◆ "If I don't have his approval, is it awful, terrible, and horrible?"
- ◆ "Do I really have to be perfect before I can accept myself?"

Ellis believes that role playing is more effective if it entails a cognitive restructuring of the attitudes revealed by the experience.

Behavioral Methods in REBT Groups

HOMEWORK ASSIGNMENTS. Earlier, I described cognitive homework assignments, which involve reading, listening to audio tapes, and doing a written A-B-C-D-E analysis. Rational emotive behavior therapists also frequently use activity-oriented homework assignments to help people behave more rationally. Group leaders assist members in doing these assignments in their head, through the imagination process, and then encourage members to carry them into real life. REBT favors *in vivo* desensitization and urges members to do repetitively the very things they are afraid of doing as a way to overcome their crippling fears (Ellis, 1993). Group participants engage in the PYA (push your ass) technique by deliberately forcing themselves to confront "dangerous" pursuits, until they can learn how to cope when they encounter fearful situations. Partly by doing the fearful thing many times, they eventually conquer their fears by carrying out their homework assignments (Ellis et al., 1992). These assignments, which are given by the leader as well as other group members, may be carried out in the group itself or outside of it; in the latter case, the person is supposed to report the results to the group. Here are some examples of in-group assignments:

◆ Members who tend to view the group leader as a superbeing who is to be believed without question are invited to challenge the leader and to deal with their attitudes toward authority figures. This assignment allows members to see how, by maintaining a helpless attitude in the presence of such figures, they keep themselves from being empowered.

◆ A man who is shy around women is encouraged to approach the female group members and systematically challenge his fears and expectations by talking about them.

◆ A woman who is very quiet during the group sessions because she is self-conscious over her accent can be asked to disclose and explore her fears and embarrassment about speaking out. She can also be challenged to work on changing her beliefs about her inability to contribute something of value because of her accent.

◆ A group member who is convinced that others in the group will reject him if they know about his shameful side can be encouraged to disclose some of the fears that are keeping him hidden.

In addition to these in-group assignments, leaders challenge members to carry out homework assignments. Individuals who are afraid of riding in the subway, flying on airplanes, or riding in elevators are encouraged to engage repeatedly in these anxiety-producing activities. For example, people with elevator fears might be encouraged to enter 20 elevators daily for one month while forcefully telling themselves that they can stand it even if the damn elevator gets stuck.

Ellis (1992b) typically begins a group session by asking members to read their homework assignments to discover whether they have done the assignment and, if not, why not. After homework is reviewed and discussed, members generally bring up some problem they want to explore, discuss their goals and plans, or report on their progress. Both Ellis and the other group members listen carefully for dogmatic "shoulds." As these dysfunctional core beliefs are identified, members are challenged to dispute them vigorously, and they learn rational coping statements. Then, another homework assignment is suggested as a way to continue uprooting dysfunctional thinking and replacing it with effective thoughts and behaviors.

REINFORCEMENT AND PENALTIES.   REBT often makes use of both reinforcers and penalties to help clients change. Reinforcements can involve reading a novel, watching a movie, going to a concert, or eating a favorite food. Clients can be taught to reinforce themselves with something they like, but only after they have carried out a specific homework assignment that they have promised themselves to do but that they tend to avoid doing. One of REBT's goals is to teach clients better methods of self-management. Members' ultimate success depends on how effectively they can take charge of their lives beyond the group sessions. Using principles of reinforcement often helps members develop consistency in applying rational principles to the new problems they encounter. In this sense, they become their own therapists and continually teach themselves how to manage their lives.

REBT also recommends the use of self-imposed penalties when members do not carry out agreed-upon homework. Ellis (1993) writes that "difficult customers" (DC's) are urged to burn a hundred dollar bill or send it to an organization they violently disagree with when they fail to keep their promises to themselves to change their behavior" (p. 24).

According to Ellis (1980), the self-management methods of REBT work best when clients control their own behavior, rather than allowing themselves to be controlled by the therapist or a teacher. Therefore, practitioners attempt to help clients select their own reinforcements and penalities.

SKILL TRAINING. REBT has long espoused the training of clients in specific skills in which they are deficient, as long as this training is done in the context of challenging them to uproot their dysfunctional thinking (Ellis, 1980). The assumption is that by acquiring skills they formerly lacked, clients will feel more confident about themselves and will experience significant changes in the way they think, feel, and behave.

Evaluation of Rational Emotive Behavior Therapy

Contributions and Strengths of the Approach

I consider several aspects of REBT valuable enough to use in my own approach to group practice. Although I do believe that events and significant persons in our past play a critical role in shaping our present beliefs about ourselves, I agree with Ellis that we are responsible for maintaining self-destructive and irrational convictions. True, we may have learned that unless we were everything that others expected us to be, we could never hope to be loved and accepted. But the fact that at one time we uncritically accepted certain premises doesn't exempt us now from the responsibility of scrutinizing these and other irrational assumptions and replacing them with more rational ones, which will lead to different and more effective behavior. In this sense, REBT is based on the existential assumption that we are ultimately free and responsible, rather than being controlled by our past conditioning. Groups are a particularly useful format both for exploring the ways in which we have bought into self-defeating beliefs and for providing a climate where we can construct new beliefs.

I often ask group members to express the beliefs or assumptions that underlie the problems they are experiencing. One of the most common answers is that making mistakes is a terrible, unforgivable thing and that we should arrange our lives in such a way that we won't make mistakes. After probing to find out how the person came to accept such a belief, I generally pursue the issue with other questions—for example: "Does this belief really make sense to you now? What would your life be like if you continued to live by these assumptions? Do you think you'd be different if you could change some of these basic beliefs? If so, in what ways? What actions can you take now, in this group and in your everyday life, that will help you change some of the beliefs you hold?"

In short, I value REBT's emphasis on thinking, because of the crucial role that conceptualizing plays in bringing about behavioral and emotional changes. Although I do find considerable value in experiencing a catharsis and expressing pent-up feelings, I've found that for an emotional experience to have a significant impact, it is necessary to attempt to understand the meaning of the experience. REBT provides a framework for this vital cognitive dimension.

Like any other action-oriented approach, REBT insists that newly acquired insights be put into action. The homework method is an excellent avenue for translating insights into concrete action programs. In my own groups I often suggest assignments that can be carried out in the group and that allow clients to practice new behaviors and experiment with a different style of being. I recall, for example, Donald, an older client who avoided women in his group because he was sure that they wouldn't want to waste their time talking with him. I asked him whether he wanted to change this pattern, and he answered that he wanted very much to initiate contact. So I suggested that during the afternoon he seek out the three women in our group with whom he most wanted to talk and start a conversation with them. The behavior I suggested was experimental and new and was meant to allow him to see what would happen and to decide whether he wanted to continue with this different style of behavior. Note that these assignments don't have to be "given" by the leader; members can be encouraged to set tasks for themselves.

REBT is most easily used with clients who are willing to accept their own responsibility for creating their difficulties. As mentioned earlier, it is very compatible with an existential approach. Furthermore, it easily incorporates specific techniques developed in other systems (such as behavior therapy and Adlerian therapy). Because it also employs emotive techniques, there are creative ways to draw on Gestalt techniques.

Ellis (1987a) admits that REBT has its limitations, but his discussion of this topic points more to limitations within the client (such as resistance) rather than any limitations in theory and practice. He mentions some benefits and strengths of REBT:

◆ It is an intrinsically brief therapy, for in a few sessions clients who are willing to work typically experience significant gains.
◆ It aims not only for effectiveness but also for efficiency, using many cognitive, emotive, and behavioral techniques that may be uniquely effective for difficult clients.
◆ REBT has been incorporated into education, business, and communications. Ellis sees it evolving from individual and group therapy

into the general field of educational and mass-media therapy. He contends that its principles are ideally suited for applications in homes, schools, social institutions, community centers, and hospitals (Wessler, 1986).

RESEARCH EFFORTS IN REBT. REBT and other cognitive-behavioral therapies have been studied experimentally, although there were methodological shortcomings in many of these studies. Some studies had inadequate control groups, and others failed to make comparisons with other forms of therapy (DeGiuseppe, Miller, & Trexler, 1979). Many studies focused either on the cognitive dimension as a key factor in emotional disturbance or on therapeutic outcomes. As Wessler (1986) notes, however, very few studies investigated group therapy per se.

One of the problems in conducting research on the practice of REBT, whether group or individual, is that the approach does not rely on employing a single technique. Therapists typically use a combination of methods within a single session with a given client. If a particular technique does not seem to be producing results, the therapist is likely to switch quickly to another. This technical eclecticism and therapeutic flexibility make it difficult to do controlled research (Wessler, 1986).

In a review of outcome studies of REBT from 1977 to 1982, McGovern and Silverman (1986) report general findings that support its efficacy. Of the 47 studies reviewed, 31 had significant findings in favor of the REBT position. In the remaining studies the REBT treatment groups showed improvement, and in no study was another treatment technique significantly superior.

In a more recent review of the outcome studies of REBT from 1982 to 1989, Silverman, McCarthy, and McGovern (1992) conclude that there appears to be some increased sophistication in the research. For example, increases were noted in the number of control groups used, as well as the number of follow-up studies. The researchers contend that the approach is "a valuable, effective therapy that warrants increased research to broaden its application. Over the past 20 years, the research that has been conducted with RET has constantly verified its role as an efficacious therapy applicable in a variety of problem situations" (p. 169). After their review of 70 REBT outcome studies, Lyons and Woods (1991) found it to be an effective form of therapy.

Limitations of the Approach

A major reservation I have with regard to REBT concerns the dangers inherent in the therapist's confrontive and persuasive stance and the possibility of imposing the leader's values on the members. Brainwashing or other forms of psychological harm are more possible in REBT than in less directive approaches.

Ellis emphasizes that clients' beliefs are "irrational" or "dysfunctional" because such beliefs (1) include absolutist "musts" and (2) don't work and are self-defeating. *If REBT is practiced correctly,* the group leader judges these elements, not the person or the person's beliefs in their own right. Value systems themselves are not attacked by properly trained therapists or by properly taught group members (Albert Ellis, personal communication, December 20, 1992). However, it is possible that some group leaders will assume that it is their function to decide if someone's beliefs are irrational, and they might then work hard at converting that member to "sound thinking." Aside from the very relevant issue of what constitutes rational thinking and who is the judge of it, I question the value of getting rid of one system of irrational beliefs only to adopt a new set of questionable beliefs, particularly if these values are pushed by the group leader or, in some instances, by other group members. Therefore, it is essential that REBT practitioners be highly aware of themselves and their own motivations. This implies that the therapist's level of knowledge, training, perceptiveness, and accuracy of judgment are particularly important. Perhaps one ethical safeguard is for group leaders using REBT procedures to discuss the issue of values openly and caution members to beware of pressure to change in a definite direction, one that might be alien to their value system.

Another potential limitation of the REBT approach to groups is the possibility of group pressure against members who resist certain changes. Although feedback is potentially of great value, ultimately it is really up to the person receiving the feedback to decide what to do about it. If members push and persuade and attempt to do the thinking for another member, the results are at least questionable, since the very integrity of the individual member is at stake.

If REBT is done in the manner prescribed by Ellis, however, these dangers are considerably lessened. He rarely questions his clients' desires, preferences, values, or morality. What he does question is their "musts," "shoulds," and irrational demands. If someone said, "I want romantic love" or "I prefer to be sexually abstinent," Ellis would rarely disagree. However, if the person said instead, "I must be loved romantically" or "I have to be abstinent under all conditions," he would challenge such *must*urbatory views and encourage the client to change them to strong preferences. It is Ellis's belief that his brand of REBT, by showing clients that even rationality is *desirable* but not *necessary,* minimizes bigotry, absolutism, and emotional disturbance, including the potential absolutism of members and leader.

Some have criticized Ellis for what they perceive as his negative views on spiritual values and his generally antagonistic stance toward religion. My concern is that he would confront clients whom he considered "rigid, devout, and dogmatic religionists." Ellis (1992a) contends that through his writings he has made it clear that religion, in its usual definition, is not irrational, nor does it lead to emotional disturbance. Instead, he maintains that "devout religiosity" (religiosity that is pietistic, rigid, dogmatic, and relies totally on a supernatural or divine power) tends to be emotionally harmful. The main point is that it is not the therapist's role to decide for the client that reliance on a higher power is irrational, unless it means that the client is devoutly believing that he or she is absolutely powerless to help himself or herself.

It is well to underscore that REBT can be done by many people in a manner different from Ellis's style. Since he has so much visibility, it is worth distinguishing between the principles and techniques of REBT and his somewhat confrontational way of using them. A therapist can be soft-spoken and gentle and still use REBT concepts and methods.

Applying Rational Emotive Behavior Therapy with Multicultural Populations

REBT has certain advantages in working with multicultural populations. If members are not challenged too quickly, they can be invited to examine the premises on which they behave. Consider a group composed of members from a particular culture. This culture stresses doing one's best, cooperation, interdependence, respect for the family, and working hard. Some members of this group may be struggling with feelings of shame and guilt if they perceive that they are not living up to the expectations set for them by their parents and families. A student may feel that she is bringing shame to her family if she gets a "B" in a course. Leaders who confront the cultural values of such clients too quickly are likely to see counterproductive results. In fact, these clients may drop out of therapy, based largely on feeling misunderstood. A sensitive REBT group practitioner can, however, encourage such clients to begin to question how they may have uncritically accepted as truth all of the messages from their culture. Without encouraging them to abandon respect for their cultural heritage, the therapist can still challenge them to examine their beliefs and understand their consequences.

Just as does the behavioral group therapist, the REBT group leader functions in the role of a teacher. This image would seem ideal for certain cultural groups, because it detracts from the stigma of being mentally ill and focuses on problems of living. Life can be more fulfilling if clients learn better ways to think about the issues that confront them. The group leader, using the A-B-C model, teaches clients how they became disturbed. One of the leader's functions is to teach them how to dispute their irrational thinking and how to change their self-defeating style of life. With the help of the therapist and other group members, clients learn new ways of thinking and behaving, which result in new feelings.

It needs to be emphasized that, since REBT is a forceful approach, the therapist must exert caution in challenging clients about their beliefs and behaviors. What may seem like an irrational belief to a therapist may be a long-cherished value that influences the individual. The client may say: "All my life I've been taught to respect my father. Although I do have respect and love for him, I'm thinking that I want to make some choices about my life that aren't in line with his choice for me. I've always told myself that I simply can't disappoint my father, so I've suppressed my wishes and followed his will." A group leader who insensitively hammered away at the irrational quality of this woman's respect would not be upholding her values. Even though it might be therapeutic for her to question some of her beliefs, the therapist must not err by imposing his or her standards on this person. An effective REBT group therapist might say to this client:

> I can well understand that you were raised to follow your father's actions and will, and that is fine if you want to still hold and follow this value. You do, however, have a choice: you can either change your own interpretation of this value or you can strongly keep it but not demand that you *absolutely must* follow it at all times, and that if you don't you are a *rotten person*. Whatever you desire, including the values that you take from your culture, is fine; but having to *perfectly* follow these values, and putting yourself *as a person* down when you slightly deviate from them, is unrealistic and self-defeating. So you'd better give some thought to that kind of allegiance to your cultural values—or, for that matter, to any of your noncultural and self-chosen values [Albert Ellis, personal communication, February 10, 1992].

A key limitation of REBT group therapy for some ethnic-minority clients is that they could become dependent on the leader to make decisions about what constitutes rationality. It would be easy for a group leader who is not well qualified to assume a highly active stance that would keep the client passive. If the therapist does most of the talking, the members do most of the listening. Therefore, it seems important that leaders teach their clients to question and to assume an active role in the therapeutic process.

Where to Go from Here

The *Journal of Rational-Emotive and Cognitive-Behavior Therapy* is published by Human Sciences Press, Inc., 72 Fifth Avenue, New York, NY 10011-8004. This journal is an excellent way to keep informed of the developments in REBT. The journal is published quarterly; subscriptions are $34.00 for a calendar year.

The Institute for Rational-Emotive Therapy in New York City offers a variety of professional training involving a primary certificate, an intermediate certificate, an associate fellowship, and a fellowship. Each of these programs has different requirements, including clinical experience, supervision, and personal therapy experience. Several affiliated branches around the world offer official programs of study in REBT. For more specific information, see Appendixes A, B, and C in Ellis and Grieger (1986) or contact the institute. You can get a catalog describing REBT workshops, books, cassette tapes, films, self-help forms, and software items by contacting:

Institute for Rational-Emotive Therapy
45 East 65th Street
New York, NY 10021-6593
TELEPHONE: (212) 535-0822

For information regarding international affiliated training centers, contact the institute. Training outside the United States is available through centers in Australia, England, Germany, India, Israel, Italy, Mexico, and the Netherlands.

Affiliated Training Centers in the United States

The New York Institute for Rational-Emotive Therapy and the affiliated centers listed below provide official training programs that qualify for the institute's Primary Training Certificate in REBT for professionals:

Southern California Institute for Rational-Emotive Therapy
3579 Arlington Avenue
Riverside, CA 92506
TELEPHONE: (714) 687-5018
Linda M. Gilbert, Ph.D.

Denver Institute for Rational-Emotive Therapy
950 Wadsworth Blvd., Suite 206
Lakewood, CO 80215
TELEPHONE: (303) 620-7198
Laura L. Knutson, M.S.W.

Institute for Rational Living—Florida
3105 W. Azeele Street
Tampa, FL 33609
TELEPHONE: (813) 281-2733
Vincent Parr, Ph.D.

Midwest Center for RET
9719 Sylvan Drive
Jamesville, IA 50647
TELEPHONE: (319) 987-2980
Ann Vernon, Ph.D.

Cleveland Institute for Rational Living
3659 Green Road, Suite 212
Beachwood, OH 44122
TELEPHONE: (216) 464-1144
James A. Bard, Ph.D.
Harold R. Fisher, Ph.D.
David R. Lima, ACSW

Pacific Institute for RET
4550 S. W. Kruse Way, Suite 325
Lake Oswego, OR 97035
TELEPHONE: (503) 635-2489
Hank Robb, Ph.D.
Rick Warren, Ph.D.

Pennsylvania Institute for Rational-Emotive Therapy
111 N. Franklin Street
Wilkes-Barre, PA 18701
TELEPHONE: (717) 826-0999
Keith Ferrell, M.A., C.A.C.
Ann Marie Kopec, M.S.W.

Center for Rational Living—Austin
3301 Northland Drive, No. 210
Austin, TX 78731
TELEPHONE: (512) 452-8116
Dana Lehman, Ph.D.

Mid-Atlantic Institute for RET
818 East High Street
Charlottesville, VA 22901
TELEPHONE: (804) 296-0606
Russell M. Grieger, Ph.D.

RECOMMENDED SUPPLEMENTARY READINGS

Handbook of Rational-Emotive Therapy: Vol. 2 (Ellis & Grieger, 1986) is a comprehensive and updated work that deals with the theoretical and conceptual foundations of REBT, the dynamics of emotional disturbance, specific techniques to promote change, and applications of the approach.

Handbook of Rational-Emotive Therapy: Vol. 1 (Ellis & Grieger, 1977) discusses both theoretical and applied aspects and contains an excellent section on techniques. I especially recommend Chapter 1 ("An Overview of the Clinical Theory of RET"), Chapter 18 ("RET in Groups"), and Chapter 29 ("The Present and Future of RET"). If you want to read further on research data, Chapters 2 and 3 are quite comprehensive.

Humanistic Psychotherapy: The Rational-Emotive Approach (Ellis, 1973) is a clear presentation of the key concepts of the model, especially its humanistic and active/directive aspects. It is a very useful book that I recommend you read in its entirety.

A New Guide to Rational Living (Ellis & Harper, 1975) is a self-help book that presents a straightforward approach to REBT, based on homework assignments and self-questioning. It is easy reading, and many of the principles discussed can be applied to group work.

REFERENCES AND SUGGESTED READINGS*

Bandura, A. (1969). *Principles of behavior modification.* New York: Holt, Rinehart & Winston.

Beck, A. T., & Haaga, D. A. F. (1992). The future of cognitive therapy. *Psychotherapy, 29*(1), 34–38.

Bernard, M. E. (Ed.). (1991). *Using rational-emotive therapy effectively: A practitioner's guide.* New York: Plenum.

Bernard, M. E. (1992). *Staying rational in an irrational world.* New York: Carol Publishing.

*Books and articles marked with an asterisk are suggested for further study.

Brabender, V., & Fallon, A. (1993). *Models of inpatient group therapy.* Washington, DC: American Psychological Association.

DiGiuseppe, R. A., Miller, N. J., & Trexler, L. D. (1979). A review of rational-emotive psychotherapy outcome studies. In A. Ellis & J. M. Whiteley (Eds.), *Theoretical and empirical foundations of rational-emotive therapy.* Pacific Grove, CA: Brooks/Cole.

Donigian, J. & Malnati, R. (1987). *Critical incidents in group therapy.* Pacific Grove, CA: Brooks/Cole.

Dryden, W., & Hill, L. K. (1993). *Innovations in rational-emotive therapy.* Newbury Park, CA: Sage.

Ellis, A. (1962). *Reason and emotion in psychotherapy.* New York: Lyle Stuart.

Ellis, A. (1969). A weekend of rational encounter. In A. Burton (Ed.), *Encounter: The theory and practice of encounter groups.* San Francisco: Jossey-Bass.

Ellis, A. (1973). *Humanistic psychotherapy: The rational-emotive approach.* New York: McGraw-Hill.

Ellis, A. (1974). The group as agent in facilitating change toward rational thinking and appropriate emoting. In A. Jacobs & W. W. Spradlin (Eds.), *The group as agent of change.* New York: Behavioral Publications.

Ellis, A. (1977a). The basic clinical theory of rational-emotive therapy. In A. Ellis & R. Grieger, *Handbook of rational-emotive therapy: Vol. 1.* New York: Springer.

Ellis, A. (1977b). *A garland of rational songs.* New York: Institute for Rational-Emotive Therapy.

*Ellis, A. (1977c). Rational-emotive therapy in groups. In A. Ellis & R. Grieger, *Handbook of rational-emotive therapy: Vol. 1.* New York: Springer.

Ellis, A. (1979a). Rational-emotive therapy. In A. Ellis & J. M. Whiteley (Eds.), *Theoretical and empirical foundations of rational-emotive therapy.* Pacific Grove, CA: Brooks/Cole.

Ellis, A. (1979b). Rational-emotive therapy: Research data that support the clinical and personality hypotheses of RET and other modes of cognitive-behavior therapy. In A. Ellis & J. M. Whiteley (Eds.), *Theoretical and empirical foundations of rational-emotive therapy.* Pacific Grove, CA: Brooks/Cole.

*Ellis, A. (1979c). The theory of rational-emotive therapy. In A. Ellis & J. M. Whiteley (Eds.), *Theoretical and empirical foundations of rational-emotive therapy.* Pacific Grove, CA: Brooks/Cole.

Ellis, A. (1980). Overview of the clinical theory of rational-emotive therapy. In R. Grieger & J. Boyd (Eds.), *Rational-emotive therapy: A skills-based approach* (pp. 1–31). New York: Van Nostrand Reinhold.

Ellis, A. (1982). Rational-emotive group therapy. In G. Gazda (Ed.), *Basic approaches to group psychotherapy and group counseling* (3rd ed.). Springfield, IL: Charles C Thomas.

Ellis, A. (1984a). Is the unified-interaction approach to cognitive-behavior modification a reinvention of the wheel? *Clinical Psychology Review, 4,* 215–218.

Ellis, A. (1984b). Maintenance and generalization in rational-emotive therapy. *The Cognitive Behaviorist, 6*(1), 2–4.

Ellis, A. (1984c). Rational-emotive therapy (RET) approaches to overcoming resistance: III. Using emotive and behavioral techniques of overcoming resistance. *British Journal of Cognitive Psychotherapy, 2*(1), 11–26.

*Ellis, A. (1985). *Overcoming resistance: Rational-emotive therapy with difficult clients.* New York: Springer.

Ellis, A. (1986a). Rational-emotive therapy. In I. L. Kutash and A. Wolf (Eds.), *Psychotherapist's casebook* (pp. 277–287). San Francisco: Jossey-Bass.

Ellis, A. (1986b). Rational-emotive therapy and cognitive behavior therapy: Similarities and differences. In A. Ellis & R. Grieger (Eds.), *Handbook of rational-emotive therapy: Vol. 2.* New York: Springer.

Ellis, A. (1987a). The evolution of rational-emotive therapy (RET) and cognitive behavior therapy (CBT). In J. K. Zeig (Ed.), *The evolution of psychotherapy* (pp. 107–132). New York: Brunner/Mazel.

Ellis, A. (1987b). The impossibility of achieving consistently good mental health. *American Psychologist, 42*(4), 364–375.

Ellis, A. (1988). *How to stubbornly refuse to make yourself miserable about anything—yes, anything!* Secaucus, NJ: Lyle Stuart.

Ellis, A. (1991a). Achieving self-actualization. In A. Jones & R. Crandall (Eds.), *Handbook of self-actualization*. Corte Madera, CA: Select Press.

Ellis, A. (1991b). The revised ABC's of rational-emotive therapy. In J. Zeig (Ed.), *The evolution of psychotherapy: The second conference*. New York: Brunner/Mazel.

Ellis, A. (1991c). Using RET effectively: Reflections and interview. In M. E. Bernard (Ed.), *Using rational-emotive therapy effectively* (pp. 1–33). New York: Plenum.

Ellis, A. (1992a). Do I really hold that religiousness is irrational? *American Psychologist, 47*(3), 428–429.

*Ellis, A. (1992b). Group rational-emotive and cognitive-behavioral therapy. *International Journal of Group Psychotherapy, 42*(1), 63–80.

Ellis, A. (1992c). My early experiences in developing the practice of psychology. *Professional Psychology: Research and Practice, 23*(1), 7–10.

Ellis, A. (1993). Fundamentals of rational-emotive therapy. In W. Dryden & L. K. Hill (Eds.), *Innovations in rational-emotive therapy* (pp. 1–32). Newbury Park, CA: Sage.

Ellis, A., Abrams, M., & Dengelegi, L. (1992). *The art and science of rational eating*. New York: Barricade Books.

*Ellis, A., & Bernard, M. E. (1986). What is rational-emotive therapy (RET)? In A. Ellis & R. Grieger (Eds.), *Handbook of rational-emotive therapy: Vol. 2*. New York: Springer.

*Ellis, A., & Dryden, W. (1987). *The practice of rational-emotive therapy*. Secaucus, NJ: Lyle Stuart.

Ellis, A., & Dryden, W. (1990). *The essential Albert Ellis*. New York: Springer.

Ellis, A., & Dryden, W. (1991). *A dialogue with Albert Ellis: Against dogma*. Stony Stratford, England: Open University Press.

Ellis, A., & Grieger, R. (1977). *Handbook of rational-emotive therapy: Vol. 1*. New York: Springer.

*Ellis, A., & Grieger, R. (1986). *Handbook of rational-emotive therapy: Vol. 2*. New York: Springer.

*Ellis, A., & Harper, R. A. (1975). *A new guide to rational living*. Englewood Cliffs, NJ: Prentice-Hall.

Ellis, A., & Velten, E. (1992). *When AA doesn't work: Rational steps for quitting alcohol*. New York: Barricade Books.

Ellis, A., & Whiteley, J. M. (Eds.). (1979). *Theoretical and empirical foundations of rational-emotive therapy*. Pacific Grove, CA: Brooks/Cole.

Grieger, R., & Boyd, J. (1980). *Rational-emotive therapy*. New York: Van Nostrand Reinhold.

Hajzler, D. J., & Bernard, M. E. (1991). A review of rational-emotive education outcome studies. *School Psychology Quarterly, 6*(1), 27–46.

Lyons, L. C., & Woods, P. J. (1991). The efficacy of rational-emotive therapy: A quantitative review of the outcome research. *Clinical Psychology Review, 11,* 357–369.

Mahoney, M. J. (1991). *Human change processes*. New York: Basic Books.

McGovern, T. E., & Silverman, M. (1986). A review of outcome studies of rational-emotive therapy from 1977 to 1982. In A. Ellis & R. Grieger (Eds.), *Handbook of rational-emotive therapy: Vol. 2*. New York: Springer.

Silverman, M. S., McCarthy, M., & McGovern, T. (1992). A review of outcome studies of rational-emotive therapy from 1982 to 1989. *Journal of Rational-Emotive and Cognitive-Behavior Therapy, 10*(3), 111–175.

Walen, S., DiGiuseppe, R., & Dryden, W. (1992). *A practitioner's guide to rational-emotive therapy*. New York: Oxford University Press.

Warren, R., & McLellarn, R. W. (1987). What do RET therapists think they are doing? An international survey. *Journal of Rational-Emotive Therapy, 5*(2), 71–91.

Warren, R., McLellarn, R. W., & Ellis, A. (1987). Albert Ellis's personal responses to the survey of rational-emotive therapists. *Journal of Rational-Emotive Therapy, 5*(2), 92–107.

Weinrach, S. G. (1980). Unconventional therapist: Albert Ellis. *Personnel and Guidance Journal, 59*(3), 152–160.

Wessler, R. L. (1986). Rational-emotive therapy in groups. In A. Ellis & R. Grieger (Eds.), *Handbook of rational-emotive therapy: Vol. 2.* New York: Springer.

CHAPTER FIFTEEN

Reality Therapy in Groups

Introduction

Like many of the other founders of therapeutic approaches described in this book, William Glasser was psychoanalytically trained. He quickly became disenchanted with this approach, however, and began to experiment with innovative methods, which later came to be called reality therapy.

Reality therapy focuses on solving problems and on coping with the demands of reality in society. Thus, practitioners concentrate on what clients can do practically to change the behavior they use to fulfill their needs. People can improve the quality of their life through honestly examining their wants and needs. Group members are challenged to evaluate the quality of their behavior, formulate a plan for change, commit themselves to their plan, and follow through with their commitment. By avoiding making excuses and blaming others and by evaluating what they are doing to get what they want, they are able to achieve increasing control over their life.

Glasser's approach assumes that people strive to gain this control of their life in order to fulfill their needs. Like behavior therapy, transactional analysis, and rational emotive behavior therapy, reality therapy is active, directive, and didactic. It does not emphasize attitudes, insight, one's past, or unconscious motivations.

Until about 1985, Glasser's work was aimed at putting a few basic concepts of reality therapy to work in a variety of settings, such as correctional institutions, schools, private practice, marital and family therapy, group work, and counseling in community clinics. The current practice of reality therapy is largely based on concepts derived from control theory. The ideas of control theory are based on a book by William T. Powers (1973) entitled *Behavior: The Control of Perception.* Glasser (1992) has expanded and clarified Powers's work so that it is now an integral part of reality therapy.

Robert Wubbolding (1988) provides a concise description of reality therapy:

Reality therapy is a method of helping people take better control of their lives. It helps people to identify and to clarify what they want and need, and then evaluate whether they can realistically attain what they want. It helps them to examine their own behaviors and to evaluate them with clear criteria. This is followed by positive planning designed to help them control their own lives as well as fulfill their realistic wants and their needs. The result is added strength, more self-confidence, better human relations, and a personal plan for a more effective life. It, thus, provides people with a self-help tool to use daily in coping with adversity, growing personally, and getting more effective control of their lives [p. 173].

Key Concepts

Human Needs and Purposeful Behavior

Reality therapy is built on the notion that human behavior is purposeful and orginates from within the individual rather than from external forces. We are motivated by innate forces, and all of our behavior is aimed at fulfilling basic needs. Glasser (1992) and Wubbolding (1991) identify five essential human needs: love and belonging, power, freedom, fun, and survival. *Belonging* is the need for involvement with people and the need for loving others and being loved. *Power* is the need for achievement and accomplishment, or the need for a sense of being in charge of one's own life. *Freedom* is the need to make choices. *Fun* involves the need to enjoy life, to laugh, and to experience humor. *Survival* is concerned with maintaining life and good health. We spend all our life attempting to satisfy these basic needs. Control theory explains our attempt to control the world around us for the purpose of satisfying one or more of our basic needs.

Although all humans possess these needs, each individual fulfills them in various ways. People develop an inner "picture album" of specific wants, which contains precise images of how they wish to fulfill their needs. Responsibility consists of learning how to realistically meet these basic human needs, and the essence of therapy consists of teaching people to accept that responsibility. People behave for a purpose: to mold their environment, as a sculptor molds clay, to match their own inner pictures of what they want. These goals are achievable only through hard work (Wubbolding, 1988).

A major goal of reality therapy is to teach people better ways of fulfilling their needs and getting what they want from life. In Glasser's words, "What we decide to do is our choice, and the goal of reality therapy is to help clients figure out and put into practice better choices than those they have been making" (1989, p. 8). The reality therapist's job is to counsel clients to choose better ways of behaving than the ones they have been choosing. It takes considerable therapeutic skill to persuade clients that they are *choosing* what they are complaining about and to demonstrate that it would benefit them to choose more effective behaviors (Glasser, 1992). We have a significant degree of control over our life, and the more effectively we put this control into action, the more fulfilled we will be.

Existential/Phenomenological Orientation

In many ways Glasser's approach is grounded on phenomenological and existential premises. He maintains that we perceive the world in the context of our own needs, not as it really is. It is important for therapists to understand that clients live both in the external world and in their own internal world.

In addition to this focus on the subjective world, contemporary reality therapy continues to have a strong existential orientation. We are viewed as choosing our own goals and as responsible for the kind of world we create for ourselves. We are not helpless victims, and we can create a better life. Glasser (1985) does not accept the notion that misery simply happens to us; rather, it is something that we often choose. He observes that clients are typically quick to complain that they are upset because people in their life are not behaving as they would like them to. It is a powerful lesson for us to recognize that we choose all of our behaviors, including feeling miserable and thinking that we are victims. We choose misery in the attempt to reduce our frustration (which is the gap, or discrepancy, between what we want and what we have at a specific moment). When people do choose misery by developing a range of "paining" behaviors, it is because these are the best behaviors that they are able to generate at the time. But why does it make sense to choose misery? Glasser (1985) answers this question by discussing four reasons: (1) to keep anger under control, (2) to get others to help us, (3) to excuse our unwillingness to do something more effective, and (4) to gain powerful control. Glasser speaks of people *depressing* or *angering* themselves, rather than being depressed or being angry. With this perspective, depression can be explained as an active choice that we make rather than the result of being a passive victim. This process of "depressing" keeps anger in check, and it also allows us to ask for help. Glasser contends that as long as we cling to the notion that we are victims of depression and that misery is something that happens to us, we will not change for the better. We can change only when we recognize and act on the reality that what we are doing is the result of our choices.

Total Behavior

According to Glasser's latest formulation of control theory (1989, 1992), we always have control over what we do. This basic premise is clarified in the context of understanding our total behavior, which always includes four components: *doing* (or active behaviors such as talking or jogging); *thinking* (voluntary thoughts and self-statements); *feeling* (such as anger, joy, depression, anxiety); and *physiology* (such as sweating, "headaching," or developing other psychosomatic symptoms). Although these behaviors are interrelated, one of them is often more prominent than the others. Wubbolding (1991) uses the "suitcase" analogy to describe the concept of total behavior. In lifting a suitcase you grab it by the easiest part, the handle. Total behavior is like a suitcase. The handle is the *doing* part. Lift the handle, and total behavior follows. The sequence is doing, thinking, feeling, and physiology. It is typically easier to force ourselves to *do* something different than it is to feel or think something different.

Control theory is grounded on the assumption that it is impossible to choose a total behavior and not choose all its components. If we hope to change a total behavior (such as experiencing the emotional and physiological consequences of depressing ourselves), it is necessary to change what we are doing and what we are thinking. For example, we might feel upset and then depress ourselves if we fail to get a job that we applied for. We do not have the ability to directly change how we are feeling, independently of what we are doing or thinking. But we have an almost complete ability to change what we are doing and some ability to change what we are thinking, in spite of how we might be feeling. Therefore, the key to changing a total behavior lies in choosing to change what we are *doing*. If we markedly change the doing component, we cannot avoid changing the thinking, feeling, and physiological components as well (Glasser, 1992).

Success Identity

A primary goal of reality therapy is to help people achieve a success identity—that is, to learn more effective need-fulfilling behaviors. Those who possess a success identity see themselves as able to give and accept love, to feel that they are significant to others, to experience a sense of self-worth, to become involved with others in a caring way, and to meet their needs in ways that are not at the expense of others.

Those who seek therapy are often people who have a "failure identity": they see themselves as unloved, rejected, and unwanted, unable to become intimately involved with others, incompetent to make and stick with commitments, and generally helpless. People seek therapy because they are in psychological pain and because they are not getting what they want from life. Typically, individuals with a failure identity meet challenges with a despairing "I can't," a self-fulfilling prophecy that leads to further lack of success, which in turn supports a negative self-view and eventually makes these people see themselves as hopeless failures in life. Because reality therapy assumes that we are ultimately self-determining beings who become what we decide to become, the system is designed to teach people how they can change behavior that fosters a failure identity and develop behavior that leads to a success identity.

The Essence of Control Theory

Control theory is based on the premise that *behavior* is the *control* of our *perceptions*. Although we may not be able to control what is actually in the real world, we do attempt to control what we perceive. According to Glasser (1989), a core concept in control theory is the "pictures in the client's head," because they are the most important part of the individual's life. Everything that we do, think, and feel is generated by what happens inside of us. Our behavior is generated by the difference between what we want, the pictures in our heads, and what we have at the time. The underlying assumption of control theory is that "our behavior is always our best attempt to control the world and ourselves as part of that world so that we can best satisfy our needs" (Glasser, 1989, p. 5).

Glasser (1989) maintains that control theory teaches that the only behavior we can control is our own. The only way we can control events in our environment is through what we choose to do. How we feel is not controlled by others or events. We are not psychological slaves to others, nor are we trapped by our past or present, unless we choose to be.

Typically, when individuals seek counseling it is because they are unable to cope with their lives. Most people believe that they are in psychological pain because they are the victims of people or external events that they cannot control. The premise of control theory, however, is that people are able to choose all the important facets of their life, including how they feel and, to a great extent, even their health. Glasser contends that what makes control theory hopeful is the fact that people choose what they are doing and how they are feeling. Therefore, with the assistance of an effective counselor, individuals can learn to make better choices. In Glasser's words:

> The message of control theory is that once we understand its basic ideas, specifically the needs, the pictures in heads, and the concept of total behavior, no matter how bad things seem, we can choose to do better with our lives—provided we are willing to make the effort to do so [1989, p. 2].

What are the implications of control theory for the practice of reality-therapy group counseling? Group leaders can help members recognize that what they are doing is not working for them, help them accept themselves as a person, and guide them in making realistic plans to do better. Practitioners provide help through skillful questioning that is aimed at getting members to assess what they want. According to Glasser (1992), if group leaders are not skillful enough to get clients to see that their total behavior is not getting them what they want, therapy will not be effective. Leaders need to challenge members continually with the basic reality-therapy question: "Is what you are now choosing to do (your actions and thoughts) getting you what you want?" Other questions often posed to members include: "Do you want to change? How would you most like to change your life? What do you want in your life that you are not getting? If you were to change, how might your life be different? If you changed, how would you feel better? What would you have in your life if you were to change? What do you have to do now to make the changes happen?" Members can more easily choose better behavior if they come to realize that what they are doing, thinking, and feeling is not simply happening to them but that they are, indeed, making choices.

Role and Functions of the Group Leader

The central task of reality-therapy group practitioners is to become involved with the individual group members and then to help them face reality.

According to Glasser, reality therapy teaches that people are most able to gain effective control of their life when they recognize and accept accountablity for their own chosen behaviors:

> The role of the reality therapy counselor is to maintain a counseling environment which does the following: (1) helps clients to avoid excuses and accept this responsibility, (2) fosters their clients' psychological strengths and (3) provides the opportunity for clients to learn and test new and more effective behavioral choices [1986c, p. 20].

This role requires the leader to perform a variety of functions:

- providing a model for responsible behavior and a model of a life based on a success identity
- establishing with each member a therapeutic relationship based on care and respect, one that encourages and demands responsible and effective behavior
- establishing a structure for the group sessions
- assisting members in setting practical limits to the duration and scope of their therapy
- encouraging members to get involved with one another, to share common experiences, and to help one another deal with problems in a responsible manner
- assisting members to define and clarify what they want to get from the group experience and showing them how a group can enable them to meet their psychological needs
- helping participants identify the commonality of their wants
- teaching members how to assist one another in a supportive manner
- encouraging participants to provide feedback to one another
- counseling in a noncriticizing and accepting way that encourages members to reveal what is in their special world
- challenging members to see that they are *choosing* to "depress" rather than being depressed
- actively promoting discussion of members' current behavior and actively discouraging excuses for irresponsible or ineffective behavior
- helping members make an inner self-evaluation
- introducing and fostering the process of evaluating which wants are realistically attainable
- teaching members to formulate and carry out plans to change their behaviors
- helping participants evaluate their level of commitment to their action plans
- adapting and adjusting the basic principles of control theory and procedures used in the practice of reality therapy to meet the unique needs of culturally diverse group members
- teaching participants ways to evaluate their individual progress as well as the progress of the group
- helping members conceptualize and summarize what they have learned from their group experience

- ◆ teaching members how to apply to everyday life what they have learned in the group
- ◆ helping members think of ways to deal with future challenges
- ◆ encouraging members to identify how to continue making the changes they want once the group ends

Reality-therapy group leaders assume a verbally active and directive role in the group. In carrying out their functions, they focus on the strengths and potentials of the members rather than on their failures. They assume that dwelling on limitations, problems, and failures tends to reinforce a client's basic failure identity and ineffective control. Therefore, they challenge members to look at their unused potential and to discover how to work toward creating a success identity and more effective control.

It is important for group leaders to develop their own individual therapeutic style. Sincerity and being comfortable with their style are crucial traits in carrying out therapeutic functions. Developing a personal style does take time and experience in working with a variety of groups. In establishing this style, effective practitioners are aware of their own value system and of the cultural differences and worldviews of the members. Group practitioners can continue their growth by being open to challenge and by exploring their own values with the groups they facilitate.

The Practice of Reality Therapy in Groups

The practice of reality therapy consists of two major components: (1) the counseling environment and (2) specific procedures that lead to changes in behavior. The art of counseling is to weave these components together in ways that lead clients to evaluate their life and decide to move in more effective directions. Wubbolding (1988) describes these two elements as the "cycle of counseling." The cycle illustrates that there is an overall sequence to translating reality therapy's theory into practice. The counseling environment, which consists of specific guidelines for implementing interventions, is the foundation from which the procedures are built.

Several points are important to keep in mind. First, although the concepts discussed below may seem clear and simple as they are presented in written form, they are difficult to translate into actual therapeutic practice, and it takes skill and creativity to apply them successfully in group work. Although the principles will be the same when used by any certified reality therapist, the manner in which they are applied does vary depending on the therapist's style and personal characteristics. Finally, although the principles are applied in a progressive manner, they should not be thought of as discrete and rigid categories. There is a considerable degree of interdependence among these principles, and taken together they contribute to the total process of reality therapy.

Glasser (1986c) has developed procedures that form the core of reality therapy. He stresses that the practice of reality therapy is a process and that it is a mistake to apply these methods in a rigid, step-by-step, or "cookbook," fashion. He adds that the practice of reality therapy is an art. The discussion that follows should be considered an aid for teaching reality therapy, but it should not be thought of as a replacement for the extensive training that is needed to counsel effectively.

My discussion of the practice of reality therapy is an integrated summary and adaptation of material from various sources (Glasser, 1980, 1981, 1985, 1986a, 1986b, 1986c, 1989, 1992; Wubbolding, 1988, 1991, 1992). The student manual that accompanies this textbook contains a chart by Wubbolding that highlights issues and tasks to be accomplished at each of the stages of a reality-therapy group.

The Counseling Environment

PERSONAL INVOLVEMENT WITH THE CLIENT. The practice of reality therapy begins with the counselor's efforts to create a supportive environment within which clients can begin to make life changes. To create this therapeutic climate, counselors need to make friends with clients, which implies getting involved in their lives and creating the rapport that will be the foundation of the therapeutic relationship. It is essential for the counselor to see the world as the clients see it. In a sense, this is the most important and demanding aspect of a group, for in the absence of personal involvement there can be no effective therapy. When reality group therapy is ineffective, it is usually because genuine involvement has not been established. Caring on the part of the group leader can go a long way toward building the bonds of trust that will be needed for clients to commit themselves to the challenges of making positive changes.

For real involvement to take place, the leader must have certain personal qualities, including warmth, understanding, acceptance, concern, respect for the client, openness, and the willingness to be challenged by others. One of the best ways to develop this goodwill and therapeutic friendship is simply by listening to clients. Yet as Wubbolding (1988) mentions, this high level of empathy is shown more by skillful questioning than by reflective listening. Involvement is also promoted by talking about a wide range of topics that have relevance for group members, topics that relate to the members' current everyday behaviors and experiences and that play down misery and past failures.

In his description of the cycle of counseling, Wubbolding (1988, 1991, 1992, 1993) identifies specific ways for counselors to create a climate that leads to involvement with clients. Wubbolding (1993) emphasizes that the cycle of counseling is not a simplistic, lock-step method that is applied in the same way with every client. Some of the approaches to establishing a therapeutic environment are using attending behavior; being consistent and courteous; suspending judgment of clients; doing the unexpected; using humor appropriately; being oneself as a counselor; engaging in facilitative self-disclosure; listening for metaphors in the client's speech; listening for themes; summarizing and focusing; allowing silences at times; demonstrating empathy; and being an ethical practitioner. In addition to these positive attributes, counselors who hope to enhance involvement do not criticize, argue, belittle, demean, find fault, or give up easily. Instead, the emphasis is on accepting clients as they are and encouraging them to focus on what they can control. Once involvement has been established, the leader encourages the group members to confront themselves with the reality and consequences of their *current* behavior. The essence of reality group therapy consists of this process of self-evaluation that the members make.

Because of the opportunity to form relationships with several other people besides the therapist, there is a definite advantage in practicing reality therapy in groups. The group milieu can do a lot to deepen caring and involvement. Fellow group members provide both support and an honest challenge to look at one's life. The nonpunitive atmosphere of the group can promote self-acceptance and the desire to make specific plans for better behavior (Glasser, 1976b). Group interaction is seen as especially important in helping individual members break the vicious circle of failure experiences, because according to reality-therapy theory, people cannot achieve a success identity and gain more effective control by isolating themselves. What they do must fulfill the need for belonging.

To provide an understanding of how the basic concepts of reality therapy are applied to the group process, I will describe a group of male adolescents who are in a detention facility for various criminal offenses. Participation in the group constitutes one aspect of these youths' treatment program, and sessions are held several times a week for at least an hour. The evolution and development of this group will be briefly described to demonstrate how reality-therapy principles actually work. For purposes of the example, assume that most of the youths in the group have a failure identity.

How does this principle of involvement apply to the case illustration just described? To begin with, we should note that many of the youths in the detention facility who are now being required to attend group-therapy sessions have never had any meaningful and positive involvements with others. Under such circumstances, how is it possible for a leader to establish a personal involvement with the youths and to facilitate involvement among the group members? First, the leader must establish his or her credibility by demonstrating a genuine concern and caring for the youths, seeing them not as they see themselves but as the successful and responsible persons they are capable of becoming. With that concern, the foundation for involvement is laid. Without this positive view of participants' possibilities—or, even worse, by harboring the belief that the youths cannot change—the leader will worsen the boys' sense of hopelessness and their inevitable resistance to seeing themselves in a more positive light.

One effective way to create a therapeutic climate for participants in involuntary groups is for the leader to explain to members some specific ways in which the group process can be of personal value to them. For example, if participants see the group as a place where they can learn to escape their particular pattern of repeated failures, they may take the first step toward involvement. Such involvement is fostered by the reality therapist, who actively participates in defining the nature and the purpose of the group as well as the limits of its activities. However, the leader encourages the members to participate in establishing the goals that guide their group, even in correctional settings.

COUNSELOR ATTITUDES AND BEHAVIORS THAT PROMOTE CHANGE. Counselors hope to teach their clients to value the attitude of accepting responsibility for their total behaviors. Thus, they accept no excuses for irresponsible behavior such as not doing what they said they would do. If clients do not follow through with their plans for change, counselors do not ask fruitless questions about why the plan failed. Instead, they teach members that excuses are a form of self-deception that may offer temporary relief but will ultimately lead to failure and to the cementing of a failure identity. As Wubbolding (1988) has pointed out, accepting excuses gives a message to clients: "Your behavior can be excused because you are weak and not in control of your behavior. It is not really possible for you to change your life." On the other hand, by refusing to accept excuses, the therapist conveys a different attitude: "You are strong and in control of your behavior. You can make a better plan, and you can change your life."

Reality therapy holds that punishment is not a useful means of effecting behavioral change. Instead of using punishment, the therapist challenges clients to see and to accept *reasonable consequences* that flow from their actions. Consequences that are reasonable are related to the offense, and as such they are for the benefit of the person breaking the rule. Consequences that are administered calmly and consistently allow less latitude for anger and recrimination. Such consequences are educational and tend to result in responsibility and rehabilitation (Wubbolding, 1988). Taking the example of the youths in the detention facility, the therapist would avoid deprecating a group member for, say, having failed to attend a meeting. The therapist might, however, lead the young man to see that his failure to attend meetings could affect his chances for eventual release. By avoiding the use of critical statements, by not accepting any excuses, and by remaining nonjudgmental, therapists can ask clients if they *really* want to change. Clients can be asked to reevaluate to determine if they still want to stick by their commitments.

It is important that counselors not give up easily in their belief in the client's ability to find a more responsible life, even if the client makes little effort to follow through on plans. Reality therapists simply do not include giving up as one of their options, for if they did, it would tend to confirm the client's belief that no one cared enough to help. Glasser acknowledges: "Clients have depended on people in the past, and many of these people have given up. Clients need from us a clear message that we are not going to do the same" (1989, p. 14). Those with a failure identity expect others to give up on them. It is a real challenge to refuse to give up easily on clients who are resistant, passive/aggressive, uncooperative, hostile, or apathetic. It is unhelpful for a therapist to assume that another person will never change or that a person is hopeless. Regardless of what clients say or do, it is therapeutically helpful for the therapist not to lose faith in their capacity to change.

The concept of refusing to give up applies well to the example of the group of adolescent delinquents. A leading factor contributing to their delinquent behavior may well be the fact that many people have given up on them and have showed little faith in their ability to succeed. The group leader who adopts a stance of refusing to give up and a commitment to keep trying to reach these adolescents challenges them to find ways to believing in themselves. Once the members believe that the leader and other members will not give up on them, the sense of belongingness is solidified, which allows for work to proceed. The members can then develop a sense of faith in themselves, for they know that they are no longer alone. Although it is up to them to make decisions about how they will live in the world, they also realize that they do have the capacity to resolve their problems and make some significant changes in what they are doing, thinking, and feeling.

In addition to the counselor's attitudes mentioned above that create an environment conducive for client change, Wubbolding (1988) emphasizes the importance of being willing to seek consultation with someone who is trained in reality therapy. Even for seasoned practitioners, there is always room for improvement, which can take place both by consultation and by developing a plan for ongoing professional development.

Procedures That Lead to Change: The WDEP System

According to Glasser (1992), the procedures that lead to change are based on the assumption that human beings are motivated to change when (1) they are convinced that their present behavior is not getting them what they want and (2) they believe that there are other behaviors they can choose that will get them closer to what they want.

Wubbolding (1991, 1992) describes an acronym, WDEP, that he sees as illustrating key procedures that can be applied in the practice of reality-therapy groups. Each of the letters refers to a cluster of strategies, as follows: W = wants; D = direction and doing; E = evaluation; and P = planning. These strategies designed to promote change are discussed in the sections below.

EXPLORING WANTS, NEEDS, AND PERCEPTIONS. Reality therapists ask, "What do you want?" Through the therapist's skillful questioning, clients are encouraged to recognize, define, and refine how they wish to meet their needs. Part of counseling consists of the exploration of clients' "picture album" and the ways in which their behavior is aimed at moving the external world closer to their inner world of wants. It is essential that this exploration continue throughout the entire counseling process, because the client's pictures change. Clients are given the opportunity to explore every facet of life, including what they want from their family, friends, and work. Furthermore, it is useful for clients to define what they expect and want from the counselor and from themselves (Wubbolding, 1988, 1991, 1992).

In a group, members explore what they want, what they have, and what they are not getting. Throughout the process, the focus is on getting members to make a self-evaluation to determine the direction in which their behavior is taking them. This assessment provides a basis for making specific changes that will enable the members to reduce their frustrations. Useful questions can help them pinpoint what they want: "What kind of person do you wish you were?" "What would your family be like if your wants and their wants matched?" "What would you be doing if you were living the way you wished?" "Is this choice to your best short-term and long-term advantage, and it is consistent with your values?" This line of questioning sets the stage for the application of other procedures in reality therapy.

FOCUS ON CURRENT BEHAVIOR.   After clients explore their picture album (wants) and needs, they are asked to look at their current behavior to determine if what they are doing is getting them what they want. Wubbolding writes that the therapist holds a mirror before group members and asks: "Will this choice get you where you want to go? Is your destination truly helpful to you?" (1991, p. 93).

Group leaders consistently attempt to focus clients on what they are *doing now*. They try not to allow clients to talk about events in the past unless these events can be easily related to present situations. Although the problems that members bring to a group may well be rooted in the past, there is little that leaders can do to remove the frustrations of the past. The solution is always in the present, because the need or needs that are unsatisfied are always in the present. What can be done is to help the members choose better behaviors to satisfy their needs (Glasser, 1989, 1992). Thus, the past may be discussed if doing so will help clients plan for a better tomorrow.

Reality therapists also avoid discussing clients' feelings or their physiological reactions as though these were separate from their total behavior. That doesn't imply that attitudes are dismissed as unimportant; rather, the approach is that change in doing is easier than attitudinal change and of greater value in the therapeutic process. The counselor relates clients' feelings or physical symptoms to their concurrent actions and thoughts, over which they have more direct control. For that reason, a client who expressed feelings of helplessness would not be questioned about the reasons for these feelings or encouraged to explore them. Although the counselor might encourage her to discuss feelings, the focus would clearly be on urging her to identify actions that were accompanying or supporting the feelings (Glasser, 1989, 1992).

The aim of this emphasis on current behavior is to help clients understand their responsibilities for their own feelings. As a way of encouraging clients to look at what they are actually doing to contribute to their feelings, these questions might be asked:

◆ What are you doing now?
◆ What did you actually do this past week?

- ◆ What did you want to do differently this past week?
- ◆ What stopped you from doing what you say you wanted to do?
- ◆ What will you do tomorrow?

Getting members to focus on what they are doing has the aim of teaching them that they can gain conscious control over their behavior, can make choices, and can change their life. Although they may want to talk in detail about how others are not living up to their expectations and how if only the world would change, they could be happy, such a tack will only solidify their victimlike position.

Thus, the leader in our example would discourage the group of juvenile offenders from dwelling on their crimes and the reasons underlying their current feelings and attitudes about themselves and others. Rather, the leader would seek to encourage the youths to discuss the behavior that led to their sentence and would challenge them to trace and face the practical consequences of their behavior—in short, to evaluate their behavior and accept responsibility for it.

GETTING CLIENTS TO EVALUATE THEIR BEHAVIOR. It is the therapist's task to confront clients with the consequences of their behavior and to get *them* to judge the quality of their actions. Indeed, unless clients eventually judge their own behavior, they will not change. After clients make value judgments about the quality of their behavior, they can determine what may be contributing to their failures and what changes they can undertake to promote success.

It is important that therapists remain nonjudgmental about clients' behavior and do not assume the responsibility for the client in making these value judgments. Instead, they best serve clients when they challenge them to stop, look, and listen. If therapists can stimulate client self-questioning— "What am I doing now?" "Is it getting me where I want to go?" "Is my behavior working for me?" "Am I making constructive choices?"—the client will be more likely to begin to make changes. Asking clients to evaluate each component of their total behavior is a major task in reality therapy.

From the reality therapist's perspective, it is acceptable to be directive with certain clients in the beginning of treatment. Reality therapists sometimes express what they think will be helpful. In treating children of alcoholics and even alcoholics themselves, for example, it is necessary to say straightforwardly what will work and what will not work. Certain clients do not have the thinking behaviors in their control system to be able to make consistent evaluations. These clients are likely to have blurred pictures and may not always be aware of what they want or whether their wants are realistic. As clients grow and continually interact with the counselor, they learn to make evaluations with less help.

Some clients insist that they do not have a problem and that their behavior is not getting them into trouble. It is essential to recognize that clients behave according to the perceptions in their internal world and that the counselor must accept that what the client perceives may be far different from what those close to the client perceive (Glasser, 1986a, 1986c,

1989). In such cases, Glasser suggests, counselors should continue to focus on the client's present behaviors and keep repeating the core question in a variety of ways. He says that patience is important, for in working with difficult clients, it may take considerable time for them to realize that certain behavior patterns are not getting them what they want.

Returning to the example of the youths in the detention facility, the group leader might ask them: "Does your behavior get you what you want? Where has your behavior led you? Does your behavior hurt you or others? Is your behavior fulfilling your needs?" More specifically, an adolescent who has been sentenced for robbing a liquor store to support a drug habit is asked to evaluate the consequences of continuing his acts and to confront the probable consequences of being caught and jailed. Further, he is directed to face the consequences of taking drugs. It is the task of the youth—with the therapist's help—to determine and evaluate the consequences of his actions and then decide whether he wants to change his behavior. It is not the task of the therapist to do his changing for him, nor can the therapist *make* him want to give up drugs and stealing and lead a more constructive life. In short, the therapist helps the client determine *what* needs to be changed, and the client determines *why*, or if, the change is needed.

PLANNING AND ACTION. Much of the work in reality therapy consists of helping members identify specific ways to change their failure behavior into success behavior. Once a client has made an evaluation about his or her behavior and decided to change it, the therapist assists the client in developing a plan for behavioral changes. The art of such planning is to establish practical short-term goals that have a high probability of being successfully attained, because such successes will positively reinforce the client's efforts to achieve long-range goals.

Planning for responsible behavior is the core of the helping process. This is clearly a teaching phase of therapy. Therefore, therapy is best directed toward providing clients with new information and helping them discover more effective ways of getting what they want (Glasser, 1981). A large portion of the therapy time consists of making plans and then checking to determine how these plans are working. In a group context members learn how to plan realistically and responsibly through contact with both the other members and the leader. The members are encouraged to experiment with new behaviors, to try out different ways of obtaining their goals, and to carry out an action program. It is important that these plans not be too ambitious, for people need to experience success. The purpose of the plan is to arrange for successful experiences. Once a plan works, feelings of self-esteem will increase. It is clear that helpful plans are modest in the beginning and specify what is to be done, when it will be done, and how often. In short, plans are meant to encourage clients to translate their talk and intentions into actions.

A plan that fulfills wants and needs is central to effective group counseling. The process of creating and carrying out plans enables people to gain effective control over their lives. Wubbolding (1988, 1991) devotes an entire chapter to the characteristics of effective planning, which are summarized below:

◆ The plan should be tied as closely as possible to the client's need in counseling. Skillful group leaders help members identify which of their plans involve greater need-fulfilling payoffs and help members assess what their plans will do for them.

◆ Good plans are simple and easy to understand. Although plans need to be specific, concrete, and measurable, they should be flexible and open to modification as clients gain a deeper understanding of the specific behaviors that they want to change. In short, it is vital that clients run their plans, not vice versa.

◆ Plans should be realistic and attainable. Leaders can help members recognize that even small plans can help them in taking significant steps toward their desired changes. This idea is captured nicely by my daughter Heidi in paraphrasing a Chinese proverb: "A journey of a thousand miles begins with the first step. So start walking!"

◆ An effective plan involves doing something, rather than not doing something. That is, the plan should involve a positive plan of action, and it should be stated in terms of what will be done.

◆ The group leader encourages members to develop plans that they can carry out independently of what others do. Therefore, the leader's task is to focus on the members, rather than on the world external to them, which is often beyond their control. Group members can learn that they have control only over their own world of wants and their behavioral and perceptual systems. If members wait for others to change, then whether they change is contingent on others. Good plans are specific and concrete. Group leaders can help members develop specificity through their skillful questioning. Leaders often ask members questions such as "What?" "Where?" "With whom?" "When?" and "How often?"

◆ Effective plans are repetitive; that is, they are performed regularly, if not daily. In order for group members to overcome their negative symptoms such as "depressing," "anxietying," negative thinking, and psychosomatic complaints, it is essential to replace them with positive symptoms. These symptoms include feelings of joy and trust, rational thinking, healthful activities, diet and exercise, and other positive qualities that are a part of one's personal growth program. People do not change by practicing new behaviors only when the spirit moves them but, rather, by continuously repeating the positive elements of their program.

◆ Plans should have a sense of immediacy; that is, they should be put into action as soon as possible. Leaders may ask their members questions such as "What are you willing to do today to begin to change your life?" "You say that you would like to have more fun. So, what are you going to do now to enjoy yourself?" The message behind these questions is that members do have the capacity to control their lives by making immediate changes.

◆ Effective planning involves process-centered activities. For example, members may say that they can do any of the following: pay their child three compliments, jog 30 minutes a day, substitute nutritious food for junk food, devote two hours a week to volunteer work, and take a vacation that they have been wanting.

◆ Before members carry out their plan, it is a good idea to evaluate the plan in the group and get feedback from other members and the leader. They should ask if their plan is realistic and attainable and if it relates to what they need and want. After the plan has been carried out in real life, it is useful to evaluate it again. Members can return to the group and talk about the degree to which their plan has been successful. With input from the group, they can figure out what the plan might be lacking, how it needs to be more specific, or how it might need to be modified in some other way.

◆ In order for clients to commit themselves to their plan, it is useful for them to firm it up—for example, by writing it down. Furthermore, both the group leader and other members can help by providing reinforcement for an effective plan.

Most members do not formulate an ideal plan like the one just described. The better the plan, however, the better are the chances that members will attain their wants. Toward this end, it is essential that they commit themselves to following through with their plans.

Although the burden of responsibility for formulating and carrying out plans for change rests with the group members, it is the task of the leader to create an accepting and nourishing atmosphere for planning. It should be emphasized that throughout this planning phase the group leader continually urges members to assume responsibility for their own choices and actions by reminding them that no one in the world will do things for them or live their life for them. Challenging members to make responsible plans calls for considerable skill and inventiveness.

COMMITMENT.   Typically, people with a failure identity have trouble making and keeping commitments. Clearly, formulating even the most reasonable and practical plan is a waste of time if the client lacks the willingness to implement it. Plans can be put in the form of a contract that will assist group members in holding themselves and others accountable for carrying them out.

Here one can readily see the value of a group, such as the one in our example. Once individual members make plans and announce them, the group is in a position to help them evaluate and review these plans and to offer support and encouragement when needed. If individual members fall short of their commitments or in any way fail to implement their plans, that fact cannot be hidden from others and, more importantly, from themselves. If some members are able to follow through with their plans, they serve as models for the rest of the group. Others may realize that if their peers can do what they have set out to do, so can they.

It is essential that members who are reluctant to make a commitment be helped to express and explore their fears of failing. Members may have many resistances and fear rejection. Therefore, the support of the group is especially critical during this phase. Members can be encouraged to begin each group session by reporting on the activities of the week, including the difficulties they encountered in sticking with their plans as well as the successes they had in trying out new behavior in the real world. Just as in behavioral groups, where the buddy system is used, reality therapy can encourage members to make contacts with each other during the week if they have trouble in sticking by their commitments.

Of course, there are always those who are unwilling to make *any* commitments. As was mentioned earlier, therapists cannot force change. But they can help such people look at what is stopping them from making a commitment to change. Sometimes people are convinced that they cannot change, that they cannot stick to any decision, and that they are destined to remain a failure. In such cases it is important that the client be helped to see clearly the consequences of not changing and then be guided to formulate very short-range, limited plans having goals that are easy to reach. Clients need to achieve some degree of success, and they need to believe that they do have the power to change. As far as this basic principle of reality therapy is concerned, the nature and scope of the plan are not as important as the commitment to some plan for change, however limited.

Commitment places the responsibility for changing directly on the clients. If members say over and over that they want to change and hope to change, they can be asked the question "Will you do it, and when will you do it?" The danger, of course, is that the member's plan may not be carried out, which leads to an increase of frustrations and adds to the person's failures. Reality therapy tries to avoid this problem by not asking for any commitment that is unreasonable or impossible.

Special Procedures in Reality Group Therapy

This section describes four special procedures that can be appropriately applied to the practice of reality therapy in group settings: (1) the skillful use of questioning, (2) self-help procedures for a personal-growth plan, (3) the use of humor, and (4) paradoxical techniques. In his book *Using Reality Therapy*, Wubbolding (1988) has extended reality therapy by adding these special procedures to the more conventionally used methods. Of course, reality therapists do not have a patent on these procedures, and all of them can be used in many of the other therapeutic approaches that we have examined. These special procedures can enhance the group process and can also assist members in attaining their personal goals. In addition to the potential value of these techniques, there are also caveats. As useful as these procedures may be, all of them have the potential for misuse by poorly trained leaders or by leaders who are more concerned with gratifying their own power needs than they are with the welfare of the members.

THE ART OF SKILLFUL QUESTIONING.   Because reality therapy makes use of questioning to a greater degree than many other counseling approaches, it is important for group leaders to develop extensive questioning skills. There are four main purposes for questioning: (1) to enter the inner world of group members, (2) to gather information, (3) to give information, and (4) to help members take more effective control of their lives (Wubbolding, 1988). The art of group counseling implies that leaders know *what* questions to ask, *how* to ask them, and *when* to ask them.

Questioning is often misused by group leaders. Some leaders' questions appear to have no point other than to keep the members talking. Those leaders use the question-and-answer technique mainly because they don't know what else to do. Such questioning can certainly be overdone and can result in client defensiveness and resistance. However, well-timed and strategic questions can get members to think about what they want and to evaluate whether their behavior is leading them in the direction they want to go.

SELF-HELP PROCEDURES FOR A PERSONAL-GROWTH PROGRAM. One of the contributions of reality group therapy is that members can learn a variety of self-help tools. As was discussed in a previous section, members make plans to carry newly acquired behaviors from the group setting into their daily lives. Wubbolding (1988) describes his version of an approach to personal growth in his *replacement program*. This program defines categories of pictures to be used in the client's inner world of wants and behaviors, which are specific and unique for each person. According to Wubbolding, "replacements" include "do-it behaviors" in place of "give-up behaviors" and "positive-symptom behaviors" instead of "negative-symptom behaviors." This replacement program helps members identify specific behaviors that fulfill both wants and needs and target specific behaviors for change. Used in the context of group counseling, this self-improvement program is a developmental process.

THE USE OF HUMOR. A number of other approaches integrate humor as an intervention to promote constructive change (Adlerian therapy, psychodrama, existential therapy, Gestalt therapy, TA, REBT). Many times group members feel so "heavy" that they fail to see any humor in their life situation. In dwelling on their negative symptoms, they make little room for levity. Of course, the use of humor must be timed appropriately. Group leaders can make mistakes by poking fun at clients before a therapeutic relationship has been developed. There must be a trusting climate within the group that allows members to become spontaneous and to laugh at themselves and with one another. Once a group has achieved a working level of cohesion, it is far more likely that humor will result in positive outcomes. Humor that is therapeutic is not sarcastic, does not ridicule clients, and does not show a lack of respect. Therapeutic humor has an educative, corrective message, and it helps clients put situations in perspective. Once members have worked through a place where they were stuck or some source of emotional pain, they may be able to see things in perspective and even laugh at the very issues they previously cried about in the group.

The group therapist can model spontaneous and good-hearted humor, can be transparently real and human, and can use humor to present an interpretation to group members. From the standpoint of group members, the use of humor has the potential to open them to new ways of self-expression and to provide the flexibility to look at themselves from a fresh perspective. A solemn and grave attitude characterizes some members, and humor can go a long way in helping them overcome their exaggerated earnestness. Furthermore, being able to laugh and to appreciate the absurdity of the human condition promotes interpersonal skills. As members are able to fully participate in shared humor, a sense of catharsis occurs, and self-disclosure frequently follows. Humor can play a key role in the life of the group as a whole by serving as a cohesive force.

USING PARADOXICAL TECHNIQUES. Clients in reality therapy are generally encouraged to change by direct and straightforward procedures. Yet there are times when certain clients seem especially resistant to making plans, or if they do make plans, they may resist carrying them out. Some of these group members may return to a session and inform others in their group that they tried their plan but it didn't work. In response, reality therapists sometimes do the unexpected. Wubbolding (1988) contends that there are paradoxes in the theory of reality therapy and that in order to perceive this approach, it is necessary to think paradoxically. At times the best way to make desired changes is to do so indirectly, by dealing with the problem in an unexpected way. This involves looking at a client's behavior in an inverse way, seeing the cause as the effect and the effect as the cause.

In one of our weeklong residential groups, Alex seemed intent on winning everyone's approval in the group. One of his concerns in his everyday life was his worry over being inadequate. He disliked working so hard for the approval and acceptance of his family and friends. Alex was indirect about seeking the approval of the members and the co-leaders, yet it was clear that he very much wanted it. As an exercise, I suggested that he try even harder to win the approval of each of us. Of course, he said that he did not want to ask others for their approval, nor did he want to so desperately need this approval. My co-leaders and I asked him to do the very thing that he said he wanted to do less of. We suggested that he might even start a conversation with "I very much want you to like me, and I need your acceptance to feel worthwhile." He was to be as open and direct as possible in soliciting approval, even to the extent of asking us what he could do that would please us. He soon grew very tired of working so hard for our approval. He vividly saw how he was indirectly doing so many things to get others to like him. By the end of the day he began to laugh at himself for being so intent on being accepted by everyone at any price. At least he was much more aware of messages he was sending to others, as well as his own internal dialogue when he sensed he was not totally approved of. Interestingly, as he became much less focused on getting everyone in the group to approve of him, he increasingly said and did things that were pleasing to him. He began the process of valuing his approval of himself more than the approval of others. Although this strategy was effective in

Alex's case, it might have been counterproductive in other cases. The leaders had established a good working relationship with him, and the trust level was increasing in the group. Although he was unsure whether he had the approval of everyone in the group, he did feel that the leaders and the members cared for him. He went along with our exercise because he did not sense that we were laughing at him, and eventually he was able to appreciate the humor in his situation.

Paradoxical procedures are powerful interventions, and thus they should be used only by practitioners who have been adequately trained in this technique or are under close supervision. Research findings on the use of paradoxical techniques reveal that they have been successfully applied in dealing with depression, insomnia, phobias, and anxiety disorders. They also appear to be especially well suited for resistant clients with specific behaviorally defined problems (Huddleston & Engels, 1986).

Paradoxical procedures are usually not used until the more conventional procedures of reality therapy have been tried. Furthermore, there are ethical and clinical issues involved in using paradoxical interventions. Ethical practice demands that group leaders know when paradoxical procedures should be avoided. These procedures are not advisable in crisis situations, suicide, homicide, violence, abuse, or excessive drinking. Paradox in these situations is likely to be counterproductive and irresponsible (Weeks & L'Abate, 1982).

In summary, the value of paradoxical procedures depends largely on the training and experience of the group practitioner. There is potential for misuse when group leaders use them for shock value or as a gimmick because everything else has failed (Weeks & L'Abate, 1982). When these procedures are used at the right time for the client and at the right stage of a group's development, however, they can be powerful therapeutic tools that promote group cohesion and lead to positive change in group members.

Used properly, paradox can have an impact similar to that of humor in helping members cast their problems in a new light. As in the case of Alex, they may actually learn how to laugh at their foibles, which can make change a much easier matter. Questions a practitioner can raise to determine when the use of paradox is appropriate include these: "As a group leader, have I established a high level of trust between myself and the members?" "What is the degree of cohesion of the group?" "Might the use of paradox have a boomerang effect, with members feeling tricked and thus becoming increasingly resistant?" "How have the members responded to the use of other techniques?" "How effective have the conventional procedures been in promoting client change?" "Do I know why I might introduce a paradoxical procedure?" "Am I clear about what I hope to accomplish, and do I have an educated sense of how a member might react to this procedure?"

If you would like to pursue the topic of the use of paradox, see Wubbolding (1988), Weeks and L'Abate (1982), Dowd and Milne (1986), and Huddleston and Engels (1986).

Evaluation of Reality Therapy

Contributions and Strengths of the Approach

A characteristic of reality therapy that I especially favor is its stress on accountability. When a group participant indicates a desire to change certain behaviors, for example, the leader confronts the member with a question about what is keeping the person from doing so. I appreciate the fact that it is the members, not the leader, who evaluate their own behavior and decide whether they want to change. It seems to me that many group leaders meet with resistance because they have suggestions and plans for how the members should best live their lives. To their credit, reality therapists keep challenging the members to evaluate for themselves whether what they are doing is getting them what they want. If the members concede that what they are doing is not working for them, their resistance is much more likely to melt, and they tend to be more open to trying different behaviors.

Once the members make some change, reality therapy provides the structure for them to make specific plans, to formulate contracts for action, and to evaluate their level of success. In most of my groups I have found it useful to employ these action-oriented procedures to help members carry what they are learning in the group into their everyday life. I also ask members to state the terms of their contract clearly in the group and to report to the group the outcome of their efforts to fulfill it.

Other aspects of reality therapy that I endorse include the idea of not accepting excuses for failure to follow through with contracts and the avoidance of any form of punishment and blaming. As I see it, if people don't carry out a plan, it is important to discuss with them what got in their way. Perhaps they set their goals unrealistically high, or perhaps there is a discrepancy between what they say they want to change and what they actually want to change. (One can generally believe behavior; one cannot always believe words.)

I also like reality therapy's insistence that change will not come by insight alone; rather, members will have to begin doing something different once they determine that their behavior is not working for them. I have become increasingly skeptical about the value of catharsis as a therapeutic vehicle unless the release of pent-up emotions is eventually followed up with an action plan. My colleagues and I have worked in groups with people who seem to have immobilized themselves by dwelling excessively on their negative feelings and by being unwilling to take action to change. Therefore, we continue to challenge such members to look at the futility of waiting for others to change. Increasingly, we have asked them to assume that the significant people in their life may never change, which means that they will have to take a more active stance in shaping their own destiny. I appreciate Glasser's insistence on teaching clients that the only person's life they can control is their own. Thus, the focus is not on what others are doing or on getting others to be different; instead, it is on helping clients change their own patterns of acting and thinking.

Group members must look inward and search for alternatives. Since other members and the group leader will not accept rationalizations for their failing behavior, the members are forced to choose for themselves whether to change. Applied to the example used in this chapter, we can readily see that the leader will not allow the detained youths to complain endlessly about their parents' rejection, about their bad breaks in life, and about their many failures. Whatever the reasons are for their being in an institution now, they will have to make a decision about where their behavior is leading them. I consider the challenging and skillful questioning by reality therapists to be a major strength of this approach. Of course, it is important for leaders to ask open-ended questions that get members to search inwardly and to avoid the "district attorney" style of questioning in which they feel grilled and bombarded.

Reality therapy encourages clients to look at the range of freedom they do possess, along with the responsibilities of this freedom. In this sense reality therapy is a form of existential therapy. As it is currently practiced, the emphasis is on the inner needs, wants, self-evaluation, and choices made by clients (Wubbolding, 1988). Because of this focus on the perceptual and behavioral systems, reality therapy can also be considered as a cognitive-behavioral approach. A strength of the approach is its emphasis on understanding the subjective inner world of clients. This phenomenological view helps the therapist understand more fully how clients perceive their world, and such a perspective is an excellent means of establishing the rapport needed for creating an effective client/therapist relationship. Understanding the personal world of the client does not mean that therapists have to adopt a "soft" approach; on the contrary, they can demonstrate their caring by refusing to give up on the client. A therapist who consistently maintains a sense of hope that clients *can* change is often the catalyst who instills and activates a sense of optimism.

One of the strengths of reality therapy is that it is a straightforward and clear approach. Although its key principles are simple, basic, and practical, you should not conclude that the method is necessarily simple to apply in group-counseling situations. Skills need to be mastered and practiced. Using the methods effectively in groups requires training and supervision.

Reality therapy's advantages can also be seen in a group of parents with "incorrigible" children. These parents may have a common bond because of their feelings that their life is being destroyed by the acting-out behavior of their adolescent daughters and sons. A therapist can teach these parents how to apply the principles of reality therapy consistently in their dealings with their children. The parents can also be taught how to focus more on their options for changing their behavior, rather than on the problems they are having in trying to "straighten out" their children.

Reality therapy has much to offer groups of parents, groups composed of children and adolescents who are having behavioral problems and who continually get in trouble at school, groups of teachers who work with a variety of students, groups of people who recognize that their lifestyle is not working for them, and groups of people in institutions for criminal behavior.

The approach is well suited to brief interventions in crisis-counseling situations. It can be useful in working with clients who see themselves as the victims of the abusive actions of others. It is also widely used in addiction counseling and in groups with substance abusers. In many of these situations with these populations, it would be inappropriate to embark on long-term therapy that delves into unconscious dynamics and an intensive exploration of one's past.

Reality therapy appears to work effectively for a variety of practitioners in a diversity of groups, and it has been successfully used in educational settings, in correctional institutions, in various mental-health agencies, and in private practice. Its principles can be used by parents, social-welfare workers, counselors, marriage and family therapists, school administrators, the clergy, and youth workers. Glasser (1992) has successfully applied reality-therapy principles and procedures with schools, youth custodial institutions, drug-addiction clinics, and rehabilitation centers.

In summary, I see some unique values and contributions of reality therapy for group leaders. Most of its principles can be fruitfully integrated into several of the other systems that have been discussed in this book. As is true of all models, the practitioner must examine the concepts of control theory and the procedures of reality therapy to determine what elements can be effectively incorporated into his or her individual therapeutic style of facilitating groups.

Limitations of the Approach

Some critics object to reality therapy as being simplistic and superficial. I have to admit that I, too, have been critical of it on those grounds; however, I no longer feel that way. I basically agree with Glasser's view that the therapeutic procedures of reality therapy are simple and clear-cut to talk about but that actually putting them into practice is not a simple matter. A concern I still have about this approach is the danger that group practitioners will abuse the theory by applying the principles simplistically in their work. There is the danger of the group leader's assuming the role of a "preacher," or moral expert, who judges for the members how they should change. Clearly, if group members accept the leader's standards of behavior instead of questioning and struggling, they don't have to look within themselves to discover their own values. From my perspective this is a very undesirable outcome.

Though I agree that an action program is essential for changes in behavior, my personal preference is to give more attention to the realm of expressing and exploring feelings than reality therapy calls for. Once involvement is attained in a group, my inclination is to give members many opportunities to express emotions that they may have kept buried for years. Therapeutic work is deepened by paying attention to the realm of feelings. Therefore, I draw heavily on techniques from the experiential approaches as a way of helping the members fully experience their feelings, rather than simply talking about them or about problem situations. Further, I go along with transactional analysis, rational emotive behavior therapy, and the other cognitive-behavioral therapies in placing emphasis on the role of thinking as a key determinant of behavior. Many problems that show up behaviorally have a connection to the self-defeating statements that we often repeat to ourselves. So in addition to encouraging members to come into full contact with the range of their feelings, I also try to get them to look at the thoughts and beliefs that are contributing to their emotional and behavioral problems.

Another limitation I see is the tendency to carry valid points to an invalid extreme. For example, although it is true that focusing on the past can constitute avoidance of present responsibility, discounting the role of the past can easily lead to a superficial treatment of certain problems. Glasser asserts: "If clients are able to satisfy their needs now, then they will gain the ability to surmount what happened in the past. It is when the present is still filled with frustration that the past remains fresh and painful" (1989, p. 12). From my perspective, this is a large assumption! As I have maintained throughout the critiques of each approach, unrecognized and unexplored issues from our past will bring a shadow to our present experiencing and behavior. Thus, I see it as critical to explore the ways in which our experiences are manifested in our present and in our future. Some reality therapists do make it a practice to talk about the past if it is tied to the present (Wubbolding, 1988). For example, they are likely to help an adult who was abused as a child to talk about it, for this is not really purely a past event, even though it happened many years ago. The event results in a present source of pain, and therefore it is present behavior rather than past behavior. Similarly, there are some advantages to focusing on the conscious aspects of behavior, yet carried to an extreme this emphasis denies the powerful place of the unconscious in human experience. I don't see this theory as adequately explaining unconscious dynamics, dealing with ways in which the unconscious affects conscious behavior, or addressing how unconscious factors are played out within a group setting.

A final criticism of reality therapy, from a behavior therapist's perspective, would be that empirical research is lacking to justify the claims that its procedures actually work. Reality therapy is most popular with practitioners (especially in the fields of education, substance abuse, and corrections), not with research centers and universities. Thus, those who are looking for empirical data rather than advocacy data will probably be critical of reality therapy for its lack of attention to research.

Applying Reality Therapy with Multicultural Populations

Wubbolding (1990b) has expanded the practice of reality therapy to both group counseling and multicultural situations. He believes that reality therapy needs to be modified to fit the cultural context of people from areas other than North America. He puts forth the following ethical principles for adapting reality therapy to culturally diverse client populations:

◆ Reality therapy is most ethically and effectively practiced in a multi-cultural setting when its principles and procedures are adapted to the individual client.
◆ Because of the need for adaptation, reality therapy should not be viewed as a rigid and closed system that is applied in the same manner to everyone or to every cultural group, but as an open system that allows for flexibility in application.
◆ The skill in this adaptation process requires more than knowing the concepts and procedures of reality therapy. It requires an understanding of how to apply these principles and procedures to the client's culture and worldview.

Wubbolding's experience in conducting reality-therapy workshops in Japan, Taiwan, Hong Kong, Singapore, Korea, India, and Europe has taught him about the difficulty of making generalizations about other cultures. Based on these experiences, Wubbolding (1990b) adapted the cycle of counseling to working with Japanese clients. He points to some basic language differences between the Japanese and Western cultures. North Americans are inclined to say what they mean, to be assertive, and to be clear and direct in asking for what they want. In Japanese culture, assertive language is not appropriate between a child and a parent or between an employee and a supervisor. Ways of communicating are more indirect. Because of this indirect style, some of the following specific adaptations are needed to make the practice of reality therapy relevant to Japanese clients:

◆ It is not necessary to have clients verbally define their specific wants or express their goals. Also, the reality therapist's tendency to ask direct questions may need to be softened, and questions could be posed more elaborately and indirectly. Confrontation will be used to a much lesser degree.
◆ There is no exact translation for the word *plan*, nor is there an exact word for the term *accountability*, yet both of these are key dimensions in the practice of reality therapy.
◆ As counselors present dimensions such as wants of the client, the evaluation process, making plans, and committing to them, it is useful to employ a more indirect style of communication than is typically practiced in the Western version of reality therapy. For example, in working with Western clients, counselors would not settle for a response of "I'll try." In the Japanese culture, however, the counselor is likely to accept an "I'll try" as a firm commitment.

These are but a few illustrations of ways in which reality therapy might be adapted to non-Western clients. Although reality therapy assumes that all people have the basic needs (survival, belonging, power, fun, and freedom), the ways in which these needs are expressed depend largely on the cultural context. What is essential is that in working with culturally diverse clients, group leaders allow latitude for a diverse range of acceptable behaviors to satisfy these needs.

Now, let's focus on some of the broader applications of the core concepts of reality therapy from a multicultural perspective. One of these key themes is helping a wide range of clients with diverse backgrounds evaluate for themselves whether their wants are realistic and whether their behavior is helping them. Once they have made this assessment, they can make realistic plans that are consistent with their cultural values. This focus clearly empowers clients. It is a sign of respect that the group leader refrains from deciding what behavior should be changed. Through skillful and sensitive questioning, the leader can help clients determine the degree to which they have acculturated into the dominant society. They can then make a personal assessment of the degree to which their wants and needs are being satisfied by having made this decision. It is possible for them to find their own balance of retaining their ethnic and cultural identity and at the same time integrating some of the values and practices of the dominant group. Again, the group leader does not determine this for these clients but challenges them to arrive at their own answers based on their own value system.

Practitioners who lead groups composed of culturally diverse members may find such clients reluctant to share their feelings during the early phase of the group. Because of their cultural values, some clients are likely to react more positively and to cooperate to a greater degree if the focus is on what they are doing and wanting, rather than on what they are feeling. For example, some clients may be experiencing depression and anxiety, and they may hope to gain relief from these symptoms by being in a group. Thinking of these symptoms from a reality-therapy perspective, the leader could guide the members to look at what they are doing (or not doing) that is contributing to their emotional state. There is no pressure to experience a catharsis and to do emotional work within the group. Yet members eventually realize that they are "depressing" and "anxietying," rather than having these things simply happen *to* them. Once they realize that certain behaviors are not functional for their purposes, they are in a better position to make changes that will lead to different outcomes.

As is true for the cognitive-behavioral approaches, reality therapy often works with contracts. In this way the group members eventually specify particular problems that are causing them difficulty and that they would like to explore in the group. Thus, group counseling is typically cast in the framework of a teaching/learning process, which appeals to many non-Euro-American clients. There is a specific focus—namely, a certain behavioral pattern that becomes the target for intervention. The reality-therapy leader is interested in helping members discover better ways to meet their needs. To its credit, this approach provides group members with tools for making the desired changes, especially during the planning phase. With the support and help of other members and the group leader, clients can develop specific and workable plans for action. Within this context, members can be assisted in taking specific steps to move the external world closer to the inner world of their wants. If their plans do not always meet with success in everyday reality, these members can then bring concrete situations back to the group sessions. This type of specificity, and the direction that is provided by an effective plan, are certainly assets in working with minority clients in groups.

One of the limitations of using reality-therapy principles with ethnic minorities, gays and lesbians, and women is that these clients may not feel that this approach takes into account some very real environmental forces that are operating against them in everyday life. For example, discrimination, racism, sexism, homophobia, ageism, and negative attitudes toward disabilities are unfortunate realities, and these forces do limit many minority clients in getting what they want from life. If the group leader does not accept these environmental restrictions or is not interested in social change as well as individual change, members are likely to feel misunderstood. There is a danger that some reality therapists may overstress the ability of these clients to take charge of their life. Such clients may interpret the group leader's line of questioning as "If you try hard enough, you can pull yourself up by your bootstraps and become anything you choose." Group members who get such messages may prematurely leave the group in the belief that the leader and other members are not fully appreciating their everyday struggles. Rather than being a fault of the reality-therapy approach, this is more a limitation of some who practice it.

As we have seen, some clients are reluctant to say what they want. Their culture has not reinforced them for asking assertively for what they desire, and in fact, they may be socialized to think more of what is good for the social group and not to be so concerned with their individualistic wants. In working with people with this cultural background, reality therapy must be "softened" somewhat, and such clients should not be pushed to declare their wants assertively.

In writing about the multicultural applications of reality therapy, Wubbolding (1990b) notes that although the basic theory has universal application, translating principles into practice needs to be geared to the individual's cultural background. The challenge is to find ways of adapting reality therapy to the diversity we encounter in our groups, rather than expecting (or forcing) these clients to adapt to and neatly correspond with the theory. As with other theories and the techniques that flow from them, flexibility is a foremost requirement.

Where to Go from Here

The programs offered by the Institute for Reality Therapy are designed to teach the concepts of control theory and the practice of reality therapy. The institute offers a certification process, which starts with a one-week intensive seminar in which participants become involved in discussions, demonstrations, and role playing. For those wishing to pursue certification in reality therapy, a supervised practicum is arranged to best meet the needs of each trainee. There is also a second intensive week and a second practicum. The basic and the advanced practicum each entails a minimum of 30 hours over at least a six-month period. For further information about these training programs, contact either of these two organizations:

Institute for Reality Therapy
Dr. William Glasser, President
7301 Medical Center Drive, Suite 407
Canoga Park, CA 91307
TELEPHONE: (818) 888-0688

Center for Reality Therapy
Dr. Robert E. Wubbolding, Director
7777 Montgomery Road
Cincinnati, OH 45236-4258
TELEPHONE: (513) 561-1911

A useful videotape, *Using Reality Therapy in Group Counseling*, has been prepared by Robert Wubbolding. The first part of this two-hour video consists of an explanation of the basic concepts of control theory and of the stages involved in a reality-therapy group. The second part is a demonstration of a group, with a commentary from the perspective of a practicing reality therapist. This tape is available by contacting Wubbolding at the Center for Reality Therapy, at the address given above.

RECOMMENDED SUPPLEMENTARY READINGS

Glasser has written little on group counseling; however, the principles and concepts discussed in the following books easily translate to group work.

Control Theory: A New Explanation of How We Control Our Lives (Glasser, 1985) is the one book that I would recommend most highly. In this popular and easy-to-read book, Glasser discusses how we can choose to change our actions and thus gain better control of our feelings and thoughts and live healthier and more productive lives. Other interesting topics that he explores include choosing misery, craziness and responsibility, psychosomatic illness as a creative process, addicting drugs, taking control of our health, and how to start using control theory.

Using Reality Therapy (Wubbolding, 1988) extends the principles of reality therapy by presenting case studies that can be applied to group and family counseling, as well as individual counseling. This book is very clearly written with many practical guidelines for using the principles of reality therapy in practice. There are many excellent questions and brief examples. The author has extended the scope of reality therapy to include marriage counseling, the use of paradoxical techniques, supervision, and self-help. He presents reality therapy as a philosophy of life rather than a doctrinaire theory or set of prescriptions.

Understanding Reality Therapy (Wubbolding, 1991) utilizes a metaphorical approach as a way to explain the basic components in the practice of reality therapy. Drawing on his therapeutic practice, the author explains how metaphors and analogies can illuminate the ways we view the world.

The *Journal of Reality Therapy* began semiannual publication in September 1981. The journal publishes manuscripts concerning research, theory development, and specific descriptions of the successful application of reality-therapy principles in field settings. Subscriptions are $12.00 a year. If you are interested in subscribing, contact:

Dr. Lawrence Litwack, Editor
Journal of Reality Therapy
203 Lake Hall
Boston-Bouve College
Northeastern University
360 Huntington Avenue
Boston, MA 02115

REFERENCES AND SUGGESTED READINGS*

*Dowd, E. T., & Milne, C. R. (1986). Paradoxical interventions in counseling psychology. *The Counseling Psychologist, 14*(2), 237–282.

Glasser, N. (Ed.). (1980). *What are you doing? How people are helped through reality therapy.* New York: Harper & Row.

*Glasser, N. (Ed.). (1989). *Control theory in the practice of reality therapy: Case studies.* New York: Harper & Row (Perennial).

Glasser, W. (1965). *Reality therapy: A new approach to psychiatry.* New York: Harper & Row.

Glasser, W. (1969). *Schools without failure.* New York: Harper & Row.

Glasser, W. (1976a). *Positive addiction.* New York: Harper & Row.

Glasser, W. (1976b). Reality therapy. In V. Binder, A. Binder, & B. Rimland (Eds.), *Modern therapies.* Englewood Cliffs, NJ: Prentice-Hall.

Glasser, W. (1980). Reality therapy. An explanation of the steps of reality therapy. In N. Glasser (Ed.), *What are you doing? How people are helped through reality therapy.* New York: Harper & Row.

Glasser, W. (1981). *Stations of the mind.* New York: Harper & Row.

Glasser, W. (1984a). Reality therapy. In R. Corsini (Ed.), *Current psychotherapies* (3rd ed.). Itasca, IL: F. E. Peacock.

Glasser, W. (1984b). *Take effective control of your life.* New York: Harper & Row.

*Glasser, W. (1985). *Control theory: A new explanation of how we control our lives.* New York: Harper & Row (Perennial).

*Glasser, W. (1986a). *The basic concepts of reality therapy* (chart). Canoga Park, CA: Institute for Reality Therapy.

Glasser, W. (1986b). *Control theory in the classroom.* New York: Harper & Row (Perennial).

Glasser, W. (1986c). *The control theory-reality therapy workbook.* Canoga Park, CA: Institute for Reality Therapy.

*Glasser, W. (1989). Control theory. In N. Glasser (Ed.), *Control theory in the practice of reality therapy: Case studies.* New York: Harper & Row (Perennial).

*Glasser, W. (1992). Reality therapy. *New York State Journal for Counseling and Development, 7*(1), 5–13.

Huddleston, J. E., & Engels, D. W. (1986). Issues related to the use of paradoxical techniques in counseling. *Journal of Counseling and Human Service Professions, 1*(1), 127–133.

Powers, W. M. (1973). *Behavior: The control of perception.* Hawthorne, NY: Aldine Press.

Weeks, G. R., & L'Abate, L. (1982). *Paradoxical psychotherapy: Theory and practice with individuals, couples, and families.* New York: Brunner/Mazel.

*Books and articles marked with an asterisk are suggested for further study.

*Wubbolding, R. E. (1988). *Using reality therapy*. New York: Harper & Row (Perennial).

Wubbolding, R. E. (1990a). *Evaluation: The cornerstone in the practice of reality therapy*. Alexandria, Egypt: Omar Center for Psychological and Academic consultations, Studies, and Services.

Wubbolding, R. E. (1990b). *Expanding reality therapy: Group counseling and multicultural dimensions*. Cincinnati: Real World Publication.

*Wubbolding, R. E. (1991). *Understanding reality therapy*. New York: Harper & Row (Perennial).

*Wubbolding, R. E. (1992). *Cycle of counseling and supervision and coaching using reality therapy* (chart). Cincinnati, Center for Reality Therapy.

Wubbolding, R. E. (1993). Reality therapy with children. In T. R. Kratochwill & R. J. Morris (Eds.), *Handbook of psychology with children and adolescents* (pp. 288–319). Boston: Allyn & Bacon.

◆ PART THREE ◆

APPLICATION AND INTEGRATION

CHAPTER SIXTEEN
Illustration of a Group in Action:
Various Perspectives

CHAPTER SEVENTEEN
Comparisons, Contrasts, and Integration

Illustration of a Group in Action: Various Perspectives

To give you a better picture of how the various approaches discussed in Part Two actually work, this chapter describes a model group in action. It explores the different ways in which practitioners of various orientations would deal with some specific issues and aspects of group work. To describe fully how all the orientations might be used in a group of ten people and two co-leaders would prove cumbersome. Thus, in order to simplify this project, I give a brief description of the group's members and their problems and then demonstrate how several therapeutic approaches might be functional for each case. For this purpose I have selected what I consider to be typical themes that emerge in many groups. I present each theme and then show how some of the approaches might deal with it. It needs to be stressed that this chapter reflects my own biases and experiences with respect to the group themes I've selected, as well as my personal interpretation of how the various leaders would work with their groups. The actual implementation of any specific model, as well as the techniques and style of the group leader, would naturally vary from my description.

The Model Group

Our model group is a closed and time-limited group with ten members (five women and five men) and two co-leaders. The setting is a community mental-health center, and our group is a part of the group-therapy program that the center offers to adults who have problems coping effectively with the demands of everyday living. These adults might be termed "normal neurotics"; although none of them is seriously disturbed, they all experience enough anxiety to seek therapy as a way of dealing more successfully with their personal problems.

All the group members have had some individual counseling, they are joining the group voluntarily, and they have agreed to come to all of the sessions, which take place once a week for two hours for the duration of the group. The group will meet for 20 weeks, during the course of which no new members will be admitted. Before making the decision to join the group and attend all its sessions, the members participated in a presession in which they met with the co-leaders to get acquainted and determine whether they wanted to have this type of group experience.

The Emerging Themes

The ten themes I've selected from among the many that typically emerge during the life of a group are the following:

1. clarifying personal goals
2. creating and maintaining trust
3. dealing with fears and resistances
4. coping with loneliness and isolation
5. resolving dependence/independence conflicts
6. overcoming the fear of intimacy
7. dealing with depression
8. searching for meaning in life
9. challenging and clarifying values
10. dealing with the termination of the group

I approach these themes by describing how they apply in concrete ways to various members of our model group. For each theme, I present the *essence* of what these members explore at different sessions. Then, I show how the co-leaders of the group, using the various theoretical approaches, could deal with these themes, the individual members, and the group as a whole. I conclude by describing how I would use concepts and techniques from these various approaches to deal with some issues characteristic of the ending stages of a group.

Theme: Clarifying Personal Goals

As you know, in most groups the initial sessions are devoted to exploring group goals and clarifying the members' personal goals. Following is the essence of what each member of our model group hopes to get from participating:

> *Emily* (age 23, single, lives at home with her parents and attends college): I hope to get up enough courage to finally attempt to make it on my own. Though I don't like living with my parents because it limits me, I must admit that it's a comfortable arrangement.
>
> *Ed* (age 60, an engineer, twice divorced and now living alone, has had drinking problems for years): I'm afraid of being isolated, but I'm also afraid that people will reject me. I want to learn to

deal with these fears and with my depression and anxiety without having to resort to drinking.

Beth (age 55, a widow with two teenage sons living at home, has devoted most of her life to taking care of her sons and others): Maybe I could learn how to ask for something for myself without feeling so terribly guilty.

Robert (age 28, single, a social worker, has difficulty forming close interpersonal relationships, is afraid of women, and tends to "use" them): Sometimes I feel dead and numb, and I wonder if I'll ever change. I expect to work on my fears of getting close to women.

Joanne (age 35, three children and a miserable marriage, has recently returned to college): I decided to stay with my husband until I finish college and get a good job and until my kids go to high school. I want to reexamine this decision and determine if the price is too high.

Sam (age 34, married, hates his work in maintenance and wants to change it but is not confident enough to do so): Besides making some vocational decisions, I hope to leave this group feeling better about myself and my possibilities.

Sharon (age 25, an executive secretary, lives with a man despite her parents' objections): I'm confused about what I really hope to get from this group. I know I feel guilty for letting my parents down, but I don't know if a group will help me or not.

Randy (age 47, a high school teacher, has been abandoned by his wife, who took the children with her): I can't concentrate. I keep thinking of her and our kids. I want to be able to deal with the anger and the pain I feel much of the time.

Judy (age 38, single, a university professor, is struggling to find new meaning for her life): I keep asking myself, "Is this all there is to life?" I think I have a lot to be thankful for, yet I often feel empty. I want to take another look at my values and see if they still fit.

Boyd (age 22, a college student, lately has experienced moments of panic, anxiety, and some bouts of depression): There have been times that I wanted to commit suicide, and it scares me. I hope to understand some of my feelings. Also, I hope to find out that I'm not the only one who feels like this.

Some Therapeutic Approaches

Co-leaders with a *behavioral, TA,* or *reality-therapy* orientation will probably begin by having each member state his or her goals as clearly and concretely as possible. They will help the members formulate specific contracts for their own work, contracts that will provide a direction for the group. For example, in working with Robert, leaders with these orientations will have him clarify what it is that he fears about women and how he sees himself as keeping distant. This effort may lead him to formulate a working contract as follows: "I agree to work with the women in this group by openly exploring my reactions to them. By dealing with the feelings I have toward women in the group, I may get a clearer understanding of the impact I have on women in general." As another example, Beth—the person who has trouble asking for what she wants—may be helped to develop a list of her specific wants and to formulate a contract to explore her feelings about trying to satisfy these wants.

One form of a behavioral group is the *multimodal* approach to therapy, which takes the whole person into consideration. Comprehensive group therapy entails the correction of irrational beliefs, deviant behaviors, unpleasant feelings, bothersome images, stressful relationships, negative sensations, and possible biochemical imbalances. The group process is characterized, from this perspective, by a broad assessment that may include questions such as the following: "What are your major strengths? What keeps you from getting what you want? What behaviors would you like to acquire, and what ones do you want to eliminate? What are some emotions that are a problem for you? How do you see yourself now? What are the values that give your life the most meaning? What are some ways in which you satisfy your intellectual needs? What is the quality of your relationships with others? What do you give to others, and what do you get from them? What is the state of your health?" This process of initial assessment brings out some central and significant themes that can be productively explored in a group. It gets clients to think about what is going on in their life and encourages them to formulate personal goals that will give the group some direction.

From the *reality-therapy* perspective, the group leaders will help members make an evaluation of what they are presently doing to determine the degree to which their behavior is getting them what they want. The leaders may ask any of the following questions of the members to stimulate this self-evaluation: "What do you have in your life now that you most value? What is at least one thing that is missing in your life? If you had what you wanted now, how would your life be different? What can you begin to do today to get what you say you want? How can you best use this group to get what you want?" The aim of this line of questioning is to get members to realize that if what they are doing, thinking, and feeling is not satisfactory to them, they have the power to change and choose better behaviors.

In an *Adlerian group* there is an emphasis on cooperatively working out the goals that will govern the direction the group takes. One leader might say: "Since this is your group, I'd like to hear from each of you what you expect from this group. What are the ways you'd like the group to function? After each of you has a chance to state your expectation, perhaps we can spend some time formulating what rules you'd like to have in place." The focus will be on identifying what members most want to accomplish. Cooperation on a common therapeutic task is essential if change is to occur.

Theme: Creating and Maintaining Trust

Trust soon becomes an issue as the group gets under way. Members will often question their ability to trust the group leaders, the other members, and even themselves.

Judy, the professor, says: "I'm concerned that what I say to the group will not remain in the group. I have no reason to distrust anybody in here; still, I know that I have some reservations about revealing myself to the group."

Sharon expresses her lack of trust in herself: "I've never been in a group before, and I don't know if I'll fit in here or what is appropriate. I mean, I don't even know how to let others know what is going on within me, and I'm afraid that if I do let people know, I'll just bore everybody."

Boyd doubts whether the leaders are competent to deal with what he calls his "heavy" feelings, such as suicidal impulses. "I'm afraid you guys will just try to cheer me up or maybe tell me I'm really crazy. Also, I'm worried about what the other people here will think about me."

Typically, groups focus on issues of trust, such as those illustrated by the examples just given, during their early stages. It is clear that if members are to drop their defenses and reveal themselves—as indeed they must if the group is to be effective—they need assurance that the group is a safe place to do this. More importantly, they need a *reason* to reveal themselves. Thus, members must see that by being open and taking risks, they will understand themselves more fully.

Helping to build trust in the group is a vital task for group leaders, and the way in which they approach the group is of crucial importance. In this section I summarize some comments that might be made by practitioners of the various orientations during the early stages of a group. Note that the leaders try to promote trust by specifying what the group is designed to do and by indicating how the group process will work. Also note how their comments clearly reveal their different orientations.

Some Therapeutic Approaches

The following are summaries of what the leaders of various group models might say to the group in attempting to clarify the general purposes and goals of the group. These statements would certainly contribute to the building of a climate of trust.

PSYCHOANALYTIC GROUP. "In this group we'll be paying a lot of attention to what is going on in the here and now, with particular attention on your reactions to one another. We'll look for patterns in the way you relate, and my job is to help you see how your earlier experiences are still relevant to the way you perceive others and react to them."

ADLERIAN GROUP. "In this group we'll be focusing on your style of life as it becomes evident through your behavior in here. We'll also be giving attention to some of your early recollections, your memories of what it was like for you to be in your family, and how your position in your family might be still affecting you. A group is an ideal place to make changes in your life, for the group is a microcosm of your social world. In here we'll encourage you to try on new behaviors and to put your insights into action by testing them in this group and in your encounters in daily life."

PSYCHODRAMA GROUP. "In this group you'll act out—not just talk about— your conflicts, and you'll reenact emotionally significant scenes. By releasing pent-up feelings, you'll gain more insight, and you'll experiment with more spontaneous ways of behaving."

EXISTENTIAL GROUP. "Here each of you can discover how you've restricted your freedom. Our main task is challenging you to assume the responsibility for your own choices and to search for a more real existence. We hope to share ourselves with you in the process."

PERSON-CENTERED GROUP. "Our job is to facilitate, not direct, this group. In part this means helping to make it an accepting and caring group. Since we assume that each of you has the capacity to know what you want, we also assume that once you see this as a safe place, you'll drop your pretenses and show your real selves. We believe that you'll eventually learn to trust yourselves and to rely on your own judgments."

GESTALT GROUP. "We'll stay as much as possible in the here and now and deal with whatever prevents you from maintaining a present-centered awareness. Our focus will be on the *what* and *how,* rather than the *why,* of behavior. With this focus, which will help you express parts of yourselves that you've denied, we expect that you'll eventually become more integrated and whole. Above all, we're here to assist you in identifying the unfinished business from your past that's impeding your present functioning."

TRANSACTIONAL-ANALYSIS GROUP. "Each of you is our colleague in your own therapy. We don't presume the right to special knowledge about you; rather, we assume that *you* will decide on the course of your work in here, largely by developing clear contracts that will specify what you want to change and how you want to do it."

BEHAVIOR-THERAPY GROUP. "We assume that if you've learned in-effective behavior, you can learn new, constructive behavior. The group will offer a context for this learning. Our task is to teach you new coping skills; your task is to practice these skills, both within and outside the group. The group will give you the support needed to reinforce any changes you make, so that they become an integral part of you."

REBT GROUP. "Although others may be largely responsible for indoctrinating you with self-defeating beliefs, we hold you responsible for maintaining such beliefs. Accordingly, we'll be active in getting you to critically evaluate your processes of self-indoctrination. Group work will be directed toward replacing your current irrational belief systems with a rational philosophy of life."

REALITY-THERAPY GROUP. "Since we believe that each of you is seeking to gain better control of your life, our main goal in this group is to assist you in determining whether your current behavior meets your needs adequately. If you discover that it doesn't and if you decide to change, it will be your responsibility to formulate a plan of action designed to promote change. The group will offer you a place to practice this plan for change, and outside homework assignments will help you carry these changes into your everyday behavior."

Theme: Dealing with Fears and Resistances

During the early stages of the group, members typically express fears about getting involved and display resistance toward any attempt at delving into deeply personal concerns. Some members keep their fears about becoming involved in the group to themselves, whereas others seem eager to express their fears and put them to rest so that they can begin to work. Whether or not the fears are expressed, they tend to give rise to some ambivalence: the desire to reveal oneself is balanced by the reluctance to expose oneself. Following are some typical expressions of the ambivalence:

- ◆ Why do I have to reveal my private feelings in this group? What good will it do anyhow?
- ◆ I'm afraid to get involved, because I may make a fool of myself.
- ◆ I'm afraid that if I say what I really think and feel, the group will reject me.
- ◆ If I see myself as I really am, I may find that there's nothing inside me.
- ◆ I'm afraid that by becoming too involved in this group, I may make my problems bigger than they really are.
- ◆ If I get too involved in the group, I'm afraid I'll become too dependent on it for solving problems that I have to handle alone.
- ◆ Right now my life is rather comfortable; if I become too involved in the group, I may open up a can of worms that I can't handle.
- ◆ I'm afraid that the group will strip away my defenses and leave me vulnerable.
- ◆ I'm somewhat afraid of disclosing myself to others, not only because of what *they* may think but also because of what *I* might find out about myself.
- ◆ I want to protect myself by not letting myself care. If I get too close to people in the group, I'll feel a real loss when it ends.

Some Therapeutic Approaches

PSYCHODRAMA GROUP. The co-leaders will encourage members to express their concerns and fears by talking directly to one another. The message could be delivered thusly: "I'd like each of you to share some of your fears about being in this group now. As you do so, look at different members in the group, and let them know how you experience your fears. I hope you'll talk to one another in this group, rather than talking about your fears and concerns. If you have a reaction to anyone in the group, again, I'd ask that you speak directly to him or her. There is a great deal more power in what we say when we encounter one another directly."

PSYCHOANALYTIC GROUP. Psychoanalytically oriented leaders see resistance as a basic part of the group process. Since in this model resistance to self-knowledge often presents itself in the form of resistance to others, dealing with resistance to the group is an essential aspect of therapy. At appropriate times the leaders may interpret the individual members' resistance to the group. The aim is to help members learn about themselves by exploring their reactions to other group members, who serve as catalysts to evoke early memories.

GESTALT GROUP. Gestalt leaders tend to deal with resistance by inviting members to rehearse their fears out loud. For example, Ed, who holds back because of his fear of being rejected by the group, may be asked to stand in front of each group member and complete the sentence "You could reject me by . . ." Next, he may be asked to make the rounds again, this time to finish the sentence "You would reject me if you knew . . ." By completing the sentence in a different way with each member, Ed can express the full spectrum of the fears of rejection that he normally keeps inside of himself. The goal is to render the fears less compelling and to take some steps toward dealing with them.

REBT GROUP. Taking the example of Ed again, leaders of this orientation may confront him with questions such as "What would be so terrible if everyone in here *did* reject you? Would you fall apart? Why do you tell yourself that rejection is such an awful thing?" The attempt here is to show Ed that he has uncritically bought the irrational idea that he will not survive if he gets rejected. The leaders may then invite other members to express similar irrational fears and then proceed to teach the group members that they are responsible for making themselves emotionally disturbed by unquestioningly accepting such irrational notions.

EXISTENTIAL GROUP. During the early stages of a group, members may express their fears that if they take a look at themselves, they may find that they are empty or that they are not the person they have convinced themselves they are. This confrontation with oneself can be terrifying for some, and in an existential group these fears are openly acknowledged and worked with. The group leaders may ask the members to close their eyes and imagine that these fears of theirs are actually occurring in this group. For example, Robert, who is afraid of women and closeness with them, can imagine his worst fears happening in the group. Judy may confront her fears that she is living without any values of her own. And Boyd can allow himself to imagine his panic over the times he has feared he might want to kill himself. This is the first step in making a commitment to themselves and the group to face and deal with their fears.

Theme: Coping with Loneliness and Isolation

Randy, the high school teacher who has been abandoned by his wife and children, is the exponent of this theme. He keeps asking himself: "Why did she leave me? Am I to blame for what happened? Will I ever be able to trust anyone again? Will I be able to get over the pain of this breakup?"

Some Therapeutic Approaches

PERSON-CENTERED GROUP. The co-leaders may invite Randy to tell his story in detail. While he does so, they pay full attention not only to what he is saying but also to his nonverbal expressions of pain over his losses and his feelings of being utterly alone and abandoned. The leaders' attention and the support of the group stimulate him to fully experience and share the intensity of his feelings.

The group leaders may notice that Ed, who has had similar experiences, appears deeply moved, and they will ask him to express what he is feeling. Ed may reveal that he is identifying with Randy and that he still feels torn up over his second divorce—a revelation that may cause Ed and Randy to spontaneously talk with each other, which in turn may provoke other members to share what they are feeling and demonstrate that they care about the two men. The support of the leaders and of the group as a whole would tend to encourage a full and open expression of both men's feelings, which previously may have been bottled up.

PSYCHODRAMA GROUP. The leaders are likely to ask Randy what he would like to understand more fully about the breakup of his marriage. Randy replies, "There are a lot of things that have gone unsaid—things that I feel stuck with, things that I'm afraid I won't ever say." Randy is then asked to go to the stage area and say what he fears he'll never to able to say. When he has done so, he is asked to "become his wife" and, in this role, to say all the things he imagines that she would say. This exchange of roles is continued until the group can get a feeling of how Randy sees his wife.

Next, Randy is asked to select a member to play his wife's role. He picks Joanne and begins by expressing his hurt—his feelings of loneliness and loss. Joanne (as his symbolic wife) responds. Eventually his pain turns to anger; he begins to release the bottled-up anger yet keeps blocking it with self-deprecating remarks. At this point Robert, the member who has difficulty with women, is selected as Randy's double and steps next to Randy, shouting many of the things that Randy seems to be cutting off with his guilt. By having someone speak in his behalf, Randy may be able to eventually release his most intense, deepest rage.

When this scene has finally served its purpose, the leader may ask Randy to fantasize a future as he would wish it, say, five years from now. In this fantasy he sees his wife and children reunited with him. He is then asked to act out a scene from this future as he would wish it to be, playing his wife's role as well as his own. During the course of this psychodrama Randy recalls how his wife's departure vividly reminded him of the scene when his mother left him after she divorced his father. The importance of this connection would be underscored by the leader, who might suggest to Randy that he could deal with his childhood experience later within the group.

REBT GROUP.   The approach of the leaders to Randy's problems will focus on getting him to stop his vicious self-blaming. Members of an REBT group are quickly taught the A-B-C model of therapy. In Randy's case, the Activating event (A—that is, his wife's leaving) is not the cause of his misery now. Rather, the cause is his response to the Activating event—namely, his irrational Beliefs (B). Specifically, his response is to keep telling himself that because his wife left him, he is rotten; that if his wife does not love him, nobody will or can; that if he had not been basically worthless and *if only* he had been different, his wife would still be with him. Thus, the emotional Consequence (C) of his emotional pain is due not to his wife's departure but to his faulty and illogical thinking. In the REBT group other members will confront Randy with his self-destructive style and persuade him to consider changing his thinking.

In the course of this work it is discovered that Randy has been avoiding making contacts with other women because he has convinced himself that no woman could *ever* want anything to do with him. Thus, the leaders challenge him to attack this self-defeating notion of basic unworthiness. He is asked to role-play asking a woman in the group for a date, and the male co-therapist coaches him in this play by showing him how to be assertive. Randy is given an opportunity to discuss his fears of getting involved again, which can lead him to begin differentiating between realistic and unrealistic fears. He receives a homework assignment, such as the task of initiating and maintaining a conversation with some women at his place of work. He is asked to keep a written record of his reactions to these encounters and to report the results to the group at its next session.

ADLERIAN GROUP.   In working with the theme of loneliness and isolation, the leaders will probably pay attention to Randy's family constellation and his early recollections. It is assumed that he wants to belong, to feel useful, and to have a place of significance in his family of origin. One leader asks: "Randy, describe each sibling as you remember the person. I'd be interested in knowing how you saw yourself in relationship to each of your siblings." Randy responds: "I can remember how alone I felt at home as a kid. My bigger brother got all the attention, and I was sure I'd never measure up to him. I often felt that I didn't belong in our family, especially when he was around. I just couldn't seem to get any of the attention no matter what I did! Just saying all this brings back the feelings of loneliness that I felt so often as a child."

The Adlerian therapists may explore with Randy ways in which he is trying to garner sympathy. One therapist could ask: "Are you aware of how you actually got attention by being neglected in your family?" Because of the assumption that all behavior is purposeful, Randy is asked to explore not only the ways he received attention but also what this attention actually did for him.

Theme: Resolving Dependence/Independence Conflicts

Emily, the group member who is living with her parents and going to college, discusses the resentment she feels toward them. According to Emily, her parents control her life, are responsible for her insecurity, and make it difficult for her to break away and live on her own. She has admitted that she finds living at home comfortable. As she begins delving further, she sees that she is frightened of taking increased responsibility for her own life and that her parents are scapegoats for her own inability to become independent. In the group she struggles with conflicting desires—a desire to remain secure by clinging to what is known and a desire to assume more responsibility for directing her own life. She is torn between wanting to become her own parent (doing for herself what she now expects her parents to do for her) and fearing the added responsibility of increased maturity.

Some Therapeutic Approaches

REALITY-THERAPY GROUP. If Emily discusses her problem in a reality-therapy group, the leaders may confront her tendency to blame her parents as follows: "You seem to be getting a lot of mileage from making your parents responsible for your dependency. Also, you seem to dwell on the past too much, almost as if you were clinging to it as an excuse for not being the free person you say you want to be. Using your past to justify your current 'inability' to make decisions keeps you from getting in touch with your power. As long as you hold onto your past and blame your parents, you never really have to take an honest look at yourself."

The aim of this approach is to get Emily to evaluate her current behavior and to accept the role she is playing now; exploring her feelings or discussing her changing attitudes is of little interest here. The pivotal question for her is "Do I want to continue my dependent behavior, or do I want to change it?" If she decides that she does want to change, she will then be asked to develop a plan of action, which will include definite steps toward behaving more independently, and a contract to change, which will include a commitment to try new behavior outside the group.

EXISTENTIAL GROUP. Assume now that Emily brings up her dependence independence conflicts in an existentially oriented group. It is probable that one of the co-leaders will ask other group members if they can identify with her. In our model group Joanne, who has a desire to leave her secure but boring marriage, Sharon, who feels guilty for not living up to her parents' expectations, and Beth, who may see herself in the parental role with respect to Emily's conflict, can all identify with Emily. In the existential group Emily, Joanne, Sharon, and Beth may be asked to form an inner circle and sit in the center of the group. The leader may instruct this subgroup to "discuss all the ways that you are unfree now, talk about how it feels not to be in charge of your own life, express your fears of giving up your security in order to gain independence, and examine the advantages of remaining dependent."

The purpose behind this exercise is to provide these four participants with an opportunity to fully explore how they feel and think about their practice of giving up their power to others. The aim is to assist them to see clearly what keeps them secure (and unfree) and to determine honestly the cost of this security.

TRANSACTIONAL-ANALYSIS GROUP. The leaders may take one or more of several exploratory paths—for example:

◆ identifying and analyzing the games that Emily is playing
◆ working on her life script to determine how she is following a plan for life drawn up by her parents
◆ assisting her in seeing the typical ego state in which she functions (probably the Child ego state, at least with respect to her parents)
◆ exploring the injunctions that she has lived by, as well as her early decisions

The exploration of Emily's injunctions can involve many group members who share similar injunctions, such as "Don't grow up"; "Don't disappoint your parents"; "Don't think for yourself"; "Don't trust yourself"; "Do what is expected of you." The sharing of Emily's injunctions can provide other members with a valuable catalyst for examining the ways in which they have incorporated parental messages without thinking about them. Similarly, the sharing of an early decision that she has apparently made— "Let your parents take care of you, because you are not able to take care of yourself"—will be used by the group to explore other instances of early decisions.

BEHAVIOR-THERAPY GROUP. Emily will probably be asked to specify ways in which she would like to change her relationship with her parents. Next, she may be invited to role-play herself with the co-leaders, who act as her parents. In this role play she is directed to tell her parents what she would like to change in their relationship.

Later, other members may be invited to give Emily feedback answers to questions such as "Was she assertive? Is her style effective for the purpose of having her parents listen to her?" If the feedback indicates that Emily comes across as being apologetic, the female co-leader may step in to demonstrate a direct style for clearly stating desires without apologies. Emily may then be asked to replay her role with the symbolic parents, using the information that she has just received. If appropriate, the group may then offer positive feedback, pointing out and supporting assertive behavior on her part.

Theme: Overcoming the Fear of Intimacy

Another theme is exemplified by Robert's difficulties in forming close relationships of any kind, particularly intimate relationships with women. As he describes his struggles, he mentions several times that often he feels numb and emotionally dead. He worries that something is basically wrong with him, because he finds it hard to care for fellow group members who express psychological pain. As he puts it: "As some of you go through 'heavy' stuff, I feel detached, sort of cold and isolated. I'm not letting myself identify with anybody in here, and that makes me wonder if I'd ever be able to care and if I have the capacity to get intimately involved with anyone. I feel sort of dead inside." The themes that are evoked and explored in the group include the fear of intimacy (and the need for intimacy), feelings of isolation and deadness, and, to some extent, feelings of hopelessness.

Some Therapeutic Approaches

GESTALT GROUP. The leaders focus on Robert's ambivalence toward intimacy. First, he is asked to face each woman in the group and state his worst fear about getting close to her. Next, he is asked to concentrate on his here-and-now fears toward the women in the group. Then, he is asked to conduct a dialogue between the two sides of himself from two chairs.

As he sits in one chair and plays the side of him that wants to care and get involved, he says: "It feels lonely and cold behind the walls that I build around myself. I work so hard to keep people out. I want to get out of the walls, but I'm afraid of what is out there." As he sits in the other chair and plays the side that wants to remain behind those walls, he says: "Stay behind those walls that you've worked so hard to build. You're isolated, but at least you're safe. You know what happens whenever you let yourself really care: you always get burned, and that pain isn't worth the effort of getting involved." This dialogue, which may continue for about five minutes, helps Robert become more aware of the polarities within him, without forcing him to choose between his two sides yet.

BEHAVIOR-THERAPY GROUP. The therapists will use relaxation and desensitization techniques to approach Robert's fear of intimacy. Relaxation techniques, which are taught to the entire group, consist of systematically tensing and relaxing all the muscles in the body. They are practiced daily at home.

A practical application of relaxation techniques to Robert's difficulties may proceed as follows: He is instructed to construct an imaginary hierarchy of interpersonal situations ranging from those that would produce the least amount of anxiety to those that would produce the most. He is then asked to use the techniques that he has learned to become extremely relaxed. Next, he is guided through a fantasy about an interpersonal situation that, according to his hierarchy, generates the least degree of anxiety—say, merely seeing a woman that he is attracted to. This is followed by fantasies of situations involving greater and greater anxiety. As soon as Robert experiences anxiety, he is instructed to "switch off" that scene and relax. In this manner he may manage to work himself up to sustaining fantasies about a high-anxiety-producing situation—for example, approaching a woman and initiating a conversation with her.

At another session Robert may practice behavioral rehearsal, putting himself into a real-life situation in the group. For example, after inviting him to assume that Sharon is a woman that he would like to date, one leader may ask him: "How would you let Sharon know that you are interested in her? Assume that you and Sharon are actually on a date. What might your conversation be like? Pretend that you are saying good-bye. What would you tell her about your feelings concerning her and your evening with her? What is it that you hope you could say?" After this rehearsal, the leader asks Robert to select a woman in his everyday life that he would actually like to make contact with and, with the help of other group members, to develop a homework assignment relating to making that contact—an assignment that he is to practice during the week and to report on during the following session.

The action-oriented behavior-therapy approach has Robert challenge his fears of intimacy, not analyze their cause. He begins in the relative safety of his fantasies as guided in the group situation, progresses to dealing with his feelings toward a female member of his group (Sharon) by role playing (behavior rehearsal), and finally applies his newly acquired skills to his everyday life.

REBT GROUP. The description of the behavioral group could easily fit the REBT group. The REBT leaders, however, are more likely to challenge Robert's perceptions about the catastrophic consequences of becoming intimate. The emphasis here is on teaching him that he is stopping himself by his fears, many of which are unfounded or based on irrational beliefs. The aim is to have him put himself in situations where he has to critically appraise his beliefs regarding emotional closeness. As in the behavioral approach, he is expected to carry out homework assignments.

TRANSACTIONAL-ANALYSIS GROUP. The leaders may well focus on exposing and working with an early decision that Robert made—for example: "If you open yourself to being loved by others, or if you let yourself care about others, you are bound to be hurt. Thus, it's best to seal off your feelings and become emotionally numb, because then you won't feel the pain." After some initial probing, the leaders may have him reconstruct a specific, relevant scene with his parents when he was 10 years old. With the help of the leaders, he attempts to experience the scene as completely as possible, including the feelings of helplessness that he felt as a child. In that manner, he may be led to see that a decision concerning closeness that he made as a helpless child served his survival needs *then* but is no longer an appropriate basis for his actions *now*.

Following this reconstruction, wherein Robert can experience the intensity of his fear of closeness, the leaders have him engage his cognitive faculties by asking him to consider *when* and *why* he made his early decision and to think about how that decision impedes his relationships in the present. Finally, some of his injunctions—for example, "Don't get close"; "Never let people know what you're feeling"; "Don't trust women"; "Don't feel"—may be challenged.

PSYCHOANALYTIC GROUP. The leaders may use Robert's response to them as a therapeutic device, and the following scenes may ensue: The male leader points out that Robert typically avoids, and appears uncomfortable with, the female leader. Robert admits his discomfort, explaining that he sees her as a dynamic and insightful woman who, he feels, could use her power to hurt him. While maintaining the focus on Robert's feelings toward the female leader, the therapists draw parallels between his responses in the group and his relationships with his mother and sisters.

Assuming that the interpretations are apt and timely, Robert may make some fruitful associations between how he behaved in his mother's presence and how he behaves in the group. He may begin to see how he is transferring some of his childhood feelings for his mother to the female leader. (This transference is encouraged, because it provides useful material that will eventually allow him to work through some of his attitudes toward women.) At the same time he may become aware of the ways in which he is competing with the women in the group for the therapists' attention—a behavior that may relate to his childhood behavior of competing with his sisters for their parents' attention. Whatever the insights, they are merely the beginning of significant work in a psychoanalytic group. In Robert's case, awareness of a connection between his childhood experiences and his current fear of closeness would be followed by an effort to use the transferences that have occurred with respect to women in the group to work through his fears of closeness.

Theme: Dealing with Depression

One common theme that emerges is exemplified by Ed (the oldest person in the group), who is chronically depressed and, like Robert, feels isolated and incapable of breaking out of his isolation. After two divorces, he sees himself as a failure in maintaining relationships; thus, he lives alone rather than risk further failure. Ed, an admitted alcoholic, describes how his drinking has ruined his personal and professional lives and how all these failures have left him feeling hopeless, helpless, and in great need of alcohol for comfort. After some limited success with Alcoholics Anonymous, he clearly sees that booze doesn't solve his problems and that he is guilt ridden by his failures in life and weakness for alcohol. Now he wants to probe deeper into the reasons that compel him to seek refuge in drinking—reasons that he realizes are merely symptomatic of personality problems. He also realizes the importance of coming to grips with his bouts of depression.

Some Therapeutic Approaches

PERSON-CENTERED GROUP. Leaders of a person-centered group will work to develop a climate of acceptance and trust in which Ed can express his feelings. By providing an example of accepting attentiveness, the leaders let him know that he has permission to feel what he feels and share these feelings with the group. In this manner someone like Ed, who punishes himself with disapproval and rejection and expects the same treatment from others, may for the first time feel that he is accepted and acceptable. Armed with this new view of himself, he is in a far better position to probe the reasons behind his drinking.

PSYCHOANALYTIC GROUP. The leaders will focus on any dependencies that Ed may develop with respect to the group—for example, dependence on the leaders for decision making and dependence on other members for support and approval. They may direct him toward exploring how he views each therapist, what he wants from them, and how he uses them (as he used his parents) to get confirmation as a person. By examining his need for approval from the group leaders, he may become aware, for instance, that he never really felt loved by his parents and that he grew up believing that not achieving perfection meant that he was a failure.

By exploring his reactions within the group, particularly with respect to the group leaders, and with the help of some interpretations by them, Ed begins to draw parallels between his interactions with his parents and family and his interactions with the group leaders and other members. For several sessions this association is explored in greater depth, and he begins working through his feelings toward each therapist. Eventually, he may find that in many ways he is making the leaders his symbolic parents (expecting them to respond to him as his parents did and keeping himself a helpless child waiting for their approval) and, more generally, that he is reliving his past in the group.

In future sessions Ed may work on his inordinate need for approval and love, on his extreme dependence on others to direct him, and on his taking refuge in drinking to blunt the anxiety of not feeling loved. Thus, he could fruitfully explore the roots of his excessive drinking and come to understand that it is both an escape from anxiety and an attempt to create the illusion of being the powerful person he would like to be.

REALITY-THERAPY GROUP. A way of describing the reality-therapy approach to Ed's problem is to contrast it with the approach of the psychoanalytic group:

◆ Since reality therapy focuses on future success, not on past failure, Ed is not allowed to dwell on his past.

◆ Whatever reactions he has toward the leaders, they are assumed to be generated by the present therapeutic relationship and not to be the result of transference or distortions from his past.

◆ The co-therapists actively work at having him look at his current behavior and decide whether this behavior is getting him what he wants. If he decides that his behavior is dysfunctional, he is challenged to develop a plan for change.

◆ The leaders discourage Ed from focusing on his feelings of hopelessness, despair, isolation, and dependence; rather, he is encouraged and directed to examine what it is that he is *doing* now that contributes to these feelings. To direct this examination of how his actions are contributing to his feelings, the leaders ask questions such as "What exactly did you do today from the time you woke up to now? You say that you feel despair and isolation; taking the last week, could you tell us specifically *what* you did whenever you had such feelings? How did your behavior contribute to your feelings? What do you see that you *can* do before our next session to begin to change your pattern? Are you willing to take specific steps that involve behaving differently? What are some constructive things that you can do when you feel a need to drink?"

◆ Regarding Ed's stated desire to penetrate the reasons underlying his drinking problem, the reality therapists will probably say: "We don't go looking for causes from the past to explain what we view as current ineffective behavior. Insight into the unconscious reasons for your behavior is not our concern. Instead, we want to talk about your options for beginning to actually decide on a course of action that will lead to responsible and effective behavior."

TRANSACTIONAL-ANALYSIS GROUP. The TA approach to Ed's "theme" will probably include the following elements:

◆ Work focuses on Ed's life script, which in his case may be captured succinctly in the phrase "drinking myself to death" and his supporting injunctions such as "Don't think!" "Don't succeed!" "Don't be competent!" In the group he may work on his process of developing his life course, so that he can come to see that his current script, "drinking myself to death," may be a self-fulfilling prophecy.

◆ The therapists may also point out the ways in which Ed is slowly killing himself psychologically by keeping himself isolated. In the group, time is devoted to examining the games he plays, along with the payoffs for these games. Eventually, he is led to see that his games are related to a purposeful plan. (That is, if he plays his games long enough, he will eventually collect enough bad feelings to justify the final ending of his script, which could be suicide. This would fulfill his basic injunction "Don't be!")

The aim of the work in the TA group is to help Ed understand *how* and under *what conditions* he formulated his original decision—for example: "Don't trust yourself, because you'll always fail. Instead, expect others to decide for you, because you're incapable of directing your own life." Once Ed sees how he made his decision, and once he becomes aware of the games he plays—even in his group—he can be led to see that he doesn't have to continue being the victim of an early decision and that he is now in a position to make a new decision.

Theme: Searching for Meaning in Life

Boyd, the 22-year-old college student who experiences much anxiety and entertains occasional suicidal thoughts, shares with the group the acute panic he feels because of his fantasies of killing himself. He says that even though he has a large quantity of life left, he cannot see that it will have much quality, and he wonders why he should go on. Like Ed, Boyd feels anxiety about making choices, and, like Ed—who is taking the slower route of alcohol—he wants to "end it all." When Boyd reveals the emptiness of his life, Judy says that she identifies with his problem. Despite her success as a professor, she is struggling to find meaning.

After making an assessment of suicidal risk and determining that there is no present danger, various practitioners may proceed as follows.

Some Therapeutic Approaches

EXISTENTIAL GROUP. The leaders may well use the fact that Judy identifies with Boyd's problems. They will ask both of them to sit in the center of the group to discuss their perceptions of how their life has lost meaning and to explore their sense of emptiness in greater depth. When this dialogue has run its course, the leaders invite other members to talk about aspects of their own life that have grown stale. Using these discussions as a basis, the leaders may then work with Judy, Boyd, or any of the other members on a variety of themes:

◆ Life doesn't have meaning by itself; it is up to us to create meaning in our life.
◆ Feelings of emptiness and a sense that life has lost its meaning may signal the need to begin building new meanings. The sense of purposelessness can be a sign that we are ready for a change.

◆ If we don't like the direction in which we are moving, we need to ask what we can do to change the direction and what we are doing to prevent change.
◆ We must accept responsibility for our own capacities and limitations and for what we are becoming.

In working with Judy, existential group leaders may focus on some of the paths she is taking to find meaning in her life—for example, her work, her relationships with others, and her leisure-time activities. In the existential view the anxiety that she is feeling over what she terms "emptiness" is not seen in negative terms; rather, it is viewed positively as a potential growth force. The fact that she is questioning her values to determine the extent to which they still hold meaning for her indicates that she is ready for change. Her anxiety is seen as a natural response to the contemplation of change.

In working with Boyd, the existential group leaders may look beyond the obvious implications of his suicidal thoughts to discover how alive or how dead he is feeling with respect to the life that he still has. Here again his anxiety over his death impulses may be seen as a positive sign, as though he were actually saying: "I want more from life than I am receiving. No longer am I content with merely existing; I want to be *alive!*" In short, his anxiety will probably be viewed as an impetus for changing his life in such a way that he will *want* to live.

BEHAVIOR-THERAPY GROUP. Behaviorally oriented leaders approaching the themes exemplified by Boyd and Judy will first help the two members define in concrete and specific terms what they want to explore. General goals, such as trying to find meaning in life, coping with emptiness, or experiencing existential anxiety over outworn projects, are far too vague for these leaders. Their focus will be on specifics, as seen in the following dialogue between Judy and one of the co-leaders, who is helping Judy define a specific area on which to focus in the group.

Judy: I have a vague feeling of hollowness, as if my life didn't have any unifying purpose. I question the meaning of life.

Co-leader: You're not being specific about this lack of meaning. Could you pinpoint what it is that you'd like to change?

Judy: What I'd like to change is the emptiness I often feel. I want to feel that what I'm doing matters, that my life has meaning.

Co-leader: I'd like to hear more about how your life is for you.

Judy: I feel that when I'm needed and appreciated, there's meaning in my life. When I'm unrecognized, I feel that my life is empty.

Co-leader: Right now, could you list some of your activities that make you feel good and also list specific things that lead you to feel unappreciated?

Judy: I think I could, but not right now. Maybe before our next group meeting.

> *Co-leader:* Fine. Let me make a suggestion. Before we meet again, try to pay attention to the conditions that tend to be associated with either a feeling of purpose or the sense of emptiness you describe. Carry a notebook, and jot down a few notes concerning what you actually *do* in situations attached to these feelings. In this way we'll have a better sense of what you're doing, and we can work on specific areas of change.

As can be seen, the behavior therapist is attempting to break down the task into manageable parts—to identify specific behaviors that can be observed and to develop specific goals that can be measured. Rather than working on broad existential concerns such as the meaning of life, the leader focuses on behaviors that contribute to Judy's feelings of emptiness and teaches her how to observe such behaviors. One can readily see how a similar approach would be taken to Boyd's case.

ADLERIAN GROUP. In the cases of Ed, Boyd, and Judy—all of whom are searching for meaning—Adlerian procedures are quite appropriate. Adlerians assume that people are motivated by goals; the function of a group is to help members identify their life goals. This is done by asking them to look at what they are striving toward. Questions that can be asked are "What are you after? Where are you going? What is your image of the central goal that gives your life meaning?" For members such as Boyd, Judy, and Ed, attention is given to their life plan, including their fictional goals. For example, Ed probably developed in early childhood a fictional image of what he would like to be in order to be safe and to feel that he belonged. His assessment of his early experiences might well be inaccurate, and his lifestyle today could be based on his striving for goals that he had as a child. Ed may have learned that drinking was a way for him to escape from painful reality. When he drank, he felt strong and superior, and eventually his whole life became centered on drinking. With alcohol he could convince himself that he was all that he wanted to be. However, this style of life is now proving to be ineffective, and Ed is seeing how empty his life is. With the encouragement of the group, he begins to challenge his mistaken beliefs, gains more awareness of how he has deceived himself by living in fantasy, and starts talking about ways to find new goals that will provide him with meaning in life.

GESTALT GROUP. Judy's declaration that she feels empty will probably be met by a question about how she experiences this emptiness. Let's postulate that Judy answers such a question as follows: "Sometimes I feel as if I'm alone and lost in a desert. In fact, last night I had a dream about just that, about being lost in a desert. I was dying for lack of water—all I could see was rocks, sand, and one cactus bush with thorns on it. Then I stumbled across a well, but when I dipped into it, the well was bone dry. I began to cry, but there were no tears."

The Gestalt leaders will probably focus on Judy's dream as a way of helping her experience her emptiness more fully. They don't interpret her dream; rather, they help her discover the meaning of her dream for herself by asking her to *become* selected parts of her dream, giving them a voice and speaking in the present. What follows is a sample of this dream work:

Co-leader: Judy, I'd like you to become the cactus with thorns and speak as if you were the cactus bush.

Judy: Nobody better get close to me; if you do, I'll stick you. I'm all alone here, and that's the way I want to be. It's taken me a long time to grow these thorns, so stay away!

Co-leader: Now let yourself become the rocks.

Judy: I'm hard; nothing can get to me. I'll last forever. Nothing can get inside me.

Co-leader: What are you experiencing now?

Judy: In many ways I'm like that rock and thorny bush. People can't really get to me. I'm hard and protected.

Co-leader: And how does it feel to be hard and protected?

Judy: Safe. Yet, at the same time I'm lonely out here on this empty desert.

Co-leader: Now I'd like you to become the well. Try to speak as if you were the well in your dream.

Judy: I look as if I could keep you from dying of thirst—as if I could nourish you. Yet, when you dip inside me, you'll find that I'm all dried up. There's really no water deep inside me—I'm just a bottomless pit, dried and empty.

This process of becoming various parts of her dream can enable Judy to make connections between the different parts of her dream and her own life. She apparently fears that although people see her as a bright and talented person with much to offer (a full well), she actually has nothing of value to offer (an empty well). Although the Gestalt technique of dream interpretation doesn't solve her problem of emptiness or end her quest for meaning, it does help her move closer to experiencing her emptiness and becoming aware of her fear that she is the one who is keeping people out of her life.

Theme: Challenging and Clarifying Values

Sharon, the 25-year-old executive secretary who is living with a man over her parents' objections, feels comfortable with her lifestyle yet is uncomfortable about her parents' strong disapproval. According to Sharon, her parents feel that she is letting them down and that unless she gets married, she is not worthy of their respect. She is in pain over the loss of their esteem: "I don't really expect them to agree with me, and I can accept their right to think as they do. What troubles me, though, is that I'm really hung up on their refusal to let me live my life as I see fit. In order to live life as I want to, I have to decide to be disowned by them."

Some Therapeutic Approaches

PSYCHODRAMA GROUP. The directors will probably want to know whether Sharon remembers any time as a child when she wanted parental approval and didn't receive it. Let's say that she recalls a time when she decided not to go to church anymore—a decision her parents could not accept, although they had no way of forcing her to continue attending church. The directors help her reenact this childhood scene with the help of two group members who play her parents. The following are a few possibilities for a psychodrama format:

- ◆ Playing herself as a child, Sharon says all the things now that she thought and felt but never said when her parents withdrew their affection.
- ◆ She asks her parents (still as the child) to respect her and allow her to have her own life.
- ◆ The symbolic parents play their roles either as rejecting parents or as accepting parents.
- ◆ Other group members stand in for Sharon and say things that she finds difficult to express.
- ◆ Sharon projects a scene with her parents in the present that incorporates an interaction with them as she would wish it to be. In this case she coaches others to be the parents she would want.

Following the psychodrama there is an effort to connect Sharon's present problem with the feelings she had as a child. The ways in which she now pleads with her parents for approval could be much like her dynamics as a child. The experience of the psychodrama could at least help her see how to deal with her parents in a more direct and mature way than she typically does.

PERSON-CENTERED GROUP. The leaders will give Sharon the freedom to express and explore her feelings about the pain she feels over the loss of her parents' esteem. If the members and facilitators can really understand her struggle between wanting to live her own life and wanting parental acceptance, she is likely to gain more clarity on this issue. The facilitators probably do not introduce any techniques; rather, Sharon is invited to talk about her feelings, values, and thoughts. The goal is not to get the group's validation, for this would be the same as her striving for her mother's and father's validation. Instead, it is hoped that as she explores her conflicts, she will come to trust her ability to find a direction in life that is acceptable to her. The primary goal in this type of group is to foster a climate in which the actualizing tendency can freely express itself. If the members and the facilitators can show Sharon respect and positive regard, if they can understand her struggle as she experiences it, and if they can show her warmth and caring, it is likely that she will profit from the group experience and move forward in a constructive manner. With the support of the group, she will find within herself the answers she is searching for, and she will probably rely less on others to confirm her worth as a person.

PSYCHOANALYTIC GROUP. From an analytic perspective, Sharon can be viewed as having a passive, dependent attitude toward her parents. In some ways she is keeping herself infantile by looking at them to feed her and nourish her as a person. She has not given up the fantasy of being the type of young girl that her parents wanted; this frustration of her need to be seen as the "ideal daughter" by her parents may bring about feelings of insecurity, disillusionment, and anxiety. The leaders, and other members as well, can interpret her behavior as seeking the parents she has always wanted. She may now be treating others in the group as she treated her parents. She may look to the leaders and some members to tell her how she should live her life and how she could win their unconditional love.

At the working stage Sharon may regress and reexperience some old and familiar patterns, which will be seen as material to be worked through in the group. How she behaves in the group sessions provides some clues to the historical determinants of her present behavior. The group therapists make timely interpretations so that some of her past can be brought to the surface. Another focus will be guiding her in working through her transferences with the leaders and other members. In the group situation it is probable that she has re-created her original family; this transference interferes with her accurate appraisal of reality, since she is now projecting onto others in the group feelings she had for her parents.

ADLERIAN GROUP. As in the psychoanalytic group, interpretation will probably be a central therapeutic technique. However, Adlerian interpretation is different from psychoanalytic interpretation in that it is done in relation to Sharon's lifestyle. No time is devoted to exploring the possible causes of her struggle to win her parents' approval. Instead, the focus is on the here-and-now behavior that she displays, on her expectations that arise from her goals, and on ways in which she can begin to challenge her thinking and thus make changes in her behavior. In the Adlerian group she is invited to consider the leaders' interpretations of her striving for parental approval. She explores her style of life to see how searching for approval may be a theme. The interpretation is focused on her goals, purposes, and intentions, as well as on her private logic and how it works. As she gains insight, through referring to her basic premises and to the ways these beliefs are mistaken, she can begin the process of modifying these cognitions and thus find ways of leading a more satisfying life. The focus of the work is typically of a *cognitive* nature, for it is assumed that if she changes her beliefs, her actions will also change.

GESTALT GROUP. The leaders will probably focus on a specific behavior related to Sharon's problems—say, the fact that she speaks in a soft and pleading voice. To help her get in touch with what she is doing, the leaders can ask her to exaggerate her mannerism—for example: "Go around to each group member, and be as apologetic as you can be. Keep your eyes fixed to the ground, and tell everyone how much you need them to approve of you; then apologize for being a bother to them."

Through this exercise Sharon may gain an awareness of how her general style expresses tentativeness and how her demeanor invites people to feel sorry for her. Since, as suggested by her statement above, she would like to deny her apologetic aspect, this exercise is aimed at exposing this aspect by exaggerating it. The leaders may then ask her to bring her parents into the room and speak to them openly and candidly, in the way she would like to. Next, she is asked to switch places and "become her parents," in order to answer what she has just told them and to disclose what they may be thinking of her yet not saying. This shifting in and out of roles—Sharon playing herself and then "becoming her parents"—continues until she can identify unfinished business from her past that is getting in her way now. In the process she may work on her feelings of resentment, anger, and fear toward her parents.

Theme: Dealing with the Termination of the Group

Up to this point I've given examples of how the various approaches to group therapy might be practiced with respect to the themes that have emerged in the model group. Although it is valuable to practice working within the framework of each theory as you learn about it, there is no need to limit yourself to practicing any one model exclusively. Instead, you can integrate various components from all these models and begin to develop your own leadership style—a style that suits your personality and the kind of group you may lead. To assist you in thinking about ways to integrate these different group models into your personal style, I will now describe how I would use concepts and techniques from the various approaches in dealing with some typical issues that I observe during the last few sessions of most groups: wrapping up, saying good-bye, consolidating learning, closing out personal issues, applying group learning to daily life, and evaluating outcomes.

Feelings of Separation and Loss

The final stage of a group is a difficult time. The members are aware that their community is about to dissolve, and they are beginning to mourn their impending separation. Some of them are pulling back; they are becoming less intense and are no longer contributing much new material to work on. Others wonder whether they'll be able to maintain the openness they have learned in the group once they can't count any longer on the group's encouragement and support. They fear that in their everyday life they won't find people who give them the kind of support they need to keep experimenting with change and, as a consequence, that they may regress to old ways.

If I were leading our model group, I would want to give its members an opportunity to fully express their feelings about the termination of the group. The *person-centered* approach, which stresses listening actively and giving permission to explore whatever feelings are present, offers a useful model for this phase of group work. Here members don't need much direction; rather, they need to be encouraged to face the reality that after sharing in an intense experience, they will soon be going their separate ways. It is necessary to allow members to talk about any unfinished business they may have concerning their own problems or other members. If participants can fully express their feelings about separation, the transition period between leaving the group and carrying what they've learned in the group into their day-to-day life will be made easier.

I have often observed the fear on the part of many group participants that they won't be able to create in their everyday life that which they have experienced within the group. Here I apply the concepts of the *rational emotive behavior* approach and encourage participants to substitute rational ideas for what appear to be unfounded beliefs about separation from the group. The following examples may shed light on this process:

◆ *Irrational belief No. 1:* "In this group I can be open and trusting, but I don't think this is possible in my everyday life."
◆ *Rational belief No. 1:* "I can be open with selected others, and I'm largely responsible for initiating trust in my relationships."

◆ *Irrational belief No. 2:* "I don't see any way I can do all of the things I learned in the group in my everyday life."
◆ *Rational belief No. 2:* "If I choose to, I can create in my daily life the kind of relationships I valued in this group; that will enable me to be the kind of person I want to be wherever I am."

◆ *Irrational belief No. 3:* "In the group I received support for the changes I made and valued; in my everyday life most people won't like many of my changes, and they won't give me the support I need to maintain them."
◆ *Rational belief No. 3:* "I probably won't receive support or even approval for the changes I have made and will make, but I'm no longer in desperate need of support from everyone."

The process of helping members challenge their beliefs about separation and about incorporating what they've acquired in the group can be most valuable. My goal is to help participants see that their group has been a place where they could learn *how* to form meaningful interpersonal relationships, a process that is not restricted to the group but that can be applied in any setting.

In this regard there is some value in helping participants understand any connections that might exist between their past and their family, on the one side, and the relationships they have developed within the group, on the other. For that purpose the *psychoanalytic* approach is useful. In some ways the group represents a new family for its members, and by relating their behaviors in the group "family" to their behaviors in their actual families, members can learn much about themselves. To assist participants in their process of making connections among behaviors, I ask them to consider the following questions:

- ◆ To whom was I drawn in this group?
- ◆ With whom did I have the most conflict?
- ◆ In what ways did my feelings and actions in this group resemble the ways in which I felt and acted as a child in my family?
- ◆ Were my reactions to the group leaders in any way similar to my reactions to my parents?
- ◆ What did I want from them?
- ◆ How did I react toward them?
- ◆ Did I experience feelings of competitiveness or jealousy within the group?

Looking Ahead

Another tool I use as the group is drawing to a close is the development of fantasies. I find that too often group members don't allow themselves to imagine creatively how they would like to experience their life. To assist them in their endeavor, I ask members to picture themselves and their life in some ideal future circumstance, a technique that is used by both the *Gestalt* and the *psychodrama* approaches. Applying the fantasy technique to the case in point, I might suggest to members the following:

- ◆ Imagine that you are attending a reunion of the group five years from now and that we are meeting to discuss how our life has changed. What do you *most* want to be able to say to us at this reunion?
- ◆ Let yourself fantasize about all the ways in which you want to be different in your everyday life once you leave this group. Close your eyes, and carry on a silent dialogue between yourself and the people who are most special in your life. What are you telling them? What are they replying?
- ◆ Imagine that a year has passed since we ended the group. Also imagine that nothing has changed in your life—that you have continued the way you have always been. Try to picture how you would feel.

I have found that some members and the group in general might benefit by sharing fantasies. For this purpose a brief Gestalt exercise that has members be themselves in the future and carry on a dialogue with significant people is useful. (In this exercise the members themselves play all parts in the dialogue.) Role-playing exercises are also helpful. For example, I sometimes ask participants to select a member of the group to role-play a person in their life. The role play begins by having the participant briefly tell the person selected what it is that he or she would like to change in their relationship and *how* he or she intends to make those changes.

Also during the final stages of the group, I ask the members to review what they have learned about their early decisions as a result of participating in this group, an approach characteristic of both *transactional analysis* and *rational emotive behavior therapy*. To stimulate this review, I typically question the members as follows:

◆ Do you want to revise any of these early decisions?
◆ Are these decisions still appropriate for you now?
◆ What new decisions do you want to make?

In addition, I ask members to review what they've learned concerning the games they play, as well as the payoffs from these games, and to think about specific ways in which they might experiment with game-free behavior outside of the group. Further, I ask members to identify, even write down, the self-defeating statements with which they continue to indoctrinate themselves, to share them, and to offer one another feedback concerning the validity of these self-statements, as well as suggestions on how to combat self-destructive thinking.

Toward the final stages of the group, I rely heavily on the cognitive and action-oriented approaches characteristic of the *behavior therapies, reality therapy, rational emotive behavior therapy,* and *transactional analysis.* I see the group as a learning laboratory in which the members have identified the specific changes that they are willing to make and have experimented with new behaviors. Assuming that this has indeed occurred, it becomes extremely important that the members carry out their own action-oriented programs outside the group. During the last session I have members work in small groups to formulate a *specific* contract—a brief statement of the plans they have concerning behavioral changes once the group ends. The aim of this small-group work is to have members clearly define what they now want to do and how they specifically intend to do it. The results of the efforts are then shared with the entire group. Finally, I try to schedule a follow-up session—usually several months after the termination of the group—for the purpose of allowing members to discuss, from that perspective, what the group meant to each of them as well as to report on the extent to which they have fulfilled their contract.

My experience has taught me that members tend to forget some of what they learned and to discount the actual value of what they did in the group. To help prevent this from occurring and to help members retain whatever they have learned—about others, about human struggling, about life, and about themselves—I ask them at the final session to review specific insights they had throughout the course of the group. It is my contention that unless one articulates and shares with others the specifics of what one has learned in the group, one's group experience may soon become an indistinct blur.

Here, again, I find the principles of the *behavioral* approaches useful during the final session—specifically, the application of feedback principles to help members strengthen the perceptions that they gained during the course of the group. For example, I often ask members to complete feedback sentences for every member in the group, such as:

- ◆ "One of the things I like best about you is . . ."
- ◆ "One way I see you blocking your strengths is . . ."
- ◆ "My hope for you is . . ."
- ◆ "My greatest concern or fear for you is . . ."
- ◆ "The way I'll remember you in this group is . . ."
- ◆ "A few things that I hope you'll remember are . . ."

Focused feedback, whether verbal or written, can give the participants a good sense of the impact they had on others in the group.

As the final session draws to a close, I give members a message to take with them—a message grounded in the *existential* approach: "I hope you have become aware of your role and of the responsibility you bear for who you are now and for who you are becoming. I hope you will no longer blame others for your problems and will no longer see yourself as a victim of circumstances outside of yourself. Many of you have become aware of the choices that are open to you; thus, you can now reflect fruitfully on the decisions you will make. Even if you decide to remain largely as you are, you now are aware that you *can* choose, that you don't need to have others design your life for you. Although choosing for yourself can provoke anxiety, it does give you a sense that your life is yours and that you have the power to shape your own future.

Behavioral approaches stress developing clear goals, working on these goals during the sessions, and then evaluating the degree to which these goals were met. I see that what members do after the group ends is as important as the group sessions. Therefore, I tend to devote ample time to suggesting ways in which members might consolidate their learning and carry it into daily living. Specifically, I encourage members to develop the habit of keeping a journal—writing down the problems they are encountering, describing how they feel about themselves in specific situations, and listing their successes and difficulties in following through with their contracts. Because I feel that an appropriate book read at an appropriate time can be a powerful catalyst in helping people make the changes they want to make, I encourage members to read as a way of continuing to work on themselves and to grow.

Finally, and as mentioned earlier, I see it as important to schedule a follow-up group meeting several months after the end of the group to allow members to evaluate the outcomes of the group experience for themselves and to evaluate the group as a whole. In this connection I offer members some guidelines for evaluating themselves and their group experience, as well as topics to discuss at the follow-up group meeting.

CHAPTER SEVENTEEN

Comparisons, Contrasts, and Integration

The purpose of this chapter is fourfold: (1) to compare and contrast the various models as they apply to issues special to group work; (2) to raise some basic questions that you'll need to answer now and throughout the course of your practice; (3) to challenge you to attempt an integration of the various perspectives that is consistent with your personality; and (4) to stimulate your thinking about ways of developing and refining group techniques that reflect your leadership style. The questions that this chapter will help you answer include these:

- Is it possible to achieve some integration of the diverse group models by focusing on their commonalities?
- How would an integrated view of the various perspectives actually help you define your own goals of group counseling?
- How do you go about blending concepts and techniques from several approaches to achieve your own definition of the leader's role and your own unique leadership style?
- How can you achieve an optimum balance between responsible leadership and responsible membership, whereby you accept your rightful share of responsibility for the direction of the group without usurping the members' responsibility?
- How much structure does a group need?
- How do you develop techniques that are consonant with your personality and style and are also appropriate for the kinds of group you lead?
- What are some of the possible abuses and misuses of group techniques?
- How can the techniques of the theoretical approaches be modified to fit the cultural backgrounds of various clients?
- What are the advantages and the dangers of an eclectic approach to group practice?

The Goals of Group Counseling: Various Perspectives

In order to impart meaningful direction to their groups, leaders need to address themselves to the issue of goals. What should be the specific goals of a given group, and who should determine them? How can the leader help group members develop meaningful goals for themselves? How does the leader's theoretical orientation influence the process of goal setting? Is it possible to set group goals based on a variety of theoretical orientations?

To help you find common denominators among the goals stressed by the various theoretical models and to guide you in your attempt to integrate these models, I've brought together in Table 17-1 (p. 487) the essential therapeutic goals of each of the group approaches discussed in the preceding chapters. As you read the table, keep in mind that the diversity of goals can be simplified by seeing the goals as existing on a continuum from general, global, and long-term objectives to specific, concrete, and short-term objectives. Existential and relationship-oriented group approaches tend to deal with broad goals, and behavioral and cognitively oriented systems focus on short-term, observable, and precise goals. The goals at opposite ends of the continuum are not necessarily contradictory; it is just a matter of how specifically the goals are defined. Thus, a convergence is possible if practitioners view concrete short-term goals as components of broad, long-range goals.

Most theoretical perspectives agree on the importance of group members' formulating their own specific goals. When leaders decide that they know what is best for the participants and force their own goals on them, they typically encounter resistance. To be sure, leaders need to have some overall goals for the group, but such goals should in no way infringe on the members' freedom to select personal goals that will give direction to their work in the group. The individual goal setting is an ongoing process that needs to be constantly reevaluated. The leader can be of invaluable assistance in this regard by encouraging members to formulate clear and specific goals for themselves and by helping them determine how they can work toward achieving these goals.

Role and Functions of the Group Leader: Various Perspectives

Should the leader be a facilitator? a therapist? a teacher? a catalyst? just another, albeit more experienced, group member? a technician? a director? an evaluator? some or all of these?

How you answer these questions will depend in part on your theoretical perspective, but ultimately your answers will be based on your own definition of the leader's role and on your own assessment of what the most significant functions of the leader are. There are also certain criteria that cut across all the theoretical approaches—for example, the type of group and its goals, the setting, the nature of the participants, and the demands of your job.

Before discussing the various perspectives on the group leader's role and functions, let's briefly review some of the tasks that I consider essential to successful group leadership:

1. Group leaders initiate and promote interaction by the way they structure the group and model behaviors. Thus, they demonstrate how to share, take risks, relate honestly and involve others in interactions. They can also share their leadership functions so that group members are able to become increasingly independent and don't need to lean on the leader to initiate and direct every action in the group.

2. Group leaders have the task of orienting members to the group process, teaching them how to get the most from their group, and helping them become aware of the group dynamics. These goals are achieved by encouraging members to look at the direction their group is taking, to determine whether there are barriers that prevent them from working effectively, and to become aware of any hidden agenda that could obstruct the flow of the group.

3. Group leaders must be capable of sensitive, active listening. Only by paying full attention to the members' verbal and nonverbal communication can they help participants move toward a deeper level of self-exploration and self-understanding. If attending skills are lacking, genuine empathy and understanding between group leader and participants are not possible.

4. Group leaders are responsible for creating a climate conducive to exploring personally significant issues. Trust needs to be established early in a group, and the leader has a crucial role in building an atmosphere in which people can reveal themselves, behave in new ways, and question their basic beliefs and assumptions.

5. Group leaders are responsible for setting limits, helping establish group rules, and protecting members. Although leaders don't have to prepare a lengthy list of "dos" and "don'ts," they do need to establish certain ground rules. They need to inform members of their rights and responsibilities, stress the importance of the issue of confidentiality throughout the group's life, and take the necessary steps to ensure the physical and psychological safety of the group members.

6. Finally, group leaders need to direct attention to ways in which people can profit as much as possible from the group experience. They can do this by clarifying, summarizing, and integrating what has gone on and what has been learned, by helping members crystallize their feelings and new insights, and by encouraging them to decide on action programs that will facilitate applying what they have learned in the group to their outside lives.

As we have seen, each therapeutic approach stresses different functions for the group leader. For example, the person-centered approach emphasizes the role of facilitator. Since in this model the group is seen as having the resources to direct itself, the leader is supposed to facilitate rather than direct group process. Other approaches see the leader as a teacher. Rational emotive behavior therapy, reality therapy, Adlerian therapy, behavior therapy, and transactional analysis are all based on the assumption that group counseling or therapy is essentially an educational and learning process, and consequently the leader's key function is teaching skills and providing a cognitive framework that will lead to reeducation and behavioral changes.

Other models, such as the psychoanalytic approach, focus on the role of the group leader as a technical expert who interprets intrapsychic and interpersonal processes as they manifest themselves in a group. Still other models, such as the existential, the person-centered, and the Gestalt approaches, stress the leader's role in helping members gain an experiential awareness of their conflicts through meaningful relationships with the leader and others in the group. As we have seen, your roles and functions as a group leader are many; which of them you choose to emphasize is partly determined by your theoretical orientation. As you review the different perspectives summarized in Table 17-2 (pp. 488–489), consider what elements you want to incorporate from each of them in defining your own role as group leader.

Degree of Structuring and Division of Responsibility: Various Perspectives

Group leaders often struggle with the question of what constitutes the optimum degree of structure in a group. It should be clear that all groups have a structure. Even the least directive group leaders, who avoid imposing a format on the group, do make the choice of having an open structure and letting the participants determine the course of the group.

Group structuring exists on a continuum, from extremely nondirective to highly directive. On the nondirective end of the continuum are psychoanalytic groups, person-centered groups, and some existential groups. In these groups the leaders tend to assume a passive stance and encourage group members to give direction to the group. One aspect of the learning value of these groups is that the members assume much of the responsibility.

At the opposite end of the continuum are those leaders who provide a high degree of structure for the group. They often use structured exercises to open the group sessions; also, they employ techniques to focus members on specific themes or problem areas and to intensify certain emotions and conflicts. Many behavior-therapy groups are characterized by a very directive group leadership. Typically, there is a progression from session to session, the meetings are organized in accordance with a predetermined agenda, and certain procedures are used to direct the group toward exploration and resolution of specific problem areas.

Like structuring, division of responsibility can be conceptualized in terms of a continuum. At one end are those group leaders who see themselves as experts and who believe that they should actively intervene to keep the group moving in ways that they deem productive. The group's outcomes are seen as very dependent on the leader's skills. Thus, explaining members' failures in terms of their insufficient motivation or lack of ego strength is considered a rationalization on the part of the leader, who, being the expert, is the one who has failed and is the one responsible for the failure of the treatment plan. Behaviorally oriented group leaders embrace this view.

The rational emotive behavior approach, too, places a large share of responsibility on the group leader. Since therapy is considered an educative process, the group leader is seen mainly as a teacher in charge of the reeducation of the group members. For effective results, group therapists are expected to employ a rapid-fire, didactic, persuasive methodology aimed at cognitive restructuring. However, despite the highly directive role REBT assigns to the leader, it also places a considerable share of responsibility for directing the group on the members, who are expected to be active, work hard, and practice between group sessions.

At the other end of the continuum are group leaders who expressly announce at the beginning of a group that the members are responsible for themselves and that what they get (or fail to get) from a group depends on them and them alone. This type of leadership is characteristic of the person-centered leader, who sees the participants as the ones who truly know what is best for them. The leader does not assume responsibility for actively directing the group process; he or she functions as a facilitator by attempting to create a trusting climate wherein members can safely explore deeply personal issues and search for the necessary resources within themselves.

Somewhat in the middle of the continuum are Gestalt group leaders. They are typically active, in that they intervene with techniques that provide the group with structure, but they also insist that group members are responsible for whatever they experience. The group process is seen as a way of helping the participants become aware of how they are denying personal responsibility and learn how to rely on themselves for their own support. Group leaders are responsible for being aware of their own experience throughout the group process and for introducing appropriate techniques to intensify group work. Members are responsible for bringing up issues that they want to investigate in the group and for making their own interpretations. Table 17-3 (pp. 489–490) gives you an idea of the variety of theoretical positions on structuring and division of responsibility.

My view is that group leaders need to achieve a balance between assuming too much responsibility for the direction of the group and assuming too little. If clients are perceived by the leader as not having the capacity to take care of themselves, they soon begin to live up to this expectation. Besides undermining members' independence, leaders who assume an inordinate amount of responsibility burden themselves greatly. They tend to blame themselves for whatever failures or setbacks the group suffers. If members do little productive work, these leaders see it as their fault. If the group remains fragmented, they view this as a reflection of their lack of skill. In short, this style of leadership is draining, and the leaders who use it may soon lose the energy required to lead groups.

On the other hand, leaders who place all the responsibility for the direction and outcomes of a group on the participants may simply be trying to avoid their own role in the success or failure of their groups. Thus, if a group seems to go nowhere, these leaders avoid asking themselves whether their leadership or lack of it is a contributing factor.

The Use of Techniques: Various Perspectives

Techniques are quite useful both as catalysts for group action and as devices to keep the group moving. But techniques are just tools, and like all tools they can be used properly or misused. When leaders fall into a pattern of employing methods mechanically, they become technicians and are not responding to the needs of the particular group they are leading. Also, indiscriminate use of techniques tends to increase the resistance level of the group instead of facilitating deeper communication. Some leaders, overly eager to use new methods, treat them as if they were a bag of tricks. Others, out of anxiety over not knowing how to deal with certain problems that arise in a group, try technique after technique in helter-skelter fashion. In general, group leaders should have sound reasons for using particular methods of intervention, and an overreliance on technique is, in my view, questionable. Techniques need to be an extension of who the leader is as a person, and group leaders should not force themselves to use methods that don't suit their personality and their unique leadership style.

My basic assumption is that techniques should facilitate group process, not artificially create action in a group. I also assume that they are most effective when the group leader learns how to pay attention to the obvious. They can deepen feelings that are already present, and they should grow out of what is going on in the group at the time. There is always something going on in a group, and this material can suggest appropriate methods. Although my colleagues and I sometimes use techniques to introduce material at the initial stage of a group and often use them to integrate what members have learned at the final stage, we generally do not have a preset agenda. We take our cues from what is occurring within the group and flow with that, rather than attempting to direct the group to pursue a specific theme. For example, if I notice that there is little energy in the room and that nobody appears willing to do significant work, I don't introduce an exercise designed to stir up feelings or promote interaction. Instead, I may let the group know that I am feeling strained from taking too much responsibility for keeping the group alive, and I try to get some assessment of what each person is experiencing.

In choosing techniques to facilitate group process, you must consider several factors. Your theory, of course, will influence what methods you employ. If it focuses on cognitive aspects, your techniques are likely to encourage clients to look for the connection between their thought patterns and their actions. If you have a Gestalt orientation, your techniques will tend to promote an awareness of present feelings and an intensification of these feelings. If you are behaviorally oriented, many of your techniques will be geared to getting members to monitor their actions and experiment with specific behaviors. Your style of leadership also has much to do with what methods you will use. Finally, the population with whom you are working, the purpose of your group, and the stage of development of the group are all factors to consider in the selection of techniques.

To avoid using techniques routinely, leaders must understand the relationship between techniques and theoretical concepts and be fully aware of why they are using certain methods; that is, they must have an idea of what they expect to occur. In addition to having a rationale for using group techniques, leaders need to continually assess their effects.

As illustrated by Table 17-4 (pp. 491–492), the various group models offer a variety of strategies for initiating and maintaining group interaction. There is no reason why group practitioners should restrict themselves to the techniques of a single approach simply because that's the approach they favor. For example, group leaders with an existential orientation can comfortably draw on techniques from the behaviorally and cognitively oriented models. In summary, leaders need to use their imagination to discover ways of adapting techniques from various theoretical models to the specific type of group they lead and of modifying them to suit their leadership style.

Group Work in a Multicultural Context: Various Perspectives

Each of the theories presented in this book has been briefly examined for its relevance to culturally diverse populations. As can be seen in Table 17-5 (pp. 492–493), each perspective has certain concepts or techniques that can contribute to effective multicultural group counseling. Yet they all have some limitations, and caution is needed in using certain techniques that flow from a given theory (see Table 17-6 on p. 494). Technical eclecticism seems especially necessary in working with a diverse range of cultural backgrounds. Harm can come to group participants who are expected to fit all the specifications of a given theory, whether or not the values espoused by the theory are consistent with their own cultural values. Rather than stretching the client to fit the dimensions of a single theory, leaders must make their theory and practice fit the unique needs of the client. This requirement calls for group leaders who possess knowledge of various cultures, awareness of their own cultural heritage, and skills to assist diverse clients in meeting their needs within the realities of their culture.

It is essential for leaders to be able to assess the special needs of clients. Depending on the group member's ethnicity and culture and also on the individual concerns that bring a member to a group, the leader will need to show flexibility in utilizing diverse therapeutic strategies. At times, some clients will need more direction, and even advice. Others will be very hesitant in talking about themselves in personal ways, especially during the early phase of a group. Leaders need to be patient and to avoid quickly pushing members to "open up and be real." Furthermore, leaders need to recognize that what may appear to be resistance is very likely to be the client's response to years of cultural conditioning and respect for certain values and traditions. What the matter comes down to is the familiarity of group leaders with a variety of theoretical approaches and the ability to employ and adapt their techniques to fit the person-in-the-environment. It is not enough to merely assist members in gaining insight, expressing suppressed emotions, or making certain behavioral changes. The challenge for leaders is to find practical strategies for adapting the techniques they have developed to enable clients to question the impact their culture continues to have on their life and to make decisions about what facets of their life they want to change. Being an effective group leader involves reflecting on how your own culture influences you and your interventions in your groups. This awareness will be a critical factor in your becoming more sensitive to the cultural backgrounds of the members in your groups.

Applications of the Integrated Eclectic Model

The term *integrated eclectic model* refers to a perspective based on concepts and techniques from the various theoretical approaches. It is the model I use in my own practice of group work. This section describes how I apply my synthesis at each stage of a group's development. This model is designed to address the three factors of thinking, feeling, and doing. As you've seen, some of the ten theories discussed in this book focus on cognition, others on the experiencing of feelings, and others on behavior. My goal is to blend the unique contributions of these approaches so that all three dimensions of human experiencing are given attention at each phase of a group. At the same time, it is important to avoid the trap of emerging with a hodgepodge of unamalgamated theories thrown hastily together. Your goal should be to develop a consistent conceptual framework that you can use as a basis for selecting from the multiple techniques that you've studied.

Theories Applied to the Pregroup Stage

The preparatory period in the formation of a group may be the most critical of all. If the group's foundation is weak, the group may never get off the ground. Effective groups do not simply "happen." The hard work and careful organization that go into planning a group are bound to have payoffs once the group gets under way. At this point it would be a good idea for you to review the major considerations in forming groups, found in Chapter 4.

The behavioral theories are particularly relevant at the pregroup stage, for they emphasize assessing both the need for a particular kind of group and the participant's readiness and appropriateness for a group. As a group leader, you must have clear expectations, a rationale for why and how a group is an effective approach, and a sense of how to design a specific group tailored to the unique needs and interests of the members. If you are clear about how a group can benefit prospective members, you'll be better able to help them decide whether to join. If members know what they are getting into, the chances are increased that they will become active and committed participants. In this regard the therapeutic approaches that structure a group on a contractual basis have much to offer. A contract can help demystify the group process, can increase the members' sense of responsibility to become active agents in their own change, and can structure the course a group takes. Contracts set forth the division of responsibility between the members and the leader, and they are a useful departure point for productive work. As you will remember, the cognitively and behaviorally oriented therapies stress contracts as a way of beginning the process. TA groups, behavioral group therapy, and, sometimes, rational emotive behavior therapy and reality-therapy groups work on a contractual basis. Whatever your theoretical orientation, open-ended and flexible contracts can be drawn up before the group actually meets as a whole.

The functions of the leader that are especially important at the pregoup phase are developing a clear proposal for a specific group; recruiting, screening, and selecting members; providing orientation to the members so that they can derive the maximum gains from the experience; and, ideally, arranging for a preliminary group session to help members get acquainted and provide some teaching about the nature and functioning of groups.

Theories Applied to the Initial Stage

BASIC CHARACTERISTICS. The early phase of a group is a time for orientation and exploration. Some of the distinguishing characteristics at this time are the following: Members are attempting to find a place in the group. They are trying to get acquainted and learn what a group is all about. They are gradually learning the norms and expectations. Interactions tend to be of a socially acceptable nature and somewhat on the surface, and there is a certain tentativeness within the group. Perhaps the most basic issue pertains to creating and maintaining trust. The attitudes and behaviors of the group leader are directly related to the creation of a level of trust that will promote significant interaction.

DRAWING ON THEORIES. The relationship-oriented approaches, especially person-centered therapy and existential therapy, provide an excellent foundation for building a community characterized by trust and the willingness to take the risks that are necessary for change. The leader's modeling is especially important, for it is my belief that members learn more from what the leader does than from what he or she says. Here is where enthusiasm about groups can be communicated to the members by a dedicated, competent, and caring group leader. A basic sense of respect for what the members are experiencing as they approach a new group can best be demonstrated by a leader's willingness to allow them to express what they are thinking and feeling in the here and now. Typically, members do have some initial anxieties. They may fear an unfamiliar situation, rejection, or close-ness. Some may fear opening up more than they will be able to manage, disrupting their life outside the group, or incurring the disapproval of others in the group. A genuine interest in listening to these feelings sets the tone for caring, attentiveness, and compassion and goes a long way toward creat-ing a climate in which members can be free to share what they feel and think.

Besides encouraging members to express their feelings, I draw on the cognitive therapies. Thus, members come to a group with certain ex-pectations of themselves and of what they think a group can do for them. Some may expect others to provide them with answers to their problems, some may expect to get from the group what they see themselves as missing in their relationships at home and work, and some may be convinced that a group will not really help them. Such expectations need to be stated and addressed at the early sessions.

DEFINING PERSONAL GOALS. It is during the initial stage that the *be-havioral* approaches and the *cognitive* therapies have special relevance. I like the behavioral emphasis on helping members identify concrete aspects of their behavior that they most want to change. From there the leader may do some teaching to show members how involvement in the group can be instrumental in attaining their goals. I see it as counterproductive for leaders to impose on members specific goals that they should work toward, for unless the members really want to change, there is little hope that change can be forced on them. For this reason I value the Adlerian concept of goal alignment. Adlerians make special efforts to negotiate a congruence of goals between the client and the therapist. TA groups are also character-ized by mutually agreed-on therapeutic goals. In reality-therapy groups there is emphasis on asking members to evaluate their wants and to de-termine whether these desires are realistic. Reality therapy also challenges members to look at their behavior and decide whether it is working for them. If members make the evaluation that their current behavior is not working, the process of making specific behavioral changes can begin. If members are not aided in making an evaluation of their wants, needs, and current behavior, they find it very difficult to know where to begin. Careful consideration of this personal evaluation is a way to engage the group members and to motivate them to do something different. Of course, the skill in group leading involves showing members how a group can help them get what they say they want. I cannot overstress the importance of inducing the members to decide if they really want to change some of their thoughts, feelings, and behaviors.

Although I am very sympathetic toward the existential goal of learning how to live more creatively by accepting freedom and responsibility, I think such broad goals need to be narrowed down so that members have a clear idea of what thoughts, feelings, and actions they are willing to change and can learn how to make such changes. A way to help members specify their goals is to ask them to write them down. Questions such as the following can be useful: "What do I want to change about myself? Do any of my thoughts lead to unwanted feelings? What would I like more of or less of? What am I willing to do to make the specific changes that I say I want to make? What are some short-range goals that I want to attain in this group?"

Theories Applied to the Transition Stage

LEARNING TO DEAL WITH CONFLICT AND RESISTANCE. One of the most challenging and often frustrating periods in the life of a group is the transition phase. Before a group can progress to the working stage, it typically must learn to recognize and deal with anxiety, defensiveness, resistance, conflict, the struggle for control, challenges to the leader, and various other problematic behaviors. Some groups reach the transitional period only to remain stuck there. This impasse can be traced either to an earlier failure to establish norms or to inept handling of resistance and conflict within the group. It is essential that conflict be both recognized and then dealt with therapeutically if the group is to move forward. One way to recognize resistance is to regularly assess the group members' level of satisfaction with their participation in the group. This can be done in a brief written evaluation, which can then be tabulated and brought back to the group. It is useful to get members used to regular assessments, for in this way problems within the group can be detected and then worked on in the sessions. Specific questions can be asked about each member's level of investment, satisfaction with the sessions, trust level, and willingness to take risks. You might refer to the student manual of this text for ideas about inventories that can be used to assess group process. Of course, this type of assessment is consistent with behavioral approaches that stress specificity of behavior, outcomes, and regular feedback about the process as a way to determine whether the group interventions are effective.

Again, the role of leader modeling is critical when it comes to accepting and dealing with resistance. At times, leaders create resistance or make it worse by what they say or do. If leaders take too personally any problems that occur within the group, they burden themselves and tend to become defensive. It is essential to give members some room to maneuver, to avoid responding sharply or defensively, and, most certainly, to avoid sarcasm. The manner in which the group leader deals with the inevitable resistance that manifests itself in various avoidances and defensive maneuvers will determine how well the group meets the developmental tasks at the transition phase. I hope you will learn how to respect resistance by seeing it as a normal and healthy sign of a group's movement toward autonomy. Rather than viewing resistance as a nuisance to be gotten around, you can help members deal with the sources of their resistance in a therapeutic way.

WAYS OF CONCEPTUALIZING RESISTANCE. Several theoretical perspectives shed some light on the dynamics of resistance and suggest methods of dealing with it constructively. From a psychoanalytic perspective, resistance is seen as anything that prevents members from dealing with unconscious material. It is the unconscious attempt to defend oneself from the anxiety that would arise if the unconscious were uncovered. It helps me to remember that members have to struggle with intrapsychic conflicts as well as interpersonal conflicts. A leader who is sensitive to the ambivalence that members experience in both wanting to be a part of the process of self-discovery and fearing self-knowledge can help participants begin to look at their fears and defenses.

I see ways of combining the psychoanalytic and Adlerian views of resistance. Group members typically reexperience some of the old feelings they had in their original family. Sibling rivalry, position in the group, acceptance/rejection feelings, strivings for attention and success, authority issues, managing of negative feelings, and childhood traumas all surface in the group experience. People are often stuck in a developmental sense because of these unfinished situations that now intrude on their ability to function effectively. In many ways the group resembles one's family of origin. By working with their projections, transferences, attractions, and other feelings toward others in the group, the members can experiment with new ways of thinking about themselves and others.

A THINKING/FEELING/BEHAVING PERSPECTIVE.   When a group is in transition, I appreciate the freedom given by the person-centered approach to express any feelings and have this expression accepted. My hope is that members will allow themselves to *feel* the ways in which they are resisting and to intensify those feelings. Here is where I draw on some of the action-oriented techniques of Gestalt therapy and psychodrama so that clients will have a way to experience as fully as possible whatever they feel. It is important to assess what clients need, however, and to work within the framework of their cultural background. Some members, because of their cultural injunctions, would have a difficult time getting involved in the emotional aspects of Gestalt experiments or emotionally intense psychodramas. It is certainly not therapeutically productive to push clients to experience emotions, but it could be helpful to explore with them their reluctance to share their emotions.

At some point I would also want to work with the belief systems and self-talk of the members. Here is where I find transactional analysis, rational emotive behavior therapy, and the cognitive therapies of value. For example, a member might participate very little in a group because she is following certain parental injunctions, such as "Don't show other people what you feel." "Don't talk in public about your family and personal problems." "Don't trust others." "Be strong, and don't give in to feelings of self-pity." I think TA provides a useful framework within which members can gain awareness of these parental messages and their early decisions. Although a group experience can help these clients eventually challenge the validity of certain messages, it is important to avoid confronting some of these values too quickly. Patience and respect are extremely important at this time.

REBT is also of value in helping members challenge some of the self-defeating beliefs that lead to an entrenchment of their defensiveness in the group. A member may say very little because of his fear of disapproval or because he has convinced himself that he must say things "perfectly" so that others will understand him. Once members allow themselves to experience their resistance on a feeling level, they are better able to genuinely challenge their cognitions. Here is where writing helps again. If members can be encouraged to keep a journal of their thoughts (and how these thoughts lead to some unwanted behaviors and feelings), they can then do some in-depth exploration of certain self-talk that is not productive. They can learn new and more functional cognitions, and they can practice them both in and out of group. Related to this is their willingness to begin to behave in different ways. I like the emphasis of reality therapy on paying attention to what one is *doing* and REBT's emphasis on the need to practice new behaviors as the basis for making lasting changes. Reality therapy provides some particularly useful questions that can lead members to make plans for change. This planning can be one way for members to actually begin to act differently.

Theories Applied to the Working Stage

During the working stage there is a commitment by members to explore the significant problems that they bring to the sessions and to express their reactions to what is taking place within the group. I find that this stage requires the least degree of structuring. In part this is because members bring up issues they want to work on, freely interact with one another, have the feeling of being a group rather than a bunch of strangers, and assume responsibility to keep the sessions moving.

CONCEPTS AND TECHNIQUES. My preference is to let the members raise the issues they are willing to pursue seriously rather than taking the responsibility for calling on them, drawing them out, or telling them what they should talk about. I still find it helpful to ask members to create their own agenda for each meeting, and I like to begin a group session by asking each person to declare in a clear sentence what he or she wants for the session. This does not imply a passive stance, however, for during the working stage I am very willing to suggest experiments and to invite members to take part in a technique that is designed to heighten whatever it is that they are experiencing. Again, my concern is with the thinking, feeling, and doing dimensions, and the techniques I suggest reflect this type of integration. Once members declare that they do want to work and we decide what it is they want to accomplish, I typically ask them if they are willing to participate in an experiment.

Generally, I prefer to begin with helping members get into contact with what they are feeling in the here and now. Gestalt techniques are most useful in focusing on present-centered awareness and bringing any unfinished business from the past to the surface. I favor the approach that asks members to bring any past issue into the present, as is true of both psychodrama and Gestalt. There is a lively quality to the work, and members rather quickly begin to experience what they feel rather than talking abstractly about feelings and thoughts. For example, if a woman becomes aware that she is afraid that she is growing up to be just like the mother she resents, a good place to begin is to ask her to "bring your mother into the group" symbolically. Again, Gestalt and psychodrama offer a rich range of techniques to help her get into focus and intensify her experience. She might experiment with assuming her mother's identity and actually speaking to others in the group "as her mother." Although I value the contact with feelings, I think it is of limited value to stop with catharsis or the mere expression of her feelings. I am likely to suggest that she identify some of the beliefs that she has picked up from her mother. Perhaps she has uncritically accepted some irrational ideas that she is stubbornly clinging to and is keeping herself upset by living by untested assumptions.

Coupled with her emotional work, some exploration of her cognitions is likely to reveal how her daily behavior is limiting her. Therefore, I see debates as productive in a group. Especially valuable are debates that members can learn to have with themselves. They can challenge untested assumptions, argue the pros and cons of a given issue, and think about how they sometimes set themselves up for defeat. Finally, working at a behavioral level is an excellent way to correct faulty thinking and emotional disturbances.

My particular emphasis during the working phase is to focus on what members are doing outside of the sessions. Therefore, I like to allow time toward the end of each session to ask every member to respond to questions such as "What did you learn about yourself in today's session? What kind of behaviors can you practice during the week? What is one specific homework assignment that you are willing to give yourself and carry out?" This approach reinforces in-group learning, and it helps members continually think about how to apply new ways of thinking and behaving in everyday situations.

Theories Applied to the Final Stage

REVIEW OF TASKS. The final stage of the group's evolution is critical, for members have an opportunity to clarify the meaning of their experiences in the group, to consolidate the gains they have made, and to revise their decisions about what newly acquired behaviors they want to transfer to their daily life. The major task facing members during this consolidation stage is to learn ways of maintaining these changed behaviors in the outside world. My focus is on getting the members to review the nature of any changes on a thinking/feeling/behaving level. Have they learned the value of expressing negative feelings rather than swallowing them? Have they learned that repressing their feelings results in some indirect expression of them? What cognitions have they modified? Have they let go of some dysfunctional cognitions that lead to emotional upsets? Have they challenged their beliefs and values and made them their own? What concrete behavioral changes have they made that they value? How did they make these changes? How can they continue to behave in ways that are productive? What plan for action can they devise now that the group is coming to an end so that they can continue to make progress?

THEORETICAL PERSPECTIVES. I tend to use the most structure during the beginning and ending phases of a group. It is not my style to hope that members will automatically transfer specific cognitive, emotional, and behavioral changes from the group to the outside world. Therefore, I provide a structure that I hope will promote this transfer of learning. I have mentioned that in ongoing groups I do whatever I can to promote action on the part of the members by getting them to create their own homework assignments and then to report of their progress at the next group meeting. This is a way of continually using the group as a place to learn how to be different and then of carrying this new behavior into life. The group is a means to an end and should never become an end in itself.

Whereas I tend to use experiential therapies and exploration of feelings during the working phase, I lean during the final stage toward the cognitive-behavioral therapies and toward putting one's learning into some type of conceptual framework. From the behavioral therapies I draw techniques such as practice and rehearsal for leaving a group, self-monitoring procedures, building a support system beyond the group, and learning methods of self-reinforcement. Since I see therapy as a teaching/learning process, I try to help members devise a conceptual framework that will ensure that they make sense of what they have experienced. Therefore, at the final stage I tend to ask over and over: "What did you learn in this group that you valued, and how did you learn it?" I don't want members attributing their changes to the magic of the group but, rather, to specific actions that they took to change. Both REBT and reality therapy are relevant models at this point in a group's history, since they stress the importance of developing specific plans for change, making a commitment to do what is needed to bring about change, and evaluating the outcomes of the therapeutic process. Although members are urged to try out a plan of action during the working phase, it is during the final stage that such a plan is essential. It is also important to help members find ways to continue to build on their newly acquired skills. Members can promote their change by deciding toward the end of the group on other paths for growth. They can make decisions about specific activities that will keep challenging them. They can make contracts to behave in certain ways once the group ends.

It should not be assumed, because of the emphasis I am placing on cognitive work and behavioral plans for action during the final stage, that feelings are unimportant at this time. I see it as critical that members deal with their feelings about separation and termination, that they express any fears or reservations they may have about making it in the world without the support of the group, and that they learn how to say good-bye. Also, the opportunity to complete any unfinished business is paramount at this time.

During the ending stage the leader needs to watch for certain dangers. Members may avoid reviewing their experience and fail to put it into some cognitive framework, thus limiting the generalization of their learning. And because of their anxiety over separation, some members may distance themselves and thus get less benefit from the group. Toward the end of a group's history there is a place for the role of the leader as a teacher. Leaders can caution members and provide them with practical strategies for dealing with setbacks once they leave a group. Members need to learn that the path toward growth is bumpy and uneven. At this time they can be taught how to evaluate the impact of the group on them as well as assess the progress they have made as a group.

Theories Applied to Postgroup Issues

After the group comes to an end, the members' main task is applying their in-group learning to an action program in their daily life so that they can function in self-directed ways. I value setting aside time for individual interviews with each member, if possible, along with arranging for a follow-up group session. Such procedures build in accountability, for both the members and the leader can more accurately assess the impact of the group. Again, the behavioral approaches stress this accountability and evaluation, which enable the leader to make modifications in future groups based on what seemed to work. Follow-up procedures also provide a safety valve, for if members left the group with unresolved or negative feelings, they can at least discuss them with the group leader.

The Pros and Cons of an Eclectic Model

As I've said many times, I'm convinced that as a group practitioner you need to find a style that fits for you as a person; the model I've described is the result of my own search for an approach to groups that fits me both professionally and personally. It reflects my view of groups as entities that express in an integrated fashion the thinking, feeling, and doing dimensions of individual members. It also combines the didactic with the experiential, since I believe that what we experience in a group needs to be supported by a conceptual framework. Without such a framework, it would be difficult for us to make sense of the experience and to understand its implications for our daily existence. My model brings together the action-oriented, the insight-oriented, and the experientially oriented approaches—that is, the cognitive, affective, and behavioral dimensions—to pursue more effectively the basic goal of any therapeutic group: change.

Although I believe that an integration of therapeutic perspectives provides the best way to develop your interventions in a group, creating an eclectic stance is truly a challenge, for it does not simply mean picking bits and pieces from theories in a random and fragmented manner. In forming an integrated perspective, it is important to ask: Which theories provide a basis for understanding the *cognitive* dimensions? How about the *feeling* aspects? And how about the *behavioral* dimension? Most of the ten therapeutic orientations I have presented focus on one of these dimensions of human experience. Although the other dimensions are not necessarily ignored, they are often given short shrift.

Developing an integrated theoretical perspective requires much reading, thinking, and actual counseling experience. Unless you have an accurate and in-depth knowledge of these theories, you cannot formulate a true synthesis. A central message of this book has been to encourage you to remain open to each theory, to do further reading, and to reflect on how the key concepts of each theory fit your personality. Building your personalized theory of counseling, based on what you consider to be the best features of several theories, is a long-term venture. Effective leaders are continually defining and refining a personalized group theory that guides them in their practice and allows them to make sense of what occurs in groups. Of course, the specific type of group that you are leading and the makeup of the clients in your group are critical variables in deciding what strategies are most appropriate. Be open to modifying your techniques so that they fit the needs of the members of the group, including their social and cultural background.

Having said all that, I wish to add that there are dangers in encouraging an eclectic approach. At its worst, eclecticism can be an excuse for sloppy practice—a practice that lacks a systematic rationale for what you actually do in your work. If you merely pick and choose according to whims, it is likely that what you select is just the reflection of your biases and preconceived ideas. At its best, however, eclecticism can be a creative synthesis of the unique contributions of diverse approaches, dynamically integrating concepts and techniques that fit the uniqueness of your personality and style.

Summary and Review Charts

At this point it would be useful for you to reflect on the major insights you have gained through taking this course and reading this book. Most of all, think about what theories seemed to have the most practical application in helping you understand your present life situation. You might consider what changes you are interested in making and which approaches could provide you with strategies to modify specific thoughts, feelings, and behaviors. This is a good time to review what you may have learned about your ability to establish effective relationships with other people. Especially important is a review of any personal characteristics that could either help or hinder you in developing solid working relationships with the members in your groups.

After you make this review of significant personal learning, I suggest that you also ponder what you have learned about group process. It has been my experience that between the first and the last day of an introductory course in group counseling, students find that what seems at first to be an overwhelming mass of knowledge and a bewildering array of theories eventually becomes a manageable store of understanding about the basis of counseling. Moreover, I hope that you will be patient enough to recognize that much of the theoretical foundation you have received in this book will take on new meanings when you gain more practical experience in leading various groups. The same is true for the many professional and ethical issues that were discussed in the book. I think it is essential that you reflect on these basic issues, that you begin to formulate your own position on them, and that you discuss them with fellow students and instructors. Even though experience will teach you many new lessons, you will be far better equipped to deal with these and related issues when you meet them if you have reflected on them now.

As you review the following charts (Tables 17-1 through 17-6) summarizing the ten theories, consider which particular approaches you would be most inclined to draw from with respect to the following dimensions: (1) goals of group counseling, (2) group leader's role and function, (3) degree of structuring and division of responsibility, (4) group techniques, and (5) adapting theories to the practice of multicultural group counseling.

I hope that this book and the manual that accompanies it have stimulated you to think productively about group process, to read more and learn more about the topics we have explored together, and to seek group experience both as a member and as a leader. I am sincerely interested in getting feedback from you regarding this textbook and the accompanying manual as well as your experience in your own training program. I'll welcome and value any suggestions for making this book more useful in future revisions. You can use the tear-out evaluation at the end of this book or write to me in care of Brooks/Cole Publishing Company, Pacific Grove, CA 93950.

◆ **TABLE 17-1** ◆

Comparative Overview of Group Goals

MODEL	GOALS
Psychoanalytic	To provide a climate that helps clients reexperience early family relationships. To uncover buried feelings associated with past events that carry over into current behavior. To facilitate insight into the origins of faulty psychological development and stimulate a corrective emotional experience.
Adlerian	To create a therapeutic relationship that encourages participants to explore their basic life assumptions and to achieve a broader understanding of lifestyles. To help clients recognize their strengths and their power to change. To encourage them to accept full responsibility for their chosen lifestyle and for any changes they want to make.
Psychodrama	To facilitate the release of pent-up feelings, to provide insight, and to help clients develop new and more effective behaviors. To open up unexplored possibilities for solving conflicts and for experiencing dominant sides of oneself.
Existential	To provide conditions that maximize self-awareness and reduce blocks to growth. To help clients discover and use freedom of choice and assume responsibility for their own choices.
Person-centered	To provide a safe climate wherein members can explore the full range of their feelings. To help members become increasingly open to new experiences and develop confidence in themselves and their own judgments. To encourage clients to live in the present. To develop openness, honesty, and spontaneity. To make it possible for clients to encounter others in the here and now and to use the group as a place to overcome feelings of alienation.
Gestalt	To enable members to pay close attention to their moment-to-moment experiencing, so they can recognize and integrate disowned aspects of themselves.
Transactional analysis	To assist clients in becoming free of scripts and games in their interactions. To challenge members to reexamine early decisions and make new ones based on awareness.
Behavior therapy	To help group members eliminate maladaptive behaviors and learn new and more effective behavioral patterns. (Broad goals are broken down into precise subgoals.)
Rational emotive behavior therapy	To teach group members that they are responsible for their own disturbances and to help them identify and abandon the process of self-indoctrination by which they keep their disturbances alive. To eliminate the clients' irrational and self-defeating outlook on life and replace it with a more tolerant and rational one.
Reality therapy	To guide members toward learning realistic and responsible behavior and developing a "success identity." To assist group members in evaluating their behavior and in deciding on a plan of action for change.

◆ **TABLE 17-2** ◆

Comparative Overview of Leader's Role and Functions

MODEL	LEADER'S ROLE
Psychoanalytic	Facilitates group interaction by helping create an accepting and tolerant climate. Remains relatively anonymous and objective, so that members will develop projections toward him or her. Signals indications of resistance and transference and interprets their meanings. Helps members work through unfinished business. Sets limits for the group.
Adlerian	Uses procedures such as confrontation, self-disclosure, interpretation, and analysis of prevailing patterns to challenge beliefs and goals. Observes social context of behavior. Models attentive caring. Helps members accept and utilize their assets. Encourages members to develop the courage needed to translate what is learned in the group to behavior outside of the group.
Psychodrama	Functions as both facilitator and director. Has the job of warming up the group, helping set up a psychodrama, directing the enactment, and then processing the outcomes with the participants. Specific tasks include facilitating, observing, directing, producing, and summarizing.
Existential	Has the central role of being fully present and available to individuals in the group and of grasping their subjective being-in-the-world. Functions by creating a person-to-person relationship, by disclosing himself or herself, and by confronting members in a caring way.
Person-centered	Facilitates the group (as opposed to directing it)—deals with barriers to communication, establishes a climate of trust, and assists the group in functioning effectively. Central task is to be genuine in the sessions and demonstrate caring, respect, and understanding. Has the primary role of creating a climate of tolerance and experimentation. Often becomes directly involved by sharing personal feelings and impressions about what is happening in the group.
Gestalt	Suggests techniques designed to help participants intensify their experience and be alert to their body messages. Assists clients in identifying and working through unfinished business from the past that interferes with current functioning. Focuses on members' behaviors and feelings.
Transactional analysis	Has a didactic role. Teaches clients how to recognize the games they play to avoid intimacy, the ego state in which they are functioning in a given transaction, and the self-defeating aspects of early decisions and adopted life plans.
Behavior therapy	Functions as an expert in behavior modification; thus, must be directive and often functions as teacher or trainer. Imparts information and teaches coping skills and methods of modifying behavior, so that members can practice outside group sessions.

◆ TABLE 17-2 ◆

(continued)

MODEL	LEADER'S ROLE
Rational emotive behavior therapy	Functions didactically: explains, teaches, and reeducates. Helps members see and rigorously confront their illogical thinking and identify its connection with self-defeating behavior. Teaches them to change their patterns of thinking and behaving.
Reality therapy	Encourages members to evaluate their behavior and make choices that will allow them to fulfill their needs in socially acceptable ways. Helps members by establishing a personal relationship with them, by firmly expecting that they will formulate and implement a plan for change.

◆ TABLE 17-3 ◆

Comparative Overview of Degree of Structuring and Division of Responsibility

MODEL	STRUCTURING AND RESPONSIBILITY
Psychoanalytic	*Leader* shies away from directive leadership and allows the group to determine its own course; interprets the meaning of certain behavioral patterns. *Members* raise issues and produce material from the unconscious; assume increasing responsibility for interacting spontaneously, making interpretations, and sharing insights about others; become auxiliary therapists for one another.
Adlerian	*Leader,* at the outset, works toward goal alignment; takes active steps to establish and maintain a therapeutic relationship, to explore and analyze the individual's dynamics, and to communicate a basic attitude of concern and hope. *Members* develop insight about themselves; assume the responsibility for taking positive measures to make changes; consider alternative beliefs, goals, and behaviors.
Psychodrama	*Director/leader* suggests specific techniques designed to intensify feelings, re-create past situations, and provide increased awareness of conflicts; makes sure that the protagonist is not left hanging and that other members of the group have a chance to share what they experienced during the psychodrama. *Members* produce the material for psychodramas and, when in the role of protagonist, direct their own psychodramas.
Existential	*Leader* may structure the group along the lines of certain existential themes such as freedom, responsibility, anxiety, and guilt; shares here-and-now feelings with the group. *Members* are responsible for deciding the issues they want to explore, thus determining the direction of the group.

(continued)

◆ TABLE 17-3 ◆

(continued)

MODEL	STRUCTURING AND RESPONSIBILITY
Person-centered	*Leader* provides very little structuring or direction. *Members* are seen as having the capacity to find a meaningful direction, of being able to help one another, and of moving toward constructive outcomes.
Gestalt	*Leader* is responsible for being aware of his/her present-centered experience and for using it in the context of the group; brings structure to the group by introducing appropriate techniques to intensify emotions. *Members* must be active and make their own interpretations.
Transactional analysis	Because of the stress on an equal relationship between leader and members, responsibility is shared, as specified in a contract. *Members* and *leader* spell out in the contract what changes members want to make and what issues they want to explore in the group.
Behavior therapy	*Leader* is responsible for active teaching and for having the group proceed according to a predetermined set of activities. *Members* are expected to be active, to apply what they learn to everyday life situations, and to practice new behaviors outside the group.
Rational emotive behavior therapy	*Leader* is responsible for challenging any signs of member behavior based on faulty thinking; structures the group experience so that members stay with the task of making constructive changes. *Members* are responsible for attacking their own self-defeating thinking and that of fellow group members; are expected to carry out self-confrontation outside the group and work hard at changing illogical thoughts.
Reality therapy	*Leader* teaches members to assume responsibility for how they live their life; structures the group by focusing on present behavior and ways of making specific behavioral changes; influences members by modeling success-oriented behavior; confronts clients who are not living realistically. *Members* decide on specific changes they want to make and are held responsible for implementing desired changes.

◆ **TABLE 17-4** ◆

Comparative Overview of Group Techniques

MODEL	TECHNIQUES
Psychoanalytic	Interpretation, dream analysis, free association, analysis of resistance, and analysis of transference—all designed to make the unconscious conscious and bring about insight.
Adlerian	Analysis and assessment, exploration of family constellation, reporting of earliest recollections, confrontation, interpretation, cognitive restructuring, challenging of one's belief system, and exploration of social dynamics and of one's unique style of life.
Psychodrama	Self-presentation, presentation of the other, interview in the role of the other and interview in the role of the self, soliloquy, role reversal, double technique and auxiliary egos, mirroring, multiple doubles, future projection, and life rehearsal.
Existential	Since this approach stresses understanding first and techniques second, no specific set of methods is prescribed. However, leaders can borrow techniques from other therapies to better understand the world of clients and to deepen the level of therapeutic work.
Person-centered	The stress is on the facilitator's attitudes and behavior, and few structured or planned techniques are used. Basic techniques include active listening, reflection of feelings, clarification, support, and "being there" for the client.
Gestalt	Many action-oriented techniques are available to the leader, all of which intensify immediate experiencing and awareness of current feelings. Techniques include confrontation, empty chair, game of dialogue, making the rounds, fantasy approaches, reversal procedures, rehearsal techniques, exaggerating a behavior, staying with feelings, dialogues with self or significant others in the present, and dream work. Exercises are designed to enable participants to become increasingly aware of bodily tensions and of the fear of getting physically and emotionally close, to give members a chance to experiment with new behavior, and to release feelings. Guided fantasy, imagery, and other techniques designed to stimulate the imagination are used.
Transactional analysis	Techniques include the use of a script-analysis checklist or questionnaire to detect early injunctions and decisions, games, and life positions; family modeling; role playing; and structural analysis.
Behavior therapy	The main techniques, which are based on behavioral and learning principles and are aimed at behavioral changes and cognitive restructuring, include systematic desensitization, implosive therapy, assertion training, aversive techniques, operant-conditioning methods, self-help techniques, reinforcement and supportive measures, behavioral research, coaching, modeling, feedback, and procedures for challenging and changing cognitions.

(continued)

♦ TABLE 17-4 ♦

(continued)

MODEL	TECHNIQUES
Rational emotive behavior therapy	The essential technique is active teaching. Leaders probe, confront, challenge, and forcefully direct. They model and teach rational thinking, and they explain, persuade, and lecture clients. They use a rapid-fire style that requires members to constantly use their cognitive skills. REBT uses a wide range of behavioral techniques such as deconditioning, role playing, behavioral research, homework assignments, and assertion training.
Reality therapy	A wide range of techniques is used, such as role playing, confrontation, modeling, use of humor, contracts, and specific plans for action.

♦ TABLE 17-5 ♦

Comparative Overview of Contributions to Multicultural Counseling

MODEL	CONTRIBUTION
Psychoanalytic	Focus on family dynamics is appropriate for working with many minority groups. Therapist formality appeals to those clients who expect professional distance. Notion of defense is helpful in understanding inner dynamics and dealing with environmental stresses.
Adlerian	Culture is viewed as a perspective and background from which meaning in life can be derived. Each individual will make a different meaning out of his or her personal cultural experience.
Psychodrama	For reserved clients, this approach invites self-expression in the present. Director can create scenes that are culturally sensitive and assist members in understanding the impact of their culture on them. Through enactment, nonverbal clients have other means of communication. Opportunities arise for developing spontaneity and creativity within the framework of one's culture.
Existential	A core value is the emphasis on understanding the member's phenomenological world, including cultural background. This approach leads to empowerment in an oppressive society. It can help members examine their options for change within the context of their cultural realities.
Person-centered	Rogers made significant contributions to breaking cultural barriers and facilitating open dialogue among diverse cultural populations. Main strengths are respect for client's values, active listening, welcoming of differences, nonjudgmental attitude, understanding, willingness to allow clients to determine what will be explored in sessions, and prizing of cultural pluralism.

◆ **TABLE 17-5** ◆

(continued)

MODEL	CONTRIBUTION
Gestalt	Focus on expressing oneself nonverbally is congruent with those cultures that look beyond words for messages. Approach provides many techniques in working with clients who have cultural injunctions against freely expressing feelings. Focus on bodily expressions is a subtle way to help clients recognize their conflicts.
Transactional analysis	Contractual method acts as a safeguard against therapist imposition of values that may not be congruent with a client's culture. This approach offers a basis for understanding the impact of cultural and familial injunctions. It provides a structure that many clients will value.
Behavior therapy	Focus on behavior, rather than on feelings, is compatible with many cultures. Strengths include preparation of members by teaching them purposes of group; assisting members in learning practical skills; educational focus of groups; and stress on self-management strategies.
Rational emotive behavior therapy	This approach provides ways of questioning one's beliefs and identifying values that may no longer be functional. Its focus on thinking and rationality (as opposed to expressing feelings) is likely to be acceptable to many clients. Focus on teaching/learning process tends to avoid the stigma of mental illness. Many clients may value the leader directiveness and stress on homework.
Reality therapy	Focus is on members' making own evaluation of behavior (including how they respond to their culture). Through personal assessment they can determine the degree to which their needs and wants are being satisfied; they can find a balance between retaining their own ethnic identity and integrating some of the values and practices of the dominant society.

◆ **TABLE 17-6** ◆

Comparative Overview of Limitations in Multicultural Counseling

MODEL	LIMITATIONS
Psychoanalytic	Focus on insight, intrapsychic dynamics, and long-term treatment is often not valued by clients who prefer to learn coping skills in dealing with pressing environmental concerns. Internal focus is often in conflict with cultural values that stress an interpersonal and environmental focus.
Adlerian	This approach's detailed interview about one's family background can conflict with cultures that have injunctions against disclosing family matters. Leader needs to make certain that the goals of members are respected and that these goals are congruent with the goals of a given group.
Psychodrama	Emphasis on experiencing and expressing feelings, on catharsis, and on enacting past problems in the present can be highly threatening for some clients. Caution needed in encouraging clients to display their intense emotions in presence of others.
Existential	Its values of individuality, freedom, autonomy, and self-realization often conflict with cultural values of collectivism, respect for tradition, deference to authority, and interdependence. Some may be deterred by absence of specific techniques. Others will expect more focus on surviving in their world.
Person-centered	Some of the core values of this approach may not be congruent with the client's culture. Lack of leader direction and structure are unacceptable for many clients who are seeking help and immediate answers from knowledgeable leader.
Gestalt	Clients who have been culturally conditioned to be emotionally reserved may not embrace Gestalt techniques. It is important not to push quickly for expressing feelings until relationship is established. Some may not see how "being aware of present experiencing" will lead to solving their problems.
Transactional analysis	Terminology of TA may distract clients from some cultures with a different perspective. Leader must establish clear contract of what client wants before challenging client's life scripts, cultural and familial injunctions, and decisions. Caution required in probing into family patterns.
Behavior therapy	Leaders need to help members assess the possible consequences of making behavioral changes. Family members may not value clients' newly acquired assertive style, so clients must be taught how to cope with resistance by others.
Rational emotive behavior therapy	If leader has a forceful and directive leadership style, members may retreat. It is necessary to understand client's world before forcefully attacking beliefs perceived as irrational by leader.
Reality therapy	Approach stresses taking charge of one's own life, yet some members hope to change their external environment. Leader needs to appreciate the role of discrimination and racism and help clients deal with social and political realities.

Name Index

Abe, T., 285–286
Abrams, M., 392
Adler, A., 186–193, 195, 199, 200
Alberti, R. E., 359–361, 377
Ansbacher, H. L., 187–188, 190–192, 200, 204
Ansbacher, R. R., 187–188, 190, 204
Arredondo, P., 18, 38
Atkinson, D. R., 19, 181

Baldwin, C., 51
Banawi, R., 40
Bandura, A., 349, 353, 367
Barrett-Lennard, G. T., 273
Beck, A. T., 364, 391
Beggs, M. S., 13–15
Bernard, M. E., 385
Berne, E., 325, 334, 343
Bion, W. R., 154–155
Bitter, J., 190–191, 194, 199
Blatner, A., 206–208, 210–212, 214, 218, 221–223, 227, 229–230, 234
Blau, W., 165, 174
Bond, L., 119–120
Bondi, A. M., 46
Borkman, T. J., 12–13, 15
Bowman, V. E., 92
Boy, A. V., 269, 284
Bozarth, J. D., 273, 276
Braaten, L. J., 268, 270–271, 273
Brabender, V., 150, 371, 389–390
Bracke, P. E., 255
Brodley, B. T., 276
Bugental, J. F. T., 237, 244, 253–255, 259, 260
Burnside, I. M., 170–171

Cain, D. J., 273, 278, 283–284, 288
Callanan, P., 41, 78, 121, 231
Casement, P. J., 181
Childers, J. H., 114
Chu, J., 19, 21, 23, 286

Clarkson, P., 318, 323
Coleman, N. C., 361–362
Coleman, V. D., 18
Comas-Diaz, L., 18, 21, 71, 174–175, 180–181
Corey, G., 8, 41, 48, 52, 61, 78, 121, 171, 231, 247, 260
Corey, M., 8, 41, 48, 61, 78, 121, 171, 231, 247, 260
Cormier, L. S., 352, 378
Cormier, W. H., 352, 378
Corsini, R. J., 188–189, 199, 201, 203, 213
Couch, R. D., 114
Coughlan, D., 268–269, 278
Cushman, P., 255

Davison, G. C., 354
De La Cancela, V., 180
DeLucia, J. L., 18, 92
Dengelegi, L., 392
Deurzen-Smith, E. van, 236, 238, 244–245, 250, 253, 255–257, 259–260
Dies, R. R., 100, 120
DiGiuseppe, R. A., 400
Dinkmeyer, D. C., 187, 189–195, 197–198, 200, 203
Donigian, J., 50
Dowd, E. T., 428
Downing, J., 316
Dreikurs, R., 187, 189–190, 193–197, 199
Duncan, J. A., 51–52
Durkin, H., 147–148
Dusay, J. M., 325–327, 337, 342

Edleson, J., 351, 353, 355, 357–358, 372, 374–375, 377
Elefthery, D. G., 230
Ellis, A., 200, 381–390, 392–403, 405
Emery, G., 364
Emmons, M. L., 359–361, 377
Engels, D. W., 428
Enns, C. Z., 15, 179, 340, 376

Erikson, E., 139, 159–162, 164–165, 167–170, 172, 179, 181

Fallon, A., 371, 389–390
Feder, B., 323
Fine, L. J., 219, 225–226, 232
Forester-Miller, H., 51–52
Foulkes, S. H., 152
Frankl, V., 200, 241, 247–250
Freud, S., 139–140, 143, 155, 159–167, 171–172, 179, 186–189, 192, 199, 207
Frew, J. E., 300
Fukuyama, M. A., 17, 22, 361–362

Gabbard, G. O., 175
Garcia, V. L., 70–71
Gazda, G. M., 84–85
Gilchrest, G., 70–71
Glasser, W., 409–421, 431–432, 436
Gleason, D. F., 13
Goethe, J. W., 250
Goldberg, I. A., 154, 183
Goldfried, M. R., 354
Goldman, E. E., 221, 226–227, 234
Goodman, P., 306
Gordon, T., 266
Goren, Y., 175
Gould, W. B., 241
Goulding, M., 326, 329–331, 337–338, 343
Goulding, R., 326–327, 329–331, 337–339, 343
Grant, S. K., 181
Greeley, A. T., 70–71
Greenberg, I. A., 209, 213–214, 221–223, 226
Greenberg, L. S., 265, 318
Greg, C. H., 18–19
Grieger, R., 403, 405
Griffith, J., 191–192, 203
Guevremont, D. C., 347, 356, 371–373, 377

Hamachek, D. F., 161–162, 164–165, 167
Hansen, J. C., 85
Harper, R., 405
Harris, M., 120
Haskell, M. R., 212–213, 219
Hedges, L. E., 173
Hefferline, R., 306
Heidegger, M., 237, 246
Herlihy, B., 52
Ho, M. K., 19, 22, 25, 92
Hobbs, N., 266
Hom, A. B., 19, 91
Huddleston, J. E., 428

Ibrahim, F. A., 18, 38, 258

Jensen-Scott, R. L., 18
Juan, G., 19, 91
Jung, C., 186

Kadis, L. B., 343
Kapur, R., 336, 341

Karpman, S., 335
Katz, A. H., 12
Kepner, J. I., 318, 323
Kernberg, O. F., 173–175, 182
Kessler, B. L., 70–71
Kierkegaard, S., 244
Kim, H. H. W., 71
Kohut, H., 173, 175–176, 182
Kolb, G. E., 155–156
Kretsch, R., 175
Kuehnel, J. M., 347
Kutash, I. L., 140, 143, 150–152

L'Abate, L., 428
LaFromboise, T. D., 287
Lakin, M., 14–15, 31, 40
Lantz, J., 242
Lazarus, A. A., 349–350, 366–372, 377–378
Lee, P. C., 19, 91
Leong, F. T. L., 19, 21, 25, 71, 91, 201, 286–287
Leveton, E., 221–223, 230, 234
Levitsky, A., 306
Liberman, R. P., 347
Lietaer, G., 271, 277–278
Locke, D. C., 17–18
Locke, N., 142–143, 147, 149, 156
Lyons, L. L., 400

Mackewn, J., 318, 323
Mahler, C. Q., 85
Mahler, M. S., 173–174, 182
Malcolm, D., 282
Manaster, G. J., 189, 203
Marmorstein, R., 316
Maslow, A., 200, 265
Mason, W. C., 13
May, R., 200, 237–239, 246–247, 253, 260
Mayne, T. J., 370
McCarthy, M., 400
McCarty, G. J., 154, 183
McDavis, R. J., 38
McGovern, T. E., 400
McIlduff, E., 268–269, 278
McLellarn, R. W., 391, 394
McNeil, K., 50
Meichenbaum, D., 350, 362–363, 365
Meissen, G. J., 13–14
Merta, R. J., 50
Miller, K., 336, 341
Miller, N. J., 400
Milne, C. R., 428
Minrath, M., 174–175, 180–181
Mohatt, G. V., 287
Mokuau, N., 19, 287–288
Morelock, J., 247–248
Moreno, J. L., 206–210, 212, 217, 222–223, 229–230, 232–233
Moreno, Z. T., 207, 210, 214–216, 220–221, 223, 225, 227–228, 232–233
Morran, D. K., 100–101, 119–120
Morrison, D. S., 221, 226–227, 234
Morten, G., 19

Mosak, H. H., 190, 195–196, 198
Mullan, H., 140, 149, 151, 155, 157, 183, 246, 254
Murayama, S., 285–286

Natiello, P., 268–269, 273
Nicholas, M. W., 208
Nojima, K., 285–286
Nye, R. D., 289

Oaklander, L. N., 259
Ormont, L. R., 115

Passons, W. R., 305–307
Pate, R. H., 46
Pedersen, P., 16–20, 39
Perls, F., 295–299, 302–303, 306, 316, 322
Pew, W. L., 187, 200
Pierce, K. A., 51
Polster, E., 296–297, 303, 306, 317–319, 323
Polster, M., 297, 303–304, 306, 317–319, 323
Powers, R. L., 191–192, 203
Powers, W. M., 409

Rainwater, J., 316
Raskin, N. J., 266–267, 278, 282
Raymond, D., 259
Reich, W., 302
Remley, T., 51
Rice, L. N., 265, 318
Riordan, R. J., 13–15
Robison, F. F., 101, 120
Rogers, C. R., 104, 263–264, 266–268, 271–273, 276–277, 279, 281–282, 285, 289
Rohde, R., 119
Ronall, R., 323
Rose, S. D., 351–359, 365, 371–372, 374–375, 377–378
Rosenbaum, M., 140, 149, 151, 155, 157, 183
Rush, A. J., 364
Russell, J. M., 41, 78, 121, 176, 231, 241, 243, 265–266

Sampson, E. E., 21
Sartre, J. P., 237, 241
Scheidlinger, S., 153
Schubert, M. A., 13
Schutz, W., 85, 104
Schwartz, E. K., 147, 149, 154, 156–158, 182–183
Shapiro, J. L., 81–82
Shaw, B. F., 364
Shepherd, I. L., 319
Sherman, R., 189–192, 203
Silverman, M. S., 400

Simkin, J. S., 318–319
Sisson, J. A., 50
Smith, E. M., 85, 301
Sonstegard, M., 194–197, 200
Sperry, L., 200
Spiegler, M. D., 347, 356, 371, 372–373, 377
St. Clair, M., 172–173, 182
Starr, A., 223, 228
Steiner, C., 326, 329, 335, 343
Stern, D. N., 172
Stevens, J. O., 306
Stockton, R., 40, 100–101, 119–120
Strupp, H. H., 158, 172, 176–177, 179–180
Subramanian, K., 351, 365
Sue, D., 19, 21, 321
Sue, D. W., 18–19, 21, 38, 71, 321
Sue, S., 19, 21, 23, 286

Tallant, S. H., 351, 365, 374, 378
Terner, J., 187, 200
Tharp, R. G., 345, 366
Thomason, T. C., 71, 321
Thompson, C. E., 181
Thorne, B., 264, 268, 283, 289
Tillich, P., 250
Tolman, R. M., 351, 365, 374, 378
Trexler, L. D., 400
Trimble, J. E., 287
Tudor, K., 340
Tuttman, S., 140

Warner, R. W., 85
Warren, R., 391, 394
Wasserman, A., 175
Watson, D. L., 345, 366
Weeks, G. R., 428
Wessler, R. L., 387, 391, 395, 400
Whitney, D., 375
Wolf, A., 140–141, 143, 147, 149–152, 154–159, 182–183
Wolfgang, L., 50
Woods, P. J., 400
Wrenn, C. G., 20–21
Wubbolding, R. E., 409–411, 415–416, 418–422, 425–428, 430, 432–433, 435–436

Yalom, I. D., 36–37, 47–48, 60, 85, 88–89, 92, 97, 100, 103–104, 111, 114, 116, 155, 166, 175–176, 236–237, 242–243, 259–260
Yang, J., 180
Yontef, G. M., 318–319
Yu, A., 18–19

Zimring, F. M., 267
Zinker, J., 294, 301, 303–306, 316–319, 323

Subject Index

A-B-C theory, 384–386, 387, 391, 450
Acceptance, 263, 270–272, 275, 393–394
Accountability, 433, 484
Active listening, 63, 273, 276
Adlerian approach, 186–202, 229, 426
  contributions to other approaches, 200
  family counseling, 200
  goal alignment, 478
  history of, 186–187
  key concepts of, 187–193
  role and functions of counselor, 198
  structuring and responsibility, 489
Adlerian groups, 5, 116–117, 193–198, 444,
    445–446, 450–451, 460, 463
  contributions and strengths of, 199–200
  contributions to multicultural counseling,
    492
  evaluation of, 199–202
  goals of, 190, 194–195, 487
  limitations in multicultural counseling,
    494
  limitations of, 200–201
  in multicultural settings, 201–202
  phases of, 194–198
  role and functions of leader, 196, 198,
    472, 488
  techniques, 491
Adolescence, in developmental model, 166–
    168
Adolescents, groups for, 4, 9, 42, 89–90,
    417–419
Adult children of alcoholics, groups for,
    11
Advice giving, 69, 97, 104, 146
African-American clients, 16, 17, 287
Alcoholics Anonymous, 13
Alliance for the Mentally Ill, 13
Aloneness, 251–253
Alternate session, use of, 157
American Counseling Association (ACA),
    32, 36, 39, 48, 49, 50, 86
American Group Psychotherapy Association
    (AGPA), 182

American Psychological Association (APA),
    19, 36, 38, 39
Anal stage, 161–162
Analysis, in Adlerian approach, 195–196
Anxiety, 77
  in beginning leaders, 58
  equilibrium/disequilibrium theory of, 144
  existential, 237, 238, 239, 244–246
  in final stage, 123–124
  in Gestalt groups, 314
  in initial stage, 95, 97, 99, 100
  neurotic, 248
  in pregroup preparation, 92
  in psychoanalytic groups, 144, 147, 151–
    152, 178
  in transition stage, 103, 107, 479
  in working stage, 122
Asian-American clients, 16, 18, 19, 91–92,
    286–287
Assertion-training groups, 4, 10, 351, 359–
    362, 366, 369, 376, 387, 391
Assessment, in Adlerian approach, 195–196
Association for Specialists in Group Work
    (ASGW), 26, 29, 30, 31, 33, 35, 37, 38,
    42, 43, 44, 45, 46, 49, 50, 52, 86
Attending behavior, as leadership skill, 274
Authenticity:
  of group leaders, 56
  search for, 250–251
Autonomy, 105, 112, 157, 162
Avoidance, 123–124, 297–298
Awareness, 143, 293, 294, 296–297, 301,
    326–327
  body, 300–302
  multicultural, 16–18

BASIC ID, concept of, 367–369
Basic mistakes, Adlerian concept of, 195–
    196
Behavior modification, 4, 306
Behavior therapy approach, 5, 12, 93, 229,
    319, 345–376, 443, 446, 452–454, 459–
    460, 467, 468

advantages of, 371–372
contracts, 477
contributions and strengths of, 370–371
contributions to multicultural counseling,
  493
and follow-up, 484
goals, 478, 487
group stages, 351–358, 483
key concepts of, 346–349
limitations in multicultural counseling,
  494
limitations of, 373–375
in multicultural settings, 375–377
multimethod approach, 351
role and functions of leader, 349–351,
  472, 488
structuring and responsibility, 490
techniques, 371, 482, 491
Behavioral assessment, 346–347
Behavioral disorders, Adlerian view of,
  192–193
Behavioral rehearsal, 346, 348, 351, 354,
  364, 369, 387, 391, 454
Behaviorism, 236
Behavior-oriented therapies, 236
Bereavement groups, 4
Bion's method of interpretation, 154–155
Blocking, as leadership skill, 69
Body work, Reichian, 302
Borderline personality disorder, 173–175,
  179
Boundary disturbances, 300
Buddy system, 356–357

"Can't" statements, 308
Career-exploration groups, 4
Caring, 113–114, 198, 263, 270, 416–417
Castration anxiety, 163
Catharsis, 11, 41, 116, 145, 162, 206, 210,
  211, 213, 221–222, 225, 229, 321, 427,
  429
Center for Studies of the Person, 282
Change, commitment to, 115
Child abuse, 32
Child-guidance clinics, 186–187, 193
Children, groups for, 9, 42, 89
Children of alcoholics, groups for, 4
Clarifying, as leadership skill, 7, 63–64,
  277
Client-centered therapy, 263, 266
Closed groups, 124
Closure, of psychodrama groups, 221
Coaching, 354, 359, 373
Coercion and undue pressure, in group
  counseling, 29–30
Cognitive-behavioral model, 117, 373, 430
Cognitive rehearsal, 355
Cognitive restructuring, 116–117, 346, 351,
  355–356, 361, 364, 369
Cognitive therapy, 200, 229, 319, 385, 478,
  483
  and belief systems, 480

phenomenological approach of, 189
techniques, 364
Cohesion, 87, 351
development of, 69, 97, 100, 110–112,
  157, 217, 221, 351–352
inhibiting factors, 29, 87
nature of, 110, 112
Co-leadership model, 61, 79–80
advantages and disadvantages of, 79–80
final-stage issues, 124–126
initial-stage issues, 97–101
postgroup issues, 127
pregroup issues, 94
transition-stage issues, 107–109
working-stage issues, 122
College students, groups for, 9–10, 11
Colorado State University, 11
Competence, of group leaders, 35, 42, 43–44
Confidentiality, 91, 92, 96
exceptions to, 32–33, 42
with minors, 33, 42
right to, 27, 31–33
state laws concerning, 32
Conflict:
learning to deal with, 479
resolution, 193
in transition stage, 103–106
Confluence, 300
Confrontation, 111, 113, 195, 313, 338,
  342
of co-leaders, 105–106
effective, 65, 105, 118–119
in Gestalt groups, 306
as leadership skill, 65, 198, 338
misuse of, 34, 105, 320
in multicultural counseling, 24–25
in person-centered groups, 280
in working stage, 117–119, 122
Congruence, 269
Consciousness-raising groups, 4, 10
Consequences, reasonable, 418
Consultation, with colleagues, 42, 419
Contracts:
contingency, 353, 391
use of, 34, 35, 93, 325, 336–337, 339–340,
  351–352, 429, 434, 443–444, 467, 477
Control:
struggle for, 103–106
theory, in reality therapy, 409–410, 412–
  413
Coping skills, 356, 363–365
Council for Accreditation of Counseling and
  Related Educational Programs (CAC-
  REP), 45–46
Counseling, multicultural, 16–23
Countertransference, 47, 61, 149–151, 158–
  159, 177–178, 209, 230
Creativity and choice, Adlerian concept of,
  189
Crisis counseling, 428, 431
Crisis-oriented groups, 4
Cross-cultural counseling, 180–182
Cultural encapsulation, transcending, 20–21

Death, 246–248
Defense, modes of, 298–300
Defensiveness, 103, 141
Deflection, 300
Denial, 124, 145
Dependence, 99–100, 167, 303
  orientation of group, 154
  vs. independence, 105, 451–453
Depression:
  dealing with, 455–458
  reality-therapy view of, 411
Desensitization, 346, 381, 391, 453
Developmental model:
  Erikson's view of stages in, 159–171
  Freud's theory of psychosexual develop-
    ment in, 159–167
  implications for group work, 159–171
Dialogues, experiments with, 310–311
Director, in psychodrama, 212–214, 216,
    217, 218, 221, 224, 225
Displacement, 146
Double technique, 225–226
Dream work, 140, 143, 152, 154, 155–156,
    195, 315–317
Dual relationships, 35–36
Dyads, use of, 100

Early childhood, in developmental model,
    161–163
Early recollections, 195, 199
Eating-disorders groups, 4
Eclectic approach, 4, 369, 382
  pros and cons of, 484–485
Eclecticism, 229
  technical, 349, 367
Ego, 159, 164
Ego-defense mechanisms, 144–147, 178,
    299–300
Ego states, 325, 326, 327–328, 337, 341
  adult, 328
  child, 328
  parent, 327–328
Elderly, as minority group, 16
Elderly, groups for, 10, 89
Electra complex, 163, 179
Empathy, 66, 98, 113–114, 189–190, 198,
    209, 216, 218, 224, 263, 267–268, 272–
    274, 319, 416
Empty-chair technique, 311, 312, 314
Encounter groups, 265, 266, 281–282, 284
Encouragement, 193, 197–198
Energy, blocks to, 300–302
Erikson's psychosocial perspective, 139
Ethical guidelines for group leaders, 26
Ethnicity, definition of, 16
Evaluation:
  of group experience, 76–77, 121, 128–129
  as leadership skill, 67
  objective, 348–349
Exaggeration exercise, 314–315
Existential approach, 5, 189, 200, 236–259,
    265–266, 318, 411, 426, 430, 446, 448–
    449, 452, 458–459, 468

contributions and strengths of, 254–256
contributions to multicultural counseling,
    492
evaluation of, 254–259
goals of, 487
key concepts of, 238–253
limitations of, 256–257, 494
in multicultural settings, 257–259
purpose of, 238
role and functions of group leader, 253–
    254, 472, 488
structuring and responsibility, 489
techniques, 491
Existential vacuum, 248
Experiments, use of, 304–305

Facilitating:
  as leadership skill, 66–67
  person-centered concept of, 276–278
Family, in Adlerian approach, 191–192,
    195, 199
Family therapy, 229, 326
Fantasy approaches, 312–313, 321, 331, 340
Fear of intimacy, dealing with, 453–455
Fears and resistance, dealing with, 447–449
Feedback:
  in behavioral groups, 346, 354, 355, 359,
    373
  in existential groups, 242
  of group members, 77, 90, 97, 100, 119–
    121, 125, 126, 467–468
  as leadership skill, 67
  in person-centered groups, 280
  in psychoanalytic groups, 145, 175
  in psychodrama, 213, 216, 220–221, 222
  in REBT groups, 388, 401
Feelings, 124, 208, 480
Fictional finalism, 192
Fight/flight groups, 154
Final stage, of group, 123–130, 482–484
Follow-up:
  of group experience, 127–129
  sessions, use of, 358
Formative tendency, 264
Free association, 140, 143, 147, 152, 155,
    156
Freedom:
  existential concept of, 238, 240–242, 258
  of exit, 29
  to experiment, 114
Freud's psychosexual perspective, 139
Future, focus on, 296
Future projection, 227–228

Games, in transactional analysis, 332–333,
    334, 338
Gay men, as minority group, 16
Generativity vs. stagnation, 169–170
Genital stage, 166–167
Genuineness, 98, 198, 263, 267, 269–270,
    318
Gestalt groups, 5, 293–322
  goals of, 487

key concepts of, 294–305
role and functions of group leader, 302–305, 472, 488
styles of, 317–318
techniques, 481–482, 491
Gestalt Institute of Cleveland, 322
Gestalt therapy, 189, 200, 229, 326, 340, 426, 446, 448, 453, 460–461, 463–464, 466
applications and techniques, 303–304, 305–317, 320–321
cautions and ethical concerns, 319–320
contributions and strengths of, 317–318
contributions to multicultural counseling, 493
evaluation of, 317–320
fantasy techniques, 466
goals of, 293, 294
limitations in multicultural counseling, 494
limitations of, 318–320
in multicultural settings, 320–322
structuring and responsibility, 490
Gestalt Therapy Institute of Los Angeles, 322
Gestalt Training Center of La Jolla, 322
Goals, therapeutic, 93, 100, 112, 336–337, 347–348, 352, 359
defining and clarifying, 98–99, 442–444, 478–479
of group counseling, various perspectives on, 470
Goal setting, as leadership skill, 67
Go-around technique, 152, 217, 305
Gossiping, 69
Group counseling:
for adolescents, 9, 42, 167–168
advantages of, 8
for children, 9, 42
for college students, 9, 10, 11
for the elderly, 10, 170–171
ethical and professional issues in, 26, 38–40
goals of, 7–8
vs. group therapy, 10–11
for minorities, 10, 15
in multicultural context, 18–23
overview of, 6–10
for the physically handicapped, 10
techniques, 40–41
Group leaders, 53–83
beginning, problems and issues of, 57–63
challenging of, 105–106
competence of, 4, 26, 35, 42, 43–44
education and training of, 44–52
effective, 26, 121
ethical guidelines for, 26
personal characteristics and behaviors of, 54–57
role and functions of, 94, 97–101, 122–123, 127, 157–159, 470–472
skills, overview of, 72–73

training and supervision of, 44–52, 268–269, 283
values of, impact on group, 37–38
Group leadership:
abuse of position, 150
co-leading model of, 79–80
legal liability and malpractice, 41–43
skills, 63–70
styles of, 81–83
Group members:
difficult, 60–61, 106–107
goals of, 7–8
orientation of, 91–94
personal relationships with leaders, 35–36
preparation of, 91–94
recruiting, screening, and selecting, 86–88
responsibilities of, 27
rights of, 26–33
Group models:
comparative view of, 469–494
illustrated, 441–468
Group psychotherapy, 6, 10–11, 88, 140, 229
vs. self-help groups, 14–15
Groups:
for adolescents, 4, 9, 42, 89–90, 417–419
for adult children of alcoholics, 11
announcing of, 86
assertiveness training, 10, 359–362
for children, 9, 42, 89
for children of alcoholics, 4
closed, 85, 124
cohesion, development of, 87, 110–112
for college students, 9–10, 11
consciousness-raising, 10, 89
dependency-oriented, 154
disequilibrium, 151
duration of, 90
early stages, 84–109
effectiveness of, 4
for elderly, 10, 89
encounter, 265, 266, 281–282, 284
equilibrium, 151–152
fight/flight oriented, 154
final stage, 123–130
follow-up session, 127–129
frequency and length of meetings, 90
HIV-positive clients, 4
homogeneous vs. heterogeneous, 89–90
for incest survivors, 12
initial stage, 95–103
later stages, 110–130
malequilibrium, 152
open vs. closed, 88–89
pairing-oriented, 154
postgroup stage, 127–130
pregroup issues, 85–95
pregroup session, 91–94
proposal for, 85, 94–95
purposes of, 3

Groups (cont.)
  reality-oriented, 171
  recruitment of members, 86–88
  re-entry students, 10
  reminiscing, 171
  remotivation-therapy, 171
  resistance in, 106–107
  responsibility, division of, 99
  screening and selection procedured, 86–88
  for self-directed behavior change, 365–366
  self-help, 6, 12–15
  setting for, 91
  size of, 90
  as social microcosms, 8, 14, 90, 238
  social-skills training, 358–359
  for special populations, 8–10
  stages of development, various perspectives on, 84–85
  stress-management, 10, 362–365
  structured, 6, 11–12, 91, 99–101
  support, 12
  test-anxiety reduction, 10
  therapeutic conditions for, 263–264, 267–268
  therapeutic factors, 113–121
  transition stage, 103–109
  types of, 3, 4, 10–15
  voluntary vs. involuntary membership, 28–29, 89
  work group, 154–155
  working, characteristics of, 112–113
  working stage, 110–123
Group sessions, procedures for:
  closing, 75, 76–78
  keeping them moving, 78–79
  opening, 75–76
Group techniques, 40–41, 43–44
Guilt, existential, 250–251

Handicapped, as minority group, 16
Here-and-now focus, 111–112, 115, 117, 140, 142, 144, 210, 214–215, 219, 242, 294–297, 305, 312, 317
Hidden agendas, 99
Hispanic clients, 16, 17, 287
HIV-positive people, groups for, 4
Holism, 188
Homework assignments, 68, 76, 77–78, 113, 278, 285, 348, 350, 354, 355, 357, 361, 364, 370, 371, 373, 381, 382, 387, 392–393, 396–397, 399, 482–483
Honesty, 97
Hope, 114
Humanistic Psychology, 264–265
Humor, 394, 426–427

Id, 163–164, 171
Identity, 95–96
  crisis, 167
  failure, 412, 415, 417–418, 424
  success, 412, 414, 415, 417
Imagery, use of, 321, 338, 391, 394
Imagination therapy, 229

Immediacy, 111, 120
Impasse, 299, 302–303
Incest, 145
Inclusion, 95–96
Individual psychology, 188
Industry vs. inferiority, 165
Infancy, in developmental model, 160–161
Inferiority/superiority, Adlerian concept of, 190–191
Informed consent, 27–28, 42
Initial stage, of group, 95–103
  characteristics of, 95, 101
  leader functions, 102–103
  member functions and possible problems, 101–102
  primary tasks of, 95–96
  theories applied to, 477–479
Initiating, as leadership skill, 67
Initiative vs. guilt, 163–164
Injunctions and counterinjunctions, 329–330, 331, 334, 342
Insight, 111, 141, 148, 152, 154, 155, 156–157, 175, 194, 196–197, 210–211, 216, 220
Insight groups, 4
Integrated eclectic model, 476–485
Integrity vs. despair, 170
Interpretation, 7, 144, 152–155, 158, 192, 197, 198, 220, 276, 293, 318
  leadership skill, 64–65
Intimacy, 115–116
  fear of, 453–455
  vs. isolation, 168–169
Introjection, 299, 310
Irrational beliefs, 391–392
Isolation, coping with, 449–451
I/Thou relationship, 304, 318, 320
"It" talk, 307

Japanese clients, 285–286, 433
Journal for Specialists in Group Work, 18
Jungian therapy, 229

Karpman Drama Triangle, 335

Language exercises, 306–307
Latency stage, 165
Learning theory, 12, 200
Legal liability, 41–43
Lesbians, as minority group, 16
Life positions, 333–335
Life scripts, 325, 326, 327, 333–335, 338
Lifestyle, Adlerian concept of, 192, 195, 196
Linking, as leadership skill, 69
Listening, active, 63, 273, 277
Logotherapy, 200, 241–242
Loneliness, coping with, 449–451

Magic shop, 227
Mahler's developmental perspective, 173
Making the rounds, 311–312
Malpractice, 35, 41–43
Meaning, search for, 248–250, 458–461

Mended Hearts, 13
Mental-health clinics, 286
Minorities, groups for, 10, 15
Minority, definition of, 16
Mirror technique, 226–227
Modeling, 208, 346, 348, 349–350, 353–354, 355, 364, 369, 372, 373, 387, 391
  as leadership skill, 68–69, 97–98
Multicultural awareness, 16–18
Multicultural group counseling, 18–23
  Adlerian approach to, 201–202
  behavior therapy in, 375–377
  challenges and rewards of, 19–20
  confrontation in, 24–25
  existential approach to, 257–259
  general guidelines for, 23
  Gestalt therapy in, 320–322
  limitations of, 22–23
  person-centered approach to, 285–288
  preparing clients for, 23–24
  psychoanalytic approach to, 180–182
  psychodrama in, 231–232
  rational emotive behavior therapy in, 402–403
  reality therapy in, 432–435
  and self-disclosure, 117–118
  touching, as issue in, 23
  transactional analysis in, 341–342
  various perspectives on, 475–476
Multicultural group counselors, 70–75
  beliefs and attitudes of, 74
  knowledge of, 74
  recognizing limitations of, 75
  skills of, 74
Multimodal therapy, 229, 366–370, 393, 444
Muscular armoring, 302
Musturbation, 384
Mutuality, 111, 112, 155

Narcissistic personality disorder, 173–175, 179
Native American clients, 16, 17, 287
Negligence and malpractice, 41
Neurosis, layers of, 298–300
New Beginnings, 13
Nondirective counseling, 263
Nonverbal language, 308–309

Object-relations theory, 172–173, 179
Oedipus complex, 163, 179
On the Street, 13
Openness, 333
Open vs. closed groups, 88–89
Oral stage, 160

"Paining" behaviors, 411
Pairing-oriented group, 154
Paradoxical techniques, 427–428
Parent groups, 4
Past, 327
  focus on, 294–296, 420
  influence of, in psychoanalytic theory, 142–143

Penalties, in behavioral therapy, 398
Personal-growth groups, 4
Personal power, concept of, 268
Person-centered approach, 5, 66, 189, 200, 263–289, 318, 446, 449, 456, 462–463, 465
  characteristics of, 279
  contributions and strengths of, 282–283
  contributions to multicultural counseling, 492
  evaluation of, 282–288
  goals of, 487
  key concepts of, 267–275
  limitations in multicultural counseling, 494
  limitations of, 284–285
  in multicultural settings, 285–288
  role and functions of group leader, 276–278, 471–472, 488
  stages of, 279–281
  structuring and responsibility, 490
  techniques, 491
Phallic stage, 163–164
Phenomenology, 188–189, 237, 265, 282, 306, 411
Physically handicapped, groups for, 10
"Picture album," 410, 419–420
Play therapy, 229
Polarities, 310, 314
Political issues, and groups, 14
Postgroup stage, 127–130
  evaluating results, 128–129
  issues for co-leaders, 127
  leader functions during, 130
  member functions and problems, 129–130
  theories applied to, 484
Pregroup stage, 85–95
  interview, 86–88, 351
  issues for co-leaders, 94
  leader functions, 94
  leader preparation, 85
  member functions and problems, 92–94
  theories applied to, 476–477
  use of, 91–94
Preschool age, in developmental model, 163–165
Presence, person-centered concept of, 268
Present, 209–210, 294–295, 327
Problem solving, 356, 391
Professional Standards for Training of Group Counselors, 44
Projection, 141, 145–146, 149, 156, 299–300, 310–311, 333
Protecting, as leadership skill, 68
Psychoanalytic approach, 140, 141, 200, 207, 236, 319, 325–326, 374, 381, 409, 445, 448, 455, 456–457, 463, 465–466
  classic, modifications of, 177, 179
Psychoanalytic group counseling, 5, 139–183
  advantages of, 141–142
  contemporary trends in, 171–177
  contributions and strengths of, 177–179

Psychoanalytic group counseling (*cont.*)
  contributions to multicultural counseling, 492
  feminist perspective of, 179
  goals of, 140–141, 487
  key concepts of, 142–151
  limitations in multicultural counseling, 494
  limitations of, 179–180
  in multicultural settings, 180–182
  regressive-reconstructive approach, 140, 141, 472, 488
  structuring and responsibility, 489
  techniques, 491
  therapeutic process, 141–142
  transference, 455
Psychodrama groups, 5, 189, 206–233, 326, 340, 426, 446, 448, 449–450, 462, 466
  audience, 212, 216
  auxiliary egos, 212, 215
  basic components of, 212–216
  contributions and strengths of, 228–229
  contributions to multicultural counseling, 492
  creativity, 207–208
  encounter, 209
  evaluation of, 228–232
  fantasy technique, 466
  goals of, 487
  key concepts of, 207–212
  limitations in multicultural counseling, 494
  limitations of, 230
  in multicultural settings, 231–232
  phases of, 216–222
  protagonist, 212, 214–215
  role and functions of group leader, 488
  stage, 212
  structuring and responsibility, 489
  techniques, 222–228, 481–482, 491
  view of human nature, 207–208
Psychological risks, 33–35, 68, 86–87, 91–92
Psychosexual stages of development, 179
Psychosocial development, 159–171, 179
Psychotherapy, for group leaders, 47

Qualifiers and disclaimers, 307–308
Questioning, 64, 69, 307, 413, 423, 425–426
Questionnaires, use of, 129, 335

Race, definition of, 16
Rackets, concept of, 332, 338
Rational emotive behavior group therapy, 5, 93, 117, 200, 229, 319, 345, 381–403, 409, 426, 432, 446–447, 448, 450, 454, 465, 467
  A-B-C theory, 384–386, 387, 391, 450
  advantages of, 387–388
  behavioral methods in, 396–398
  and belief systems, 480, 481
  cognitive methods of, 391–393
  concerns about, 400–401
  contracts, 477
  contributions and strengths of, 398–400
  contributions to multicultural settings, 493
  disputation, 385
  as educational model, 387
  evaluation of, 398–403
  feedback, 401
  goals of, 386–387, 487
  homework assignments, 392–393, 396–397
  irrational beliefs, 385–386, 391–392
  key concepts of, 382–386
  limitations in multicultural, 494
  limitations of, 400–402
  in multicultural settings, 402–403
  musturbation, 384
  rationale for, 387–388
  role and functions of group leader, 389–390, 472, 489
  role playing, 395–396
  self-acceptance, 386
  self-rating, 386
  skill training, 398
  structuring and responsibility, 490
  techniques and procedures, 390–398, 492
  unconditional acceptance in, 393–394
Rationalization, 146, 296
Reach to Recovery, 13
Reaction formation, 146
Reality testing, 211
Reality-therapy groups, 4, 5, 93, 189, 200, 229, 319, 345, 409–436, 443, 444, 447, 451–452, 467
  change, procedures leading to, 419–425
  commitment, 424–425
  contracts, 477
  contributions and strengths of, 429–431
  contributions to multicultural counseling, 493
  counseling environment, 416–419
  current behavior, focus on, 420–421
  cycle of counseling, 415–416
  failure identity, 412, 415, 417–418, 424
  goals, 478, 487
  humor, 426–427
  key concepts of, 410–413
  limitations in multicultural counseling, 494
  limitations of, 431–432
  in multicultural settings, 432–435
  paradoxical techniques, 427–428
  personal involvement with clients, 416–418
  planning and action, 422–424
  replacement program, 426
  responsibility, 418, 424
  role and functions of group leader, 413–415, 472, 489
  self-help procedures, 426
  special procedures in, 425–428

structuring and responsibility, 490
success identity, 412, 415, 417
techniques, 492
WDEP system, 419–424
Recording, of sessions, 32
Recreational/vocational therapy groups, 4
Recruitment, of group members, 86–88
Redecision therapy, 326–327, 329, 337
Re-entry students, groups for, 10
Reflecting feelings, as leadership skill, 7,
    65, 277
Regression, 145, 151
Rehearsal, in Gestalt therapy, 313–314
Reinforcement, in behavioral therapy, 352–
    353, 372, 397–398
Relatedness, 251–253
Relaxation:
    exercises, 369, 453–454
    progressive, 363
    training, 346, 351, 391
Remotivation groups, 4
Reorientation, in Adlerian groups, 194
Repression, 144, 145, 163–165
Research:
    in behavioral group therapy, 370–371
    in Gestalt therapy, 319–320
    in groups, 32
    on group structure, 100–101
    in person-centered therapy, 277–278,
        283–284
    on pregroup preparation, 91–92
    in rational emotive behavior therapy,
        400
    in transactional analysis, 340–341
Resistance:
    and anxiety, 144
    causes of, 94, 106, 147, 231, 279, 299,
        300–301, 309–310, 425
    conceptualizing, 143, 147–148, 177
    dealing with, 60–61, 106–107, 141, 147–
        148, 152, 153, 156, 158, 178, 197, 301,
        363, 398, 424–425, 427, 447–449, 479–
        480
    to intimacy, 115
    vs. reluctance, 23
    in transition stage, 106–107
Respect, 68, 98, 119, 193, 194, 198, 230,
    319, 350
Responsibility:
    assuming, 296–297, 309–310
    division of, 99, 303, 472–474
    in reality-therapy groups, 418, 424
Restating, as leadership skill, 63
Retroflection, 300
Reversal techniques, 314
Rights and responsibilities, of group mem-
    bers, 26–33
Risks, in group counseling, 33–35, 68, 86–
    87, 91–92
Risk taking, 110–111, 218, 387
Role playing, 7, 114, 206, 211–212, 359,
    364, 369, 373, 387, 391, 395–396, 466
Role reversal, 223, 224–225

Scapegoating, 69
School age, in developmental model, 165–
    166
Screening and selection of group members,
    86–88
Script analysis, 334–335
Self-acceptance, 269, 280, 386
Self-actualization, 53, 263, 265
Self-awareness, 53–54, 238–240, 269
    groups, 4
Self-concept, 167, 310
Self-confidence, 54, 214
Self-confrontation, 55
Self-control, 162
Self-deception, 146, 418
Self-determination, 187, 189, 240–244
Self-directed behavior change, 365–366
Self-disclosure:
    by group members, 93, 111, 117–119,
        161, 196, 221, 388
    as leadership skill, 58–60, 68, 99, 101,
        123, 198, 218, 270, 274–275, 277
    research findings on, 60, 101
Self-esteem, 175–176, 301, 422
Self-exploration, 112, 236, 238, 269
Self-help:
    groups, 6, 12–15
    procedures, for personal growth, 426
Self-knowledge, 214
Self-object, Kohut's concept of, 176
Self-presentation, in psychodrama, 224
Self-psychology, 172, 179
Self-rating, 386
Self-reinforcement, 353
Self-responsibility, 357
Self-talk, 355
Self-trust, 269
Self-understanding, 141, 222, 272, 327
Senior citizens, groups for, 4
Sexual identity, 163, 165, 167
Sexuality, 163–164
Sexual relationships with clients, 36
Shame-attacking exercises, 394–395
"Should" and "ought" statements, 308, 327–
    328, 329–330
Sibling rivalry, 149
Silence, 23, 97
Skills, of group leaders, 63–70
Skill training, 398
Social interest, 189–190
Socialization, among group members, 33,
    36–37
Social-learning theory, 346, 367
Social microcosms, groups as, 8, 14, 90, 238
Social skills:
    training, 354, 358–359, 373, 391
Sociopsychological view of development, 186
Socioteleological approach, 187
Soliloquy, 226
Spontaneity, 208, 213, 214, 216, 218, 230
Stages, of group, 84–130
Standards of practice, 35
Storytelling, 69

Stress-inoculation training, 363–365
Stress-management training, 365
Stress-reduction groups, 10
Strokes, 328–329, 332, 334
Structured exercises, 305
Structured groups, 11–12
Structuring, 99–101, 472–474
Suggestion, as leadership skill, 67–68
Summarizing, as leadership skill, 64, 277
Superego, 163
Superiority, striving for, 187
Supervision, of group leaders, 44–52, 274, 283
Support groups, 12
Supporting, as leadership skill, 65–66

Taking off Pounds Sensibly (TOPS), 13
Techniques:
    abuse of, 319
    in behavioral therapy, 348–350, 352–357, 358–366
    coping-skills, 356
    in existential therapy, 253–254, 255
    in Gestalt therapy, 305–317, 318, 321
    overview of, 7
    in person-centered approach, 276, 283–284
    in psychodrama, 217, 222–228
    training in, importance of, 43–44, 255
    in transactional analysis, 334–335
    use of, 283–284
    various perspectives on, 474–475, 491–492
Tele, 209
Teleology, 188
Termination, of group, 70, 123–130, 350, 464–468
Test-anxiety reduction groups, 4, 10
Theater of Spontaneity, 206
Touching, in multicultural counseling, 23
Training, of group leaders, 44–52
Transactional-analysis approach, 5, 117, 200, 229, 319, 325–343, 345, 409, 426, 432, 443, 446, 452, 454–455, 457–458, 467
    basic assumptions, 326–327
    and belief systems, 480
    classical (Bernian) approach, 325–337
    contracts, 477
    contributions and strengths of, 339–340
    contributions to multicultural counseling, 493
    depression, as issue in, 457–458
    evaluation of, 339–342
    goals, 478, 487
    historical background, 325–326
    key concepts of, 327–335
    limitations in multicultural counseling, 494

    limitations of, 340–341
    in multicultural settings, 341–342
    rationale for, 326–327
    redecisional school of, 326, 337–339
    role and functions of group leader, 336, 472, 488
    stages of, 337–339
    structuring and responsibility, 490
    therapeutic procedures and techniques, 336–339, 491
Transference, 47, 105, 140, 144, 146, 148–149, 150, 152, 154, 156, 158, 178, 209, 299–300, 455
Transition stage, of group:
    characteristics of, 103–107
    leader functions, 108–109
    member functions and problems, 107–108
    theories applied to, 479–481
Treatment plan, use of, 348, 352
Trust, 92, 104, 110, 217, 321, 333, 426, 428, 458, 465, 477
    creating and maintaining, 96–97, 101, 104, 113, 279–280, 328, 350, 416, 445–447
    inhibiting situations, 29
    vs. mistrust, 160–161
    person-centered concept of, 267

Unconditional positive regard, 198, 267–268, 270–272, 275
Unconscious, 143–144, 147–148, 150, 152, 155–156, 158, 163, 177, 207, 236
Unfinished business, 11, 28, 29, 124, 125, 149, 155, 156, 167, 210, 221–222, 247–248, 293, 295, 297–298, 303, 321
University of Texas at Austin, Counseling-Psychological Services Center, 11

Values:
    challenging and clarifying, 461–464
    of group leader, 37–38
Voluntary vs. involuntary group membership, 28–29, 89

Warmth, importance of, 263, 275
Western orientation, core values of, 21–22
White ethnics, 16
Women, as minority group, 16
Women clients, 340
Working stage, of group development, 110–123
    characteristics of, 112–113, 121–122
    leader functions, 122–123
    member functions and problems, 122
    theories applied to, 481–482
Working-through, 141, 156–157, 207, 222

"You" talk, 307

TO THE OWNER OF THIS BOOK:

I hope that you have enjoyed *Theory and Practice of Group Counseling* (fourth edition) as much as I enjoyed writing it. I'd like to know as much about your experiences with the book as you care to offer. Only through your comments and the comments of others can I learn how to make this a better book for future readers.

School: _____

Address of school (city, state, and zip code): _____

Your instructor's name: _____

1. What did you like *most* about *Theory and Practice of Group Counseling?*

_____

_____

2. What did you like *least* about the book? _____

_____

_____

3. Were all the chapters of the book assigned for you to read? _____

(If not, which ones weren't?) _____

4. How interesting and informative was the last chapter (Chapter 17)? _____

_____

5. What material do you think could be omitted in future editions? _____

_____

6. If you used the student manual, how helpful was it as an aid in understanding concepts and theoretical approaches? _____

_____

7. In the space below or in a separate letter, please let me know what other comments about the book you'd like to make. (For example, were any chapters or concepts particularly difficult?) Please recomend specific changes you'd like to see in future editions. I'd be delighted to hear from you!

Optional:

Your name: _____ Date: _____

May Brooks/Cole quote you, either in promotion for *Theory and Practice of Group Counseling* (fourth edition) or in future publishing ventures?

Yes: _____ No: _____

Sincerely,

Gerald Corey

FOLD HERE

NO POSTAGE
NECESSARY
IF MAILED
IN THE
UNITED STATES

BUSINESS REPLY MAIL

FIRST CLASS　　　　PERMIT NO. 358　　　　PACIFIC GROVE, CA

POSTAGE WILL BE PAID BY ADDRESSEE

ATT: *Dr. Gerald Corey*

Brooks/Cole Publishing Company
511 Forest Lodge Road
Pacific Grove, California 93950-9968

FOLD HERE

Brooks/Cole Publishing is dedicated to publishing quality books for the helping professions. If you would like to learn more about our publications, please use this mailer to request our catalogue.

Name: _____

Street Address: _____

City, State, and Zip: _____